An Introduction to Human Resource Management

An Introduction to
Human Resource
Management

Wendy Bloisi
London Metropolitan University, UK

The McGraw·Hill Companies

London Boston Burr Ridge, IL Dubuque, IA Madison, WI New York San Francisco
St. Louis Bangkok Caracas Bogotá Kuala Lumpur Lisbon Madrid Mexico City
Milan Montreal New Delhi Santiago Seoul Singapore Sydney Taipei Toronto

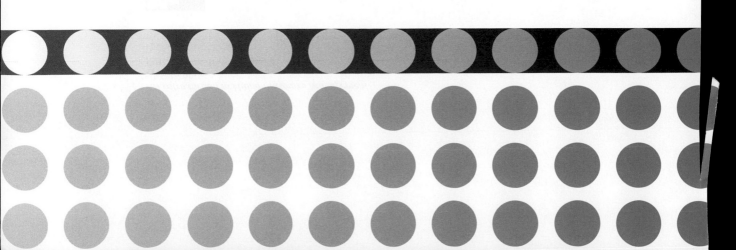

An Introduction to Human Resource Management
Wendy Bloisi
ISBN-13 978-0-07-710968-4
ISBN-10 0077109686

Published by McGraw-Hill Education
Shoppenhangers Road
Maidenhead
Berkshire
SL6 2QL
Telephone: 44 (0) 1628 502 500
Fax: 44 (0) 1628 770 224
Website: www.mcgraw-hill.co.uk

British Library Cataloguing in Publication Data
A catalogue record for this book is available from the British Library

Library of Congress Cataloging in Publication Data
The Library of Congress data for this book has been applied for from the Library of Congress

Commissioning Editor: Rachel Gear
Head of Development: Caroline Prodger
Senior Marketing Manager: Alice Duijser
Senior Production Editor: James Bishop

Text design by Hard Lines
Cover design by Ego Creative
Typeset by Wearset Ltd, Boldon, Tyne and Wear
Printed and bound in Spain by Mateu Cromo Artes Gráficas

Published by McGraw-Hill Education (UK) Limited an imprint of The McGraw-Hill
Companies, Inc., 1221 Avenue of the Americas, New York, NY 10020. Copyright © 2007 by
McGraw-Hill Education (UK) Limited. All rights reserved. No part of this publication may be
reproduced or distributed in any form or by any means, or stored in a database or retrieval
system, without the prior written consent of The McGraw-Hill Companies, Inc., including, but
not limited to, in any network or other electronic storage or transmission, or broadcast for
distance learning.

Dedication

To my son Alexander. Thank you for your patience.

Brief Table of Contents

Preface ix

Guidelines for study xv

Guided tour xix

Technology to enhance learning and teaching xxii

Acknowledgements xxv

PART 1

The role of human resource management 1

1 Introduction to human resource management 3

2 Human resource planning and resourcing 41

3 Work and job design 74

PART 2

Acquiring and rewarding staff 103

4 Recruiting the right people 105

5 Selecting the right people 138

6 Remuneration and reward 176

PART 3

Developing people 213

7 Learning, training and development 215

8 Managing and developing performance 252

9 Employee relations, participation and involvement 286

PART 4

Effective human resource management 321

10 Health, safety and employee well-being 323

11 Equal opportunities and managing diversity 361

12 Strategic human resource management 399

13 Current issues and new developments 435

Index 471

Detailed Table of Contents

Preface ix
Guidelines for study xv
Guided tour xix
Technology to enhance learning and teaching xxiii
Acknowledgements xxv

PART 1 The role of human resource management 1

1 Introduction to human resource management 3
The history of HRM 6
The rise of HRM 10
Personnel management versus human resource management 10
Distinguishing between HRM and PM 12
Defining HRM: soft versus hard HRM 14
The context of human resource management 25
The role of the HR manager 28

2 Human resource planning and resourcing 41
The human resource planning process 43
Types of organisational plan 48
Forecasting 50
Analysing HR needs 50
Supply of and demand for labour 52
The impact of the internal labour market on the planning process 56
Planning for and managing talent 58
Planning and the external labour market 61
Strategies for responding to the supply of and demand for labour 62
Forming a resourcing strategy 64
The changing nature of work 64
Planning for a flexible workplace 65

3 Work and job design 74
The analysis and design of work 75
Organisational structure 78
The changing nature of jobs 79
Job design 81
Task depth and scope 85
The psychological contract 87
New ways of working 88
Developments in flexible working 88
The role of teams in the design of work 92

PART 2 Acquiring and rewarding staff 103

4 Recruiting the right people 105
Recruitment: the question of definition 106
The recruitment sequence 108
Job analysis 109
Job descriptions, person specifications and competency frameworks 113
The competency alternative 114
The legal context of recruitment 116
Recruitment: sources and methods 119

5 Selecting the right people 138
The traditional selection process 140
Application forms 141
Shortlisting 143
The interview 144
References 148
Contemporary methods of selection 151
Making the appointment: cognisance of the legal framework 163
Induction 165

6 Remuneration and reward 176
Definitions of remuneration and reward 178
Payment structure 179
Payment concepts 185
Reward and motivation 188
Legal aspects 201
Low pay 204
Transparency and equity 204

PART 3 Developing people 213

7 Learning, training and development 215
The advantages of learning, training and development 218
How do people learn? 219
Designing effective training programmes 228
The learning organisation 239

8 Managing and developing performance 252
Performance management 253
Performance appraisal 259
Feedback 263
Staff retention strategies 268
Empowerment 272
Coaching 276

9 Employee relations, participation and involvement 286
Employee relations 288
Employee representation 289
Employee participation and involvement 291
Dealing with conflict 294
Negotiation 301
Grievance and discipline 306

PART 4 Effective human resource management 321

10 Health, safety and employee well-being 323
Introduction 325
Health through safety 328
Health through well-being 339

11 Equal opportunities and managing diversity 361
Who manages diversity? 364
The problems with policies 365
Definition of equal opportunities and diversity 366
Managing diversity 372
The legal framework 376
Diversity awareness 378
The competing forces in decision-making 381

Diversity initiatives 382
Legal aspects 389

12 Strategic human resource management 399
Introduction to strategic human resource management (SHRM) 402
Strategic management 403
The development of SHRM 410
Implementation of HR strategies 416
Resource-based SHRM 416
Creating competitive advantage 419
High-performance work systems 422
Identifying bundles of HR practices 424

13 Current issues and new developments 435
Employment costs 437
Changes in working roles and career progression 438
Globalisation and international human resource management 444
Outsourcing 447
Virtualising 452
Employee relocation 454
The role of HRM in takeovers and mergers 456
Communicating takeover decisions 459

Index 471

Preface

This first edition of *An Introduction to Human Resource Management* introduces students to the role of human resource management in organisations. It can be used either in conjunction with *Management and Organisational Behaviour* by Wendy Bloisi, Curtis Cook and Phillip Hunsaker (also published by McGraw-Hill), or as a stand-alone text.

This book concentrates on the practice of HR in the UK and many of the examples used in the book are UK-based since, apart from brief experiences of working in Germany and Thailand, that is where my working life has been spent. However, I have included several global case examples, which I hope overseas students will be able to relate to. I have also included examples of cases from the voluntary sector, education, local authorities and the police, since human resource management is not the prerogative of big business. Colleagues at London Metropolitan University have also kindly agreed to contribute chapters that relate to their areas of expertise: Chapters 4, 5 and 10 were contributed by Margaret May and Edward Brunsdon, Chapter 11 by Gil Robinson and Chapter 13 by Michael Flagg.

Many students who study human resource management may not have much work experience and I have tried where possible to relate the theory to practice in an attempt to make the book more meaningful.

A textbook should hold the interest of the reader and draw him or her into learning the subject field. It should also provide the lecturer with an inviting and useful text, by providing rich pedagogical features and ancillary support. I hope this book does that.

Wendy Bloisi
London, 2006

Student needs

At present the student reader is likely to be taking an Introduction to Human Resource Management module as part of an undergraduate degree course. My vision is that most students who use this text will not be in HR roles for, say, another three years. Therefore they need to know how to be effective performers both individually and in teams within organisations. They also need to know how the HR department functions in preparation for the time when they will play a part. Part of their success requires understanding the macro aspects of human resource management, such as strategy and current issues, as well as the functions of the day-to-day environment.

Student-centred learning

With cutbacks in class contact, certainly in the area of higher education, students are expected to spend more time on independent study. The teacher is seen as a facilitator guiding the students, rather than as an instructor. This edition with its wealth of cases allows the student to gain an insight into what is happening in organisations. The 'Stop and reflect' exercises, discussion questions and case questions allow students to contribute to their own learning.

What makes this text a multidimensional learning resource?

Thanks to the constructive feedback received from academics in the UK, *An Introduction to Human Resource Management* is a text designed to achieve several goals. The text and instructional ancillaries are a learning package with a balance of concepts, examples and practical applications. Included are pedagogical alternatives that help students develop personal skills and organisational insights into the role of the human resource manager. It also promotes an understanding of how human resources function, and why they do the things they do, within applied contexts that are highly visual and interesting to read.

Each chapter incorporates a repertoire of features and pedagogical aids aimed at holding reader interest and encouraging the student to bridge an understanding of concepts and theories with skill-building capabilities and applications. This multidimensional-resource approach provides the teacher with several options to use the text features most compatible with his or her personal approach to stimulating learning. Chapters include the features described below.

Learning outcomes

As an introductory overview, learning outcomes help students quickly grasp the essentials they are expected to learn from each chapter. Outcomes are reinforced by directly linking them to the study and discussion questions at the end of the chapter. At the end of each chapter there is a learning checklist, which again links back to the learning outcomes and allows students to check that they have understood the relevant chapter before moving on.

Opening vignettes

To provoke preliminary thought about the practical lessons of the chapter, an opening real-world scenario or issue introduces students to the value of learning chapter material. For example, Chapter 3 opens with insights into why the Virgin Group needs to think about succession planning for the time when its founder, entrepreneur Richard Branson, steps down.

Stop and reflect

Students encounter self-reflective exercises designed to apply the lessons of the chapter to themselves. The objective is to encourage the student to reflect upon personal preferences and behaviours, or other factors that reveal something about how he or she functions on one or more dimensions explained in the chapter. For example, in Chapter 12 students are asked to answer questions on how strategic they think they are.

Boxed features

To enable students to grapple with real-world key issues facing managers and organisations, five types of boxes appear throughout the text. Two kinds of boxed materials link chapter content to the themes of 'Managing diversity' and 'International perspective'. Students are also given an opportunity to evaluate their own thoughts and ideas through 'Stop and reflect' exercises within each chapter. There follows an up-close review of each type of box.

Managing diversity

The 'Managing diversity' features detail a situation in which factors of gender, race, ethnicity or disability call for managerial sensitivity and/or change. The box in Chapter 9, for example, focuses on strategies that Hallmark Cards has introduced to eliminate age discrimination and develop a more flexible workplace.

International perspective

The 'International perspective' features bring world events, people and organisations into focus for the purpose of learning about life in other cultures and to reduce the tendency to judge others through the filters of one's own culture. For example, the box in Chapter 10 looks at the construction industry in Lithuania and the issues of health and safety, which are a concern for other countries as well as the UK.

Exhibits

Tables, charts and diagrams remain time-tested ways of summarising comparative data, the relationships among variables or the actions that lead to a desired outcome. Typically each chapter includes a half-dozen or so colour-enhanced exhibits to provide the visual learner with a break from text reading and an easy summary of ideas conveyed in a graphical form.

Margin definitions

The technical language of human resource management is summarised in key terms. These appear with definitions in the page margins beside the point in the text where they are introduced and discussed.

Summary

Some students find it helpful to turn from the chapter objectives immediately to review the summary. They then begin reading the text and features. Those who do this will find that the summaries provide highlights that relate back to chapter objectives and key topics.

Areas for personal development

Each chapter provides six to eight instruction sets on how to bridge concepts with development of personal skills appropriate to effective human resource management. These development areas provide guidance on how to initiate actions that enable students to practise several principles of managing the human resource. For example, the 'Areas for personal development' section for Chapter 8 advises readers about behaviours essential for managing the performance of oneself and of others.

Questions for study and discussion

Wherever appropriate, main headings within the chapters are presented as questions to be answered by reading the text, exhibits, boxes and cases. End-of-chapter questions provide ways to help students ensure that chapter outcomes are learned.

List of key concepts

At the end of each chapter is a list of key terms and details of the page on which each is introduced and defined.

Experiential exercises

Many human resource management faculties like to use selected in-class exercises as a way of
encouraging students to learn from direct experiences. Two exercises at the end of each chapter
provide variety in how different types of activity can be used to stimulate experiential learning
behaviours.

Individual task

The individual learner is given an opportunity to work through an issue, process or technique
that stimulates experiential learning. (Some personal skills exercises extend individual learning
by incorporating a dyad or small group follow-on to either demonstrate individual differences
or add complexity to the assignment.) In Chapter 4, students are asked to apply the information
provided in the chapter on formative recruitment and recruitment sources and methods to a
practical work situation.

Team task

Because so much of what happens in organisations occurs with people interacting, the team
exercises stimulate learning by first having a group of students work through the content issues
of an activity, then debriefing the behavioural dynamics and processes that facilitated or inter-
fered with task accomplishment and learning. In Chapter 8, the team exercise is a role-play that
gives all class members an opportunity to carry out an appraisal and discuss the problems as
part of an in-class discussion.

Cases

Business education has a long history of engaging students in discussion of cases as a way of
learning from experience. End-of-chapter cases provide vivid descriptions of an organisation's
experience, followed by a few questions to encourage students to think critically about the case
situation in relation to concepts explained in the text. The examples chosen aim to reflect a
range of contexts, including international business, like Virgin or O$_2$, small businesses and
public-sector examples from organisations such as the police and the NHS. The case in Chapter
3, for example, invites students to consider problems with work and job design in St Lucia's
secondary school.

WWW exercise: Manager's Internet tools

These end-of-chapter exercises link use of the Internet to organisations described in the chapters. Students are guided to certain websites, directed to selected pages and asked to search for
answers to a set of questions that connect with concepts in the chapter. For instance, Chapter
5's WWW exercise asks students to visit the CIPD website and assess the advice it provides on
choosing and using psychological tests.

References

For the research minded, full details of all texts cited are collected at the end of each chapter. These conform to the Harvard system of referencing, which is the preferred method in many universities. They also help direct further reading.

For a quick at-a-glance guide to all of these features, see the illustrated *Guided tour* on pages xix–xxi which is designed to help you navigate through the textbook.

Online supplements

Online Learning Centre

This new book offers an accompanying Online Learning Centre (www.mcgraw-hill.co.uk/textbooks/bloisi). This is an added resource for lecturers and students alike. Included here are:

- an overview of information about the text
- professional resources
- downloadable supplements (for teachers)
- learning outcomes
- chapter self-test quizzes
- key terms
- Internet exercises
- a business skills area
- message board, and much more.

Visit the OLC to make use of these valuable resources for your course.

For more information, see the guide to 'Technology to enhance learning and teaching', on pages xxii–xxiv.

Supplements for lecturers

Lecturer's manual

No lecturer's manual (LM) is intended to supplant the creativity and perspectives on learning that each lecturer brings to his or her class. However, lecturers often find the LM a helpful guide in planning class sessions. The lecturer's manual for this text was written in collaboration with the contributing authors themselves, based on their combined 60-plus years of teaching this material in diverse learning environments. For preparing the course syllabus, the lecturer's manual provides suggestions for human resource management-focused courses. The LM also suggests shortcuts to making decisions – for example, about which cases or exercises to assign and how to sequence chapter assignments. To offer teaching suggestions, the LM provides the following elements for each chapter:

- chapter overview
- key terms from the text, with definitions
- learning outcomes
- answers to study and discussion questions
- synopsis of the experiential exercises and debriefing questions/answers

- synopsis of the case and perspective answers to questions
- a summary of each boxed item

PowerPoint slides

Supplemental exhibits and teaching points (as well as visuals for the exhibit drawings that appear in the text) are available as a Microsoft PowerPoint presentation. They review each chapter's key topics or summarise key points likely to be taught as a mini-lecture. Overall, the combination gives instructors considerable choice in drawing upon resources beyond those they have personally created for the classroom.

Supplements for students

A range of resources for students accompany this book on the Online Learning Centre (www.mcgraw-hill.co.uk/textbooks/bloisi). Tailored specifically to the book, they are organised by chapter to make learning and revising easier. Chapter-by-chapter resources include:

- learning objectives
- Internet exercises
- multiple-choice quizzes
- true or false questions
- web links.

There is also a general Glossary, and a Business Skills area offering a practical context for students to apply their human resource management skills.

Guidelines for study

Time management

As a student, whether full time or part time, you are likely to have a lot of constraints on your time. You may be fitting your study around work, or vice versa, you may have family responsibilities. Whatever the constraints, you need to decide how much time you can devote to study.

Here are some tips, identified by students, on managing time.[1]

- **Be consistent.** How much time can you realistically devote to study? Timetable it in your diary.
- **Be realistic.** Set aside time, divide time equally for everything – socialising, study, part-time work, family, hobby and community.
- **Allocate activities.** If you know you have assignment deadlines or seminar activities, write it in your diary.
- **Rest is important.** If you work instead of sleep occasionally, make provision to catch up – have a 'power nap'. Do not stay up too late before exams as this is likely to affect your performance. If you have planned properly you shouldn't have to.
- **Who will benefit?** Are you studying for yourself? If so, ask people to respect your time-management goals, and provide encouragement and support. It will not last for ever.
- **Ask for help.** If you get stuck, don't leave work until the last minute, ask your tutor, peers or friends for help. You will be glad that you did. Go for it, don't be lazy, you can do it!
- **Stay flexible.** Take account of changing circumstances and adjust accordingly.
- **Don't get stressed.** Stay calm, make a priority list, be self-disciplined and *enjoy*!

Academic writing

As part of your study you will be expected to engage in a variety of academic writing tasks including essays, reports, projects, case studies and examinations.

Before you start make sure you know what is required. Are you writing an academic paper, essay or report? Look for key words in the question. Highlight them to make sure you understand what is required. Plan your outline with an introduction, which should include an outline of what you are doing and how you are going to do it. The main body should include your arguments, ideas and evidence, and a conclusion to summarise your main points. Make sure you refer back to the main question to ensure that you have answered it. You will also need to include references and a bibliography (see below).

When writing, students should take care not to mix fact and opinion. You need to think about what is a fact and what is an opinion – especially in this day and age, when more and more information is obtained from the Internet. You need to think about who put it there, what their background is; in other words, do they have an axe to grind? Are they trying to sell something? Sometimes, opinions can be stated as fact, even when they have been based on research. Academic journals are often peer reviewed, which means that other academics will have looked at published research and either tried to replicate it or offered alternative research arguments that either prove or disprove the research. When referring to journals check if they have been peer reviewed.

Take care when writing as it is often difficult to express absolute certainty and you should be careful to monitor your use of language.[2]

Sources/referencing

Whenever you are required to write a piece of coursework – either as an essay or academic paper – you will be expected to make references (also known as citations or a bibliography) to the books and articles that you have drawn on to produce your coursework.

Referencing is important as it helps to trace the history of an idea and identifies where the work came from. It provides evidence that you have knowledge of the subject you are discussing; it identifies the perspectives and research of different writers; it provides evidence to support your argument and it will show that you are able to produce work of acceptable academic practice.

When you start your background reading and researching in order to produce an assignment, write down the bibliographic details of the books, articles and other sources that you consult or take notes from. 'Bibliographic details' are those details about a book or article that enable the reader to identify and, if necessary, get hold of or access the book or article that you are referring to. Many people use index cards to record bibliographic details.[3]

Proper referencing also protects you against charges of plagiarism. Essentially, plagiarism is about using the expressions of an author you have read as if they were your own personal voice, or failing to give credit to the ideas, theories and opinions of other writers by presenting them as if they were (written) reflections of your own thinking. Plagiarism is cheating and most academic institutions take it very seriously and may fail students.[4]

Referencing systems

There are a number of referencing systems used in academic writing.

The *Harvard system* uses the name of the author and date of publication in the body text. The Bibliography or References at the end of the book (or chapter, as here) will then list the authors' names in alphabetical order with the date of publication, followed by the title and publisher. You will find that we have used this system throughout the main part of this book, with the full details given at the end of each chapter.

The *numeric system* (as used in this section) gives a number at the end of each quote. A corresponding numbered list is then provided at the end of the book or chapter, giving full publication details. This list helps the reader to identify the source of the information provided in the text.

The difference between a reference list and a bibliography

A reference provides the full bibliographic details of the citation of an author's work that you have actually consulted and specifically referred to in your coursework. This may be by quoting an author in the body of your coursework, or by referring to the theories, ideas or opinions of an author in the body of your coursework. At the end of your coursework there should be a list of references in alphabetical order, if you are using the Harvard system, or in numerical order, of all the citations you have made in the body of your coursework.[5]

Strictly speaking, a bibliography is a list of all the texts you have consulted as part of your background reading or researching that have *influenced* your writing, but that have not been cited *directly*. So some of the references in your bibliography may not be to work that you have *specifically* cited in your coursework. If, in practice, your reference list and bibliography amount to the same thing there is no need to produce an additional bibliography. This is why the Harvard system is so popular, as often only one list is needed.[6]

Do not forget to ask your tutors about their expectations regarding the referencing practices they require for the particular coursework they have set for you to do.

Make a record of who and what you are reading. Get into the habit of making a note of the bibliographic details of what you are reading at the time of your reading, and you will begin to find that writing up coursework is not a punishment – it's a personal, and rewarding, challenge.

Using case studies

Case studies are a description of a situation in an organisational context over a particular period of time. They are used in education as a means of acquiring knowledge and developing various skills. It is for this reason that I have included a case study in each of the chapters of this book. Many students find case studies difficult, as they are not being taught but instead are having to use their problem-solving skills alone. You may be using case studies in class as a means of clarifying your understanding of a topic area, or in an exam as a summative assessment of your learning. Analysing case studies can often strike fear in the hearts of students, especially if they are used to right or wrong answers. There is also no set method of analysing the case – it is very much up to the individual to find the method they prefer. However, the more you deal with case studies the better you will become.

Geoff Easton recommends the following in his seven-step approach.[7]

1 Understanding the situation: What is happening in the case? Is it relevant? Is it all there? What is missing? Can I make decisions based on the information?

2 Diagnosing the problem areas: What is the situation now? What should it be? The difference between the two is the problem. You will need to identify the factors involved and the different relationships to find out if you have the right cause, as not all the symptoms may lead to the problem.

3 Generating alternative solutions: Be creative. You may want to produce a mind map or decision tree to identify various solutions. Could you use one of these methods, or another, for your case study? You are unlikely to implement all your solutions, but it will enable you to examine them and make decisions.

4 Predicting outcomes: What would happen if you implemented a particular solution? You need to try to predict all possible outcomes and think about what happens to other problems if you solve one problem and not another. You need to weigh up the risks with the benefits.

5 Evaluating alternatives: You will need to choose your alternative solutions. They need to be qualified and quantified before you justify your choice.

6 Rounding out the analysis: How much detail do you need to include? You may need to go back to the case and go through the stages again. This will add breadth and depth to your analysis.

7 Communicating the results: How are you going to report the results? Is it a written or an oral presentation? You need to spend time on this – especially if you are going to be marked for it. Think about professionalism – especially if you are looking for a future in management.

Exam techniques

You will notice in each chapter that there are questions for study and discussion; some of these questions may be similar to those you may encounter in an exam. The better prepared you are for exams the less stress you are likely to feel. When you start an exam, read the instructions carefully. Do you have to answer every question? How many marks are allocated to each question? Divide up your time to make sure that you will be able to answer the required questions, also allowing some time to check through the paper at the end.

Check the wording of the exam. Are you being asked to – describe, discuss, evaluate, analyse, etc. Before you start your answer draw up a brief plan; this often helps the thought processes and can be crossed out afterwards.[8]

Make sure your writing is legible. Perfectly able students have been known to fail exams because their handwriting couldn't be read.

When the exam is over forget about it. Don't dwell on what you may or may not have done; and it is often better not to discuss it with others, as this can often cause anxiety. You can't do anything until the results are published so you may as well relax and chill out.

Finally, if you feel you need more help with your study skills, there are many useful books available to help you to develop specific skills in exams, writing, research or other aspects of student life. Some of McGraw-Hill/Open University Press' books appear on page xxiv – go to www.openup.co.uk/sg for a discount!

Notes

1 Thanks to BX 101 undergraduates at London Metropolitan University who provided the study tips (2002).

2 Unpublished paper on academic writing by Linda Johnson at London Metropolitan University (1998).

3 Egan, S. (1978) 'Citation Indexes: Background, Description and Evaluation with Special Reference to SSCI', MA thesis, University of Sheffield.

4 Ibid.

5 Kaplan, N. (1965) 'The Norms of Citation Behavior: Prolegomena to the Footnote. *American Documentation* 16(3), pp. 179–184.

6 Martyn, J. (1966) 'Citation Indexing', *The Indexer* 5(1), pp. 5–15.

7 Easton, G. (1982) *Learning from Case Studies*. Prentice Hall, Chapter 2.

8 Study Skills and Learning Materials Booklet (unpublished). London Metropolitan University, (2002).

Further reading

Buzan, T. with Buzan, B. (1995) *The Mind Map Book*. London, BBC Books.

Cameron, S. (2002) *The Business Student's Handbook* (2nd edn). Prentice Hall.

Levin, P. (2004) *Sail Through Exams!* Open University Press/McGraw-Hill.

Levin, P. (2004) *Write Great Essays!* Open University Press/McGraw-Hill.

Learning outcomes

Each chapter opens with a set of learning outcomes, helping students to quickly grasp the essentials they are expected to learn from each chapter.

Opening vignettes

An opening realworld scenario introduces students to the issues and practical lessons of the chapter. The short questions are designed to provoke some initial thoughts about the HRM issues that will follow.

Bringing out the Branson

Virgin Atlantic has emerged from the airline industry's... shape. But is the business fit enough to fly if its charismatic... Branson in 1984, the company started out with one... people expected the venture to fail, but by the end of t... passengers.

Virgin Atlantic celebrated its twentieth birthday on 2...

Stop and reflect

These short self-reflective exercises are designed to help readers to apply the lessons of the chapter to their own situation. They ask students to take the theory in the chapter and consider it in relation to their own thoughts, emotions or experience.

Stop and reflect

Planning your HR career

How many of you actually consider how to get ahead in hu... below to identify what you could do.

■ Can you identify companies with a good reputation for c... future?
■ Have you joined a professional body such as the CIPD?
■ Do you plan to get a broad base of knowledge, rather than...
■ Are you proactive in developing yourself?
■ Do you network to build a base of useful contacts?
■ Can you measure your performance accurately to identi... strategy?
■ Can you show yourself as an authority figure?
■ Can you apply what you have learnt to developing others?

If you can answer yes to the majority of the above questio... forward to a high-flying career in HR. If your answers are mai... you need to do to to get ahead and link it into your career plan.

Managing diversity

Throughout the book students will find boxed examples where factors of gender, race, ethnicity or disability play a part in the case study. They are designed to develop students' awareness of the need for managerial sensitivity or change in order to accommodate diversity in the workplace.

managing diversity

Prison scheme gets back to work

A scheme to address local skill shortages by prov... has been set up by HMP Lindholme. Billed as th... construction site, with the space to build three prison. Inmates selected for the scheme will w... while gaining work experience.

The initiative if convinced to the broader aim... alive, which links prison training and skills. 'We... ages. It is then up to the local establishment and source told PM.

Fiona Ross, education, training and emplo... scheme, said it may encourage other prisons to... may act as an example.'

The centre, funded until 2007 via Yorkshire F... to add local employers to its steering group wh... ex-offenders annually into employment or more qualifications.

Ken Parker, area manager for Yorkshire and... project would benefit both ex-offenders and the... This innovative project aims to support ofte... giving them craft skills that will enable them to fi...

A recent CIPD report, *Employers and Offend...* Employment has a major part to play in red... lions of pounds a year. Government needs to eng... grammes to get ex-offenders into work were geat... have been given the relevant skills,' said Dianah V...

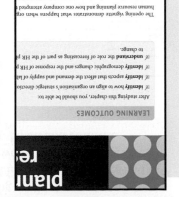

...nanks and raged through the town, businesses were wiped o... In such a situation, past data will not be for any use as HR ma... This is where judgement plays a part in the process: the man... and intuition to predict future needs.

Discussion questions

These questions encourage review and application of the knowledge acquired from each chapter. They can be used for individual learning or as discussion points in a seminar or assignment.

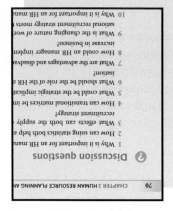

Chapter summary and Personal development section

The summary briefly reviews and reinforces the main topics covered in each chapter to ensure a solid understanding of the key topics. The Personal development section then takes these conclusions and bridges the gap to the student, providing guidance on development and skills of the student, applying ideas to HRM in practice.

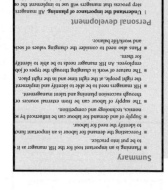

Margin definitions

Key terms are defined in the margin, and a list of key concepts is also provided as a revision tool at the end of chapters. The margin notes are designed to help students to recall key definitions as they learn.

International perspective

While the legal, social and cultural contexts of HRM in the text relate primarily to the UK, students need to be aware of the ever increasing globalisation of the working world. Examples are designed to help students learn about life in other cultures and to consider HRM issues in the wider world. Countries featured include India, Australia, South Africa, Japan and countries within the European Union.

Further reading

Brewell, S. (2003) *Staff Retention*. London: Chartered Management
Cotton, J.L. and Tuttle, J.M. (1986) 'A meta analysis and rev
Academy of Management Review 11, pp. 50–70.
Eannon, M. (2004) 'Britain's real working lives', *People Manage*
Garret, A. (2005) 'Crash course in exit interviews', *Managemen*
Handy, C.B. (1989) *The Age of Unreason*. London: Business Boo
Higginbottom, K. (2003) 'Tesco seeks mountain of youth', *Peop*
Huselid, M.A. (1995) 'The impact of human resource mana
McEvoy, G.M. and Cascio, C.F. (1985) 'Strategies for reducing
Journal of Applied Psychology 70, pp. 342–353.
Schein, E.H. (1985) *Organisational Culture and Leadership*. San
Schmit, M.J. and Allscheid, S.P. (1995) 'Employee attitudes and
retical and empirical connections', *Personnel Psychology* 48, p
Sheridan, J.E. (1992) 'Organisational culture and employee
Journal 35, pp. 1036–1056.

References

Alder, R. (2006) 'Beware the risks of job share schemes', *Personn*
Atkinson, J. (1985) 'Manpower strategies for flexible organisati
pp. 28–31.

Further reading and References

Each chapter closes with a comprehensive list of key readings referred to in the text. Using the Harvard style, the references serve as a useful starting point for students to undertake wider reading or research around a particular topic.

Web exercises and learning checklists

Online exercises encourage students to use the Internet as an effective research tool. Students are directed to specific websites and asked to search for answers to a number of questions connected to concepts in the chapter. Learning checklists recap the central themes of the chapter.

Case studies

The book includes end-of-chapter case studies, providing vivid descriptions of an organisation's experience, followed by a set of questions to encourage critical thinking around the issues raised in the case.

Individual and team tasks

This end-of-chapter feature offers the perfect way to practise HRM techniques and to play out some of the issues in a discussion with other students. These experiential exercises aim to develop learning through direct experience of a situation, issue or debate.

Technology to enhance learning and teaching

Online Learning Centre (OLC)

After completing each chapter, log on to the supporting Online Learning Centre website. Take advantage of the study tools offered to reinforce the material you have read in the text, and to develop your knowledge in a fun and effective way. These resources are designed to make your learning easier and to act as a useful revision tool for exams and tests – we hope you find them useful!

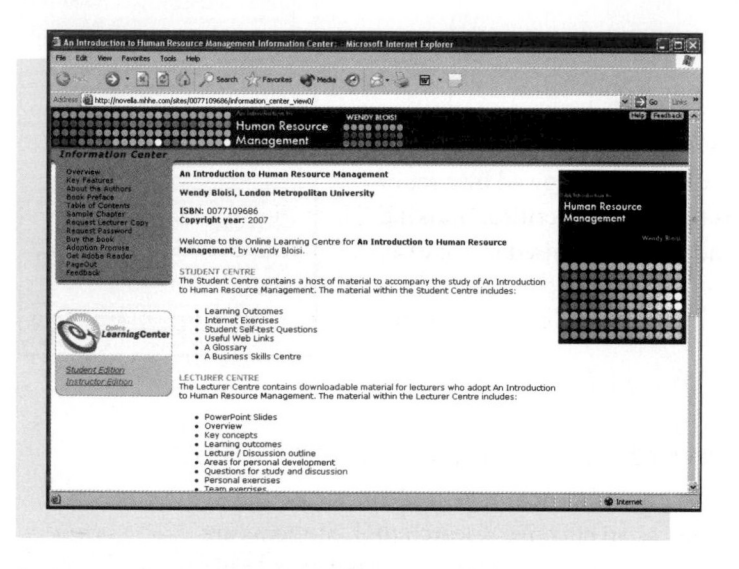

Resources for students include:

- *business skills area, for your personal development and learning*
- *self-testing MCQs with feedback – good practice for exams!*
- *web links for useful organisations and companies*
- *learning outcomes to guide you through each chapter*
- *true-or-false questions for a quick test of your understanding*
- *Internet exercises to employ your online research skills*
- *online glossary of key terms for a quick revision of definitions.*

Visit **www.mcgraw-hill.co.uk/textbooks/bloisi** today

Also available for lecturers:

- *a variety of resources to help you use this book effectively to deliver your HRM course*
- *PowerPoint presentations, which can be edited for use when you deliver your lectures or supplied to students as seminar handouts*
- *a lecturer guide containing chapter overviews, learning outcomes and key concepts from the text, with definitions*
- *guide answers to discussion questions*
- *synopsis of the personal development exercises and debriefing questions/answers*
- *case analysis and perspective answers to questions from each case study in the book*
- *a summary of each boxed item*
- *lecture outlines for each chapter*
- *guidance notes for the web exercises, individual and team tasks.*

EZ·Test

EZ Test, a new computerised testbank format from McGraw-Hill, is available with this title. EZ Test enables you to upload testbanks, modify questions and add your own questions, thus creating a testbank that's totally unique to your course! Find out more at: *http://mcgraw-hill.co.uk/he/eztest/*, or ask your McGraw-Hill representative for more information.

Lecturers: customise content for your courses using the McGraw-Hill Primis Content Centre

Now it's incredibly easy to create a flexible, customised solution for your course, using content from both US and European McGraw-Hill Education textbooks, content from our Professional list including Harvard Business Press titles, as well as a selection of over 9000 cases from Harvard, Insead and Darden. In addition, we can incorporate your own material and course notes.

For more information, please contact your local rep, who will discuss the right delivery options for your custom publication – including printed readers, e-Books and CD-Roms. To see what McGraw-Hill content you can choose from, visit *www.primisonline.com.*

Study skills

Open University Press publishes guides to study, research and exam skills to help undergraduate and postgraduate students through their university studies.

Visit *www.openup.co.uk/sg/* to see the full selection of study skills titles, and get a **£2 discount** by entering the promotional code **study** when buying online!

Computing skills

If you'd like to brush up on your computing skills, we have a range of titles covering MS Office applications such as Word, Excel, PowerPoint, Access and more.

Get a £2 discount on these titles by entering the promotional code **app** when ordering online at *www.mcgraw-hill.co.uk/app*.

Acknowledgements

Our thanks go to the following reviewers for their comments at various stages in the development of the text:

Nick Bacon, University of Nottingham
Debarpita Bardhan-Correia, University of Buckingham
Guy Brown, Northumbria University
Nick Creaby-Attwood, University of Teesside
Louise Doyle, National College of Ireland
Samantha Lynch, University of Kent
Brian Good, University of Surrey
Julian Gould-Williams, Cardiff University
Kirsten Krauth, Coventry University
Maureen Royce, Liverpool John Moores University
John Summers, Anglia Ruskin University

The reviewers' comments and suggestions were invaluable in bringing this new text to fruition and we hope they will be pleased to see their suggestions implemented throughout the textbook.

We would also like to thank Dr Edward Brunsdon and Dr Margaret May for their contributions in the form of chapters on Recruitment, Selection, and Health, safety and employee well-being and Gill Robinson for contributing the Equal opportunities chapter. Thanks also to Michael Flagg for his chapter on Current issues and new developments.

The publishers would also like to thank the following organisations and individuals that granted their permission for us to reproduce their material in this textbook:

Michael Beer and Bert Spector, p. 17
Blackwell Publishing, p. 15, p. 16, p. 425
Business in the Community, p. 436
Emma Clark, p. 356
Philly Desai, Turnstone Research and Consultancy, p. 317
Paul Donovan, p. 178
The Financial Times, p. 217, p. 230
Catherine Hakim, p. 467
Harvard Business School Press, p. 419
Haymarket Direct for the extract from *Management Today*, p. 324
Human Resource Management Journal, Blackwell Publishing, p. 425
Independent Newspapers, p. 38
Makbool Javaid, p. 19
Journal of Management Studies, Blackwell Publishing, p. 13, p. 20
Sarah Murray, p. 248
Palgrave Macmillan, p. 422
People Management, p. 5, p. 19, p. 30, p. 43, p. 56, p. 62, p. 75, p. 106, p. 139, p. 175, p. 210, p. 239, p. 268, p. 288, p. 309, p. 336, p. 356, p. 389, p. 395, p. 402, p. 455, p. 467

Joy Persaud, p. 56
Reed Business Information, for the extract from *Personnel Today*, p. 72
Peter Reilly, p. 30
Zoe Roberts, p. 288
Jane Simms, p. 43, p. 309
Roger Trapp, p. 395
John Wiley Publishing, p. 23, p. 25

Every effort has been made to trace and acknowledge ownership of copyright and to clear permission for material reproduced in this book. The publishers will be pleased to make suitable arrangements to clear permission with any copyright holders whom it has not been possible to contact.

Thanks also go to the first-year undergraduates at London Metropolitan University, who tried some of the activities.

PART 1

The role of human resource management

Part contents

1 Introduction to human resource management   3

2 Human resource planning and resourcing   41

3 Work and job design   74

Chapter 1

Introduction to human resource management

LEARNING OUTCOMES

After studying this chapter, you should be able to:

- ☑ **identify** the historical developments and their impact on HRM
- ☑ **outline** the development and functions of HRM
- ☑ **understand** the differences between HRM and personnel management
- ☑ **evaluate** 'hard' and 'soft' approaches to HRM
- ☑ **understand** how diversity is an issue in HR practice
- ☑ **consider** HRM as an international issue.

The opening vignette gives a somewhat pessimistic view of the role of people in the workplace. Often it is the job of the human resource manager to develop policies and practices that serve the organisation, but she or he also needs to think about the people. If the people are nurtured then the organisation can develop. As can be seen below, this was not the case with Enron.

Enron: something's got to give

Human beings are not governed purely by their own self-interest, so our management and HR systems should not assume they are.

For more than a year, Andrew Fastow – the erstwhile chief financial officer of Enron and the key architect of the off-balance-sheet entities that caused Enron's sudden death – ran rings around the prosecutors investigating the collapse of the energy giant.

Suddenly, he has pleaded guilty to charges that are likely to land him in prison for 10 years, forfeited $29 million he personally made from operating the off-balance-sheet entities, and agreed to fully co-operate with the prosecutors.

What caused Fastow's about-turn was the likely indictment of his wife, Lea Fastow. The only condition he made for his plea bargain was that he and his wife should not go to prison at the same time. He wanted to ensure that his two children had at least one parent at home. Basically, he sacrificed his self-interest, as he saw it, to protect the interests of his children and, to a lesser extent, those of his wife, who was also his high-school sweetheart.

This was the same Andrew Fastow who designed Enron's entire management system around a firm faith that employees pursued only their own self-interest. 'You must allow people to eat what they hunt,' he used to say, 'only then will they hunt well.' It was this philosophy that made Enron adopt one of the most extreme systems of individual incentives: when you started a new venture within Enron, you got phantom stocks relevant only to your venture. As long as your efforts made money, you got rich, irrespective of what happened to other parts of the company. As a result, everyone in Enron, including Fastow, acted like hunters – looking out only for themselves. The results of such behaviour are now well known.

This is an interesting contrast, and it is by no means unusual. Most managers know that they themselves, and most other people, care about others close to them in their personal lives – their children, old friends, perhaps even some of their neighbours – and that they would happily incur some costs to help these people. At the same time, they also believe that, at work, people care only about their own self-interest. Even if they do not explicitly believe that, they design their companies' organisational and managerial processes as if the motivation to voluntarily help others has no role in the office or the factory.

The facts are clear. Most people pursue their self-interest. At the same time, except for a pathological few, most people also have an innate preference for helping others. And they like to help others not just as a means to further their own self-interest but also as an end in itself. This is equally true for people's personal and work lives. Also, this is not something as grand as altruism; it's much more mundane than that – it's just how all of us ordinary folks are.

What would happen if senior managers recognised that it was possible to build an organisation in which people derived as much joy from the success of others as from their own success, and designed their management processes accordingly? It would vastly change those processes.

As an example, make a quick inventory of your HR processes and put them into two categories: those that reinforce the self-interest-seeking behaviours of people, and those that support their helping others. Look at concrete processes and mechanisms, not abstractions like values which, unless translated and embedded in specific practices, have little effect on behaviours. How long are the two lists? Can you do something to rebalance them?

One possible difficulty you may face is that you do not quite know what you can do to support the more co-operative behaviours. For example, what specific kind of incentive systems might you use? What kind of decision-making processes can you adopt? Structurally, too, what can you do to hardwire non-selfishness – which is not at all the same thing as becoming a saint and not the obverse of self-sacrifice – in your organisation?

These are among the key questions that we, fellows of the Advanced Institute of Management Research, will be trying to answer. Much of the existing management research makes the same assumption as Fastow made about what motivates people at work. We will question and broaden these assumptions with the aim of coming up with rigorously researched theories that are not victims of pessimism about people, and that will, we hope, help you build high-performance organisations that are also delightful to work in. Watch this space.

Source: Sumantra Ghoshal, *People Management*, 12 February 2004, p. 23.
Reproduced with kind permission of *People Management*.

Discussion questions

1 What is the point of HR if employees are only out to serve themselves?

2 What role could the HR manager play in building an organisation that celebrates the success of others rather than individuals?

The opening vignette gives a disturbing view of management practices. Enron encouraged employees to lose sight of organisational goals, in an attempt to serve their own goals. The chief financial officer of Enron, Andrew Fastow, encouraged self-interest by offering employees shares, which reflected the value of the business they brought to the company. The result: a culture of selfishness, which encouraged greed and ultimately destroyed the company. As an HR manager, your role in organisations will not be solely related to the concrete mechanisms of human resource management, such as the functions, but also abstract values, such as culture.

Whether you work as a supervisor in a supermarket with responsibility for the checkout operators, the general manager of the local branch of a multinational bank, the union representative for a major airline or the director of HRM in a technology organisation, you will be responsible for managing people. You may have decided to choose people management because you have a love of people, but empathy for people is not necessarily what makes human resource practitioners effective. According to Hunt (1999), what is important for HR managers is an understanding of the structures and climate in which people's potential can be released, developed and rewarded. Andrew Fastow of Enron, although misguided, discovered this in his famous quote: 'You must allow people to eat what they hunt – only then will they hunt well.' However, he failed to understand the necessity of developing the whole organisation and the results are history. The Enron view of people management is not the view taken by all organisations. The John Lewis Partnership, for instance, also believes in giving its employees, or 'partners' as they are referred to by the company, a stake in the organisation. It achieves this by encouraging workers to co-operate to fulfil the company's aims. In turn, employees are rewarded with a share of the profits.

This book introduces you to the role of the people manager and human resource specialist. It also should be useful for general managers wanting to successfully manage and develop their employees. The book is designed not only to introduce you to the underlying theories and concepts that inform human resource practitioners but also to current practices necessary for the functions of HRM. At the moment, human resources (HR) is in a constant state of change, with Hunt (1999) suggesting that one of the following could happen.

■ Human resources goes into decline – outsourcing and downsizing has removed the HR specialist from organisations and placed the HR role with the overworked line manager.

vision
The view of how the organisation sees itself developing and achieving its objectives.

■ Human resource management is an important function, which will begin to play an important role in top management. The HR function will be closely integrated into the **vision** and strategy of the organisation.

■ Human resources will continue as it has done in the past, due to the limitations of labour markets, unions, legislation, etc. This implies that it stands still and does not develop.

Whatever the view of HR and how it develops in the future, it is important to understand where it has come from and what has influenced it. To set the scene of where we are today, we will now take an overview of the historical development of the profession. A historical time line is illustrated in Exhibit 1-1.

The history of HRM

The late nineteenth century

Wherever people have needed to be employed there has been some form of people management, although it has only been in recent years that a consistent view has emerged on how to develop people.

At the end of the nineteenth century many workers were employed in the manufacturing sectors, where they had to put in long hours and conditions were often harsh. The welfare state did not exist and no work could mean destitution. However, even in such unenlightened times some employers did value their workers and took on a **paternalist** role for their employees. Such famous names as Cadbury, Rowntree and Bournville, all chocolate manufacturers, and Lever, a soap manufacturer, all

paternalist
An employer viewed as a father figure in the organisation.

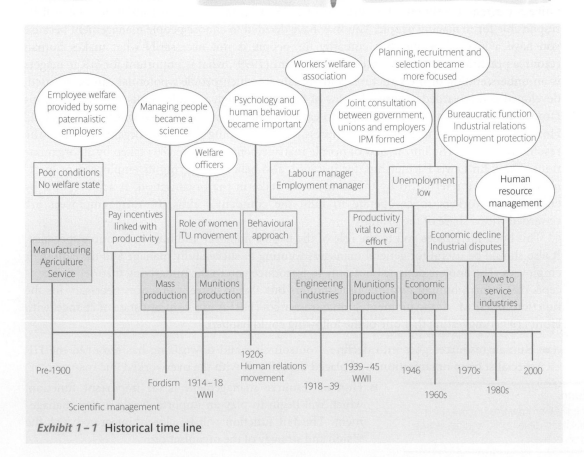

Exhibit 1 – 1 Historical time line

took their employees' welfare very seriously and established the provision of health and education as part of their role as a responsible employer. These enlightened employers tended to be Quakers and were some of the first employers to employ welfare officers. The welfare officers were often women and were concerned not only with visiting sick employees but also with supervising moral welfare. Pressures were also coming from an emerging labour movement and trades unions were gaining influence with a campaign for 'industrial betterment' (Cannel, 2004).

The 1900s also saw the development of personnel management as a professional body, with the formation of the Welfare Workers' Association, a forerunner to the CIPD.

Scientific management

Human resource management as we know it today also developed from a range of theories from sociologists, psychologists, and management and organisational behaviourists. One of the earliest can be traced back to the United States in the early 1900s with the development of 'time and motion' studies, which would find the 'one best way' of performing a task. The father of what became known as scientific management was Frederick Taylor. Taylor replaced haphazard rules of thumb with precise measure principles. He was one of the first to emphasise the prediction of behaviour and encouraged the use of training and other management techniques to influence work outcomes. Taylor identified the skills needed for a particular job and would hire and train workers to perform to the required standards. Employees were rewarded with a 'differential piece rate' pay system that rewarded work output. Many managers took on the ideas of Taylor, often without the pay incentives. Although Taylor publicised his ideas as a success, the reality was threats of industrial action, redundancies and disgruntled management (Rose, 1975).

scientific management
An early 1900s movement, which held that the scientific observation of people would reveal the one best way to do any task.

Fordism

The USA was also leading the way in developing large-scale industrialisation with car manufacturers such as Henry Ford. Ford continued with the scientific management approach and developed an assembly line where the workers were allowed a minimum amount of time to complete a task before the car moved to the next stage in the production process. Employees unable to keep up were fired; this led to a high level of absenteeism as well as high employment turnover. To counteract the high staff turnover Ford introduced 'the five dollar day' bonus, which would double workers' wages. However, the bonus was payable only to employees whose moral and work ethic was seen as appropriate both at home and at work. Management control was also increased, through the use of job evaluation and a pay system that was matched to the difficulty or status of the job. Workers had to be with the company six months to qualify for the scheme, and young people under 21 and women were not eligible (Benyon, 1973). With mass production the role of managing people became a science and managers were expected to have not only technical expertise but also managerial ability. In the UK, however, reliability and the ability to impose discipline were seen as far more important than technical knowledge.

The human relations movement

human relations
The movement which proposed the view that the social side of work was important for improving performance.

The human relations movement began to grow in the 1920s with Elton Mayo and the famous Hawthorne experiments. This shifted the view of people management away from the mechanistic principles of scientific management and towards a behavioural approach of satisfying the social needs of workers. The results of the Hawthorne approach taught managers that concern for people did not mean lower production, but the reverse. This was seen as an anti-Taylor perspective as it argued against Taylor's 'one best way', although it agreed with Taylor's idea of sufficient rest breaks for workers.

Research in the UK was also emerging from the National Institute of Industrial Psychology (NIIP). It investigated methods of work and its relation to fatigue, and concluded that fatigue was not only psychological but also physiological. The resulting research, by what became known as the human relations school and other work psychologists, identified the importance of the human factor of work. They discovered that people were more effective if they were allowed a say in how to perform tasks and that social relations were often more important than money in maintaining morale.

The First World War

The war years of 1914–18 saw major developments in personnel management. The Munitions of War Act 1915, passed to ensure a sufficient supply of labour to munitions' factories, made the provision of welfare services compulsory. This led to a large increase in the number of welfare officers, many of whom were men as it was considered more appropriate for them to oversee the welfare of boys.

However, women were also being recruited in large numbers to replace the men sent to the trenches. This led to some bitter disputes with trades unions, which saw craftsmen's jobs being filled by unskilled women. It led to the government having to enter into discussion and consultation with the unions (Cannel, 2004).

Another development was the role of 'labour officers', needed to assist in the recruitment, selection, discipline and industrial relations on the shop floor of unionised workers. Labour officers also had to interpret the many government directives concerning the employment of civilians in wartime and aspects concerning discipline and dismissal. Many labour officers were male and came from an engineering and works management background (Evans, 2003).

Between the wars

The engineering industries developed the role of the personnel manager, and job titles such as 'labour manager' or 'employment manager' became more common. Their role was to handle recruitment, dismissal, absence and pay. Pay negotiations were becoming more common and officials appointed by employers' federations negotiated national pay rates with the unions.

The inter-war years also saw the emergence of the title 'personnel manager', in companies such as Marks & Spencer. The personnel manager dealt with many of the functions of the human resource that we know today. However, senior management more often dealt with any industrial relations problems (Cannel, 2004).

Personnel was not the only name to change: the Worker's Welfare Association, after evolving through several name changes, finally became the Institute of Labour Management in 1931, and eventually the Institute of Personnel Management (IPM) in 1946.

The Second World War

The 1939–45 war saw more government regulations introduced to regulate employment and increase morale in a bid to boost the war effort. The role of the welfare and personnel manager was seen by government as a vital part of the drive to greater efficiency. Strikes were also made illegal and productivity improvements became part of a joint consultation and negotiation between unions and the government. By the end of the war the personnel profession had expanded and had approximately 5300 practitioners; many of the HRM practices in use today can trace their origins back to the war years.

The post-war years

With the post-war years came a time of economic boom, with manufacturing at its peak. Unemployment was low and personnel practices such as planning, recruitment and selection became important aspects of the personnel manager's role. During the war much of the personnel role had been to implement government rules, and the emerging personnel profession tended to be very bureaucratic and based on function (Cannel, 2004).

Industrial relations also took on a new role. During the war years negotiations were centralised and often government led. With large companies now developing their own employment policies, negotiations became more and more decentralised with local shop stewards and local bargaining. Official and unofficial strikes became damaging to the economy and the UK became notorious for its poor industrial relations. Eventually, a report by Lord Donovan in 1968 criticised employers, managers and unions for their failure to negotiate and failure to plan for industrial relations strategies. Much of the criticism of the failure of industrial relations was directed at the failure of employers to give personnel management a high priority. The higher profile of personnel today can partly be seen as a response to the criticism made by Donovan (Cannel, 2004).

The 1960s also saw the introduction of new legislation, such as contracts of employment, training and redundancy payments. The 1970s saw the introduction of equal opportunities legislation and employment protection, but there were also attempts to control trades union activity. The economy was also in decline and personnel departments were not only expected to implement the new legislation, but also directives on pay regulations to curb the spiralling inflation. New techniques needed to be developed to improve performance and much of the work done by social scientists and management and organisational behaviour theorists in the USA, such as Herzberg's theory of motivation, found their way into the personnel departments.

The main features of personnel management as it is today were in place by the end of the 1970s and are summed up by Cannel (2004) as follows.

- **The collective bargaining role** – centred around dealing with trades unions and the development of industrial relations strategies.
- **The implementer of legislation role** – implying understanding and implementing a growing amount of legislation.
- **The bureaucratic role** – implementing a series of rules about behaviour at work, dealing with recruitment, managing absence, and so on.
- **The social conscience of business role**, or 'value champion' – a residue from the welfare worker function.
- **A growing performance improvement role** (in some organisations and sectors) – about integrating the personnel function with business needs and taking a more strategic view.

Looking at the historical context can help us to understand how human resource management has developed into a profession and how it is continuing to increase in importance.

The rise of HRM

The election of a Conservative Government under Margaret Thatcher in 1979 marked a change in shift from collectivism to individualism. Legislation was introduced to control the perceived abuse of union power by banning sympathy strikes and removing the concept of the 'closed shop', where union membership was compulsory. High unemployment of over three million, and the decline of the manufacturing industries, also led to decline in the strength of the unions.

The 1980s also saw the term 'human resource management' (HRM) introduced to the UK from America. The meaning of the term has led to many debates and academic discussions, as can be seen below. To some, it was seen as a way of minimising the trades unions' influence, and the name change from 'personnel' symbolised this. Others saw HRM as a more strategic role in the achievement of organisational objectives, with an HR director at board level. Before moving on to the personnel management versus human resource management debate, developments through the 1980s and 1990s, such as the rise of the training specialist, as well as the reward, resourcing and diversity specialists that exist in many large organisations, are now seen as an important part of the personnel function.

As can be seen throughout the last century, the role of the HR professional continues to evolve, develop and have a significant impact on the effectiveness of organisations although the debate between personnel and HRM has continued into the twenty-first century and this is discussed in the following section.

Personnel management versus human resource management

Personnel management is often considered an old-fashioned name for human resource management, and in some organisations there may well be little difference between the old personnel department and today's HR department. But HRM can also mean a particular philosophy of the role of HRM in organisations, and how people are developed and nurtured to achieve organisational goals.

The foundations of HR activity

The traditional view of HRM can be explained by the four objectives that form the foundation of the human resource activity. These can be identified as staffing, performance, change management and administration objectives, and are illustrated in Exhibit 1-2.

These are the underlying objectives that support the HR function and enable managers not only to ensure compliance with legislation but also to enable a move towards strategic development, which will be discussed in the next chapter. An explanation of why they are important is given below.

Staffing objectives

Staffing ensures that the right staff are available at the right time in the right place. This involves identifying the nature of the job and implementing a recruitment and selection process to

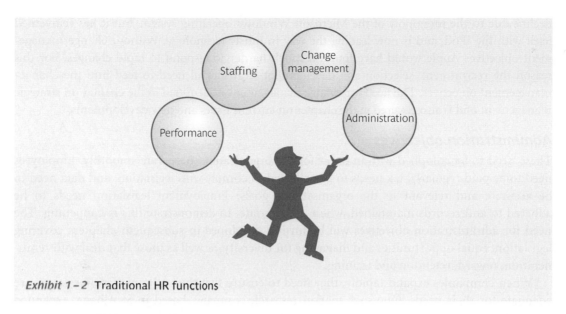

Exhibit 1–2 **Traditional HR functions**

ensure a correct match. Staffing objectives also need to ensure that once the people are recruited they can be retained, through either a reward package and/or development process. There is nothing new about this, as can be seen from the overview of the history of HRM: even Henry Ford had to offer an incentive of the 'five dollar day' in an attempt to reduce staff turnover, and today many workers in the financial sector eagerly await their end-of-year bonuses. How these objectives are achieved will be revisited in subsequent chapters on planning and resourcing, recruitment and selection, and retention.

Performance objectives

These are a continuation of the staffing objectives. Once the staff are in place they need to be motivated to perform. This can take place through the development processes. Performance targets may be introduced through an appraisal system where employers invite members of staff to discuss their performance and future ambitions and develop strategies to enable them to be met. House of Fraser stores use the appraisal system not only to identify future managers but also to enable sales staff to receive training, either in work-related issues such as customer care, or personal development areas such as improving IT skills. Training and development are often used to close the gap between current performance and expected future performance. But, as House of Fraser identified, they can also be used for maintaining commitment and empowerment, which in turn will improve performance. Performance objectives can also identify the disengaged worker, who for whatever reason no longer feels committed to the organisation. Again strategies can be put in place to return these workers to fuller participation in the workplace. Many of these issues will be discussed in later chapters on learning, training and development, and managing and developing performance.

Change-management objectives

These are required if organisations are to be effective in developing an innovative and fast-moving organisation that can keep up with the fast pace of development in a modern society. Organisations need to be adaptable and flexible, which means that policies and objectives need to be in place to manage change. Many of the IT industries need to be adaptable and fast changing to keep up with changes in modern technology. For example, Apple Computers' market share was in decline due to the monopoly of the Microsoft Windows operating system, but it has reinvented itself with the iPod, and is now leading the way in music technology. Without change-management objectives Apple would have found it much harder to respond to rapid changes. For this reason the recruitment, selection and development strategies all need to feed into the change-management objectives. The need for change management is identified in the chapter on strategic management and is also covered in the chapter on current issues and new developments.

Administration objectives

These need to be complied with in order for the organisation to operate smoothly. Employees need to be paid regularly, tax needs to be collected to comply with legislation, and data need to be accurate and relevant to the organisation's goals. Employment legislation needs to be adhered to and records maintained, where appropriate, to demonstrate this is happening. The need for administration objectives will be further developed in subsequent chapters covering legislation, equal opportunities and managing for diversity, as well as those that deal with remuneration, reward, retention and training.

When companies expand rapidly, they need to ensure that their administration systems are adequate for their needs. One such market research company, based in St Albans, expanded from a team of two people to an organisation employing 20 people. There were no systems in place to deal with the increase, and this resulted in poor allocation of tasks, not knowing who was on duty and at what time, as well as staff not being paid on time. The result: demotivated staff and a high staff turnover, which eventually affected business performance.

Distinguishing between HRM and PM

workforce centred
Refers to personnel managers who concentrate on protecting the workers from managers.

All the above objectives need to be taken into account, whether personnel management or HRM. However, personnel management is viewed as **workforce centred** and more operational in focus. Personnel managers recruit, select and carry out administrative procedures in accordance with management's requirements. They act as a bridge between the employer and the employee. As a result, personnel managers were seen as functional specialists rather than strategic managers and often had little power or status in the organisation. The personnel manager needed to understand the needs of the manager and the employee, and articulate those needs to both sides.

Some organisations, however, see HRM as a particular approach in the management of people. HRM can be seen as a radical new approach linked to strategy and viewing people as assets who need to be actively managed as part of the long-term interests of the organisation. HRM can be viewed as a radical integrated approach to the management of people in an organisation and, as such, can be seen as a general management function. Where personnel managers can be viewed as specialists, HRM can be seen as the responsibility of *all* managers, particularly senior managers, and as such is proactive rather than reactive. Guest (1987) identifies the differences in his model (see Exhibit 1-3).

Guest (1987) shows a model of HRM that is commitment based, which is distinct from compliance-based personnel management. According to Guest, HRM is:

- linked to the strategic management of an organisation
- seeks commitment to organisational goals
- focuses on the individual needs rather than the collective workforce

	Personnel	HRM
Time and planning	Short-term, reactive, ad hoc, marginal	Long-term, proactive, strategic, integrated
Psychological contract	Compliance	Commitment
Control systems	External	Self-control
Employee relations	Pluralist, collective, low trust	Unitarist, individual, high trust
Structures and systems	Bureaucratic/mechanistic, centralised, formal	Organic, devolved, flexible
Roles	Specialist/professional	Largely integrated into line management
Evaluation criteria	Cost minimisation	Maximum utilisation (human asset accounting)

Exhibit 1 – 3 **The differences between personnel and human resource management**
Source: Guest (1987), 'Human Resource Management and Industrial Relations', *Journal of Management Studies* 24(5), pp. 503–521. Reproduced with permission of Blackwell Publishing.

- enables organisations to devolve power and become more flexible
- emphasises people as an asset to be positively utilised by the organisation.

Guest (1987) sees HRM as a distinct approach to managing the workforce and argues that, although personnel management will also select and train staff, it is the distinct approach in the selection and training that matters. HRM's approach should be linked to high performance and commitment rather than compliance. Guest (1997) recognises that, although empirical evidence is only just beginning to show the link between HRM and performance, evidence is already suggesting that HRM works. The view from industry is also suggesting that HRM is taking on a strategic role in industry. The CIPD (2003) HR survey identified HR issues as now being regularly discussed at executive boards and HR managers seeing their role as that of a strategic business partner, with the HR function now focused on achieving key business goals and developing employee capabilities.

Storey (1992) defines the elements that differentiate HRM as follows.

- Human capability and commitment: Storey argues that this is what differentiates organisations.
- Strategic importance of HRM: it needs to be implemented into the organisational strategy and considered at the highest management level.
- The long-term importance of HRM: it needs to be integrated into the management functions and seen to have important consequences for the ability of the organisation to achieve its goals.
- The key functions of HRM: seen to encourage commitment rather than compliance.

Storey (1992) identifies a model with 27 points that differentiate HRM from personnel and industrial relations (IR) practices. Storey's model is based on an ideal type of organisation and is a tool used to present what Storey sees as the essential features of personnel and HRM in an exaggerated way.

Storey identifies four categories in which the 27 points fit. These are: beliefs and assumptions, strategic concepts, line management, and key levers, which include the functions of HR such as selection, pay, and so on.

Storey's model can be viewed as an 'ideal type' of HRM and has been used as a tool for research and analysis of organisations. In practice, HRM would use some elements of his 27 points but would be extremely unlikely to include all of them. As such the model is useful as a research tool but does not reflect what happens in practice (see Exhibit 1-4).

Storey's (1992) 27 points of difference identify personnel management as being bureaucratic, based on rules and procedures and seen as a separate function from general management. On the other hand, HRM is seen as related to the business need, central to the corporate plan and the responsibility of all managers.

Storey (1992) proposes another model as a means of comparative analysis, for identifying the shift organisations may take from personnel management to HRM. This is illustrated in Exhibit 1-5.

Storey (1992) suggests in the model depicted in Exhibit 1-5 that, for an organisation to gain competitive advantage, a strategic response needs to be given to the beliefs and assumptions of the organisation and that line managers should take on part of this role. Line managers would have a responsibility for the change in key levers, which would move the organisation away from being locked into bureaucratic procedures towards becoming a flexible organisation that would encourage commitment through performance-related goals.

Storey not only identified the shift towards human resource management, he also described two approaches to HRM as 'hard' and 'soft'; these approaches are discussed below, after the 'Stop and reflect' exercise.

Stop and reflect

Where would you prefer to work?

Consider the main differences between personnel and human resource management. Would you prefer to work in a company that follows personnel management practices or HRM practices?

Defining HRM: soft versus hard HRM

hard HRM
Views people as a resource used as a means of achieving organisational goals.

soft HRM
Encourages employers to develop strategies to gain employee commitment.

Within the HRM view, two approaches have been identified. Storey (1989) labelled these two approaches **hard HRM** and **soft HRM**. The 'hard' approach, rooted in manpower planning, is concerned with aligning human resource strategy with business strategy, while the 'soft' approach is rooted in the human relations school, has concern for workers' outcomes and encourages commitment to the organisation by focusing on workers' concerns.

Soft HRM

The soft view of HRM, developed by Storey (2001), popularised a distinctive approach to managing the human resource. Beer *et al.* (1984) proposed the Harvard model as a means of improving managers' methods of managing people. Walton (1985) argued that the role of

Dimension	Personnel/IR	HRM
Beliefs and assumptions		
1 Contract	Careful delineation of written contracts	Aim to go 'beyond contract'
2 Rules	Importance of devising clear rules/mutuality	'Can-do' outlook; impatience with 'rule'
3 Guide to management action	Procedures	'Business need'
4 Behaviour referent	Norms/custom and practice	Values/mission
5 Managerial task vis-à-vis labour	Monitoring	Nurturing
6 Nature of relations	Pluralist	Unitarist
7 Conflict	Institutionalised	De-emphasised
Strategic aspects		
8 Key relations	Labour management	Customer
9 Initiatives	Piecemeal	Integrated
10 Corporate plan	Marginal to	Central to
11 Speed of decision	Slow	Fast
Line management		
12 Management role	Transactional	Transformational leadership
13 Key managers	Personnel/IR specialists	General/business/line managers
14 Communication	Indirect	Direct
15 Standardisation	High (for example, 'parity' an issue)	Low (for example, 'parity' not an issue)
16 Prized management skills	Negotiation	Facilitation
Key levers		
17 Selection	Separate, marginal task	Integrated, key task
18 Pay	Job evaluation (fixed grades)	Performance related
19 Conditions	Separately negotiated	Harmonisation
20 Labour management	Collective bargaining contracts	Towards individual contracts
21 Thrust of relations with stewards	Regularised through facilities and training	Marginalised (with exception of some bargaining for change models)
22 Job categories and grades	Many	Few
23 Communication	Restricted flow	Increased flow
24 Job design	Division of labour	Teamwork
25 Conflict handling	Reach temporary truces	Manage climate and culture
26 Training and development	Controlled access to courses	Learning companies
27 Foci of attention for interventions	Personnel procedures	Wide-ranging cultural, structural and personnel strategies

Exhibit 1–4 27 points of difference between personnel and IR practices and HRM practices

Source: Storey (1992) *Developments in the Management of Human Resources: An Analytical Review,* p. 38. Reproduced with permission of Blackwell Publishing.

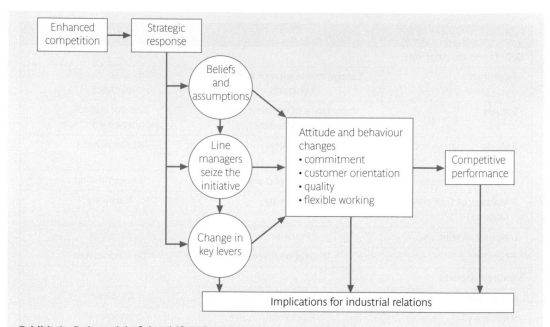

Exhibit 1–5 A model of the shift to human resource management

Source: Storey (1992) *Developments in the Management of Human Resources: An Analytical Review*, p. 38. Reproduced with permission of Blackwell Publishing.

HRM was to develop strategies to gain employees' commitment, not to be a means of controlling them.

Beer *et al.* (1984) suggest that managers need to be more responsible for HRM. The Harvard model opened the debate in the 1980s and proposes four human resource categories, as is demonstrated in Exhibit 1-6.

The issues proposed by Beer *et al.* (1984) argue that managers need to take responsibility for employee influence, human resource flow, reward systems and work systems, regardless of the size of the organisation. They recognise that different stakeholders have different interests and, for an organisation to be effective, managers need to take these interests into account.

Employee influence

This refers to how managers disperse their power and authority throughout the organisation while ensuring that the organisational goals are met.

The human resource flow

This refers to issues of recruitment, selection, development and ending the contract for the people in the organisation. The model argues that managers must work together to ensure that the right people are in the right place at the right time.

Rewards systems

These are concerned with how employees are rewarded for their work. They include monetary reward such as pay, bonuses and profit sharing, and non-monetary rewards such as holidays and health insurance. They are also concerned with intrinsic rewards such as job fulfilment and empowerment, which help to maintain a motivated and productive workforce. The **Harvard model**

Harvard model

A soft model of HRM to encourage employee commitment through employee influence, HR flow, reward and work systems.

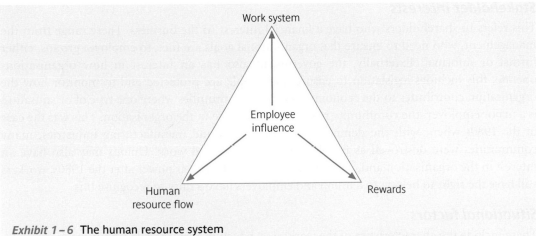

Exhibit 1–6 The human resource system
Source: Beer *et al.* (1984) *Managing Human Assets*, The Free Press. Reproduced with permission of the authors.

recommends that employees are involved in the design of the reward system, while managers must ensure it is consistent with the organisation's goals.

Work systems

This refers to the organisation of work to ensure that it is efficient and productive and, again, can meet the organisation's goals. Work systems need to ensure that the communication channels work and the correct technology is in place at the various levels of the organisation.

As can be seen from Exhibit 1-7, the human resource system forms one part of the Harvard model and cannot be considered without taking into account stakeholder interests, situational factors, HR outcomes and the long-term consequences of decisions.

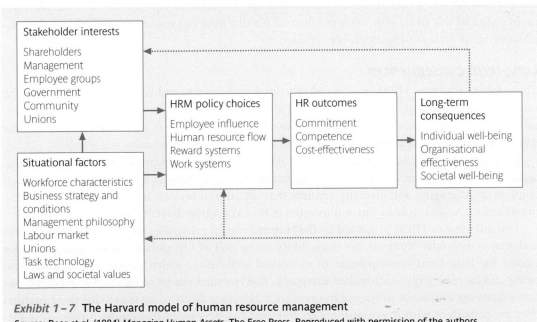

Exhibit 1–7 The Harvard model of human resource management
Source: Beer *et al.* (1984) *Managing Human Assets*, The Free Press. Reproduced with permission of the authors.

Stakeholder interests

This refers to shareholders who have a financial interest in the business. These range from the management, who need to ensure that organisational goals are met, to employee groups, either formal or informal. Externally, the government also has an interest in how organisations operate; this includes legislation to ensure that people are protected and to monitor how the organisation contributes to the economy. Often in communities where one type of organisation is a major employer, the community may also have a stake in the organisation. This was the case in the 1980s when, with the demise of the coal mines and manufacturing industries, many communities were destroyed as people moved away to find work. Unions may also have an interest in the organisation and, although many unions lost their power after the 1980s, workers still have the right to belong to a union and employers have a duty to recognise this.

Situational factors

These include the characteristics of the workforce, which in turn include labour markets, union representation, laws and societal values. Questions need to be asked such as: Who are they? Where do they come from? What is the culture? The business environment also needs to be considered, such as the economic conditions, strategic issues as to the direction of the organisation, and the management philosophy that drives the organisation. The technology and work systems also need to be taken into account to ensure that the workers can be effective.

These lead to the HRM policy choices of employee influence, human resource flow, reward systems and work systems, which were illustrated in Exhibit 1-6.

HR outcomes

These follow on from the HRM policy choices and are concerned with commitment, competence, congruence and cost-effectiveness. Managers need to ask: How can we gain commitment from our workers to enable the achievement of organisational goals? How can we ensure we have a trained and competent workforce who are able to perform productively? How can we sustain congruence; in other words, ensure that our workers are compatible with the management style and will fit in with other employees? Finally, how can managers ensure they are cost-effective while maintaining employee satisfaction?

Long-term consequences

These follow on from HRM policy and outcomes and refer to individual well-being. Will the outcomes ensure that individuals are looked after and their needs considered? Will the organisation still be able to be effective and compete or provide a service in the external market? How will the HR outcome satisfy the wider needs of society and the community as a whole?

Managing diversity is another important issue for managers today, which is why HR managers need to be aware, not only of legislation, but also how it can affect the morale of employees. Managing for diversity ensures that all employees can feel valued as part of the organisation. An example of this is illustrated in the 'Managing diversity' box.

The soft view of HRM proposed by the Harvard model recognises the importance of people and that stakeholder interests are more likely to be met if HR policy choices and outcomes ensure the long-term consequences of individual well-being, which impact on societal well-being and increase organisational effectiveness. The Harvard model suggests that organisations that encourage employee influence in decision-making are likely to be more effective provided they are consistent with organisational goals. Guest has developed this model further as is discussed below.

A pain in the neck: tied-down dress codes

In a significant judgment in January 2004 (Thompson vs Department for Work and Pensions – unreported, EAT 0254/03), the EAT (Employment Appeal Tribunal) overturned a tribunal decision that Matthew Thompson, who works for JobCentre Plus, had been treated less favourably on the grounds of his sex by being required to wear a collar and tie at work. Another 6950 other male JobCentre workers have lodged similar complaints.

All JobCentre staff were required to dress 'in a professional, business-like way'. Men were required to wear a collar and tie, women to 'dress appropriately and to a similar standard'. Thompson said this was unlawful sex discrimination.

The tribunal's decision was based on men being required to wear clothing of a particular kind, whereas women were not, and on a 'higher standard' being imposed on men than on women. The EAT said the question for the tribunal should have been whether the level of smartness required for all could be achieved for men only by requiring them to wear a collar and tie. The appeal from the Department for Work and Pensions (DWP) was allowed and the case was remitted to a differently constituted tribunal. Both sides were given permission to appeal.

Although the employer's appeal was successful, the case serves as a timely reminder to employers to avoid any allegations of unlawful discrimination by applying a sensible approach to dress codes and to be flexible in trying to accommodate individual needs. Employers are entitled to request their staff to dress in an appropriate manner and, while there can be different rules to reflect the conventions of dress for men and women, there must be an even-handed approach so the 'package' as a whole is not discriminatory.

With legislation against religious discrimination now in place, employers should have already reviewed their dress codes to ensure provisions do not constitute indirect discrimination – for example, preventing Muslim women from wearing a *hijab* (headscarf). In some cases, dress codes can be adapted to allow employees to wear the required items/adornments. Where indirect discrimination is concerned, employers may be able to objectively justify applying the dress standard – for example, when religious dress requirements conflict with health and safety or hygiene rules.

Source: Makbool Javaid, *People Management*, 12 February 2004, p. 19.
Reproduced with permission of *People Management* and Makbool Javaid.

Discussion questions
1 Do you think the JobCentre uses personnel management or HRM?
2 How would you deal with such an issue to prevent it going to a tribunal?

Development of the soft HRM model

Guest (1987) extended the Harvard model's four HR policy choices of employee influence, human resource flow, reward systems and work systems to a total of seven. These seven policy areas (illustrated in Exhibit 1-8), included: organisational job design; policy formulation and implementation, and management of change; recruitment, selection and socialisation; appraisal, training and development; manpower flows; reward systems; and communication systems. The correct policy choices will lead to HR outcomes of commitment, competence and cost-effectiveness, and result in the long-term consequences of individual well-being, organisational effectiveness and societal well-being.

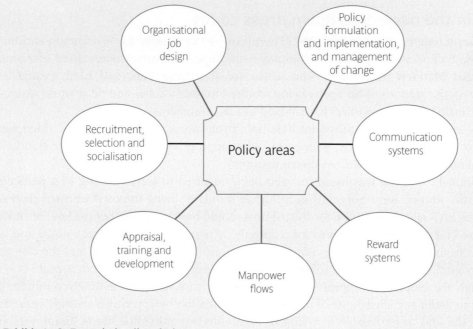

Exhibit 1–8 **Extended policy choices**
Source: Guest (1987) 'Human Resource Management and Industrial Relations', *Journal of Management Studies* 24(5), pp. 503–521. Reproduced with permission of Blackwell Publishing.

Organisational and job design

This is similar to the Harvard model's *work systems* and includes how the design of a job fits into the organisational design. It takes into account the suitability of the tasks and technology used to achieve organisational goals. The design of organisations should reflect a high commitment model to HR and demonstrate how work design can be related to organisation strategy. For example, workers would be empowered to take control of their work as a means of increasing commitment to the organisation. The organisational structures would be designed to enable this to happen, power is more likely to be dispersed and management would be less authoritarian.

Policy formulation and management of change

This means using HR policy to identify and manage change in a business environment. This extends from the Harvard model, which had not identified change as a separate policy. It is especially important in a fast-changing business environment to manage change effectively to ensure competitiveness. Apple computers managed to develop the iPod and gain competitive advantage by having policies for managing innovation and change.

Recruitment, selection and socialisation

This is covered in the Harvard model's **human resource flow**. As the name suggests, it covers aspects of how and where employees are recruited, selected and inducted into the organisation, to ensure that they will be suitable in achieving organisational outcomes. However, this is more than just having the right people in the right place at the right time: it also needs to ensure that the workforce will be involved in the achieving of organisational goals.

human resource flow
The movement of people through the organisation, from recruitment and selection to termination of employment.

Appraisal, training and development

This is not covered in the Harvard model as a separate policy. Guest (1987) argues that policies are necessary to ensure that employee performance is evaluated, which in turn ensures that the appropriate training and development take place. The aim is for a motivated, skilled, involved and contented workforce. Competing commitments, such as union involvement and work/life balance, would be identified and strategies would be developed to ensure that workers are able to be fully committed.

Manpower flows

These ensure that systems are in place to monitor employees throughout their life in the organisation. They can provide information on how staff are promoted or why they may leave the organisation. The Harvard model covers this in its *workflow* policies. It is important, as high staff turnover can indicate a problem with morale. Poor morale leads to poor productivity and low commitment to the organisation.

Reward systems

As with the Harvard approach, these cover the type of monetary and non-monetary rewards the organisation uses to maintain employee commitment. It needs to ensure that appropriate rewards are available, desirable and achievable. For example, if performance-related pay is part of the reward system then the criteria for achieving qualifying targets need to be transparent and achievable. If targets are imposed that are perceived to be out of reach, employees are less likely to feel committed to achieving them.

Communication systems

This refers to the processes the organisation has in place to ensure that efficient communication takes place and that information can be shared between employees and managers. Communication is seen as a vital part of ensuring employee participation and commitment. In a high-commitment organisation communication would be open and effective. Employees need to feel they are listened to and their opinions and concerns taken into account. Employers cannot be expected to meet the goals of the organisation if these have not been communicated to them, which is important for a high-commitment organisation. Poor communication also often leads to a disgruntled and dissatisfied workforce and poor employee relations.

Guest (1987) continued with the theme of a soft HRM model, but argued that policies and practices should be designed to achieve the organisational outcomes of strategic integration, employee commitment, workforce flexibility and quality. This is demonstrated in Exhibit 1-9.

The distinguishing feature of Guest's model is that HR policies should be designed to achieve the following outcomes.

Strategic integration

strategy
The process of envisioning and planning to create a match between organisational competencies and goals.

This ensures that the HR policies and business policies are integrated. It argues that HR strategies and planning form part of a manager's role and that the HR **strategy** should form part of the business strategy and not be treated as a separate entity. This means that managers take responsibility for the human resource and need to ensure that they have the right people in the right places to ensure that the business strategy can be achieved.

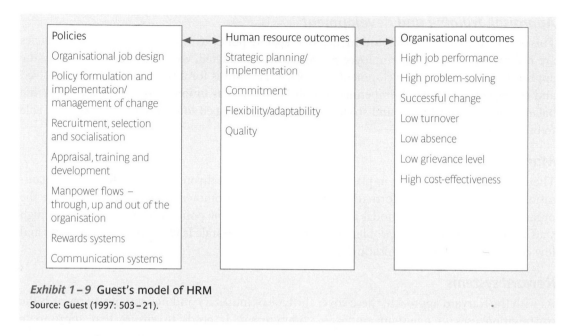

Exhibit 1–9 Guest's model of HRM
Source: Guest (1997: 503–21).

Employee commitment

This encourages employees to have 'buy in' to the organisation, which in turn encourages high levels of productivity. Commitment is gained through 'winning their hearts and minds', rather than imposing management sanctions. This means that the employment relationship should be more than an economic exchange where employees receive a financial reward for their services. It should also include a psychological relationship of shared goals and values, and a sense of belonging.

Workforce flexibility

This ensures that the workforce is adaptable and flexible; this in turn will mean that the organisation can respond to changes. Training to enable increased flexibility will be integral to the HR strategy and will be designed to encourage a motivated, skilled and involved workforce.

Quality

A high-quality workforce will ensure that the products and services provided are of the highest standards. The drive for quality will be encouraged through a high-commitment model, which also encourages effective commitment to the organisation.

Guest (1987) argued that the HR outcomes will result in organisational outcomes of high job performance, high problem-solving ability, a greater ability to adapt to change and improved cost-effectiveness. The HR outcomes will also reduce employee turnover, absence and grievances. However, Guest proposes that this will happen only if a strategic approach is taken to integrate HRM policies into business policies and they have the support of all the managers in the organisation.

Keenoy (1990) criticises Guest's model as being too simplistic and unrealistic in that it would be hard to implement in a realistic working environment. In response, Guest (1997) argues that progress in the UK in integrating HR policies has been slow and, for soft HRM to work, managers need to take into account social market attitudes and develop long-term thinking through consultation within the workforce. Many managers do not take a long-term view for their organisations and, as a consequence, many HRM policies are also short term and follow fashion rather than ensuring long-term commitment to the organisation through its people.

Both the Harvard model and Guest's model represent the soft approach to HR. The ideas they propose should create highly committed workforce managers who have concern for workers' outcomes and are able to link these to the organisation's outcomes. In conclusion, the soft approach to HR ensures that employees are competent to perform, are committed and that this is congruent with organisational goals, which in turn should result in cost-effective HRM and lead to the organisation achieving competitive advantage.

An alternative approach to HRM identified by Storey is the 'hard' approach which is discussed below.

Hard HRM

Michigan model
The model that develops hard HRM as a means of using people as an organisational resource to achieve organisational goals.

Storey (2001) identifies the 'hard' model of HRM as that proposed by Fombrun *et al.* (1984), also referred to as the **Michigan model**.

The 'hard' model of HRM emphasises that employees should be treated as a means of achieving the organisation's goals. This means that employees are a business resource and successful organisations are those that best deploy their human resources.

'Hard' HRM assumes that increasing performance will be the manager's main reason for improving HRM. Fombrun *et al.* (1984) argue that the external environment of increased competition and market instability will necessitate HRM strategies be designed to achieve the goals of the organisation.

Fombrun *et al.* (1984) also argue that organisations exist to accomplish a mission or achieve objectives, and strategic management takes into account three interconnected issues of mission and strategy, organisation structure and human resource systems. See Exhibit 1-10 to find out how these fit together.

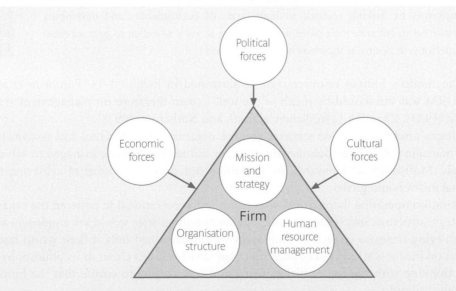

Exhibit 1–10 Strategic management and environmental pressures
Source: Fombrun *et al.* (1984: 41) © 1984 John Wiley & Sons. Reprinted by permission of John Wiley & Sons, Inc.

Mission and strategy

mission
The fundamental purpose of an organisation that defines the nature of its business and provides strategic direction unifying human and other resources.

This refers to the organisation's reason for being. The **mission** articulates the organisation's fundamental purpose and defines the nature of the business. It is there to unify human and other resources. Organisations exist to achieve a mission and managers need to think strategically about how people are managed and deployed to this end.

Organisation structure

This refers to the requirements and tasks needed to achieve the organisation's goals. These include accounting systems and communication networks, as well as the personnel required at the different levels and the tasks to be accomplished.

Human resource management systems

These establish the need for people to be recruited and developed, which in turn will enable them to achieve the organisational goals and maintain performance.

The Michigan model shown in Exhibit 1-10 recognises the external and internal forces of HRM as a triangle. Management decides the mission and strategy, it designs the organisational structure to meet the strategy and mission, and integrates and organises HRM to fit in with the structure and to fulfil the mission and strategy. The mission, strategy, organisational structure and human resource management cannot operate in isolation. They also need to respond to the external forces of politics, economics and culture. Once these have been taken into account, managers can begin to design the human resource system.

Devanna *et al.* (1984) describe the four functions of the cycle as follows:

> Performance is a function of all of the human resource components: selecting people who are best able to perform the jobs defined by the structure, appraising their performance to facilitate the equitable distribution of rewards, motivating employees by linking rewards to high levels of performance, and developing employees to enhance their current performance at work as well as to prepare them to perform in positions they may hold in the future.

The Michigan model's human resource cycle is illustrated in Exhibit 1-11. Fombrun *et al.*'s concept of HRM was influenced by much of the well-known literature on management style, such as Mayo (1933), Chandler (1962) and Galbraith and Nathanson (1978).

The Michigan model is based on strategic control, organisational structure and systems put in place for managing people. It identifies the need for human assets to be managed to achieve strategic goals. Motivation and rewards are important but only as a means of achieving the organisational mission and goals.

An organisation operating 'hard' HRM would aim to have a rational fit between the organisation's strategy, structure and HRM systems. The management style would see employees as a means of achieving business goals, and employees would be valued only if their worth had a positive effect on business strategy. The hard model of HRM is much closer in its philosophy to free market thinking with the use of hiring, firing and cost-cutting to ensure that the human resource is fully utilised.

Empirical research by Truss *et al.* (1997) into large organisations such as BT, Lloyds TSB and Hewlett-Packard has not produced evidence of organisations' systematic and consistent practice

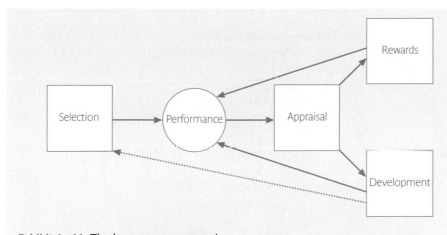

Exhibit 1–11 The human resource cycle
Source: Fombrun *et al.* (1984: 41) © 1984 John Wiley & Sons. Reprinted by permission of John Wiley & Sons, Inc.

of HRM. However, it did find that employees were strategically controlled in order for them to achieve organisational goals, which is consistent with the hard approach. Strategic human resource management is developed in more detail in Chapter 2. Whatever definition of HRM is used it needs to be explored in the context of the organisation and in the context of how the human resource is managed.

The context of human resource management

Human resource management cannot take place in isolation from the internal organisation or the external environment where the political, economic, societal, technological and international context can have an impact on how the organisation operates and how HRM is managed within that context. The **context** within which HRM takes place will impact on organisational policies and have implications for the functions of HR. One example is the Beardmore Conference Hotel, whose flexible benefits reflected the local society and culture as well as the economic environment, where managers recognised the need to attract and retain staff at that time.

context
The external and internal environment within which HR operates.

Context has many layers, which build up to impact on how the organisation does business. Exhibit 1-12 demonstrates how organisations operate within a given context.

The organisational context

To operate successfully the organisation needs to ask itself the following questions: What business are we in? How can we carry out our business to be as effective as possible and to meet our **stakeholders**' needs? The organisational context is also influenced by the external context; it interacts with its environment and this in turn impacts on HR. For this reason, HR practices need to be designed to reflect the organisational context. However, in a fast-changing working environment this is often difficult to achieve: new technologies are developed, governments and attitudes change. Policies should inform practice, but these need to be flexible enough to

stakeholders
Identifiable clusters of people who have an economic and/or social interest in the performance of an organisation.

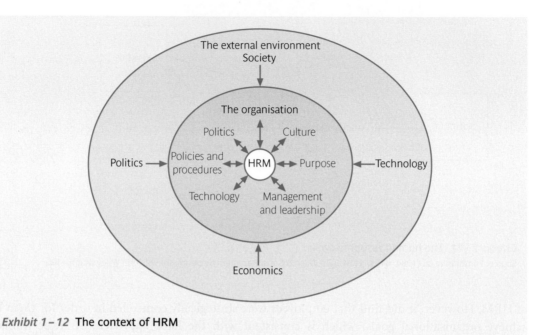

Exhibit 1 – 12 **The context of HRM**

respond to the influences of the external environment. For example, changes in working hours have meant changes in policies, which in turn have led to changes in practice, which in theory should have meant a reduction in working hours for some workers.

The external context

The external environment influences the external context of the organisation. An organisation would not be effective if it ignored the external context of politics, economics, society and technology. In London and the south-east of England, there is a shortage of key workers, such as nurses and teachers, and many workers have been employed from abroad to fill the vacancies. For organisations, this means a review of policies to ensure that new workers' needs are considered. On the practical side, new aspects of training may have to be delivered to meet language needs. To do this an organisation needs to operate as an open system, which can change to meet the needs of its external environment. Katz and Kahn (1966) identify open systems as those that interact with the environment; this makes them complex and difficult to control.

---

open system
System influenced by the external environment and inputs, making it complex and difficult to control.

The political context

The political context not only refers to the type of government in power at the time, but also whether the country is democratic or not. In the UK the political context changes depending on which political party is in power. In the past, the Conservative Government has tended to favour the employer over the employee; an example of this was the removal of the minimum wage. Traditional Labour Governments have focused on the employee and have had close links with the unions. With New Labour the lines have become somewhat blurred: although they have reintroduced the minimum wage, they have also formed close links with industry by encouraging public/private partnerships. With every change of government the HR practitioner needs to identify the impact on the organisation and the HR department.

The economic context

The economic context refers to the health of the nation. If business is booming and unemployment is low, it may be harder to find and retain staff. In times of economic decline, unemployment increases and a greater choice of labour is available to the employer. However, economic decline may also mean that your organisation has to 'downsize' and the HR department will then face the dilemma of dealing with redundancies. An organisation may also need to answer to shareholders, who expect to see a healthy return on their investment. For the HR professional this could mean developing operations overseas where labour is cheaper, such as Prudential moving its call centres to India. It may also mean outsourcing some or all of the functions of HR, as the organisation pursues its competitive advantage.

The social context

The social context refers to the culture, politics, leadership and management style that influence the organisation. The example of Enron in the opening vignette is an example of how culture, politics, leadership and management style can influence an organisation. An HR manager must be able to identify the culture within which the organisation operates. This means she or he needs to recognise and understand the values the organisation is trying to promote. However, they also need to understand the **culture** and society from which their employees are recruited. Schein (1985) offers the following as a definition of culture:

culture
The pattern of learned behaviours shared and transmitted among the members of society.

> a pattern of basic assumptions – invented, discovered or developed by a given group as it learns to cope with its problems of external adaption and internal integration – that has worked well enough to be considered valuable and therefore, to be taught to new members as the correct way to perceive, think and feel in relation to those problems.

Many industries in the past have grown up in particular regions. For example, coal mining in the north-east of England, steelworks in Wales, pottery in the Midlands, financial services in London. Even though many of these industries have now gone, society often clings to the past tradition. As new industries move in, the HR manager needs to adapt and change the culture to match the new organisation.

An HR manager should not underestimate the importance of the societal context of business as, in many instances, businesses have foundered due to a lack of understanding of the culture. Examples are EuroDisney Paris, whose lack of understanding of European culture and its failure to embrace all things American, had a serious impact on business, or Wal-Mart in Argentina, which failed to understand how the Argentines liked to shop, and could not understand why business was not booming in its bright and shiny new supermarkets.

The technological context

The technological context refers to the technology available for the organisation to use. In today's world, technology has a major impact in ensuring an organisation can maintain competitive advantage. For the HR manager it means keeping up to date with the technology available and the implications for using that technology. Thirty years ago the HR manager would have kept paper records, probably with the minimum of information. Today, the HR manager is expected to collect tax and national insurance, administer pensions and keep the information secure to comply with legislation such as the Data Protection Act. The HR manager also needs to ensure that staff are trained and developed to allow the company to embrace a fast-changing technological environment. Then there are the implications of technology replacing people or using technology to relocate sectors of the organisation such as customer services. There are also the new ways of working made possible through the use of email, videoconferencing and the Internet, where organisations can exist virtually. The HR manager needs to understand how to manage in the context of technology.

The global context

Today, many organisations operate in a global context. Globalisation is directing HR managers to develop an international strategy, which can impact on the activities of the HR department. Managers need to work across cultures and direct activities either externally from the home country or internally in the host country. This means the HR manager needs to have an understanding of international issues; each chapter of this book includes an 'International perspectives' feature to give the reader an insight into global issues.

The 'International perspective' box below gives an insight into the changing nature of HR in an international context.

The role of the HR manager

The 'International perspective' feature talks about the functions of HR and how they need to be organised to achieve a sufficiently integrated approach to management. The role of the manager is to enable individuals to achieve organisational goals and objectives. Managers get things done through people. To do this successfully, they need to know who these people are, where they are from, how they can be developed not only for personal fulfilment but also to help achieve the organisational goals, and the impact of external constraints such as legislation, competition, employee relations, and education and training. The HR manager needs to know how these come together to form the function of HRM (see Exhibit 1-13).

organisational goals
The desired outcomes of an organisation that enable managers to assess and measure performance.

The different functions of HR

Exhibit 1-13 demonstrates how the HR manager has to juggle the different functions of HR in the internal environment of the organisation while keeping an eye on what is happening in the external environment. The functions of HR will be dealt with in more detail in later chapters. Below is a brief overview of each of these functions.

Planning, resourcing and retention

Managers need to know how many staff they will need in order to achieve the organisational goals. They need to identify where the staff will be needed, how many and at what times. This is especially important in organisations where business fluctuates, such as the retail and hospitality sectors. Managers also need to be able to identify the level of skills required. The general manager of your local Tesco knows that Friday and Saturday are likely to be the busiest days. S/he can look back at the past sales history and identify peak times. The store manager will ensure that s/he has trained checkout operators available, extra customer service staff and shelf

Into Africa

A move to shared services has transformed HR in a major South African bank. Could its new service centre handle back-office work for other countries?

South Africa offers a sophisticated business community, a large labour pool, relatively low wage costs, and a language and cultural fit with potential key buyers in Europe and North America. But its fledgling offshoring industry faces tough competition from India, China and other countries where labour costs are lower, or those such as Ireland, where the technological infrastructure is more developed. Until recently, as the chief executive of one company told a local financial magazine, the country had failed to land a 'big, recognisable brand name'. But the laying of a fibre-optic cable connecting Europe to South Africa in February 2003 is making a difference.

One company that has started down the offshoring path, by taking over the back-office processing work of an American insurance company, is Absa. Absa was formed in 1991–92 out of four existing banks. With around 30,000 employees, it is South Africa's leading bank and has, for two years running, been voted the best company to work for in the country. Absa's decentralised business model gives strategic business units (SBUs) freedom to operate in a corporate governance framework, although there are enterprise-wide management processes and standardised practices. SBUs have access to a number of specialist functions, including HR.

Under a new structure for the function, launched in November 2002, account executives provide business-aligned, strategic advice to SBU management teams. If they need specialist help they turn to a 'design and development group' that has expertise in OD, employment equity, learning and development, 'employee wellness' and other specialist areas. Staff organised along similar functional lines in five centres across the country implement strategy – for example, by delivering development programmes or supporting line managers in difficult disciplinary cases.

The first port of call for both managers and employees on any people management issue is the employee self-service and manager desktop application on the bank's people management portal. If this does not provide an answer to their query they can make a telephone call or send an email to the contact centre in Johannesburg. There are currently 20 people working in this shared service centre, with 14 taking routine first-tier calls and the rest handling more complex second-tier queries. Between them they deal with 800 calls per day.

Unlike many HR service centres in the UK, which opt for people with good interpersonal skills rather than HR knowledge, Absa employs HR professionals in its contact centre. It has found that staff without an understanding of HR issues struggled. This could be because first-tier calls are more complex than those taken by HR service centres in the UK.

Another contrast with UK practice is that those taking second-tier calls are organised along functional lines. They specialise in OD, learning and development, employment relations, recruitment and reward or performance management. This arrangement seems to work well where there are questions on regulations or standard processes to answer. It works less well where the question is more philosophical or context-specific.

Employee wellness does not have its own specialist agent, as this activity has been outsourced. In the past the emphasis was on face-to-face counselling, and there has been criticism of the switch to a more impersonal telephone service. Similar criticism has been levelled at telephone helplines in the UK. But at Absa, where employees have to deal with such things as discovering they have AIDS or the trauma stemming from a bank robbery, this is clearly a matter of some seriousness.

international perspective

▶ Finally, as part of the new people management structure, a number of personnel activities have been devolved to line managers. The bank has pursued this policy quite vigorously, emphasising the move from a 'support' to a 'specialist' role for the function. Yet people management has helped managers through the change process.

The shared services approach to HR that Absa has created leads South African practice. Absa starts with a competitive edge over its South African counterparts. It can compete on economies of scale with other call centre facilities, given that it has the largest call centre in the country, with 1500 operating seats. And, with respect to HR, it is unusual in already having a shared services operation up and running.

But the bank is not getting too distracted by the thought of generating profits from selling HR services externally. It is still looking critically at ways of improving the current model. A review recently initiated by the people management executive committee, and facilitated centrally, gathered the opinions of both the function's own staff and its internal customers.

Overall, this process revealed a very positive response to the new HR model. Some of the feedback was inevitably backward looking and many employees thought that communication could have been better. More pertinent perhaps is the view that there was too much emphasis on structure and not enough on the skills in the HR community necessary to operate it.

The skills needs of both generalist and specialist people management staff in their new roles clearly need to be examined. This links to the question of career paths. The switch to a shared services environment disturbs traditional development routes and they need to be reinstated in a new form.

There is plenty to do to improve Absa's existing HR model. But with the foundations of a world-class operation now in place, the bank would be in strong position to jump on the off-shoring bandwagon if it really does arrive in South Africa.

Source: Peter Reilly, *People Management*, 15 January 2004, p. 36.
Reproduced with permission of *People Management* and Peter Reilly.

Discussion questions

1 What is your view of companies that outsource their HR practices?

2 As an international HR manager do you see any problems in offshore HR operations?

---

planning
The method used to achieve organisational goals.

resourcing
The pool of resources available for the manager to use to fulfil the plan and achieve objectives.

packers to replace items. This is part of the **planning** and **resourcing** process. The retention of staff is also important, as recruiting staff is an expensive and time-consuming process. A manager needs to ensure that staff are happy in their work as not only will they be more productive, they will also be more likely to remain with the organisation.

Recruitment and selection

When the need for people has been ascertained, the next task is to find them, and ensure that the right people are selected and recruited for the organisation. If the wrong people are recruited then there could be difficulties in achieving organisational goals and business could suffer. Employees may be over-qualified for jobs and leave, or under-qualified and not be able to perform adequately. This could have serious implications for the organisation. Think of the last

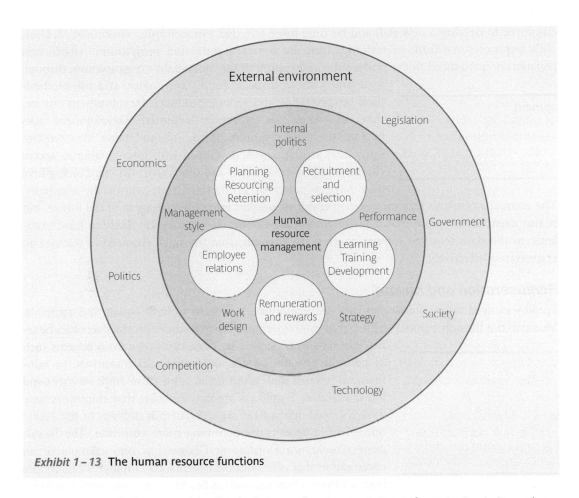

Exhibit 1–13 The human resource functions

time you took a flight in an aircraft, whether on a low-cost carrier such as easyJet or Ryanair, or on one of the larger airlines such as British Airways, the company representatives you came in contact with all projected a company image. The **recruitment** and **selection** process would ensure that only those candidates compatible with company goals would be recruited. The methods used could be IQ tests or psychometric tests, or as is often the case with airlines, guidelines for acceptable weight and height. If the wrong people had been recruited there could be serious implications for passenger safety and ultimately company reputation. Recruitment and selection will be dealt with in more detail in Chapters 4 and 5.

recruitment
The procedure used to attract staff to an organisation.

selection
The methods used to identify suitable staff who will match the requirements of the organisation.

Training and development

In order to get the best from employees they need to be trained. **Training** is done to fill any gap between the skills and knowledge they have at present and the skills and knowledge the organisation wants them to have in order to fulfil set goals. It ensures that employees are able to perform to the required standard. Whenever someone new is employed they need to be trained; this may take the form of an induction programme to make the new employee feel welcome and orientate them to the culture and working methods of the organisation, or it may be to enable the

training
The methods used to bridge the gap between where the employee is now to where the employer wants them to be.

employee to develop a new skill and become more effective. For example, working at McDonald's requires some form of training from the company induction programme, where new recruits are introduced to the philosophy and culture of the McDonald's organisation, through to learning about hygiene, health and safety, and the methods used for preparing and serving products. **Development** ensures that employees can fulfil their potential. Development goes beyond the skills required for the job and takes into account individual aspirations. A developed workforce is able to accept change and is more fulfilled and motivated. An engineering firm may have a policy of promoting from within the company.

development
Continuous learning to enable employees to fulfil themselves in their careers, which in turn increases commitment and motivation.

The company needs to recognise which employees aspire to be the managers of the future, but it also needs to recognise that if the engineers are not developed they are likely to have problems, as the skills required for engineering are different from the skills required to manage an organisation effectively.

Remuneration and reward

Employees need to be paid so that they are able to live. **Pay** needs to be adequate and equitable. Money is not the only **reward** and may not motivate employees to be more productive; other benefits also need to be looked at. These can range from benefits such as pensions, healthcare and other financial incentives, to non-financial rewards such as those that come from empowerment and job satisfaction. Employers are now realising that employees have different needs and a fixed reward system is unlikely to suit everyone. Flexible benefits are becoming more common. The Beardmore Conference Hotel, near Glasgow, is one example of an organisation that offers flexible benefits. Its employees can choose from a range of benefits, such as flexible hours, childcare vouchers,

pay
The monetary reward for providing a service.

reward
A monetary or non-monetary reward used as an inducement to increase performance or gain commitment.

pensions or driving lessons. With flexible benefits, an employee who needs childcare could choose childcare vouchers as part of their reward package, while older workers may prefer a company pension. The ability for employees to be able to choose their rewards means that they feel valued as individuals, which in turn means that they are more likely to stay with the organisation. Remuneration and reward are dealt with in more detail in Chapter 6.

Employee relations

Healthy relations need to be maintained with employees to ensure a productive workforce. In the event of disputes and conflict arising, managers need to be able to manage the situation successfully in order to ensure win–win outcomes. They need to be able to communicate and negotiate with unions and other employee representatives to ensure that a stable working environment is maintained. In 2003 British Airways check-in staff at Heathrow staged a walkout over new working practices. The result was hundreds of flights cancelled, summer holidays ruined and chaos at Heathrow, one of the world's busiest airports. Representatives from the union and BA then conducted angry exchanges in front of the media. Could it have been avoided?

employee relations
The relationship an employer builds with its employees to encourage a satisfactory working environment.

The role of effective **employee relations** will be dealt with in Chapter 9.

The functions of human resource management cannot be carried out in isolation from the wider context of the organisation, or the society in which the organisation operates. The external environment can impact on how the functions are designed and implemented. This is why an HR manager needs to understand developments and changes in economics, politics, government, legislation, technology, external competition and society, and be able to manage change to respond to them effectively. An effective HR manager needs to able to respond to current issues and new developments. Some of these are discussed in Chapter 13. The internal environment also needs to respond to external influences. To do this it may develop a more strategic approach to HRM, which is discussed in Chapter 2.

Strategy can filter through the organisation, through the managing and development of performance, discussed in Chapter 9, and by increasing employee participation and empowerment, discussed in Chapter 10.

An HR manager also needs to consider issues of work and job design in response to the demands of society and the legal implications of health and safety, stress and employee welfare, discussed in Chapter 11. Society also demands fair treatment, which means the HR manager not only has to be familiar with equal opportunities to comply with the law but also must know how s/he can value diversity to ensure employees are valued, as discussed in Chapter 12.

Human resource managers have a complex role in the organisation and, while people management is the role of all managers, it is the role of the HR specialist to develop a holistic and systematic approach to the management of people to enable the organisation to achieve its goals.

Summary

- An HR manager needs to recognise that human resource management is in a constant state of change and they need also to recognise the importance of their role as a management professional.
- HR management has progressed from an ad hoc role to the professional body of the CIPD. It can trace its routes from the paternalistic principles of the nineteenth century, through to the era of scientific management and human relations, to its current state.
- The terms personnel management and HRM are part of the debate that informs the role of the HR manager. HRM is viewed as a means of moving people along to achieve organisational goals through staffing, performance, change management and administrative objectives. Personnel management has often been seen as a bridge between employer and employee.
- 'Hard' HRM, characterised by the Michigan model, is seen as viewing people as a resource needed to achieve organisational goals.
- 'Soft' HRM, characterised by the Harvard model, is seen as a method of developing strategies to encourage employee commitment through employee influence, human resource flow, reward and work systems.
- The functions of HR include: planning and resourcing; recruitment and selection; training and development; pay and reward; employee relations. These enable the HR manager to achieve organisational goals.
- Understanding the HR context in relation to the organisational and external context is important for an effective HR manager. The organisational context refers to the structures, processes, culture and systems in the organisation, while the external environment refers to the external politics, economics, technology and society that influence the organisation and, in turn, impact on the HR professional.

Personal development

1 **Understand how HR is divided into different functions.** If you work for an organisation, look at its functions. When you applied for the job did you fill in an application form? How were you interviewed? Did you know what the selection criteria were? How are you motivated? Is it through pay or are there other rewards on offer? What type of training have you been offered? Could you develop a career with this organisation? This should give you an idea of how the functions of HR are carried out.

2 **Identify how history has contributed to the current state of HR.** A knowledge of historical developments can help us to understand the present. Do you know any organisations or managers that view people as machines required to perform to their maximum capacity? Can you see problems in the operation of this type of organisation?

3 **Recognise the implications of the HR vs personnel debate.** Identify a company with which you are familiar, either somewhere you work or have contact with. Does it have an HR department or a personnel department? Can you identify how the departments view themselves? Look for clues such as policies, practices, control and rewards. Do they give an indication of the importance of people management?

4 **Determine the impact of the 'hard' and 'soft' approaches to HR.** Which model would you use as a manager? Which would be more effective for organisational performance and competitive advantage? Can you identify any organisations that follow either the 'hard' or 'soft' approach of HR? Is it effective?

5 **Recognise the importance of the context of HR.** Identify and describe the external environment that surrounds your organisation. How does this affect the internal organisation? What is the role of HR in both the internal and external context? Are there specific recruitment policies? Are there diversity issues that need to be addressed? Is there high labour turnover? Is the HR department effective in managing in context?

❓ Discussion questions

1 What are the functions of human resource management?

2 Explain what the term 'personnel management' means.

3 Why are staffing, performance, change management and administration objectives important to HRM?

4 How does Storey define the elements that differentiate HRM from personnel management?

5 What does the term 'hard' HRM mean?

6 Guest (1987) argues that 'policies and practices should be designed to achieve organisational integration, employee commitment and workforce flexibility'. How can the HR manager implement policies and practices to achieve the above aims?

7 Critically analyse the Harvard model of HR. What implications does it have for the HR manager?

8 The Michigan model of HRM identifies the need for human assets to be managed to achieve strategic goals. What are the implications for an HR manager?

9 Why is it important for an HR manager to understand the context in which s/he operates?

10 What is the impact of technology on the practices of an HR manager in an organisation?

🔑 Key concepts

vision, *p. 5*	stakeholders, *p. 25*
paternalist, *p. 6*	open system, *p. 26*
scientific management, *p. 7*	culture, *p. 27*
human relations, *p. 8*	organisational goals, *p. 28*
workforce centred, *p. 12*	planning, *p. 30*
hard HRM, *p. 14*	resourcing, *p. 30*
soft HRM, *p. 14*	recruitment, *p. 31*
Harvard model, *p. 16*	selection, *p. 31*
human resource flow, *p. 20*	training, *p. 31*
strategy, *p. 21*	development, *p. 32*
Michigan model, *p. 23*	pay, *p. 32*
mission, *p. 24*	reward, *p. 32*
context, *p. 25*	employee relations, *p. 32*

Individual task

Purpose To develop an approach to strategic thinking.

Time 40 minutes

Procedure Many employers require HR professionals to think strategically. Study the job advertisement below for an assistant HR manager. Draft an application in which you persuade the employer of your strategic capabilities. You may also want to include your CV.

Alternatively, if you are just starting out in the HR field, identify the skills you would need to develop to be in a position to apply for such a job and write down the strategies needed in order to develop the identified skills.

Walco Supermarkets plc
Assistant Human Resource Manager

Salary £25K + benefits

As a member of Walco's management group, you will assist the HR manager in identifying strategic business issues and will ensure that implementation of appropriate HR solutions results in enhanced operational capability and an increase in customer focus. The role requires an individual who is capable of assisting in the pioneering of leading-edge approaches to people development and driving significant culture change.

The successful applicant will have a good honours degree in Human Resource Management or a related field and be a member of the CIPD with a view to attaining graduate status and will have one year's experience in a strategic HR/OD role. You will be resilient and flexible in handling competing priorities and will have some experience of managing change.

To apply, visit 'job vacancies' at our website: www.walco.co.uk

Walco is an equal opportunities employer

Team task

Purpose To gain an understanding of how HR professionals develop strategic thinking.

Time 40 minutes

Procedure You are part of an HR team for Walco plc, a large chain of supermarkets. Your director of HR has just come back from an MBA management weekend and has decided that the HR team needs to be more strategic. The team has decided to get together and link the functions of HR to strategy. The problem is that the organisational strategy is unclear. You looked at the mission statement on the company's website and it says 'Walco – leading on price, leading on quality'. But it says very little about how it proposes to do this, although it does mention that Walco's people are a valuable asset.

Each one of the team members is responsible for a different function, such as planning, resourcing, recruitment, selection, training, development, pay, reward and employee relations.

- Decide who will be responsible for which areas.
- Choose a group member to chair the meeting.
- Outline the strategies that could be developed for each of the functions.

Case study: **Police – marching to a modern beat; massive investment and a clear framework will increase the performance of all police forces**

'The police service is going through a period of radical change,' says Jane Stichbury, chair of the Association of Chief Police Officers for the Personnel Management Business Area. 'Reform is improving and enhancing the professionalism of the service and there are now better opportunities for staff than ever before.'

Indeed, the first National Policing Plan for England and Wales was published by the Home Secretary last year. This three-year plan sets out a clear framework for raising the performance of all forces, delivering improved police operation and greater public reassurance.

Coupled with an investment increase of £1.8bn over the last three years into the service, conditions for employees have greatly improved. The pay system is being modernised to improve rewards for the most difficult and demanding front-line posts, as well as increasing basic pay to boost recruitment and retention. Following extensive training, a new recruit can now expect a starting salary of £26,000 in London. A recent allocation of £20m has also been provided specifically to improve police stations, modernise officers' working surroundings and update technology.

'We're also delivering an environment now that is far more supportive, where there is strong leadership and a range of new policies that offer people flexibility,' says Stichbury. Indeed, mentoring programmes, part-time working and job sharing are increasingly common options in many forces. Support networks and welfare provisions, such as counselling, have also been extended.

In a climate where public confidence in pensions is low, police staff can also be assured of a secure retirement. 'You can pull your police pension after 30 years, regardless of how old you were when you joined,' says Bob Carr, head of recruitment for the Metropolitan Police Service, who will be eligible for retirement at just 49. 'The vast majority of people go on to serve their full term. So you have security of tenure when you're in the job and when you've finished.'

Police officers frequently cite the satisfaction and challenge of the varied workload as the most rewarding aspects of their jobs. Indeed, police in Britain deal with about six million 999 emergency calls a year and have cut overall crime by 22 per cent in the last five years. They are, however, faced with more and more complicated crimes, often high profile and in the public eye.

'When a police officer comes to work they have no idea what they are going to be faced with over the next eight hours,' says Jan Berry, chair of the Police Federation of England and Wales and a serving police officer with 28 years' experience. 'It can be tough as you are dealing with life and death situations, but this is part of the attraction, the challenge of being able to turn your hand and deal with a small child who is lost one second to a raging fire or shootout the next.'

There are now a record number of police officers employed by the 43 forces across England and Wales, with 5400 more officers than two years ago. However, the good news is that recruitment is still highly active. Indeed, numbers are set to increase, with a government target of 132,500 police officers by 2004. In addition, a further 4000 Community Support Officers are being recruited by forces who have limited powers to deal with low-level crime and disorder. Measures are also being introduced to increase the numbers and effectiveness of Special Constables.

When joining the police service, whether as a school leaver, a graduate or later in life as a second career, the same basic training programme will apply, lasting for 15 weeks at a National

Police Training Centre or 18 weeks within the Metropolitan Police Service. This is followed by a two-year probationary period as a patrolling Police Constable in a borough, dealing with local events such as road accidents, public order and crime incidents. Once the two years is up, promotion and specialism into one of the many areas, such as Firearms, Drugs Squad, Criminal Investigation Department (CID), Traffic Patrol or Underwater Search Teams, is a popular route.

For those with the potential to rise quickly to Inspector level or higher, there is the choice of applying for the new High Potential Development Scheme (HPD), which if successful will offer a fast-track route into some of the most challenging managerial jobs. The scheme, although tough, gives a thorough grounding in police work, with an emphasis on substantial responsibility early on. There is no age limit, and some recent successful candidates have been in their late thirties.

Competition for joining the police service is fierce, with more than 35,000 people in England and Wales applying every year. Of these, only about 5000 are successful.

Unlike many jobs, no formal qualifications are required, although an educational standard is required to pass the initial recruitment tests. Recruiters will be looking for candidates who show self-confidence, good levels of fitness and the ability to think on their feet. 'Personal qualities are more important than qualifications,' says Bob Carr. 'You need to be resourceful, determined and flexible. It's not a nine-to-five job, so someone who is willing to go out of their way to make a difference is likely to be successful.'

Source: Jacqueline Freeman, *The Independent*, 30 January 2003, p. 1.
Reproduced with permission of Independent Newspapers.

Discussion questions

1 If you were responsible for HR in a local police force, how would you organise the HR function?

2 What role would the HR manager have in managing change in the police force?

3 How important do you think job satisfaction is in maintaining morale?

4 How would you devise a policy to attract new recruits to a police force?

WWW exercise

Choose a company that you would be interested in working for in the future. Go to the recruitment section of its website.

1 What information is available?

2 Are you able to make an informed choice about your future career prospects?

3 Does the website give an indication of how the company views the HR function?

4 Why are you interested in working for this company?

Specific web exercise

The Chartered Institute of Personnel and Development (CIPD) is the professional body that represents HR professionals in the UK. Visit its website at: www.cipd.co.uk

1 How does the CIPD support the HR professional?

2 How can you use the CIPD to gain a better understanding of the HR profession?

LEARNING CHECKLIST

Before moving on to the next chapter, check that you are able to:

☑ outline the development of HRM

☑ understand the differences between HRM and personnel management

☑ evaluate 'hard' and 'soft' approaches to HRM

☑ understand the role of strategic HRM

☑ understand how diversity underpins HR practice

☑ understand the international forces that drive HRM.

Further reading

Hendry, C. (1994) 'The Single European Market and the HRM response', in P.S. Kirkbride (ed.) *Human Resource Management: Perspectives for the 1990s*. London: Routledge.

Hendry, C. and Pettigrew, A. (1990) 'Human resource management: an agenda for the 1990s', *International Journal of Human Resource Management* 1(1), pp. 17–43.

Legge, K. (1995), *HRM: Rhetorics and Realities*. Basingstoke: Macmillan Business.

Rothwell, W.J., Prescott, R.K. and Taylor, M.W. (1998) *The Strategic Human Resource Leader: How to Prepare your Organisation for the Six Key Trends Shaping the Future*. Palo Alto, CA: Davies-Black Publications, p. 5.

References

Beer, M., Spector, B., Lawrence, P.R., Quinn Mills, D. and Walton, R.E. (1984) *Managing Human Assets*. New York, NY: The Free Press.

Benyon, H. (1973) *Working for Ford*. Harmondsworth: Penguin.

Cannel, M. (2004) *Personnel Management: A Short History*. London: CIPD.

Chandler, A.D. (1962) *Strategy and Structure: Chapters in the History of American Industrial Enterprise*. Cambridge, MA: MIT Press.

Devanna, M.A., Fombrun, C.J. and Tichy, N.M. (1984) 'A framework for strategic human resource management', in C.J. Fombrun, N.M. Tichy and M.A. Devanna (eds) *Strategic Human Resource Management*. New York, NY: John Wiley & Sons.

Evans, A. (2003) *The History of the CIPD*. London: CIPD.

Fombrun, C.J., Tichy, N.M. and Devanna, M.A. (1984) *Strategic Human Resource Management*. New York, NY: John Wiley & Sons.

Galbraith, J.R. and Nathanson, D. (1978) *Strategy formulation: analytical concepts*. St Paul, MN: West Publishing Company.

Guest, D.E. (1987) 'Human resource management and industrial relations', *Journal of Management Studies* 24(5), pp. 503–521.

Guest, D.E. (1997) 'Human resource management and performance: a review and research agenda', *International Journal of Human Resource Management* 8(3), June, pp. 263–276.

Hunt, J. (1999) 'The shifting focus of the personnel function', *Personal Management* 16(2), February, pp. 14–19.

Katz, D. and Kahn, R.L. (1966) *The Social Psychology of Organizations*. New York, NY: Wiley.

Keenoy, T. (1990) 'HRM: Rhetoric, Reality and Contradiction', *International Journal of Human Resource Management* 1(3), pp. 363–384.

Mayo, E. (1933) *The Human Problems of an Industrial Civilization*. New York, NY: Macmillan.

Rose, M. (1975) *Industrial Behaviour: Theoretical Development Since Taylor*. Harmondsworth: Penguin.

Schein, E. (1985) *Organization Culture and Leadership*. San Francisco, CA: Jossey-Bass.

Storey, J. (1989) *New Perspectives on Human Resource Management*. London: Routledge.

Storey, J. (1992) *Developments in the Management of Human Resources: An Analytical Review*. Cambridge, MA: Blackwell.

Storey, J. (2001) *Human Resource Management: A Critical Text* (2nd edn). London: Thomson Learning.

Truss, C., Gratton, L., Hope-Hailey, V. and McGovern, P. (1997) 'Soft and hard models of human resource management: a reappraisal', *Journal of Management Studies* 34(1), p. 53.

Walton, R.E. (1985) *Human Resource Management: Trends and Challenges*. Harvard Business School Press.

Human resource planning and resourcing

LEARNING OUTCOMES

After studying this chapter, you should be able to:

- ☑ **identify** how to align an organisation's strategic direction with HR planning

- ☑ **identify** aspects that affect the demand and supply of labour

- ☑ **identify** demographic changes and the response of HR planners

- ☑ **understand** the role of forecasting as part of the HR planning process and its response to change.

The opening vignette demonstrates what happens when organisations have not thought about human resource planning and how one company attempted to redress the issues.

Bringing out the Branson

Virgin Atlantic has emerged from the airline industry's post-9/11 turbulence in reasonable shape. But is the business fit enough to fly if its charismatic founder should depart?

Virgin Atlantic celebrated its twentieth birthday on 22 June 2004. Set up by Sir Richard Branson in 1984, the company started out with one aircraft flying one route. Many people expected the venture to fail, but by the end of the decade it had carried a million passengers.

▶

Over the years Virgin Atlantic continued to grow organically, cherry-picking routes, taking risks and snapping at its rivals' heels. Provocative advertising and the considerable PR clout provided by Branson helped to fuel this growth. But the airline had no cohesive long-term strategy, according to Moira Nangle, director of organisational development.

Branson recently announced plans to double the size of Virgin Atlantic over the coming five years as part of its continued effort to surpass BA. The company will acquire 26 new aircraft and has started recruiting 1400 people, with up to another 5000 jobs expected to be created by the end of 2010.

This expansion marks the beginning of Virgin Atlantic's next phase, which Nangle describes as 'growing up with style'. The focus, she explains, has switched from 'the big sexy projects' towards getting the day-to-day basics right, including speed of check-in, accuracy of baggage delivery and punctuality of service.

The new emphasis on these basics means that staff need to be better trained and more accountable for delivering services to the customers. This has big implications for HR processes such as performance management, development planning and recruitment.

'After 9/11,' she says, '20 per cent of our market dropped away, which meant we would have to lose 25 per cent of our staff. We didn't even have a redundancy policy. For the first time we had to lay people off, which sent out a completely different message. In the past they had always been "loved up".'

Despite its lack of experience in this area, Nangle says that the company handled the redundancies pretty well – a claim backed up by the fact that it has recently been able to re-hire some of the people who left.

The airline was honest and moved swiftly, according to Nangle. On the first Monday after 11 September 2001, Branson broke the news to employees that many of them would have to leave. 'He also declared that he would create "a mission to bring our friends back". You could have heard a pin drop,' she recalls. 'It brought a real lump to many people's throats.'

Within a month people had started leaving, after extensive discussions between the board and the staff committees that contributed to the selection criteria, package details and union consultations.

'We trained all our managers and staff representatives in how to break bad news and deal with the reactions,' says Nangle. 'We held a daily "war cabinet". I used our recruitment and training teams to give outplacement counselling. We called the programme "Changing Places" and set it up like a job club, with access to phones, the Internet, newspapers, trade journals and so on. We also brought other employers in to talk about job opportunities. People were trained in CV writing, interview skills and job search techniques.'

Although they did things 'intuitively' and 'with heart', Nangle thinks with hindsight they would have handled the redundancy programme differently.

Because those who left found other jobs fairly easily, some remaining employees wondered whether they should have volunteered for redundancy. They were having to do bigger or different jobs with little support or training, because many of the training functions had closed. 'People also needed space and help to talk about the difficulties, share their "war" stories and plan how to get through their new experiences. We hadn't thought that through as well as we could have,' Nangle admits.

Virgin Atlantic countered this problem by encouraging dialogue about what had happened, communicating a new sense of purpose and building a vision of the future. Management consultant Kjell Nordström was brought in to reinforce the importance of the company's new focus on the day-to-day business, while stressing that people rather than products or services – which can quickly be replicated – are the one remaining source of competitive advantage.

The company is also testing some new management development concepts. These include training managers to give high-quality developmental feedback. It is also piloting new learning and personal development programmes and considering how to make these more widely accessible.

The airline is also refining its recruitment practices. Several months ago the business was experiencing high staff turnover among cabin crews. To determine the reasons, it interviewed groups of new recruits before they joined, the day they joined, at the end of their training, at the end of their first flight, and then after three months and six months in the job.

'The feedback we got suggested that we talked up the job a bit, and people were surprised that it was actually less glamorous and much harder work than they expected,' Nangle says. 'We are now trying to be more realistic in our advertising and job specs, focusing more on the need for emotional resilience, for example. What's more, the kind of people who tend to be attracted to us are self-starters. The problem is that they tend not to finish things, and you need a balance. We are now more rigorous in terms of selecting people with experience in the service sector.'

Branson is still the key inspiration behind the business, but what would happen if he were to leave? There is a growing recognition in business of the value of low-profile leaders such as Tesco's Sir Terry Leahy, and there is also a realisation that success is about teamwork rather than the exploits of one heroic, transformational leader with bags of charisma and style.

Nangle argues that Branson's dominance of the business motivates, rather than demotivates, the top team, but admits: 'It can be difficult when someone writes to Richard about a problem and their manager hadn't realised it was an issue.'

There will clearly come a point when Virgin Atlantic needs to cut the apron strings from Branson and fly off on its own into the big wide world. The separation may prove painful for both sides, as it was when Anita Roddick loosened her ties with Body Shop. Branson currently owns 51 per cent of the business, while Singapore Airlines owns 49 per cent, but if he decides to take the airline public again, that would be an obvious time to pull back and let the professional managers take over.

Then Virgin Atlantic really will have grown up.

> Source: Jane Simms, *People Management*, 14 October 2004, p. 36.
> Reproduced with permission of *People Management* and Jane Simms.

Discussion questions

1 How could Virgin Atlantic have used planning to manage its redundancies?

2 Virgin Atlantic has recognised the need for succession planning. How could it implement this?

The human resource planning process

When an organisation has decided on a course of strategic action, it is the role of the HR department to find and develop its people to enable the strategies to be achieved. This does not happen in isolation – it needs to take into account factors in the external environment such as availability of labour, skills, education and employment costs. It also needs to look at the internal environment inside the organisation. Where does it need the labour? What skills do staff need? What training and development is important for the organisation?

To do this an organisation needs to forecast. This means it needs to look ahead to establish its future human resource needs. As can be seen in the opening vignette, Virgin not only had to plan for expansion but it also needed to put a plan in place in case Richard Branson should leave the organisation. This has meant that the HR manager for Virgin needed to have a plan of where to recruit labour, but also a plan for succession and the development of talent.

A major part of a manager's job is to plan. The question is what type of planning should an HR manager be doing and how can this be linked back to the strategic plan of the organisation. Exhibit 2-1 gives an example of the type of planning an HR manager should do. How this can be achieved will be discussed in the following chapters. However, HR managers need to be aware that, whatever part of the HR function they are concerned with, plans need to be formulated and implemented.

Human resource planning

Macaleer and Shannon (2003) suggest that the human resource planning process is intended to help guide the organisation to plan in any of the following general areas that involve staffing:

- growth and disengagement
- replacement and re-staffing
- job rotation and cross-functional training
- the design, implementation and management of supporting programmes such as benefits and compensation.

One way of planning for staffing needs is through the standard planning approach.

Standard planning

This is the most common approach and is used by HR managers to assess who their employees are and what they are doing. This information is used to help predict staffing levels for the following year. However, according to Macaleer and Shannon (2003), the disadvantages of this approach are as follows.

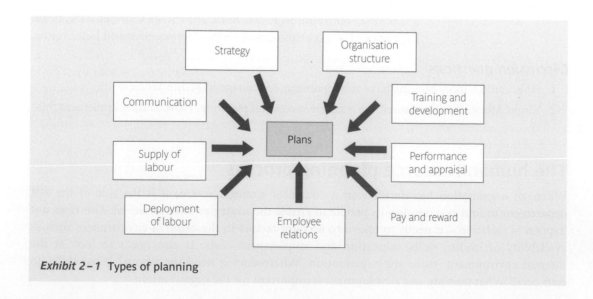

Exhibit 2 – 1 **Types of planning**

- It implies that all existing business activities will be continued and are as important as new strategies and plans.

- It assumes that the current business activities are the foundation for reaching the organisation's business goals and are being performed effectively.

- It can unnecessarily increase staff levels and not consider the specific competencies that are needed to achieve the strategic objectives.

- It will not uncover, within the organisation, those who continue to want to increase the level of employees to preserve power and compensation without looking at productivity.

- It often tends to institutionalise the existing planning process and systems beyond their usefulness.

- It short cuts important communications from line and staff managers on their goals and support requirements.

- It supports an outdated concept, tying compensation and recognition programmes to rewarding those with the largest staffs.

- It supports the non-productive concept that one must have sufficient staff to respond immediately to any request, regardless of its importance.

This means that HR managers need to understand the link between productivity and the human resource and how productivity measures can be used to bring about, improve and maintain competitive advantage. Output per head is no longer suitable as a basic measure, as was once prescribed by Taylor in his approach to scientific management (see Chapter 1). This is especially so with the move to knowledge workers. A more acceptable measure would be output per unit of staff cost.

One of the most vital sources of information is the manpower planning process itself.

Information about the past and present can help guide the manpower planning process for the future. HR managers need to understand manpower growth, promotion flows and labour turnover, and how they form the basis of plans.

Monitoring data against the plan can help clarify what is happening and why. If HR managers want a strategic place in the organisation then, at the very minimum, they need to be armed with an understanding of these data.

The process of planning is a continuous one and feeds from one cycle to the next. Changing demographics can have an impact here. For example, a reduction in the number of school leavers can have a dramatic impact on the recruitment of trainees for certain jobs. This may mean that the plans have to be designed to look for alternative sources, such as immigrant labour, or encourage other sectors of the population by changing the nature of work, such as providing term-time employment for single parents, or flexible working arrangements.

HR managers need to understand the business and technological goals and line managers need to understand the constraints of manpower.

To be able to plan effectively HR managers need to understand the business they are in and the relevance of human resource management to it. Once this is understood then they will have a chance to contribute fully to the business plan. HR managers also need to work co-operatively with colleagues from other departments and understand data from areas such as marketing and finance. To do this effectively they need to take a more strategic approach.

Strategic human resource planning

Planning should be linked to the strategic aims of the business. This means that the planning and resourcing strategies need to support those strategies of the organisation that lead to competitive advantage. For the human resource planner this means making decisions about resource allocation, and the priorities and action steps necessary to meet the strategic goals of the organisation. One criticism of HR managers, by Hammonds (2006), is that they are neither strategic nor leaders and they prefer to pursue efficiency in lieu of value. This needs to change if HR managers want to become strategic partners with a 'seat at the top table'.

To ensure effective links to strategy, an organisation should review the need for having the following plans:

- job or role competency planning
- manpower planning
- training and development planning
- career development planning and process
- planning for and managing terminations, downsizing and attrition.

An example of strategic planning can be found at the Britannia Building Society. At the turn of the new millennium, it had no people strategies and dealt with people problems as they arose. The appointment of a new director, Karen Moir, put people firmly on the agenda. She found that HR was incidental rather than critical and, for the organisation to move forward, it needed to be more proactive.

Moir believed that people policies should not be separated from other aspects of business strategy and that commitment should come from the top. The strategy at Britannia was to 'maintain and improve its place in the market'. To move forward, Britannia needed to develop its performance management, reward and communication strategies as this would link into the change in values it required from its employees, to meet the organisational goals. To move the strategy forward, it introduced measurements for every aspect of the business, which included employee satisfaction, customer satisfaction, individual performance and business perform-ance. The results have been that employees understand the organisational values and are able to commit to them.

organisational values
The principles that guide an organisation's behaviour.

The example of Britannia demonstrates the importance of having an HR strategy and how linking it back to business can improve performance.

As discussed earlier, the disadvantages of the standard planning approach have led HR managers to develop a strategy-based human resources planning process, which can meet the business objectives of the organisation and is therefore seen as a more effective approach. This approach is based on past analysis but also focuses on the future staffing needs that will help to achieve the strategic aims of the organisation.

Macaleer and Shannon (2003) suggest that strategic planning can be achieved by:

- understanding the specific business priorities by department and business unit, based on the overall strategic objectives
- understanding the internal and external factors that may affect the achievement of the objectives that will ultimately impact the programmes and services to be provided
- understanding who has the responsibility and accountability for achieving each of the objectives, where they are shared, and who is to absorb the associated costs (this will identify who your internal customers will be and what they expect)

- determining if alternatives for the achievement of each business objective have been developed and what impact this will have on services
- translating these business objectives into specific human resource programmes and services
- determining the trade-offs in terms of resources needed and timing
- analysing the impact if each business objective is not achieved in terms of HR services
- testing each priority, starting with the lowest one in terms of the return versus the expenditure of time and money
- determining where efficiencies can be achieved
- determining the staffing requirements to meet the business objectives, including level of staffing required and timing; types of employee and specific competencies required; current complement versus your zero-based staffing requirements; where surpluses and gaps exist.

If human resources managers want to be strategic partners, they will need to be involved in the business planning process, and must thoroughly understand the plans and be able to translate them into actions. This will ensure that the organisation has the right people with the right strengths in the right roles at the right time. HR should also challenge the business assumptions and plans and bring to the business table innovative ideas for how the organisation can compete in the future. An HR department must take a leadership role, linking the business objectives to the required culture and staffing of the organisation.

To be able to achieve strategic partnership, the HR department must receive answers to the following questions.

- What does success look like in our organisation and how can we identify and measure it?
- What is considered a high-performing team in our company?
- Have we developed a business plan in which everyone understands their respective roles in achieving the results and buys into it?
- What do we need to deliver for the company to achieve its strategic objectives? (Consider the areas of culture, recruitment, compensation, benefits, training and organisational development, and outside competition. Consider the audiences of senior management, middle management, employees and regulatory agencies.)
- What specific actions do we need to take in each area?
- What resources will be required? Are they available?
- What specific competencies are required to deliver these results? Are they currently available? How can they be developed?
- Are we competing effectively for knowledge-based talent?
- What are the competency strengths of our competitors and how can we better compete against those strengths?
- How will we address the identified competency gaps in the organisation?
- To what level should we have a developed succession plan?
- How well do the team members understand the strategy and what it means to them? What can we do to enhance their understanding?
- What performance objectives do we need to establish to drive results on a group level as well as an individual level?

- How will we measure those results and how often?
- What external benchmarking will we use to measure our results against those of other firms?
- How will we reward employees for achieving those results?
- How will we communicate our progress and success?

Human resource management should be a partnership between both line and staff managers. To create a high-performance work environment, human resources professionals need to evolve into a strategic role and become a business partner.

Types of organisational plan

As can be seen from Exhibit 2-2, organisations should have several different types of plan. The strategic plan links to the tactical plan, which links to the operational plan. There should also be a contingency plan in case of unexpected events; this can direct any changes necessary to achieve the preceding plans.

Strategic plans

As discussed earlier, these are developed to achieve strategic goals, and need to be linked with the overall strategy of the organisation. The strategic plan will outline the resource allocations, priorities and action steps necessary to meet the strategic goals. The board of directors and top management usually establish **strategic plans**. These tend to be long term and to focus on the strategic direction of the organisation. The long-term focus means that these plans often focus from five to ten years; however, the fast-changing nature of the work environment often means that these plans need to be flexible enough to respond to change. The strategic human resource plan will align itself with the strategic plan.

strategic plans

General plans outlining priorities and actions needed to implement the strategic goals of an organisation.

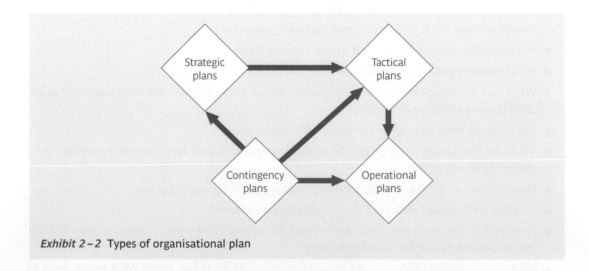

Exhibit 2–2 Types of organisational plan

Tactical plans

tactical plans
Plans aimed at achieving tactical goals and implementing parts of a strategic plan.

Tactical plans are aimed at achieving the tactical goals of the organisation. They implement the specific parts of the strategic plan. They are usually the responsibility of upper and middle management and tend to have a mid-term focus; they are more specific and concrete than strategic plans. Tactical plans are more concerned with getting things done than with deciding what to do.

Operational plans

operational plans
Plans that focus on implementing the tactical plans in day-to-day procedures in the organisation.

Operational plans focus on the implementation of tactical plans and are concerned with the day-to-day running of the organisation, such as staffing rotas. Middle and lower-level managers develop these plans. They tend to be short term and narrow in focus. Each plan usually deals with a small set of activities.

Contingency plans

As with all good plans, sometimes things need to be changed and this is where contingency planning comes in. **Contingency plans** consider alternative courses of action that can be taken if plans are disrupted or deemed inappropriate. Some organisations have contingency plans for positive or negative performance, often based on economic forecasts.

contingency plans
Plans for alternative courses of action to be taken if an intended plan is suddenly disrupted.

The process of contingency planning is demonstrated in Exhibit 2-3. In HR, the manager needs to develop basic plans, which detail staffing levels, pay levels, redundancies, and so on. These may include strategic, tactical and operational plans. It is then useful to identify events that could affect the feasibility of the plans. An example of this can be seen in the opening vignette, where Virgin was suddenly in a position where it had to consider redundancies and yet had no plans or policies in place. One method of contingency planning is asking 'What if?' questions. Virgin could have asked itself: What could we do if we lost 25 per cent of our market? What plans should we have in place? This might have helped it to develop alternative methods to making staff redundant.

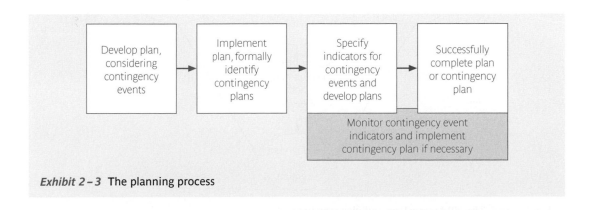

Exhibit 2-3 The planning process

Forecasting

Forecasting is the first step in the planning process when ascertaining the need for labour in an organisation. How it is done can vary. Statistics are one method that can be used, but this often only tells one side of the story. The Post Office, for example, uses statistics to predict when it will need extra people. By analysing past volume, it knows that the two months before Christmas are likely to be a busy time, and it will aim to increase recruitment to meet this demand. However, it does not predict unforeseen conditions, such as postal strikes resulting in loss of business or competitors moving into the market. This is where a subjective approach on the part of human resource planning experts is needed to make judgements about the future demand and supply of labour.

forecasting
The identification of the need and demand for, and supply of, labour in an organisation.

Exhibit 2-4 gives an overview of the forecasting and planning process. Ideally, a balanced approach to forecasting is best, with the expertise of the human resource planner aided by quantitative methods. Organisations that do not forecast their HR needs are unlikely to be able to respond to fluctuations in business, which could result in them losing any competitive advantage they may have.

Analysing HR needs

How does the HR planner know where, when and who to recruit? One method is to use **trend analysis**. This involves examining the past employment data of an organisation so as to predict future needs. Often, a five-year period is looked at, although the actual time span can be decided by the planner. Trends identified can be broken down into departments, especially if particular areas of the organisation have different trends. For example, a hotel may have an established core of staff in its kitchen, restaurant and accommodation areas. By looking at past trends a manager will be able to identify, say, the need to increase staff numbers in the kitchen and restaurant in the run-up to Christmas. However, extra staff may not be needed in the

trend analysis
Examining an organisation's past employment levels, say, to predict future needs.

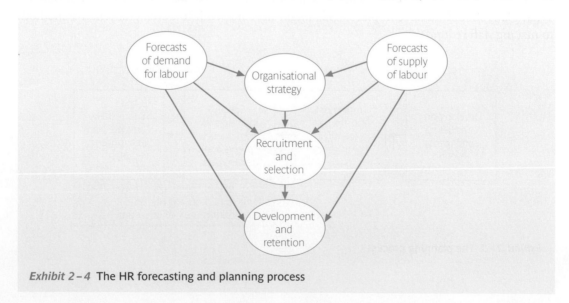

Exhibit 2–4 The HR forecasting and planning process

accommodation or administration departments, and may even be able to be re-deployed to other areas. By looking at trends, managers can decide if they need to recruit more staff, either on a permanent or temporary basis, or lay off staff.

ratio analysis
Making forecasts based on relationships between volume of business and staff levels.

Another method of forecasting the demand for labour is ratio analysis. This means predicting future labour needs by identifying a link between a causal factor and the number of employees. For example, a waiter may be able to serve 20 customers at each meal time, but at weekends when the restaurant is full, extra staff will be needed. The manager looks at the bookings and acts accordingly. Therefore, when 100 customers are booked in for an evening meal, the manager knows he will need five waiters. An example of what affects demand for labour can be seen in Exhibit 2-5.

This appears to make forecasting easy, and statistical packages are useful when business is stable, but what about the unexpected? The freak floods in the summer of 2004 in Boscastle, Cornwall, would not have been predicted by an HR planner, yet as the river swelled, broke its banks and raged through the town, businesses were wiped out along with the tourism industry. In such a situation, past data will not be any use as HR managers try to predict future needs. This is where judgement plays a part in the process: the manager will have to rely on experience and intuition to predict future needs.

Stop and reflect

Planning your HR career

How many of you actually consider how to get ahead in human resources? Use the checklist below to identify what you could do.

- Can you identify companies with a good reputation for developing the HR directors of the future?
- Have you joined a professional body such as the CIPD?
- Do you plan to get a broad base of knowledge, rather than specialise straight away?
- Are you proactive in developing yourself?
- Do you network to build a base of useful contacts?
- Can you measure your performance accurately to identify how it could be linked to an HR strategy?
- Can you show yourself as an authority figure?
- Can you apply what you have learnt to developing others?

If you can answer yes to the majority of the above questions, you can more than likely look forward to a high-flying career in HR. If your answers are mainly no or maybe, think about what you need to do to get ahead and link it into your career plan.

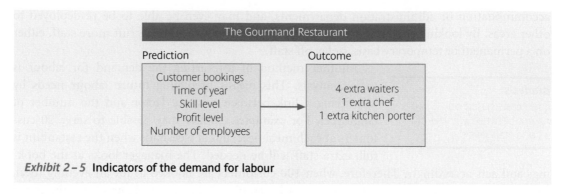

Exhibit 2-5 **Indicators of the demand for labour**

Supply of and demand for labour

Once the need for labour has been established the HR manager needs to identify where that labour will come from.

labour supply
The amount of labour available to employers in the workplace.

labour demand
The amount of labour required by organisations.

Labour supply refers to the number of people either in or seeking work. It also refers to the type of labour available, in terms of, say, qualifications, age and time available to work.

Labour demand refers to the number of jobs available and the types of job. In times of economic decline there are likely to be more people available for work than there are jobs, which means employers can choose who works for them and may even be able to pay them a lower rate. Of course, if the rate is too low, or the job is considered too menial, then potential applicants may not consider it worth taking.

In the past, major industries were often closely connected with local towns and the local schools would supply the necessary labour. Examples of this could be seen in the coal industry, which usually had a reliable pool of local labour, as did the manufacturing industries. When these industries went into decline, the redundant workers were left with the prospect of long-term unemployment. Government initiatives encouraged new businesses to develop, but these often required new skills that the redundant workers did not have. This led to other government training initiatives to equip potential workers with the relevant skills. Government policy is often used to alter the demand for and supply of labour. Initiatives today include tax credits to enable people to move from benefits to work, and child tax credits and help with childcare costs to enable parents to get back into work.

HR managers need to be able to identify the factors that are likely to influence the supply of and demand for labour. They also need to be aware of the impact of competitive forces, which will enable them to attract the best people. Information on where to identify trends can be seen in Exhibit 2-6.

Society

'Society' is to do with how we live our lives. In the UK we tend to have an individualist culture rather than a collective culture. This means that managing people has become increasingly complicated. There is a lot of emphasis on climbing the corporate ladder; people entering the workforce do not place the same value on having long-term careers with one organisation as their predecessors perhaps did. Not only that, many families may have to rely on a dual income and this could mean a change in the work dynamics: while some may choose a dual career path, others may want to reduce their hours or become more flexible. These issues are predictable

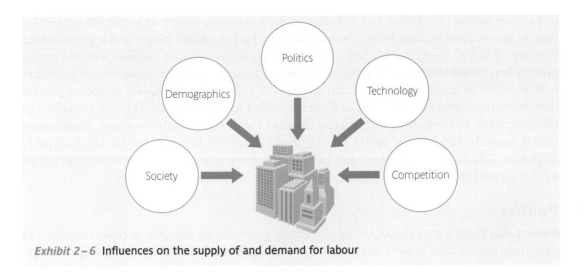

Exhibit 2–6 Influences on the supply of and demand for labour

and managers need to assess where their employees are in their life stages, and allow them the flexibility to grow and develop.

Another problem involves trying to encourage people to enter the labour market through social inclusion rather than social exclusion. **Social exclusion** is concerned with the underemployment of certain groups of people, often single mothers. One way to combat this is through government initiatives, and childcare is currently a central plank of both the economic efficiency and the social exclusion agendas. The government's welfare-to-work policies aim to address the underemployment of low-income parents as well as the social exclusion of working-class children in certain parts of British cities. The focus is on the expansion of paid work for women, especially for single mothers, and so childcare has become a key economic issue.

social exclusion

When potential workers are excluded from the labour market due to lack of support for caring responsibilities or a lack of skills.

You may wonder what this has to do with human resource planning. But, with a shrinking labour market, employers either need to concentrate on keeping employees who want to become parents or attracting others to their jobs. The obstacle to attracting single parents into the workplace is the lack of affordable childcare and, although there are state initiatives to provide funding for childcare, employers could also play their part by providing in-house nurseries or allowing flexible working. Across the UK, only 53 per cent of lone parents are in work.

Schein pointed out that certain changing dynamics in the workplace increase the importance of effective human resources planning. Research by Macaleer and Shannon (2003) confirms that change is having an impact on human resource planning through the changing managerial role and changing social values.

Demographics

When an HR manager is looking for sources of labour it is important that he or she takes into account the social trends in the area. These are likely to give an indication of the expectations of the workforce and their desire to fill available jobs. Information about this can be gleaned from the national census and also from social trend surveys. Demographics is information that illustrates the conditions of life in an area, and will identify the number of people available for work, their age and gender. The census is a useful source of information.

The UK and the rest of the European Union can expect a demographic change in the form of an ageing population and a decline in the workforce, as well as a split labour market that is characterised by high levels of unemployment for low-skilled people and a simultaneous shortage of skilled workers. This lack of flexible, high-skilled workers coupled with the ageing process has created the image of an immobile labour force. In response, governments may have to implement an immigration policy that attempts to address these issues via a selective process that discourages unskilled migrants and attracts skilled foreign workers. This will revitalise the labour market, foster growth and increase demand for unskilled native workers. Zimmerman (2005) suggests that Europe should take up the challenge by harmonising the single-country migration policies across Europe, and become an active player on the international labour market by providing competitive institutional settings for European companies.

Politics

Politics also plays a part in labour supply. Often, governments will put in place initiatives to encourage people back to work either through training schemes, welfare to work, or by encouraging businesses through the allocation of grants to invest in particular areas (these are often known as regeneration zones; information about them can be obtained from the Department of Trade and Industry).

Technology

The technology and degree of skilled labour an organisation requires also need to be taken into account when planning for labour. Is the local area likely to have the necessary skills? What type of training will need to be given? Is the industry seen as desirable? Will it meet the labour force's expectations? These issues all need to be taken into account if people are to be attracted into an organisation. It is also a good idea for HR managers to be aware of the competition, both in the same industry and other industries. Is your organisation competing for the same skills? What can you offer that competitors do not, to attract the best workers?

Competition

HR managers need to ensure that they have an understanding of the skills needed for future markets, technology and economic situations, and work with other managers to explore the skills capabilities needed.

Organisational design may also mean a need to change the structure of an organisation. Knowledge workers may not need the same type of supervision as manual workers, therefore rigid structures of authority and control need to be changed to a matrix system. HR needs to look at organisational design from two perspectives, as follows.

1 Is there a need to alter the way work is performed in order to secure a supply of workers?
2 Is there a need to alter the authority structure because of greater needs to use the skill of knowledge workers and improve flexibility?

HR's role in the first category would be to look at the supply of all the labour available, look at their requirements and decide how best these can be fitted into the organisation. This could be through the use of part-time workers, job share or flexible hours.

Current trends indicate that, although some industries such as manufacturing are losing jobs, the construction industry, service sector, public-sector health and education are all increasing jobs. Unemployment is falling and many employers will be increasing their staffing levels (Philpott, 2004).

International rescue

It wasn't so long ago that commentators were predicting that globalisation and skills shortages would spark a massive upsurge in international recruitment advertising. But has it actually happened? Well, the experience of advertising agencies at the front line suggests that it hasn't – at least not yet.

When you ask agency bosses whether the international scene is booming or not, some do say that the market is mobile and in expansion mode, but just as many others believe that caution still reigns and that any plans for global recruitment are still very much in their infancy.

Andrew Wilkinson, UK chief executive at TMP, says there is a limit to the amount of international recruitment that can be done to attract talent from developing countries. By contrast, he says that the most prevalent trend is to place the jobs in countries where the skills exist. 'In IT, the jobs go to where the skills are because the costs are lower. If you bring labour in, you end up paying higher rates.'

Wilkinson believes that it's relatively easy to attract, say, German, Spanish or French nationals to the UK because the established EU member states are seen as one marketplace. But some companies recruit only within their national borders because of the costs involved in advertising further afield.

The Internet, however, is one medium that can allow recruiters to minimise these costs. Ed Larder, group media director at Euro RSCG Riley, agrees that online advertising has many benefits. But he thinks that the Internet is not yet sophisticated enough to be used as a single medium for advertising.

Despite this, Larder adds that advertising on the Internet is good only for attracting those who are actively seeking a job. And he points out that many clients do not look outside the UK pool when hunting for talent.

'A lot of research needs to be done before recruiting globally. It's not a step to be taken lightly – it's expensive. There is the cost of seeing the candidate in person. It can cost an awful lot if it goes wrong,' he says.

So what are the practical considerations for employers who are willing to search for talent across national frontiers? Wilkinson says that the best approach is to drive applications online because you can set up questions to screen prospective employees from afar and test their English-language skills at the same time. But he admits that difficulties can arise where a UK company's HR practitioners lack the inside information that tells them how weighty a foreign qualification is or how good a particular university is.

Wilkinson gives the example of adverts that Hewlett-Packard and IBM have run across Europe recently. But even where such campaigns are successful, there can be practical problems when recruiting from an international pool. These range from catering for time differences to dealing with the demands of local legislation. Another consideration is that the data protection laws governing what employment information can be transferred vary from country to country.

In addition to all these tangible complications, there is the constant threat of more subtle problems, such as communication difficulties between operations based in different countries, according to Robert Peasnell, managing director of Barkers London. He stresses that any team handling international recruitment needs to be aware of any relevant cultural sensitivities.

'You don't want the managers in one country revolting because they haven't been consulted at the outset,' he says. 'You have to ensure that stakeholders across territories are kept up to speed and are involved continually.'

international perspective

▶ Overall, recruiting internationally does seem to be a fledgling activity, except where employers are seeking highly specialised skills. And any companies that do go down this route must be prepared to pay a premium.

Wilkinson says that relocating individuals and their families from one country to another creates significant challenges and considerable costs. 'You need to set up local induction tours for the areas you are hoping to recruit for. You need to look both at the job and also the whole environment, bearing in mind all the extra costs. If you don't prepare the ground in this way they may still join – but you mustn't be surprised if they leave you soon afterwards.'

Source: Joy Persaud, *People Management*, 25 June 2004, p. 20.
Reproduced with permission of *People Management* and Joy Persaud.

Discussion questions

1 What are the implications for human resource planners if organisations were to take jobs to the workers, rather than import workers to the jobs?

2 What are the advantages and disadvantages of using the Internet for global recruitment?

The impact of the internal labour market on the planning process

Before recruiting into the organisation from external sources, it is a good idea to examine the internal labour supply. Who is currently in the organisation, what are they doing and what happens to them?

As with forecasting the demand for labour, the internal labour market can be examined through the use of statistical packages or experienced judgements. Transitional matrices are one example that can show where employees are in the organisation at different times. An example of a transitional matrix for a department store can be seen in Exhibit 2-7.

transitional matrices
Charts showing which employees are in which job at a given time.

The transitional matrix tells us not only who is in the organisation but also what has happened to them. For example, 80 per cent of administration staff were still in the organisation in 2004, whereas 20 per cent had left. Of the retail assistants, again 80 per cent were still in the same job, 10 per cent had left and 10 per cent had been promoted to department supervisor. There had been no change in store manager, but there had been a big change in the assistant management position, which had been filled by internal promotion.

Matrices are useful for analysing turnover trends in an organisation. They can also identify where internal promotions occur and can be an aid to identifying training, development and retention issues.

When identifying the internal supply of labour, a qualifications inventory can be useful. This may contain an employee performance record, and details of educational background and any training undertaken. This can help identify potential candidates for promotion as well as potential gaps in performance that may need to be closed. (How this is done will be dealt with in more detail in Chapter 7.) Charts can be developed that show the potential for promotion of proposed candidates for future positions. The appraisal system can be linked in to ensure that candidates are aware of their future potential in the organisation. (This will be dealt with in Chapter 8.) An alternative to identifying potential candidates for replacement is to create a

2000		2004							
		1	2	3	4	5	6	7	8
1	Store manager	100							0
2	Assistant manager		50						50
3	Retail manager		50	50					0
4	Warehouse manager				100				0
5	Department supervisor			5		85			10
6	Retail assistants					10	80		10
7	Administration							80	20
8	Left organisation								

Exhibit 2–7 Retail store transitional matrix

position replacement system. This shows the availability of possible replacements, with details of promotion potential and training needs, to ensure their suitability. Small organisations may well be able to maintain these records manually but there are computerised systems available that, once a database of all employees has been created, can identify suitable candidates. These can be especially useful for succession planning.

succession planning
Planning the availability of internal candidates for promotion into key positions.

Succession planning is important as it ensures that there are suitable candidates to take over key positions in the event of strategic changes or replacement of individuals. It is most often used in senior executive positions, such as replacement of the chief executive. However, Pomeroy (2004) reports that, of senior executives polled in a recent survey, more than 39 per cent had no succession management plan in place for senior leadership positions. This is despite the fact that 88 per cent of CEOs think talent management is important and 93 per cent that succession planning is important to an organisation's success. So why is there a difference in what senior managers think is important to what is actually happening? According to Pomeroy (2004), senior managers in 45 per cent of organisations were unclear about how to identify and develop leadership talent. They felt that HR should be playing a more active role and yet was playing either no role in the process or was adding little value to succession practices. However, when HR did play an active role, succession planning was found to be more effective than without any input. The views of senior managers were that, for HR managers to play a greater role, they needed to understand executive challenges and demonstrate a strategic understanding of the business.

Carnworth (2004) suggests that company boards should spend time on succession planning before they are confronted with a gap. Forward-thinking companies will have identified contenders and they may well also have benchmarked the internal candidates against external candidates headhunted from other organisations. When considering succession planning, especially for a senior position, it is necessary to consider not only the personal effectiveness of the candidate, but also the type of industry and where the organisation is in its life cycle – in other words, how mature it is and the expectations of external stakeholders.

Successful succession planning includes the following activities:

- an analysis of the skills and functions of employees at each level of the organisation
- an audit of existing senior managers and the identification of future supply from both internal and external sources
- planning of individual career paths through the appraisal system
- fast-track promotion paths for potential high-performing candidates, in line with future organisational needs
- planned training and development interventions for internal candidates.

Planning for and managing talent

talent management
Managing processes to ensure that the best staff are recruited and retained.

Talent management is another method that can be used to ensure that an organisation keeps or attracts the best staff. The head of HR at Yahoo!, Libby Sartain, recognised this as an issue when Yahoo! was expecting a recruitment boom and needed to keep and retain its best people in a competitive business environment.

Sartain (2004) suggests that organisations need to have an effective talent management strategy that takes into account the following steps:

- attract top talent
- source targeted talent
- select and hire talent.

In the past, Yahoo! had undergone a number of changes in its business strategy and staffing needs, and although it had hired staff, it had also fired them. Rather than firing employees, they could have been moved to other sectors of the organisation. Sartain developed strategies that would train managers in recruitment and retention activities, and change the culture of 'hire and fire'. A broader talent initiative was also implemented to improve the work flow and HR metrics and enhance HR's function in the company. Senior management were involved in the implementation of the plan, which can be seen in Exhibit 2-8.

The company also sought to develop a seamless integrated talent function to hire, develop and retain. The steps involved in this plan can be seen in Exhibit 2-9.

Talent management should form part of the planning system and link into its resourcing and retention strategies. The implementation of plans needs to be monitored and linked into the financial budget. Yahoo! does this by using a profiling tool that can plan headcount by levels, and develop job descriptions and pay ranges. Another tool available to the manager is known as enterprise resource planning software, although it is important to make sure that this system is appropriate for the organisation's needs.

ERP
Enterprise resource planning – a system used to integrate information systems in the organisation.

Enterprise resource planning (ERP) software is used in the planning process in such a way that it will integrate most departmental information systems into a single computer system that can be used across the organisation. This means that it should serve the needs of human resource planners by also linking in to payroll, customers, distribution, finance, and so on. In the past, each of the different

1	Develop a recruitment and development strategy, instead of simply filling jobs as they become available
2	Enhance the internal and external employment brand
3	Improve internal and external communication
4	Improve sourcing
5	Improve screening
6	Enhance learning and development
7	Improve the process
8	Institute workforce planning
9	Create a structure for talent management
10	Use metrics

Exhibit 2 – 8 Yahoo!'s talent management plan

1	Plan who and how many to hire, including filling 'gaps'
2	Attract those you want
3	Recruit those you want
4	Assess correctly
5	Develop carefully
6	Retain only those you want

Exhibit 2 – 9 Yahoo!'s integrated talent function

departments would have had its own system and they would not be able to talk to one another. An integrated model would mean that someone in finance could access the database to see how much finance was needed for staffing needs. Or the HR manager could access sales data to identify when extra staff would be needed. This may seem ideal for busy departmental managers, but Doran (2004) suggests that ERP systems do not always have a good track record as they are nearly always over budget, the return on investment is poor and training is needed to get people to change the way they work. If employees feel that their current working methods are better than ERP, then they won't want to change. One university found such a difficulty when it implemented PeopleSoft to manage its HR and student systems. According to Gage (2004), the staff and students found the system so disruptive that they had to do more of the work manually, and the university spent months trying to solve existing problems and identify potential problems.

Using plans to attract the best talent

A talent management plan should be able to identify and develop strategies that create the right psychological contract for employees, identify corporate values, and link these to the individual's personal values and behaviours. Plans for attracting talent could also identify how coaching could be used, how people relate to your organisational brand, as well as plans to allow for flexibility and work/life balance.

Create the right psychological contract

Respecting individuals and making them feel valued is one of the most important things an employer can do, and often one of the hardest. Although money helps to attract employees, a sense of achievement and recognition is more likely to ensure they stay.

Know and live corporate values

Corporate values are often reflected in the mission statement of the organisation. These need to be communicated to employees so that they can become their values too. When an organisation has determined its values it needs to decide how to ensure buy-in from its employees. This means that reward strategies need to be consistent with the values.

Assess individuals' values and behavioural styles

By understanding what drives and motivates people and how they relate to the world around them, the right resourcing, recruitment and selection strategies can be put in place. This helps to ensure that people are in the right roles in the organisation. Having good feedback systems can help ensure this happens.

Create a coaching culture

In flatter, leaner organisational structures there is less emphasis on climbing the career ladder. This means that people need to develop both personally and professionally in their work teams. Organisations that allow for new learning opportunities are more likely to increase employee satisfaction.

Brand people processes

Find out what people like and dislike about your organisation. Interview new entrants to identify why they chose your organisation, and ask those who declined positions why this was. Then build a 'people brand' that reflects the picture employees have of the organisation. This means that new employees will know exactly what to expect.

Offer flexible benefits

This will be discussed in more detail in Chapter 6. Since people are motivated by different things, it makes sense to develop a reward package that reflects these differences. Flexible benefits allow this to happen.

Encourage a better work/life balance

Can flexible ways of working be made accessible to all? Work/life balance can help improve performance in organisations, as it can reduce stress and enable employees to follow outside pursuits. This means that when they are at work they should be refreshed and invigorated. Work/life balance should be reflected at all levels of the organisation, from board level downwards.

Be realistic and market driven

In some organisations the competition for talent can be very strong. Thought needs to be given to how this issue can be addressed. This means looking at job design to make jobs more appealing and also thinking about how to create loyalty, through either teamwork or promotion strategies.

Build a sense of community

Encourage employees to relate to each other through social interaction. Put in place team-building events, which encourage loyalty. Promote enjoyment through social activities to improve bonding.

Improve positive energy

Remove those things that irritate people at work. Ask each department what it is that annoys them, and get it fixed. Often this will be something minor, like a faulty photocopier, but it could also be a bureaucratic system that is hindering creativity.

Planning and the external labour market

It is not always possible to recruit only from internal sources as it may be that the company is expanding and needs to recruit large numbers of extra employees. This is where the external labour market needs to be investigated. This means that the HR specialist also needs to be aware of the general economic conditions outside the organisation. Government statistics are often a useful aid in guiding employment strategies. Areas of high unemployment are more likely to have a larger pool of labour to choose from, but often high unemployment can also mean social deprivation and lower educational achievement. This means that although more people may be available for work, they may not have the skills necessary for the organisation. This in turn will create issues with regard to training and development.

However, in areas of low unemployment, there may well be a shortage of unskilled workers. London and the south-east of England are examples of this. Property is expensive to buy here, and there is a shortage of cheap rental accommodation. This means that the people who can afford to live in the area tend to be in professional and higher-paid jobs. The result is that there is a shortage of low-paid professionals, such as teachers and nurses, and a shortage of unskilled service-sector workers. To overcome this, employers need to find strategies to encourage workers to move into the area. These may be in the form of enhanced pay, such as London weighting, or subsidised housing, such as key worker accommodation. Employers also need to be aware of alternative labour sources. Some hospitals have used agencies to recruit nurses from countries such as Spain, where there is oversupply, or the Philippines, but here there are also ethical considerations such as depriving developing countries of key workers.

Czerny (2004), in the examination of a survey by the CIPD, indicates that 28 per cent of employers expect to recruit migrant workers as a result of labour shortages. Once the source of supply has been established then organisations also need to ensure that they can compete with other organisations for employees.

However, Richbell (2001) suggests that there is a significant pool of labour in the UK in the 16 to 24 age group, but these people are unskilled and lack formal qualifications. This means that the organisation has not only to provide an induction and training scheme, but also must develop commitment. Although the government is addressing this with the introduction of the 'New Deal', it is still often more cost-effective to recruit people who are already trained.

managing diversity

Prison scheme gets back to work

A scheme to address local skill shortages by providing prisoners with hands-on work experience has been set up by HMP Lindholme. Billed as the first project of its kind in the prison service, a construction site, with the space to build three houses, and a bakery have been set up in the prison. Inmates selected for the scheme will work towards industry-recognised qualifications while gaining work experience.

The initiative is connected to the broader aims of the government's 'Custody to Work' initiative, which links prison training and skills. 'We are focusing on sectors with serious skill shortages. It is then up to the local establishment and prison to work together,' an HM Prison Service source told *PM*.

Fiona Ross, education, training and employment co-ordinator for charity Sova and the scheme, said it may encourage other prisons to do the same: 'It is not a national rollout, but it may act as an example.'

The centre, funded until 2007 via Yorkshire Forward, a regional development agency, hopes to add local employers to its steering group when the project is launched. It aims to assist 125 ex-offenders annually into employment or more training, and to provide around 600 accredited qualifications.

Ken Parker, area manager for Yorkshire and Humberside CITB-ConstructionSkills, said the project would benefit both ex-offenders and the construction industry.

'This innovative project aims to support offenders in their rehabilitation and resettlement by giving them craft skills that will enable them to find jobs,' he said.

A recent CIPD report, *Employers and Offenders*, said the government needed to ensure programmes to get ex-offenders into work were geared towards employers' needs.

'Employment has a major part to play in reducing re-offending, which costs the country billions of pounds a year. Government needs to engage with employers to ensure that ex-prisoners have been given the relevant skills,' said Dianah Worman, CIPD adviser, diversity.

Source: Katie Hope, *People Management*, 14 October 2004, p. 11.
Reproduced with permission of *People Management*.

Discussion questions

1 How can employers be encouraged to use such a scheme where there are skill shortages?

2 What type of planning will an organisation need to undertake to ensure recruiting from the scheme is a success?

Strategies for responding to the supply of and demand for labour

Often it is left to the HR manager to respond to labour changes in the workplace. It may be that poor economic conditions or competitive reasons dictate the need to reduce the pool of labour. Whatever the reason, there are several strategies available to the HR manager that can be used, although their impact on employees should not be overlooked.

To reduce an oversupply of labour the following tactics can be considered.

■ Downsizing: reducing the size of an organisation to enhance competitiveness. This can be done rapidly, but it often results in negative publicity and poor morale among the remaining employees.

- Pay reductions: reducing the amount of pay employees receive. This can also be done rapidly, but can have a serious effect on employee relations and morale.
- Demotions: moving people to a lower-level job, either as the result of a middle-management layer being removed or to save money. This can affect morale by making workers feel undervalued.
- Transfers: relocating employees to different roles or different locations. This can be organised quickly, but can impact on family life if the move is to a different location. Often, relocation packages have to be introduced.
- Work combining: involves combining jobs. This is quick to implement, but can mean employees become overloaded and less effective.
- Recruitment freeze: new employees are no longer recruited. This may not help if specialisms are required and the current workforce cannot provide the skills.
- Natural wastage: this is where the employer relies on people to leave and does not replace them. This can take time but is unlikely to affect staff morale, unless those remaining feel overburdened with work.
- Early retirement: where older members, usually aged 55 and over, are encouraged to retire. Depending on pension package and family commitments, this can be seen as a popular option for employees, although it can be expensive for the employer.
- Retraining: training an employee for an alternative position. This can take time and resources, but is less likely to have an impact on staff morale.

There are also times when the HR manager needs to consider increasing the supply of labour, due to improved economic conditions, expansion or an increased share of the market. To decide which strategies to use, the HR manager also needs to think about whether increases in labour are likely to be temporary or permanent.

The following strategies can be considered to increase labour supply.

- Overtime: can be introduced quickly, is often popular with employees as it involves extra pay and can be removed equally quickly when economic needs dictate.
- Temporary employees: can be implemented fairly quickly, depending on the skill level required of new recruits. They can also be removed quickly when their contracts expire.
- Outsourcing: where certain aspects of a job are given to another company to do. Customer service, for instance, may outsource to other countries where labour is cheaper. It is also easy to end the contract if circumstances change. Problems may arise with a lack of understanding of the organisation's or home country's culture.
- Retrained transfers: this is where an oversupply of staff in one area of an organisation are relocated and retrained to take on a different role. This can take time, but flexible employees can be more beneficial to the survival of the workplace.
- Turnover reduction: involves examining why employees are leaving and developing strategies to reduce loss. This is especially important as high staff turnover is often an indication of poor morale and also adds to recruitment costs.
- New recruits: this can take time as it will involve job analysis, job design and the employment procedure. It is also not as easy to reverse if conditions change.
- Technological innovation: introducing new technology to replace people. This can take time and resources to implement as the most appropriate technology needs to be investigated.

Whichever strategies are used it is important to ensure that they are the right ones for the organisation. In other words, the strategies used should help maintain or increase the company's competitive advantage while fitting in with the overall business strategy.

Forming a resourcing strategy

An organisation with a coherent resourcing strategy is more likely to be able to respond quickly in times of growth or recession. HR needs to identify how to attract the most talented people at the best cost in a realistic time frame. According to Cornish (2003), 'A strategic approach to resourcing will help you recruit in the most cost-effective way and move the HR function closer to a pivotal role at the heart of planning the future of the organisation.'

Cornish recommends working outside the established channels by following the guidelines listed below.

1 **The employee value proposition (EVP)** – to attract talent, make your vacancy the best option. Think about added value beyond pay and conditions. Communicate to internal staff. The EVP should be part of the employee experience and help create a psychological contract.

2 **Requisition and approvals** – use technology to enable the recruitment process to be user friendly. For example, a bank of generic job descriptions that can be altered when needed. This will ensure costs are controlled.

3 **Channel strategy** – analyse recruitment information. This ensures that the HR department will know from where it recruits both internally and externally and at what cost.

4 **Building communities** – identify internal candidates first. Be proactive in identifying career opportunities for your employees. Pre-screen internal candidates as this can negate the need to use external agencies.

5 **Screening and selection** – be clear as to what the organisation wants and ensure that the procedures used reflect those needs.

6 **Management information** – ensure that information is available to inform decision-makers. This can help identify which methods give you the best talent at the best price.

The changing nature of work

At the beginning of the twentieth century, the majority of jobs in the UK were either in manufacturing, heavy industry or agriculture. Throughout the century manufacturing went into decline, heavy industry disappeared and technology took over. The changes in jobs also led to changes in leisure practices: people had more money to spend. The result was a growth in the service sector. It has also meant an increase in the number of jobs for knowledge workers. Demographic and social changes have also meant that there is an increasing number of part-time jobs, often filled by women. The privatisation of the public sector has also removed the idea of a 'job for life'. Changes in the organisational and economic context of work have also led to increased job insecurity. The resulting insecurities can also impact on job performance in the form of dissatisfaction, poor performance and high staff turnover.

transferable skills
Generic skills that can transfer from one job to another, such as IT and communication skills.

The changing nature of work has meant that employees need to be flexible and to have **transferable skills** that can be moved from one job to another with ease. Employers also need to ensure that employees can be moved around the organisation in order to meet labour needs.

The changing nature of work means that HR managers need to be able to respond to required changes in an organisation. This will include working with managers at the initiation stage and also at the implementation stage. For example, an HR manager working for an organisation that wants to introduce new technology needs to ensure that the staff will have the skills available to use the new systems. This can be done either through the recruitment of new employees or the development of the existing workforce. It is for these reasons that the HR specialist needs to demonstrate strategic thinking in organisational decisions. In practice, however, this is often ignored. At the implementation stage, the HR manager is needed to advise on negotiation strategies, as well as to encourage employee involvement and continued development. A summary of findings by White *et al.* (2004) states that the labour market has developed in ways that are not only beneficial to employers but also for employees, and HR is playing a more important role (as noted in the list below).

- **The uses of flexible labour** – used in all types of organisation, although its use is slowing down.

- **Career opportunities** – most workplaces are attempting to offer career opportunities to all employees.

- **Extensive use of HRM practices** – a high-performance 'strategy' has been identified in about one in three workplaces.

- **Extensive use of ICT** – the use of technology has been found in one in five workplaces and attempts to link up with a high-performance HRM strategy.

- **Recruitment and retention** – becoming a high priority, with more women being recruited to formerly male-dominated jobs.

- **Increasing diversity** – more recruitment from groups who have formerly faced employment barriers, such as those of different ethnic origin, or people with disabilities.

- **A 'high benefits strategy'** – used to strengthen recruitment and retention. This has been found to include significant fringe benefits and family-friendly practices.

- **Trades unions** – unionised workplaces are more likely to have family-friendly practices and use flexible labour.

Planning for a flexible workplace
Work/life balance

An HR manager needs to be aware that employees often have many demands on their time and, although they are employed to do a job, employers should not be so rigid as to assume this is the employee's number one priority. Hence the requirement by the government that employers should recognise the need for **work/life balance**, in consideration of the duties and responsibilities that employees have outside their work situation. The call for acknowledgement of the need for flexibility in working hours could, in the longer term, actually result in greater job satisfaction and a reduction of the need for absence. Furthermore, this could nurture a more positive employer–employee relationship, thereby encouraging greater commitment to

work/life balance
The need for employees to balance their commitments outside the workplace with their availability to work.

the firm. These suggestions are now being backed by industrial practice and are already in place at organisations such as Lloyds TSB, Littlewoods, Barclays plc and Asda, who have all reported positive outcomes. Such practices pave the way for EC directives that include increased maternity leave, together with the introduction of paternity leave in the UK. Proposals for work flexibility claim that there are benefits for employer as well as employee. Such a condition is a different employment relationship from being laid off, a practice used in seasonal service industries. It encourages individual negotiation and agreements between employee and employer rather than across-the-firm collective agreements. At an individual level this would form the basis of the 'psychological contract'. It is understandable that certain EC partners with industry-wide and government-backed agreements have traditionally been opposed to individually based agreements, on the grounds that they are inequitable. Furthermore, as a consequence, this would lead to the erosion of conditions and payment systems long established by statute in particular industries.

Atkinson (1985), of the then Institute of Manpower Studies, presented a paper that highlighted the flexibility of work employment patterns in firms in the UK, which was already well established. This was attributed to the continuing requirement for a more efficient use of all resources, including human resources, which included employment costs and improved employment efficiency (see Exhibit 2-10).

Flexible working means that organisations need to focus on outputs rather than on how long someone has been sitting at their desk. BT Global Service is one organisation that does this, and it has found that the application of flexible working actually allows employees to be

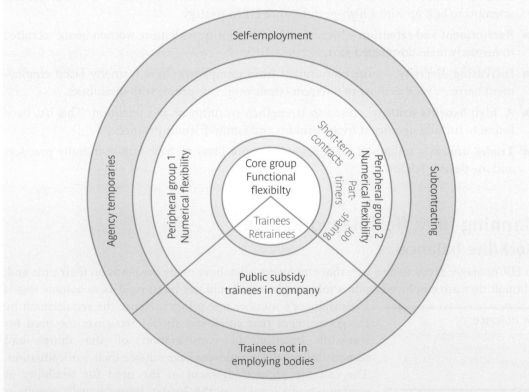

Exhibit 2–10 **Flexible working patterns**
Source: Adapted from Atkinson (1985).

more efficient. This adds a new dimension to the planning process. To be flexible, employees need to have the technology to be able to do their job effectively. For Julie Woods-Moss, vice president of marketing at BT, this means using her BlackBerry to keep in touch with the office and make sure she doesn't miss out on any vital decisions. It also means using wi-fi technology, which enables her to link to her computer from anywhere in the world. The benefits to Julie are that she can limit the time she spends travelling to and from work, which means it can be used more productively, and she can also spend more time with her family.

For the planners to enable Julie to do this, she needs to be provided with the appropriate technology.

Flexible working benefits both the organisation and its employees. Organisations that fail to embrace mobile working will pay the price as employees will seek to move to alternative organisations that do.

Being freed from the straitjacket of nine-to-five, five days a week, and allowed to adapt your working life to your other needs used to be a rarity, but is now increasingly commonplace. Flexible working is now often part of the package, and companies that do not offer it may lose out.

To move to a flexible working culture managers should change to:

- a culture focused on output, not how long employees sit at their desks
- flexible working that benefits both the organisation and its employees, and provide support to help people adapt to the change
- encourage people to consider the balance between convenience and effectiveness, and not always trade the latter for the former.

Planning for agile workers

Agile workers need to have the transferable skills to be able to move and adapt easily to different jobs. However, it is not only the employer that should encourage agile working; employees also need to change their mindsets. Research by Jonathan Winter, director of the Ci Group, found that:

> Employers are restricted by traditional mindsets, budgeting methods and a fixation with headcount. But it's not just employers who need to change. Our research found that frustrated workers lack the skills to negotiate imaginative career deals with their employers. What's needed is an entirely new kind of career partnership, between employers and workers.

One method of encouraging flexibility and agility is through the use of annual hours.

Annual hours

One method of flexible working is through annual hours: rather than pay for a 40-hour week, employees are paid for a set amount of hours per year.

According to Gregory (2006), 5 per cent of employees now work in this way. For the HR planner this means that working hours are matched to the needs of the business. This also allows a strategic approach as staff are allocated when and where the business needs it most, and it enables a set salary to be paid without overtime. One company that uses such a scheme is Armstrong Metal Ceilings. Here, it has been welcomed by both staff and employers. Employees are given two weeks' notice of a change in work patterns and a computer program tracks the hours that employees work.

Job sharing

One example of job sharing has recently been introduced by McDonald's with its 'family contracts'. McDonald's employs one family on a single contract and, according to Alder (2006), these contracts allow husbands, wives, children and grandparents to job share and swap shifts without notifying management in advance. The contracts have been introduced to tackle the problem of absenteeism.

Absent workers can be a particular problem and certainly cost businesses vast sums of money, but employing a whole family on one contract could cause other problems. Alder (2006) suggests that the following problems could arise.

- If there was a dispute, employment tribunals could argue that each person is entitled to be treated as an individual person rather than all being treated as one entity.

- The poor performance of one worker could mean the employer terminates the contract: the others might claim unfair dismissal.

- It may be difficult for employers to discipline poorly performing workers without penalising the others, given that they are all sharing the same contract.

- Workers could dispute how shifts are allocated, giving rise to a situation where nobody turns up for work.

- Each part-time worker might be entitled to the same benefits as a single full-time worker, despite perhaps only working occasional shifts. As a result, employers' costs in relation to benefits could be higher than if one worker was employed to do the job.

- There may be instances in which one of the family members requires closer management or perhaps needs to be excluded from working with other employees.

HR can act as an agent for change, not only as part of the change in organisational design but also as an aid to cultural change as a means of assisting an acceptance of new working practices.

Communication is an important part of the change process and this offers a role for the HR specialist. Top management need to be convinced, as also do employees further down in the organisation:

- reward structures will need to change
- career development will need rethinking
- status levels may become an issue in flatter organisations
- HR planning has great opportunities to guide organisational change and enable a business to achieve its objectives.

Organisations are becoming more complex in structure and technologies, and are operating in more complex economic, political and diverse cultural environments, meaning that managers cannot safely make decisions alone. They cannot get enough information within their own head to be both integrator and decision-maker. Instead, they become the managers of the decision-making process. This means that HR managers need to ensure that, as part of the decision-making process, they align their plans with the strategic goals of the organisation.

Summary

- Planning is an important tool for the HR manager as it enables the organisational strategy to be put into practice.

- Forecasting the demand for labour is an important function of HR as it enables a manager to identify the need for labour.

- Supply of and demand for labour can be influenced by society, demographics, politics, economics, technology and competition.

- The supply of labour can be from external sources or developed from internal sources through succession planning and talent management.

- HR managers need to be able to identify and implement strategies to ensure that they have the right people, at the right time and in the right place.

- The nature of work is changing through the types of jobs available and the expectations of employees. An HR manager needs to be able to identify trends in the workplace and plan for them.

- Plans also need to consider the changing values of society and allow for flexible working and work/life balance.

Personal development

1 **Understand the importance of planning.** All managers have to plan. This is the step-by-step process that managers will use to implement the organisation's strategy. As you start out on your career path, you may already have an idea of where you want to be in five or ten years' time. What practical steps do you need to take to fulfil your aims? How can you measure if your plan is effective?

2 **Identify how trends are measured, and the tools available.** There are several tools available to the HR manager, either as software packages or through quantitative formulas. Familiarise yourself with what is available and what the limitations are. Think about how an HR manager can plan for the unexpected.

3 **Recognise the role of the external and internal environment in the demand for and supply of labour.** This is also important for developing your own career path: will you have to move to another area to find the job of your choice, or will you need additional qualifications and skills if competition is tough? How can you ensure that you have competitive advantage in the recruitment stakes?

4 **Understand the importance of developing and retaining talent.** Would you like to work in an organisation where your skills are not appreciated, and you are not developed or encouraged to gain skills that would enable you to be promoted? For most people this would leave them feeling devalued. Think about the strategies an HR manager could use to develop and train staff to ensure that he/she has a pool of talent to pick from when promotions are available.

5 **Identify the factors that can help an organisation to retain its staff.** A high turnover of staff in an organisation may be linked to poor management practices, which could also affect organisational performance. This costs organisations money and time. As a manager how can you ensure that you keep your staff?

❓ Discussion questions

1 Why is it important for an HR manager to plan?

2 How can using statistics both help and hinder an HR manager's resourcing plan?

3 What effects can both the supply of and demand for labour have on an organisation's recruitment strategy?

4 How can transitional matrices be implemented by an HR manager?

5 What could be the strategic implications for an organisation without a succession plan?

6 What should be the role of the HR manager in developing and retaining talent in an organisation?

7 What are the advantages and disadvantages of ERP for the HR manager and the organisation?

8 How could an HR manager implement strategies to increase the supply of labour with an increase in business?

9 What is the changing nature of work and how can an HR manager ensure that the organisational recruitment strategy meets these changes?

10 Why is it important for an HR manager to develop staff retention strategies?

🔑 Key concepts

organisational values, *p. 46*	labour demand, *p. 52*
strategic plans, *p. 48*	social exclusion, *p. 53*
tactical plans, *p. 49*	transitional matrices, *p. 56*
operational plans, *p. 49*	succession planning, *p. 57*
contingency plans, *p. 49*	talent management, *p. 58*
forecasting, *p. 50*	ERP, *p. 58*
trend analysis, *p. 50*	transferable skills, *p. 64*
ratio analysis, *p. 51*	work/life balance, *p. 65*
labour supply, *p. 52*	

Individual task

Most people have a general idea of what they want from life and where they expect their career to go in the future, but few take the time to identify a plan to help them achieve their goals.

1 Make a list of five goals that you would like to achieve in the next 10 years. These could be work-related goals or personal goals.

2 Write a plan for each of the goals, breaking it down into time elements, resource issues and training issues (for example, what you would expect to achieve after one year, two years, five years, and so on).

3 How is this planning process similar to that of an HR manager?

Team task

Purpose To understand the impact poor human resource planning can have on an organisation.

Time 40 minutes

Procedure Divide into groups of six. You have each been allocated a role as part of the strategic planning team for British Airways.

After a disastrous bank holiday weekend, where poor workforce planning caused flight cancellations, which in turn affected thousands of customers, you as a team need to ensure that it never happens again.

Each person in your team is allocated a role, such as human resources director, recruitment and selection manager, training manager, a trades union representative from the Transport and General Workers Union, finance director and customer services manager.

You have identified the following problems:

- staffing levels were too low
- more staff had left in the past year than had been anticipated
- there is a lack of new recruits
- criminal records checks are being delayed
- a new policy of absence management has been introduced
- staff are threatening industrial action
- you need wage cost stability due to industry pressures such as rising fuel prices and increasing competition.

As a team, develop a human resource plan that can help BA achieve its strategic aims without causing workforce dissatisfaction.

Case study: St Albans Council praised for workforce planning success

Local government minister Nick Raynsford has praised St Albans City and District Council for its success as part of a government pilot scheme to investigate how local authorities can make their workforce planning more effective.

The results of the St Albans project, which was co-ordinated by the human resources department, are now being used as a basis for implementing good practice in local authorities throughout England.

Raynsford said the initiatives had resulted in an extensive management development programme, flexible working, a new apprenticeship scheme and a revised appraisal scheme.

Councillor Chris Oxley, the council's portfolio holder for resources, said: 'It is our firm policy to think creatively to ensure our council continues to retain and recruit the very best staff and, at the same time, help students who find funding their degree courses a challenge. We want to help them so they can help us.'

The project covered the following areas.

- Managers were asked to look ahead and identify how their staffing needs would develop in light of the priorities over the next five years, and what skills those people would require. In St Albans, workforce considerations are now part of every senior manager's annual strategic review.

■ The project identified immediate and long-term staffing needs, and highlighted skill shortages, particularly in planning and environmental health. Using these findings and those from other councils that took part in the pilot scheme, meetings have taken place with universities to make them aware of the skills that are in short supply.

■ The council has also been raising its profile among planning students by introducing a bursary scheme at Oxford Brookes University, and is offering holiday work placements to students interested in taking up careers in planning.

■ The council has also made use of the Modern Apprenticeship scheme to address the national shortage of benefits staff and to encourage young people into specific areas of local government such as environmental health, HR and customer services.

■ Placements were advertised in the local media and targeted young people aged 16 to 24. Candidates gain work experience and participate in a programme of NVQ qualifications. The council's objective is to create a team of trained and qualified employees, able to fill vacancies as they arise.

Source: M. Miller, *Personneltoday.com*, 8 October 2004, www.personneltoday.com.
Reproduced with permission of *Personnel Today*. © Reed Business Information.

Discussion questions

1 If you were a department manager, how would you identify your short-term and long-term staffing needs?

2 How can an HR manager ensure that she or he is aware of government initiatives and professional developments?

3 What implications is their plan likely to have on other functions of HR?

WWW exercise

Specific web exercise

There are several websites on the Internet that enable you to test your motivation and commitment to work. One such exercise can be followed through the link below.

Go to the website of www.personneltoday.com. Click on the link to self-test. Click on the link 'Are you doing enough to keep your job?'

You may like to compare your answers with those of colleagues. If your motivation is poor, could this lead to a problem of staff retention?

LEARNING CHECKLIST

Before moving on to the next chapter, check that you are able to:

☑ identify how to align an organisation's strategic direction with human resource planning

☑ identify aspects that affect the demand for and supply of labour

☑ understand the role of forecasting as part of the HR planning process and its response to change

☑ evaluate staff retention strategies.

Further reading

Browell, S. (2003) *Staff Retention*. London: Chartered Management Institute, Hodder & Stoughton.

Cotton, J.L. and Tuttle, J.M. (1986) 'A meta analysis and review with implications for research', *Academy of Management Review* 11, pp. 50–70.

Emmott, M. (2004) 'Britain's real working lives', *People Management*, 30 June, p. 14.

Garrett, A. (2003) 'Crash course in exit interviews', *Management Today*, December, p. 18.

Handy, C.B. (1989) *The Age of Unreason*. London: Business Books.

Higginbottom, K. (2003) 'Tesco seeks mountain of youth', *People Management*, 23 October, p. 11.

Huselid, M.A. (1995) 'The impact of human resource management practices on turnover, productivity and corporate financial performance', *Academy of Management Review* 38(3), pp. 635–872.

McEvoy, G.M. and Cascio, C.F. (1985) 'Strategies for reducing employee turnover: a meta-analysis', *Journal of Applied Psychology* 70, pp. 342–353.

Schein, E.H. (1985) *Organisational Culture and Leadership*. San Francisco: Jossey-Bass.

Schmit, M.L. and Allscheid, S.P. (1995) 'Employee attitudes and customer satisfaction: making theoretical and empirical connections', *Personnel Psychology* 48, pp. 521–536.

Sheridan, J.E. (1992) 'Organisational culture and employee retention', *Academy of Management Journal* 35, pp. 1036–1056.

References

Alder, R. (2006) 'Beware the risks of job share schemes', *Personnel Today*, 28 February, p. 15.

Atkinson, J. (1985) 'Manpower strategies for flexible organisations', *Personnel Management*, August, pp. 28–31.

Carnworth, A. (2004) 'In my opinion', *Management Today*, October 2004, p. 12.

Cornish, A. (2003) 'How to form a resourcing strategy', *People Management*, 4 December, p. 44.

Czerny, A. (2004) 'UK's foreign trawl continues', *People Management*, 14 October, p. 7.

Doran, A. (2004) 'ERPs: a good idea for HR to take and pass on', *Canadian HR Reporter* 17(19), 12 July, p. 9.

Gage, D. (2004) 'Hard lesson; when Stanford university installed new financial and human-resources systems, it nearly flunked out. Can tighter controls earn it a passing grade?', *Baseline* 1(31), p. 56.

Gregory, A. (2006) 'Flexible working is on the cards', *Works Management* 59(3), March, pp. 20–22.

Hammonds, K.H. (2006) 'Why we hate HR', *Leadership Excellence* 23(2), p. 20.

Macaleer, B. and Shannon, J. (2003) 'Does HR planning improve business performance?', *Industrial Management* 45(1), January/February, pp. 14–20.

Philpott, J. (2004) 'Quarterly HR trends and indicators', survey report, CIPD.

Pomeroy, A. (2004) 'Succession planning lags', *HR Magazine* 49(9), September, p. 12.

Richbell, S. (2001) 'Trends and emerging values in human resource management: the UK scene', *International Journal of Manpower*, pp. 261–268.

Sartain, L. (2004) 'How a talent management plan can anchor your company's future', *HR Focus* 81(10), October, p. 7.

White, M., Hill, S. and Smeaton, D. (2004) *Managing to Change? British Workplaces and the Future of Work*. ERSC Future of Work Programme.

Zimmerman, K.F. (2005) 'European labour mobility: challenges and potentials', *De Economist* (Leiden) 153(4), December, p. 425.

Chapter 3

Work and job design

LEARNING OUTCOMES

After studying this chapter, you should be able to:

- ☑ **examine** the role of HR in the analysis of jobs
- ☑ **understand** the importance of job design
- ☑ **understand** new developments in the world of work
- ☑ **understand** the importance of team working.

The opening vignette illustrates the importance of job design and how, when implemented with proper consultation, it can be a powerful tool in improving performance.

The National Crime Squad

The design and measurement of work can be seen to have far-reaching effects in an organisation. It not only links into recruitment and selection processes but also pay, reward and performance. Therefore it is vital to get it right.

This opening vignette offers an example of how, with proper consultation, traditional job descriptions can be changed to encourage employee commitment, which in turn leads to improved performance.

Between May 2003 and March 2004 the National Crime Squad (NCS) dismantled or disrupted 190 businesses involved in class-A drug trafficking, and 40 organisations connected to immigration crime. The squad's other achievements included the seizure of nearly £4 million under the Proceeds of Crime Act 2002.

With such good results, why worry about performance management? According to Dave Hays, HR manager at the NCS, there was a desire to achieve even better results and demonstrate the significant contribution that HR was making. 'We wanted to show how HR has a direct impact on the bottom line, which in our case is to reduce the undermining effect of serious and organised crime on the fabric of society,' he says.

After consultations with police officers and staff, the organisation developed a competency framework. This consisted of behavioural competencies, activities and national occupational standards. It also took account of the Home Office's own national framework.

The vehicle for introducing the competency framework was a set of role profiles focusing on behavioural skills and role-specific accountabilities. Hays admits that the breadth of these role profiles has caused some concern because the old-style job descriptions that they replaced were seen to have clear performance parameters. However, he adds, they had been treated as to-do lists, which were often a substitute for management interaction.

'One of the benefits of introducing role profiles is that their perceived breadth actually encourages managers to sit down with members of their teams to discuss what is expected of them – the first step towards performance management,' Hays explains.

The new framework has also led to some significant changes concerning reward. Traditionally, pay progression throughout the police service has been on a time-served basis – part of the terms and conditions negotiated at national level through the Police Staff Council (PSC). 'A new starter would enter on the first point of a pay band and, come each April, would move to the next point until they hit the top of the band,' Hays explains.

He says that it generally didn't matter whether employees were good, bad or indifferent – every April they would get a pay rise.

The NCS decided to challenge this approach by capitalising on the wording of the PSC handbook, which states that progression 'may be accelerated within the scale for excellent performance' and 'delayed in case of poor performance'. But, instead of linking pay to performance, the focus is now on contribution. 'It's about what you bring to the job; not what you produce at the other end,' Hays says.

Source: A. Baron and D. Hays, *People Management*, 14 October 2004, p. 44.
Reproduced with permission of *People Management*.

Discussion questions

1 Why do managers need an understanding of work design?

2 Why was it important to consult with employees rather than impose the new job profiles on them?

The analysis and design of work

How jobs are designed is an important part of the organisation of work. This is not just the design of individual jobs, but also how the jobs link to each other in the structure of the organisation. This in turn links back to strategy, as the fit between jobs, organisational structure and external environment can have a major impact on how successful an organisation is. The mission and strategy of a company should determine how jobs are designed. For example, an organisation interested in efficiency is more likely to have centralised systems of functional clusters, such as a centralised HR or finance department, whereas an organisation that wants to encourage innovation and creativity may well organise work into self-managed teams, each with their own support services. There is not necessarily 'one best way' of organising jobs or designing organisations, it is usually contingent on the environment, structure and reasons for being, but what is important is that these are aligned to its design of work.

Walton (1996) and Wood and Albanese (1995) suggest that organisations wanting to enhance performance need to develop high performance and high commitment management, which needs to be linked into the specific design of work in the organisation.

A summary of Walton's and Wood and Albanese's work by the CIPD (2001) identifies the main features of a high commitment organisation as:

- the development of career ladders to encourage commitment
- emphasis on training at all levels of the organisation
- a high level of functional flexibility with the abandonment of potentially rigid job descriptions
- the reduction of hierarchies and the ending of status differentials
- a heavy reliance on team structure for disseminating information (team briefing), structuring work (team working) and problem-solving (quality circles)
- job design as something management consciously does in order to provide jobs that have a considerable level of intrinsic satisfaction
- a policy of no compulsory lay-offs or redundancies, and permanent employment guarantees with the possible use of temporary workers to cushion fluctuations in demand for labour
- new forms of assessment and payment systems and, more specifically, merit pay and profit sharing
- involving employees in quality management
- developing strategies to show staff they are valued.

This means that managers need to have appropriate techniques in place for the analysis and design of jobs. Guest *et al.* (2000) suggest that job design should 'ensure flexibility, commitment and motivation, including steps to ensure that employees have the responsibility and autonomy to use their knowledge to the full'.

Although job analysis and job design are separate, they are interlinked and it is difficult to do one without the other. **Job analysis** focuses on existing jobs and is used for gathering information for other human resource management practices, such as recruitment, selection, training, development and remuneration (this will be discussed in more detail in Chapter 4). Job analysis is the gathering together of information about skills, activities and levels of performance required to do a job. Job analysis leads to the job descriptions and person specifications necessary for the recruitment and selection process. Job design focuses instead on redesigning existing jobs to make them more efficient or more interesting. However, to do this, jobs still have to undergo some form of analysis. This chapter explains how this can happen.

job analysis

The process of obtaining detailed information about jobs.

Work flow design

organisational structure

The formal network of allocation of tasks in an organisation, which includes vertical and horizontal lines of communication.

This is the process of analysing the tasks necessary in the production of a product or service. Once we understand how the work is to flow, we can then decide how to group jobs into various tasks and who is to do these tasks. The **organisational structure** refers to how the work is distributed in the organisation and includes lines of communication as well as showing how different work roles relate to one another. This includes showing the allocation of tasks and levels of supervision at departmental level and also how different departments or parts of the organisation relate to one another and the chain of command above departmental level.

Work flow analysis

To understand the work flow process, we need to identify all the outputs of work and analyse the processes necessary to produce the outputs. It is only then that we can identify the inputs needed to produce the final product or service. This is illustrated in Exhibit 3-1.

All work outputs will be working towards the final output, whether it is a product or service to be delivered. For example, by ensuring the HR department has the right recruitment and selection strategies, the people employed are able to produce a product or service of an acceptable quality. Sometimes it is not easy to see how particular jobs link into the completed product, but if a job enables the final output to be delivered more efficiently, then it is important to the flow of work. An office cleaner may not be seen as necessary to the output of a department, but without a clean work environment people are unlikely to be efficient. Once outputs have been identified it is necessary to specify standards for the quantity or quality of these outputs. It is important for an HR manager to understand how the different work units in an organisation fit together and how having the right people, in the right place at the right time, ensures that a high-quality output can be produced.

Once the work outputs have been analysed, it is necessary to identify the work processes used to produce the outputs. The work processes are all the activities necessary to produce a given output. For each stage of production of goods or services an operating procedure can be produced. These will include all the tasks necessary in a work unit and how they will be divided among the work group.

To aid efficiency a manager needs to understand the processes required in the development of the product or service for that unit. He or she also needs to understand the implications of an increase or decrease in workload and when it is in the interests of efficiency to increase the size of the work group. An understanding of the work tasks enables a manager to specify which tasks are to be done by which individual, and to eliminate tasks that are not necessary to the job.

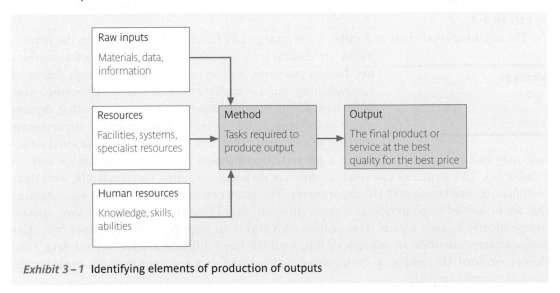

Exhibit 3 – 1 **Identifying elements of production of outputs**

Microsoft is an example of an organisation that follows this strategy in an attempt to ensure that it has a lean organisation with high levels of motivation – a combination, it argues, that helps it maintain competitive advantage. It does this by deliberately understaffing its teams to maintain a sense of 'small bands of people with a mission' (Fefer, 1992). However, this strategy could backfire. If people feel they are being overworked this could result in high levels of stress, which ultimately makes the organisation less effective. Technology also needs to be taken into account in the design of work. Although new technology may not be received positively by all employees, it is a significant aspect of job design in the twenty-first century and is important in increasing effectiveness. However, the wrong technology could increase problems in the workplace.

Analysing work inputs such as raw materials, resources such as equipment and technology, and human resources such as the technical skills and ability level of employees, is the final stage in work flow analysis. Have a look at the 'Stop and reflect' exercise and apply it to your college or university. Where the work is complex it may be that one person is not able to complete a particular task. This is where the team can come into play, as team members back each other up by having a wide range of skills. (Teams are becoming an increasingly important part of the workplace and will be discussed in more detail later in this chapter.)

Stop and reflect

In your college or university faculty, can you identify:

- who does what
- which roles are vital for the department
- who are the unseen workers that could affect productivity if they were removed?

Organisational structure

The structure of an organisation provides an overview of how it fits together. It is often displayed through the use of organisational charts. An example of an organisational chart is given in Exhibit 3-2.

The organisational chart in Exhibit 3-2 is arranged by function. In other words, the departments are divided into specialised divisions of finance, marketing, human resources, and so on. This enables a high degree of **centralisation**, but due to departmental specialisation employees often have a limited understanding of the role of other departments in the organisation, a factor that can lead to departments working against each other. Other types of organisational structure may be by division, such as in a property development organisation, as can be seen in Exhibit 3-3. This structure can result in different divisions operating independently, with their own finance, marketing and HR departments. The same can also be the case for organisations that are organised in geographical regions. Although they belong to one company, they operate independently in each region. This enables each region to respond to the customer base. Car manufacturers are often an example of this. Ford UK has a different market to Ford Asia, Ford Europe or Ford US, and as a consequence is structured as a semi-autonomous organisation from its parent company.

centralisation
An organisational structure that concentrates authority and decision-making towards the top.

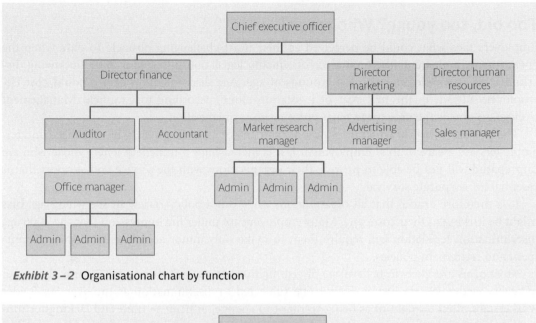

Exhibit 3 – 2 **Organisational chart by function**

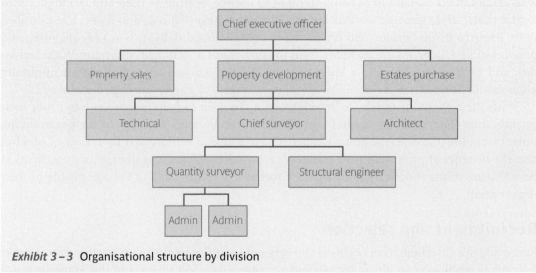

Exhibit 3 – 3 **Organisational structure by division**

Although function is one way of designing work, managers also need to think about who their employees are and how they can best fit into the design of the workplace. Ignoring workers could soon have serious consequences for employers and this is illustrated by the 'Managing diversity' box.

The changing nature of jobs

During the 1980s and 1990s there was a move away from the idea of jobs for life and a move towards employing people on short-term or fixed-term contracts. Organisations also moved towards using contract workers for certain functions, such as cleaning or catering.

This can lead to problems with job analysis, as many job analysis techniques tend to view jobs as static, whereas jobs in fact tend to change and evolve. Therefore, a job analysis can easily become out of date, which also results in the job description and specification being out of date. As the

managing diversity

Too old, too young? Who cares?

Employers face what could be perceived as their most challenging obstacle to date when the government implements the final piece of equality legislation in October 2006 outlawing discrimination in employment on the grounds of age. Age discrimination claims could cost UK employers £193m in the first year of legislation alone, according to Cranfield Management College, so now is the time to start age-proofing your organisation.

The legislation has far wider implications than any of us could possibly have realised and few employers are aware of this. Employment law is increasingly a minefield where those who are unprepared will not be able to provide their organisations with the service and support that is essential for corporate survival.

It is therefore crucial that all organisations carry out a policy review to see where age bias might be lurking in their company. Many employers are under the impression that the 2006 age discrimination legislation will require them to make only minor adjustments to their recruitment and retirement policies.

Most of us are likely to believe age discrimination affects only those aged 50 and above, yet in reality under 18s are just as likely to be subjected to discrimination as the over 50s. Older workers are often thought of as being resistant to change, difficult to train and lacking technological skills, while younger workers are thought to be inexperienced, unreliable, irresponsible, more likely to throw 'sickies' and lacking basic organisational skills such as time planning and prioritisation. Under 18s are excluded from the provisions of National Minimum Wage legislation and 18–21 year olds have a lower minimum wage attached to them. Surely a minimum wage should be exactly that – a minimum wage payable to all employees regardless of age?

With these issues in mind, we have devised a checklist to help employers age-proof their organisation. The need for greater age diversity brings many benefits to an organisation, notwithstanding the expertise and life experience of a diverse workforce with a range of ages but also the benefits of protecting your business's reputation and keeping discrimination claims at bay. Organisations should monitor age as a method of understanding the age profile of their organisation.

Recruitment and selection

Removing age discrimination begins at the very outset of the employment relationship. Thankfully many employers are already removing age criteria from job adverts but the 'graduate training scheme' is still prevalent. From October 2006 this will be indirect age discrimination as those candidates under 20 or over 65 are unlikely to have obtained a degree. The selection criteria for all roles will need to focus on the skills and competencies that are essential to perform the role. Making unsubstantiated requirements such as 'at least 10 years' experience' may fall foul of the new discrimination legislation. Age considerations must no longer be a central part of the application process as a method of judging a candidate's suitability for the role.

Promotion

Criteria based around having a minimum number of years of experience will be outlawed. Selection for promotion must be assessed using the same open and objective criteria used for external selection and devoid of anything that could be construed as direct or indirect age discrimination.

Training and development

Age must not be a barrier to training. Businesses need to consider the different learning styles of delegates – not everyone likes computer-based training (CBT) or is comfortable using it. Blended learning, with a mixture of formal classroom tuition, CBT and coaching, may be the most appropriate delivery method for an age-diverse organisation.

Redundancy

Be very careful when constructing redundancy criteria. Only objective criteria should be used. This might entail making people re-apply for their jobs if this is the only way to remove discrimination barriers.

Retirement

Many companies force people to retire anywhere between the ages of 50 and 65, regardless of their health and ability or desire to work. This will no longer be acceptable or legal, and organisations need to ensure that contracts of employment have no specified contractual retirement age. Why make people with highly valued skills and experience leave your organisation simply because they have reached a certain age? By all means include a clause that says they may continue to work for as long as they are fit and able.

Employee benefits

As yet there has been no concrete instruction from the UK Government as to whether pension schemes (and their age-related contributions) will be exempted from the new legislation. Consider how your business's pension schemes will be affected if pensions are not exempted and age-related contributions become outlawed. Watch this space as this legislation may well have an enormous impact upon the insurance industry and premiums for employer-paid insurance benefits!

Source: Gareth Emmons, *Business Europe.com*, http://bcs.businesseurope.com.

Discussion questions

1 What impact could the new legislation on age have on the design of work?

2 How should job and person specifications reflect an organisation's ability to manage a diverse workforce?

working environment becomes more flexible so too do job descriptions. This means that job descriptions are becoming broader and more flexible, and encourage generic transferable skills rather than job-specific skills. This also means that organisations need to be proactive in the design of jobs to ensure they meet the needs of the organisation and encourage competitive advantage.

Job design

job design
The method of identifying the tasks and levels of performance needed for a job.

Job design is the practical process of deciding how the job will be done and the tasks needed as part of the job. To do this an understanding is needed about the role of the job in the flow of work and an analysis of tasks needed as part of the job, as has been discussed earlier. For example, workers at McDonald's putting together burgers will have had their job analysed to decide the best way to do the job. Above their workstations are clear instructions for a step-by-step approach to assembling each product.

In the past job design has been the responsibility of managers and industrial engineers, who emphasised productivity over meaningfulness or satisfaction. However, research into the relationship between motivation and performance has identified the need for different approaches to job design.

Four basic approaches to job design have been identified by Campion (1987). These include the mechanistic approach, the motivational approach, the biological approach and the perceptual-motor approach to job design.

The mechanistic approach to job design

The **mechanistic approach** has its roots in the scientific school of management. This approach focuses on the most efficient way of doing a job. Taylor (1914), the father of the scientific approach, believed that the scientific **observation** of people at work would identify the 'one best way' to do a task. The McDonald's approach mentioned above is an example of mechanistic job design. Taylor was one of the first to develop the idea of time and motion studies to identify the most efficient movements during a work task. Workers were selected and trained to perform their jobs using Taylor's approach and were offered monetary incentives to ensure that they performed to their maximum efficiency. The problem with this approach to job design is that it is too preoccupied with productivity and ignores the worker's social needs. Although it was later recognised that employees had other needs, many managers use and continue to implement the scientific approach. A recent example is sports clothing manufacturer Nike, which was found to be employing labourers in its Chinese factories on a piece-rate system for as little as 10 pence an hour (Shook, 2001). It was not only the worker's jobs that changed under the **scientific management** approach, so did the manager's job. The manager now had to use scientific precision to divide work into tasks, to select and train people to do the tasks, and to ensure that procedures were in place to enable workers to separate work needs from individual needs.

mechanistic approach
A job design method that focuses on the most efficient way of doing the work.

observation
Watching people at work to understand what they do.

scientific management
Developed by Taylor as the 'one best way' to do a task.

The mechanistic approach takes the view that high-quality service is reliable service and, although today's managers have realised that involvement from the workers also has to be taken into account in the design process, many companies still base their job design on the mechanistic approach. For example, Disney theme parks, whether in Paris or Orlando, have carefully scripted roles for their employees. Not only do staff members have to learn how to deal with every eventuality, they also have to learn and rehearse a variety of phrases to prevent them sounding like robots. This is the reason they are known as 'cast members' rather than employees, as it gives the idea of an actor performing on stage rather than a worker doing a job.

The motivational approach to job design

human relations approach
A method of job design that focuses on the social behaviour of the person.

This stems from the **human relations approach** to management, where the focus shifted from a rational economic picture of employees to a social behavioural perspective. It also stems from the assumption that jobs can be designed to stimulate employee motivation and increase job satisfaction. This moved the focus away from the scientific approach of management and focused instead on the psychological effects of work. Theorists such as Herzberg (1993) asked two questions: 'What makes you feel good about your work?' and 'What makes you feel bad?' From the answers received, Herzberg concluded that job satisfaction was one of the key elements of motivational job design. Herzberg developed a 'dual factor theory' of motivation. He identified the 'hygiene factors' of a job. These referred to practices at work that could cause dissatisfaction, but if corrected would not motivate. For example, you could be given a laptop computer to do your job: it may stop you moaning about lack of IT facilities but you would not be motivated to work harder. Herzberg identified the 'motivator factors', which originate from the focus of the job, as those that can create job satisfaction and hence increase motivation. These tend to come from the social relationships at work and recognition of good performance.

From these findings different models of job design were developed, such as Hackman and Oldham's (1980). They developed a job characteristics model that identified the motivational factors of a job from the following aspects:

- skill variety – the variety of skills needed to complete the task
- task identity – how much of the complete product or service is completed by the worker; how much they feel they have ownership of the task
- task significance – how important the task is to the lives of others
- autonomy – how much of a decision-making role the person has while doing the job
- feedback – how much feedback an employee is given about their job performance.

The job characteristics proposed by Hackman and Oldham (1980), shown in Exhibit 3-4, are used to evaluate the meaningfulness of a job by its effect on the critical psychological states of:

- experienced meaningfulness
- responsibility
- knowledge of results.

When the critical psychological characteristics are high, then employees will have a high level of internal work motivation. This should then lead to greater productivity and help create competitive advantage through people.

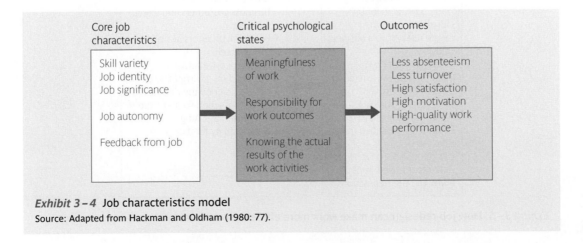

Exhibit 3–4 Job characteristics model
Source: Adapted from Hackman and Oldham (1980: 77).

job enlargement
Expanding the job to make it more meaningful.

horizontal loading
The process of enlarging jobs by combining separate work activities into a whole job that provides for greater task variety.

For a manager this means that work needs to be designed to make it more meaningful.

This is done through job enlargement, where the job is broadened to include different types of task. One method of doing this is through horizontal loading, where more duties are added with the same type of task characteristics. An example of this could be a car manufacturer where, in the past, workers had been responsible only for one element of the job, such as putting the wheels on a car. Enlarging the job could mean that as the car moved along the production line they moved along with it. The result would be that they would have more ownership of their task and therefore it would be more meaningful. Although this approach may increase skill variety, it could cause resentment if an employee thinks their work-load is being increased.

job enrichment
Empowering workers by involving them in the decision-making processes and design of their job.

vertical loading
The process of structuring a greater range of responsibility for planning, control and decision-making authority into the job.

job rotation
Moving people to different jobs to enrich their experience.

Another method of increasing the motivating potential of a job is through job enrichment, where workers are empowered by being more involved in the decision-making process. This uses vertical loading of responsibility, where workers can be involved in the planning, organisation and control of work. An example of this can be through self-managed teams, where workers are given a goal to achieve but it is their teams that decide how tasks are allocated to achieve their goal. Job rotation can also be used as part of the motivational approach; here, workers are moved from one job to another over time. When job rotation is used, most of the jobs tend to be similar and narrowly defined. However, it can increase skill variety and help boost job identity. Exhibit 3-5 illustrates how job redesign can improve work and make it more meaningful.

After the redesign of the cashiers' jobs, their new jobs were found to be more motivating and as a result their job performance increased significantly.

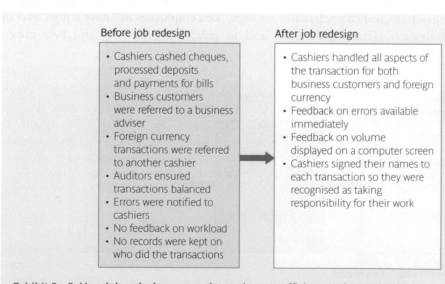

Before job redesign	After job redesign
• Cashiers cashed cheques, processed deposits and payments for bills • Business customers were referred to a business adviser • Foreign currency transactions were referred to another cashier • Auditors ensured transactions balanced • Errors were notified to cashiers • No feedback on workload • No records were kept on who did the transactions	• Cashiers handled all aspects of the transaction for both business customers and foreign currency • Feedback on errors available immediately • Feedback on volume displayed on a computer screen • Cashiers signed their names to each transaction so they were recognised as taking responsibility for their work

Exhibit 3 – 5 **How job redesign can make work more efficient and meaningful**

Research has shown that if work is seen as meaningful and important to the individual then they are likely to be more committed to the organisation and more productive.

The biological, or human factor, approach to job design

The biological, or human factor, approach to job design has developed from the study of ergonomics, where the employee's physical work environment is studied to minimise physical strain. This approach focuses on the health of the workforce and causes of physical fatigue. For example, it could mean providing the correct type of chair to ensure correct posture is maintained, providing wrist rests for computer operators, or screen guards to protect eyes from the glare of computer screens. The idea is that equipment can be designed that fits the physical features of the working population. Many of these issues could be seen as part of providing a healthy and safe working environment. A recent example of a biological approach to job design was carried out by a bank that needed to identify why a group of workers was always off sick. On investigation it was found that the office had no air conditioning, no windows and all the desks were bunched together, which meant not only sharing space but also germs. By changing the work environment, sickness was reduced.

ergonomics
The study of efficiency of people in their work environments.

When using the biological approach the demographics of the workers also need to be taken into account, such as the age of employees. Older employees may need to work at a different pace than a younger workforce, and women and men have different body shapes, which means the height and size of equipment may have to be adjustable.

Employers need to be concerned about the biological aspects of job design as not only is it a health and safety issue, but it could also affect job performance and leave them open to expensive litigation from employees, especially with recent legislation to protect workers with disability.

The perceptual-motor approach to job design

perceptual-motor approach
An approach to job design that has its origins in work psychology, and focuses on mental capabilities and limitations.

The perceptual-motor approach has its origins in work psychology and focuses on human mental capabilities and limitations. This approach is designed to design jobs so that they do not exceed the capabilities of the least capable person. It is useful for jobs in which an error could have serious consequences, such as air traffic control. A study by Buffardi *et al.* (2000) identified the relationship between ability requirements and job error, and suggested that all managers should be aware of the information-processing requirements of all jobs and design them to ensure that they could be performed by the least capable employee. In many respects this is returning to the mechanistic approach of job design, where jobs are de-skilled to reduce the cognitive demands. In jobs that require a high degree of information processing this would make sense, as it could reduce stress and potential burnout.

Task depth and scope

Two typical dimensions used for defining or describing all types of jobs, from general manager to routine production operator, are task scope and depth. Task scope describes the horizontal characteristics of a job, or the degree of variety in the activities a person is expected to perform. A job narrow in scope has few activities. A court reporter, for example, transcribes verbatim what is said during a trial; a lab technician draws blood samples eight hours a day. A cleaner who only empties waste bins has a narrower task scope than one who also mops, vacuums, dusts and washes windows.

Task depth addresses how much vertical responsibility or individual accountability is expected in a job. Depth increases when the employee is given responsibility to schedule the sequence of work, to initiate self-control if activities or output begin to get out of balance, to identify and solve problems as they occur, or to originate innovative ways of improving the process or the output. Task depth is shallow when managers determine what job-holders are to do, when they are to do it and in what quantities, and then monitor results to determine if work output matches the standards handed down.

Combining scope and depth into four job profiles

Task scope and depth can be considered ways of 'loading' work into jobs. When combined into a 2×2 matrix, high or low loadings on each of the two variables identify four types of broad job classification. Exhibit 3-6 illustrates how these job features produce different work experiences.

Ultimately, managers should ask themselves the following questions. Do our job structures and technology fit the capabilities of the people we employ? Do these jobs promote high-quality work, satisfying to those who produce it? Too often, the answer to both questions will be no. Despite all the media attention showered on high technology and dotcom start-ups, many jobs still incorporate narrowly defined requirements that were common 20 or more years ago. Routine jobs that are low in scope and depth are prone to under-utilise the mental competencies of employees, and thus reduce the quality level attained by the organisation.

Routine jobs

These are programmed to be repetitive and narrow in scope, and are often restricted by technology. People in these simplistic and repetitive jobs are expected not to do much independent thinking, instead just paying attention to detail. Examples of routine jobs include data entry, assembly, clerical and cashier jobs. Skills are mastered in a matter of hours or days; there is no expectation of career growth unless one becomes a supervisor over those performing these routine jobs.

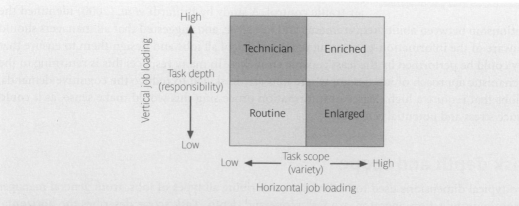

Exhibit 3 – 6 Four combinations of task scope and task depth
Source: Bloisi *et al.* (2003).

Technician jobs

These offer greater opportunities for independent thinking and deciding what to do when, but provide employees with little variety in their daily tasks. The technician may have a university education or need professional training to learn how to perform the job of, say, a pharmacist or stockbroker. The work may be valued by the client, but research suggests that people such as medical technicians find their jobs become meaningless over time because their job tasks are repetitive and there is little growth opportunity.

Enlarged jobs

These provide an expanded variety or diversity of tasks. At times jobs are deliberately expanded, either by adding on sequential tasks or by allowing employees to rotate among different jobs. Decreasing the number of separate job classifications or titles in a traditional industry typically affords employees enlarged variety or a change of pace.

Enriched jobs

These enable an individual to feel responsible for whole tasks. Most professional jobs that require analysis and manipulation of symbolic data (managers, scientists and teachers, for example) are enriched to give the individual responsibility for doing whatever is necessary to get the job done. The work presents challenges and novelty, with the incumbent empowered to solve problems and find innovative solutions to shifting performance demands.

Scope and depth are at the most basic level of job design. Other dimensions of jobs are equally important and can have an effect on the attitudes of workers and their willingness to perform successfully. These elements form part of the psychological contract.

The psychological contract

psychological contract
The expectation that an employee will be rewarded for their contribution to the organisation.

The **psychological contract** refers to the expectation that an employee will be rewarded for their contribution to the organisation. This does not refer to a written contract of employment, which would include the rights and duties of both the employer and employee: it is an unwritten psychological contract that in the past could have included expectations about job security and promotion prospects. With the changing nature of work a new psychological contract is emerging that includes employers' expectations of creativity, flexibility and innovation. Employees are recognising that the responsibility of employability resides with them and not with the employer. This can create problems for the organisation, as it needs to create commitment from its employees while still being flexible enough to restructure in response to changing markets.

An example of what might be included in a psychological contract can be seen in Exhibit 3-7.

So what happens if we put in the work and our employer doesn't come up with the expected rewards? According to Briner and Conway (2004), this makes us question whether it is worth putting in that extra effort in future. If we decide it isn't, then we may end up doing the bare minimum, or even question if we are in the right job.

The psychological contract was first identified by Argyris (1994), who on observing a foreman and his employees noticed that the workers were motivated to achieve providing they had a fair wage and control over their work. The idea of a psychological contract was developed by Rousseau (1995), who recognised that it was subjective and individual, and could vary from

Employees promise to:	Employers promise to provide:
■ work hard	■ pay commensurate with performance
■ uphold company reputation	■ opportunities for training and development
■ maintain high levels of attendance and punctuality	■ opportunities for promotion
■ show loyalty to the organisation	■ recognition for innovation or new ideas
■ work extra hours when required	■ feedback on performance
■ develop new skills and update old ones	■ interesting tasks
■ be flexible – for example, taking on colleagues' work	■ an attractive benefits package
■ be honest	■ respectful treatment
■ come up with new ideas	■ reasonable job security
	■ a pleasant and safe working environment

Exhibit 3 – 7 Example of a psychological contract
Source: Adapted from Briner and Conway (2004: 43).

one person to another. Rousseau's work highlighted the impact the psychological contract could have on an organisation's performance and noted that it should be more measurable and concrete. In some cases this has meant that employers have specified in more detail what is expected of employees, although they have not always been explicit about what they will give.

New ways of working

As a response to the new psychological contract employers are changing the nature of work arrangements. Many jobs may be outsourced to other organisations, either in the UK or abroad, such as call centres dealing with customer services, which are often outsourced to India. Alternatively, contract company workers are used. This is where one organisation provides workers to do a job for another, such as hospital cleaners, who work for a cleaning firm rather than directly for the hospital. There is also the use of agency workers, where an organisation will use temporary workers when needed rather than employ people within the organisation. This is the case with agency nurses and supply teachers, who work for the agency rather than the hospital or school. Many workers choose these working arrangements as they allow flexibility and enable them to ensure they have an acceptable work/life balance. Many employers also choose to use contract or temporary workers as it enables them to respond to change more readily. However, research has shown that many such jobs provide very few employee benefits, and many organisations that use these workers need to ensure that they are able to do the job and meet the needs of the customers. It has also been suggested that the use of temporary or agency staff can be demoralising for permanent staff, as although the temporary staff may be competent in their skills they are often not familiar with the organisational culture, which means they require constant monitoring.

Developments in flexible working

With developments in technology and increased use of the Internet, as well as the demise of the nine-to-five, five-day week, many employers are requiring workers to be more flexible. This means that where many employees would only have worked during weekdays, they are now required to work evenings, night shifts or at weekends. New technology also means that employees are no longer able to switch off from work at the end of a day: they can be contacted by email or mobile phone wherever they are in the world. All this is leading to increased employee stress, which ultimately leads to employee dissatisfaction and less productive workers.

To counteract these problems many employers are developing flexible working patterns and aiming to use employees' time at work more productively. Some employers, such as British Telecom, encourage staff to work more flexibly. Following a workstyle analysis it now has 7500 of its workforce formally based at home and another 40,000 have remote access. This has meant that, not only does it save £180 million in property costs, but it has also improved productivity by 20–40 per cent, as staff no longer have to waste time travelling to work. It also sends a strong message that the company trusts its employees, which is also seen as an important motivator. The 'International perspective' box illustrates how the reality of teleworking affects both employers and employees.

Telecommuting: a Canadian perspective

Telework arrangements can save employees time and companies money. A number of larger multinationals have adopted it in their operations, but fewer than you'd expect. Yet it really does make sense. The challenge is doing it right, with the right people, on the right schedule.

Like so many innovative business management concepts, telecommuting is often hailed as a wonderful idea but remains under-used in real life. Employers across Canada talk about the importance of work/life balance but when it comes to actually instituting systems to address that, they hesitate.

Quebec is considered an exception in Canada. The province has the most family- and employee-friendly policies and practices in the country, according to a November 2003 study. This includes not only the option of telework but also decent pay, less overtime, personal days off with pay, flexible hours and on-site day care. People from the province of Ontario, on the other hand, are the highest paid in the country but are the most unhappy and least satisfied with their jobs. Telecommuting is only a small piece of the larger work/life balance issue but it can be a useful tool for both employees and management.

Diverse needs

The core concept behind telecommuting unquestionably makes a lot of sense. Many people are exhausted by daily commutes in ever more congested cities. In fact, 2.5 hours was the average amount of commute time indicated by respondents in one study conducted by Derrick Neufeld CMA, a professor at the Richard Ivey School of Business (University of Western Ontario). By equipping employees with sophisticated technology at home, you can keep them in as good or better touch with co-workers and superiors. This can reduce stress, increase job satisfaction and improve workforce retention – along with productivity.

The technological advances in the past 10 years have clearly made a difference in the telecommuting landscape. IBM launched its mobility and telecommunications programme in 1996 with a nine-month pilot in the company's Ottawa offices. Even in a short eight years, there's a world of difference in the technology available, says Susan Turner, IBM Canada's diversity and workplace programs executive.

'Any company starting now has the advantage of more flexibility,' she notes. 'We have a system now that transfers our phone calls to wherever we are. At the same time, with Same-time instant messaging and messenger service, anyone in our organisation can access remote conferencing from wherever they are.'

'There is still lots of resistance everywhere but at the same time everybody is getting more comfortable with the technology and the work anywhere, anytime mentality,' says Bob Fortier, a telework pioneer in Canada, and founder and principal of InnoVisions Canada, a telework consulting company. 'And now, we're seeing a lot more strategic business drivers – real estate costs, contingency planning, improved recruitment and retention, and leveraging labour forces from other time zones. I believe that telework is really still in its infancy.'

But telecommuting isn't for every organisation or everyone in an organisation. For instance, while IBM maintains an innovative programme, only between 25 and 30 per cent of its employees are full-time telecommuters. This includes obvious candidates such as consultants and employees who remain on-site at client offices. However, 80 per cent of the other employees do have the flexibility to work from home occasionally.

Charting realities

Employees have their own reasons for wanting to telecommute. The primary reason appears to be an increased sense of personal control and flexibility. Many like the idea of setting their own hours, eliminating a frustrating daily commute, dressing more casually or having fewer workday interruptions so they can focus on output.

'The point for most employees, in my experience, isn't to shirk their job responsibilities but rather to do their jobs more efficiently and effectively, while at the same time better balancing their work and personal lives,' says Neufeld. Turner also points out some employees' need for flexible work hours to care for elderly family members or children.

But although many approach the telecommuting concept with enthusiasm, the reality can sometimes be mixed. The fact remains that such an arrangement doesn't suit everyone or every work environment.

'I've spoken to individuals who were very enthusiastic about telecommuting initially but then found that their boss's needs or their team's culture required them to be in the office every day,' says Neufeld. 'Or, distractions at home proved to be too great. I've spoken to others who were initially sceptical but quickly warmed to it after a bit of experience.'

A telecommuting relationship, however, also creates expectations on both sides. For instance, employees typically expect that any commute time savings belong to them, whereas managers often feel that the firm should be entitled to at least some time 'kickback'. There are other blurry issues raised by such an arrangement, such as who should pay for the remote technology; who should pay for home office space renovations; or whether in-office employees would have career progression advantages over telecommuters.

'The bottom line is that the effects of telecommuting for firms and individuals will depend on many factors,' says Neufeld. 'Any telecommuting programme must first assess the suitability of individuals case by case and work out the details with them before committing to the idea.'

Neufeld stressed the importance of reviewing the personal, relational, resource and function factors of anyone interested in telecommuting. Do they have the motivation, job commitment, focus on deliverables, interpersonal communication capacity and distraction-free environment to thrive in such an arrangement? Do they have relationships with managers and peers that will facilitate distance communication? Is their job independent or interdependent? Do clients or customers expect regular physical access to the employee? And is the telecommuter properly equipped for such an arrangement?

At IBM, employees are given a self-assessment tool, to determine whether or not telecommuting is a good fit for their personality and their job. Included with the tool are online tutorials and an employee's guide to working at home.

'If you have a failing performance at work, it's unlikely you're going to have the chance to telecommute,' says Turner. 'But at the same time, we look at personal circumstances. It may be that working from home would improve certain individuals' performance.'

Proper models

Larger firms considering adopting telework arrangements have to take a look at the bigger picture of the organisation and consider a number of issues.

'A few years ago, I sat in on a task force that evaluated telecommuting for a large firm, prior to the development of a national programme,' says Neufeld. 'A team of approximately 20 senior executives with deep functional expertise met over a six-month period, examined published information and assessed the suitability of telecommuting to the organisation. They developed a planning framework. They surveyed the workforce to understand people's attitudes towards the idea and invited employees to join project teams to design a programme that would work for them.'

What impressed Neufeld most about the programme wasn't so much the particulars of the technique but rather the three components that are critical to any successful implementation: public commitment from senior leaders; employee involvement (via primary advanced research on attitudes and involvement with protocols); and project management excellence (clear and realistic objectives, stated milestones, contingency planning, etc.).

Companies will get resistance from employees if they aren't clear on any of these levels, and honesty, clearly, is an asset. Management needs to be clear about its objectives in making such a move.

It's important to have employee buy-in before a big push is made to introduce any such programme. The intentions of the programme should be explicit too. Employees are more receptive when they are given the big-picture view.

Once a programme is accepted by employees, of course, the work isn't done. There is also a risk-management component in telework that companies have to consider. 'If companies aren't taking steps to protect the technology that employees are using at home, they are opening themselves up for attacks on their system,' says Fortier. 'It's also cavalier to send lots of employees home without considering home ergonomics, the kind of equipment they're using. Without considering these issues, companies aren't doing their due diligence.'

Source: R. Coleman, *CMA Management* 78(15), August–September 2004, Society of Management Accountants of Canada, p. 23(5).

Discussion questions

1 What recommendations would you give to an organisation that wanted to develop teleworking?

2 How would you implement a job analysis for workers without a physical presence in the organisation?

The role of teams in the design of work

With flatter and leaner organisations, teams are having a greater impact on the design of work. Many employers are realising the role a team can have in increasing productivity and they are moving away from a hierarchical management structure to a flatter, team-based structure. This means that managers need to design jobs to fit in with teams. With increasing job complexity it is often the case that no one person has all the skills to do a specific job, therefore the task is allocated to a team rather than an individual. Team working means that a wide set of skills is available and team members can back each other up when necessary. To be effective, managers need to identify the level of task interdependence with the level of outcome interdependence. For example, a surgical ward in a hospital would consist of doctors, nurses, administrators, and so on. The staff all have different skills and different responsibilities, and yet without all of these the ward would not be able to function. Therefore it is the role of the manager to identify how these individuals should feed into the team process and be rewarded as a team. The role of teamwork is especially important in high-pressure work environments and it means everyone is responsible for ensuring that mistakes are identified and rectified.

Organisations also need to be more flexible and, according to Guile and Fonda (1999), this means managers need to integrate individual tasks into team-based, horizontal work structures. In the past, many approaches to job design have been concerned only with the design of the job for the individual rather than the team.

The contemporary team approach to job design takes into account:

- the needs of individuals
- the constraints of technology, and
- the role of these in the team.

In designing work around teams, job rotation, job enlargement and job enrichment may be used to enable workers to move from different tasks or to follow the whole process as part of the team. For example, a car manufacturer using teams may allocate its teams to certain parts of the manufacturing process, or the team may follow the car through the entire manufacturing process. Any decisions that need to be made as part of the work process will include all members of the team. The results are that team working enables team members to satisfy their achievement needs through task completion, and their social needs through team interaction.

Functional group roles

role

An expected set of behaviours that are expected from a member by others in a group.

According to Kolb *et al.* (1991), a **role** is an expected set of recurring behaviours that is expected from a team member by others in the group. Some group roles are functional in that they help the group achieve its goals. Other roles, which are usually motivated by specific individual needs, are dysfunctional and interfere with group effectiveness. After a group has matured to the 'performing' stage, personal behaviours detrimental to the group are mostly eliminated and members adopt behaviours beneficial to group performance.

Belbin's team roles

Belbin (1993), in a study of business game teams at the Carnegie Institute of Technology in 1981, found that for a group to be effective there are eight necessary roles, shown in Exhibit 3-8, which

Role	Characteristics	Strengths	Possible weaknesses	Contributions to work team
Co-ordinator	Calm Self-confident Disciplined Controlled	Optimist Self-disciplined Common sense Organisational skills	Average intellect or creative ability	Presides and co-ordinates, good at working through others
Shaper	Highly strung Dominant Extrovert	Challenges inertia Dynamic	Impatient Irritable Argumentative	Passionate about the task and good at inspiring others and spurring to action
Plant	Introvert Individualist Imaginative	Intellectual Creative thinker Unorthodox	Disregards practice or procedure Doesn't take account of reality	An innovative person full of imagination and ideas
Monitor-evaluator	Prudent Unemotional Unbiased	Discreet High intellect Rational Analytical	Uninspiring A 'jobsworth' Tactless	Analyses project and spots possible flaws, keeps the plant in check
Resource investigator	Popular Sociable Extrovert Relaxed	Good social skills Communicative	Not an originator of ideas Can easily lose interest	Good for networking and making contact outside the team
Implementer	Trustworthy Efficient Practical	Administrator Conscientious Systematic	Not a leader Inflexible	Transforms plans into action; often performs tasks others may consider boring
Team worker	Supportive Sensitive Diplomatic	Shows concern for others Team player	Indecisive in a crisis	Maintains team spirit and helps reduce conflict; often only noticed when absent
Finisher	Conscientious Thorough Anxious	Perfectionist Pays attention to detail	Worries over small details	Ensures the team concentrates on the necessary tasks to achieve deadlines; not always popular
Specialist	Independent Single-minded	Dedicated	Protective of expertise	Provides knowledge and skills when needed

Exhibit 3–8 Belbin's team roles
Source: Belbin (1993).

ideally would be spread evenly among the team. These were known as the co-ordinator, the shaper, the plant, the monitor-evaluator, the resource investigator, the implementer, the team worker and the finisher. Belbin also identified a ninth person, the specialist, who would join the group when required; this person may be a legal expert, IT specialist or accountant.

Belbin (1993) noticed that when a group's task changes, individuals may move from one role to another and, in small groups, people may occupy more than one role.

Independent research confirms that groups that have a balance of member roles are the most effective, although there has been some argument as to whether it is necessary to have as many as nine members in order for a group to be effective.

The research by Belbin, and the subsequent self-perception inventory developed by Belbin and his colleagues, enable team members to be identified prior to team formation, and can be useful when teams need to be assembled quickly. However, care needs to be taken when using this technique, to ensure that the appropriate people are selected as roles are not necessarily static.

task roles
Roles that directly help to accomplish group goals.

maintenance roles
Roles that help establish and maintain good relationships among group members.

personal roles
Roles that only meet individual needs and may be detrimental to the group.

Earlier research by Benne and Sheats (1948) also found that it is necessary for two types of functional role to emerge for a group to continue to exist and accomplish its objectives in a satisfactory manner. They called these task roles and maintenance roles. **Task roles** are those that directly help accomplish group goals, while **maintenance roles** help establish and maintain good relationships among group members. Examples of these roles are listed in Exhibit 3-9, along with some frequent **personal roles**, which are sets of behaviours that meet individual needs and are usually detrimental to the group's interaction. Personal roles need to be replaced with maintenance and task roles before a group can become an effective team.

Self-managed teams

Providing employees with more autonomy with regard to how to do their jobs has been found to be particularly effective in maintaining high worker commitment, which in turn improves performance. Job autonomy is proving to be the way forward, as many employees value the responsibility this entails. One method of increasing autonomy is through self-managed teams.

self-managed teams
An autonomous group of workers responsible for planning, scheduling, monitoring and staffing themselves.

Self-managed teams are those that are given responsibility for their own authority for planning, scheduling and staffing.

Task roles	Maintenance roles	Personal roles
Initiating	Encouraging	Blocking
Giving information	Harmonising	Recognition seeking
Seeking information	Setting group standards	Dominating
Summarising	Gatekeeping	Avoiding
Elaborating	Compromising	Seeking help
Consensus testing	Providing feedback	

Exhibit 3 – 9 Group roles

The car manufacturer Volvo was one of the first to implement autonomous work teams. In the 1970s it built a new engine plant that was designed in such a way as to allow work teams to decide how to assemble engines, establish their own pace of work and schedule breaks. The result, according to Barker (1993), was that staff turnover and absenteeism reduced to virtually nil, and productivity was increased to one engine every 30 minutes. However, as technology has moved on, the Volvo plant has now ceased to exist as more efficient means of production have been found.

Since the 1970s many multinational companies, such as Hewlett-Packard and General Motors, have established self-managed teams, and this has generally had a positive impact on productivity and responsibility.

There has also been criticism of relying on teams, where some organisations have felt that this has not produced the desired increases in production that were originally envisaged. Much of this is down to unrealistic expectations. Scott and Harrison (1997) argue that team working is not a 'quick fix', which can be used to improve performance if there are other more serious organisational problems, but it can help improve motivation by empowering employees to take responsibility for their own work.

Self-managed teams can have varying levels of responsibility. They may have responsibility for setting their budget, or they could be given a budget that they have to work within. Either way, they have to decide how to use their resources – both financial and human – and organise the work tasks to achieve their goals. Self-managed teams have no traditional hierarchy, with everyone in the team having the same status and being involved in the management function. Although a team leader may be identified to represent the team either by senior management or within the team itself, this role is one of facilitation rather than monitoring and control.

Although the idea of self-managed teams is to increase ownership and therefore increase control, problems can arise if the implementation of teams has not been adequately thought through: for instance, problems with resistance to change within both the team and the organisation at large, or peer pressure. The implications for providing autonomy at work are more than changing the design of the job; other aspects of human resource management also need to be taken into account and aligned to fit the new jobs.

Kerr (1993) found that organisations with a high degree of autonomy, which are more likely to use self-managed teams, usually have the following characteristics:

- detailed recruitment and selection processes that ensure new recruits are able to work autonomously
- a flat organisational structure
- flexible guidelines and parameters to enable workers to make decisions
- accountability for their results; it is the achievement of results, rather than the process, that is important
- high-quality performance is an expected part of the measurement
- open and effective communication structures
- employee satisfaction as a core value.

For these reasons, organisations wanting to redesign work and move to a more team-based approach may need to think beyond job redesign and focus on organisation redesign. To make such a change takes time, and to enable effective team working and organisational success takes planning. Usually the process starts with teams making a few decisions, such as when to perform routine functions and assigning daily tasks. As they become more empowered they can take on responsibility for quality control and selection of team members, and eventually teams can begin to develop workplace methods and procedures, monitor team performance and prepare budgets.

Johnson (1993) identifies the following as tasks for which self-managed teams can make decisions:

- routine maintenance and cleanliness
- stop production if there are quality problems
- assign tasks to team members
- select team members
- identify and provide training
- develop work methods
- ensure health and safety is enforced
- monitor, report and evaluate workplace performance
- set production goals
- liaise with suppliers and customers
- carry out disciplinary procedures
- conduct team appraisals
- plan budgets and forecasts.

Barriers to teamwork

Although individuals can create barriers to effective change, quite often the major obstacle is the organisation itself. Therefore, for teams to be successful, it is the organisation that needs to change. To reduce barriers to team working, organisations need to:

- develop compensation systems that reward teams rather than individuals
- develop appraisal systems that focus on group involvement and achievement, rather than the individual
- enable teams to access information; many organisations are fearful of allowing sensitive information to be shared with employees in case of industrial espionage
- develop team-working skills through training
- develop team-management skills for line managers and employee representatives.

Summary

- The design and flow of work is important to the functioning of an organisation, as it identifies how tasks are allocated, who is responsible and how the organisation communicates. The organisational structure can be used to identify the flow of work.

- Work flow analysis identifies how the tasks are distributed in an organisation to enable it to fulfil its aims. An analysis of the flow of work is useful to ensure that the organisation's strategy and mission are being achieved.

- Job analysis is the process of obtaining detailed information about individual jobs. It is used as part of the HR planning and recruitment and selection process.

- Job analysis methods involve examining job descriptions and person specifications, observing workers, using questionnaires and interviews.

- Job descriptions identify the basic requirements of a job, the key tasks, responsibilities and attributes.

- The person specification identifies the skills and attributes a person needs for a job. Frameworks developed by Rodger (1952) and Fraser (1978) outline attributes, such as physique, mental abilities and personality.

- Job design refers to how work is organised. Campion (1987) identified four methods based on mechanistic, motivational, biological and perceptual-motor approaches.

- The psychological contract refers to expectations that an employee will be rewarded for his or her contribution to an organisation. The fulfilment of the psychological contract is important in encouraging commitment.

- In designing jobs it is important to understand the impact of new ways of working and designing jobs, such as outsourcing, teleworking and work/life balance.

- Work and job design also need to identify the expanded roles of teams, and their importance for task completion and employee commitment.

- Team working involves people taking on different roles in the organisation, and work design needs to reflect such roles.

Personal development

1 **Understand how the design of an organisation is linked to the flow of work.** Identify an organisation with which you are familiar: what does the structure of the organisation look like? Draw a diagram, identifying who is in charge, who talks to whom, and so on. How and where are the tasks accomplished? Does this link back to the aims of the organisation?

2 **Identify how job analysis can be used to obtain information about a job.** Where would you start if you needed to carry out a job analysis for recruitment purposes? If it is with the job description, is it up to date and still relevant? Who could you ask for more information? How could you ask them? What are the advantages and disadvantages of the various techniques used for job analysis?

3 **Identify the different approaches used in job design.** What are the implications of the four different approaches proposed by Campion (1987)? Which one do you think would encourage employee commitment? How could managers ensure they use the right approach for their organisation?

4 **Understand the impact of the psychological contract.** What would you expect from an employer you are working for? If your expectations are not met, how would you feel? What expectations should the employer have from you, or does the psychological contract operate only in one direction?

5 **Understand the implications of new ways of working for job and work design.** Would different approaches to job design be used for a call centre in the UK and one in India? How could job descriptions reflect people's desire for flexible working or working from home? How can managers measure job performance if they no longer see their workers?

6 **Understand the importance of team working and self-managed teams in the design of work.** How could you design work tasks around teams rather than individuals? What are the implications of pay and reward for self-managed teams? What is the impact of team working on the structure of the organisation?

❓ Discussion questions

1 Why does the analysis of the flow of work involve an initial examination of the organisational structure?

2 How do job analysis and job design link to the functions of HR?

3 Why is it important for an HR manager to be able to use job analysis techniques?

4 What is the difference between a job description and a person specification?

5 What should be included in a job description?

6 Examine in detail the different approaches to job design and the implications of each approach for managers.

7 Why is it important to managers to understand the role of the psychological contract at work?

8 How can job descriptions reflect the new ways of working?

9 What are the implications of team working for managers in the design of jobs? How can this impact on other areas of the HR function?

10 As an HR manager, how can you ensure that design of work responds to the needs of a diverse workforce?

Individual task

Purpose To understand the implications of the psychological contract.

Time 40 minutes

Procedure What would be expected from the psychological contract, from both the employee and employer perspective?

Once an outline has been developed, compare the expectations of both employer and employee, and answer the following questions.

1 How can they be combined to ensure that the employee's expectations and the organisation's expectations are harmonised?

2 Should the psychological contract be explicit or implicit?

❶ Key concepts

job analysis, *p. 76*	vertical loading, *p. 84*
organisational structure, *p. 76*	job rotation, *p. 84*
centralisation, *p. 78*	ergonomics, *p. 85*
job design, *p. 81*	perceptual-motor approach, *p. 85*
mechanistic approach, *p. 82*	psychological contract, *p. 87*
observation, *p. 82*	role, *p. 92*
scientific management, *p. 82*	task roles, *p. 94*
human relations approach, *p. 82*	maintenance roles, *p. 94*
job enlargement, *p. 84*	personal roles, *p. 94*
horizontal loading, *p. 84*	self-managed teams, *p. 94*
job enrichment, *p. 84*	

Team task

Purpose This exercise involves using the principles of scientific management and applying them to the design of work.

Time 60 minutes

Materials Sheets of plain paper, scissors.

Procedure Divide the class into groups of four. Each group will be assigned one of the following goal-setting conditions.

1 *No minimum:* the group sets its own standard.

2 *Low minimum:* the group is told to produce 15 paper chatterboxes per 15-minute production run.

3 *High minimum:* the group is told that it is expected to produce 30 chatterboxes per 15-minute production run.

Making chatterboxes

Cut a piece of paper into an even square. Fold the four corners to the centre. You will now have another smaller square. Repeat to make another smaller square. Turn the paper over and again fold all corners to the centre. Place a finger and thumb under each flap on the underneath and push the points together to form a pyramid. You should now be able to open and close the 'mouth' of the chatterbox.

Scoring

- All paper must be obtained before the beginning of the production period.
- Each sheet is worth £1.
- Each chatterbox can be sold for £5. However, they must all meet specified quality standards (see below).

Production standards

- The paper must not be torn.
- All points must meet exactly.
- The folds must not overlap one another.
- If the chatterboxes are torn, they are worthless.
- If the points do not meet or the folds overlap they can be sold as seconds for £3.
- At the end of the 15-minute production period, deduct the cost of materials from the sales price of the chatterboxes and calculate the total profit.

Discussion questions

1 Did any of the groups use scientific principles such as task specialisation and division of labour?

2 What were the effects of the different goal-setting conditions on the groups' performance of the task?

3 Is this the most effective way to design work?

Case study: St Lucia's secondary school

St Lucia's is a secondary school of 800 students in an affluent suburb of London. It has recently recruited a new head, who has a vision of making the school one of high academic achievement, while maintaining a caring ethos.

The school office is staffed by two secretaries: one, Cara, who is full-time and works from 9 am to 5 pm and another, Julie, who works from 9 am to 4 pm term time only. Cara and Julie feel they are at breaking point: the office is situated at the entrance to the school, therefore any visitors have to report to the office (these could be parents of children, suppliers and so on). Cara and Julie also have to answer the main telephone line into the school and record any absences. If any of the students need to buy stationery or make phone calls home they also have to do this via the school office. This means that, for much of the day, they are dealing with interruptions, which means they are unable to do their main jobs of typing out exam results, compiling school reports, drafting newsletters and monitoring attendance. The outcome has been that Cara often starts work at 8 am and does not finish until 6 pm, and Julie often has to take work home with her to do in the evening.

The new head is keen to reorganise the office and would like to ensure that there is cover from 8 am until 6 pm Monday to Friday, including holidays. Cara and Julie are now fed up, there has been no consultation, and they feel they are overworked, underpaid and undervalued. They feel that, rather than increasing their hours, they should be employing another member of staff. Both have now given notice to leave.

You have been approached as an HR consultant to try to resolve the situation.

Discussion questions

1 How would you identify the work flow and its fit to the organisational structure?

2 What tools would you use to analyse the different jobs?

3 What recommendations would you make to the headteacher?

4 Why is job analysis and design important to the effectiveness of an organisation?

WWW exercise

Choose a company that you would like to work for when you have completed your studies. Visit its website and look at the vacancies it has available. Choose one of the jobs, and view the job description and person specification for that job.

1 What are the tasks, skills and qualifications required for the job?

2 Does the person specification give a fair representation of the person requirements for the job?

3 What are the gaps you have, if any, in meeting the person specification?

4 What do you need to do to close those gaps?

Specific web exercise

The Virgin company has a very clear idea about what it expects one of its employees to be like. Go to the Virgin website at www.virgin.com/aboutus/jobs.

From the information provided, what would you expect to be in the person specification if you were to apply for a job with this company?

LEARNING CHECKLIST

Before moving on to the next chapter, check that you are able to:

☑ examine the role of HR in the analysis of jobs

☑ understand the importance of job design

☑ understand new developments in the world of work

☑ understand the importance of team working.

Further reading

Fisher, H., Hunter, T.A. and Macrosson, W.D.K. (1998) 'The structure of Belbin's team roles', *Journal of Occupational and Organizational Psychology* 71(3), pp. 283–288.

Flanagan, J.C. (1954) 'The critical incident technique', *Psychological Bulletin* 51, pp. 327–358.

Fleishman, E. and Mumford, M. (1991) 'Ability requirements scales', *The Job Analysis Handbook for Business, Industry and Government*, pp. 917–935.

Fleishman, E. and Reilly, M. (1992) *Handbook of Human Abilities.* Palo Alto, CA: Consulting Psychologists Press.

Harvey, R.J. (1993) 'Job analysis', in M.D. Dunnette and L.M. Hough (eds) *Handbook of Industrial Organisational Psychology* (2nd edn, Vol. 2). Palo Alto, CA: Consulting Psychologists Press, pp. 71–163.

McCormick, E.J., Jeanneret, P.R. and Mecham, R.C. (1972) 'A study of job characteristics and job dimensions as based on the position analysis questionnaire', *Journal of Applied Psychology* 56, pp. 347–367.

Scarborough, H., Swan, J. and Preston, J. (1999) *Knowledge Management: A Literature Review.* London: Institute of Personnel Development.

Schmitt, N. and Chan, D. (1998) *Personal Selection: A Theoretical Approach.* London: Sage.

References

Argyris, C. (1994) 'Good communication that blocks learning', *Harvard Business Review* 72, July–August, pp. 77–85.

Barker, J.R. (1993) 'Tightening the iron cage: concertive control in self-managing teams', *Administrative Science Quarterly*, September, pp. 408–437.

Belbin, R.M. (1993) *Team Roles at Work.* Oxford: Butterworth Heinemann.

Benne, K.D. and Sheats, P. (1948) 'Functional roles of group members', *Journal of Social Issues* 4(2), Spring, pp. 41–49.

Bloisi, W., Cook, H. and Hunsaker, P. (2003) *Management and Organisational Behaviour.* Maidenhead: McGraw-Hill.

Briner, R. and Conway, N. (2004) 'Promises, promises', *People Management*, 25 November, pp. 42–43.

Buffardi, L.C., Fleishman, E.A., Morath, R.A. and McCarthy, P.M. (2000) 'Relationships between ability requirements and human errors in job tasks', *Journal of Applied Psychology* 85, pp. 551–564.

Campion, M.A. (1987) 'Job design, approaches, outcomes and trade offs', *Organizational Behaviour*, Winter.

CIPD (2001) *The Case for Good People Management: A Summary of Research.* London: CIPD.

Fefer, M. (1992) 'Bill Gates' next challenge', *Fortune*, 14 December, pp. 30–41.

Fraser, J.M. (1978) *Employment Interviewing* (5th edn). Macdonald and Evans.

Guest, D., Michie, J., Sheehan, M. and Conway, N. (2000) *Employee Relations, HRM and Business Performance: An Analysis of the 1998 Work Place Employee Relations Survey.* London: Institute of Personnel Development.

Guile, D. and Fonda, N. (1999) *Managing Learning for Value Added.* London: Institute of Personnel Development.

Hackman, R. and Oldham, G. (1980) *Work Redesign.* Boston: Addison-Wesley.

Herzberg, F. (1993) *The Motivation to Work.* Transaction Publications.

Johnson, S.T. (1993) 'Work teams: what's ahead in work design and rewards management', *Compensation and Benefits Review*, March–April, p. 37.

Kerr, J. (1993) 'The best small companies to work for in America', *Inc.*, July, p. 63.

Kolb, D.A., Rubin, I.M. and Osland, J.M. (1991) *Organisational Psychology: An Experiential Approach* (5th edn). Prentice Hall.

Rodger, A. (1952) *The Seven Point Plan.* London: National Institute of Industrial Psychology.

Rousseau, D. (1995) *Psychological Contracts in Organisations: Understanding Written and Unwritten Agreements.* London: Sage.

Scott, W. and Harrison, H. (1997) 'Full team ahead', *People Management*, 9 October.

Shook, D. (2001) 'Why Nike is dragging its feet', *Business Week Online*, 19 March.

Taylor, F.W. (1914) *The Principles of Scientific Management.* New York: Harper & Row.

Walton, R.E. (1996) 'From control to commitment in the workplace', *Harvard Business Review* 63, pp. 76–84.

Wood, S. and Albanese, M. (1995) 'Can we speak of high commitment on the shop floor?', *Journal of Management Studies*, March, pp. 215–247.

PART 2

Acquiring and rewarding staff

Part contents

4 **Recruiting the right people**   *105*

5 **Selecting the right people**   *138*

6 **Remuneration and reward**   *176*

4

Recruiting the right people

Margaret May and Edward Brunsdon

LEARNING OUTCOMES

After studying this chapter, you should be able to:

- ☑ **identify** 'broad' and 'narrow' definitions of recruitment in the HR literature

- ☑ **provide** outline descriptions of the procedures involved in 'formative' recruitment

- ☑ **understand** recruitment within its employment law context

- ☑ **recognise** the range of possible sources and methods of recruitment, and assess their comparative strengths and weaknesses

- ☑ **offer** an account as to why organisations use a multisource and multimethod approach to recruitment.

The opening vignette demonstrates how an employer can increase its recruitment pool by getting in touch with the needs of the local community.

NHS Greater Glasgow

Matching people without jobs to employers with vacancies has long been the dream of policy-makers, but has proved surprisingly difficult to achieve. Now a project in Scotland has shown how it can be done. Working for Health in Greater Glasgow, a training and recruitment pro-gramme for long-term unemployed people, has not only succeeded in getting 85 per cent of participants through the programme, but has also placed the majority in jobs. Most of these are among the 2000 or so vacancies the NHS in Greater Glasgow struggles to fill, such as hospital porters, technicians and domestic assistants. This has saved thousands of pounds in recruitment costs, cutting the lead time for filling basic grade hospital jobs from 18 weeks to nothing.

Last year the project involved 149 participants – three-quarters of whom were from deprived areas and had been unemployed for at least six months, some for more than 10 years. The participants spent up to six weeks on a pre-employment programme, which involved life-skills development to build their confidence, support in identifying suitable jobs, job application training and an introduction to the NHS. This included hospital visits, work placements and training in skills such as patient confidentiality and basic hygiene. The programme has now been extended to a maximum of 15 weeks for 2005–06 and aims to cover 350 people, including recent immigrants.

The project is the result of a partnership between NHS Greater Glasgow, JobCentre Plus, the Wise Group (a Glasgow-based charity that helps unemployed people back into work) and other agencies, with the involvement of trades unions. Funded by Scottish Enterprise Glasgow and JobCentre Plus, it arose from the problems facing local hospitals, which were struggling to compete for recruits in an increasingly tight labour market. NHS managers saw the programme as an opportunity to improve health in the community by tackling unemployment. They also aimed to improve staff diversity – 31 per cent of Glasgow's population, but only 12.5 per cent of NHS Greater Glasgow's workforce, live in deprived areas.

Annette Monaghan, care careers programme manager at NHS Greater Glasgow, who leads the project, says all its targets have been met or exceeded, including those on community health; 56 per cent of participants reported an improvement in their general health as a result of the programme, and 82 per cent felt more optimistic.

She stresses the importance of long-term commitment to the health service: 'We're not just looking at jobs, but careers,' she says. 'It's always been theoretically possible for people to work their way up in the NHS, but we are putting a more robust structure and resourcing into that in the coming years.'

Source: adapted from CIPD Annual Conference newspaper,
from *People Management*, 27 October 2005, p. 12.
Reproduced with permission of *People Management*.

Discussion questions

1 Should it be the role of the NHS to reduce local unemployment?
2 Are there differences in recruiting for a job or a career?

Recruitment is an understated and undervalued feature of the HR portfolio. It is given limited space in most publications and, where it is considered, it usually acts as a summary prelude to more detailed discussions of selection. This is something of an irony because, whatever the achievements of selection procedures, they are heavily influenced by the success or otherwise of recruitment. Recruitment supplies the candidates for selection but, more than this, it is very difficult for selection techniques to overcome the failure or limitations of recruitment (Marchington and Wilkinson, 2005). It is therefore of some importance that students of HR understand recruitment procedures in their own right, and be aware of and try to redress their limitations. The opening vignette illustrates how a local hospital can link with the local community for its recruitment needs. This has benefits for both the hospital and the community.

Recruitment: the question of definition

One has only to read the chapters of two or three standard HRM textbooks to recognise that there is no agreed definition of what is meant by the term 'recruitment'. The variations that exist fall into two main types: the 'narrow' and 'broad' definitions, both of which formulate

recruitment

The different activities of attracting applicants to an organisation, and the selection of people to fill vacancies.

recruitment in terms of constituent activities and in relation to selection. The 'broad' definition views **recruitment** as embracing both the different activities of attracting applicants to an organisation and the selection of people to fill vacancies. The 'narrow' definition limits the range of activities to those involved in attracting people to apply for employment in an organisation.

Maund exemplifies the broad definition when she describes recruitment as: 'the term given to ... choosing suitable applicants for job vacancies'. Thus, '[i]ncluded in this process is selection ... [it is] [t]he last part of the recruitment process when the organisation decides who to employ from the candidates available' (Maund, 2001: 151). Bratton and Gold (2003) provide an illustration of the narrow definition when they portray recruitment as: 'the process of generating a pool of capable people to apply for employment to an organisation'. Selection, in their view, is a discrete and subsequent process, 'by which managers and others use specific instruments to choose from a pool of applicants a person or persons most likely to succeed in the job(s), given management goals and legal requirements' (Bratton and Gold, 2003: 221). This division pervades the academic and professional literature. For instance, in similar vein to Maund, several professional writings – for example, the CIPD (2005) article on recruitment and retention and the Acas advisory booklet on the same topic (Acas, 2005) – incorporate selection within a broad conception of recruitment. Against them, a number of academic publications (e.g. Taylor, 2002; Sisson and Storey, 2003; Marchington and Wilkinson, 2005) operate with slightly different formulations of the narrow definition.

It is the narrow definition that will be employed in this chapter, primarily because it is more robust. The broad definition, as it is used by Maund, contains conceptual ambiguities. She wants to use the term 'recruitment' to describe all the activities involved in filling a job vacancy but then see selection as the final part of the process. What is not clear beyond the assertion of this superordinate/subordinate link however is *how* these activities are to be differentiated. It cannot, for example, be in terms of their respective 'goals', since the general goal of filling a job vacancy must incorporate the specific selection goal of 'decid[ing] who to employ from the candidates available'. Again, it cannot be in terms of their constituent activities since the activities of selecting are, in her own terms, also part of recruitment. Again, to try to create a time criterion, as when she describes selection as 'the last part of the recruitment process' (Maund, 2001), does not help because if it is not retrospective, it is too imprecise to allow differentiation.

The narrow definition used by Gold is not subject to these ambiguities. He does not invoke superordinate and subordinate conceptions; recruitment and selection represent distinct but related clusters of activities that *ideally* exist in a temporal sequence. Organisations recruit by generating a pool of suitably qualified applicants for a post or posts; **selection** consists of sifting through that pool and making decisions about the appropriateness of those applicants. This is not to suggest, however, that his definitions cannot be compromised by real-world situations. For instance, while explicitly designed for selection, it may well be that managers try to use employment interviews to 'sell' their organisation – that is, as a tacit form of recruitment (Taylor, 2002). Again, given that recruitment and selection take place over a period of time, their activities in certain situations could overlap – that is, selection activities could be under way before recruitment has been completed. Such issues, however, are of a different status to those in the Maund type of formulation. They do not undermine the formal definitions so much as convey a warning about the limitations of all definitions and the need to work with them in a cautious, analytical manner.

selection

Consists of sifting through the pool of applicants and making decisions about their appropriateness.

The recruitment sequence

Within the narrow definition, recruitment is typically seen as occurring in two main stages: the formative work and the recruitment practices (sources and methods) that end with the arrival of applications. Each contains a cluster of activities usually portrayed as a linear sequence (see Exhibit 4-1).

Formative recruitment activities

What triggers the recruitment process? The simple answer is the possibility of acquiring new staff. Whether an organisation is considering additional staff (through expansion or restructuring) or replacing existing staff members who are leaving, the initial phase of formative recruitment involves reviewing the options. What alternatives are there to employing new staff and are they worth pursuing? These might involve restructuring the workforce, changing the technological base, outsourcing the work activities and/or changing the existing working-time arrangements (see Exhibit 4-2).

The alternatives are ideally addressed in broader intra- and extra-organisational contexts. In the case of the former, it is a matter of linking the question of new staff to the organisation's wider human resource strategy and business plans to develop or alter its production and services. With regard to extra-organisational contexts, the focus switches to the question of current labour and product markets and, among other things, ascertaining the availability of people with suitable qualifications and skills at wage levels the organisation is prepared to pay. If, having considered these questions, there is a decision to appoint new staff, the next step is to consider how the vacancy is to be managed.

Managing the vacancy

The work at this point is in deciding who, within the organisation, is going to be responsible for the recruitment and selection activities. Is it to be the line manager, someone within the HR department or a shared activity between the two? Who will provide the administrative support

Major stages	Activities within each stage
Stage 1: Formative recruitment	■ Reviewing the possibility of acquiring new staff and the identification of a vacancy ■ Deciding the management of the vacancy ■ Job analysis, producing a job description and person specification
Stage 2: Recruitment sources and methods	■ Decisions on recruitment sources and methods to be employed ■ Determining the application format (e.g. electronic or paper, formal application or CV) ■ Putting the job vacancy and other publicity materials into the public domain ■ Applications arrive

Exhibit 4–1 Stages and activities in recruitment

Option	Consideration
■ Restructuring the workforce	Can the activities and responsibilities of *current* workers be altered or redefined in order to fill the vacancy?
■ Additional/new technology	Is there a case for buying in additional or new technology to undertake the work rather than employing a new member of staff?
■ Outsourcing	Is it worth outsourcing the work to freelance staff or a third-party organisation?
■ Working time	Can the work be covered with more flexible working arrangements, e.g. allowing some staff to begin earlier/later to provide cover for a longer part of the day? Can it be covered by overtime?

Exhibit 4–2 Possible alternatives to employing new staff

and who will make the final decisions? Once these matters are resolved, a team can be put together, and a realistic time schedule can be set for the completion of recruitment as well as dealing with answers to more specific questions such as who is to undertake the job analysis.

Job analysis

The need for job analysis has been explained by the CIPD in the following way:

> Before recruiting for a new, or existing position, it is important to invest time in gathering information about the nature of the job. This means thinking not only about the content (i.e. tasks) making up the job, but also the job's purpose, the outputs required by the job holder and how it fits into the organisation's structure. It is also important to consider the skills and personal attributes needed to perform the [tasks] effectively.
>
> (CIPD, 2005: 2)

Exhibit 4-3 shows how the different recruitment activities link together and will ultimately lead to the successful selection of the right candidate for the job.

job analysis
Identifying the tasks and skills that make up a job.

Job analysis is important because it provides the information on which two significant recruitment documents are based: the job and person specifications. The *job description* summarises the job's purpose and the activities contributing to that purpose together with lines of responsibility. The *person specification* identifies the characteristics deemed necessary for someone holding that job. In organisations with either buoyant product and service markets and/or high levels of staff turnover it may not be necessary to undertake a job analysis for every vacancy that occurs. In such circumstances, however, it can nonetheless be useful to engage in the more restricted activity of checking whether the existing job description and person specification are appropriate for future needs (Marchington and Wilkinson, 2005).

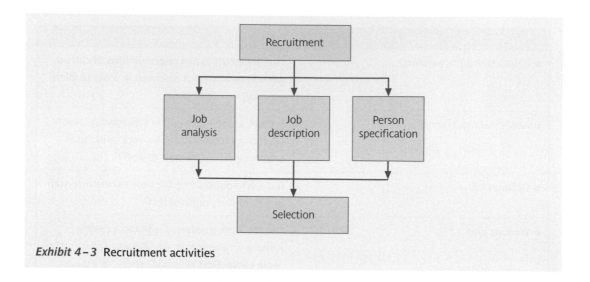

Exhibit 4 – 3 Recruitment activities

Methods of job analysis

So how is job analysis undertaken? Essentially, it involves collecting systematic information about the job from current incumbents and/or their colleagues (Newell and Shackleton, 2000). The techniques used to gather such information spread across the methodological spectrum from diaries and logs, observations and interviews at the qualitative end, through to the more quantitative forms of analysis such as questionnaires, hierarchical task analysis and repertory grid assessments. Given the range and requirements of each of these methods, it is inevitable that they will differ in terms of their costs, ease of use, sensitivity and sophistication (Searle, 2003). The HR professionals or line managers undertaking the job analysis are thus forced into a 'trade-off' in deciding which of the techniques (or which combination of techniques) to employ. Costs, for example, are a potentially important feature of the calculation in terms of the time, effort and money to be invested. The ability of the techniques to elicit the required information (sophistication) and their accuracy also need to be considered carefully, as do the availability of trained analysts or consultants (convenience), and the willingness of staff to participate (sensitivity). The choice of technique/s is thus determined by the assessed importance of these criteria when evaluated in terms of the jobs to be analysed and the work environment in which the jobs function.

Of the range of techniques, this chapter provides brief synopses of five simply to illustrate what can be involved and the issues that pervade job analysis. (More detailed accounts of all the techniques commonly used can be found in Cooper and Robertson (2002), Cooper *et al.* (2003) and Searle (2003).) Diaries and logs, observation and interviews will be employed as examples of qualitative techniques, and questionnaires and hierarchical task analysis as illustrations of their more quantitative counterparts.

Diaries and logs

These are self-reporting techniques that involve current job-holders recording their activities over a period of time – for example, every working hour over the course of a week. They are simple and non-intrusive ways of collecting information that, in financial terms, can also be relatively cheap. Once the job-holders agree to complete the diaries or logs, the main issues of self-reporting concern the information focus, the process of collecting the information and its accuracy. What, for instance, is being recorded? Is it everything that the employee does or simply specific types of activity? Is there a checklist being employed to aid the employee or do the job-holders log the information in their own terms? Are they to use an actual or electronic diary? Is training being provided? In terms of accuracy, the employees may not complete their log at the required time and, as a consequence, may over- or understate aspects of the tasks. In some instances, they may also choose to exaggerate particular job aspects (perhaps to emphasise their expertise or importance). Diaries and logs rely heavily on the commitment and accuracy of the post-holder completing the record and, as a consequence, have led some job analysts to argue that the technique is best employed in analysing comparatively stable and higher-level managerial or executive posts.

Observation

This is a traditional approach to job analysis in which a trained observer watches the tasks being undertaken and how they are being undertaken. Usually a checklist of factors is employed to ensure that data are gathered against relevant tasks and that there is consistency between observations. This is particularly important if there is a team of observers and/or the observations are carried out over a period of time. The technique is regarded as one of the more accurate ways of obtaining job information and it is generally assumed that it does allow an analyst to detect some required skills (e.g. manual dexterity, computer usage) and aptitudes (e.g. attention to detail, concern for the end-user and safety awareness). However, it is not without its issues. Observation is time-consuming and when employed as the solitary method of analysis may not be able to detect many of the cognitive and intellectual skills invested in some tasks nor provide an insight into their relative level of difficulty. Again, dependent on the period of observation, it may not capture the myriad of tasks involved in some jobs (think, for instance, of firefighters, ambulance personnel, police officers or retail assistants) and observers may well influence the conduct of the job-holders being observed (the 'Hawthorne effect'), leading to inaccurate data. In consequence, observation is often used with other techniques of analysis such as interviewing in order to provide a supplementary source of information.

Interviews

The third form of analysis, these range from structured interviews (with fixed question schedules) through to unstructured interviews (with open-ended question schedules). Fixed question schedules mean that the same questions are asked of each job-holder, thereby enabling easier comparability of the answers. The open-ended questions of unstructured interviews give the interviewer the opportunity to probe for more detailed responses and enable staff to elaborate particular points and, as a consequence, are seen to permit greater accuracy. Trying to draw on the benefits of both types of interview, most job analyses use semi-structured question schedules with some fixed and some open-ended questions. The major strength of interviewing in job analysis is its limited cost, its convenience and the opportunity for rapport to develop between interviewer and job-holder. The major limitations concern the potential variability of interviewer skills and the possible unreliability of the data elicited.

Structured questionnaires

These form one of the more popular ways of obtaining quantitative information about key tasks and aptitudes, and are especially valuable where there is a large job-holder population to cover. While some employers devise their own questionnaire(s), many others will buy in a commercially developed package involving the questionnaires and associated training in their use and analysis. One example of a commercial option is the Work Profiling System (WPS). WPS collects two different sets of job information. The first set concerns the main duties of the job and gathers detailed data about the tasks, their frequency of occurrence and job-holder evaluations of their significance. The second collects information on training and qualification levels, responsibilities, the physical context and the remuneration package (Searle, 2003). Like other structured questionnaires, the WPS provides a systematic way of collecting information and the resultant numerical data can be easily collated and compared using computer analysis. It has a higher reliability than the qualitative job analysis techniques and, once training is completed, can be both cheaper and less time-consuming than, say, interviewing. However, structured question-naires can also have problems. Clearly the quality of data is only as good as the questions asked and the predetermined range of answers. It is therefore vital that the questions are understood by employees and the categories of answer are comprehensive (i.e. they cover all the options).

Hierarchical task analysis

This is a second quantitative technique. Developed some 40 years ago by Annett and Duncan (1967), it defines jobs in terms of their outcomes. The job analyst works with the job-holder to break the job down into its constituent parts – namely plans, subtasks and tasks. The overall aim is to provide a sequential series of activities that will achieve the desired outcomes, whether it's a matter of forklift driving or catering management. The technique involves following a defined set of rules to ensure a clear analysis of the job, the level of performance and the con-ditions under which the tasks are carried out. It is neo-Taylorist in nature and, while producing a methodical picture of the job in terms of a sequence of tasks and subtasks, it is, for many ana-lysts, inflexible and unable to represent the interpretative and situational factors that can influ-ence the achievement of tasks (Cooper *et al.*, 2003; Searle, 2003).

Limitations of the techniques

The limitations of each of these techniques are indicative of more pervasive issues, namely:

- the (empiricist) conception of method underpinning orthodox job analysis
- the assumption of the stability of work.

The empiricist conception of scientific method assumes that there is an objective world to be inves-tigated and that research techniques (such as those employed in job analysis) can be used to gather information from that world in a neutral or value-free way. Thus the job analysis techniques described above are construed as data-gathering instruments that, in themselves, need not and should not have an impact on the information collected. What writers such as Taylor (2002) suggest is that there are major flaws in this viewpoint. Not the least of these is its failure to recognise that all research methods are inherently *social processes*, and are continually subject to the interpre-tations, actions and reactions of researchers, research subjects and others in the context(s) in which data are collected and analysed. In the specific case of job analysis, Searle (2003: 44–48) describes a wide range of potential social influences that include: the respective calculations of job-holder and analyst; the differential skills, work experience and/or social backgrounds within and between researcher(s) and subject(s); the organisational context in which the analysis is undertaken; and even the interpretation of the measurement formats employed in the various job analysis techniques. Empiricism wants to maintain

---

empiricism
Aims to maintain techniques that are inherently neutral and, where social influences exist, considers that they should be treated as 'contamination' or 'bias', and controlled or repressed.

that its techniques are inherently neutral and that, where social influences exist, they should be treated as 'contamination' or 'bias' and controlled or repressed through, for instance, research training or the use of more advanced techniques. Its critics suggest that this is not possible and that the data produced by job analysis are always going to contain levels of inaccuracy because of such social factors.

This problem of inaccuracy is compounded by the second pervasive issue – namely the assumption of stability in job analysis. Job analysis techniques take it for granted that 'jobs are relatively stable and subject to limited or no change' (Searle, 2003: 48). This stance basically conflicts with the globalisation of markets and technological change in a number of work areas where jobs are in a continual state of flux with regard to 'content, character and complexity' (Taylor, 2002: 103). The fact that such change is neither unidimensional or unidirectional, simply adds to the case that the products of job analysis – job and person specifications – can quickly become obsolete and thus lose their recruitment and selection value. While there is a counterargument – namely that this should lead to more regular job analysis (for example, through six-monthly or annual appraisals) – it still leaves organisations in a quandary. On the one hand, job analysis is considered central to the recruitment and selection process, often involving a sizeable investment of time, finance and other resources; on the other, its products can quickly become dated and are often based on only partially accurate information. So, what do organisations do? Abandon job analysis and use its resources in a more 'productive' way elsewhere or persevere with a known fallible procedure? Most organisations take the latter course: they see the significance of job analysis and decide to work within its limitations to produce job and person specifications (although in the latter case there has been some enhancement in the form of competency frameworks).

Job descriptions, person specifications and competency frameworks

If written job descriptions and person specifications are the main products of a job analysis, how are they utilised? A **job description** is used to set out the basic details of the job. It defines its primary purpose, reporting relations, the main activities or tasks carried out, and any special requirements or features. Typically, a job description contains: a job title; a grade and/or rate of pay; a main location; a line manager's name/post; details of any subordinates; summary of the main purpose of the job; a list (and possibly brief descriptions) of principal duties, together with reference to other documents (see the example in Exhibit 4-4 of a job description for an administrative post).

job description
Summarises the job's purpose and the activities contributing to that purpose, together with lines of responsibility; used to set out the basic details of the job.

person specification
Converts the job specification into human terms, specifying the kind of person needed to perform the job described.

Whereas a job description portrays the duties to be undertaken, a **person specification** 'convert[s] the job specification into human terms, specifying the kind of person needed to perform the described job' (Newell and Shackleton, 2000: 115). Inferences are made about the experience, qualifications, skills and psychosocial characteristics that are necessary for a candidate to become a successful job-holder. The classical versions of person specifications are the seven-point plan constructed by Rodger (in 1952) and its subsequent adaptation by Fraser (1966); these are outlined in Exhibit 4-5. An example of a person specification is given in Exhibit 4-6.

Job description	
Job title	Section secretary
Grade of appointment	Administrative Grade C
Section	Accounts (Moorgate)
Reports to	Administrative manager
Staff responsibilities	None
Job purpose	To provide a full and professional secretarial support service for the three accounts managers in the section including: shorthand, word processing, spreadsheet analysis, diary management, organising meetings, conferences and travel itineraries

The main responsibilities are to:

■ produce letters, reports, presentations and other documentation on Word, Excel and PowerPoint from audio tapes, shorthand and copy
■ answer telephone queries, redirect or take messages where appropriate
■ maintain an effective filing system
■ sort and distribute incoming post
■ manage three managers' diaries, organise meetings, conferences and travel itineraries
■ ensure timely payment of all section invoices and bills
■ organise departmental journals and maintain subscriptions
■ provide cover for the administrative manager.

For more general working conditions please see the enclosed staff handbook or go to our website at www . . .

Exhibit 4 – 4 Example of a job description

These specifications have several uses that include: establishing both the essential and desirable criteria against which candidates will be judged; providing a template for subsequent selection procedures; and, together with the job specification, forming the basis for drafting recruitment materials. For successful applicants they are also likely to feature in their future appraisals.

The competency alternative

The inadequacies of the person specification and, in particular, the growing recognition that it is not socially or politically neutral in its construction, have led to attempts to replace it with a competency-based approach. This pays far less attention to personal qualities, characteristics, dispositions or interests, and places much greater weight on what it sees as the effective actions or conduct that are likely to lead to successful individual and organisational performance. **Competency**, then, when employed in recruitment is concerned with *inputs* – in particular, the conduct, skills, knowledge and capacities that applicants

competency
Looks at the effective actions or conduct that are likely to lead to successful individual and organisational performance, rather than qualifications or experience.

Rodger's seven-point plan

1 *Physical make-up*: physical attributes such as ability to lift heavy loads or differentiate between colours

2 *Attainments*: educational or professional qualifications considered necessary for undertaking the work

3 *General intelligence*: ability to define and solve problems, and use initiative in dealing with issues that have arisen

4 *Special aptitudes*: skills, attributes or competencies that are specifically relevant to the particular job

5 *Interests*: both work-related and leisure pursuits that may be relevant to the particular job

6 *Disposition*: attitude to work and to other members of staff and customers, as well as friendliness and assertiveness

7 *Circumstances*: domestic commitments, mobility and family support

Fraser's five-point plan

1 *Impact on others*: this covers much the same sort of issues as 'physical make-up' (above), but is more focused on impact on other employees and customers

2 *Acquired knowledge and qualifications*: see Rodger's second category, above

3 *Innate abilities*: see 'general intelligence', above

4 *Motivation*: a person's desire to succeed in particular aspects of work, and their commitment to achieve these goals

5 *Adjustment*: characteristics specifically related to the job, such as the ability to cope with difficult customers or work well in a team

Exhibit 4–5 Classical views of person specifications
Source: Adapted from Rodger (1952), Fraser (1966).

must possess (or be capable of acquiring) in order to maximise the benefit to the organisation (CIPD, 2004b). Thus, where the person specification for the secretary's post (Exhibit 4-6) may simply ask for someone who is trustworthy, the competency approach would want to express it as a measurable performance such as 'someone capable of dealing with confidential information in an appropriate and sensitive way'. Again, where a person specification for a lectureship might include the requirement of 'self-confidence', the competency approach would seek a measurable input – for example, 'the ability to deliver a cogent and informative lecture to 200 undergraduates'.

The difference between the approaches may, as some suggest, be a matter of emphasis rather than substance (e.g. Newell and Shackleton, 2000). It could, for example, be argued that a secretary needs to be trustworthy if he/she is going to handle confidential information in a sensitive and appropriate manner. Again, a lecturer needs a level of self-confidence if she/he is going to deliver a cogent and informative lecture. Proponents of the competency approach to recruitment, however, maintain that this is not the point. Job and person specifications may well be used in tandem with competency approaches but what the latter provides is the possibility of a clearer statement of expectations of performance that in turn makes the recruitment process fairer and more open. It also enables a clearer set of benchmarks for use in subsequent performance appraisals.

One company that has identified the need to diversify its recruitment strategy is Expedia, as illustrated in the 'Managing diversity' box.

	Job title: Section secretary
Experience	Essential: three years' experience of working in a secretarial role within a large complex organisation; must have provided secretarial support for a team of managers Desirable: previous experience of an accounts department
Qualifications and knowledge	Essential: excellent knowledge of Word, PowerPoint, Excel, shorthand and audio typing Desirable: RSA secretarial qualifications, knowledge of finance/accounts functions
Skills	Essential: accurate typing and well-practised shorthand (60 wpm) Good written and oral communication skills Demonstrates good attention to detail, along with professional presentation and layout of documents Presents a professional and positive image of self and department at all times through written and verbal communication; uses appropriate language and medium when producing written documentation Is good at planning and organising Manages own and others' time and resources effectively, including diary management, a clear filing system and budgetary management A good team worker; works with managers and other administrative staff to ensure the section operates efficiently
Personal qualities and aptitudes	Essential: supportive – capable of demonstrating commitment to the managers and the wider team in the section Proactive: capable of anticipating problems and showing initiative in resolving them and generating new ideas Trustworthy: able to deal with confidential information in an appropriate and sensitive way Flexible: is willing to undertake a range of tasks to ensure the effective running of the section; is willing to work the hours required for the successful completion of tasks

Exhibit 4–6 An illustration of a person specification

The legal context of recruitment

Pertinent to the construction of job, person and competency specifications, and the subsequent processes, is the legal context in which recruitment takes place. When discussed in the HR literature, the focus tends to be on anti-discrimination or equal treatment at work legislation (see, for example, Martin and Jackson, 2002). Prior to 2000, the major initiator of this legislation was the UK Government, which introduced laws, regulations and codes of practice to prohibit direct and indirect discrimination on the basis of someone's gender, disability, race, 'spent' criminal record and trades union membership (see Exhibit 4-7). The abundance of legal activity

Expedia

Expedia is now the largest online travel service in the world, with Expedia.com in the USA and local versions in Europe and Canada. It prides itself on its excellent reputation, both as a profitable business and quality employer, which continues to grow and this, it suggests, makes it an exciting company to have a career with.

It offers a wide variety of career paths with compensation packages that include a competitive salary and excellent benefits. In addition to receiving comprehensive benefits, Expedia suggests that its people enjoy the reward of working for a respected industry leader that continues to innovate and advance.

If this is so, why is it that it finds it so difficult to fill vacancies?

'We're not really making the most of our brand as we still fill 90 per cent of our vacancies through third parties,' Alison Hodgson told *PM*.

Hodgson, who is also chairwoman of the Association of Graduate Recruiters, said the organisation needed to diversify its recruitment strategy by relying less on recruitment agencies to source candidates, and instead conducting research into potential talent pools and advertising more. This year, the company spent on advertising only one-tenth of what it spent on third-party recruitment.

The company, originally set up by Microsoft, currently has 1000 employees in Europe and 3000 in the USA.

'We need to get a healthier balance between the various recruitment methods, and map out how we can access and attract the people we want,' said Hodgson. But she admitted that finding the right people would be a challenge because Expedia operates in the online travel sector.

Hodgson said there was a shortage of candidates with the right combination of merchandising knowledge and online technological acumen that most of Expedia's posts required. 'You don't find the kinds of skills and calibre of people we want in traditional travel firms,' she said.

Another of Hodgson's responsibilities in the newly created role will be to link up separate strands of HR at Expedia, including talent acquisition and succession planning.

Source: Adapted from: 'Expedia needs to use its brand to attract staff', *People Management*, 24 November 2005, p. 14, www.expedia.com.

Discussion questions

1 Could Expedia's inability to recruit be due to its stereotyping of its ideal candidate?
2 How could Expedia make its jobs appeal to a wider audience?

in the first five years of the new millennium, however, has largely emanated from the European Council of Ministers' adoption of the Employment Directive on Equal Treatment in 2000. This required all EU member states to introduce laws prohibiting direct and indirect discrimination at work on grounds of age, race and ethnic origin, sexual orientation, religion and belief, and disability. For the UK this has, in some instances, involved the government in amending existing legislation. In others it has been a matter of creating new legislation as, for example, in the case of the law on age discrimination which will come into force from December 2006.

This is not the place to elaborate on the detail or complexities of these laws, what they cover, their operation or 'policing' nationally and in Europe. What is important for our purposes is to know that the legislation makes it unlawful for organisations to utilise someone's gender, marital status, colour, race, 'spent' criminal record, nationality, disability, religious beliefs,

Equal Pay Act 1970

Rehabilitation of Offenders Act 1974

Sex Discrimination Acts 1975 and 1986

Race Relations Act 1976

Trade Union and Labour Relations (Consolidation) Acts 1992

Disability Discrimination Act 1996

The Sex Discrimination (Gender Assignment) Regulations 1999

The Part-time Workers (Prevention of Less Favourable Treatment) Regulations 2000

The Employment Equality (Amendment) Regulations 2003

The Employment Equality (Religion and Belief) Regulations 2003

Equal Pay (Questions and Answers) Order 2003

The Race Relations Act 1976 (Amendment) Regulations 2003

Disability Discrimination Act 2005

The Age Discrimination Regulations 2006

Exhibit 4–7 UK equal treatment at work legislation since 1970

sexual orientation, trades union membership (and, from December 2006, age) as the basis for making employment decisions. The implications for recruitment are immense. Among the things affected will be: the language and processes of job analysis; job and person specifications; marketing strategy; advertising and application procedures. Managers and HR professionals will be required to reflect on their recruitment strategies, their literature and their performance. Failure to do so adequately could lead to claims of discrimination or unfair treatment, which in turn could mean costly legal cases, fines and damage to the organisation's reputation.

As important as it is in both nature and consequence, equal treatment at work legislation is but one area of employment law impacting on recruitment. There is a range of other UK and European legislation, for instance, on asylum and protection (affecting who can be recruited), health and safety, and the recruitment practices of employment agencies as well as statutes on privacy, access to and the disclosure of information that HR professionals must also understand and observe. To take just one instance of the latter, the Data Protection Act 1998 came into force in March 2000. It is designed to regulate personal data and give effect in UK law to the European Directive on Data Protection (95/46/EC). The Act is concerned with information that employers might collect on any individual who may wish to work, does work or has worked for their organisation. It covers personal data in an electronic, manual or any other format that is readily accessible, as well as all aspects of processing data from collection, holding, access, use and disclosure through to its destruction. There are eight data protection principles that are central to the Act. In brief, they state that personal data should be: processed fairly and lawfully; processed for limited purposes and not in any manner incompatible with those purposes; adequate, relevant and not excessive; accurate; not kept for longer than is necessary; processed in line with applicants' and employees' rights; kept secure; and not transferred to countries that don't protect personal data adequately (www.informationcommissioner.gov.uk).

The Act also gives applicants and employees the right to have a copy of the information that an employer holds about them. It allows them to apply to the courts to obtain an order requiring an organisation or its data control manager to correct inaccurate data, and to seek compensation where damage and distress have been caused as a result of any breach of the Act. Employees may also object to the processing of personal data about them. In some circumstances they can stop employers from keeping certain types of information or from using it in particular ways. Of particular importance here is what is termed 'sensitive personal data', included within which is someone's race or ethnic group, their political opinions, religious or other beliefs, whether they are a member of a trades union or not, their physical or mental health, sexual life, and any court record or allegations of such. Organisations must ensure that both applicants and employees give them explicit consent to process this type of information and/or that the processing has a necessary purpose (for instance, it is a legal requirement or important for monitoring equality of opportunity).

So, what are the implications of this act for recruitment? As with the equal treatment at work legislation, the Data Protection Act has practical consequences for a number of different activities. In terms of recruitment, for example, applicants providing personal information in response to a job advert need to be advised who they are giving the information to and how it will be used. If it is a recruitment agency that is advertising on behalf of an employer, it must explain how the personal data it receives will be employed and disclosed. On receiving identifiable personal details from an agency, an organisation must ensure that applicants become aware that it is now holding their information. With regard to selection, application forms (and subsequent interviews) must seek only personal data that are deemed relevant to the decision to appoint. Organisations must advise applicants how they will verify the information supplied in an application form (or on a CV) and, if sensitive data are collected, explain why this information is sought and how it will be used. The period for retaining personal information in recruitment (and selection) records is not specified in the Act; it simply states that it should not be kept any longer than business need requires and should take account of relevant professional guidelines. The Information Commission (2002), which drew up the Codes of Practice for the Act, recommends that data collected in applications and for checking applications should be kept for no more than six months before being destroyed (although this does not rule out organisations storing information to protect themselves against possible legal action).

This brief discussion of the Data Protection Act has sought to establish that:

- there is a realm of employment law beyond anti-discriminatory legislation that also impacts on aspects of recruitment
- the legislation permeates most aspects of the recruitment process
- a sound knowledge of this area is imperative (non-compliance could lead to legal action – in this instance, to the organisation being prosecuted and/or being subjected to claims for compensation).

Recruitment: sources and methods

With the job analysis completed, and the job description and person specification written up, the next stage of the process is recruitment – that is, considering ways of attracting people who meet the job requirements (Newell and Shackleton, 2000: 116). The HR literature talks in terms of two central types of recruitment: 'internal' and 'external'. The activities contained in each of these categories can be further subdivided in terms of 'source(s)' and 'methods'. This is a subclassification drawn from the employer's perspective in which sources are the differing domains of applicant supply – that is, the part or parts of labour markets from which applicants are sought. 'Methods' are the actual techniques employed both to make individuals aware of vacancies and to make those vacancies attractive to them. They are, in other words, the mechanisms for creating demand for vacancies.

Stop and reflect

Refer to Rodger's seven-point plan and Fraser's five-point plan in Exhibit 4-5. What would be the personal specification of a student? How do the two plans compare in identifying suitable attributes?

Internal recruitment

Internal recruitment methods involve creating a pool of applicants to fill a vacancy from current employees – that is, the organisation operates as its own source of supply. Research suggests that, as a matter of course, most commercial employers attempt to fill vacancies from within their organisation before they consider looking for people outside. The CIPD recruitment survey (2004a), for example, found that 84 per cent of UK organisations surveyed looked to internal applicants in the first instance. They did so by using such methods of communication as internal email or intranet (69 per cent), notice and bulletin boards (68 per cent), team meetings (18 per cent), their staff newsletters or magazines (14 per cent), and by memos, circulars and direct approaches.

internal recruitment
Involves creating a pool of applicants to fill a vacancy from current employees.

According to Taylor (2002: 126), there are several recognised advantages to internal recruitment.

- It is a relatively cheap way of recruiting, vacancies can be advertised at little cost and it can also save time.
- It can lead to a robust internal labour market, and boost employee morale through the opportunities for career development and progression.
- It means that applicants have a better knowledge of the way the organisation operates and what to expect in the job.
- Selection will be based on a better knowledge of the individuals' merits and prospects and is thus less of a risk than external recruiting.

The arguments against internal recruitment are as follows.

- It perpetuates existing ways of thinking and carrying out tasks; external recruits, it is argued, would be more likely to bring in new ways of undertaking tasks.
- It assumes that the 'best' person for the job is currently working for the organisation.
- It recruits in the organisation's current image, hence if ethnic minorities or other disadvantaged groups are not currently well represented, promoting from within will do nothing to create greater diversity.
- Rejecting current employees in an internal recruitment exercise can lead to major morale and confidence issues, possibly leading to further staff turnover.

Exclusive or even regular use of internal recruitment is much less common in public and voluntary sector agencies where stronger equal opportunities policies consistently prevail. In these agencies, whatever the 'strengths' of the internal field, it is considered 'good practice' to create a level playing field in which internal and external candidates can apply for posts.

External recruitment

As Exhibit 4-8 illustrates, an abundance of methods can be employed in external recruitment.

---

external recruitment

Identifies possible candidates for recruitment from the labour pool outside the organisation.

Some are used in conjunction with particular labour sources (e.g. employee referral schemes use current staff to refer their friends, family and associates), while others (e.g. advertising) have a broader application. The choice of where and how to look for applicants is related to a range of criteria, such as the organisation's HR strategy, cost and time constraints, the likelihood of the method reaching its anticipated audience, and the volume of applications that each method is likely to yield.

The organisation's own resources

It is common practice, particularly in the commercial sector, for organisations to utilise their own current resources – that is, their employees, their records and databases, and their websites – to create a pool of external applicants for a vacancy. In terms of current staff, the primary method of recruitment is employee referrals – that is, encouraging employees to nominate 'potential recruits through their personal contacts' (Marchington and Wilkinson, 2005: 172). Staff are typically offered a financial incentive to recommend friends or former colleagues for a vacancy in the organisation. Payments for successful recruitment can range from £25 to £5000, and are usually dependent on the type of vacancy. Amazon.com, for instance, pays its staff £200 for new warehouse associates and up to £1500 for managers or 'critical hires', while Capgemini's referral payments range from £500 to £3000, depending on the grade of the person recruited (Income Data Services, 2004).

Employee referral is a narrow search technique in that details of the vacancy are limited to specific individuals or groups known to its staff. Slightly broader are the searches involving the organisation's use of its archives, records and databases. Here it can seek applicants from any combination of prior candidates for posts, its own retirees, former employees working for other organisations (Carrington, 2005), and people who have previously 'walked in' to ask if there are vacancies and left a completed application form or CV. The method involves HR or managers assessing the paper or electronic records against the person or competency specification and inviting the appropriate persons to apply.

According to CIPD research (2004a), a large proportion of the organisations surveyed used these methods of recruitment in the private sector. Employee referral schemes were particularly popular in commercial services, where 71 per cent of companies surveyed and 66 per cent of manufacturing companies used them. In more recent research, some organisations used their schemes to fill as many as 95 per cent of their vacancies (Industrial Relations Services, 2005b). The re-hire of former (or 'boomerang') employees, although not as widespread a practice as in the United States, is also a growth recruitment area. PricewaterhouseCoopers, for instance, has developed its own 'talent bank' that includes former employees with whom it remains in contact through an alumni association. Its use of this bank has led to a 30 per cent reduction in the use of third-party agencies for seeking experienced staff (Carrington, 2005).

However, while the use of organisational sources appears to be popular, opinion is divided among both managers and academics about their value. Some HR management research (e.g. Iles and Robertson, 1997; Income Data Services, 2004) suggests that they can:

- yield a better pool of well-qualified applicants
- contribute to a lower turnover of staff

Sources	Methods
The organisation's resources Current employees Archives and records (past applicants; former employees; retirees and 'walk-ins') Organisation's website	Employee referrals Manual/electronic search of HR records, subsequent HR/manager's decision to inform and/or invite applications Posting the vacancy on its generic or dedicated recruitment site
Educational sources Schools, colleges and universities, careers advisers/Careers Service, tutors	Careers fairs; 'milk-round interviews'; use of student 'work experience/work placements' to assess potential; employer presentations; student sponsorships; advertising in specialist graduate recruitment directories and magazines
Government employment agencies JobCentre Plus Connexions Forces Resettlement Agency	Display cards at the local JobCentre, a quick-call telephone service (Jobseekers Direct) and a website linked to JobPoint; electronic circulation of local, regional, national and international vacancies; focusing on 13–19 year olds, establishing links with 'partnership' employers; two-way information base of available staff and agency searches
Commercial employment agencies Recruitment advertising agencies and consultants Temporary and contract staffing agencies Permanent employment and executive search agencies Cyber agencies	Organisational databases, newsprint advertisements, websites Organisational databases, newsprint advertisements, websites Organisational databases, newsprint advertisements, websites, agency networks Job boards
Professional and industry contacts Professional associations and trades unions; suppliers; customers; works contractors	Conferences, networking, individual contacts
Newsprint sources National and local newspapers Trade and professional journals	Newsprint (often combined with Internet) advertising Newsprint (often combined with Internet) advertising
Other media sources Television, cinema and radio	'Live' advertising

Exhibit 4–8 The sources and methods of external recruitment

- lead to higher levels of employee performance
- contribute to cost reductions (Nationwide, for instance, claims to have saved between £2000 and £10,000 of advertising costs per job by using an employee referral scheme).

Set against these views is the general case that, by using these sources:

- an organisation will only ever reach a limited audience, which is unlikely to reflect the diversity of the wider community
- there is no guarantee that they will generate the best pool of candidates.

In the specific case of employee referral schemes, it is argued that:

- unsuccessful referrals may lead to demotivated staff
- referral schemes can involve an additional administrative HR burden as they have to track both the referrer and applicant, and ensure payment is made correctly and in a timely manner (Income Data Services, 2004).

These critical views seem to hold particular sway in the voluntary and public sectors, where only 34 per cent and 26 per cent of organisations respectively use referral schemes to recruit staff (CIPD, 2004a). The main reason for their aversion seems to be the fact that they tend to favour groups already well represented in the workforce.

A much wider and more speculative use of organisational resources, across the sectors, involves posting vacancies on a generic or dedicated website. This, according to the CIPD survey, is becoming an increasingly popular means of staff recruitment. An estimated 72 per cent of respondents used their own websites to publicise vacancies (CIPD, 2004a). The amount an organisation invests in this source will depend on its e-strategy, available funds and competitor activity. A basic option would simply involve providing a list of vacancies and contact details. A more detailed approach would provide the information normally posted to applicants (e.g. job and person specifications, organisational facilities and benefits, and online application forms). Linked to the person specification, organisations might also provide self-assessment questionnaires or quizzes to assess fitness for the job and cameos of a 'day in the life' nature. Larger organisations often have dedicated sites for particular types of applicant, such as graduates and technical specialists, or have a search facility to view particular types of vacancy.

The main advantages to organisations of recruiting from their websites include the potential to:

- reduce recruitment costs and speed up the recruitment cycle; Woolworths, for example, claims to have reduced its cost per hire by 70 per cent and its time to hire from an average of eight weeks to as little as two days (Smethurst, 2004)
- devote as much space as they wish to 'selling' the job
- make applying easier
- shorten the recruitment cycle
- reach a wide pool of potential applicants
- offer a global audience access to vacancies 24 hours a day, seven days a week
- provide an image of a modern, forward-looking organisation (Industrial Relations Services, 2004).

It is, however, likely to be well-known corporations or organisations with a good reputation within specific labour markets that are likely to reap these benefits as 'small and medium-sized employers will not attract sufficient numbers of hits to their websites to be able to rely on this as a means of finding new recruits' (Taylor, 2002: 138).

Among the possible disadvantages are:

- it tends to be a supplementary rather than first-choice recruitment source for most job-hunters and this may limit the applicant audience

- it obviously excludes those who either cannot access the Internet or do not have software compatible with the website

- organisations may be bombarded with unsuitable applicants because it is so easy to apply online (Industrial Relations Services, 2004)

- the recruitment process becomes impersonal, deterring some applicants

- websites that are not of the highest standard may turn potential applicants away.

Educational sources

Of the wide range of other external sources, educational institutions provide a primary locale for potential recruits. According to the CIPD survey (2004a), links with schools, colleges and universities are used more by the commercial sector (56 per cent of respondents) than the public (38 per cent) and voluntary sectors (40 per cent). This picture might look a little different, however, if data on subgroups of each sector were available. Public agencies (e.g. the Armed Forces, and government departments such as the Inland Revenue and the Treasury), as well as large commercial organisations, invest heavily in national campaigns for university graduates. Because of the costs and relatively small number of recruits required, medium-sized and smaller firms and local authorities are more likely to focus at the area or regional level, seeking young people leaving school, from colleges of further education and local universities.

In seeking graduate applicants of the best calibre, large commercial organisations and national public agencies are prepared to invest in time-consuming and expensive activities such as sending representatives round the country, participating at careers fairs, undertaking presentations for groups of students, performing initial interviews and briefing careers advisers. They are primarily looking for 'management material', and seeking well-qualified, well-motivated, intelligent and mobile graduates. They come 'armed' with glossy literature about their organisation, DVD and PowerPoint presentations, and website addresses with information about future points of contact. It is essentially a 'sales pitch' in a 'war for talent' (Willcock, 2005) in which the representatives attempt to create demand for their jobs by showing students the benefits of working for their organisation. Alongside such methods, the companies and agencies will also advertise in specialist graduate recruitment publications such as the *Prospects* directories, offer work placement opportunities (either as vacation work or as part of a degree programme), and sponsor some students during their studies (on condition that they subsequently join the sponsoring organisation).

Many companies use a global recruitment strategy, as is demonstrated in the 'International perspective' box.

Small and medium-sized organisations operate from a somewhat different platform, with a less direct, lower-cost strategy when looking at schools, further education colleges and local universities (Income Data Services, 1998). Although they offer work experience to students and, in some instances, industry placements for staff, much of what they undertake is designed as a prelude to actual recruitment – that is, they primarily aim to raise the status of the organisation in the community and particularly among the students seeking work in the near future. To this

Shell reaps benefits of global recruitment strategy

Global recruitment initiatives can be transferred to markets around the world while remaining culturally sensitive to local needs, according to Sherri Sheehy, Shell's recruitment manager for Europe, the Middle East, Africa and Russia.

Speaking at the Global Recruiting Forum in Brussels, Sheehy told delegates that Shell's recruitment system was aligned around the world so that it could treat candidates with 'equal fairness'.

She advised companies to develop a global marketing strategy with strong employer branding, designed to give job candidates a clear impression of the firm. 'Companies need to ask themselves: "What do we know about our candidates? Can we offer them what they are looking for?"' she said.

Although there are advantages to working with one global brand and recruitment process, Sheehy said there could be 'creative tension' between headquarters: 'You have to be careful not to be too US-orientated or Eurocentric when dealing with departments in other regions of the world.'

Source: Adapted from S. Overan, 'Shell reaps benefits of global recruitment strategy', *PM Online*, 19 December 2005.

Discussion questions

1 What are the problems with creating a global brand when recruiting locally?

2 Should the head office impose its recruitment strategy on the home country?

end, they undertake activities such as sponsoring school/college events, assisting students with projects, running workshops on business understanding, and supporting employees looking to work as school or college governors.

Government agencies

As a resource for other employers, the work of government agencies is primarily a matter of facilitating recruitment. Utilising both direct and indirect methods, this involves providing communication links between employers and their prospective employees, as well as providing training, skills development and, in some instances, financial support to enable people to become either employable or more suitable for a wider range of occupations. The primary institutional vehicle for these activities is the JobCentre Plus network, which, since 2002, has been the lead government agency dealing with jobless people of working age and whose core aim is to put more people into work by helping employers fill their vacancies.

Among the direct methods that it employs are: a one-to-one personal advisory service with benefit claimants; a telephone service, Jobseekers Direct; and a dedicated website listing vacancies linked to JobPoints. Jobseekers Direct sets out to offer a quick and easy telephone service to help the jobless find a temporary or permanent, full- or part-time job. The service advises people of vacancy details and how to apply. It will send them application forms and, wherever possible, will ring the employer to arrange an interview. JobPoints are touch-screen kiosks located in JobCentre Plus offices as well as in supermarkets and libraries. They offer a search facility for different categories of work, and details of local, regional, national and international vacancies. The indirect methods used by the network are typically targeted at those out of work for longer than 26 weeks, although this does vary with the different groups on New Deal schemes. The nature of the assistance ranges from advice and support programmes (e.g. helping people to develop a CV, prepare for an interview, apply for jobs and supplying stamps, stationery and newspapers), through to educational courses (e.g. literacy, numeracy and skills development), sponsored training (e.g. accountancy, computing) and courses leading to qualifications in different trades and services.

Similar programmes geared to a younger age group are provided by another agency – Connexions. Set up in 2001 with a much broader remit, it offers young people between the ages of 13 and 19 information, advice and guidance on health, housing, money, education, work and career topics. In terms of recruitment, it utilises both direct and indirect methods. It helps with applications and CVs, and will organise interviews, but will also offer advice on skills development, guidance on training opportunities and, in partnership with local employers, the opportunity for work experience and careers guidance. Connexions works closely with the Learning and Skills Councils to develop 'work-based routes' for young people looking for vocational qualifications.

More specialist government agencies operate for particular occupational groups. A case in point is the Forces Resettlement Agency, which, as part of its role, offers education, retraining and job opportunities for people retiring from or leaving the Armed Forces. While there is a differentiation of support based on rank and length of service, all service personnel have access to an employment consultant's advice, a job-finding service and access to websites (such as 'Questonline' and 'courses4forces') offering information on jobs and retraining. Those with more than five years' service also have access to career transition workshops and training centres, and the opportunity to gain work experience with civilian employers and receive regular information about job opportunities. Officers have their own job-finding service via the Officers Association.

In addition to providing its own recruitment resource services, the government also sponsors or part-sponsors voluntary agencies. An example here is the Shaw Trust, which is a leading national charity that seeks to create work opportunities for people with disabilities. According to the Office for National Statistics (ONS), over seven million people, or 19 per cent of those of working age, are disabled, of whom only 50 per cent are currently working (ONS, 2004). To increase the number of disabled people in the workforce the Shaw Trust offers a range of work-related services, many of which are funded, under contract, by JobCentre Plus. These services include financial support to buy specialist equipment, advice on training, support in job search and interviews, and arranging 'work tasters' and placements.

Commercial recruitment agencies

Unlike government agencies, whose main aim is to facilitate employment and offer a recruitment service that is free at the point of access, commercial recruitment agencies are companies that undertake part or all of the recruitment process (on behalf of employers) in return for a fee. They form an industry that is heterogeneous in nature, with differing:

- ranges of activity (some agencies specialise in advertising posts, others in the supply of staff, yet others in a complete recruitment package)
- types of staff placement (temporary, fixed-term or permanent staffing)
- ranges of staff supply (from a narrow to a wide variety of occupations)
- catchment areas (e.g. local, regional, national or global suppliers)

- company size, small independent to large multinational (e.g. Reed or Kelly Services)
- business strategy (some agencies have a business model that is high volume/low margins, others a low volume/high margins model).

Recruitment advertising agencies and consultants

Advertising and recruitment consultants are private companies that offer particular sets of services to employers. In the case of the former, recruitment advertising agencies can design, write and place advertisements, produce recruitment materials, advertise on the Internet, build websites and handle responses. Recruitment consultants, by contrast, can take over a larger part of the recruitment process. As well as the advertising, they will also undertake other outsourced aspects of vacancy management, such as getting information to applicants and sifting initial applications to provide employers with a shortlist. The issue always for employers is balancing the costs of outsourcing recruitment activities against the gains of saving company time and using agency expertise, especially in unfamiliar labour markets (Taylor, 2002).

Temporary and contract staffing agencies

The phrase 'temporary and contract staffing agencies' covers the organisations that seek to meet the short-term recruitment needs of employers. The demand for staff may be a consequence of increased productivity, the need to cover a period of extended absence, filling a post while a permanent member of staff is sought or simply the desire to seek a more flexible workforce. Temporary staff are typically selected and paid by the supply agency and offered to employers at an hourly rate. Their length of service may vary from a few days to several months. Contract workers' assignments tend to be longer than those of temporary staff; they are typically taken on for a fixed period of months or on renewable annual contracts. They are usually paid by the employer, with the supplying agency receiving a commission or fee.

There is little in the way of systematic data on temporary and contract staffing agencies; the industry is fragmented and contains both large national and international companies (such as Reed Executive, Adecco and Manpower), and small high-street operations. The majority of agencies are small with fewer than five employees, while the largest in the UK have over 250 employees each (Keynotes, 2004). Traditionally, agencies operated in the clerical and light industrial sectors and, while these areas still provide nearly one-third of their placements, temporary and contract staff are now also supplied to the building and construction, computing/IT, education, financial services, hotel and catering, medical, technical/engineering and professional/managerial sectors. Estimates suggest that there are 12,500 agencies working in the UK temporary and contract staffing market, which placed over one million people in the financial year 2003–04 and generated a turnover of approximately £23 billion (Keynotes, 2004).

The main benefit to employers of recruiting via temporary and contract agencies is the provision of a relatively reliable source of qualified personnel who are available at short notice and can also be laid off relatively cheaply if no longer required. They are 'flexible' both in this sense and in that unsatisfactory or inappropriate workers can quickly be replaced. Employers are outsourcing much of the cost and effort of recruiting, while getting an opportunity to assess staff who might later be offered permanent appointments. Temporary or contract employees similarly get the chance to 'road test' the work environment rather than simply accepting a job based on impressions given at interview or through a tour of the facilities (Taylor, 2002). The main disadvantage of recruiting through temporary and contract agencies is the cost:

> Hourly rates for agency workers are invariably double those paid to regular employees. In addition, the agency will incorporate charges into the contract that place a financial penalty on employers who make permanent offers of employment to their temps – a practice that is now limited as a result of . . . government regulations [introduced in 2003].
>
> (Taylor, 2002: 145)

Permanent employment and executive search agencies

The third group of commercial agencies providing recruitment services are those dedicated to identifying candidates for permanent posts. They operate in a smaller market than their temporary and contract counterparts with aggregate annual placements of approximately half a million in 2004 and a turnover of approximately £1.7 billion (Industrial Relations Services, 2005a). Half of these placements were secretarial or clerical staff. Like the temporary and contract market, that for permanent agencies is also fragmented although, in this instance, it has fewer national and international firms and significantly more smaller agencies operating within fairly narrow geographical areas. Adecco (with a UK turnover of £572 million in the year to December 2002) and Brook Street (with a UK turnover of £133 million in the year to December 2003) are the leading permanent employment agencies, but 95 per cent of companies in this sector had turnovers of less than £5 million and half had turnovers of less than £250,000. In terms of staffing, 60 per cent of the VAT-based agencies had fewer than five employees (Keynotes, 2005). They all tend to operate on a 'no sale, no fee' basis. Fees for successful placements typically increase with the seniority, status and salary being paid for the post, and are usually expressed as a percentage of the first year's earnings. They are in the region of 15–17.5 per cent for more junior posts, and can go up to 25–30 per cent for senior posts.

The main benefit that permanent employment agencies offer employers is the opportunity to restrict the cost and outsource the effort of recruitment. To be economically viable, these agencies must therefore be more cost-effective than in-house recruitment options and/or be capable of offering additional services, such as specialist knowledge of the industry sector, advice on the current state of the candidates' market, and pay and benefits packages. Beyond the immediacies of cost, the major issues confronting employers using these agencies are:

■ the necessary formative investment in ensuring that job descriptions and person specifications are as accurate as possible

■ ensuring that candidates supplied meet both these specifications and the organisation's expected standards of performance

■ that delays in the supply of applicants are kept to a minimum (Industrial Relations Services, 2005a).

Executive search agencies (often called 'headhunters') are a subsection of the permanent recruitment market. They focus on supplying suitable candidates for permanent roles as senior directors, managers and executives. They are primarily engaged when:

■ the post is of such a senior and sensitive nature that it would be detrimental to the client organisation if it was known to be searching for a senior manager or executive

■ there are very few people who could fill the vacancy and the client organisation needs a go-between to see if senior staff in other companies are interested in moving

■ the post is at a level where suitable candidates are unlikely to wish to make direct application through normal procedures and may well not read job advertisements.

The major advantage of executive search agencies is that they offer a service that client organisations are unwilling or unable to undertake themselves. In effect, it is a form of soliciting that involves enticing the employees of one organisation to consider moving to another. Each search has its own parameters and is usually undertaken against a strict set of instructions from the client organisation and within an agreed time frame (normally a matter of months). The agencies are expected to remain in continual rapport with their clients, to work speedily and to have the ability to help successful candidates negotiate terms of severance from their current place of employment. Given that the situation is potentially damaging to candidates, their existing companies and the client organisation, discretion and advice on negotiations are of immense importance.

The main issues with engaging executive search agencies are: the problem of poaching; the search consultant's expertise and knowledge of the market; and the pressures of conducting the search within an equal opportunities context. In the case of the first of these, the headhunting agency will get to know one or more of the senior executives of the organisation for which it is working and they, in turn, may be of interest to a third party. Client organisations attempt to preclude this with a 'no poaching' or 'off limits' policy in their contractual agreement with the agency, but this is rarely fireproof. In terms of the second, companies have been known to express their concern about whether search consultants know the market to an appropriate standard and/or whether working within tight time parameters they are capable of finding the *best* possible candidates to shortlist (Industrial Relations Services, 2005a). To counter these types of concern, many of the agencies have adopted a Code of Practice (devised by the Association of Search and Selection Consultants) through which they seek to assure client organisations of the highest standards of service embodied in the code. The third issue, equal opportunities, is a more general matter, and of as much concern to the client organisation as the search agency. In an IRS survey of employers (Industrial Relations Services, 2005a), twice as many public-sector employers as private-sector organisations cited the agency's commitment to equal opportunities as grounds for choosing it to undertake the search for applicants. Although it features in the Code of Practice, if equal opportunities is not a clear commitment for the client, it is unlikely to be a central feature of the agency's search. It is a complex issue for, other than the minimalist stance of refusing to engage in overt discrimination, how can an agency assure a client of equity in what is essentially a closed form of searching?

Cyber agencies

Many permanent and temporary contract agencies also run websites advertising the vacancies of their clients. These compete in the digital world with newspaper websites like Fish4jobs (which is owned by four of the UK's largest newspaper companies – Trinity Mirror, Newsquest, Guardian Media Group and Northcliffe) and what have been termed 'cyber agencies' (Taylor, 2002). Cyber agencies (such as Monster.com) are commercial web companies that operate job boards. In the CIPD survey (2004a) they were used by 39 per cent of respondents primarily to recruit to managerial positions but also to encourage applications to graduate traineeships. Some job boards target specific work sectors – for example, Jobsgopublic – while others are designed for particular occupations (as in the case of people management for HR professionals) or niche markets – such as Jobswithdogs.co.uk, 'your free and friendly destination for all the latest vacancies and news on working with dogs in the UK' (Kent, 2005). Current job boards, however, are not just a service creating an applicant pool by matching job-seekers' CVs with employers' job and person specifications: recent changes in software mean that board operators, or indeed their employer clients, can engage in applicant tracking, skills matching, competency testing and, with the increasing use of broadband, virtual office tours and 'live' employee profiles. They can create, in other words, a much more effective, more informed and informative digital recruitment process than previously possible (Kent, 2005).

The disadvantages of job boards are not dissimilar to those of other websites (see above), however in employers' eyes their primary problem is that they are still not delivering the required quantity or quality of applicants (Industrial Relations Services, 2004). As a consequence, organisations are changing the way they use these boards, employing them more as portals for their own corporate websites. In this way, they gain the marketing potential of the board itself but also have greater control over the quantity and quality of candidates progressing through the recruitment process (Industrial Relations Services, 2004).

Newsprint and other media sources

Newsprint sources offer a more traditional but nonetheless popular way of attracting applicants. Indeed in the CIPD research (2004a), 61 per cent of respondents said that they used national newspapers to advertise some of their vacancies, while an even greater number, 87 per cent, indicated that they advertised in local newspapers – the most frequently used recruitment source in the survey. These aggregate figures do, however, mask quite marked variations in sectoral usage, particularly in the case of national newspapers. Where, for instance, 78 per cent of the sampled public-sector organisations and 72 per cent of the voluntary sector took out advertisements in national newspapers, only 55 per cent of private-sector manufacturing, production and service companies employed the same channel. With local newspapers the variations were narrower, but there was still a difference between public, voluntary and private manufacturing and production, where over 90 per cent of organisations used this recruitment source (94 per cent in the case of public-sector organisations), and the 81 per cent of private-sector services advertising their vacancies in this way.

The choice between national or local newspapers seems to depend largely on the available funds and the target audience. For most posts, local newspapers are considered preferable as they are typically less expensive and reach an audience within travelling distance of the organisation. It is only necessary to meet the higher costs of advertising nationally for relatively specialised posts for which there is a national market (e.g. chief executive of an organisation) or in circumstances where wide trawls of potential applicants are considered desirable (e.g. graduate traineeships for government agencies or national companies). The CIPD survey (2004a) provides supportive evidence. Its research found that local newspaper adverts were primarily utilised in recruiting to administrative, secretarial and manual/craft posts, while those in the national press targeted senior managerial and professional vacancies. It also found that the nature of the advert, in both sources, was beginning to change. To meet with competition from the Internet, 'ads are starting to look different. They are now promoting the employer brand and directing people to their websites' (cited in Arkin, 2004). Thus, rather than being a purely informational base for potential applicants, they are also being employed as a means of marketing the organisation, suggesting why it should be viewed as a 'preferred employer' or 'employer of choice', and how people that apply would benefit from joining.

Trade and occupational journals form the third significant newsprint source, with usage ranging from 71 per cent in private-sector services up to 87 per cent in the public sector (CIPD, 2004a). They provide the medium of choice for advertising professional vacancies in, for instance, engineering, accountancy, legal practice, social work, surveying and human resource management. They are particularly important where the target audience is scattered over a wide geographical area and where the cost of advertising in national newspapers is considered prohibitive. Beyond cost, the major benefit of using this source is that it is aimed at the appropriate professionals and thus the likelihood of responses from unsuitable candidates is reduced. The downside is that such publications often appear only on a fortnightly or monthly basis and, given the time required for creating and placing the advertisement, may lead to costly delays.

Non-newsprint media sources, such as television, cinema and radio, are much less frequently used in recruitment. On average, only 9 per cent of sampled organisations employed these media (CIPD, 2004a). The primary reason is cost: '[t]he cost of preparing and screening a television advertisement is on a par with the whole HR budget for many organisations' (Roberts, 2003: 132). The length of preparation time, however, and the limited availability of 'peak' advertising slots also work to reduce its suitability. Where television advertising has been employed in recent years it has been in government-sponsored campaigns that form part of longer-term recruitment strategies as, for example, in looking to meet the UK shortfall of teachers and nurses, and in attracting personnel to the Armed Forces.

Cinema advertising has also been used in these campaigns and can often provide a lower-cost option than television. It 'is particularly suitable for a younger general target audience and [again] where time is not a problem (for example, the pre-planned recruitment to new businesses). It also offers [more of] an opportunity to localise the advertisement' (Roberts, 2003: 132). Radio recruitment advertising is generally cheaper to prepare and broadcast than its cinema or television equivalents. It is seen to be particularly effective as a complementary form of advertising as, for instance, in prompting people to attend a particular recruitment open day. Like the other non-newsprint sources, it is seen to have a wider coverage than newspapers, and gains attention in ways that newsprint sources cannot. Newspaper advertising: 'will usually be read only by those who are seeking another job, whereas radio advertising at peak commuting time may catch the attention of . . . listener[s] driving to and from work and may spark their interest to find out more' (Roberts, 2003: 133). Against this, it is much easier to respond to written advertisements, where all the information on response details are to hand, than to garner the same information from the 'live' advertisements of radio, cinema and television.

Summary

- What this chapter has sought to describe and assess are the major features of formative recruitment and the range of available recruitment sources and methods.

- It should be clear from the discussion that, in both recruitment stages, there are a series of calculations and decisions to be made. These range from how to identify the vacancy, and whether to employ new staff, through to which recruitment sources and methods to deploy to best effect.

- In each instance, the calculations and decisions are linked to both general operational conditions (e.g. the employment law parameters, the competitive nature of the labour market, the organisation's HR strategy), as well as the known imperfections of the methods (in both job analysis and recruitment practice) and the specific circumstances that the organisation faces (e.g. the urgency with which it needs the new staff).

- Other considerations include the amount it can spend on recruiting them, the likelihood of its recruitment methods hitting their anticipated audience and the volume of applications they might yield.

- The explicit risk associated with these calculations and decisions is that they may not generate the best (most appropriate) applicant field for the post – the tacit risks are the problems to which this can lead (e.g. the cost of re-advertising the post or accepting the need to select from a less adequate field with all the potential problematic outcomes this might yield).

- In an attempt to control these risks many organisations, in practice, have turned to multiple recruitment sources and methods in the firm belief that, collectively, they are likely to produce stronger applicant fields (Arkin, 2004).

Personal development

1 **Think about the definitions of recruitment.** In your own words, describe what is meant by the 'broad' and 'narrow' definitions of recruitment. Using HR publications (other than those employed as illustrations in that section of the chapter), try to identify examples of each type of definition in the literature.

2 **Examine how job analysis could be implemented in an organisation.** If you were to engage in job analysis for an organisation, which of the techniques would you choose to employ and why?

3 **Recognise the limitations of job descriptions.** Have you been given job descriptions and person specifications in the jobs for which you have applied? Look at the examples provided in the chapter. Do you think they provide potential applicants with the appropriate information? What more might you want to know about a post before you would consider applying?

4 **Identify how different recruitment methods are implemented by organisations.** Choosing an organisation with which you are familiar, what sources and methods of recruitment does it employ? What other recruitment sources should it consider?

5 **Identify the sources of potential candidates for recruitment.** In your experience of recruitment practices, what sources and methods of recruitment are effective and why?

❓ Discussion questions

1 What alternatives are there to recruiting new staff?

2 Why is job analysis important?

3 In what ways might competency frameworks be seen as an improvement on person specifications?

4 How does employment law impact on the recruitment process?

5 On what grounds do employers use internal recruitment methods? What are the limitations of using these methods?

6 What are the strengths and weaknesses of online recruitment?

7 When might an organisation consider using 'headhunters' in its recruitment practices?

8 In what circumstances might 'live' advertising (e.g. on television and radio) provide an effective form of recruitment?

🔒 Key concepts

recruitment, *p. 107*

selection, *p. 107*

job analysis, *p. 109*

empiricism, *p. 112*

job description, *p. 113*

person specification, *p. 113*

competency, *p. 114*

internal recruitment, *p. 120*

external recruitment, *p. 121*

Individual task

Purpose To apply the information provided in this chapter on formative recruitment and recruitment sources and methods to a practical work situation.

Time 40 minutes

Procedure You are part of a regional HR team for a national DIY company that is planning to open a new branch in Leeds in six months' time. You have been asked to oversee the task of recruiting shopfloor, warehouse and administrative staff for the branch.

- How would you go about this process?
- Describe the sources and methods you would use to recruit the staff.
- What problems might you anticipate in meeting the opening-day deadline?

Team task

Purpose To identify alternatives to the recruitment process.

Time 40 minutes

Procedure Your HR team of four people has been approached by a well-known fast-food burger chain, which is having problems with staffing levels. It operates 24-hour opening, although peak times are during breakfast, lunch and dinner. It is not sure if it can better utilise existing staff or whether it needs to recruit more.

1 Using the chart below, work through the options and identify possible solutions to the problem.

2 What impact could changing the staffing patterns have on the existing workforce?

Option	Consideration
■ Restructuring the workforce	Can the activities and responsibilities of *current* workers be altered or redefined in order to fill the vacancy?
■ Additional/new technology	Is there a case for buying in additional or new technology to undertake the work rather than employing new members of staff?
■ Outsourcing	Is it worth outsourcing the work to freelance staff or a third-party organisation?
■ Working time	Can the work be covered with more flexible working arrangements, e.g. allowing some staff to begin earlier/later to provide cover for a longer part of the day? Can it be covered by overtime?

Case study: Hotels and resorts tap global workforce through immigrant visas and sponsorships

Imagine receiving dozens of applications from qualified, eager help for line-level positions. One need not only dream of such a pleasant predicament. If a property is willing to hire from overseas, there's an ever-expanding pool of qualified labour eager and able to take extra steps to shore up one's employment outlook.

Just ask Mike Scholz, former chairman of Best Western International, whose Best Western T-4 Lodge in Big Sky, Montana, employs 10 to 12 foreigners during the summer and now is looking to do the same during peak winter months. Many students can obtain J1 visas to work in the United States for four months (with an additional month allowed to explore the country and experience the culture).

'We're using Workexperienceusa.com to fill many of our open positions from abroad,' Scholz said. 'The vendor posts our positions online, handles all the pre-employment screening, and arranges for all the visas and flight details once we have selected a candidate.

'Last year, we hired several international applicants who were already in the area working at a local ski resort but wanted second jobs,' he said. 'These students are so eager to visit America for a few months and gain work experience that they will hitchhike and/or walk 10 miles from the resort after cleaning rooms all day just to wash dishes or wait tables for us at night.'

'It's a tall order and may take some time, but the more visas available to hospitality, the more opportunities there will be to fill positions from abroad,' said H.P. Rama, a past chairman of the

Asian American Hotel Owners Association (AAHOA). 'We're in the midst of a serious labour crisis, and good help is getting harder and harder to find. Why not open our doors to more international applicants and fill these vacant positions?'

Dennis Hatch, Sonesta's corporate human-resources director, said the company doesn't have quite the turnover problem that some of its competitors have because the company takes great care of its own.

However, Hatch said some of Sonesta's 18 properties and three cruise lines do hire foreigners from time to time, either on a temporary or permanent basis, depending on whether the individual is visiting on a short-term visa or is an immigrant with established permanent residence. Some Sonesta employees hail from as far away as Bosnia, Haiti, Romania, and Central and South America, and feel privileged just to have the opportunity to set foot on US soil, he said.

'We have some hotels and resorts located where the labour shortage is particularly evident or where pockets of immigrants have settled, such as our Cambridge, Massachusetts, property,' Hatch said.

'It's truly refreshing to receive applications from people who are eager to work hard and please,' he said. 'When someone comes from war-torn Bosnia, you can imagine how happy they are just to be in America and to have a place to work and gain experience.'

Employing foreigners need not be a short-term solution to deal with the current labour shortage. Rama said many AAHOA members have sponsored family and friends immigrating from India to the United States, giving them secure jobs and a roof over their heads while filling open frontline and back-of-the-house vacancies for many years to come.

'Thousands of sponsorship visas are issued every year to spouses, parents and siblings of immigrants with permanent residence, and many of these individuals end up working, and living, for at least a short time, at lodging properties across the country,' Rama said.

'At the same time, many hotels and resorts can solve seasonal labour crises by working with international employees to obtain short-term educational training and student work visas,' he said. 'These creative hiring practices are becoming increasingly popular as hoteliers become more aware of cross-border employment opportunities and accustomed to related hiring policies.'

Buggsi Patel, president of Buggsi Hospitality and chairman of AAHOA, said the tight labour market requires hoteliers to plan far in advance for employment needs, and explore and use all recruiting options at their disposal. Several properties that currently don't provide housing might be able to invest in such services and still save dollars on the bottom line through reduced recruiting, training and turnover costs.

'Like many things in business, hiring from abroad and possibly even providing help with housing isn't for everyone,' he said. 'Having said that, just because a property or company has never done this before doesn't mean it doesn't make good business sense to change tradition and adapt to today's tough hiring times and increasingly global market.'

Source: Adapted from M. Whitford, 'A world of hiring opportunities', *Hotel and Motel Management* 216(3), 19 February 2001, p. 4.

Discussion questions

1 Does it make good business sense to use short-term labour?

2 Are employees going to be committed to an organisation when they know the employment is likely to be short term?

3 What could the impact be for the local employment market?

4 How can employers ensure that they integrate employees from such diverse cultures?

WWW exercise

Go to the www.monster.co.uk job board and examine the services on offer to (a) employers and (b) job-seekers. How can the job board, or the employers it is working for, make improvements?

LEARNING CHECKLIST

Before moving on to the next chapter, check that you are able to:

- ☑ describe the difference between the 'broad' and 'narrow' definitions of recruitment
- ☑ identify the key activities of 'formative recruitment' and the subsequent recruitment procedures
- ☑ recognise the importance of employment law in the recruitment context
- ☑ list the range of sources and methods of recruitment
- ☑ assess their relative strengths and weaknesses, and the reasons why employers tend to use multiple sources and methods in recruiting.

Further reading

People Management (2005) 'The ex factor', *People Management*, 10 February at www.peoplemanagement.co.uk.

Ward, K. (2002) 'The UK temporary staffing industry: an overview', mimeograph, Manchester: University of Manchester.

Useful websites

Association of Online Recruiters: www.onrec.com

CIETT (International Confederation of Private Employment Agencies): www.ciett.org

CIPD (Chartered Institute of Personnel and Development): www.cipd.co.uk

Department of Trade and Industry (DTI): www.dti.gov.uk

Information Commissioner: www.informationcommissioner.gov.uk

JobCentre Plus: www.jobcentreplus.gov.uk

People Management magazine: www.peoplemanagement.co.uk

Recruiter: www.professional-recruiter.co.uk

Recruitment and Employment Confederation: www.rec.uk.com

RI5 (provides market intelligence for the recruitment industry): www.ri5.co.uk

UK Recruiter: www.ukrecruiter.co.uk

References

Acas (2005) *Recruitment and Induction*, advisory booklet, www.acas.org.uk.

Annett, J. and Duncan, K.D. (1967) *Task Analysis and Training Design*. Hull: Hull University, Department of Psychology.

Arkin, A. (2004) 'Multiple Choice', *People Management*, 30 June, www.peoplemanagement.co.uk.

Bratton, J. and Gold, J. (2003) *Human Resource Management: Theory and Practice* (3rd edn). Basingstoke: Palgrave Macmillan.

Carrington, L. (2005) 'The ex factor', *People Management*, 10 February, pp. 36–38.

CIPD (2004a) *Recruitment, Retention and Turnover 2004*, www.cipd.co.uk.

CIPD (2004b) 'Competency and competency frameworks', factsheet, www.cipd.co.uk.

CIPD (2005) 'Recruitment', factsheet, www.cipd.co.uk.

Cooper, D. and Robertson, I. (2002) *The Psychology of Personnel Selection*. London: Thomson.

Cooper, D., Robertson, I. and Tinline, G. (2003) *Recruitment and Selection: A Framework for Success*. London: Thomson.

Fraser, M. (1966) 'The five-point plan for person specifications', London: National Institute of Industrial Psychology.

Iles, P.A. and Robertson, I.T. (1997) 'The impact of personnel selection procedures on candidates', in N. Anderson and P.H. Herriot (eds) *International Handbook of Selection and Assessment*. Chichester: John Wiley & Sons, pp. 543–566.

Income Data Services (1998) 'Business partnerships with schools', *IDS Study* 658, November. London: IDS.

Income Data Services (2004) 'Employee referral schemes', *IDS HR Studies Update* 782, September, pp. 10–14.

Information Commission (2002) *The Employment Practices Data Protection Code, Part 1: Recruitment and Selection*, www.informationcommissioner.gov.uk.

Industrial Relations Services (2004) 'Recruiters march in step with online recruitment', *IRS Employment Review* 792, 23 January, pp. 44–48.

Industrial Relations Services (2005a) 'Agencies, employers and the new regulations: one year on', *IRS Employment Review* 819, 11 March, pp. 42–48.

Industrial Relations Services (2005b) 'Recruitment and retention: yesterday, today and tomorrow', *IRS Employment Review* 825, 10 June, pp. 39–48.

Kent, S. (2005) 'Get on board', *People Management*, 28 July, p. 38.

Keynotes (2004) *Recruitment Agencies (Temporary and Contract)*, www.keynote.co.uk.

Keynotes (2005) *Recruitment Agencies (Permanent)*, www.keynote.co.uk.

Marchington, M. and Wilkinson, A. (2005) *Human Resource Management at Work: People Management and Development* (3rd edn). London: CIPD.

Martin, M. and Jackson, T. (2002) *Personnel Practice* (3rd edn). London: CIPD.

Maund, L. (2001) *An Introduction to Human Resource Management: Theory and Practice*. Basingstoke: Palgrave.

Newell, S. and Shackleton, V. (2000) 'Recruitment and selection', in S. Bach and K. Sisson (eds) *Personnel Management* (3rd edn). Oxford: Blackwell.

Office of National Statistics (2004) *The Labour Force Survey*, Autumn.

Roberts, G. (2003) *Recruitment and Selection*. London: CIPD.

Rodger, A. (1952) 'The seven-point plan', London: National Institute of Industrial Psychology.

Searle, R. (2003) *Selection and Recruitment: A Critical Text*. Milton Keynes: Open University Press.

Sisson, K. and Storey, J. (2003) *The Realities of Human Resource Management*. Maidenhead: Open University Press.

Smethurst, S. (2004) 'The allure of online', *People Management*, 29 July, p. 38.

Taylor, S. (2002) *People Resourcing*. London: CIPD.

Willcock, R. (2005) 'Employer branding is key in fight for talent', *Personnel Today*, 17 May, p. 4.

Chapter 5

Selecting the right people

Margaret May and Edward Brunsdon

LEARNING OUTCOMES

After studying this chapter, you should be able to:

- ☑ **outline** the key components of the traditional selection process

- ☑ **review** the grounds for their usage, and their relative merits and drawbacks

- ☑ **discuss** the main contemporary selection instruments

- ☑ **understand** and explain their strengths and limitations

- ☑ **recognise** the value of induction to the selection process.

The opening vignette identifies some of the problems that can be encountered when relying on certain selection methods.

Artificial intelligence and gender bias

Early in 2005, sparks flew when research was published claiming that men were more intelligent than women. The study, by Dr Paul Irwing and Professor Richard Lynn, showed that men were, on average, five points ahead of women in IQ tests. The authors said these results were 'conclusive', as their findings were based on data from 57 other studies that assessed IQ using tests of 'general cognitive ability', which included questions about spatial and verbal ability, among others.

So is it true? And does it matter in a work context? This bias in favour of men is nothing new. For years, research has suggested that traditional IQ tests of general intelligence (rather than assessments of specific aspects of intelligence) often tend to favour certain groups, with white European men frequently outperforming other groups. This suggests an element of bias in the way intelligence is being measured. Often these tests focus on abilities such as spatial awareness, a type of reasoning where men have often been found to outperform women as a result of genetic or educational influences.

The results from Irwing and Lynn's study are therefore not surprising, given the abilities assessed and the format of the tests used. Beyond showing that men are better at general intelligence tests, what use is this information when considering job performance? Not a great deal. IQ is not a good predictor of how someone will perform. Indeed, the authors cite recent statistics indicating that women are increasingly outperforming men, both academically and in the workplace. Their explanation for these statistics is that women have higher levels of motivation and a more conscientious approach to work. They say it is these characteristics, rather than their IQ, that enable women to achieve. This in itself suggests that IQ test results tell us little about how people actually apply their intelligence in 'real life'.

Organisations looking to recruit good performers should therefore use IQ tests at their peril, as they provide only limited information on how an individual is likely to perform.

In our work with organisations, we regularly use a competency-based approach. This gives more valuable information by measuring specific skills, abilities and attributes, such as problem-solving or decision-making. The organisation can then focus on the competencies relevant to the job.

So what differences arise when we assess men and women using a competency-based approach? One client in the pharmaceutical industry asked us to analyse results from an assessment process we designed to recruit salespeople. In contrast to the IQ test study, we found no significant gender differences for any of the 10 competencies against which the managers were assessed. This was despite the roles requiring a range of very different skills, from being hard-nosed and target-driven to being able to display outstanding interpersonal skills. This suggests the assessment process and competencies were free of gender bias and measured attributes that really mattered to these roles.

This carries an important message for assessment, recruitment and selection. We appear to find gender differences only when we look at broad measures – such as those in IQ tests – that do not relate directly to performance. By breaking down intelligence into specific competencies, we can gather more detailed, relevant information and avoid gender bias.

Source: B. Martin and N. Mindell, 'Artificial intelligence',
People Management, 29 December 2005, p. 7.
Reproduced with permission of *People Management*.

Discussion questions

1 Do you think IQ tests should be used as a method of selection?

2 How can employers ensure that selection methods are free from bias?

The opening vignette demonstrates how problems can arise when relying on one selection method.

selection

The process 'by which managers and others use specific instruments to choose from a pool of applicants'.

Selection has been described in the previous chapter as the process 'by which managers and others use specific instruments to choose from a pool of applicants ... [individual(s)] most likely to succeed in the job(s)' (Bratton and Gold, 2003: 221). Like recruitment, selection is a core HRM activity whose importance resides in its consequences. Good selection decisions can provide managers with valuable new members of staff who can contribute additional skills, increase productivity and, perhaps, even change the working ethos. Poor selection decisions can be costly: 'in terms of the management time required to deal with disciplinary cases, in retraining poor performers, and in having to recruit replacements for those individuals who have been selected and/or who quit soon after starting' (Marchington and Wilkinson, 2005: 157).

The traditional selection process

The **traditional selection** process, or 'classic trio' as it has been called by Cook (1993) and more recently by Taylor (2002, 2005), describes the combined use of three methods of selection: application forms, interviews and references. The key elements of this process are the application form and the interview. References play an important but subsidiary role, operating as either an information and evaluation source for shortlisting and interview questions, or as a check on the interview decision. Sequentially, the process would operate in the following way (see Exhibit 5-1). Having been encouraged by the recruitment material, individuals would apply for details of the vacancy and, by return, receive an application form and additional information such as the job and person specifications. A pool of applicants would be created from those returning the forms (and usually citing one or two referees). These forms would be screened and a shortlist of interviewees created. The appointee would be the candidate considered the best person for the job as ascertained by the application form and interview (and endorsed by references if they had not been used in the shortlisting).

In spite of the growth of an increasingly critical literature, the traditional selection process remains popular. This chapter begins by outlining its constituent instruments, pointing out their drawbacks and thus identifying the grounds for replacing or complementing them. Their limitations centre on what is termed their **predictive validity**. Selection operates from the assumption that applicants can be

traditional selection
Describes the combined use of three methods of selection: application forms, interviews and references.

predictive validity
The appropriateness of the chosen selection method for finding the right candidate.

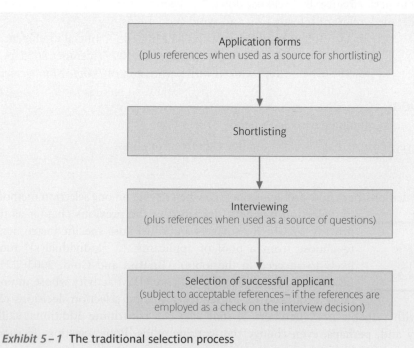

Exhibit 5–1 The traditional selection process

differentiated in terms of their qualities, skills and experience for a particular post. The task of selection instruments, such as application forms, interviews and references, is to facilitate this process – that is, to enable a choice to be made between candidates in terms of who will be most suitable for the job. They should, in other words, act as good 'predictors' of future work performance. Commentators, mainly academic occupational psychologists, maintain that the traditional methods are poor predictors of job performance and, further, that there are better selection methods available today.

Application forms

In its 2005 recruitment survey, the CIPD found that application forms or CVs were still used by over 80 per cent of its sample of organisations. A typical form includes questions asking for personal data, such as name, residence and phone number, 'previous work experience, educational background, vocational training … and future career aspirations' (Taylor, 2005: 204). They can also include questions seeking information on an applicant's state of health and whether they have criminal convictions. On what is usually a detachable section of the form, there tend to be further questions concerning gender and ethnic background. These are basically for monitoring purposes and are usually removed from the form prior to engaging in the shortlisting procedures.

Application forms are seen to have a number of purposes. Their key functions are to:

- act as the reference document used for the contact address, phone number, and so on, of the candidate
- capture the basic candidate data that enable employers to shortlist for interview
- provide information that can be used in the interview.

Among their supplementary roles, application forms can:

- supply data for good but unsuccessful candidates, which can be stored on a database for future recruitment trawls (providing this meets Data Protection Act 1998 requirements)
- (with the appropriate questions) be used as a means of assessing the effectiveness of the recruitment media
- through their clarity, design, guidance information and questions, convey a positive public image of the organisation (Pioro and Baum, 2005).

Application forms are used extensively in the public and voluntary sectors. They are less prominent in the commercial sector where many companies, particularly smaller firms, encourage applicants to submit a curriculum vitae (hereafter CV) as an alternative (Taylor, 2005). From an employer's viewpoint, there are both benefits and limitations to using application forms and CVs. Among the benefits of using CVs are the following.

- Their design, production and costs are the candidate's rather than the organisation's.
- Applicants can communicate with the prospective employer in their own terms, 'to create a positive impression … market themselves, indicate [they're] job fit and impress the reader with their skills and abilities' (Searle, 2003: 76).
- They demonstrate the candidate's ability to marshal their thoughts and put together a clear document for a designed purpose (Roberts, 2003: 140).

Among their limitations are that they:

- 'enable ... candidate[s] to construct the application to inflate their strong points and obscure or omit any weakness or concerns' (Roberts, 2003: 140)

- give applicants control over what is presented, which can make shortlisting difficult in terms of both the quantity and comparability of information

- can be written in a style that makes them difficult to verify as, for instance, in claims of the nature that someone is 'an organised manager with good team working skills and proven track record in delivering targets to tight deadlines'

- make the presentation of false information easy – 'CV fraud is rife in all sectors and at all levels' (Smethurst, 2004); among the most common forms of fraud are changing the grade of degrees achieved, claiming qualifications that have not been awarded, and changing employment histories to avoid mentioning dismissals or periods spent in jail; the CIPD recruitment survey (2005a) found that 'one in four companies had to withdraw a job offer because of CV fraud last year, and a similar proportion sacked someone for the same offence' (Smethurst, 2004: 35); to limit such risks, many organisations are now having to pay companies to check the claims made on CVs.

In comparison, the main benefits of application forms are that:

- employers are able to control the information presented to that relevant to the post

- it is harder for applicants to avoid addressing areas of weakness

- they can assist an organisation's equal treatment and fairness policies by creating a 'level playing field' as regards the nature and type of information required and, additionally, the opportunity to provide supportive guidance notes

- it is much easier to assess applicants' answers to questions in this format than via the uneven spread and quality of information submitted in CVs.

Their limitations are as follows.

- Organisations have a choice of either designing a specific form for their vacancy or using a standard application form. Both methods have disadvantages. The first is an expensive route to take and is time-consuming, while the latter may not capture important information about a candidate.

- Poorly designed application forms can appear intimidating and discourage applicants from applying.

- While there is less opportunity than with CVs, there is still a chance of fraudulent claims and thus the cost of vetting application forms.

- Like the CV, much of the information elicited is biographical in nature and commentators question whether it is possible to predict future job performance from such data (Searle, 2003).

Online application forms

Partly in response to the issues of cost and design, many firms have now adopted electronic application forms. Online applications mean that forms can have a more flexible format, overcoming fixed space allocations for particular answers and, once added to the organisation's website, can lead to reduced costs of production and distribution, and improved candidate and employer response times.

Shortlisting

Having obtained the application forms (or CVs), the next stage of the traditional approach is to reduce the applications received to a shortlist of candidates for interview. Shortlisting practice fluctuates from the highly informal to the systematic. On grounds of fairness, most commentators maintain that the systematic approach is the better option (see, for example, Torrington *et al.*, 2005). Drawing shortlisting criteria from the person specification, each application form is assessed and scored against each criterion. The preferred method is for a panel of selectors, operating independently of each other, to scan all the applications and produce their own shortlists. Anyone chosen by all the shortlisters is then invited for interview, while anyone discarded by all is rejected. The panel members then consider the merits of the remaining candidates until they reach an agreement on who should and should not be interviewed (Taylor, 2005).

Police force under fire for axing white males

A soldier who fought in the second Gulf War has spoken of his anger after he claimed he was rejected for a job as a police officer because of his race and sex. Mark Gough, aged 25, who has fought in Iraq and Bosnia, was one of 109 white male recruits cut from Gloucestershire police's recent selection process

The force attracted criticism last week after it emerged that it had given priority to 'females and applicants from minority ethnic backgrounds'.

The move was part of its programme to boost the number of minority ethnic officers within its ranks.

The recruitment drive attracted 301 applicants, of whom 192 could be sent to the police officer assessment centre.

The 109 would-be officers rejected were those who in a questionnaire scored the lowest marks out of the 172 white males who applied.

Mr Gough, a father-of-one from Quedgeley, Gloucestershire, has served in the 3rd Regiment Royal Horse Artillery for six years. He said he had always wanted to become a police officer and had left the Army after the second Gulf War in 2003 so he could prepare for the role.

He said he was shocked at the force's decision to reject him: 'I'm surprised that I quite possibly have been judged on the fact that I am a white male.

'I served with the Army for six years and as a part of my resettlement training I undertook a week with the police and had to take tests at the end, which I passed with ease.'

Civil liberties group Liberty and Law last week reported Gloucestershire Constabulary to the Commission for Racial Equality (CRE) and the Equal Opportunities Commission (EOC) after the men were rejected.

The pressure group also reported Avon and Somerset Constabulary to the CRE and the EOC last November after it emerged that nearly 200 white men had been turned down for jobs with the force because of their skin colour and gender.

A Gloucestershire police spokeswoman said she could not discuss individual applications but all deselected recruits could reapply in the future. Mr Gough will apply again to join the force.

Source: 'Police force under fire for axing white males', *Birmingham Post*, 7 February 2006, p. 6.

managing diversity

Discussion questions

1   Should this type of discrimination be allowed in order to redress the diversity balance?

2   How can an organisation such as the police appeal to the diverse groups that represent society?

The interview

As intimated above, the primary purpose of the interview is to enable selectors to choose the person best suited to the post from among the shortlisted candidates. It should therefore offer a means of both eliciting information and differentiating candidates. What follows discusses three core dimensions of this process – interview structures, contents and modes of delivery – before addressing the problems associated with this selection instrument.

Interview structures

Presented as a continuum, interviews range from the 'unstructured' to the 'structured' (see Exhibit 5-2). Interviews are unstructured when they are unplanned, non-directed, exchanges that allow free-flowing discussion between applicants and interviewers without pre-set topics or questions. To achieve anything from this interview style requires an immense amount of training, energy and skill on the part of interviewers, who are required to follow up interesting leads or important details that the applicants reveal as the interview unfolds. It seeks to encourage rapport and enable open and frank discussion, but it can also descend into disorder and leave no more than a residue of information for making consistent comparisons between candidates.

At the other end of the continuum are structured interviews. Here the interactions are controlled by the interviewers, who ask pre-set questions, in a particular sequence, on a specific range of topics. Through the structuring the aim is to offer a standardised form of questioning that is reliable and gathers comparable information about candidates. Its downside is that it is

Unstructured →	Semi-structured/focused →	Structured
■ Unplanned	■ Pre-scheduled	■ Pre-planned
■ Non-directed	■ Interviewer-directed but	■ Interviewer directed
■ 'Uncontrolled'	flexible	■ Standardised
■ Unformatted	■ Major topic areas formatted	■ Pre-formatted topics and
■ Bilateral communication flow	(focused) and some questions	questions
■ Flexible	(semi-structured)	■ Unilateral communication
	■ Communication flows	flow
	develop to facilitate interview	■ Inflexible
	objectives	
	■ Some flexibility	

Exhibit 5–2 Interview structures
Source: Adapted from Anderson and Shackleton (1993, in Searle, 2003: 104).

inflexible and does not allow for probing or follow-up questioning. Between the two extremes are semi-structured and focused interview structures. Their main difference is that, in focused interviews, the topics for discussion (but not the specific questions) are prescribed, whereas in semi-structured interviews both topics and questions (whether 'closed' or 'open-ended') are prepared in advance. What they share, however, is more than their differences. They possess directed but flexible forms that permit some open and candidate-specific questions, and thus offer the opportunity to explore ambiguous or uncertain features of CVs, application forms or references, as well as giving candidates the chance to ask questions about the job and/or organisation.

Interview content

Within these interview structures, the types of question asked of candidates can also vary. Clearly there is little or no control in unstructured interviews, where much is left to the spontaneity of the situation and the development of the interviewer–applicant rapport. With focused, semi-structured and structured interviews, however, there is an opportunity to plan and control contents, and this has enhanced the development of particular forms of questioning. The four main types are as follows.

biographical questioning
Confirms personal details about candidates and is also employed as a way of putting candidates at their ease.

1 **Biographical questioning** is often used as the opening gambit in interviews. Other than confirming previous education and qualifications, describing current work experience and exploring the rationale for wanting the post, it is also employed as a way of putting candidates at their ease. Indeed, for some analysts, this latter function is its main value as to ask about: 'hobbies, family background, early childhood and so on [does] not seem to help select the best candidate' (Smith and Smith, 2005: 246).

situational questioning
Requires candidates to respond to hypothetical work-based scenarios.

2 **Situational questioning** requires candidates to respond to hypothetical work-based scenarios. They are presented with a verbal description of some aspect of the job and asked what they would do in those circumstances. Examples for an HR post might include cameos about sexual harassment or absenteeism in which the applicants are asked how they would go about resolving the problems. The candidates' answers are noted and compared with model answers in a carefully devised marking scheme (Smith and Smith, 2005).

behavioural questioning
Asks questions about problems candidates may have faced in work-based situations.

3 **Behavioural questioning** comes in slightly different variants. One subtype employs job-relevant cameos and then asks applicants about the nearest situation they have faced to the one described, followed by a series of analytical questions such as ' "What led to the situation?", "What did you do?", "How successful was your response?", "What was the reaction of others?", "What did you learn about the situation?" ' (Smith and Smith, 2005: 246). The second subtype bypasses the cameo and draws on critical incidents from the candidate's experience as the platform for discussing her or his responses to such circumstances. Taylor uses an illustration in which selectors looking to assess candidates' decisiveness, do so by asking them about 'an occasion in which they took a particularly difficult decision or were forced to make an important decision without having as much information as they would have liked' (2005: 216).

stress questioning
A type of questioning that aims to put candidates under pressure, in order to observe how they respond.

4 **Stress questioning** is less frequently used than the other types of questioning. It is designed to put candidates under pressure by, for instance, deliberately contradicting something they say. The claim by those who use it is that this form of questioning is necessary to observe how applicants *actually* respond to stressful situations rather than listening to them *describing* how they would respond.

Delivery formats

In addition to differences in structure and content, interviews can also vary in terms of their delivery format. In face-to-face interviewing, there are at least four variations linked to the number of selectors and candidates. The *one-to-one interview*, as the name suggests, is where the interview takes place between a single interviewer and the applicant. The *tandem* or *small-group interview* occurs where two or three people interview a candidate together. There may be a division of labour in terms of the aspects of the job they explore, or they may even adopt specific roles for the interview, but they are using the same social interaction to observe the candidate at first hand and reach a joint decision. The *panel interview* operates in a similar way, but with a larger number of assessors – in the case of some senior executive posts there are up to 12 people on the panel. The *candidate group interview* is where several applicants are interviewed together, usually by several assessors. Rarely used in isolation, it is typically employed in conjunction with one-to-one or panel interviews, and to assess social skills and performance in group or team-work settings.

An alternative to the face-to-face delivery format is telephone interviewing (and, in a more advanced form, videoconferencing). Used more as an addition to, than a substitute for, face-to-face interviewing, this has seen considerable growth in the last few years. The CIPD's survey found that, on average, 30 per cent of organisations made use of telephone interviews, a figure that rose to 40 per cent in private-sector services (CIPD, 2005a). This format is employed mainly as a screening procedure and considered particularly valuable in:

■ high-volume selection

■ filling vacancies where telephone manner and customer contact are an important part of the job (e.g. call and contact centres)

■ shortlisting from an international field of applicants (CIPD, 2005f).

Analysts and employers who favour telephone interviewing argue that it is of mutual benefit to applicant and assessor in that: neither has to travel to interview (a particularly important cost consideration when it comes to international selection); the interviews can be arranged and undertaken more speedily; and, it is claimed, 'people are less inhibited than in face-to-face interviews and so the quality of information can be higher' (Martin and Jackson, 2002: 129). Countering these gains, however, are the difficulties of judging how applicants are responding to questions, managing the context in which the interview takes place and the set-up costs (CIPD, 2005f).

There is no logical limit to, or automatic correspondence between, the telephone and face-to-face delivery formats, the contents of interviews and the types of interview structure. It is, for instance, possible to have an unstructured interview conducted by a panel of selectors over the telephone (or via videoconferencing) and a structured interview conducted by a single assessor in a face-to-face situation. In practice, however, there are more, or less, likely combinations.

For example, there is a much greater chance of an unstructured interview being conducted as a one to one (in either delivery format) because it lends itself to relative informality, thus encouraging rapport and producing more open and frank discussions. In similar vein, small groups and panels are more likely to be used in asking situational, behavioural and stress questions in semi-structured, focused and structured interviews. What they lose in informality and flexibility, they gain in control and the likelihood of yielding comparable data.

Problems with interviews

Most commentators agree that there is no such thing as a problem-free interview. Whatever the interview's structure, content or mode of delivery, bias and errors occur that render it an unreliable selection instrument with low predictive validity. In the HR literature, the key sources of these issues are the interviewers themselves. They are the more active and influential party in the conduct of the process but, more than this, it is their interpretations and judgements that determine the selection outcomes. Drawing on the work of Anderson and Shackleton (1993), Taylor lists some of the main errors and sources of bias and distortion that can occur in these interpretations (see Exhibit 5-3).

Stop and reflect

Wanted: Santa

Father Christmas: £8 – £10 an hour; elves or characters in costumes, £6 – £8 an hour
   You are responsible for interviewing candidates for the role of Santa and the elves for a shopping centre's Christmas grotto. What would be your selection criteria? How can you ensure you are not breaking any employment laws?

Given this litany of potential bias and distortion, it's surprising not to see interviewing discarded as a major risk to objective selection, but this has not happened. It continues to be a popular instrument, with some 68 per cent of organisations still employing it within the traditional selection process (and 80 per cent in the case of commercial manufacturing and production firms). Some heed has been paid to the assessment of its practice, however, with organisations turning to the more structured types of interviewing and to training their selection teams. The CIPD survey (2005a), for instance, found that 56 per cent of its sample of organisations used structured, panel, interviewing (84 per cent in the case of voluntary sector agencies) and, in terms of content, 41 per cent employed behavioural questions in their structured interviews.

The decline in the use of unstructured interviewing in favour of its more structured counterparts is argued on the grounds that the greater the freedom given to interviewers in terms of structure, content and delivery, the higher the probability of bias and distortion occurring. Unstructured interviews maximise freedom and minimise control; the more structured alternatives delivered by trained individuals, small groups and panels provide greater control and thus better reliability and higher predictive validity. Interview questions can be planned carefully, candidates can be asked a comparable set of items focusing on attributes, skills and competencies, and the answers scored according to agreed rating systems (Taylor, 2005). Training (particularly in the principles of 'fair selection') is seen to be an important ingredient here, both enabling interviews to be conducted appropriately, and controlling the interpretations and

The expectancy effect	When the reading of information in CVs, applications (and perhaps references) may lead assessors to develop (positive or negative) expectations of candidates that influence interview questions and the interpretation of answers
The self-fulfilling prophecy effect	Occurs when interviewers' impressions of candidates are formed in the early stages of interviews, and these permeate subsequent questions and/or evaluations
The attribution (or 'stereotype') effect	Happens when interviewers associate particular groups with specific characteristics and judge individual candidates in these terms; although in the light of recent anti-discrimination legislation much of this stereotyping may be illegal, it is still thought to be widespread
The prototyping effect	When interviewers are impressed by a particular type of person(ality), regardless of job-related factors
The universalist effect	Occurs when interviewers, on the basis of responses to particular questions, rate candidates as 'good' or 'bad' across the board and thus reach very unbalanced decisions
The 'similar to me' effect	Describes situations in which interviewers give preference to candidates they perceive as having a similar background, career history, personality or attitudes to themselves
The information overload effect	Happens when interviewers form judgements based on only a fraction of the data available to them about each candidate
The temporal extension effect	When interviewers assume that candidates' behaviour at interview (e.g. their nervousness) is typical of their general disposition

Exhibit 5 – 3 Problems that can arise in interviews
Source: Adapted from Taylor (2005: 211).

evaluations of the information provided by candidates (Marchington and Wilkinson, 2005). Nonetheless, whether such measures actually eradicate (or even the degree to which they inhibit) interviewer distortion is still a controversial matter. Greater control is sought in the names of fairness and objectivity, but it is far from clear that it can overcome the interpretative (and some would say inherently intersubjective) nature of interviewing (Newell and Shackleton, 2001).

References

References form the final element of the traditional selection process. They differ from both application forms and interviews in that they seek a third-party assessment of the applicant's skills, abilities and character. As with interviews and application forms, they are employed by large numbers of organisations. The CIPD recruitment survey (2005a) revealed that 96 per cent of the sampled organisations asked for references for at least some of their vacancies, while 77 per cent always asked applicants for references.

As suggested earlier in the chapter, references can be employed in different ways at different stages of the selection process.

- They can be requested and used pre-interview, in conjunction with the application form to shortlist and hone interview questions.
- They can be used post-interview as a means of checking: the information provided on the application form, that supplied during the interview and the general impression created by the candidate.

In practice, the survey (CIPD, 2005a) found that 34 per cent of the organisations it sampled took up references pre-interview and thus were able to use them to shortlist and/or as a means of sharpening the interview questions. The majority of the sample, however, chose to employ references post-interview, and primarily as a means of checking the data and impressions of interviews and application forms.

Types of references

References come in many different forms, and include the following.

Employment references

These are requested from current or previous employers, although references from current employers should be sought only with the permission of applicants. This type of reference can either be an open request for information about candidates or, in a more structured form, can ask particular questions about, for example, employment dates, attendance record, responsibilities, competencies and performance.

Personal references

Prospective employers use personal references to ask for assessments of the applicant's character. Again, this can either be an open assessment request or structured in terms of the nature of the job and working conditions, and/or by asking referees to rank or rate particular personal qualities.

Academic references

These normally combine a request to confirm academic achievements with a personal assessment of the candidate's suitability for the post.

Specialist references

Examples of these are credit or medical histories. Credit references are typically undertaken for positions where cash handling or other financial transactions are important. It is now obligatory under the Financial Services and Markets Act 2000 for companies covered by this legislation to provide references for current and past employees. All employers can seek medical references from prospective employees but, as this is considered sensitive personal data by the Data Protection Act 1998, they must obtain the applicant's consent before making such a request.

Problems with references

In spite of their wide usage, references can present problems for both providers and prospective employers. In terms of prospective employers, the following issues apply.

- **Accuracy.** Because a job applicant is being asked to give the names of referees, they are highly unlikely to choose anyone who will give them a bad reference, and therefore inaccuracies or so-called 'leniency errors' may well arise.

- **Authenticity.** Cases of 'fake' references are not unusual. Instances have been recorded in which friends of applicants have posed as line managers and, again, where references have been sent from bogus companies (Smethurst, 2004).

- **Interpretation.** References may require 'interpretation': an exemplary reference could be given because an employer is trying to get rid of a member of staff, a non-committal reference because a line manager is trying to keep a member of staff, and so on.

- **Time delays.** Employers are generally disinclined to invest effort in writing references for former employees or current employees looking to leave the organisation. These are consequently seen as low priority, often leading to delays in the prospective employer's selection schedule (Taylor, 2005).

- **Non-response.** Response rates for reference requests vary between 35 and 85 per cent (CIPD, 2005c) and can cause particular problems for organisations using the references to shortlist or support interviews.

- **Poor prediction of future job performance.** According to Cooper *et al.* (2003: 154), references are 'highly subjective' and 'open to error and abuse'.

In terms of providers, the issues arise primarily from the changing legal status of what is written. The Data Protection Act 1998, and the growth in discrimination legislation and case law have resulted in an increasingly cautious approach to writing references. Referees are seen to owe a 'duty of care' to both prospective employers and applicants. In other words, they are considered culpable if they knowingly deceive recruiting organisations or mislead them into hiring people that they know to be unsuitable. They may also be held liable for losses by applicants if their references contain negligent or defamatory statements.

Attempts to improve references

Most organisations will request written references; this gives referees more time to reflect on the questions, the wording of answers and on the information provided about the job vacancy. Occasionally, however, when it's a senior post, when ambiguities have arisen in the written reference or where references are late, prospective employers may well resort to seeking references by telephone. Doing so is less anonymous, increases the chances of a balanced assessment and, more pointedly, makes it more difficult for ex-employers to avoid giving a reference. A second improvement is the more widespread use of structured questionnaires based on the job and person specifications. While these are seen to require more preparatory work than an 'open' reference, with separate forms for different types of job, they are easier for referees to complete, and permit a more focused and detailed response.

Contemporary methods of selection

Despite their continued usage, the perceived limitations of the traditional selection methods have led both employers and academics to consider alternative ways of selecting. For a few organisations these alternatives act as substitutes; for the majority, however, they are employed to shore up or strengthen the traditional methods. They are seen to:

- reduce the risk of subjective decision-making by increasing the levels of reliability and predictive validity, and

- offer a more comprehensive selection process by measuring factors that could not be adequately assessed using application forms, interviews or references.

Three methods of **contemporary selection** deserve special consideration: biographical profiling, psychological testing and assessment centres.

contemporary selection
Includes biographical profiling, psychological testing and assessment centres.

biographical profiling
The biographic detail of successful job-holders can be used to predict who will be effective in the job in the future.

Biographical profiling

Biographical profiling is held to be both an extension of, and an improvement on, the traditional selection process. It gathers more comprehensive and systematic data than application forms and references and, at the same time, is considered to have greater predictive validity than the interview. This selection method works from three key assumptions:

1 the historicist assumption that the future will be like the past; in other words, that past human action is the best predictor of future human action

2 that individuals differ from each other and these differences can be measured

3 that individual biographic profiles can be matched to job performance.

On this basis, it is argued that the biographic detail of successful job-holders can be used to predict who will be effective in the job in the future. The method starts from the question 'What is it about past and current incumbents that has enabled them to excel at their job?' The answer is sought in demographic, experiential and attitudinal data. This can include anything from simple age, gender and residential information through to 'more intricate details of personal life history and other experiences such as early and late personal relationships, personal habits and attitudes, recreational interests, self-impressions or opinions' (Searle, 2003: 82). Collected through research instruments as varied as structured surveys and qualitative 'life history' essays, the task is to analyse the data in order to establish a link between personal history and successful job performance.

Once this is achieved, the analysis is then used to draft a questionnaire for new job applicants, which sets out to measure whether, and to what extent, they possess the appropriate biographical attributes. The questions used are typically a mixture of hard – in the sense of eliciting easily verifiable information – and 'soft' items – that is, asking for 'judgements, aspirations ... attitudes and expectations' (Searle, 2003: 84). Included within the latter are questions designed to capture the applicant's reactions to specific situations as well as projections on how they would conduct themselves in particular circumstances. As the questions are largely a matter of self-assessment, questionnaires can either be sent to applicants through the post or, as is increasingly the case with other selection tools, presented in an online format.

Although bioprofiling has a long history in the United States (it has been in use there since 1894), only a small number of organisations currently use this method in the UK. It is, however, becoming more popular here (Taylor, 2005). Attracting employers is the fact that bioprofiling:

- is more extensive than an application form and enables information to be collected more economically than by interviewing
- has greater predictive validity than the classic selection format – 'Research evidence indicates that biodata has substantial and generalisable validity. This means that it measures what it claims to measure and is therefore a good predictor of performance (Searle, 2003: 88)
- incorporates independently verifiable data and is thus more difficult for applicants to fake
- is a very efficient way of assessing large numbers of applicants (especially if it is offered as a multiple-choice questionnaire)
- promotes fairness by asking all candidates the same questions and, in large part, assesses their answers on the basis of predetermined responses, thus curtailing the opportunities for assessors to impose their own judgements.

Deterring its use in some instances, however, are specific concerns about:

- the high set-up costs and, in particular, the time and money that would need to be devoted to developing the questionnaire on which the method is based
- its low portability – that is, each type of job would require its own questionnaire; 'A questionnaire that is good at predicting the performance of airline stewards will be very different from one that aims to forecast how effective pilots are likely to be' (Taylor, 2005: 229)
- the speed with which bioprofile questionnaires can become obsolete and thus the need to replace them every few years if they are to retain their predictive value
- how the very nature of the data collection denies the exploration of issues that is available with some other selection methods, such as interviews and assessment centres.

Two more general concerns are also of importance:

- bioprofiling's inherent promotion of the status quo
- the ease with which it could fall foul of anti-discriminatory legislation.

In the case of the former, it is clear that, given the method's use of past and current employees to develop criteria for assessing the likely success of future applicants, it is effectively promoting a very conservative selection strategy. If, for example, a City finance firm has a predominantly young, white, male, Anglo-Saxon employee population, bioprofiling would not, of itself, support greater gender, ethnic or age diversity in selection. With the latter, given the broad-based anti-discriminatory legislation that has developed in the UK and European Union over the last 10 years (see Chapter 11), it is extremely important that the biodata sought are sensitive to the legislative parameters, and to the sense of justice and social fairness on which they are based. Of course, if one is working in another culture then other problems can arise, as can be seen from the 'International perspectives' box.

Juapong Textiles, Ghana

Sometimes, problems can be more to do with local politics than with appropriate selection techniques, as can be seen at Juapong Textiles.

Recruitment of personnel to work at the rejuvenated Juapong Textiles Limited (JTL), scheduled to re-open in April 2006, seems to have created an unprecedented level of anxiety in Juapong, in the North Tongu district of the Volta region, and its immediate environ of Atimpoku in the Eastern Region. This was in consequence of a controversy over who should be responsible for the recruitment of workers and where it should be conducted. While some traditional authorities feel it is the sole right of indigenes of Dorfor traditional area, where the factory is located, some political leaders have maintained that all qualified Ghanaians can be recruited.

The problems seem to stem from the Minster for Trade, who feels that people can be recruited from other regions along the Volta, while the local chief thinks that only people from Juapong should be employed. As a result, he has suggested that local people boycott the factory.

The Deputy Minister for Employment reported that, 'I do not know the criteria for the selection of the right calibre of people. Whatever list anybody is compiling is not automatic because it will have to be screened by a panel', adding that any Ghanaian has the right to seek employment at the factory, irrespective of his or her origin.

The Deputy Minister said that the rejuvenation of the factory should rather be a source of good news to the people of Ghana, and was worried that some leaders had already started judging the good development along ethnic and political lines.

Some of the youth at Juapong said that, in the past, they had enjoyed some sort of priority for work due to the factory's location, expressing the fear that somebody, somewhere, was trying to change the status quo.

Some of them also said that they were staff at the company before its closure, adding that, even though they were paid all their entitlements, they think their friends and colleagues should be considered first in order to maintain the priority reserved for the area.

Source: Adapted from 'Row over job recruitment at "rejuvenated" Juapong Textiles',
Ghanaian Chronicle (Africa News), 3 February 2006.

Discussion questions

1 When working in different cultures, managers often have to adopt different selection procedures. How can they do this and still recruit the right people?

2 How can a manager ensure that selection criteria are transparent?

Psychological testing

___

psychological testing
Works from the assumption that people differ from each other and that these differences can be measured.
___

The term 'psychological testing' is usually employed as a synonym for occupational or psychometric testing. Like bioprofiling, it works from the assumption that people differ from each other and that these differences can be measured. Again like bioprofiling, it is rarely used as the exclusive means of making a decision and is typically employed in conjunction with interviewing and assessment centres (see below). It differs from bioprofiling, however, in the range and nature of tests it can call upon and in its popularity. Current estimates suggest that over half a million psychological tests are completed each year by candidates in the UK applying for graduate positions alone (Income Data Services, 2004), and that 70 per cent of firms (Searle, 2003) and 81 per cent of FTSE-100 companies (*People Management*, 2005b) use them in selection. Discussed in much of the HR literature in terms of the selection of managers or graduate applicants, they are in fact employed across a broad spectrum of occupations. B&Q, Vodafone and Asda, for example, utilise them in the selection of their retail staff (*People Management*, 2003; Income Data Services, 2004), while National Car Parks does the same in choosing its parking wardens (*People Management*, 2005a).

Psychological tests can be divided into two main types: those designed to measure applicants' ability and those that set out to assess their psychological disposition (see Exhibit 5-4). Measures are tests of intellectual performance and are usually 'maximal tests' in the sense that 'they aim to find out what is the *best* the test-taker can do' (Searle, 2003: 137). Tests are typically taken under examination conditions with a set time limit and standard instructions. The questions asked have a right answer, and candidates are usually required to select this answer within a multiple-choice format. The goal is to answer the questions as quickly and accurately as possible in the time allowed. In the pen-and-paper version of the tests, they are then marked by trained administrators and the score obtained is matched against a norm group (that is, compared with results gathered from existing employees, applicants or the general population) in order to assess how well the candidate has done. The tests are designed to offer a standardised, objective and structured assessment that is easy to measure and affords simple comparisons.

In contrast, tests of psychological disposition are not usually taken under examination conditions nor are they concerned with maximal performance. Rather, in a structured and standardised way, they seek to gauge and codify the traits or characteristics of applicants with a view to predicting how they will 'fit', perform in or manage a particular work environment. These tests are usually of the self-report type – that is, applicants are asked to record how they see themselves in terms of a range of criteria or characteristics that are typically presented in a questionnaire with multiple-choice or open-ended questions. Answers are plotted on a profile chart and, again, matched against an occupational norm group. Each outcome is typically fed back and discussed with the particular applicant before being reported to the selectors. Selectors are advised by the test administrators as to where there are strong and weak correlations between the applicants' profiles and those described in the job's person specification. They then have the opportunity to decide whether the weak correlations are grounds for rejection or to pursue them with the candidate during the remainder of the selection process.

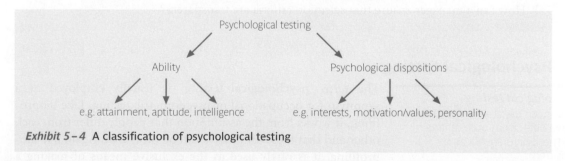

Exhibit 5–4 A classification of psychological testing

Testing ability

Ability is frequently stratified into different fields. Searle (2003) and Roberts (2003), for example, divide it into attainment, aptitude and intelligence. The tests used to measure ability tend to reflect this division primarily in terms of their level of specificity (see Exhibit 5-5). Those measuring attainment operate in particular domains and seek to assess 'present performance, irrespective of how the present capability was acquired or how it might progress ... [These] tests are most useful when the selection is made on the basis of who will be the best candidate as soon as they start work' (Smith and Smith, 2005: 192). They are particularly suitable in selection for posts that are unlikely to change in a significant way. Unlike attainment tests, those measuring aptitude gauge the *potential* or propensity to acquire knowledge, competencies or skills in the future. Their aim is to make inferences about future work performance by assessing how well applicants learn a job-related task. They are used in work situations where candidates cannot be expected to possess the requisite skills. In effect, aptitude tests measure the applicant's suitability for training. As an illustration, the psychological test supplier, SHL, has developed the 'Customer Contact Aptitude Series', which is designed to assess whether individuals possess 'the verbal and numerical reasoning required for effectiveness in sales, customer services and call centre roles' (Income Data Services, 2004: 80).

ability
Frequently stratified into different fields, such as attainment, aptitude and intelligence, and indicates the capability a candidate will have to do a job.

Where attainment and aptitude tests measure specific and often job-related knowledge and skills (see Exhibit 5-6 for illustrations), those tests designed to assess intelligence seek to gauge broad cognitive skills or provide a measure of an individual's overall ability. In Toplis *et al.*'s terms, they assess 'the capacity for abstract thinking and reasoning within a range of different contexts and media (1994: 17). These tests (for example, Raven's Progressive Matrices or the Watson-Glazer Test of Critical Thinking) are usually aimed at graduates, managers or executives (Smith and Smith, 2005). They measure abstract reasoning either through the aggregation of a battery of test scores from specific verbal and non-verbal maximal tests, or by employing a single test that presents complex problems (in words, numbers and diagrams) and then requires candidates to solve them by using logical or lateral thinking.

According to the CIPD survey (2005a), approximately 40 per cent of employers use general ability tests in selection; 50 per cent test for job-specific skills and competencies, and 39 per cent use literacy and/or numeracy tests in choosing at least some of their employees. In both the fields of attainment and aptitude, tests of literacy and numeracy are more likely to be used as

Tests of:	Temporal focus	A measurement of	Breadth
Attainment	Current	Known and controlled experience/knowledge/skills	Specific test domains
Aptitude	Future potential	Unknown and variable experience/knowledge	Narrow specific skills, often job-related
Intelligence	Current	Underlying reasoning ability	Broad cognitive skills

Exhibit 5–5 Tests of ability
Source: Adapted from Searle (2003: 144).

Type of test	Application
Verbal/communication	Ranging from attainment tests of spelling and grammar for clerical jobs to tests of verbal/critical reasoning for managers and graduates
Numerical	Ranging from basic arithmetic tests for process workers and clerical administrators to numerical critical reasoning tests for managers and graduate entrants where inferences need to be drawn from business data
Diagrammatic	Tests of logical reasoning presented in the form of shapes and diagrams; often used in occupations involving data processing, and where analytical and problem-solving skills are prevalent
Mechanical	Problem-solving tests, usually in pictorial form; employed in a wide range of apprenticeships and in engineering occupations
Spatial	Used to assess aptitude for posts in design and in occupations that require an understanding of how components fit together
Dexterity	Measure hand speed and fine precision skills and are employed in assessing process and assembly workers, as well as in co-ordination tests (e.g. in the selection of pilots)
Sensory	Measures near or far acuity, sound or colour discrimination; used, for instance, in assessing recruits for the Armed Forces and in construction
Administrative	Measures IT, word-processing speeds, filing and classification skills; used for a range of administrative posts

Exhibit 5 – 6 The application of measures of attainment and aptitude

'threshold tests' – that is, to eliminate the weaker candidates rather than as a means of choosing between those appointable. The household-to-healthcare company Kimberly-Clark Europe, for instance, uses a numerical reasoning test very early in its selection process for graduate entrants. Those applicants who fail to reach at least the 31st percentile in this test (when compared with an undergraduate norm group) do not progress to the next stage of selection (Income Data Services, 2004: 25).

Advantages of ability tests

Advocates of ability tests suggest that they carry many advantages. Among these are that they:

- measure factors that cannot be assessed using the traditional selection process
- offer a more systematic and more objective selection instrument
- provide organisations with a means of discriminating between large numbers of applicants in a rapid and often cost-effective manner (Searle, 2003)
- are among the best predictors of subsequent job performance (Robertson and Smith, 2001)
- reveal how close an applicant is to the requisite skills level, how much training they might need to reach an acceptable standard and, thus, provide a useful insight into post-hire training costs and on-the-job experience requirements (Searle, 2003)

- are transportable (i.e. they do not have to be constructed for each job)
- once established, they are cheap to run and can be used in a wide variety of selection contexts.

Disadvantages of ability tests

Of their drawbacks, the following are particularly worthy of note.

- The start-up costs are high. These costs would include, for instance:
  - initial training for staff administering and interpreting the tests; ability test training (to British Psychological Society Certificate of Competence Level A) can take up to five days with further one-day training enhancements
  - start-up kits, including one-off costs such as the test user's manual and/or computer software
  - consumables, such as answer sheets for candidates and normative data
  - software packages and licences, where online or computer administration is used (Income Data Services, 2004).

- There is a concern about the validity of the tests themselves, and specifically the degree to which variations in test performance are the product of factors other than ability. Searle (2003: Chapter 6), for instance, suggests that the choice of language, the use of time limits in tests, the emotional state and previous test experience of the test-taker and the environment in which the test occurs can all influence test scores.

- Kandola *et al.* (2000) raise doubts about the universal application of ability testing. They maintain that ability (and particularly intelligence) tests are not suitable for selecting senior managers primarily because factors other than mental ability tend to determine successful job performance at that level of operation.

- At a more overt political level, some analysts have also claimed that ability tests can possess unfair discriminatory features and have an adverse impact on the selection of members of particular social groups. Taylor, for instance, suggests that '[s]ome tests appear to disfavour members of lower socio-economic groups and some ethnic minorities, while others are biased against people whose first language is not English because of the requirement to complete them speedily' (2005: 233–234). Searle expresses her concern in a more focused way, questioning why there has not been more research on the reliability and validity of these selection instruments given the findings indicating 'differences between the performance of Caucasians and African-Americans' (2003: 165).

Testing psychological disposition

Like ability, **psychological disposition** is also divided into different fields of study. The main areas include interests, motivation and values, and personality. Tests employed in these areas (see Exhibit 5-7) look to provide standardised, objective and structured measures that afford simple comparisons of individual applicants. Those assessing interests (e.g. the Rothwell-Miller Interest Inventory) are designed to gauge a person's preferences for specific types of work-related activity. Those measuring motivation and value (e.g. Gordon's Survey of Interpersonal Values and Tarleton's Motivational Styles Questionnaire) are used to map the 'drive' or likely commitment of candidates and to gauge their 'fit'

psychological disposition
Measures are tests of intellectual performance and are usually 'maximal tests' in the sense that 'they aim to find out what is the *best* the test-taker can do'.

within an organisation's culture. Personality assessments also aim to measure applicants' 'fit' along with their likely performance as a team member and their 'match' with the perceived ideal personality for the post. Of the three fields, it is personality assessments that have proven to be the most controversial. There have been disputes about the conception of personality itself and how it is tested (see Smith and Smith, 2005: Chapters 4, 15, 16) and the effectiveness of those tests (see the criticisms below). For some analysts (e.g. Blinkhorn and Johnson, 1990) and employers, the disputes are sufficient reason to avoid current personality assessments in selection procedures. For others, they are grounds for caution in both the application of tests and interpretation of results (Searle, 2003; Taylor, 2005). Figures quoted by the Industrial Relations Services Employment Review (2002) estimated that 26 per cent of employers used personality tests when choosing managers, while the most recent CIPD survey (2005a) indicated that 36 per cent of organisations employed this instrument in selection.

The dominant model of personality in current selection procedures (Cooper *et al.*, 2003; Smith and Smith, 2005) is the 'big five' trait-based framework developed from the conceptual work of McDougall and Norman (Digman, 1990), and the conceptual and methodological work of Eysenck and Cattell (Smith and Smith, 2005). It suggests there are five basic factors, or traits, on which personalities are built and that account for the differences between individuals. Based on Searle (2003: 207–208), these are:

1 emotional stability (measures of which assess the degree to which someone is susceptible to psychological distress)

2 extroversion–introversion (tests here gauge levels of sociability)

3 agreeableness (measures of which assess the extent to which individuals are philanthropic and avoid conflict)

4 conscientiousness (tests here gauge the degree to which individuals are well organised, concerned with meeting deadlines, and the making and implementation of plans)

5 openness to experience (measures of which assess the extent to which individuals are imaginative and show independence of judgement).

Type of test	Purpose
Interests	To identify applicants' preferences for specific types of work-related activity
Motivation and values	To ascertain what 'drives' applicants and what values they think are important; by using these tests, employers look to discover how suitable an applicant is for the job profile and how they might fit within the organisational culture
Personality assessments	To gauge and codify the personal characteristics of applicants in order to predict how well: ■ their personalities match that believed to be ideal for the job, and fit within the organisational culture ■ their disposition complements those of existing team members (Taylor, 2005)

Exhibit 5–7 Tests of psychological disposition

Even among the advocates of personality assessments, these five factors are not assumed to be equally relevant in all selection situations or for all occupations (see Barrick *et al.*, 2001) nor, therefore, are they uniformly strong in predicting job performance (Cooper *et al.*, 2003). Supporters of the tests do, however, see them as providing the basis, the 'building blocks of our personality and explain[ing] the differences between us' (Taylor, 2005: 236).

The uncertain atmosphere surrounding personality assessments has led to a largely solicitous HR literature (e.g. Marchington and Wilkinson, 2005; Taylor, 2005). Replete with warnings about poorly designed tests, the dangers of using untrained analysts to interpret them and unscrupulous test suppliers, it looks to practical guidance from the CIPD and the British Psychological Society (BPS). Both these sources stress the need to train staff in the implementation and interpretation of these tests (to level B of the BPS certificate of competence), urge caution in the inferences drawn from them and recommend that the tests feature as part of a multi-instrument selection process. In their present state of development, their primary role is to enable a more complete picture of an applicant than would otherwise be possible (CIPD, 2005d).

Advantages of tests of psychological disposition

Supporters of the use of tests of psychological disposition maintain that they:

- bring greater objectivity to selection than that afforded by traditional selection methods (Income Data Services, 2004)
- offer employers insights into their candidates that are not available using interviewing, application forms and references
- supply higher predictive validity than the traditional methods
- are relatively easy to use, by a trained administrator, allowing structured comparisons of individuals.

Disadvantages of tests of psychological disposition

Critics of the use of these tests:

- question whether individual jobs can usefully be analysed in terms of more or less desirable personality traits and, relatedly, whether there are ideal personalities that correspond to particular jobs (Newell, 2005)
- ask if a questionnaire that takes 30 to 60 minutes to complete can provide sufficient information about an individual's personality to make meaningful inferences about their suitability for a job
- maintain that the data on which inferences are based are open to faking and distortion by applicants seeking to create a better image and increase their chances of selection (Arthur *et al.*, 2001)
- argue that their predictive validity, although higher than that of traditional methods, is nonetheless relatively low – particularly when compared with ability testing (Robertson and Smith, 2001)
- express concern that some assessments of disposition, particularly those of personality, could discriminate against particular groups, most notably ethnic minorities and women (Newell and Shackleton, 2001; Searle, 2003)
- maintain that initial investment costs are very high for what, essentially, is a supplementary selection instrument.

Online testing

The high initial investment costs for tests of both ability and psychological disposition have led many organisations to seek economies from the outset and opt for an online version of psychological testing. This has particularly been the case with commercial organisations with large numbers of applicants. The perceived benefits include the following.

- **Greater flexibility** for both the organisation and applicants. Applicants can complete their tests at any time and anywhere. Asking them to complete the tests alongside an online application form gives employers access to more information on which to base their short-listing or screening decisions.

- **Time and cost savings.** Without the need for test administrators or finding suitable test venues, the costs of testing and time involved can be greatly reduced. In addition, tests can often be scored automatically, again giving organisations and candidates access to results almost immediately.

- **Improving test content.** Using online technology allows employers to introduce multimedia items into the selection process, permitting both more interactive tests and virtual office tests that are more closely linked to the actual work environment than paper-based methods.

- **Better information management.** Storing test information on computers or CD-Roms provides a much more efficient way of recording test results. Databases make it easier to search and access candidate data, while email technology allows results to be quickly and easily communicated.

- **Feedback.** A number of online tests produce computer-driven narratives that can be supplied to applicants as feedback (Income Data Services, 2004).

The potential drawbacks of online testing include the following.

- **The integrity of candidates' responses.** A major issue confronting employers using online testing is how to ensure that candidates are not cheating (i.e. that they are completing the test themselves and do not have access to reference materials). One way of checking is to re-test those applicants that successfully complete the online screening, although this would clearly counter at least some of the gains of moving to online testing in the first place.

- **Security concerns.** Some employers fear that online tests compromise data security.

- **Regulating test conditions.** Although online tests allow greater standardisation of the instructions given to candidates, test users have no control over the test environment. To help increase consistency, the test instructions should inform candidates of the preferred test conditions (e.g. work area, lighting and noise levels, minimum PC specifications and how the computer should be set up (Income Data Services, 2004).

Assessment centres

assessment centre
Refers to the process of employing a range of work-related tests to assess the aptitude and skills of a group of candidates applying for a position.

The term **assessment centre** does not refer to a single selection method or to a specific location, but to the process of employing a range of work-related tests to assess the aptitude and skills of a group of candidates applying for a position. It is a multi-method, evidence-based, approach to selection that involves '[T]he utilisation of a number of different selection methods over a specified time period (typically one to four days) in order for multiple assessors to assess many candidates on a range of identified competences or behavioural dimensions' (Newell and Shackleton, 2001: 127).

First used during the Second World War as a tool for selecting military officers, assessment centres have grown in popularity in the UK, particularly for graduate and management selection. In the CIPD recruitment survey (2005a), some 34 per cent of sampled organisations said that they used them for selection purposes (41 per cent in the case of public-sector organisations). Among graduate recruiters, they are used by 52 per cent of employers, while in large organisations with more than 10,000 employees the figure rises to 95.2 per cent (Suff, 2005). Employers' support for assessment centres is in large measure because they allow them to get closer to the selection ideal of observing how applicants *perform* the sort of tasks actually found in the job for which they are being assessed (Income Data Services, 2005a).

Among the exercises utilised for this purpose are group work, written exercises, role-plays and presentations – these are often complemented by interviews and psychological tests (see Exhibit 5-8).

Group work

Group work includes leaderless group discussions, projects and business simulations, and is designed to assess effective communication, problem-solving abilities and interpersonal and

Types of exercise	Competencies and skills
Group exercise (e.g. leaderless projects and discussions, business simulations)	Effective communication; creative problem-solving; leadership; team working; flexibility; organisation skills
Written exercises (e.g. in-tray exercise)	Planning and organising ability; time management; reading and assimilating information; delegation skills; problem analysis; prioritising; decision-making
Presentations (e.g. planned or unplanned)	Effective communication; persuasion skills; ability to work under pressure; knowledge of their topic or the field of presentation
Role-playing (e.g. irate customer exercise, disciplining staff, counselling staff, negotiating with hard-bargaining suppliers, fact-finding interviews)	Communication, listening and interpersonal skills; ability to react in a changing situation; negotiation and problem-solving skills
Complementary activities	
Psychological testing	Usually personality tests, often supplemented with numerical and verbal reasoning exercises
Interviews	Employed for a range of purposes from de-briefings to seeking candidates' assessments of their previous work experience and performance

Exhibit 5 – 8 Types of assessment centre exercise and their targeted competencies and skills

leadership skills. An example of this type of exercise involves setting a group of applicants a problem to resolve in a specified time period, and monitoring the process of how they set about this task and produce a solution. HM Prison Service, for instance, has used a problem-solving group exercise for its management applicants in which each is allocated an 'employee' for whom they have to negotiate a fair proportion of the organisation's training budget while finding an overall distribution of funds that is acceptable to the rest of the group (Income Data Services, 2005a: 4).

Written exercises

Written exercises are typically individual tests that involve giving candidates a data set and/or information pack about a particular problem or situation, and asking them to produce a written report containing their analysis and recommendations for action. This form of general exercise is seen to provide selectors with a valuable assessment of both analytic and written communication skills. A specific variant of it is the so-called 'in-tray' or 'in-basket' exercise. Here, candidates are given a range of information sources, such as memos, letters, records and other documentary items, and may be asked, for example, to plan and organise their day, prioritise and/or delegate work or respond to enquiries. Some organisations have modernised it by making it an online or 'e-tray' exercise, adding 'a level of reality ... by providing candidates with their own PCs and telephones and simulating the exercise in "real-time"' (Income Data Services, 2005a: 5).

Presentations

Presentations are used to assess applicants' verbal communication skills, their ability to work under pressure and their persuasiveness. The subject matter for this type of activity can range from topics that are highly job specific through to topics of personal interest. For example, an accountant may be asked to present her/his findings on the management accounts or talk about corporate social responsibility, or alternatively, be asked to do a presentation on a topic of their choosing. How much time applicants are given to organise their presentations can also vary. Thames Water advises candidates days or weeks in advance of their assessment centre, whereas applicants to HM Prison Service get just 25 minutes to choose and prepare a topic (Income Data Services, 2005a).

Role-plays

Role-plays offer assessors the opportunity to look at candidates in the kind of situation the latter might encounter in the job for which they are applying. Typical scenarios include asking the candidate to undertake a performance appraisal with an underachieving employee, dealing with an irate customer and negotiating with a hard-bargaining supplier. An assessor usually plays the other role, although some companies bring in actors in the hope of achieving a greater consistency of performance.

Complementary activities

Although not essential, some assessment centres also incorporate psychological tests and interviews as part of their portfolio. Where psychological tests are used, they tend to be personality assessments supplemented by numerical and verbal reasoning tests. In the case of interviews, they range from de-briefings that take place after specific exercises through to the more standard interviews seeking to address candidates' evaluations of their past experience and performance.

The number and types of exercise are always tailored to the job in question, but the assessment centre literature (e.g. Income Data Services, 2005a; Suff, 2005) suggests that, as a general rule, each key skill or competency (as described in the job and person specifications) should be assessed in at least two different exercises and, in each instance, by at least two assessors.

The strengths and limitations of assessment centres

Assessment centres are considered to have a number of advantages over the other modern selection instruments as well as their traditional counterparts. Among the benefits for employers are:

- the consistency and enhanced objectivity they are considered to bring to the selection process through the use of trained assessors employing multiple methods and an evidence-based approach (Income Data Services, 2005a)
- the comprehensive picture of applicants' skills that these methods provide
- the predictive value arising from the use of work-simulation exercises
- their flexibility as selection instruments – 'They are not purchased "off-the-shelf" like [many] psychological tests, and are not as time-restricted as interviews. There is therefore plenty of scope to introduce exercises that are of specific relevance to the job and the organisation involved' (Taylor, 2005: 244)
- the opportunity to convey realistic expectations of the nature and activities of the job.

The potential drawbacks of assessment centres include:

- the expense; 'An effective centre requires a considerable investment in time and resources – the design process alone can take months. The administrative workload can also be heavy and centres are particularly demanding in terms of the time required from assessors, many of whom are relatively senior managers' (Income Data Services, 2005a: 2)
- the opaque nature of how the results of individual exercises are turned into an overall decision; for example, the so-called 'wash-up' process, the aggregation of assessors' candidate scores, can be highly political; it is rarely a straightforward calculative process and much more a meeting of assessors in which the power of individual members prevails
- the quality of training of the assessors, and their ability to assess specific competencies within overall task performance.

However, when these drawbacks are set against the cost of making the wrong recruitment decision, the substantial investment required may seem more reasonable.

Making the appointment: cognisance of the legal framework

Having made the decision on who to appoint and an offer (verbal or written) to the successful candidate, it is then incumbent upon employers to undertake a further set of related activities. It is important, for example, that all the documents pertaining to the selection process are retained for 12 months. This is to enable the organisation:

- to respond to any requests for information under the Data Protection Act 1998 or, where appropriate, the Freedom of Information Act 2000

■ to deal with any complaints about the decision or its selection procedures; a number of agencies (e.g. the CRE and the DTI) advise employers to record and store all relevant details, such as their shortlisting schemes, the scores from tests or assessment centres, the interview schedule, interviewers' notes and their ranking of each candidate, discussions and decisions.

Once the offer is accepted by the successful applicant, it becomes a legally binding agreement. While this can be agreed informally, a written statement is clearly of benefit to both parties, not least because it reduces the likelihood of future disputes. In practice, most employers provide a written **contract of employment**. The details of such contracts vary with the nature of the post, with the organisation and, where collective agreements apply, with the terms agreed with the relevant trades unions. For the majority of employees, their terms of engagement are a matter of individual negotiation subject to the employer's compliance with the relevant statute and common law (Lewis and Sargeant, 2004).

contract of employment
The legal contract between employer and employee.

Employers do, however, have a statutory duty to provide new employees with a written statement of **employment particulars** within two months of their start date. Their obligations in this respect are set out in the Employment Rights Act 1996, although in specifying individual terms and conditions, they must also take cognisance of other legal measures, the most important of which are listed in Exhibit 5-9. Collectively, these require employers to provide employees with a written statement detailing:

employment particulars
Details of duties and conditions the employee can expect from the organisation.

■ the employer and employee's names
■ the date from which the employee's period of continuous employment commenced
■ the title of the job or a brief description of the employee's work
■ the place of work
■ the scale or rate of remuneration and the method of payment
■ terms and conditions relating to hours of work and normal working hours
■ terms and conditions relating to holiday entitlement and pay.

Equal Pay Act 1970

Rehabilitation of Offenders Act 1974

The Pension Schemes Act 1993

Employment Rights Act 1996

Asylum and Immigration Act 1996

Patents Act 1997

National Minimum Wage Act 1998

The Working Time Regulations 1998

Employment Act 2002

The Information and Consultation of Employees Regulations 2004

Exhibit 5–9 Key legislation relating to employment terms and conditions

In addition, they are also required to provide either in the written statement or in an accompanying document details of:

- the period of notice to be given by the employer and the employee
- the period for which any non-permanent employment is expected to continue or, if it is for a fixed term, the date when it is to end
- the terms and conditions relating to incapacity for work due to sickness or injury, including any sick pay provisions
- pensions and pension schemes
- any collective agreements that directly affect the terms and conditions of employment
- the length of time, the currency in which the salary will be paid, additional remuneration and benefits (e.g. flights home, schooling), and the terms and conditions for returning to work in the UK where an employee is required to work outside the UK for more than one month
- dismissal, disciplinary and grievance procedures.

In terms of good practice, many employers provide more detailed specifications either in the contract or in accompanying documents, such as, for instance, staff handbooks. Such documents cover particular organisational practices, including restrictive covenants protecting intellectual property, probationary periods, business travel and expenses, and Internet and email use. While these, as employment lawyers emphasise (Lewis and Sargeant, 2004), may not form part of the contract, they nonetheless frame the employment relationship. Ensuring that employees are fully aware of the terms and conditions of their employment and what is expected of them is thus a key element in successful selection. The major tool in this familiarisation process is the final phase of selection: induction.

Induction

Induction comes into play once the successful applicants have been chosen, offers made, and the contractual terms and start dates agreed. Its general purpose is 'to ensure the effective integration of staff into or across the organisation for the benefit of both parties' (CIPD, 2005e: 1). Starting a new job can clearly be stressful. New recruits need to learn about their employing organisation, employment conditions, their colleagues, line managers and 'the way things are done'. Induction provides the employer with the opportunity of welcoming new colleagues, giving them the information they require to operate in their new work environment and to support their acclimatisation. From an employer's or manager's perspective, it is a critical phase. Poor induction could wipe out all the potential selection gains, leading to:

induction
'To ensure the effective integration of staff into or across the organisation for the benefit of both parties.'

- discord within work teams
- low morale, particularly for new employees
- loss of productivity and, in extreme cases, the avoidable costs of finding further staff if the new recruits leave or are dismissed.

The latter is not a point to be underestimated, the CIPD recruitment survey (2005a) estimates that some 13 per cent of leavers had less than six months' service.

The nature of induction varies in content, length and ethos according to the size of the organisation and type of recruit. 'Good practice' guides (e.g. Acas, 2005; CIPD, 2005e) suggest that they should, at a minimum, include:

- details of the organisation's history, its products and services
- a site map/description, describing the location of different facilities
- an organisational orientation, showing how the employee(s) fit into team and wider organisational structures
- job requirements
- terms and conditions
- health and safety information – required by law under the Health and Safety at Work Act 1974.

Reid *et al.* (2004: 225–227) add two further items, suggesting that the portfolio should also include:

1 company rules and policies (e.g. disciplinary and grievance procedures, equal opportunities policies)

2 employee development opportunities, sports and social amenities, and other employee benefits.

How this information is conveyed will also vary. For small- and medium-sized organisations, induction might involve a combination of one-to-one discussions with senior and line managers, an information pack, staff handbook, job shadowing and perhaps the allocation of a mentor or 'buddy' over the first few weeks. In larger organisations there is a greater likelihood of a formal induction programme, over days or weeks, combining an induction event with classroom-based training, presentations from senior managers and existing staff, support literature (e.g. information pack, staff manuals and handbooks), job shadowing, mentoring and e-learning facilities such as the organisational intranet (see the 'Team task' on Arup at the end of this chapter).

The main advantages of formal induction programmes (Income Data Services, 2005b) are that they:

- enable a spread of information inputs over a longer period, allowing a more gradual assimilation by the new recruits
- enable economies of scale in terms of time and costs in dealing with group rather than individual inductions
- ensure a consistency of information and enable a common positive message to be conveyed in a variety of media
- facilitate the development of work relationships through team-building events and more informal socialising (CIPD, 2005e).

Among their potential drawbacks are that:

- good inductions are difficult and time-consuming to achieve (Taylor, 2005; 261)
- they can be impersonal and remote if they rely heavily on HR and senior managers rather than colleagues and line managers (Industrial Relations Services, 2003)
- there is a continual danger of information overload if the induction programme is too intensive

- they can raise expectations beyond that which the organisation and/or the specific job can deliver, leading to low morale or disillusionment

- recruits may well vary in what they need from induction programmes, so putting everyone through a standardised programme could well be counterproductive (Taylor, 2005: 262).

Whether it's a matter of inappropriate programmes or simply negligence, the damage that poor induction can do means that organisations should regularly:

- review what they think new starters need

- attempt to tailor induction programmes where possible and appropriate

- deliver them in the right way and according to the right time scale.

Summary

- This chapter has focused on a core element of HRM: the use of effective selection instruments. Given the manifold costs of an inappropriate appointment, it is clearly important that HR advisers are aware of the relative merits and drawbacks of the selection tools available to them.

- To this end the chapter has outlined the main components of the traditional selection process and reviewed contemporary selection instruments such as bioprofiling, psychological testing and assessment centres.

- As should be clear from the discussion, none of these is problem free.

- Some, however, are seen to possess greater predictive validity than others, or to be more appropriate for certain types of job or levels of employment.

- They also vary in the costs, training and time involved.

- Employers are therefore faced with a series of decisions as to what best meets their operational exigencies and sustains their competitive edge within a complex legislative framework.

Personal development

1 **Understand the selection process.** Define the term 'selection' in your own words and summarise why it is a core HRM task. How would you explain the concept of 'predictive validity' to a colleague? Can you identify the different methods of selection? Reflect on the ways in which an organisation can ensure that it operates a fair selection process.

2 **Develop an understanding of how interviews are conducted.** What are the main constituents of (a) traditional and (b) contemporary methods of selection? How would you account for the emergence of the latter?

3 **Identify when psychological tests can be used.** What are the main types of question used in structured interviews? Using the typology provided on pp. 145–146, draw up an interview schedule for a sales representative for a pharmaceutical company. To further your understanding of these types of questions, look at several graduate traineeship application forms (either online or via your institution's Careers Service). How would you classify the questions used? How would you draw on your own experience to answer them?

4 **Identify the limitations of psychological testing.** What are the main types of psychological test used by selectors? Review the differing perspectives on the testing of psychological dispositions. Why do you think such tests are so controversial? Summarise in your own words what is meant by maximal and typical response tests, giving examples of each and the types of employment for which they might be used as selection tools.

5 **Identify how selection tools are used in organisations.** Revisit your responses to question 1 of the 'Personal development' section at the end of Chapter 1. Think again of an organisation with which you are familiar, either through your own employment or that of a friend or a member of your family. What selection tools does it utilise? Were you (or they) aware of the selection criteria for the post? Was an application form required? How was it structured? Did you/they also submit a CV? Were you/they interviewed? Who conducted the interview and what types of question were asked? Were references required? When and in what form? Looking back at the experience, how would you/they evaluate it? In the light of your reading of this chapter what could have been done to improve the process?

6 **Identify an organisation's selection strategy.** Thinking about a workplace with which you are familiar, consider whether it uses contemporary methods of selection. If so, which ones and for what type of job? How would you explain its selection strategy?

7 **Understand how interviewees can improve their performance.** Have you, or someone you know, ever been unsuccessful in your application for a job? Were you given feedback as to why you were unsuccessful and how you might have improved your chances? Consider why organisations are often advised to provide feedback, particularly if they use assessment centres as a method of selection.

8 **Identify effective induction techniques.** Have you ever attended an induction programme, either as an employee or a student? How effective did you find the arrangements? Think about your ideal job. If you were about to start it, what information and support would help you to settle in?

Discussion questions

1 What are the most important aspects to consider when designing an application form? What questions would you place on an application form for a graduate traineeship?

2 What are the advantages and disadvantages of asking applicants to complete an application form rather than submit a CV?

3 What are the main drawbacks of face-to-face interviews? Why, despite these drawbacks, have they retained their popularity as a selection tool? How might organisations seek to maximise their effectiveness?

4 What are the main ways in which references might be sought? Which would you recommend and why?

5 In what circumstances would you recommend the use of bioprofiling in the selection process?

6 What are the main types of ability test? What types of job could these tests be used for? What are their main merits and drawbacks as selection tools?

7 Why would a selector want to know about an applicant's personality? What problems do personality tests present? How can these be minimised?

8 What selection criteria and methods would you recommend to an NHS Hospital Trust wishing to recruit an HR adviser? Why?

9 Draw up a business case for induction, and design an induction checklist for (a) management-level staff and (b) sales assistants in a supermarket chain. How would you organise an induction for each group?

10 What are the main areas of law affecting selection and appointment? How does an organisation ensure that its selection and appointment processes are within the law?

🔒 Key concepts

selection, *p. 139*	biographical profiling, *p. 151*
traditional selection, *p. 140*	psychological testing, *p. 153*
predictive validity, *p. 140*	ability, *p. 155*
biographical questioning, *p. 145*	psychological disposition, *p. 157*
situational questioning, *p. 145*	assessment centre, *p. 160*
behavioural questioning, *p. 145*	contract of employment, *p. 164*
stress questioning, *p. 146*	employment particulars, *p. 164*
contemporary selection, *p. 151*	induction, *p. 165*

Individual task

Purpose To understand the role and constituents of an assessment centre, and the issues confronted in designing and using it in the selection process.

Time 60 minutes

Procedure Construct an assessment centre for UK firefighters, summarising and justifying the selection instruments you would employ.

Team task

Graduate Induction at Arup

Arup, the consulting engineering group, recruits some 200 graduates each year, half of whom are destined for its different European operations. For their induction, this European-based cohort are expected to undertake:

- a three-day general event, supported by
- a skills week
- a local induction, and
- online induction material.

The three-day event is devoted to two goals: developing an understanding of the company, its history, global operations and values; and team-building activities designed to facilitate work networks that will help the graduates through both their first few months and subsequent Arup careers. The introduction to the company has involved the chairman of Arup Group welcoming the new recruits to the event and describing the global nature of the company and its values. The team-building activities have centred on problem-solving. The cohort is divided into different groups, each with a mix of engineering disciplines. Each group is set a construction task (e.g. building a bridge from planks and barrels or making a hot-air balloon to a client's brief). The supportive environment in which these tasks are undertaken is expected to enable the formation of social networks that are going to be of benefit to both the individuals and the company.

Following the three-day event, the graduates attend one of six skills weeks. This predominantly classroom based element of the induction looks to provide the graduates with the means of translating their academic engineering base into a practical project-based contribution through the acquisition of the software, tools and processes employed in Arup: 'Typically, the week is built around a specific project seen through from beginning to end to put their learning into context' (Income Data Services, 2005b: 26).

After their skills week, the new recruits are allocated to posts in Arup's European offices. The local HR managers are responsible for ensuring that the core workplace induction activities (e.g. health and safety) are covered. Once they have settled in their new locations, the recruits are then encouraged to take some responsibility for the furtherance of their education and training at their own pace. The company provides a 'Welcome to Arup' website that has an array of information sources on company values, and information on pay and benefits. The website also provides access to e-learning modules and in-house courses.

Source: Adapted from Income Data Services (2005b: 26).

Discussion questions

1 If you were responsible for designing an induction scheme for graduate recruits at a multi-national legal services firm, what lessons could you draw from this case study?

2 What would you do differently?

3 How would you convince senior managers of the importance of having an induction scheme?

4 How would you evaluate it?

Case study: **Blast for bosses who don't have a clue how to hire right**

Small business employers have a big problem: they can't find the workers that they want and, to make matters worse, two out of three bosses don't even know how to hire properly.

Research indicates businesses that recruit smarter tend to be better growers. A report from accounting body CPA Australia and the Monash University's Family and Small Business Research Unit (FSBRU), found the human resource management (HRM) practices used by small businesses, and in particular their hiring methods, were unprofessional.

'Very few small businesses take a systematic approach to recruiting, training or developing staff,' CPA Australia's business policy adviser Judy Hartcher says.

'They are also less likely to align their HRM practices with their overall business strategy. Unless they formalise their HRM practices and include them as part of their business plan, they are less likely to reap the benefits of growth.' The damning report on the competency of bosses found 65 per cent of small businesses have little structure or formality in employment practices. While there has been progress on business plans, with more than 54.3 per cent using formal plans, only one in five had a staffing plan with a budget.

The 400 businesses examined in the research showed small business employers recruit using unimaginative, informal and ad hoc methods such as word of mouth or newspaper advertisements. Rowena Barrett, the director of the FSBRU, believes these methods are easy to use and convenient but not always effective in reaching a larger pool of suitable recruits and finding the right employee.

▶

Other mistakes included interviewing candidates without using a written list of skills and qualifications in the selection process. This not only leads to poor selection but leaves bosses exposed to accusations of indirect discrimination if the best person for the job is not selected.

The Recruitment and Consulting Services Association's (RCSA) Business Confidence and Labour Market Report found that recruitment business confidence in 2005 slipped to its lowest levels since the September 2001 terrorist attacks. The report looked at December 2004 to December 2005 and found a key factor contributing to the drop in business confidence was a lack of appropriate candidates in a tight labour market. 'The softening of recruitment business confidence may be due to a shortfall in the quality and quantity of applicants in the jobs market,' said Julie Mills, CEO of the RCSA.

'In 2005, the economy had adequate demand for employees; however, the available pool of candidates, particularly skilled ones, did not meet demand.'

Employer group Australian Business Limited says 60 per cent of its members believe the skill shortage is affecting their business viability now and in the near future.

Matthew Nolan, managing director of Provident Inventory Finance, which provides working capital to small business, recently outlined the main sources of growth. In addition to the predicable planning, financial stability and marketing strategies that have to be pursued to ensure growth, Nolan highlighted sophisticated HRM practices. 'Human resource planning including management, staffing and training are essential to growing a business,' he said.

Hartcher agrees that unprofessional bosses with poorly planned staff-handling practices undermine business growth.

'They could benefit by improving their HR practices to maximise the investment in their most important asset – their staff,' she said. 'Good policies and procedures will help increase productivity and grow the business.'

US academic Jim Collins, in his best-seller *Good to Great*, analysed many US corporate giants to see what was critical in their success of turning their good business into a great business.

One of the standout reasons for businesses of the calibre of Kimberly-Clark and Wells Fargo, which outperformed the stock market's rise by substantial factors between 1985 and 2000, was their employment policies. Working with a team of graduates for something like 15,000 hours, they found it was not hiring the right people for the job so much as hiring the right people. And, unbelievably, these companies saw the people as being even more important than the vision and strategy. 'We found, instead, that they first got the right people on the bus, the wrong people off the bus, and the right people in the right seats,' Collins said. 'And then they figured out where to drive it.'

This is a massive finding and will surprise the 65 per cent of employers who are approaching hiring in an unprofessional way. The reliance on ads – newspaper or Internet – and the unwillingness to use recruiters can often be driven by a cheapskate mentality, and can be a false economy. Consider another of the major findings from the CPA's research: one of the key employment concerns for small business was finding the right staff – 69.4 per cent of businesses owned up to this one.

Source: Adapted from P. Switzer, 'Blast for bosses who don't have a clue how to hire right', *The Australian (Finance)*, 7 February (2002), p. 22.

Discussion questions

1 Why is it so important to have appropriate selection policies?

2 If managers recognise that selection is one of the most important concerns for a business why do so many of them get it wrong?

3 How can managers improve the selection procedure?

4 How can managers find the workers they want?

WWW exercise

Choose several organisations for which you might be interested in working. Go to the recruitment section of their websites or to your institution's Careers Service and find out what selection tools they use and what advice, if any, they provide for applicants. Look at the application form. What types of question are being asked? How do they differ from post to post? What does this tell you about the design of application forms? Try to find out what other types of selection tool they use. Can you gauge why? What advice might be helpful to applicants to enable them to decide whether and how to proceed?

Specific web exercise

Visit the CIPD website (www.cipd.co.uk). What advice does it provide on choosing and using psychological tests? Why?

Visit the CRE, EOC and DRC websites (www.cre.gov.uk, www.eoc.gov.uk, www.drc.gb). Look at the 2005 *Code of Practice on Racial Equality in Employment*. What advice does it provide on selection? What advice do the EOC and DRC provide? What is the legal status of a code of practice?

You could also consider the value of different types of selection test by visiting your institution's Careers Service or testing yourself online and looking at the advice proffered on the following:

- www.monsterjob.com (constructing CVs)
- www.shldirect.com.uk (psychological/psychological disposition tests)
- www.ase-solutions.uk (psychological/psychological disposition tests)
- www.graduaterecruitment.co.uk (general information on graduate entry selection processes)
- www.prospects.ac.uk (general information on graduate entry selection processes).

You could also visit the British Psychological Society's Testing Centre website at www.bps.org.uk, and www.psychtesting.org.uk/default.asp.

LEARNING CHECKLIST

Before moving on to the next chapter, check that you are able to:

- ☑ distinguish between traditional and contemporary selection methods
- ☑ list their main components, and evaluate their relative strengths and weaknesses
- ☑ explain why employers tend to deploy a combination of selection methods
- ☑ outline the business case for and key features of effective induction
- ☑ summarise the role of the law in the selection process.

Further reading

Cook, M. (2004) *Personnel Selection: Adding Value through People* (4th edn). Chichester: Wiley.

Cooper, D. and Robertson, I. (2002) *The Psychology of Personnel Selection*. London: Thomson.

Industrial Relations Services (2003) 'Induction to perfection', *Employment Review* 772.

Sisson, K. and Storey, J. (2003) *The Realities of Human Resource Management*. Maidenhead: Open University Press.

References

Acas (2005) *Induction Training. Getting it Right*. London: Acas, www.acas.org.uk.

Anderson, N. and Shackleton, V. (1993) *Successful Selection Interviewing*. Oxford: Blackwell.

Arthur, W., Woehr, D. and Grazione, W. (2001) 'Personality testing in employment settings: problems and issues of typical selection practices', *Personnel Review* 30, pp. 657–676.

Barrick, M., Mount, M. and Judge, A. (2001) 'Personality and performance at the beginning of the new millennium: what do we know and where do we go next?' *International Journal of Selection and Assessment* 9, pp. 9–30.

Blinkhorn, S. and Johnson, C. (1990) 'The insignificance of personality testing', *Nature* 348, pp. 671–672.

Bratton, J. and Gold, J. (2003) *Human Resource Management: Theory and Practice* (3rd edn). Basingstoke: Palgrave Macmillan.

CIPD (2005a) *Recruitment, Retention and Turnover*. London: CIPD.

CIPD (2005b) 'Recruitment and Selection', factsheet, www.cipd.co.uk.

CIPD (2005c) 'References', factsheet, www.cipd.co.uk.

CIPD (2005d) 'Psychological testing', factsheet, www.cipd.co.uk.

CIPD (2005e) 'Induction', factsheet, www.cipd.co.uk.

CIPD (2005f) 'Telephone interviewing', factsheet, www.cipd.co.uk.

Commission for Racial Equality (CRE) (2005) *Statutory Code of Practice on Racial Equality in Employment*. London: CRE.

Cook, M. (1993) *Personnel Selection and Productivity*. Chichester: John Wiley.

Cooper, D., Robertson, I. and Tinline, G. (2003) *Recruitment and Selection: A Framework for Success*. London: Thomson.

Digman, J.M. (1990) 'Personality structure: emergence of the five-factor model', *Annual Review of Psychology* 41, pp. 417–440.

Income Data Services (2004) *Psychometric Tests, HR Study Plus* 770, March. London: IDS.

Income Data Services (2005a) *Assessment Centres, HR Study* 800, June. London: IDS.

Income Data Services (2005b) 'Helping new recruits to find their feet', *IDS HR Studies* 807, October 2005, pp. 23–36.

Industrial Relations Services (2002) 'Psychometrics: the next generation', *IRS Employment Review*, 28 January, pp. 36–40.

Industrial Relations Services (2003) 'The best conditions for the start of a beautiful friendship', *Employment Review* 771.

Kandola. B., Stairs, M. and Sandford-Smith, R. (2000) 'Slim picking', *People Management*, 28 December, p. 28.

Lewis, D. and Sargeant, M. (2004) *Essentials of Employment Law* (8th edn). London: CIPD.

Marchington, M. and Wilkinson, A. (2005) *Human Resource Management at Work: People Management and Development* (3rd edn). London: CIPD.

Martin, M. and Jackson, T. (2002) *Personnel Practice* (3rd edn). London: CIPD.

Newell, S. (2005) 'Recruitment and selection', in S. Bach (ed.) *Managing Human Resources*. Oxford: Blackwell.

Newell, S. and Shackleton, V. (2001) 'Selection and assessment as an interactive decision-action process', in T. Redman and A. Wilkinson (eds) *Contemporary Human Resource Management*. London: Financial Times/Prentice Hall.

People Management (2003) 'You can do it . . .', *People Management,* 20 February, pp. 42–43.

People Management (2005a) 'Psychometric testing for parking wardens', *People Management*, 7 April.

People Management (2005b) 'FTSE-100 firms turn to psychometrics', *People Management*, 11 August, p. 12.

Pioro, I. and Baum, N. (2005) 'Design better job application forms', *People Management*, 16 June, pp. 42–43.

Reid, M., Barrington, H. and Brown, M. (2004) *Human Resource Development: Beyond Training Interventions*. London: CIPD.

Roberts, G. (2003) *Recruitment and Selection: A Competency Approach* (3rd edn). London: CIPD.

Robertson, I.T. and Smith, J.M. (2001) 'Personnel selection', *Journal of Occupational and Organisational Psychology* 74, pp. 441–472.

Searle, R. (2003) *Selection and Recruitment: A Critical Text*. Milton Keynes: Open University Press.

Smethurst, S. (2004) 'The allure of online', *People Management* 10(15), 29 July, pp. 38–40.

Smith, M. and Smith, P. (2005) *Testing People at Work*. Oxford: BPS Blackwell.

Suff, R. (2005) 'Centres of attention', *IRS Employment Review* 816, pp. 42–48.

Taylor, S. (2002) *People Resourcing*. London: CIPD.

Taylor, S. (2005) *People Resourcing*. London: CIPD.

Toplis, J., Dulewicz, V. and Fletcher, C. (1994) *Psychological Testing: A Manager's Guide*. London: Institute of Personnel Management.

Torrington, D., Hall, L. and Taylor, S. (eds) (2005) *Human Resource Management* (5th edn). Harlow: FT/Prentice Hall.

Chapter **6**

Remuneration and reward

LEARNING OUTCOMES

After studying this chapter, you should be able to:

- ☑ **understand** the role of pay and reward, and its link to performance
- ☑ **evaluate** the different aspects of the reward package
- ☑ **understand** legal issues affecting pay and reward
- ☑ **discuss** the importance of ethics in remuneration and reward.

The opening vignette reflects one of the debates around pay and reward today. Although the government sets the national minimum wage, many people realise that it is not always a living wage and, to attract the best employees, they need to take action.

The rise of the living wage

HSBC has become the second big bank to agree to pay cleaning staff a 'living wage'. Could this signal the start of a trend and the end of the national minimum wage?

Last month HSBC followed Barclays to become the second big east London employer to agree to pay cleaning staff a 'living wage'. The living wage is being campaigned for by community action group The East London Communities Organisation (Telco), and trades unions including Unison. Telco commissioned research to find out the level required to enable a family of two parents and two children, with one parent working full-time and one part-time, to live above the poverty line without state benefits. The initial level was set at £6.30, and is now £6.70 an hour.

The concept seems to be gathering pace. The latest move has seen Ken Livingstone, Mayor of London, agreeing to set up a living wage unit at the Greater London Authority (GLA) and set a £7.70 per hour living wage level for those employed in the GLA's workforce.

These moves have potentially far-reaching consequences for employers with outsourcing contracts. The packages set a new standard for cleaning contractors. And by providing better basic pay, plus other benefits such as pensions, holiday and sick pay, these organisations have made it clear that they see good employment conditions for contractors as their responsibility.

This was not HSBC's stance earlier this year. In January 2004, Adrian Russell, public relations officer at the bank, said: 'We are sympathetic towards Telco's ultimate objective, which is better lives for the people they represent, but we cannot support the way they are trying to achieve it. We support the minimum wage, which is £4.50, but believe it is for the government, not HSBC, to set that level.'

Indeed, when cleaner Abdul Durrant appealed to HSBC's chairman, Sir John Bond, to renegotiate the contract with cleaning contractor OCS, Bond replied: 'We are sympathetic but we are running a business and to do that we have to get the best deal for our shareholders. What OCS pays staff is its own matter.'

But the organisation's most recent announcement shows how far its standpoint has moved. 'Corporate social responsibility (CSR) runs through much of what we do as an organisation. Certainly, we wish to be viewed as a good neighbour and a responsible employer and purchaser of contracts,' said an HSBC spokesperson in June 2004. 'We are happy to support the living wage and what OCS is willing to do for their cleaning staff. They deserve credit for listening to their staff and being prepared to make changes.'

Barclays told *PM* that the bank recognised the business benefits of paying a living wage. 'It is a CSR issue in that we want to be fair across the board, but it's also an HR issue because we want to attract the right people as well. It's about getting the right people to work for us,' said spokesman George Hulbert.

Paul Sellers, policy adviser at the TUC, believes the establishment of the living wage by the Mayor's office moves the campaign to a new level. 'It should enable the concept to spread to other parts of the country,' he said.

Barclays is already extending the deal across its London branches, with plans to go UK-wide before long, but Sellers believes that, while the initiative is so new, the private sector may be worried about how the deal will go down with shareholders looking for the biggest return on their investment – usually reflected in employing the cheapest labour.

'Once the benefits can be seen and the case can be defended against any shareholder criticism, companies will be keen to advertise the living wage as a real part of their CSR armoury,' said Sellers.

And he believes that this will come very soon. The business case for the living wage is that it brings a better standard of employee who will be more satisfied with his or her work. This leads to lower staff turnover and less absenteeism. Productivity levels rise and the higher morale means a greater commitment to the company.

So does this mean, as some campaigners have argued, that a national minimum wage is redundant?

Telco believes that the latest developments, particularly Livingstone's active involvement, will lead to the minimum wage becoming redundant in London at least.

'The Mayor's action should ensure that the minimum wage becomes irrelevant, with all good employers in London following his civic example. It will be up to the Mayor to then use his procurement powers to police the living wage,' said Neil Jameson, a co-ordinator with Telco.

▶   He believes that the living wage is now seen as a real social responsibility issue. 'People are looking at what low pay does to British people in comparison to the effects of, say, bad labour practices on children making trainers in Thailand,' said Jameson.

Telco is keen for the issue to move up the CSR agenda. The next stage would see firms agree to sign up to a CSR contract of employment. Some companies, such as Richer Sounds, an independent UK hi-fi retailer, have already shown interest. Telco also says that Stephen Timms, the minister responsible for CSR, has met with them and given his support to the project.

As a result the group plans to draw up, with the involvement of these stakeholders, a three-tier benchmark of low, middle and good performance in employment conditions of support services contracts. This would include wages, at least some employer contribution to pensions, sick pay, bank holidays and training.

This, combined with the examples of HSBC and Barclays, suggests that a living wage is now seen as a CSR policy that other firms, particularly in the financial services sector in London, will consider adopting in the not too distant future.

Source: Paul Donovan, *People Management*, 15 July 2004, p. 14.
Reproduced with permission of *People Management* and Paul Donovan.

Discussion questions

1 Who do you think should take responsibility for ensuring that employees are paid a living wage?

2 As an HR manager, how could you persuade senior managers about the benefits of a living wage as opposed to paying the minimum wage?

Definitions of remuneration and reward

Remuneration and reward are an important part of the HR function and can link directly to the organisation's strategic goals. Many organisations view compensation as one of the strategies that drives their business. The remuneration and reward package offered can not only help to attract and retain employees, it can also be used as a powerful tool to motivate staff, which in turn can increase competitiveness, profitability and competitive advantage. **Reward** can be either monetary or non-monetary, and is something that is given or received in exchange for services. In the case of employees, this means being rewarded for work performed. **Remuneration** refers to the monetary aspect of rewarding an employee for their performance. Monetary rewards are clearly important, as few people can afford to work for no pay; however, it is also important that any remuneration is fair and equitable. Yet money does not necessarily make people work harder. In other words, it is not necessarily a motivator.

reward
Compensation given to an employee in return for performance. It can be monetary, in the form of remuneration, or non-monetary.

remuneration
The monetary aspect of rewarding an employee for performance.

It is often the non-monetary awards that employees value more, such as career and social awards. Opportunities for job security, career growth, praise and recognition may be far more important to an employee than a high income in a boring, repetitive or undervalued job.

Therefore, it is important for employees to be aware of the total reward system that can be offered to an employee, as can be seen in Exhibit 6-1.

Monetary compensation is important, however, as it ensures that:

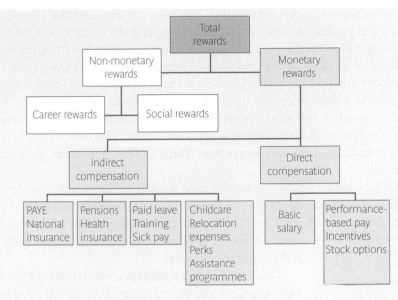

Exhibit 6 – 1 The total reward system

- the pay is sufficient to attract the right people to the organisation
- the pay is perceived as equitable so that good employees can be retained
- the rewards ensure that the organisation can maintain its competitive advantage
- the rewards are available to increase productivity and profitability
- legal obligations are met, such as equal pay for equal work
- the organisational pay structure is clearly defined and transparent to avoid criticism that could lead to legal action.

The appropriate monetary compensation can ensure harmony in several aspects of the organisation and can also have wider implications. Through the external environment it ensures that employees can be attracted to the organisation and good relationships with employee unions can be maintained while ensuring that pay is competitive. In the internal environment, pay can be linked to increased performance through performance-related pay, which can link into the business strategy. The human resource functions of job analysis, recruitment and selection, and performance management can all be linked to the type of monetary rewards on offer.

Payment structure

How much to pay staff is an important consideration for managers. In most organisations pay, benefits and staffing costs often total 23 per cent of income and, in some organisations, this can be as much as 50 per cent. This is especially true in organisations requiring a high level of personal service, such as the hotel industry.

For employees, the wages they are paid affects their standard of living and also their status in the eyes of their community, therefore it is important for pay decisions to be managed carefully. Employees also evaluate their pay decisions against awards made to other employees in an organisation.

When deciding pay levels the organisation also needs to consider the competition in the marketplace for the product or services it is providing and the competition for the labour it requires. The competition for the product means that organisations have to compete on several dimensions, such as quality, service and price. Therefore, production costs are likely to be important. If an organisation has higher labour costs than its competitors then it will more than likely have to charge higher prices for its product, which means it could be less competitive. Competition for labour is also an important factor, as organisations have to compete against each other for the best employees. Organisations that fail to offer competitive salaries will be unable to attract and retain the best employees, which in turn may affect the quality of their product or service.

When deciding what to pay, organisations need to analyse the competition for labour and decide whether it is in their interests to pay above the market average in an attempt to attract the top talent, at the risk of adding to their costs. Information about pay per sector can be obtained from the Equal Opportunities Commission and on the website statistics.gov.uk.

pay structures

The criteria used to establish the worth of a job and how much should be paid.

One method of establishing **pay structures** is through job evaluation, which, according to Acas (2003), is the process of 'determining the relative worth of a job to the organisation'.

The CIPD (2004a) suggests that job evaluation is used when:

- determining pay and grading structures
- ensuring a fair and equal pay system
- deciding on benefits provision (e.g. bonuses and cars)
- comparing rates against the external market
- undergoing organisational development in times of change
- undertaking career management and succession planning
- reviewing all jobs post-large-scale change, especially if roles have been changed.

Job evaluation needs to be based on detailed job descriptions, as discussed in Chapter 4.

job evaluation

The process of measuring the size and significance of a job in an organisation.

points rating

A system of breaking a job into key elements, factors and components, and awarding points based on the complexity of tasks.

factor comparison

A system of basing a job on an assessment of factors involved.

Job evaluation is important in ensuring that a fair payment system is in place, which is transparent and can be communicated to all employees. When there are no pay structures in place, employees may see themselves as being treated unfairly if they are paid less than their colleagues. This will be discussed in more detail later in this chapter.

Two methods of job evaluation are **points rating** and **factor comparison**. Points rating is the most commonly used method and breaks the key elements of the job into factors, which are in turn broken down into components. Each factor is allocated points according to the level needed for the job. The more demanding the job, the higher the number of points it is allocated, and therefore the higher the pay. Examples of factors that are measured frequently can be seen in Exhibit 6-2.

The factor comparison, on the other hand, is based on an assessment of factors without the allocation of points. The use of factor analysis is not as widespread as that of points rating, as most jobs have to be done on an individual basis, while the allocation of points allows a large number of jobs to be ranked at one time.

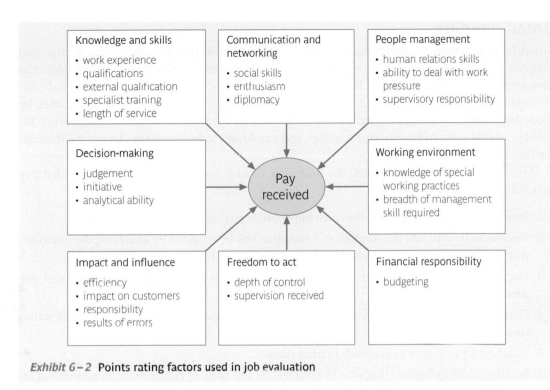

Exhibit 6-2 Points rating factors used in job evaluation

Other methods of job evaluation, which are seen as less objective but cheaper to implement, are job ranking, paired comparisons and job classification.

job ranking
Placing jobs in order of importance in a hierarchy. Pay is then matched to task difficulty.

- **Job ranking** involves ranking jobs in order of their importance to the organisation. This would include level of difficulty and their value to the organisation. Sometimes these are clearly defined, such as in a hairdressing salon – the stylist who cuts hair would be paid more than the person who does only washing and drying, however the latter may be paid more than the person who is on reception. Judgements are made about the skill level, task complexity and level of autonomy used to do the job. The jobs are then ranked in a hierarchy, which is made transparent to all employees.

paired comparison
Uses a ranking form to allocate points to jobs, which are then compared to other jobs.

- **Paired comparisons** uses a ranking form to allocate points to a job to compare each job with others in an organisation. It is more transparent than job ranking but takes longer. When comparing jobs with each other, two points will be allocated if a job is considered of higher value, one if of the same value and none if of lower value. The points are then added up and an overall ranking given.

job classification
Also known as job grading, based on the requirements of the job and levels of responsibility.

- **Job classification** (also known as job grading) involves allocating jobs to an agreed number of grades (usually between four and eight) based on the requirements of the job and levels of responsibility.

Broad banding

Broad banding refers to classifying jobs into a broad banded pay structure, with a large gap between the bottom and top rates of pay. Pay progression through each band is often related to performance or market pay rates. Broad banding is used when organisations decide to redesign or modernise pay structures, and want to address recruitment and retention difficulties by grouping jobs into a job family or moving employees to a team-based approach to work. This enables related tasks to be grouped together and employees to be encouraged to move through the band by acquiring new skills.

Armstrong (2000) suggests using the following 12 steps for developing a broad banded pay structure.

1   Reach an agreement that it is the most appropriate pay structure for progression.

2   Provisionally estimate the number of bands that will be required by analysing the organisation's structure and the various roles carried out at each level.

3   Decide on the width of bands, the degree of overlap (if any), the anchor points and pay zones.

4   Carry out a job evaluation exercise to define band boundaries, and revise the band structure as appropriate.

5   Conduct a pay survey to establish market rates.

6   Position roles in bands (singly or in clusters) on the basis of relative size as established by job evaluation results and market.

7   Decide on the basis for progressing pay within zones and for adjusting pay levels following a change in role.

8   Decide on the role of job evaluation in defining band boundaries, guiding band positioning decisions and dealing with new roles or equal value queries.

9   Examine existing rates of pay for employees, identify any increases and establish any cases where pay protection may be necessary.

10   Draw up procedures for managing the structure, including the allocation of roles to bands. Include the use of job evaluation, the conduct of pay reviews, fixing salaries for recruitment purposes or following a change in role, maintaining data on market rates and the use of performance management processes to assist in making pay review decisions.

11   Brief and train managers on the new structure and their roles in managing pay.

12   Communicate to staff the details of the new structure and how it affects them.

The advantages of broad banding are that it is more suited to flatter and leaner organisations, giving more scope for career development and more flexibility for organisations. It can simplify pay systems by grouping more jobs within the same band, which can reduce problems of inequity. It is ideal for linking with performance, which means it can in turn be linked to strategic goals.

However, there are also disadvantages with such a system, in that it needs to be carefully monitored to ensure awards are not made on the subjectivity of managers, and to guard against discrimination. Rates of pay also need to be monitored continually to ensure that they are in keeping with market rates, especially if broad banding is in response to recruitment and selection problems. There is also a resource issue, as time is needed to train managers in its implementation to ensure that it is not seen as producing inequity.

Job families

Job families group jobs with similar characteristics into categories. The job families reflect different levels of responsibility and have an individual pay structure.

Jobs within families can be linked by:

- occupation
- nature of work
- function.

The CIPD (2000) identified four key reasons as to why organisations use job families. These are:

1 to map career paths
2 to achieve greater flexibility
3 to identify groups of employees that can be linked to the market
4 to provide rewards based on personal contribution and progress.

The distinction between job families and traditional grading schemes is that each job family has completely separate pay arrangements and is allowed to set its own pay and grading bands. This means that separate families are able to compete with market expectations. For example, the accountancy department of an organisation would have a different pay structure from that of the purchasing department and this would reflect the market expectations of employees in that department. Job families can, therefore, be linked to broad banding and the market: employers have the scope to place jobs in families that reflect market conditions and provide a broad banded pay structure that allows the employee to progress either through further training or improved performance.

Market competition

Organisations need to be able to sell their goods or services at a competitive price in the market-place. Therefore, the cost of labour will be an important factor in developing pay levels. Organisations with higher labour costs than their competitors will have to charge higher prices for their products. For example, a company selling family cars with a labour cost of 30 per cent will either need to sell more cars than a company with labour costs of 25 per cent, or will have to be prepared to make less profit. The loss of profit may be unacceptable to shareholders, which could mean that the organisation's value decreases. Therefore, it is important for managers to ensure that they get it right. At the other end of the scale managers also need to ensure that they do not pay too little, otherwise they may be unable to attract staff.

Deciding what to pay

Since employees are a resource it is important for managers to ensure that they are able to get a return on their investment. Pay policies are one of the most important resource tools available to HR managers to enable them to encourage desirable behaviours and discourage undesired ones. Therefore, it is important that managers evaluate their reward system not just in terms of cost but also in terms of return on investment: in other words, how they attract, retain and motivate a high-quality workforce.

Although organisations need to take into account external competition they still have some discretion in setting their pay levels. Deciding whether to pay higher or lower than average, or average wages needs to be decided at strategic level. Paying above the market average has the benefits of being able to attract and retain top talent, which should lead to an effective and productive workforce despite the extra cost. To determine how beneficial paying higher wages could be when compared to the higher costs, researchers Lambert and Larcker (1989) developed the efficiency wage theory, which compares wages paid and productivity. They found that, where organisations need highly skilled employees or where employees are responsible for managing themselves, organisations may wish to pay an above-average wage as an incentive to maintain or improve performance. The theory suggests that employees who are paid more will want to retain their salary and will therefore work harder, although it should be remembered that pay is not the only motivator and the quality of the working environment is often more important than an increased pay packet.

efficiency wage theory
The comparison of wages to productivity.

Market surveys

benchmarking
Comparing aspects of performance with the same aspects in other organisations.

Pay surveys are a useful tool to enable organisations to benchmark their practices against those of the competition. Benchmarking is typically carried out through the use of pay surveys, which provide important insights into the average rates of pay for different sectors. When using surveys it is important to identify:

- which employers should be used as a comparison
- which jobs should be used for the comparison, and are they similar in function, level and market segmentation
- if different surveys are used, how are they applicable to the organisation concerned?

What organisations are paying may be only one side of the story. It is also useful to compare ratios such as turnover to employees and turnover to labour cost, although it should be remembered that different sectors are likely to have different labour ratios and therefore like should be compared with like.

Rate ranges

Many jobs in the public sector, such as nurses, teachers and clerical officers, are attached to a salary scale. The employee starts at a fixed point on the scale, often dependent on qualifications, experience and age. They then progress annually until they reach the top of the scale. Promotion usually enables them to move on to a different scale. The advantages of such schemes are that they are transparent, everyone knows what the scale is and colleagues of equal status will be paid the same. The disadvantage is that there is no incentive to work harder as extra effort is not rewarded with increased pay.

Both nurses and police enter at an initial level and receive incremental pay rises each year until they reach the top of their grade. They can move to different grades through examination and/or training and promotion. It is also interesting to note that, while both nursing and the police are funded by the public sector, there is a great discrepancy between the pay scales of jobs that have in the past been seen as traditional female jobs (nursing) and traditional male jobs (policing). These pay scales also demonstrate the value society places on such jobs. For example, a police constable commencing service in 2005 could expect to receive £19,803 while an auxiliary nurse would expect £10,375.

Some organisations are attempting to bridge the gap with enhanced pay for enhanced performance, usually linked to an appraisal system. There is considerable debate at the moment concerning public-sector pay reform, with government economists arguing for pay to be set at the local level in line with that of private companies. However, this is not always the case, with large national employers such as Barclays and Tesco often using nationally set pay scales but enhancing them in areas where there is a higher cost of living, such as London and the south-east.

Research by Hatchett (2004) suggests that there are several myths about how regional and national pay is set, as can be seen in Exhibit 6-3.

Payment concepts

When determining which payment system to use, an organisation needs to decide whether payment will be linked to the reward system or not. As all aspects of reward will ultimately be a cost to the organisation, the employer needs to decide whether the type of reward offered will lead to improved performance.

Myth 1

There is a significant amount of regional variation in pay outside London and the south-east. In fact, the average earnings data show that differences are minimal

Myth 2

Pay in large private-sector companies is set by myriad individual-level decisions, when in fact there are national structures and systems. Firms frequently often allow variation from the norm, under certain controls, but within defined systems and budgets

Myth 3

There is minimal influence on pay from collective bargaining, with most pay decisions set at management's discretion, based on local cost of living factors. In fact, unions have significant influence in large organisations

Myth 4

Local cost of living factors now outweigh skill levels or competencies. In fact, managers look at skill levels and grading across their organisations rather than just locally. There are complex versions of what might have been termed a 'rate for the job', whether set by job evaluation or job weight, or by sectoral or national benchmarking

Myth 5

Pay in the public sector is set by rigid national agreements, with no scope for flexible interpretation. In reality there is scope for local flexibility to deal with recruitment and retention issues, although these have not always been well funded. Some of the new measures in London, such as pay spines for school teachers, are an example. The recent report of the Local Government Pay Commission found there was adequate flexibility in local determination within a national framework

Exhibit 6–3 Myths about regional and national pay
Source: A. Hatchett, 'What next for local pay?', *People Management*, 12 February 2004, p. 15.

Traditional pay

Traditional pay follows the principles of scientific management developed by Taylor (1914)

traditional pay
Pay linked to task complexity and completion time.

and discussed in more detail in Chapter 1. To Taylor, measuring work meant that the job could be broken down into steps that could be timed and rated for difficulty and expertise. This allowed pay to be linked directly to performance and became the basis of pay systems, especially for low-skilled manual labour. Managers had overall control, and pay would be linked to performance in an attempt to increase productivity. However, there were consequences for the social aspect of work, which was ignored by Taylor and often meant that the workforce became demotivated. This was characterised by Wood (2000), who felt that this type of performance-related pay could alienate the workforce and cause workers to disengage.

New pay

New pay is a term coined by Lawler (2000), and developed by Zingheim and Schuster (1995),

new pay
Pay linked to personal development and task performance, and ultimately organisational goals.

popular in the USA. New pay involves using a combination of traditional pay and non-traditional elements such as skill-based pay and/or recognition for training and performance. This could mean that employees who are keen to develop their skills would be compensated. New pay can also include an element of variable pay, where employees are compensated for achieving organisational goals. It may be paid in the form of a cash bonus or share options.

According to Heery (1996), new pay should also be linked to both organisational performance and individual performance.

Heery (1996) characterises new pay as follows:

- an increased awareness of the need to link pay to organisational strategy
- the use of reward systems to reflect the flexibility of the organisation
- the use of variable pay based on both individual performance and personal development.

The concept of new pay is gaining ground in the USA, with many large companies now offering compensation packages that include elements of basic pay and variable pay, often linked to performance appraisal. Although not as popular in the UK some companies are now exploring its benefits.

Merit pay

Merit pay ties performance to add-on rewards. Often a base salary or hourly wage is provided

merit pay
Increasing pay by adding on rewards based on improved performance.

and then an incentive or bonus offered, based on output. Output could be measured by volume, quality of production or cost savings. Sales representatives and call centre operators often have a basic salary with commission for sales or successful calls. To improve performance the rewards have to be seen to be achievable and desirable, and when tied to performance should be seen as motivational. However, where every employee is out to make their targets, merit pay can detract from teamwork, and there could also be the problem of employees' expectations differing from the employer's. Therefore, merit pay needs to be clear and measurable to avoid problems.

Bonuses and profit sharing

Compensation plans are often based on the overall performance of the organisation rather than an individual's performance. **Profit sharing** is one method of ensuring that employees are rewarded when a company does well. One such organisation, the John Lewis Partnership, rewards business performance by distributing profits back to its employees. For John Lewis, profit sharing is a major part of the employee compensation package. To qualify for the scheme, employees need to have spent at least a year at the organisation; they are then eligible for a percentage of profit. The John Lewis scheme makes the organisation one of the leading employers in the retail sector, and this is often reflected in the quality of customer service found in its stores.

profit sharing
A method of rewarding employees when an organisation does well, through issuing shares or paying bonuses.

In many other organisations it is the director's compensation package that is loaded with **bonuses**, share options and other additions, often totalling several times the base salary, and incurring much criticism from employees and shareholders, although some companies do attempt to distribute rewards throughout the workforce. Both Body Shop and Johnson & Johnson have devised schemes that compensate employees with share options. Research by Crystal (1995) into 15 high-performing and 15 low-performing companies suggested that there was no positive relationship with performance between directors who received substantial shares and those who did not.

bonuses
Additional rewards, usually monetary, paid to employees for improved organisational performance.

When implementing share plans organisations need to be clear about how they are implemented. Fergusson (2003) suggests that they can do this by ensuring that:

- their share plans are operated in accordance with any employee contractual rights
- share plan discretions are exercised fairly and reasonably
- share plan rules have a full exclusion clause to rule out implied contractual rights
- all communications relating to share plans contain appropriate exclusion wording
- employment contracts do not give employees a contractual right to participate in share plans.

Gainsharing plans

Gainsharing encourages employees at all levels of the organisation to be responsible for improving organisational efficiency. Gainsharing plans link financial rewards for all employees to improvements in business performance. It is being seen as an increasingly popular motivational tool to improve performance and is summarised in Exhibit 6-4.

gainsharing
A pay-for-performance system that shares financial rewards among employees, based on performance improvements for the organisation.

The idea is that gainsharing can make employees more cost conscious. One example of its success was found in the post room of a gas company, where an employee noticed that by changing delivery times to 10.30 am the next day instead of 10 am postal costs could be cut by 43 per cent. This resulted in a 2 per cent bonus for all employees.

HR managers also need to be aware of the impact of rewards on motivation, as a motivated workforce is likely to be more productive.

Survey research has revealed seven fundamental reasons why gainsharing continues to grow as a method of rewarding performance.

1 The basic design of jobs is undergoing a fundamental change from individuals into teams
2 Other performance-related pay systems often lead to disappointing results, especially those that reward individuals; this is because it is often difficult to untangle individual performance from the contributions of other employees
3 Gainsharing is easy to sell to top management because payouts are often modest and any gains are shared with the organisation
4 Gainsharing has a long history, which makes it easy to imitate successful plans
5 There are many specialist consultants who can help implement such plans
6 Gainsharing provides flexibility in choosing pay-off criteria from such diverse factors as profitability, labour costs, material savings, safety records, reject rates, meeting deadlines and customer satisfaction
7 Gainsharing complements the move towards participative management and employee involvement, as many plans incorporate committee structures to evaluate and act on employee recommendations

Exhibit 6–4 The popularity of gainsharing plans
Source: Adapted from Welbourne and Gomez-Mejia (1995).

Reward and motivation

Equity theory

The **equity theory** of motivation demonstrates what can happen when employees perceive their treatment to be inequitable. Equity theory puts forward the idea that motivation can be affected by perceived fairness or discrepancies between the contribution and rewards of employees. Adams (1965) popularised the idea that employees would work better if they perceive a fairness among effort, performance and reward relationships. There are two basic dimensions to the equity process: the ratio of personal outcomes to inputs, and external comparisons.

equity theory
The idea that motivation is moderated by perceived fairness or discrepancies between contributions and rewards.

Ratio of personal outcomes to inputs

People often think in terms of the ratio of their personal outcomes to work inputs. In other words, their perceptions of fair treatment depend on how they answer the question 'What is the pay-off to me in terms of money, status, benefits, recognition, promotion and job assignments, relative to my inputs of effort exerted, skills, job knowledge and actual task performance?' Although this applies to all aspects of employee reward, payment is a major factor in assessing equitable treatment.

External comparisons

Employees are also likely to compare their own outcomes and inputs ratio to those they perceive for other people doing comparable work. These comparisons are often made on three levels.

1 Comparisons to specific individuals: if two people are performing at the same level, then they could both expect to receive the same pay and recognition.

2   Comparisons to another reference group: workers in one department may compare themselves to workers in another department. If they are getting the same deal then treatment may be seen as equitable, however if their deal is perceived to be not as good, then it is seen as inequitable and is likely to lead to dissatisfaction.

3   Comparisons to general occupational groups: people may compare themselves to other people in similar positions in other organisations, or with those of a similar educational level. For example, nurses, who are now often university graduates, may compare themselves with accountants and find discrepancies in pay and conditions inequitable.

Equity issues are not just concerned with undercompensation, they can also apply when employees see themselves as being overcompensated compared with their reference group. Attempts are then made to close the equity gap. For example, those who feel they are overcompensated may increase their performance to justify increased compensation levels, while those who perceive themselves to be undercompensated may reduce effort, leave the organisation or find alternative comparisons.

Perceived fairness

Perceived fairness is a powerful motivational tool and involves a focus on both distributive justice, which refers to the amount of compensation an employee receives, and procedural justice, which refers to the perceived fairness of how managers arrive at decisions with regard to pay and reward. Folger and Konovsky (1989) identified that distributive satisfaction has a major influence on job satisfaction and attitudes to pay and promotion decisions, whereas procedural justice reflects more on organisational outcomes such as employee commitment and trust in management. When the distribution of rewards is perceived to be inequitable and the criteria to arrive at that distribution are believed to be unfair then mounting feelings of injustice are likely to arise at work, which can easily lead to resentment. Equity therefore begins with fair procedures, which means that the pay and reward system must be seen as transparent. Even if employees are dissatisfied with levels of pay, as long as the organisation's procedures treat them fairly they are more likely to remain committed to the organisation.

distributive justice
The perceived fairness of the amount and allocation of rewards among individuals.

procedural justice
The perceived fairness of the means used to determine the amount and distribution of rewards.

Expectancy theory

The expectancy theory of motivation focuses on a person's beliefs about the relationships among effort, performance and rewards for doing a job. Vroom (1982) suggests that people will be motivated to achieve a desired goal as long as they expect that their actions will achieve that goal.

Expectancy theory was originally expressed as a probability relationship among three variables labelled expectancy, instrumentality and valence.

expectancy theory
A theory of motivation based on a person's beliefs about effort–performance–outcome relationships.

- Expectancy is the probability from 0 to 1 that an individual believes his or her work effort directly affects the performance outcome of a task.

- Instrumentality is the probability from 0 to 1 that an individual anticipates that an attained level of task performance will have personal consequences.

- Valence is the value from positive to negative that a person assigns to the personal consequences that follow work performance.

Using expectancy theory, an employee will decide whether the expected reward is available and worth it. Wanous *et al.* (1980) argue that this measurement, while useful for psychologists, can not always be implemented by managers.

To help implement his theory Vroom developed the following equation:

$$\textbf{Force (F)} = \textbf{Valence (V)} \times \textbf{Expectancy (E)}$$

For employees to understand their motivations, according to Bloisi *et al.* (2003), they need to ask themselves three questions.

1 **Does how hard I work really affect my performance?** Vroom argues that, to be motivated, you must have a positive answer to this expectancy question. Employees need to believe that their personal efforts make a positive performance difference. The employee must have the capacity for internal attribution, or a willingness to take personal credit or blame for their performance. Positive task motivation begins when employees see the link between personal effort and task performance.

2 **Are personal consequences linked to my performance?** To answer this instrumentality question, you must believe that task performance results enable you to attain pay-offs. Increased motivation is possible when an employee perceives they will receive a positive personal consequence arising from satisfactory task performance.

3 **Do I value the consequences available to me?** Answers to this valence question will depend on how much you value a particular expected outcome or pay-off. If employees really do not care about the potential reward then they will have little incentive to work harder. A person must value the pay-off if the expectancy loop is positive and motivational.

Vroom recognises the importance of individual needs and motivations, and that individuals have personal goals that may differ from those of the organisation. Managers need to understand that, to achieve a motivated workforce, organisational and individual goals need to be harmonised.

Another theory of motivation, developed by Herzberg, recognises that other aspects of work can be motivators, and managers need to be aware of this as part of their strategy for motivating employees.

Herzberg's dual-factor theory

A needs-based model intended to provide direct managerial applications evolved from Frederick Herzberg's research into the sources of job-related satisfaction and dissatisfaction. Herzberg (1966) carried out 203 interviews with accountants and engineers using the critical incident method. They were asked two questions: What made them feel good about their job and what made them feel bad. The interviewees were asked to relate the sequence of events leading up to the feelings. The responses revealed that there were two different factors affecting motivation and work. From the research Herzberg concluded that:

- job satisfaction and job dissatisfaction derive from different sources
- simply removing the sources of dissatisfaction will not cause a person to be motivated to produce better results.

dual-factor theory
Herzberg's motivation content theory, based on two independent needs: hygiene and motivator factors.

Herzberg blended these two premises into a dual-factor explanation of motivation. **Dual-factor theory** refers to two different types of need:

1 hygiene factors, which involve working conditions and can trigger dissatisfaction if inadequate

2 motivator factors, which originate from the nature of the job itself and can create job satisfaction.

Dissatisfiers as hygiene factors

hygiene factors
Job context factors such as working conditions and benefits that cause dissatisfaction if inadequate.

Herzberg drew the term hygiene factors from his public health experience. **Hygiene factors** are those basic factors surrounding the job – job security, working conditions, quality of supervision, interpersonal relationships, and adequacy of pay and fringe benefits – that, if lacking, can cause dissatisfaction. Such factors are largely *extrinsic*, or external to the nature of the job itself, and can therefore be thought of as job context features.

Hygiene factors do not produce job satisfaction. If adequate, they simply produce neutral feelings with the realisation that basic maintenance needs are taken care of. Like a city's water and sanitation systems, these factors do not cause people to be healthy and robust; they simply prevent disease and unhealthy conditions – they provide good hygiene.

Satisfiers as motivator factors

According to Herzberg (1993), only when a person feels the potential for satisfaction is he or she able to muster significant work motivation. **Motivator**

motivator factors
Job content factors such as responsibility and achievement that provide feelings of satisfaction when experienced.

factors such as job challenge, responsibility, opportunity for achievement or advancement, and recognition, provide feelings of satisfaction. These are associated with job content and are *intrinsic*, or unique to each individual in his or her own way.

Herzberg's dual-factor theory suggests that if motivators are not present in a job, a person will not necessarily be dissatisfied. However, that person will simply not be in a position to experience satisfaction, since nothing about the work itself is a motivational turn-on. When motivator factors are inherent in the job, satisfaction is perceived as possible and work-directed energy is aroused or sustained. Only then can a person be consistently motivated, according to Herzberg. Exhibit 6-5 presents the four alternative combinations of hygiene and motivator factors derived from the theory.

To improve motivation to work, managers are first advised to provide an adequate job context of working conditions and benefits for their people. This will satisfy lower-level hygiene needs, which, if not met, cause dissatisfaction. But to arouse work interest and promote self-directed task motivation, managers also need to ensure that the content of the job itself is reasonably satisfying – that jobs contain responsibility, challenge, and the opportunity to learn and advance.

The 'Stop and reflect' box gives you the opportunity to think about what you would like from your job.

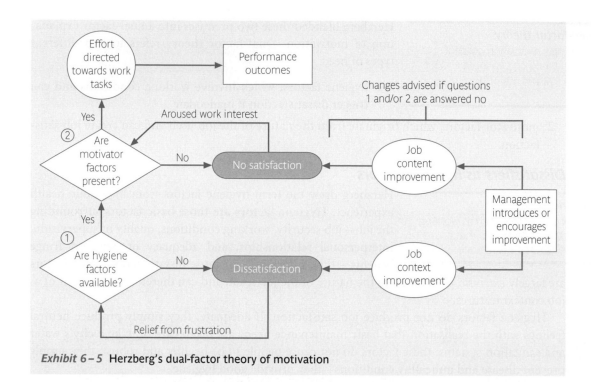

Exhibit 6 – 5 Herzberg's dual-factor theory of motivation

Stop and reflect

What do you want from your job?

Rank the following 16 work-related rewards and outcomes from 1 (most important) to 16 (least important) to you.

Good health insurance and other benefits	_____
Interesting work	_____
Job security	_____
Opportunity to learn new skills	_____
Having a week or more holiday	_____
Being able to work independently	_____
Recognition from co-workers	_____
Regular hours (no weekends, no nights)	_____
Having a job in which you can help others	_____
Limiting job stress	_____
High income	_____
Working close to home	_____
Work that is important to society	_____
Chances for promotion	_____
Contact with a lot of people	_____
Flexible hours	_____

Which of these rewards do you receive now?
Which of them can you control to increase your probability of satisfaction?

Source: Adapted from Bloisi *et al.* (2003).

A reward strategy

Research by the CIPD (2004a) found that two-thirds of organisations took a strategic approach to reward and had a written reward strategy. One of the main concerns for managers was the ability to pay the market rate in order to attract and retain the best people. For most organisations, the top priorities of a reward strategy are as follows:

- reward business goals
- recruit and retain high performers
- control pay costs
- ensure equity.

The 'International perspective' box illustrates how a reward strategy can improve employee performance.

Total rewards

total rewards
The reward strategy that brings together all components of reward, including monetary, non-monetary, learning and development.

Total rewards is a strategy which recognises that pay, although important, is not the only motivator, and that there are other tangible and non-tangible rewards that can encourage a more committed workforce. HR professionals need to recognise that total reward can be a powerful tool for aligning HR with business strategies and ensuring competitive advantage.

According to the CIPD (2004a):

> Total reward is the term that has been adopted to describe a reward strategy that brings additional components such as learning and development, together with aspects of the working environment into the benefits package. It goes beyond company culture, and is aimed at giving all employees a voice in the operation, with the employer in return receiving an engaged employee performance.

The advantages of a total reward scheme are, according to Thompson and Milsome (2001):

- easier recruitment of better-quality staff
- reduced wastage from staff turnover
- better business performance
- enhanced reputation as an employer of choice.

However, there can also be problems in creating a total reward package, in that it is always bespoke and needs to be specially designed for the organisation. Although there are consultants who specialise in developing total reward packages, they can be very expensive to set up. The cost of such a scheme needs to be matched with the potential benefits of increased employee commitment and increased competitive advantage.

Exhibit 6-6 demonstrates how financial rewards and non-financial rewards link together to form total rewards.

There are several total reward models. However, according to Thompson and Milsome (2001), they tend to share the following characteristics.

- Holistic: they focus on all aspects of the organisation, from recruitment to selection, retention, pay and reward, and are designed so that employees can contribute to the success of the organisation.

international perspective

In corporate India, it pays to reward performers

Gone are the days of across-the-board pay hikes. Today, Indian companies are going in for performance pay structures, a norm that has been in practice for several years among multinational companies (MNCs) operating in the country.

A recent study by Hewitt bears out this fact. It shows that almost 87 per cent of Indian companies are looking at retaining top talent and are using performance pay to do it. 'The results of the study, in fact, reveal that an outstanding performer earns on an average twice the salary increase earned by an average performer,' says Mr Nishchae Suri, measurement practice leader, Hewitt Associates.

According to him, Indian companies are practising the concept of performance-linked rewards widely. 'While the outstanding performers of these companies got a hike that was almost 4.7 per cent higher than the low performers last year, this year the percentage grew by 6 per cent.'

Mr Suri adds, 'As corporate revenues and budgets stagnate or even reduce, the companies are also realising the need to retain their best talent in order to drive better business results.'

Agreeing with Mr Suri, Mr Sunit Mehra, managing director of Hunt Partners, says, 'Almost all progressive companies that I am aware of have a performance pay plan in place or are implementing it. Instead of remunerating everyone equally, the Indian companies have started remunerating the performers more. The advantage to both parties is that overall salary costs are contained and it also helps to motivate the better performers.'

Mr Mehra also points out that, although this structure has definitely helped to improve the efficiency of employees, in order to make the plan effective, companies need to have simple, effective, realistic and transparent metrics to evaluate performance.

Mr Ulhas Deshpande, vice-president, human resources, IDBI Bank, says, 'Ever since we switched over to the performance-reward structure, it has helped in enhancing the efficiency and effectiveness of our employees. Just as a large number of employees have exceeded expectations, quite a few underachievers have also worked in earnest and shown significant change for the better. Overall, it has helped to improve employee productivity and quality.'

Mr Deshpande says across-the-board hikes not only result in a wider distribution of rewards but also dilute the quantum for each employee and this results in building a mindset of complacency. He adds, 'Moreover, contributors who add significant value are left with a feeling that there is no premium on performance and hence either get demotivated and leave or start underperforming. As far as the non-performer is concerned, he continues to get some increase, which is a good enough incentive to continue in the system and not improve. Therefore, the Indian companies are rightly focusing on differentiation and targeted rewards linked to results.'

Source: Ajita Shashidhar, *Hindu Business Line*, 14 March 2000, New Delhi.

Discussion questions

1 How can organisations encourage non-performers to improve their performance?

2 Does performance-related pay reward a few at the expense of the majority?

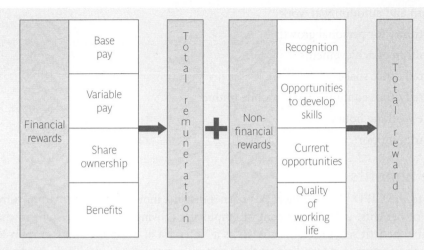

Exhibit 6–6 Total reward management
Source: Armstrong and Brown (2001).

- Best fit: they are adapted to fit the organisation, therefore different organisations will design their total reward packages to meet the needs of their individual business goals and organisational climate.

- Integrative: rewards are integrated into policies and practices according to the needs of the employees.

- Strategic: reward is linked to business strategy with the view that the total rewards on offer will improve performance.

- People centred: as people form the basis of organisations, it is important that the reward packages not only meet their needs but also encourage greater commitment.

- Customised: flexible rewards offer choice and meet the needs of employees. Younger employees often have different needs and aspirations to those of older employees and this is reflected in the package they are offered.

- Distinctive: the total reward package sets the organisation apart from others and therefore can be used as a powerful tool in attracting and retaining employees.

- Evolutionary: the total reward process should evolve over time to meet the needs of the organisation.

In the past the promise of a job for life was often enough to attract and retain workers, and financial benefits may have included shares or bonuses linked to company performance. However, with a more diverse workforce, employees are requesting different returns at work, which not only need to be varied but also flexible, so that when circumstances change the employee is able to pick and mix different benefits.

The elements included in the total reward package may, according to the CIPD (2004a), include some of the following aspects:

- flexible benefits
- access to training courses
- a challenging work role

- freedom and autonomy at work
- opportunity for personal growth
- recognition of achievements
- preferred office space
- preferred office equipment and mobile phone
- flexible working hours
- secretarial support.

Flexible benefits

According to the CIPD (2004c), there has been a distinct move towards providing a more flexible system of benefits, with 10 per cent of employers moving to such a system in the last five years. Flexible benefit schemes, also known as a 'cafeteria of benefits', allow employees to pick and choose their rewards, depending on their circumstances.

Flexible benefits form part of the total reward package and are beginning to take off as a key element of the reward package despite having been around for the last 20 years. The reason for such an interest is that employers have finally recognised that their employees prefer to choose their benefits rather than have a scheme imposed on them, and there are several consultants with sufficient expertise to enable organisations to design and deliver such schemes. Employees can now decide if they want a company car, private medical insurance, pension contributions or extra holiday. An example of one such successful scheme has been implemented in the public sector by housing association Poplar Harka, which wanted to be able to distinguish itself from other public-sector organisations to enable it to attract and retain high-calibre staff. Under the scheme employees are able to choose a mix of benefits such as medical and dental insurance, health checks, extra holiday or a home computer. Other reasons for a move to flexible benefits are the changes in tax benefits to encourage pension plans and increase in taxes to discourage company car use.

flexible benefits
A pick and mix of rewards that employees can choose depending on their wants and needs.

The advantages and disadvantages of implementing a flexible benefits scheme can be seen in Exhibit 6-7.

Incentives

Incentives are one method of recognising good performance and showing employees that they are valued and appreciated. In the past they were often linked to targets but now they are seen much more as an expected part of the rewards system. To be effective, incentive schemes need to be flexible and exciting and able to motivate a diverse workforce. However, if handled badly, they can cause serious dissatisfaction.

incentives
Mechanisms to encourage and recognise good performance.

Whatever incentives are used, they need to be suitable for the recipients. Tony Kilcoyne, a corporate gifts manager from Fraser Hart Awards and Incentives, suggests that organisations need to look at the diversity of their workforce. A young workforce, such as often found in call centres, is more likely to prefer electrical goods, while older workers may prefer holidays or gift vouchers. Employers, however, do need to remember that many incentives come with tax implications for employees which, to avoid any negative impact, they would have to pay.

Advantages of flexible benefits schemes
■ Employees choose benefits to meet their needs, and value these benefits more highly
■ Employers and employees share the responsibility for providing benefits
■ During periods of change (including mergers and acquisitions), flexible benefits help to harmonise rewards
■ Employers provide benefits at a known cost that is fixed regardless of the choices that employees make, so allowing them to cap future benefit costs
■ Employees have a true idea of the full worth of the benefits package they receive and employers do not provide benefits that are not valued
■ Employees are given a sense of control and involvement by having a choice
■ Dual-career couples avoid having benefits duplicated by their respective employers
■ Employers are seen to be more responsive to the needs of an increasingly diverse, demanding and ageing workforce
■ A competitive benefits package is valuable in attracting and retaining key personnel
■ The awarding of benefits such as company cars becomes less divisive
■ Employers' demands for flexible working practices are more justifiable if employees enjoy flexible benefits
■ Helps to align the total reward strategy to the HR and business strategies
Disadvantages of flexible benefits schemes
■ Employers find them complex and expensive to set up and maintain (although new technology is reducing both the cost and administrative burden)
■ The choices made may cause problems, both for employers and employees

Exhibit 6–7 Advantages and disadvantages of flexible benefits

Individual pay

This focuses on rewarding the right people for the right things. The idea is that pay can be a motivator and that, to motivate:

- a reward must be perceived as worth working for
- the reward must have a clearly perceived connection with the work results
- work goals must be seen to be achievable.

Traditional pay schemes are rarely able to do this and tend to pay employees regardless of their performance. One way round this is to link pay to performance through an appraisal and performance-related pay system. However, this must be robust and employees need to have a high level of trust in the appraisal system.

Performance-related pay

Performance-related pay (PRP) is often linked to performance appraisal: employees are rewarded for meeting targets, set either by themselves or their managers. PRP enables organisations to link an employee's performance to the organisational strategy and reinforce strategic goals. Often, this is an attempt to change the culture of an

performance-related pay
Pay linked to performance to encourage greater productivity.

organisation in order to improve productivity. The problem with performance-related pay is that it sends a message to employees that, to earn more they have to perform. Often, this means that it is the strongest who survive, which could result in lower performers underachieving as they have no incentive to try.

To avoid this, PRP can be linked not only to performance objectives but also to development objectives. If employees undertake training or skills development they too can be rewarded. In implementing PRP managers need to ensure that they have evaluated the need for improved performance and identified the following issues.

- Do employees value pay?
- What are the objectives of a PRP system?
- Does implementing PRP conform to the organisational values already in place?
- How can employees be encouraged to accept the system?
- What training will be given to managers on implementing the system?
- How will performance be measured and will it be accurate?
- Will there be different levels of reward depending on achievement of targets?
- How will differing contributions be assessed?
- Are there sufficient financial resources to allow payments to be made?
- How will the system be monitored?
- What happens if increased performance does not increase competitive advantage?
- How will the organisation ensure that awards are fair and equitable?

Effective PRP can substantially improve performance; however, poorly implemented systems can alienate employees. As one education union announced: 'We've performed, you pay.' In other words, we are already doing our job to the best of our ability and therefore should be rewarded properly. To be effective, PRP should specify and measure performance, specify the reward and gain employee acceptance.

One example of the negative impacts of PRP was found by a study at Aston University, where 22 organisations were examined. It was found that in the majority of cases PRP was used to encourage staff to make as many transactions in the shortest time possible. The result was that customers who went over the three minutes were cut off. Another example was a directory enquiries company, where one member of staff gave out the number of the local pizza restaurant to every caller in an attempt to minimise call times. Kent County Council, in an attempt to overcome such problems, has attempted to redress the balance by rewarding staff for their customer care, instead of whether they answer the phone in four rings. The advantages and disadvantages of PRP are summarised in Exhibit 6-8.

Team pay

Although few organisations implement team-based pay, according to the CIPD (2004b) managers who believe that their teams make a significant contribution to performance believe the teams deserve to be rewarded financially as well as being given scope to manage themselves. If the workplace is moving towards self-managed teams, then it makes sense that managers reward the team rather than the individual. Research suggests that senior managers are the ones most likely to be rewarded for their team's performance and that the rewards are not always filtered down to other employees.

Advantages	Disadvantages
■ It can retain and attract good performers	■ Reinforces management control
■ If properly implemented, it can improve both individual and organisational performance	■ Can cause pay inequality
	■ Reinforces power hierarchies
■ Job roles and duties are clarified by linking PRP to job descriptions and performance outcomes	■ Difficult to implement effectively in practice
	■ Undermines team working as it is individually based
■ It can improve communication	■ Can involve subjective rather than objective evaluations by managers
■ It can improve motivation	
■ It reinforces management control where in the past it may have been weak	■ External factors may mean employees are unable to control or achieve desired performance
■ It identifies developmental objectives	
■ It reinforces the individual employment relationship rather than the individual	■ Fast-changing work environments may mean objectives become obsolete
■ It rewards individuals without the need to promote them	■ It can discourage creative thinking
	■ Budgetary constraints can affect ratings
	■ Employees may ignore their weaknesses in order to receive increased pay, and therefore not develop
	■ Managers may reward all staff regardless of performance in order to remain popular
	■ The pay bill increases but productivity may not

Exhibit 6 – 8 Advantages and disadvantages of performance-related pay

The CIPD (2004b) believes that **team pay** works best if teams:

team pay
Rewarding the team rather than the individual for team performance.

- stand alone with agreed targets and standards
- have autonomy
- are composed of people whose work is interdependent
- are stable
- are well established and make good use of complementary skills
- are composed of flexible, multiskilled team players who are capable of expressing a different point of view if it is for the good of the whole.

For team pay to be accepted as a reward, the CIPD (2004b) also suggests that:

- everybody must understand and accept the targets
- the reward must be clearly linked to effort and achievement
- the reward must be worth striving for
- performance measures must be fair, consistent and acceptable
- everybody must be able to track performance in relation to targets and standards
- the team must influence its performance by changing behaviour or decisions
- the incentive formula must be easily understood

- reward must closely follow accomplishment
- the scheme must be appropriate
- the scheme should be carefully designed, installed, maintained and adapted to meet changing circumstances.

Another question for managers is what type of reward should be offered that would be acceptable for all members of the team. This could be monetary rewards, or team-based rewards such as away-days in luxury hotels. Research suggests they prefer team rewards, such as recognition and celebrations, rather than monetary rewards. Whatever type of reward is offered it is important to ensure that there is the right mix and that employees are aware of the distinction between individual rewards and team rewards. To be successful, both managers and teams need to understand that they have responsibilities, as can be seen in Exhibit 6-9.

Team-based pay has both advantages and disadvantages (see Exhibit 6-10) and needs to be managed carefully to ensure its success.

Organisations that have consulted thoroughly with their employees and that have a well-thought-out system will find that team pay may well enhance the performance of organisational teams, but they need to remember that there are alternatives to team-based pay that may work equally well.

Managers need to:	Teams need to:
■ conduct an initial needs analysis	■ participate in the scheme's design and modification
■ analyse current practice	■ define critical success factors and performance measures
■ define individual and team reward philosophies	■ set objectives
■ consider team pay reinforcement and non-financial rewards	■ identify accomplishments
■ create a collaborative climate	■ monitor and evaluate team performance
■ identify critical success factors	■ establish priorities
■ involve all employees	■ analyse the financial rewards and decide on improvements
■ communicate the benefits	■ conduct peer reviews of individuals
■ train employees and team leaders to optimise team performance	■ identify training and development needs
■ provide team-building training	■ suggest improvements to the scheme
■ help individuals improve their skills	■ promote non-financial rewards
■ monitor and evaluate	
■ audit the costs and ensure the scheme is self-financing	
■ promote the value of non-financial rewards	
■ recognise team accomplishments with appropriate action	

Exhibit 6–9 Manager and team responsibilities
Source: CIPD (2004b).

Advantages	Disadvantages
Team pay can:	Team pay can:
■ encourage co-operative work and behaviour	■ diminish individual self-worth
■ clarify goals and priorities at team and organisational level	■ mask individual team contributions
■ emphasise a flatter and more process-based organisation	■ compel individuals to conform to oppressive group norms
■ act as a lever for organisational change	■ result in low output that is sufficient only to gain a reasonable reward
■ encourage flexible working and multiskilling	■ cause difficulties when developing performance measures that are fair
■ offer a fairer perceived payment system	■ shift problems of unco-operative behaviour from individuals in teams to the relationships between teams
■ collectively improve performance and team processs	■ prejudice organisational flexibility – cohesive and high-performance teams may be unwilling to change
■ encourage the less effective to meet team standards	
■ develop self-managed and directed teams	

Exhibit 6 – 10 The advantages and disadvantages of team-based pay
Source: CIPD (2004b).

Legal aspects

In the UK there is a variety of legislation in place to protect the worker and ensure that they are treated fairly. This includes the:

- Equal Pay Act 1970
- The Equal Pay Amendment (Regulations) 1983
- Employment Rights Act 1996
- Social Security Contributions and Benefit Act 1992
- National Minimum Wage Act 1998

Equal Pay Act 1970

The purpose of this act is to ensure that women and men doing the same or broadly similar work, receive the same pay. The Act states that there is a right to equal pay between men and women. Although in most instances prosecution under the Act has been on behalf of women, it applies equally to men.

The Equal Pay Act 1970 applies to all employees and is not only concerned with the equality of pay but also with the provision of equal benefits such as bonuses, holidays and hours of work.

The tests used to check whether a person is entitled to equal pay are where:

- a person is employed in like work with a person of the opposite sex in the same employment
- a person is employed on work rated as equivalent to that of a person of the opposite sex in the same employment
- a person is employed in work of equal value to that of a person of the opposite sex in the same employment.

The Equal Pay Amendment (Regulations) 1983

The Equal Pay Amendment (Regulations) 1983 added to the Equal Pay Act 1970 a further category of work of 'equal value'. This came about from European Law, Article 119, and the Equal Pay Directive, as the 1970 Act did not fully comply with work of 'equal value'. The procedure involved in bringing a complaint under this act can be time consuming. It involves an independent expert, usually appointed by Acas, to visit the place of work and observe the complainant at work. This involves negotiation with the employer to access the premises, and interviewing managers and employees. The burden of proof is on the complainant to show that comparable jobs are of equal value.

Employment Rights Act 1996

The Employment Rights Act 1996 consolidates much of the previous employment rights legislation. This includes the right to an itemised pay statement for every employee who works more than eight hours. The pay statement should include details of:

- the gross amount earned
- any tax and National Insurance deductions
- any fixed deductions agreed by the employee such as pension payments
- the amount of net pay.

The Act also protects employees from unlawful deductions. For example, they cannot have their pay docked for breakages or missing stock unless it is an agreed part of their contract, but they can have their pay docked if the deductions are a result of strike action or of an overpayment in wages.

The Act also covers guarantee payments where an employee who has been paid for more than one month has the right to be paid if they are temporarily laid off due to a diminution in the employer's requirements for labour.

Social Security Contributions and Benefits Act 1992
Sick pay

All employees are entitled to receive a basic amount of sick pay. Often employees provide increased benefits, and these need to be written into the terms and conditions of employment.

Under the Social Security Contributions and Benefits Act 1992 all employees are entitled to receive statutory sick pay for the first 28 weeks of their illness. To qualify for sick pay the employee must be:

- suffering from some disease/physical or mental disability that renders him/her incapable of work, and
- the period of incapacity must be a period of four or more consecutive days.

Statutory sick pay is the responsibility of the employer and cannot be claimed back unless the sick pay exceeds 13 per cent of their National Insurance contributions each month. Some organisations, such as Tesco and British Airways, in an attempt to discourage absences, do not pay employees for the first three days of sickness, which although unpopular with staff and unions does nevertheless comply with legislation.

Tesco acts to reduce staff sick days

Britain's biggest private-sector employer has launched an experiment to reduce sick days with a mixture of sticks and carrots (or at least vouchers to buy them). One pilot scheme launched by Tesco rewards those staff who have an exemplary record for turning up with extra holiday. Another one gives them reward vouchers, and another fails to give them sick pay for their first three days off.

The supermarket chain's initiative reflects a belief among many employers that a large proportion of sick days are not caused by genuine illness: 51 per cent of human resource professionals believe that more than half the days employers lost to stress were not genuine, a survey by the Health & Safety Executive and *Personnel Today* magazine suggested last year.

A survey of GPs published this year by Norwich Union, the insurer, found that more than a third of the sick notes they issued every year might be bogus.

The CBI employers' organisation has estimated that staff absence costs business £11.6bn a year.

There are even signs that fear of 'sickies' may be exacerbating the problem of genuine sickness. More than four in ten private-sector businesses in the HSE/*Personnel Today* survey said they did not want to raise the profile of stress in case this encouraged increased reporting of it.

Under Tesco's extra holiday scheme, all staff are given three more days over the year. For every day off sick, they lose one of these extra days – though they can never lose more than three. Tesco said no worker had been compelled to take part in the pilots.

Usdaw, the shopworkers' union, which represents Tesco workers, is co-operating with the pilots. Its acquiescence contrasts sharply with the bitter opposition from the Public and Commercial Services Union to plans by management at the Department for Work and Pensions for a crackdown on sick days.

Under a proposed bonus scheme, workers whose general performance qualified them for extra cash would lose some of it if they took five days off a year, apart from annual holiday.

Source: David Turner, *Financial Times*, 17 May 2004, p. 4.

Discussion questions

1 What impact do you think these different schemes could have on employee motivation?
2 Which scheme, if any, would motivate you to work harder and which would demotivate you?

National Minimum Wage Act 1998

The National Minimum Wage Act 1998 became effective in 1999 and was designed to alleviate poverty in the low-earning sector of the workforce. The national minimum wage is the same regardless of job location, job type, size or industrial sector. Therefore someone living in London would be paid the same as someone living in Newcastle, despite substantial differences in living costs. The reasons put forward to support a national minimum wage (NMW) cover three broad areas:

1 **social** – a minimum wage would attack low pay and poverty
2 **equity** – a minimum wage reduces exploitation, protects employers against undercutting on wages, and cuts the cost to taxpayers of topping up low incomes via the social security system

3 **economic** – extra demand in the economy would increase employment; a minimum wage could also boost investment and productivity.

In commenting on the report of the Low Pay Commission, the then Secretary of State emphasised four key messages. The NMW (2004) would:

1 begin to end the 'scandal of poverty pay'

2 form part of an overall package to make work pay

3 produce a more committed and productive workforce

4 encourage competition based on quality not 'sweatshop labour'.

To comply with legislation, employers have to display details of the hourly minimum wage on the payslip and in the workplace (LPC, 2004).

The NMW has established the following rates:

- **standard rate £5.35** – payable to people aged 22 and over
- **development rate £4.45** – payable to people aged 18 to 21 years, whether or not they are receiving 'accredited training'; payable to people aged 22 and over who start a new job with a new employer and receive 'accredited training' for first six months
- **youth rate £3.30** – payable to 16 and 17 year olds (above the compulsory school leaving age); this new rate was introduced on 1 October 2006.

Low pay

The minimum wage has increased by 50 per cent since its introduction in 1999, and while some employers, such as Asda, welcome it, the Confederation for British Industry (CBI) has criticised it for stifling British industry and making it hard for businesses to be competitive. The minimum wage, as it suggests, is a minimum and many people still find it hard to make ends meet, especially if they live in London. As discussed in the opening vignette, some organisations have moved on from the minimum wage to the idea of a living wage.

The idea of a living wage originated in the USA where cities including Boston, Los Angeles and Chicago have adopted living wage ordinances, meaning that they will not employ people or contract with those who pay their staff less than a living wage. The idea is now gathering pace in the UK and already the cleaners at the Houses of Parliament are paid a living wage as are staff at Barclays and HSBC. Although some jobs are contracted out, some local authorities, such as the Greater London Authority (GLA), are implementing rules which mean that contractors will have to commit to pay the living wage if they want to work for the GLA.

Transparency and equity

To avoid any unpleasantness from employees, it is good practice for employers to ensure that an organisation rewards employees fairly. In other words, employers provide equal pay for equal work. Employers are responsible for ensuring this happens and therefore it is desirable that pay systems are clear and transparent. A structured pay system is more likely to provide such transparency than a system that relies on an employer's discretion.

In building a pay system, it is necessary for the organisation to carry out an equal pay review that involves all levels of staff, management and their representatives. According to the Equal

Opportunities Commission (EOC), 'an equal pay review involves comparing the pay of women and men doing equal work, investigating the causes of gender pay gaps and closing any gaps that can not be satisfactorily explained on grounds other than sex'. The EOC recognises that the equal pay review is concerned only with a narrow aspect of sex discrimination at work and does not take into account other aspects of inequality such as the glass ceiling. Nevertheless it does try to address the issue of disparity of a 19.5 per cent pay gap between men and women working full-time and the 40 per cent gap between men working full-time and women working part-time.

The EOC suggests following a five-step process, as illustrated in Exhibit 6-11.

Employers who ignore such advice do so at their peril. In a recent case an employee was awarded a £1,000,000 settlement that was largely the result of management's 'behind closed doors' bonus culture. Even if payouts are less substantial, an employer could still be liable for six months' back pay if found guilty of discrimination.

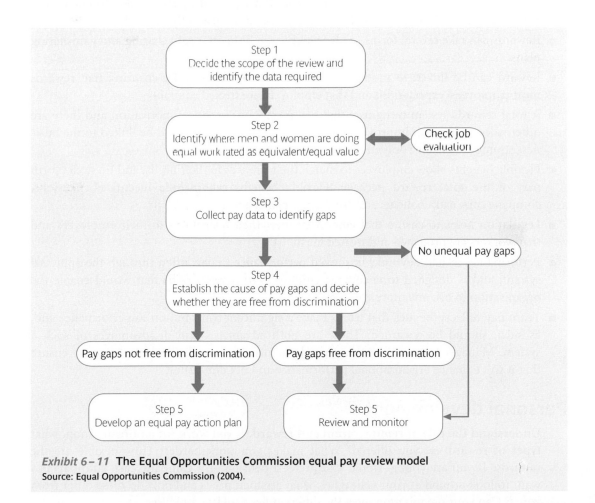

Exhibit 6–11 The Equal Opportunities Commission equal pay review model
Source: Equal Opportunities Commission (2004).

Summary

- Remuneration and reward are an important part of the HR function, as they link directly to an organisation's strategic goals. Remuneration refers to the monetary aspect, whereas rewards can be monetary or non-monetary and should be designed to show employees that they are valued.

- Payment structures are developed to ensure that employers pay the market rate, which enables them to attract and retain employees, and to demonstrate that employees are rewarded fairly and equitably.

- There are various methods that can be used to evaluate jobs, such as job ranking, paired comparisons and job classification. Information about deciding what to pay can be gathered from market surveys.

- Traditional pay was linked to the principles of scientific management and was closely controlled by managers. New pay combines traditional pay with personal development, and recognises that it should be linked to both the organisation and the individual.

- Rewards can take several forms, such as merit pay, bonuses, profit sharing and gainsharing plans.

- Reward can be linked to motivation to improve performance by ensuring that rewards meet employees' expectations and that employees are treated equitably.

- A total rewards system recognises that pay is only one aspect of motivation and there are other rewards that can improve performance. These rewards should be linked to the business strategy to enable competitive advantage.

- Flexible benefits allow employees to match their rewards to their needs, and these can form part of the total reward package. Flexible benefits can include incentives, pensions, company cars, extra holiday, and childcare vouchers.

- Legislation helps to ensure that employers meet their obligations to their employees and that workers are protected and treated fairly.

- Performance-related pay links improved performance to pay, often through the appraisal system, and is designed to encourage employees to develop skills that would enable the organisation to become more effective.

- Team pay reflects the idea that teams make a significant contribution to performance and, as such, should be rewarded. There are both advantages and disadvantages of such a system. Managers considering team-based pay need to consult their employees to ensure that it will enhance organisational performance and not diminish it.

Personal development

1 **Understand the role of remuneration and reward.** If you work for an organisation, what types of reward are you offered? What makes you work harder? How flexible are the rewards? If you are young, would you prefer a pension or a company car? You may also want to look around at your colleagues: what are their needs and how do these differ from yours? Can your organisation meet the different needs of its employees?

2 **Recognise the importance of payment systems.** Does the organisation you work for have a payment structure? Can you identify how this has been developed? Does this reflect the market conditions? If yes, how does this make employees feel? If no, why are people still working there? Does the payment system allow for recognition of achievement or perform-

ance, and who is responsible for recognising the achievement? Is it at the whim of the manager or more consistent? Do you progress because of your ability or on length of service, and is this fair?

3 **Determine the impact of bonus systems.** If you had a good idea at work and it saved the company a considerable amount of money, would you like to be rewarded? Should it only be you who receives the reward, or should it be evenly distributed? Gainsharing is one example of how employees can benefit by improving organisational efficiency. Alternatively, would you prefer a profit-sharing plan? Which scheme would encourage greater commitment to the organisation?

4 **Understand the impact of motivation on employee performance.** If you were paid less than your colleague for doing the same job, how would you feel? Would you want to work harder in the hope that your pay would be increased, or would your performance deteriorate as you became less motivated? Managers need to understand the importance of motivation to performance. Treating employees equitably not only ensures fairness, it also ensures that organisations protect themselves from legal action. Employees also have expectations: in other words, if they work harder then they may well expect promotion; if this doesn't happen, is performance likely to increase or decrease?

5 **Recognise the need to work within the legal framework.** HR practitioners need to familiarise themselves with their legal obligations. This means ensuring that employees are not discriminated against on the grounds of race, gender or disability. Other legal obligations relating to pay are concerned with the types of deduction an employer can make, and ensuring that minimum wages are paid. Legislation provides a minimum requirement. Many employers go beyond legislation to value diversity or ensure employees are paid a living wage, rather than a minimum wage.

6 **Recognise the implications of team pay.** Many people today work in leaner and flatter organisational structures, where teamwork is valued. You may well work in such a team. If so, would you like to be rewarded as part of the team or as an individual? It may be that you play sport; if so, how would you feel if every time a goal was scored, the scorer received extra pay despite it being a team effort? Team pay aims to reward team effort as opposed to individualism.

❓ Discussion questions

1 Define the terms 'reward' and 'remuneration'.

2 'We perform, you pay.' What are the arguments for and against performance-related pay?

3 What does an organisation need to consider when developing a pay structure?

4 What is the difference between 'new pay' and 'traditional pay'?

5 How could gainsharing plans be implemented as part of the reward system?

6 Why is it important for managers to have an understanding of motivation when rewarding employees?

7 What are the characteristics of a total reward system?

8 How can managers successfully implement flexible benefits while meeting the needs of the organisation?

9 What are the advantages and disadvantages of team pay?

10 How can pay and performance be linked to the strategic aims of the organisation?

ⓘ Key concepts

reward, *p. 178*

remuneration, *p. 178*

pay structures, *p. 180*

job evaluation, *p. 180*

points rating, *p. 180*

factor comparison, *p. 180*

job ranking, *p. 181*

paired comparison, *p. 181*

job classification, *p. 181*

efficiency wage theory, *p. 184*

benchmarking, *p. 184*

traditional pay, *p. 186*

new pay, *p. 186*

merit pay, *p. 186*

profit sharing, *p. 187*

bonuses, *p. 187*

gainsharing , *p. 187*

equity theory, *p. 188*

distributive justice, *p. 189*

procedural justice, *p. 189*

expectancy theory, *p. 189*

dual-factor theory, *p. 191*

hygiene factors, *p. 191*

motivator factors, *p. 191*

total rewards, *p. 193*

flexible benefits, *p. 196*

incentives, *p. 196*

performance-related pay, *p. 197*

team pay, *p. 199*

Individual task

Purpose To gain an understanding of job evaluation, one of the techniques available for determining pay.

Time 40 minutes

Procedure A points ranking system can be one method of job evaluation used to determine the level of pay. Note down the following headings:

Knowledge and skills
Decision-making
Impact and influence
Communication and networking
Freedom to act
Working environment
People management
Financial responsibility

(More detailed descriptions can be found in Exhibit 6-2.)

Now rank the following jobs in order of importance, using 1 to denote the most important and 20 the least.

Nurse	_____	Childcare assistant	_____
Cleaner	_____	Paramedic	_____
Secretary	_____	Police officer	_____
Receptionist	_____	Soldier	_____
Porter	_____	Shop assistant	_____
Doctor	_____	Call centre operator	_____
Teacher	_____	Computer technician	_____
Artist	_____	Accountant	_____
Lawyer	_____	Journalist	_____
Postman/woman	_____	HR manager	_____

What influenced your decision?

How does this compare to the rankings given by other members of the group and why are there differences?

Team task

Purpose To identify the different wants and needs people have in life, and to link them to a flexible reward system.

Time 50 minutes

Procedure Working individually, develop a list of approximately 10 rewards you would like from a job. Try to include those you would like now and those you may want later in life. Decide which rewards are essential and which desirable.

Divide into groups of four and compare which needs are similar and which different.

What are the implications for organisations who want to design a flexible benefits system?

How would you decide whether the types of reward were equitable when compared to each other?

What could happen if people see their rewards as inequitable to those given to others?

Case study: **Performance-related pay at O$_2$**

Mobile phone company O$_2$ has reduced staff turnover by introducing performance-related pay for new workers in its UK call centres.

Sally Ashford, director of compensation and benefits at O$_2$, said the new pay structure, which includes a performance-linked bonus and a revised career and pay progression framework, had 'dramatically reduced' staff attrition rates and the company's reliance on temporary staff.

O$_2$ introduced the reward structure as part of a larger transformation programme to increase employee commitment and customer satisfaction following customer complaints about the complexity of its billing tariffs.

'Previously pay rises were linked to service and length of time in the role. There was no performance element and some of the salaries we were paying were higher than the market rates,' said Ashford.

Staff pay rises are now based on individual performance, monitored via phone-call observations and productivity levels. Employees can receive a target bonus of up to 10 per cent of their salary per annum, paid out twice yearly. They also sit down every month with their line managers to discuss their performance.

Currently only 30 per cent of O_2's 3300 UK call centre staff are on the new pay structure, with the remainder on a set salary up to £5000 higher than those on the new pay scale. The difference is a result of O_2's de-merger from BT in 2001, because transferred staff were on the same terms and conditions that BT originally set in place.

'Our next big project is how to merge the existing employees onto the new terms and conditions,' said Ashford. 'Currently existing staff are at or near the maximum of the new pay scale we have introduced.'

Ashford said that, so far, the different pay scales had not caused problems between employees. 'We have been very open about the two levels of pay and have not tried to hoodwink people,' she said.

Source: Katie Hope, 'Making reward work 2004', *People Management*, 14 October 2004, p. 12. Reproduced with permission of *People Management*.

Discussion questions

1 How can performance-related pay be fairly linked into the appraisal system?

2 Why can a properly implemented pay structure improve staff retention?

3 What problems could there be with perceived equity when staff are employed on different contracts?

4 Do you think pay should be linked to length of service or to performance?

WWW exercise

Choose an organisation that you would be interested in working for in the future.

1 What information does it provide about its reward and remuneration packages?

2 Is this what you would expect from this organisation?

3 Are there any benefits that you would want that are not offered?

4 Is the pay structure transparent or is it secretive?

5 Would you be able to negotiate a better package if you were offered a job, or is it rigid?

Specific web exercise

Visit the website of the Equal Opportunities Commission at: www.eoc.org.uk and follow the links to pay and statistics for the different employment sectors.

1 Why do you think different pay in different sectors varies so much?

2 Why, despite 30 years of legislation, is there still a gap between male and female earnings?

3 How, as a manager, could you try to bridge the gap?

LEARNING CHECKLIST

Before moving on to the next chapter, check that you are able to:

☑ understand the role of pay and reward, and its link to performance

☑ evaluate the different aspects of the reward package

☑ understand the legal issues affecting pay and reward

☑ discuss the importance of ethics in remuneration and reward.

Further reading

Armstrong, M. and Ryden, O. (1996) *The IPD Guide on Team Reward*. London: Institute of Personnel and Development/CIPD.

Coles, S. (2002) 'Team building', *Employee Benefits*, June, pp. 31–35.

DSS (1998) *A New Contract for Welfare Partnership in Pensions*. London: Department of Social Security/Stationery Office.

Garvey, C. (2002) 'Steer teams with the right pay', *HR Magazine* 47(5), May, pp. 71–74, 77–78.

Herzberg, F. (1987) 'One more time: how do you motivate employees?', *Harvard Business Review* 46, September–October, pp. 109–120.

IRS (2001) 'Whatever happened to team reward?', *IRS Employment Review: Pay and Benefits Bulletin* 732, July, pp. PABB2–7.

Lawler, E.E. (1990) *Strategic Pay*. San Francisco, CA: Jossey-Bass.

Lawler, E.E. (1995) 'The new pay: a strategic approach', *Compensation and Benefits Review*, July/August, pp. 46–54.

McClurg, L.N. (2001) 'Team rewards: how far have we come?', *Human Resource Management* 40(1), Spring, pp. 73–86.

Reilly, P. (2003) *New Reward 1: Team, Skills and Competency Based Pay*. Brighton: Institute for Employment Studies.

Schuster, J.R. and Zingheim, P.K. (1992) *The New Pay: Linking Employee and Organisational Performance*. New York, NY: Lexington Books.

Scrimshaw, A (2000) *Stakeholder Pensions: A Guide to Implementation and Practice*. CIPD Executive Briefing.

Taylor, F. (1964) *Scientific Management*. New York, NY: Harper & Row.

Turner, A. (2004) *Pensions Commission Report*, www.pensionscommission.org.uk.

References

Acas (2003) *Job Evaluation: An Introduction*. London: Advisory, Conciliation and Arbitration Service (Acas).

Adams, J.S. (1965) 'Inequity and social exchange', in L. Berkowitz (ed.) *Advances in Experimental Social Psychology 2*. NY: Academic Press, pp. 267–269.

Armstrong, M. (2000) *Employee Reward*. CIPD publication.

Armstrong, M. and Brown, D. (2001) *New Dimensions in Pay Management*. London: Chartered Institute of Personnel and Development.

Bloisi, W., Cook, C. and Hunsaker, P. (2003) *Management and Organisational Behaviour*. Maidenhead: McGraw-Hill.

CIPD (2000) 'Study of broad-banded and job family pay structures', CIPD Survey Report.

CIPD (2004a) 'Total Reward', factsheet, CIPD, February.

CIPD (2004b) *Reward Management 2004: A Survey of Policy and Practice*. London: CIPD, available at http://www.cipd.co.uk/surveys.

CIPD (2004c) 'Flexible benefits', factsheet, CIPD, March.

Crystal, G. (1995) 'Paying directors in company stock doesn't boost performance', *Los Angeles Times*, 12 March.

Equal Opportunities Commission (EOC) (2004) *The Pay Review Model*. London: Equal Opportunities Commission.

Fergusson, E. (2003) 'Fair share', *People Management*, 11 September, p. 19.

Folger, R. and Konovsky, M.A. (1989) 'Effects of procedural and distributive justice on reactions to pay raise decisions', *Academy of Management Journal* 32, March, pp. 115–130.

Hatchett, A. (2004) 'What next for local pay?', *People Management*, 12 February, pp. 14–15.

Heery, E. (1996) 'Risk, representation and the new pay', *Personnel Review* 25(6), pp. 54–65.

Herzberg, F. (1966) *Work and the Nature of Man*. Cleveland: World.

Herzberg, F. (1993) *The Motivation to Work*. Transaction Publications.

Lambert, R.A. and Larcker, D.F. (1989) 'Executive compensation, corporate decision making and shareholder wealth', in F. Foulkes *Executive Compensation*. Harvard Business School Press, pp. 287–309.

Lawler, E.E. (2000) 'Pay and strategy: new thinking for the new millennium', *Compensation and Benefits Review*, January/February, pp. 7–12.

LPC (2004) *The National Minimum Wage: Protecting Young Workers: Fifth Report of the Low Pay Commission*. Norwich: Low Pay Commission, Stationery Office.

Taylor, F.W. (1914) *The Principles of Scientific Management*. New York: Harper & Row.

Thompson, P. and Milsome, S. (2001) *Reward Determination in the UK*, research report. London: Chartered Institute of Personnel and Development.

Vroom, V.H. (1982) *Work and Motivation*. Krieger.

Wanous, J.P., Keon, T.L. and Latack, J.C. (1980) 'Expectancy theory and occupational/organisational choices: a review and test', *Organisational and Human Performance*, August, pp. 66–86.

Welbourne, T.M. and Gomez-Mejia, M.J. (1995) 'Gainsharing: a critical review and a future research agenda', *Journal of Management*, 21 September, p. 559.

Wood, A.W. (2000) 'Alienation', in *Concise Encyclopedia of Philosophy*. London: Routledge.

Zingheim, P. and Schuster, J. (1995) 'Introduction: how are the new pay tools being deployed?', *Compensation and Benefits Review*, July/August, pp. 10–14.

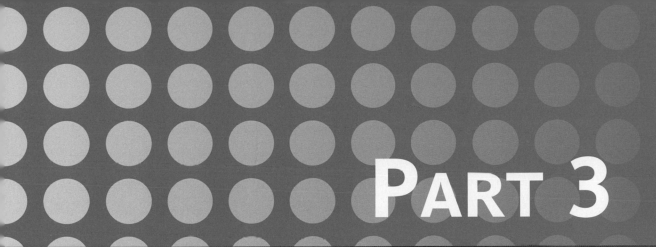

PART 3

Developing people

Part contents

7 Learning, training and development 215

8 Managing and developing performance 252

9 Employee relations, participation and involvement 286

Chapter 7

Learning, training and development

LEARNING OUTCOMES

After studying this chapter, you should be able to:

- ☑ **understand** the nature and process of learning
- ☑ **identify** different styles and approaches to learning
- ☑ **understand** the education and training debate
- ☑ **identify** strategies for training
- ☑ **understand** the relationship between competence and performance.

The opening vignette demonstrates the importance of training as a means of improving business performance.

Education can keep the car industry ahead: Japanese customers' demands have sparked a training explosion

When Nissan asked to see the training centre at a small Sutton Coldfield toolmaking company, it threw Colin Sarson, the managing director, into a panic.

Negotiations for Mr Sarson's business to become a supplier to the Sunderland plant of Japan's second largest car maker were at a delicate stage – and enormously important to the company.

But, as with hundreds of similar companies in the West Midlands vehicle heartland, it had never occurred to the toolmaker to have a training centre, something expected by the Japanese car maker.

▶

However, after identifying a suitable room, the company won the contract, but Mr Sarson got rather more than he had bargained for. 'Somehow, word got round the plant that we had a proper learning centre,' he says, slightly guiltily. 'And all of a sudden, entirely on their own initiative, there were people off the shopfloor coming into the room actually looking for training.'

After this incident in 1991, training programmes are now embedded in the business. The Japanese-inspired culture of continuous improvement permeates every activity. Mr Sarson intends virtually all his 400 employees to have earned a National Vocational Qualification (NVQ) before long.

All this is music to the ears of Mike Beasley, former managing director of Jaguar Cars, Graham Broome, a former Rover executive who since 1996 has been chief executive of the Society of Motor Manufacturers and Traders' (SMMT) Industry Forum, and David Cragg, head of the Learning and Skills Council's own Automotive Forum in the Midlands.

The trio are spearheading the biggest ever initiative – backed by industry leaders, government departments, regional authorities and the academic establishment – to increase skills within the UK's 250,000-strong vehicle industry workforce and help it to sustain global competitiveness.

They are not undertaking it in isolation from those who set the benchmarks for competitiveness: the car makers of Japan. The chairman of the SMMT's Industry Forum is Alan Jones, the long-time managing director of Toyota's manufacturing operations in the UK. Nissan and Honda, the UK's other Japanese 'transplants', are also represented.

'Supply them and you can supply anyone' is the message delivered, to the components sector in particular, by the initiative.

Under the title of Skills4Auto, the venture also aims to convince the young that the motor and engineering industries can provide enjoyable and attractive careers.

It has already created a task force with the Engineering Employers' Federation (EEF) in the West Midlands to promote the industry in schools. The scale of the problem is outlined by Ian Smith, the regional EEF's managing director. He estimates that a minimum of 2000 apprentices a year are needed in the region's manufacturing and engineering centres.

Skills4Auto itself is the first product of another initiative: an 'automotive academy' first outlined in mid-2003 by Sir Nick Scheele, the former Jaguar chairman who is now chief operating officer of parent company Ford.

'To stay ahead in the future we need people who are trained to the highest level and we aim to make that happen,' says Nick Barter, former development head at Jaguar and Land Rover, who last year was named launch director of the academy.

Skills4Auto is already identifying and evaluating training opportunities and making education and training providers more aware of the industry's needs. Chosen training schemes are being prepared as further 'spokes' are created.

Mr Beasley says: 'For the first time we have a training and development plan devised by the industry for the industry; training materials accredited by the industry; and training providers to work to the highest global standards.'

Programmes under development are at many levels: the academy itself, for example, has teamed up with the University of Cambridge to help train and educate some of the next generation of industry chief executives. But the main thrust is the creation of a range of so-called Business Improvement Techniques NVQs.

That there is a need for the initiative is not in doubt, observes Kevin Whale, Vauxhall's chairman and managing director: 'We have a shortage of application skills at technical levels as well as higher-level engineering support. So we critically need to improve training at that level.'

The seriousness of the issue in its international context is underlined by Digby Jones, director-general of the Confederation of British Industry, who warns that there is a real risk of investment in training, research and development slipping behind that of China and India.

So far, five colleges in the region, the SMMT's Industry Forum and the Sector Skills Council have collectively developed and launched more than 50 NVQ modules on business and process improvement techniques. Some 500 businesses have already been exposed to the skills programmes.

The Learning and Skills Council's David Cragg points to one company's reduction in lead times from 16 days to 12 hours, and what he describes as 'huge upskilling' at BMW's nearby Hams Hall engine plant.

As for widely aired business views critical of the quality of much of the country's NVQ programme, Mr Broome insists that the motor programmes have achieved what he regards as the three essential ingredients for NVQ integrity: 'Get the content right [and] the trainers properly validated and make sure the assessors are competent.'

Source: Adapted from John Griffiths, in the Financial Times, 16 March 2004, p. 12.
Reproduced with permission of the Financial Times.

Discussion questions

1 What does this case suggest about the importance of training for an organisation?

2 Many organisations fail to train their workers. Why do you think this happens, and what are the implications for the organisation and for the country?

The opening vignette shows the importance of a planned training programme. Many organisations fail to see the significance of this and as a result suffer from a lack of skills, which ultimately leads to an inability to compete in the global marketplace. This chapter focuses on the importance of training and gives an insight into how organisations can implement training strategies.

In some people's minds there is a clear distinction between training, education and development. To others the processes become blurred. Even if there is no formal training process all new members coming to an organisation will go through some form of socialisation.

Socialisation refers to teaching the organisational culture and philosophies to enable an employee to fit in and operate effectively. On entry to a new organisation an employee needs to 'learn the ropes' – in other words, how things are done in the new environment. This would include not only written policies and procedures, which can often be found in employee manuals, but also unwritten expectations, which an employee would need to understand in order to survive and progress in the organisation. Socialisation follows the recruitment and selection process and, as part of this process, applicants may already have gone through rigorous vetting procedures to ensure they are suitable for the organisation and the job. Before starting work, employees are often required to take part in a socialisation, also known as work orientation or induction, process. This often involves an introduction to the organisation's norms and values, where employees are introduced to company folklore, stories and symbols that form part of the organisational culture.

Whether training is planned or ad hoc, organisations that have a coherent training and development policy are more likely to be at the cutting edge and able to develop competitive advantage through their people.

The advantages of learning, training and development

Organisations that encourage learning, training and development make an intentional effort to improve not only current performance but also the future performance of employees.

By encouraging an employee to learn new skills and develop, employers can:

- ensure that their staff have the capabilities and skills to enable them to be more effective in the workplace
- create an understanding of how to work more effectively as part of a team, and the employee's role in contributing to the organisation
- ensure that the organisation's culture emphasises innovation, creativity and learning
- increase their knowledge of competitors and how employees learning new skills can lead to competitive advantage
- ensure employees are flexible and able to respond to change, which in turn provides them with increased job security as they can move around the organisation when their jobs become obsolete
- encourage acceptance of diversity so that employees have a greater understanding of each other.

The education and training of employees not only helps them to learn new skills but is also essential for their motivation, and will help organisations to attract and retain a highly motivated workforce.

---

education

The behavioural process of learning that applies to the whole person rather than specific skills.

Education versus training

Education and training both involve the process of learning and have been given the following definitions by the MSC (1981).

Education is defined as:

> activities which aim at developing the knowledge, skills, moral values and understanding required in all aspects of life rather than a knowledge and skill relating to only a limited field of activity. The purpose of education is to develop an understanding of the traditions and ideas influencing the society in which [people] live and to enable them to make a contribution to it. It involves the study of their own cultures and of the laws of nature, as well as the acquisition of linguistic and other skills which are basic to learning, personal development and communication.

---

training

The process of change used to develop specific skills, usually for a job.

Training is defined as:

> a planned process to modify attitude, knowledge or skill behaviour through learning experience to achieve effective performance in an activity or range of activities. Its purpose, in the work situation, is to develop the abilities of the individual and to satisfy the current and future needs of the organisation.

This means that training refers to a planned intervention by an organisation to improve an employee's job-related competencies. The role of training is to enable employees to master the necessary knowledge, skills and behaviours that will enable them to improve their performance on the job, whereas education is more general and provides the conditions to enable learning to take place.

The distinction between education and training is becoming increasingly blurred as qualifications such as National Vocational Qualifications (NVQs) and General National Vocational Qualifications (GNVQs) have been developed to enable parts of the education system to be more vocationally orientated.

High-leverage training links training to strategic business goals. It is used to encourage a learning organisation, where employees are required not only to acquire new skills and knowledge, which can then be applied to their job, but are also expected to share this information with other employees.

Before deciding on what type of education or training programme to offer it is a good idea to gain an understanding of how people learn.

How do people learn?

Individuals must be able to learn new knowledge and skills in order to survive in both society and the workplace. In today's fast-changing world, everyone who works is periodically required to learn new knowledge and skills. This is even more apparent from the mushrooming uses of the Internet, as it changes the ways people perform routine functions and discover new ways of obtaining and acting on information.

An important distinguishing characteristic of human beings is their ability to store information and to learn. **Learning** is the acquisition of knowledge, skill or values through study, practice or experience. Learning is usually considered to lead to relatively permanent changes in behaviour, as the learner develops capabilities for functioning in his or her environment.

learning
The acquisition of knowledge or skill through study, practice or experience.

The learning process takes place primarily in the brain. One useful metaphor for the brain is a computer. It has the capacity to receive inputs, organise and store them, and respond to some calls for retrieval. New data can be entered and existing data can be reorganised or deleted. Memory is similar to computer files, and perception and learning are the processes through which new data are added and old data revised.

intelligence
The ability to adapt to novel situations quickly and effectively, use abstract concepts effectively, and grasp relationships and learn quickly.

Computers differ in their capacity to receive, store, process and retrieve information quickly, and to manipulate the data in order to solve problems. These differing capacities are somewhat analogous to different individuals' intelligence and ability to think. Intelligence is a fuzzy concept. Generally, **intelligence** includes three different aspects:

1 the ability to adapt to novel situations quickly and effectively
2 the ability to use abstract concepts effectively
3 the ability to grasp relationships and to learn quickly.

Goleman (1994) has identified another aspect of intelligence, which he labels 'emotional intelligence'. It reflects the functioning of a person's emotional brain, which generates and regulates

feelings. Goleman suggests that emotional intelligence relates to a person's ability to get along with others, exert control over their own life, and think and decide clearly.

Individuals differ in terms of their memory, intelligence and ability to learn. Now you have the opportunity to learn some of the basic theories of how individuals learn. The main theories we will consider are:

1 behavioural conditioning

2 social learning

3 cognitive discovery.

We will also look at different individual styles of learning, because people tend to differ from one another in how they learn.

Behavioural conditioning

The development of learning theory began in the early twentieth century when the Russian physiologist Ivan Pavlov found he could condition dogs to salivate in response to the sound of a tuning fork, a previously neutral stimulus. Pavlov's work led to the development of **classical conditioning**, which is an experimental approach that associates a conditioned stimulus with an unconditioned stimulus to achieve a conditioned response.

classical conditioning
An experimental approach that associates a conditioned stimulus with an unconditioned stimulus to achieve a conditional response.

Dogs and other animals naturally salivate (*unconditional response – R*) when they are hungry and food (*unconditional stimulus – S*) is present. Pavlov experimented by preceding the presentation of food with the sound of a tuning fork (*conditional stimulus – S'*) and, over time, taught the dogs to salivate (*conditional response – R'*) at the sound alone. His experiments provided the intellectual basis for an empirical approach to the study of learning.

People experience classical conditioning in their everyday lives without realising it. For example, assume you frequently walk by a bakery early in the morning and smell (*S*) the freshly baked bread. If you have not had breakfast, you are likely to salivate and feel hunger pangs (*R*). The odour is an unconditioned stimulus, and your physical reaction is an unconditional response. Assume this happens frequently. Then one day you drive by the bakery and cannot smell the bread, but you salivate and feel hungry anyway. The sight of the shop (*S'*) has become a conditioned stimulus and your physical response, which now occurs without the actual odour, is also conditioned (*R'*) (Pavlov, 1927).

Conditioning through management of reinforcement

The psychologist B.F. Skinner (1964) extended the work of Pavlov and others to develop **operant conditioning**, which is learning in which reinforcement depends on the person's behaviour. In operant conditioning, the critical learning element is the direct linkage of significant contingent consequences to an operant behaviour.

operant conditioning
Learning in which reinforcement depends on the person's behaviour.

A *contingent consequence* is a reinforcer; it may be positive, negative or neutral. The term *operant* simply means that the individual 'operates' in his or her environment to obtain some desired consequences and avoid adverse or negative consequences. Individuals learn to anticipate or expect a certain consequence following specific behaviours. They learn to behave in ways that achieve positive consequences. The more frequently we get the desired consequences or avoid undesirable ones, the firmer the learning.

For example, assume Donna works extra hard on a special project to meet a tight deadline. Her boss is appreciative of her efforts, gives her special praise and celebrates by treating her to lunch at an upmarket restaurant. Donna enjoys the recognition and is likely to work hard again to receive the desired compliments. If she gets no response at all, she will probably feel less inclined to work hard. If Donna is late with her report and is reprimanded, she is likely to work harder the next time to avoid the negative consequence.

According to Thorndike (1913), the basic assumption underlying conditioning theory is simple: people tend to repeat those behaviours that lead to desirable consequences and avoid those that lead to negative results. Conditioning theory underlies many of the behaviours managers and teachers use in an attempt to motivate people and teach them to behave in certain ways. Today, Skinner's principles of operant conditioning are commonly applied in organisational settings to help change many types of human behaviour: drug addicts, students with learning disabilities, smokers, sex offenders and phobics, as well as employees.

Self-management of contingencies

It is possible for a person to manage his or her own contingencies. For example, one principle of time management has evolved from the premise that a person will complete 'have to' tasks quite expediently if the reward (positive reinforcement) is engaging in tasks that are more creative, enjoyable or satisfying. The psychologist, Premack (1959), formalised this self-management strategy of pairing tasks or events.

Premack principle
The pairing of disagreeable tasks with enjoyable tasks or events to hasten their completion.

The **Premack principle** is based on the finding that, when tasks are paired, the more probable (more pleasurable) behaviour will tend to reinforce or bring about the less probable behaviour. For example, complete the report, then play football or tennis. Well-organised students and workers may find they have adopted the Premack principle without even knowing it had a name. If you have not used it for self-management, try it.

Social learning theory

Behaviourist psychologists believe that operant conditioning or reinforcement theory is the most valid explanation for how people learn. However, many researchers disagree with Skinner's (1971) contentions that humankind is simply an instrument of society, and that people are passively subject to shaping by environmental events and by those in control.

Unwilling to accept the fact that reinforcement alone is the answer, Bandura (1974, 1977) and others have researched the social learning aspects of human development. **Social learning theory** is based on the process of observational learning through modelling and imitation. It holds that, rather than learning exclusively through reinforcement and the shaping of successive approximations towards a desired behaviour, we acquire much behaviour simply through imitation. Imitation is especially strong when the learner identifies with and desires to be like the role model or mentor. Imitators are in conscious control of whether or not to act like the model. As one application, research has found that the success of corporate ethics programmes is most strongly linked to top management's commitment to ethical behaviour – employees will model what they see in leaders.

social learning theory
The belief that we learn many behaviours by observing and imitating others.

anticipatory control
Bandura's suggestion that people are capable of choosing how they will respond in various situations.

Bandura (1974) suggests that people are capable of **anticipatory control** – of choosing how they will respond in various situations. Because people are capable of observing the effects of their behaviours, they can anticipate consequences across a variety of circumstances. For example, George's boss may say something in a meeting that angers him. George can choose whether or not to express his anger publicly. He is capable of anticipating his boss's response, based on his experiences with the boss and others in authority positions. He may let it pass based on anticipatory self-control.

Even though the organisational world acts on them, adults at work still choose what situations to get involved in and how to act in them to produce a desired outcome. We learn through social observation to expect that certain socially desirable behaviours will be reinforced, and we learn the value of the reinforcer. While social learning theory acknowledges and builds on many principles of reinforcement, it moves closer to the concept of learning cognitively through insight and self-discovery.

The cognitive view: new patterns of thought

The perceptual-cognitive view of learning focuses on what happens within the individual: motives, feelings, attitudes, memory and cognition (thought). Sensory mechanisms are of primary importance in the key cognitive activity, which is observation based. Through speech and knowledge of language, humans form abstract concepts for organising perceptions and manipulating ideas. Thus, **cognitive learning** involves selective interpretation of perceptual data organised into new patterns of thoughts and relationships. A manager who asks a subordinate if he has a few minutes to talk illustrates this kind of learning. The latter says, 'Well,... OK [voice dropping].' Although the words indicate consent, the boss notices a look of frustration and reads into the pause and tone of voice a strong unwillingness. The boss's ability to observe multiple stimuli and to interpret the non-verbal along with the verbal communication can be learned through training and experience.

cognitive learning
Selective interpretation of perceptual data organised into new patterns of thoughts and relationships.

Human beings are capable of rearranging thought patterns into new configurations, or gestalts. **Gestalt** is a German word meaning 'shape, configuration or the arrangement of relationships in a total situation.' Patterns of concepts and relationships may occur suddenly, through insight, or they may evolve gradually as elements are linked together with new data.

gestalt
A German word meaning 'shape, configuration or the arrangement of relationships in a total situation'.

Insight

Often known as the Eureka! ('I've found it!') or aha! experience, **insight** is best described as the sudden discovery of the answer to a problem. We achieve insight into a situation, relationship or problem when we suddenly grasp an idea or see a relationship that helps us to understand the situation better or solve the problem. Insight often comes while doing something and observing what happens.

insight
The sudden discovery of the answer to a problem.

Kohler (1925) presented the first experimental evidence on insight in the 1920s, when he demonstrated the results of his work with a chimpanzee named Sultan. The turning point in Kohler's research occurred when he enclosed Sultan and a short stick inside a barred cage, outside of which he placed a longer stick and a banana – both too far away for Sultan to reach.

Sultan first picked up the short stick and attempted to rake in the banana. However, the elusive banana remained beyond the chimp's extended reach. Unable to obtain results, Sultan sat cowering in the cage, gazing at the objects around him. Suddenly he jumped up and reached for the short stick. With it he raked in the long stick, then he used the long stick to rake in the banana. Eureka! The chimp had discovered a solution. Today we know that two of the learning processes involved in the phenomenon of insight are discrimination and generalisation.

Discrimination

Sometimes called differentiation, **discrimination** is the process by which universal or previously unstructured elements are placed into more specific structures. People learn to read by discriminating among symbols – first individual letters, then groupings of letters (words), and finally meaningful groupings of letters separated by spaces and punctuation. Discrimination also occurs when three cars are seen as a Mercedes, a Volkswagen and a Porsche, or considered in terms of their components: tyres, engines, doors, seats. Managers discriminate a general concept such as 'organisation' into people, positions, structures, policies, power, leadership, and so on (Bloisi *et al.*, 2003).

discrimination
The process by which universal or previously unstructured elements are placed into more specific structures.

Generalisation

When concepts, functions, objects and events are grouped into categories, generalisation is at work. **Generalisation** is the means through which we transfer learning from one situation to another as well as categorise information. Whereas discrimination breaks down the general into the specific, generalisation unites previously separate elements into meaningful universal themes or clusters. Generalisation helps people map out and programme their memories so that not every event has to be experienced as something totally new.

generalisation
The means through which we transfer learning from one situation to another, as well as categorise information.

Managers generalise when they categorise an organisational behaviour problem as one of communication, for example, or of conflict, motivation, job design or leadership. Then they differentiate its possible causes and probable solutions. They remember the consequences of attempted actions and apply that learning when diagnosing current problems and deciding how they will act. The ability to discriminate, generalise and develop insight is vital to conceptual skill, which is critically important for successful managers, accountants, analysts, scientists and other knowledge workers.

Because insight is a human resource, a manager may draw others into a group problem-solving process. An idea offered by Simon may trigger a thought by Sheila, which prompts a creative suggestion from Susan. One insight tends to generate another in the search for an effective group solution.

How do people differ in how they learn?

One of the most important abilities an individual can possess is the ability to learn. A manager's long-term success depends more on the ability to learn than on the mastery of specific skills or technical knowledge. However, people learn in different ways. We now discuss two ways of differentiating how people learn: one based on behavioural styles, the other on brain dominance.

Experiential learning styles

What is now a research classic by Kolb (1976) indicates that managers favour a style of learning that differs from that of many other professionals. Managers learn most readily from direct experience and by actively testing the implications of concepts to new situations. Kolb's findings are based on a model of learning that involves four different abilities; these combine to form four distinct styles.

Kolb's experiential learning model distinguishes two primary dimensions of the learning process. If we visualise his model in the form of a compass, one dimension ranges from north (the concrete experiencing of events) to south (abstract conceptualisation of ideas). The other dimension extends from west (active experimentation or testing) to east (reflective observations).

These two dimensions are combined to suggest four main learning abilities or processes. As shown in Exhibit 7-1, a complete pattern of learning flows in a circular direction. Beginning at the top: (1) the learner becomes actively involved in new concrete experiences, and (2) through reflective observation examines these experiences from different perspectives (3) to form abstract concepts and generalisations, which (4) lead to theories or assumptions that can be used for active experimentation in problem-solving and decision-making.

Most people become highly skilled at one or two processes rather than all four. When two adjacent processes are emphasised, a dominant learning style emerges. The four characteristics identified in Exhibit 7-1 – divergence, assimilation, convergence and accommodation – represent distinct personal learning styles.

The diverger

Divergers learn best by reflecting on specific experiences and drawing new inferences. The diverger tends to be highly imaginative, excels at brainstorming and likes involvement in the generation of creative ideas. Divergers have an uncanny ability to view concrete situations from many perspectives. Academically, such learners are often interested in the liberal arts, humanities and fine arts. Human resource managers are often divergers.

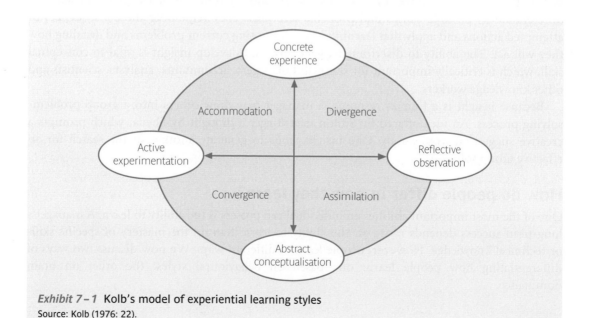

Exhibit 7–1 Kolb's model of experiential learning styles
Source: Kolb (1976: 22).

The assimilator

With their capability to combine reflective observation and abstract conceptualisation, assimilators are good at creating theoretical models. Inductive reasoning is the forte that permits integrating diverse observations into a coherent explanation. Dealing with abstract ideas is the assimilator's domain, more so than seeking practical applications or working with people. Individuals who adopt this learning style are attracted to basic research; in business, you may find them staffing corporate research and planning departments.

The converger

Convergers use abstract concepts as a basis for active experimentation. They focus on specific problems, looking for answers and solutions. Like the assimilator, the converger prefers working with ideas and specific tasks to working with people. Convergers tend to do well in the physical sciences and engineering.

The accommodator

This style focuses on doing. The accommodator's domain is active experimentation and the carrying out of plans that lead to real experiences. Such people are risk takers, able to adapt quickly to new situations. If a theory does not fit the situation, the accommodator discards the concept and works from the facts. Although at ease with people, accommodators tend to be impatient and assertive. Accommodation is often the dominant style of individuals trained for the business world, especially those who gravitate towards action-orientated management or sales jobs.

The need to combine skills and styles

Kolb's research finds that managers tend to be orientated towards learning by active experimentation and concrete experience. Many managers are accommodators. By contrast, many business school faculties tend to be strong on reflective observation and abstract conceptualisation. This makes them assimilators. Because accommodator managers tend to make fewer inferences from data and are less consistent in their actions than assimilators, both learning styles are necessary within organisations. To blend styles within an organisation, Kolb (1976) offers two recommendations.

First, managers and organisations should value and consciously seek learning from experience by budgeting time for the learning process. Second, managers and organisations should value and include those with different learning styles and perspectives. Action-orientated people should be combined with those who are reflective, and those involved in concrete experience should be joined with those who are analytical. Learning can be enhanced when style differences are valued, just as it can by integrating people from different cultures and ethnic backgrounds. (To increase your own awareness of learning style preferences and the need to develop complementary abilities, complete the 'Individual task' at the end of this chapter.)

Honey and Mumford (1992) built on Kolb's theory and defined four major categories of learning. As can be see from Exhibit 7-2, these correspond with Kolb's learning styles.

Honey and Mumford (1992) describe the people strong in the four styles of reflector, theorist, pragmatist and activist as follows.

Reflector

Prefers to stand back and think about experiences and observe them from many different perspectives. These people will collect data, analyse it and look at all angles before coming to a decision. They tend to be cautious and thoughtful, and when they act it is as part of the wider picture.

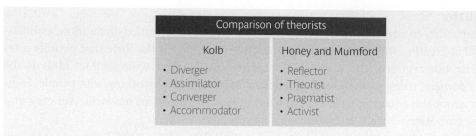

Comparison of theorists	
Kolb	**Honey and Mumford**
• Diverger	• Reflector
• Assimilator	• Theorist
• Converger	• Pragmatist
• Accommodator	• Activist

Exhibit 7-2 Comparison of Kolb and Honey and Mumford's learning styles

Theorist

Thinks problems through in a logical step-by-step sequence. These people assimilate disparate facts into a coherent theory. They tend to be perfectionists and prefer logic and rationality to reach a decision.

Pragmatist

Keen to try out new ideas, theories and techniques to find out if they work in practice. These people respond to problems and opportunities as a challenge. They tend to be impatient and will act quickly to try out new things that interest them.

Activist

Activists involve themselves in new experiences. They are open minded and tend to be enthusiastic about anything new. They tend to act first and consider the consequences later. They move quickly from one activity to another, and are often considered outgoing and gregarious.

The concept of learning styles is important as it helps us plan how different people are likely to respond to training programmes. This is illustrated in Exhibit 7-3.

Depending on the preferred style of the individual they will start at different points in the learning cycle. For example, a salesperson may start with experience and accompany a person

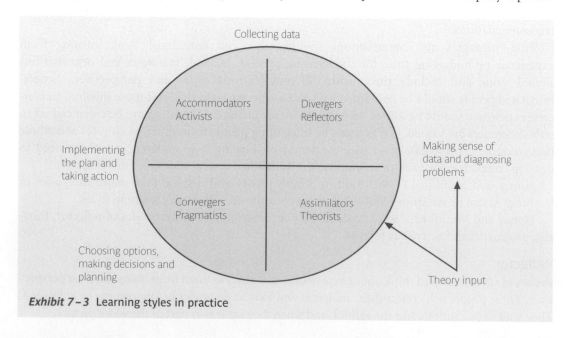

Exhibit 7-3 Learning styles in practice

making a sale; this will involve collecting data. Once they have made a sales call they may reflect on it and think about: What went well? What didn't go well? The next stage would be referring to theory either as directed by their trainer or from their own deliberations. They would then move on to planning the new behaviour: How will they make the sale next time? From here it moves back to experience. The learning cycle is continuous and as new experiences are tried out, so they are reflected on, refined and re-evaluated.

An understanding of learning styles can be really helpful for managers designing training programmes, although this is not the only explanation for differences in learning, as can be seen from studies of the two hemispheres of learning.

Two hemispheres of learning

Another explanation of differences in learning is based on brain-hemisphere dominance. Neurologists and psychologists have long known that the left hemisphere of the brain controls movements on the right-hand side of the body, and vice versa. Ornstein (1973) and others have carried this further by suggesting that our dominant brain hemisphere may play a significant role in how we learn.

The linear/systematic left

The brain's left hemisphere assimilates information in ordered, systematic ways. The process of analysis and planning (usually a central theme of the business school curriculum) is linear in structure. Accounting systems and management-science quantitative models are based on rational logic. Their underlying assumption is that if data are channelled into a formula or model, a working solution can be found.

The left hemisphere of the brain handles quantification and written language. Many organisational activities are well served by predictability and logic. In stable environments, structured, planned behaviour is likely to be effective. However, organisations do not survive and grow without creativity and change.

The holistic/relational right

Mintzberg (1976) suggests that, when it comes to running organisations, planning occurs on the left side, managing on the right. He writes, 'it may be that management researchers have been looking for the key to management in the lightness of logical analysis whereas perhaps it has always been lost in the darkness of intuition'. In drawing insights from observing managers' behaviours, Mintzberg adds, 'effective managers seem to revel in ambiguity; in complex, mysterious systems with relatively little order'.

The world of the right-hemisphere-dominant manager involves holistic, simultaneous, creative learning. In addition, it emphasises learning from face-to-face verbal exchanges rather than from written reports. Through verbal communication, managers can interpret non-verbal cues and act simultaneously on real-time data. Synthesis of soft data – impressions, feelings, intuition – provides the basis for acting more than hard-data analysis does.

Hunches and judgement are mental processes from which insights and new possibilities spring forth. With brief time sequences for processing information, action – not reflection – is more the executive norm. Orderly agendas are atypical in a world beset with interruptions and unplanned activities.

In an article on why and how to develop right-hemisphere intuitive powers, Agor (1984) cited the experiences of a number of executives who relied heavily on intuitive decisions.

Stop and reflect

Looking at the table below, rank in order of importance the skills that you think are necessary for an HR manager.

Then, looking at the right-hand column and using a scale of 1 to 5, where would you rate each skill?

	Order of importance				
	I am good at this			I need to improve	
Verbal communication	1	2	3	4	5
Managing time and stress	1	2	3	4	5
Managing individual decisions	1	2	3	4	5
Recognising, defining and solving problems	1	2	3	4	5
Motivating and influencing others	1	2	3	4	5
Delegating	1	2	3	4	5
Setting goals and articulating a vision	1	2	3	4	5
Self-awareness	1	2	3	4	5
Team building	1	2	3	4	5
Managing conflict	1	2	3	4	5

Lifelong learning

Both the Kolb and Honey and Mumford models of learning styles and the notion of brain-hemisphere specialisation emphasise the ongoing nature of individual learning. Life is a series of learning episodes and processes. Those who are managers will find that their jobs involve knowing both how to learn themselves and how to influence the learning of others.

Now that you are familiar with the different ways of learning, you can probably see for yourself why no one theory works all the time across all situations. Applied behaviour modification principles, for example, are best used in situations in which reinforcing environmental consequences can be structured. Those who learn best through direct experience are not likely to become reflective/conceptual learners. Each approach and style has its essential place in organisations.

Designing effective training programmes

To be effective, training needs to follow a systematic process, as can be seen in Exhibit 7-4.

- **Assessing needs** identifies the type of training needed; this may be through an organisational analysis, a person analysis or a task analysis.
- **Trainee acceptance** involves the employee accepting the need for training, and having the motivation and basic skills to be able to master the training content.
- **Learning environment** refers to identifying whether the factors are available to enable learning to occur. This will identify the learning aims and objectives to be achieved, the materials available, feedback, evaluation processes and other administrative processes.
- **Training methods** identify how the training will take place, such as on or off the job. The training method needs to be appropriate for the learning environment.

Changing attitudes in a business culture that is often endemically corrupt is an ongoing campaign and a challenge for Mexico City's Business School

Few business schools have as clear or as distinct a mission as Mexico City's Ipade. Part of the Panamerican University, it provides senior executives with training to US standards, but has always had a broader agenda: aiming to make the nation competitive on a global level and instilling ethics in a business culture that is often endemically corrupt.

As head of Ipade's marketing department, Mr Gutierrez has already begun promoting the school differently. He is working on raising its media profile, encouraging faculty to participate in conferences outside the traditional business arena. The primary aim is to demonstrate the data's relevance to businesses.

'Often the client of a researcher is another researcher, and the client of an academic is another academic,' Mr Gutierrez says. 'For the businessman, what matters is: "What am I going to do [to find solutions] with marketing or finance or control or accounting?" It's for that reason that they come to Ipade. We are very close to our clients.'

This is in line with the mission of the school, which trains mostly managers and executives, and graduates approximately 70 MBA students per year.

The MBA course was the last to be added, and the training of higher executives is a clear priority. 'Our mission isn't to sell more, it's to sell better. It's not to train lots of people, it's to train them well,' Mr Gutierrez says. 'It's not informative, it's formative, designed to sustain enthusiasm.'

Within Mexico's largest companies, 20 to 25 per cent of chief executives report having taken a course at Ipade.

Ipade sees the rounded development of executives as part of its mission. 'We look for more human development of executives than other business schools, to develop them as a whole person, with integral training,' Mr Gutierrez says, proposing more supplementary seminars in music and arts appreciation.

Within his own marketing classes, Mr Gutierrez has discussed the ethics of raising the price of umbrellas during rain storms or that of cold drinks during heatwaves. 'When students say "It's supply and demand", I ask them: "Are the laws of supply and demand and its results ethical?" and that makes students freeze.'

The national election in 2000 brought new business opportunities and ethical challenges. While President Vicente Fox promised to increase tax collections, open the energy sector to private investment and make social spending more effective, such change has been elusive.

He pledged to combat corruption in all its forms, hiring Ipade graduates to help him, but principled stances are not always easy when doing business in Mexico.

Much of the culture of doing business is unchanged and corruption is considered the oil that keeps the wheels moving.

Mr Gutierrez believes Ipade has a role to play in bringing change to Mexican business culture and in helping Mexico become an entry point for doing business in the rest of Latin America.

Along with other schools, Ipade is contributing case studies to a database at the Latin American Research Center at Harvard Business School. 'Even if a company doesn't export, we can learn from the cases and experience of other companies in other nations,' he says.

▶ The school is also active in promoting small and medium-sized businesses, especially as part of the US–Mexico Partnership for Prosperity, which promotes the economic development of those rural areas in Mexico where there is a high proportion of Mexican migration to the USA.

Source: adapted from Sara Silver, in the *Financial Times*, 22 September 2003, p. 16.
Reproduced with permission of the *Financial Times*.

Discussion questions

1 This example refers to education rather than training. What are the differences between them?

2 Ethics is seen as an important part of the education programme. Do you think ethical behaviour can be taught?

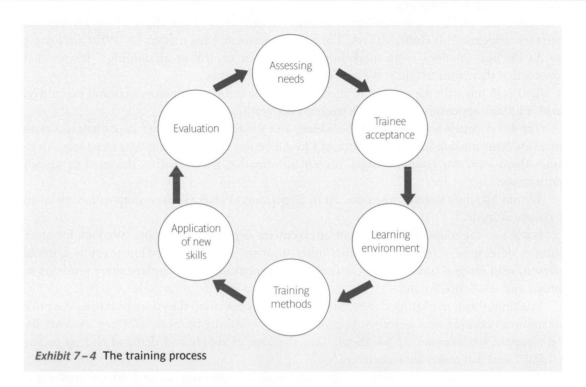

Exhibit 7 – 4 The training process

- **Application of new skills** ensures that trained employees are able to apply their new skills to the job, and should involve self-management strategies and peer and management support.

- **Evaluation** determines whether training has achieved its objectives of changed behaviour and improved performance.

Steps in training

The needs analysis

The needs analysis identifies the specific skills required for performance and productivity, as can be seen in Exhibit 7-5.

The needs analysis looks at the organisation and identifies reasons that could affect the performance of the organisation. The next step is to identify whether training is the most appropriate solution for the organisation. This would involve determining the appropriateness of

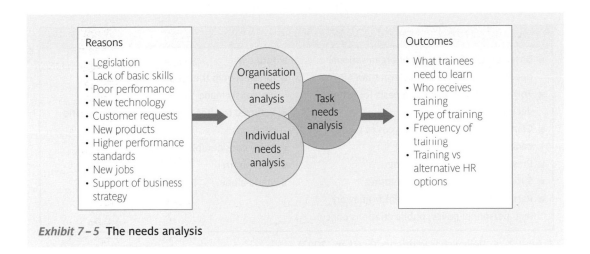

Exhibit 7–5 The needs analysis

training in relation to the organisation's business strategy, the financial and physical resources available and the support for training from both managers and employees.

The individual needs analysis helps to identify:

■ current performance against desired performance, and the gaps in ability, skills and knowledge

■ whether poor performance is a result of lack of knowledge, skill ability, or a motivational or work design problem

■ who it is that needs training

■ the readiness of the employee to accept training, as resistance may mean training interventions are ineffective.

The task analysis includes identifying the elements that make up the task, in terms of the knowledge, skill and behaviours that need to be emphasised in the training process.

Training is expensive, therefore managers need to ensure that they have fully assessed the situation to establish whether training is the answer. Once they have decided on a training strategy then training policies are the next stage.

Training policies

The training policy should be linked to the organisation's strategy and can have the characteristics demonstrated by Hackett (2003) in Exhibit 7-6.

Whether the training policy is implicit or explicit, most organisations have an underlying philosophy or belief about the value of training and will decide what type of training will be implemented, to whom, and where the training will be undertaken. This may also be in response to government initiatives such as development of a national skills base through Learning and Skills Councils (LSCs), which are responsible for achieving national training targets, through initiatives such as Investors In People (IIP) or National Vocational Qualifications (NVQs).

National Vocational Qualifications (NVQs)

National Vocational Qualifications (NVQs) were developed from a government initiative dating from 1985, as an attempt to rationalise and co-ordinate qualifications, which would

Either	Or
■ Based on careful analysis of organisational needs, best practice and relevant law ■ Formally written down as a basis for future decisions ■ Communicated to all employees to guide decision-making ■ Prescriptive and all embracing ■ Supported by operating procedures ■ Part of an internally consistent framework (e.g. personnel policy, public relations policy)	■ Intuitive ■ Inferred from the pattern of decisions previously made ■ Referred to after the event to justify specific decisions ■ Allow considerable discretion ■ Unsupported ■ Stand-alone

Exhibit 7–6 Policy characteristics (Hackett, 2003)

enable employers to have a greater understanding of the levels of qualifications and make them more skills-relevant. By 1999 a framework of over 800 NVQs had been developed covering 500 occupations. This was further developed by offering General National Vocational Qualifications (GNVQs), which covered general occupational areas rather than specific industry skills. This enabled them to be delivered in schools and colleges as part of the curriculum. **NVQs** are offered over five performance levels, which can be seen in Exhibit 7-7. The qualifications and standards are monitored by the Qualifications and Curriculum Authority (QCA).

NVQs
National Vocational Qualifications, used to measure competence in specific skills in the workplace.

NVQs focus on competencies, which is the ability to do something, rather than broader-based knowledge or behaviours. This means that training can be carried out in the workplace rather than traditional education establishments. Many large employers implement NVQs in liaison with their industry lead body or professional association. This means that the role of training has become more integrated into organisational life, with employees at different levels working towards different levels of NVQs, as well as supervisors and managers gaining training qualifications to enable them to assess candidates. This also links into National Learning Targets.

National Learning Targets

National Learning Targets
Targets set by the government to increase the achievement of skills both at school and in the workplace.

The **National Learning Targets** are one way of measuring the progress of the Department for Education and Skills (DfES). They help focus efforts to increase participation and achievement in both school and workplace learning.

The aim is to ensure that all young people gain the necessary abilities for a secure foundation for lifelong learning. There is a particular focus on improving literacy and numeracy skills in primary schools and pupil achievement in secondary schools.

The Targets also aim to develop a general commitment to lifelong learning, and to encourage employers to invest in the training and development of their employees.

Level	Performance
1	Competence that involves the application of knowledge and skills in the performance of a range of varied work activities, most of which may be routine and predictable
2	Competence that involves the application of knowledge and skills in a significant range of varied work activities, performed in a variety of contexts. Some of the activities are complex or non-routine, and there is some individual responsibility or autonomy. Collaboration with others, perhaps through membership of a work group or team, may often be a requirement
3	Competence that involves the application of knowledge and skills in a broad range of varied work activities performed in a wide variety of contexts, most of which are complex and non-routine. There is considerable responsibility and autonomy, and control or guidance of others is often required
4	Competence that involves the application of knowledge and skills in a broad range of complex, technical or professional work activities performed in a wide variety of contexts and with a substantial degree of personal responsibility and autonomy. Responsibility for the work of others and the allocation of resources is often present
5	Competence that involves the application of skills and a significant range of fundamental principles across a wide and often unpredictable variety of contexts. Very substantial personal autonomy and often significant responsibility for the work of others and for the allocation of substantial resources feature strongly, as do personal accountabilities for analysis and diagnosis, design, planning, execution and evaluation

Exhibit 7–7 Levels of NVQ performance
Source: QCA's *Data News* (May 1998).

The Learning and Skills Council

The Learning and Skills Council (LSC) has been in place since March 2001. It replaced the training functions of Training and Enterprise Councils (TECs) and the funding responsibilities of the Further Education Funding Councils (FEFCs) within England.

It brings a new coherence to all post-16 education and training, excluding higher education. The LSC is governed by a National Council, which is advised by two statutory committees (one covering adult learning and one covering young people), and operates through 47 local offices.

The Learning and Skills Council has an annual budget of around £6bn and the responsibility for funding around five million learners each year in England.

The Learning and Skills Council is responsible for the funding, planning and quality assurance of further education, school sixth form, work-based training for young people, workforce development, adult and community learning, information, advice and guidance for adult learners, and education business links.

The role of the Learning and Skills Council is to:

■ assess national learning and skills needs, and advise the government on the National Learning Targets

■ develop plans and strategies to meet the National Learning Targets

- set a clear agenda for workforce development, working with business, trades unions and Sector Skills Councils (SSCs)
- tackle adults' poor basic skills, accessibility of learning for the socially disadvantaged and those with learning difficulties, and promote equal opportunities
- develop national partnerships to understand needs and agree strategies for working together
- allocate budgets to the local Learning and Skills Councils.

Local Learning and Skills Councils

Local Learning and Skills Councils are responsible for annual budgets of £100m and for the funding of over 100,000 local learners. Their role is to ensure that the needs of local communities, businesses and individuals are met through Learning and Skills Council-funded provision and, for delivering national priorities at local level, to allocate Learning and Skills Council funding within a national framework with local flexibility, and deploy significant local discretionary budgets including funds to:

- increase the quality of local provision and support local initiatives that otherwise would not attract mainstream funding
- develop local workforce development plans that direct local action to encourage employers and small firms to invest in developing their workforce, and promote business benefits to work with SSCs in the development of the sector workforce development plan
- work closely with Regional Development Agencies (RDAs), local authorities, learning partnerships, the Connexions service, Small Business Service (formerly Business Links), University for Industry (UFI) and others to ensure coherent action is taken to achieve goals.

National committees

The Learning and Skills Council is advised by two national committees: the Young People's Committee and the Adult Learning Committee.

The Young People's Committee is responsible for advising the national council on the best means of achieving the National Learning Targets for young people. This includes strategies for increased participation from young people to remain in education until the age of 19. The committee also works alongside the Connexions service (formerly the Careers Service) to improve employability and personal development.

The Adult Learning Committee is responsible for advising the Learning and Skills Council on achieving National Learning Targets for adults, and for raising attainment and improving basic skills among adults. The Committee also works closely with the Small Business Service to encourage businesses to invest in their workforce.

Identifying training needs

As stated earlier, training is the bridge that fills the gap between where an individual is and where the organisation wants them to be. To identify such gaps, Boydell and Leary (2002) suggest that the organisation needs to identify three levels of performance, which are:

Level 1   **implementing** – bridging the gap between present and desired performance, measured against existing standards

Level 2   **improving** – to enable a continual raising of standards

Level 3   **innovating** – doing new and better things to enable change and a continuous learning organisation.

A good place to start is by examining job descriptions and job specifications, which are discussed in Chapter 3, along with techniques for analysis. These can then lead into a training specification, which, according to the Manpower Services Commission (MSC, 1981) is a 'detailed statement of what a trainee needs to learn, based on a comparison between the job specification and the individual's present level of competence'. This can be identified through comparison with expected performance standards or through the appraisal system, which is discussed in Chapter 8.

Determining training objectives

Reid and Barrington (1999) suggest that the first step in implementing training is to identify training objectives. Once the objectives have been established the next step is to identify how best to achieve them, select a strategy, then plan, implement and evaluate the training. The training objectives should identify the learning or behavioural objectives to be achieved. It is not enough just to identify the training; this must be linked to the expected change in behaviour.

This means that, in compiling the objectives, thought needs to be given as to how they will be measured, under what type of conditions and to what standard.

Determining the training strategy

Once the training objectives have been established, the type of training needs to be identified. This will usually fall into the following main categories:

- on-the-job training
- in-house programmes
- external courses
- external bespoke programmes
- self-managed learning.

On-the-job training

This might involve 'sitting next to Nellie', where a new employee is trained by an existing employee. This often means that training is not regulated and that bad habits are passed on as well as good ones. Alternatively, on-the-job training can include detailed training procedures, in line with Modern Apprenticeship schemes. On-the-job training accounts for half of all training carried out in organisations. The success of such schemes depends on:

'sitting next to Nellie'
A method of training where a trainee learns new skills by copying a more experienced worker.

- the competence of the trainers, not only in the job skills but also their training skills
- the recognition of the need for trained trainers
- adequate preparation of structured training sessions
- health and safety issues being adequately incorporated into the sessions
- regular monitoring and evaluation of performance against targets.

In-house programmes

In-house training programmes are run by the organisation. These may be provided to enhance understanding of specific topics or as development for future managers. Many organisations also run competence-based programmes, such as NVQs, that are specifically designed for their organisation. The advantage of in-house programmes is that they can be designed solely to meet organisational needs and can be delivered at a time convenient to the employer. Problems with in-house training can involve the initial cost of suitable resources and the development of trainers. There is also the need for support from management to allow employees time for training.

External courses

There are many further and higher education colleges that offer a variety of courses, often vocationally related. The advantages of external courses are that they allow participants to mix with people from other organisations and share ideas. As they are delivered outside the organisation they do not involve internal resources such as in-house specialist staff or rooms and equipment. Often, employees are able to work towards qualifications that can enhance their own development and career prospects. As with all training, if the company is prepared to allow employees to attend a course, it also needs to ensure that they are given time to study.

External bespoke courses

Many training organisations will offer tailor-made programmes for organisations. Some of these courses may also be externally recognised by examination or professional associations. Before embarking on such a scheme, managers need to ensure that the course:

- is organised by people qualified to deliver such a course
- meets the organisational objectives
- meets a training need that can be measured and assessed
- has a cost that is related to the expected benefits
- is being run by a training organisation that can provide references from other satisfied organisations.

Self-managed learning

Self-managed learning needs to be part of the overall organisational strategy. To be effective, the following conditions need to be present:

- learning must be seen to be valued by the organisation
- opportunities are made available for employees to learn through their work
- individual appraisal helps to identify development opportunities, which are then supported by the organisation
- managers, coaches, mentors and colleagues also provide assistance for the development of learning.

Reid and Barrington (1999) suggest that:

> The culture of a learning organisation recognises that any learning is beneficial to the development of the whole person, and that the gain would ultimately be fed back to the organisation in the form of [the] increased maturity and learning capacity of its personnel.

As can be seen from the 'Managing diversity' box, training needs to reflect the need of the people in the organisation and it is the organisation who can help direct employees to achieve new skills when in the past they may not have thought this possible.

Training techniques can take several different forms and managers need to ensure that they constantly evaluate their training objectives, policies and practices.

Evaluation of training

Training is about improving performance, and therefore training programmes need to be measured to ensure that this is what they have done. Training evaluation should look at four basic categories.

1 **Reaction** – the trainee's views on the programme. Did they find it useful? Was it worthwhile?

2 **Learning** – have they learned the skills they were supposed to learn? Will they now be able to do their job better?

3 **Behaviour** – has this now changed due to the training programme? Are they able to work more effectively with colleagues and customers?

4 **Results** – are the trainees now more productive? Has performance improved? Is it of better quality?

Managers who fail to evaluate training will never know if the training has been effective. As has been said before, training is expensive and managers need to know that they are getting a return on their investment.

Nearly three million UK workers may be affected by dyslexia, but there is still widespread ignorance about the condition; what are employers doing to break down the barriers?

His teachers considered him slow, unsociable and a dreamer, and he apparently didn't learn to read until he was eight or nine. Yet Albert Einstein went on to make some of the most important scientific discoveries of the twentieth century – even though it is widely believed that he was dyslexic.

He is certainly not alone. The list of successful dyslexics includes the likes of children's author Hans Christian Andersen, entrepreneur Sir Richard Branson and actor Tom Cruise.

The British Dyslexia Association (BDA) estimates that between 4 and 10 per cent of the population is dyslexic and, according to a recent report by the TUC, *Dyslexia in the Workplace*, up to 2.9 million workers may be affected. Nevertheless, the report claims that many employers do not appreciate the link between dyslexia and common performance problems. As a result they often judge dyslexic employees unfairly, even though the condition is recognised as a disability under the Disability Discrimination Act, which since October 2004 has covered all employers, regardless of size.

While most people have heard of dyslexia, there are misconceptions about what it entails. This became apparent to Aaron Tyler, a machine supervisor at Konica Minolta, when he first told his colleagues he had been diagnosed as dyslexic.

The BDA describes dyslexia as a 'combination of abilities and difficulties' – the key word here being 'abilities'. Aside from often having high IQs, dyslexics can be very creative and good at practical tasks, while also showing strengths in areas such as problem-solving, innovation and lateral thinking. Carol Youngs, policy and communications director at the BDA, says dyslexic

managing diversity

people can often see the bigger picture, even though they may not be as good at certain processes.

But if dyslexia has not been diagnosed, or if an employee is afraid to disclose their problems, then all too often any resulting poor performance is dealt with as a disciplinary matter. 'There are people who don't know they are dyslexic and are struggling. Then there are those who are trying to hide their condition because of fear they will lose their job. We need to break down both of these areas,' explains Shirley Cramer, chief executive of the Dyslexia Institute.

Peter Purton, policy officer at the TUC, agrees. He says that if employers are to benefit from the many strengths that dyslexic people can offer, they need to become more knowledgeable about the condition and take steps to harness individuals' strengths, rather than penalise them for their weaknesses. With the right support, it is possible for dyslexic people to develop strategies and alternative methods to overcome what weaknesses they do have.

Of course, the common fear among many employers, especially smaller ones, is that additional support will cost them money. But this is not necessarily the case. Kirsten Knight, a producer at BBC Radio 4, explains that some of her support will be funded by Access to Work, which she describes as the 'best piece of hidden disability support the government provides'.

Peter Purton agrees it is a key initiative that needs to be more powerfully promoted. Administered by JobCentre Plus, Access to Work can provide a grant of between 80 and 100 per cent towards any approved extra employment costs that result from a person's disability.

With or without external funding, many of the adjustments employers can make do not need to be costly. According to specialist training company Dyslexia Works, supporting a dyslexic employee may mean as little as offering some flexibility in working environment and practices – and small things can make a difference. For example, providing information on coloured paper will enable some dyslexic people to read it more easily.

Judy Greevy, head of diversity and corporate responsibility at Centrica, says that about 18 months ago the company became aware that it needed to do more around the issue of dyslexia. It now provides guidance on the subject as part of the general information made available for managers.

Centrica is also looking to put in place an e-learning package on diversity for all staff, which uses dyslexia as an example. Greevy explains that this will help people to move away from the idea that disabilities involve only physical or mobility issues.

Hampshire Constabulary, meanwhile, is delivering awareness training for one particular group of managers who have dyslexic staff reporting to them.

The plan is to ensure that all line managers and tutor constables eventually go through this training. Recruitment manager Valerie King says the Constabulary is also working hard to ensure that dyslexic applicants are treated fairly during the recruitment process. The organisation has forged links with a local further education college to help people with dyslexia or other learning difficulties prepare for their police entry assessments – for which they are also given extra time.

One employee who has particularly benefited from Hampshire's positive approach is Sarah McCabe, a recruiting assistant in the personnel department. She didn't reveal she was dyslexic until two weeks into the job because she was afraid of what the reaction would be. But McCabe explains that her colleagues responded positively and are more than willing to help her with things like emails and letters.

'If someone had told me a few years ago that I would be working in recruitment administration, I would have laughed,' she says. 'Now I think, if I can do this, what else can I do?'

Source: Catherine Edwards, *People Management*, 24 March 2005, p. 38.
Reproduced with permission of *People Management*.

Discussion questions

1 How can training programmes meet the needs of dyslexic employees?

2 Why is diversity an important issue when developing education and training programmes?

The learning organisation

Learning organisations, according to Senge *et al.* (1995), are organisations that focus energy and resources on learning from mistakes as well as opportunity seeking. They are likely to 'learn faster than the competition, change before they're forced to, and always try to marry personal and financial performance'. Senge has popularised the concept of the learning organisation. A learning organisation develops tools and methods to analyse, change and re-evaluate its organisational systems so that employees respond more effectively and quicker to the same work-related stimulus than they did in the past, and to novel stimuli almost as quickly.

learning organisation

A deliberate effort by organisational members to develop models, tools and techniques for their organisation to change and grow faster than competitors.

One successful learning organisation, Royal Dutch Shell, became committed to systematising learning when its research into older companies found that learning was their key to survival. Christensen and Overdorf (2000) suggest that the alternative is to be plagued with 'learning disabilities', which retard adaptiveness to change and can be fatal, causing organisations to prematurely shorten their life span. Like individuals, organisations that do not know how to learn to maximise the effectiveness of appropriate capabilities may survive but never live up to their potential. Those firms that become effective learners are the ones most likely to succeed in increasingly turbulent, competitive global markets.

Garvin (1993) suggests that a learning organisation is skilled at creating, acquiring and transferring knowledge, and at modifying its behaviour to reflect new knowledge and insight. Below are examples of how two managers view the power of learning within their organisations.

- Ron Hutchinson, vice president of customer service for Harley-Davidson Motor Company, Inc., says: 'To be effective long term, we must have an organisation in place that understands what caused prior mistakes and failures – and most importantly what caused successes. Then, we need to know how we can inculcate the successes and inculcate the preventive measures to avoid additional failures.'

- Human resources manager Laura Gilbert says her Educational Computing Company has become 'a place that has a proactive, creative approach to the unknown, encouraging individuals to express their feelings, and using intelligence and imagination instead of just skills and authority to find new ways to be competitive and manage work.'

The characteristics of learning organisations

Senge (1990) identified five characteristics required for a learning organisation. These are summarised in Exhibit 7-8. They are personal mastery, mental process models, shared vision,

- **Systems thinking:** members perceive their organisation as a system of interrelated processes, activities, functions and interactions. Any action taken will have repercussions for other variables in the system. It is important to see the entire picture in the short and long run
- **Shared vision:** belief and commitment towards a goal deeply desired by all. Sublimation of competing departmental and personal interests for the achievement of the shared vision
- **Personal mastery:** continual learning and personal growth by all organisational members. Individuals are willing to give up old ways of thinking and behaving to try out possible better ones for themselves and the organisation
- **Mental process models:** shared internal images of how individuals, the organisation and the world work. Willingness to reflect on the reasoning underlying our actions and to change these assumptions when necessary to create a more appropriate process for doing things
- **Team learning:** organisation members openly communicate across departmental and hierarchical boundaries to help all members solve problems and learn from each other. Decreasing the need for personal wins in order to increase the search for the truth for the good of the entire team

Exhibit 7–8 Characteristics of a learning organisation

team learning, and systems thinking. Systems thinking is the most important because all the others are a part of it. In a learning organisation, people are willing to let go of old defences and ways of behaving in order to learn with others how their organisation really works. Then they can form a common vision of where they want to go, develop mental models of how organisational processes work, design a plan to get there, and implement it as a committed team.

Armed with these characteristics, learning organisations are better equipped to cope with the traditional organisational constraints of fragmentation, competition and reactiveness. Instead of separating different organisational functions into competing fragments, learning organisations emphasise the total system and how each function contributes to the whole process. Instead of competing for resources and trying to prove who is right or wrong, learning organisations promote co-operation and sharing of knowledge for the benefit of all. Finally, instead of reacting to problems like a firefighter, learning organisations encourage innovativeness and continual improvement so that problems don't occur in the first place, or will not recur in the future.

Types of organisational learning

As discussed in the previous chapter, individuals prefer different learning styles. So do organisations. Research by Rheem (1995) has identified four basic types of organisational learning: competence acquisition, experimentation, continuous improvement, and boundary spanning.

1 **Competence acquisition:** organisations that learn by competence acquisition cultivate new capabilities in their teams and individuals – capabilities including resources, processes and values. They demonstrate public commitment to learning by continuously seeking new ways to work, and by promoting learning as a fundamental part of their business strategies.

2 **Experimentation:** organisations that learn by experimentation try out new ideas. They are innovators who attempt to be the first to market with new processes or products.

3 **Continuous improvement:** organisations that learn by continuous improvement strive to master each step in the process before moving on to the next. Their goal is to become the recognised technical leader for a particular product or process.

4 **Boundary spanning**: organisations that learn by boundary spanning continuously scan other companies' efforts, benchmarking their processes against those of competitors. Like many organisations that learn from others, Porsche sent engineering teams to Japanese car factories to compare assembly times and discover how to improve its own processes.

Rheem (1995) found that, in general, companies that learn by experimentation are better able to compete and change than those that rely on the other learning methods. This doesn't mean that experimentation is best for all companies. To maximise competitiveness, an organisation's dominant type of learning should match its culture. For instance, a bureaucratic organisation proud of tradition would have a difficult time trying to learn by experimentation.

Creating learning organisations

How can a traditional reactive organisation be changed into a continual learner? Richards (1994) suggests that instituting any process that enlarges the organisation's knowledge base and improves the way knowledge is interpreted and put to use will help. Four specific actions are to establish a learning strategy, redesign the organisational structure, infuse enterprise resource planning systems, and modify the organisation's culture.

1 **Establish a learning strategy**: management needs to develop and make explicit a strategic intent to learn. This includes a commitment to experimentation, a willingness to learn from experiences, and a willingness to implement necessary changes in the spirit of continuous improvement. One strategy worthy of elaboration in the closing part of this section is the stimulation of double-loop learning rather than conventional single-loop learning.

2 **Redesign the organisational structure**: traditional hierarchical organisational structures, which emphasise authority, separate departments into competing domains and enforce formal communication networks, impede organisational learning. To enhance organisational learning, communication can be increased by encouraging informal face-to-face interaction and electronic distribution to all concerned parties. Competition can be replaced with co-operation through the establishment of common performance measures and rewards. Authority levels are reduced by instituting cross-functional teams and eliminating departmental boundaries.

3 **Infuse enterprise resource planning systems**: enterprise resource planning (ERP) systems are software packages (such as SAP-R3 or Peoplesoft) that integrate all facets of a business, including manufacturing, accounting, procurement, human resources and sales. ERP and other forms of integrative software are increasingly web-based, designed to permit anyone who has a need to know to call up real-time information. Such instant access to data sources of information promotes learning by enabling people throughout the organisation to analyse situations and to make timely, more informed decisions. Peters (2000) refers to enterprise software as 'white-collar robots', saying that they will transform organisational productivity in the early twenty-first century, much as robots and mechanised automation transformed blue-collar efficiency in the latter half of the twentieth.

4 **Modify the organisation's culture**: learning happens best in the context of organisational cultures that value growth, openness, trust and risk taking. Known as the regenerative climate, emphasis is on high openness, trust and owning of responsibility. Managers

promote experimentation, trying new things, constructive criticism, learning from past mistakes and bringing functional disagreements into the open. Management establishes regenerative climates by publicising what is desired, acting accordingly themselves, and rewarding desired behaviours. The organisational development process is concerned with developing learning organisations to improve individual and organisational effectiveness.

Single-loop to double-loop learning

From research involving 6000 people across a wide variety of countries, ages, ethnic identities, educational levels, power levels, experience and from both sexes, Argyris (1994) concluded that many modern techniques that promote communication between managers and employees are dysfunctional. Techniques such as total quality management, management by walking around, focus groups and organisational surveys inhibit learning if used in a one-dimensional way.

Single-loop learning displaces employees' responsibility

According to Argyris (2000), when learning is of a single-loop character, the responsibility for learning and action shifts from subordinate to manager. Argyris emphasises: '**single-loop learning** asks a one-dimensional question to elicit a one-dimensional answer' wherein outcome responsibility resides with the manager doing the asking.

single-loop learning

Occurs when a manager shifts responsibility from employees to himself or herself by asking simple, unidimensional questions that produce simple, impersonal responses.

For example, the manager who asks others to identify the major obstacles to faster product innovation actually shifts accountability for innovation from the employee to the manager. Although on the surface it may appear as if employees are being empowered because their opinions are being asked for, the implication is that the manager takes responsibility for acting on the advice.

Double-loop learning keeps accountability on followers

To enter into double-loop learning, the leader would have to shift accountability back to employees. This might be done by asking tough questions, such as: How long have you known about these problems? What goes on in this company that prevented you from questioning these practices and getting them corrected or eliminated? **Double-loop learning** turns questions back on people in the form of follow-ups – to ask not only for facts, but also for the motives and action implications behind the facts, with the implication that changing the situation is their responsibility.

double-loop learning

Shifts accountability for actions and learning to employees by having a manager ask complex questions about the employee's motivation for solving a problem.

Managers often contribute to the problem if they have been trained to emphasise positive regard of others, being considerate and employee morale. Such motives and attitudes deprive employees of the opportunity to take responsibility for their own behaviour by learning to understand it. According to Argyris (2000), because double-loop learning depends on questioning one's own assumptions and behaviour, 'this apparently benevolent strategy [of single-loop learning] is actually *anti-learning*'.

All too often, managers use socially 'upbeat' feedback and behaviour to unconsciously inhibit learning, when honesty and candour would produce more responsible behaviour. Organisational members learn a set of rules to deal with difficult situations in ways that do not embarrass or threaten psychological well-being. Managers end up sending mixed messages when they reply along the lines of 'your recommendation is a good one, but I have to overrule it because...'. By saving face with subordinates while nevertheless thinking the idea is not a good one, managers are telling employees that their job is to make suggestions, and the manager's job is to make decisions and act. Rather than confront others with candour and forthrightness, managers who absolve others are talking the talk but not walking the walk. Rather than promoting the empowerment of others, they are creating dependence. Argyris (2000) writes:

> Once employees base their motivation on extrinsic factors – [such as] the CEO's promises – they are much less likely to take chances, question established policies and practices, or explore the territory that lies beyond the company vision as defined by management. They are much less likely to learn.
>
> A generation ago, business wanted employees to do exactly what they were told, and company leadership bought their acquiescence with a system of purely extrinsic rewards ... Today ... managers need employees who think constantly and creatively about the needs of the organisation. They need employees with as much intrinsic motivation and as deep a sense of organisational stewardship as any company executive.

Summary

- Socialisation refers to the process an employee goes through to fit into an organisation.

- Education is the development of knowledge and skills, as well as moral values related to all aspects of life.

- Training is the planned acquisition of particular skills to perform an activity.

- Training managers need to know how people learn, as different learning styles and preferences can have an impact on the success of training schemes.

- Lifelong learning means that people continue to learn throughout their life and managers need to ensure that employees also have an opportunity to develop new skills and knowledge.

- Training programmes should fill the gap between present performance and desired future performance.

- Competence refers to the ability to perform a task or job. NVQ qualifications test competence to set standards.

- Training strategy needs to be linked to business strategy to ensure the organisation's goals are met.

- Organisations should aim to develop a learning organisation that, by definition, will be flexible and more able to respond to change.

Personal development

1 **Recognise the difference between education and training.** Think about the different methods of learning you use when studying at college or when learning a skill for a new job. What processes do you use? How are they different and how are they the same?

2 **Match abilities to aptitudes.** Develop a list of your abilities and a list of your aptitudes (where you have the capacity to learn). Where you have aptitudes that are not yet fulfilled with abilities, write a plan of what you need to do to develop abilities. Distinguish between what you can do while still a student and what you can better learn while working over the next five years or so.

3 **Apply the Premack principle of reinforcement.** When deciding on the sequence of your 'to do' list, pair tasks and do the less satisfying one first. Do something that is more enjoyable or fulfilling as reinforcement for having done the one that is more of a chore.

4 **Follow the flow of experiential learning styles.** Refer back to Exhibit 7-1 and using the descriptors for Kolb's four styles of learning, identify the one that is most characteristic of you. As each style represents the combination of two learning abilities, observe the two alternative abilities you seem to use less frequently. Practise following the flow of the model when you are learning something complex. That way, you will include the less developed abilities and complete the learning loop.

5 **Plan for lifelong learning.** How can you plan for continuous development throughout your career? What is the impact for the individual and the organisation when learning is not valued?

6 **Develop competence.** It is one thing to know what tasks involve but another to carry them out effectively. How do you know when you are competent? How can you develop competence?

❓ Discussion questions

1 Describe the process a new employee may go through as part of socialisation into an organisation. What can be planned and what can be unplanned?

2 What are the differences between training and education?

3 Why should a manager be concerned with lifelong learning?

4 What does a training manager need to consider before implementing a training programme?

5 What are the advantages and disadvantages of the following: (a) on-the-job training; (b) in-house programmes; (c) external courses; (d) external bespoke programmes?

6 How can managers encourage self-managed learning?

7 Why is it important for the training strategy to link with the business strategy?

8 Give an example of how the manager of an e-commerce unit might apply each of these three learning theories: (1) behavioural conditioning, (2) social learning theory, and (3) cognitive theory.

🔑 Key concepts

education, *p. 218*	gestalt, *p. 222*
training, *p. 218*	insight, *p. 222*
learning, *p. 219*	discrimination, *p. 223*
intelligence, *p. 219*	generalisation, *p. 223*
classical conditioning, *p. 220*	NVQs, *p. 232*
operant conditioning, *p. 220*	National Learning Targets, *p. 232*
Premack principle, *p. 221*	'sitting next to Nellie', *p. 235*
social learning theory, *p. 221*	learning organisation, *p. 239*
anticipatory control, *p. 222*	single-loop learning, *p. 242*
cognitive learning, *p. 222*	double-loop learning, *p. 242*

Individual task

Reflections on learning styles

Continual learning is fundamental to functioning successfully within organisations. Therefore, those who aspire to careers in organisations should be aware of how they prefer to learn, and work to develop complementary learning skills where those abilities are low. To think more personally about learning processes, begin by answering the following questions. Circle the number that best describes you for the eight questions below. (This entire activity can be completed in about 5 to 7 minutes.)

1 I enjoy venturing into new experiences and relationships to see what I can learn.
This describes me   *This does not describe me*
1   2   3   4   5

2 I actively participate in here-and-now experiences that enable me to become aware of how I affect my environment and others.
This describes me   *This does not describe me*
1   2   3   4   5

3 I am a careful observer of events and people, and find myself reflecting on what I see and hear from what goes on about me.
This describes me   *This does not describe me*
1   2   3   4   5

4 I find myself talking with others about our recent experiences so that I can make sense of what people say and do, and of why events turn out as they do.
This describes me   *This does not describe me*
1   2   3   4   5

5 I like to manipulate abstract ideas and symbols to visualise how concepts and things are related.
This describes me   *This does not describe me*
1   2   3   4   5

6 I find myself engaging in 'what if?' forms of reasoning and synthesising ideas into hypotheses for future testing.
This describes me   *This does not describe me*
1   2   3   4   5

7 I enjoy taking risks by testing my ideas on others or in actions to see if they work.
This describes me   *This does not describe me*
1   2   3   4   5

8 I am decisive, a practical problem-solver who enjoys putting plans into action.
This describes me   *This does not describe me*
1   2   3   4   5

There are no right or wrong answers to the above questions. The questionnaire is not intended to be a scientifically valid instrument, but simply to serve as a stimulus to your thinking and learning. To interpret your answers, add your 'scores' for each pair of questions (1 + 2, 3 + 4, etc.) in the table below:

Scores from questions	Learning processes (abilities)
1 _____ + 2 _____ = _____	Concrete experience
3 _____ + 4 _____ = _____	Reflective observation
5 _____ + 6 _____ = _____	Abstract conceptualisation
7 _____ + 8 _____ = _____	Active experimentation

Your lowest score(s) suggest the learning processes that you tend to favour. The higher the score, the less inclined you are to use that process or ability.

Now turn back to Exhibit 7-1 and write your total scores on each of the four processes next to the appropriate label in the diagram. Are your two lowest scores adjacent to one another in the flow process (for example, 'concrete experience' and 'reflective observation')? If so, circle the learning style indicated by the combination of the two (such as 'divergence' for the above example). This is suggestive of your dominant style of learning. Read again the description of this style and reflect on whether you believe that it appropriately describes you.

If you do have a dominant style, is the total of your other two processes at least twice as high as your two lowest scores? If so, you might want to strengthen them as this suggests they are seldom used. Write down three action steps you could take to activate learning using these process alternatives. Then seek to practise them.

You may want to compare results with those of a classmate. If the two of you differ in learning styles, you can learn from one another how to strengthen your less used abilities.

Team task

Purpose To encourage students to think about how they learn, and their role in the learning experience.

Time 40 minutes

1 Think about past learning experiences, which (a) made you feel good, and (b) made you feel bad. Write down what it was that made it a good or bad learning experience.

2 In pairs, share good/bad learning experiences and see if there are any similarities or differences.

3 In fours, collectively write notes on a flip chart under the following headings: 'Things that encourage learning' and 'Things that inhibit learning'.

4 Feed back your findings to the whole group. How do these items relate to what you know or expect from your current course?

Case study: Bigger profits are the prize for education – successful training now needs to show on the company's bottom line

One criterion for measuring the success of an organisation is to gauge the value of its investment in learning.

'Return on investment is what's being measured in organisations today,' says Crystal Shaffer, director of knowledge and development at Les Fontaines, a Cap Gemini Ernst & Young company, 'because that's the determining factor in future investment.'

'Previously we saw a lot of learning organisations in companies measure things like days or hours spent on training,' she says.

'But that doesn't tell you very much about the value of the learning. Companies need to be able to link training to the company's objectives and the bottom line.'

Accurately assessing ROI for training and development is tricky. Intel Ireland, for example, measured how training contributed to performance improvements for business units that had undergone the training compared with those that had not.

A similar approach is being taken at Old Mutual, where the corporate university uses performance consultants, who meet regularly with their business units to identify requirements for performance improvement.

Another way to measure return on training investment is to evaluate its influence on employee satisfaction and levels of retention.

Michael McGinley, Intel Ireland Fab Operations training manager, identifies achieving a happier, more fulfilled workforce as one of the most important gains for an employer investing in corporate education.

Staff satisfaction is something that Lloyds TSB has also seen rise as a result of its training programmes.

'Evaluation of programmes has shown us that the learning we provide does have a real impact on the bottom line, but in addition significantly enhances intangible factors such as motivation and job satisfaction,' says Eric Linin, senior HR manager.

'In our internal staff attitude surveys, we have seen a significant positive swing for those questions relating to training since 1999.'

The increasing use of partnerships to enhance corporate education is also reflected in the awards.

'There's a growing trend to focus on what's strategic within your organisation and to partner with other organisations that can provide expertise in these areas,' says Mark Allen, president of CUX.

Intel Ireland maintains links with Dublin universities as well as with several technology institutes.

At Rolls-Royce, corporate learning is structured around 'faculties' – communities of learning represented by interest groups such as engineering, or by corporate applications such as leadership – and each has an academic partner. For example, the quality faculty works with Leicester University, engineering with Cambridge, the programme management faculty with the University of Manchester, and leadership with London Business School.

At Johnson & Johnson, the education process is extended to external partners – the healthcare providers that use its products.

'What they've done is to create an amazing alliance structure, plus an innovative learning approach, and that has become a source for medical content and theoretical training,' says Shaffer.

'They're saying: "Training is so important, we want to give it not just internally but to anyone who's dealing with this product base."'

Whether it is internal or external education, e-learning plays a prominent role in many company programmes. E-learning not only saves time and money, by using online forums and chat rooms, but trainees can also interact with each other remotely, making the face-to-face sessions more productive.

'People come from all over Europe for our programmes and each time we meet we want them to get the best from it,' says Hervé Borensztejn, vice president and head of the Corporate Business Academy. 'Through e-learning, they can work as remote teams, then when they meet physically they already know each other.'

Of all the aspects of learning and development, leadership has proved a crucial item on the agenda of all the participating companies.

'We did a survey earlier in the year of 250 organisations and asked them to list the areas of interest to them and the greatest challenges they were facing,' says Allen. 'Leadership development was at the top of the list.'

The University for Lloyds TSB has recently launched a leadership and management development curriculum. 'The real challenge is to develop the next generation of leaders – because in the next few years we'll have a lot of retirees,' says Borensztejn.

It is already becoming clear that organisations with a commitment to invest in education recognise it as a strategic investment and, even if there was an economic downturn, it is unlikely that training will be removed from the agenda.

Source: Adapted from Sarah Murray, in the *Financial Times*, 13 October 2003, p. 13.
Reproduced with permission of Sarah Murray.

Discussion questions

1 Why do you think training is important for the economic survival of an organisation?

2 How can the value of training be measured?

3 E-learning is becoming increasingly important for international organisations. What are the benefits?

4 Should training be initiated by the employer or the employee?

WWW exercise

According to the Learning and Skills Council, Modern Apprenticeships have the following advantages.

- **Improved productivity:** apprenticeships equip young people with the skills and knowledge to do the job better. And, because they are motivated, they work harder and more effectively for your business.

- **Motivated people:** apprentices are motivated people who are keen to learn. By offering apprenticeships you will find it easier to recruit and retain able young people.

- **Relevant training:** apprenticeships are designed by businesses in your sector to meet the needs of your business. This means the training is always relevant and it is tailored to the needs of your sector by people who genuinely understand what you do.

- **Avoid skills shortages:** apprenticeships allow you to invest in your business's future. By taking on an apprentice you can acquire specialist skills for your business that allow you to keep abreast of new technology.

Follow the link to www.realworkrealpay.info/Partner/default.htm and click on 'case studies'. There are several examples here of how organisations have benefited from Modern Apprenticeships.

1 What do you consider are the advantages of such a scheme to (a) the employer and (b) the employee?

2 Do you think you would be able to develop a career through such a scheme?

LEARNING CHECKLIST

Before moving on to the next chapter, check that you are able to:

☑ understand the nature and process of learning

☑ identify different styles and approaches to learning

☑ understand the education and training debate

☑ identify strategies for training

☑ understand the relationship between competence and performance.

Further reading

Bandura, A. and Walters, R. (1963) *Social Learning and Personality Development.* New York: Holt, Rinehart & Winston, p. 2.

Solomon, C.M. (1994) 'HR facilitates the learning organization concept', *Personnel Journal* 73(11), November.

References

Agor, W.H. (1984) 'Using intuition to manage organisations in the future', *Business Horizons* 27, July–August, p. 51.

Argyris, C. (1994) 'Good communication that blocks learning', *Harvard Business Review* 72, July–August, pp. 77–85.

Argyris, C. (2000) *On Organisational Learning.* Oxford: Blackwell.

Bandura, A. (1974) 'Behavior theories and models of man', *American Psychologist* 29(12), pp. 859–869.

Bandura, A. (1977) *Social Learning Theory.* New York: General Learning Press.

Bloisi, W., Cook, C. and Hunsaker, P. (2003) *Management and Organisational Behaviour.* Maidenhead: McGraw-Hill.

Boydell, T. and Leary, M. (2002) *Identifying Training Needs.* London: CIPD.

Christensen, C.M. and Overdorf, M. (2000) 'Meeting the challenge of disruptive change', *Harvard Business Review,* March–April, pp. 66–76.

Garvin, D.A. (1993) 'Building a learning organization', *Harvard Business Review* 71(4), pp. 78–91.

Goleman, D. (1994) *Emotional Intelligence.* New York: Bantam Books.

Hackett, P. (2003) 'Continuous improvement: is it a "journey with no end"?', *Training Journal,* November, pp. 18–22.

Honey, P. and Mumford, A. (1992) *The Manual of Learning Styles.* Maidenhead: Honey.

Kohler, W. (1925) *The Mentality of Apes.* New York: Harcourt Brace and World.

Kolb, D.A. (1976) 'Management and the learning process', *California Management Review* 18(3), Spring, pp. 21–31.

Mintzberg, H. (1976) 'Planning on the left side and managing on the right', *Harvard Business Review* 54, July–August, p. 53.

MSC (1981) *A New Training Initiative: A Consultative Document.* London: MSC.

Ornstein, R.E. (1973) 'Right and left thinking', *Psychology Today,* May, pp. 87–92.

Pavlov, I.P. (1927) *Conditional Reflexes,* trans. G.V. Anrep. London: Oxford University Press.

Peters, T. (2000) 'Visions 21: what will we do for work?', *Time,* 22 May, pp. 68–71.

Premack, D. (1959) 'Toward empirical behaviour laws: 1. positive reinforcement', *Psychological Review* 66.

Reid, M. and Barrington, H. (1999) *Training Interventions.* London: IPD.

Rheem, H. (1995) 'The learning organization: building learning capability', *Harvard Business Review,* March–April, pp. 3–12.

Richards, G. (1994) 'Organizational learning in the public sector: from theory to practice', *Optimum* 25(3), 22 December, p. 3.

Senge, P. (1990) *The Fifth Discipline: The Art and Practice of the Learning Organization.* New York: Doubleday.

Senge, P., Roberts, C., Ross, R.B., Smith, B.J. and Kleiner, A. (1995) *The Fifth Discipline Fieldbook: Strategies and Tools for Building a Learning Organization.* New York: Currency Doubleday.

Skinner, B.F. (1964) *The Shaping of a Behaviorist.* New York: Harper & Row.

Skinner, B.F. (1971) *Beyond Freedom and Dignity.* New York: Bantam-Vintage Books.

Thorndike, E.L. (1913) 'Law of effect', in *Educational Psychology: The Psychology of Learning.* New York: Columbia University Press.

Chapter **8**

Managing and developing performance

LEARNING OUTCOMES

After studying this chapter, you should be able to:

- ☑ **understand** the role of appraisal systems in the management of performance

- ☑ **examine** the importance of participation and involvement

- ☑ **recognise** the role of empowerment and its relationship to performance

- ☑ **understand** the concept of a learning organisation.

The opening vignette highlights some of the problems with 360-degree feedback.

Lloyds TSB: squaring the circle

When HR and training units in the Lloyds TSB Group introduced 360-degree feedback, it was because they saw its potential. But it was launched – as new initiatives so often are – in the spirit of exploration, and this left it open to interpretation by the group's differing cultures.

For 3000 retail managers, the process became part of performance management and was incorporated into their twice-yearly reviews. Managers shared the same role and function, so implementation was relatively easy and the data could be used to form an overview of people's strengths and development needs. This worked well within a prescriptive and hierarchical structure.

The same process was implemented in another part of the company where there was, in contrast, a diversity of managerial roles. In this case individuals accessed the process as and when they wanted to focus on self-development.

It would be inappropriate to comment on the specific results of these two approaches, other than to acknowledge the emerging issues. The first example demonstrates a structured approach, integral to the review process. The outcomes, however, were relevant only to that department and did not transfer across the business.

The success of the second, more ad hoc, approach was reliant on commitment to the process from the head of that function and subject to people's personal experiences of the process. Although it could aid individuals, there was no method to measure the benefits for the department, let alone across the whole business.

In both examples, the culture of the two departments determined the level of success, while neither system was measurable or transferable. They also suffered from a lack of consistency, moderation or the existence of a shared framework. In the end what proved key to a more successful implementation of the 360 process lay in another initiative: leadership development.

To give a consistent approach to leadership behaviours across the whole organisation, a 'leadership capability framework' was established. This proved to be the ideal forum in which to implement 360; from an organisational perspective the framework identified the best fit, providing a common language against which to measure capability, and it was also transferable across the organisation.

From the individual's perspective, 360 captured a self-review and boss review, while peer reviews identified their leadership capability in the context of the whole company.

Source: Adapted from J. Wilson, 'Whose round is it?', *People Management*, 24 February 2005, p. 46.

Discussion questions

1 Do you think all stakeholders – for example, staff or customers – should be involved in appraising a manager's performance?
2 How can the HR department ensure 360-degree reviews are objective?

The opening vignette identifies some of the problems with evaluating performance. 360-degree feedback is just one of the mechanisms open to managers as a method of evaluating and managing performance, and this will be discussed later in the chapter. The chapter begins, however, with setting the scene as to why performance management is important.

Performance management

Performance management is the process by which managers ensure that their employees'
outputs match the organisation's goals. Therefore performance management is vital if an organisation is to gain competitive advantage.

performance management
The process by which managers ensure employees' outputs match the organisation's goals.

A performance management system should consist of three parts.

1 It specifies which aspects of performance are relevant to the job. This can be achieved through the use of a job analysis, as discussed in Chapter 4.
2 It measures the relevant aspects of employee performance. One method of doing this is through the performance appraisal system.
3 It provides feedback to employees so that they can adjust their performance to match the organisation's goals.

Managing performance

Armstrong and Baron (2004) define performance management as:

> a process which contributes to the effective management of individuals and teams in order to achieve high levels of organisational performance. As such, it establishes shared understanding about what is to be achieved and an approach to leading and developing people which will ensure that it is achieved.

They go on to stress that it is:

> a strategy which relates to every activity of the organisation set in the context of its human resource policies, culture, style and communications systems. The nature of the strategy depends on the organisational context and can vary from organisation to organisation.

This means that performance management should be linked to the strategic aims of the organisation and should be integrated into all aspects of organisational life. It should not only be concerned with performance but also with development, which in turn will enable performance to be improved.

De Nisi (2000) argues that performance management is a range of activities engaged in by an organisation to enhance and improve organisational effectiveness. One of the biggest problems with performance management is that it means different things to different people. HR administrators often focus on the appraisal process, ensuring that managers conduct reviews on time and follow through on development needs. Line managers are often more conscious of meeting production targets. The finance department looks at factors such as performance-related reward and profitability, and the head of HR might examine performance in the context of development programmes, and assessing how effectively skills, competencies and knowledge are being deployed across the organisation.

Performance management is a combination of all these functions. However, while each approach has merit in its own right, the approaches are most effective when closely aligned to bring together performance management, human capital management and financial disciplines. This includes incentive and compensation management, learning and development, competency management and individual performance appraisals. According to Den Hartog *et al.* (2004), managing organisational and employee performance is seen as critical for the development and survival of organisations. Performance management is coming to mean a set of integrated processes in which managers work with employees to set expectations, measure and review results, and reward performance.

Functions of performance management

Performance management has three functions for the organisation: strategic, administrative and developmental, as illustrated in Exhibit 8-1.

Strategic function

Baron and Armstrong (1998) emphasise the strategic and integrated nature of performance management. They see it as a continuous process focusing on the future rather than the past. Therefore, taking a strategic approach to performance management involves aligning HR practices to both current and future performance.

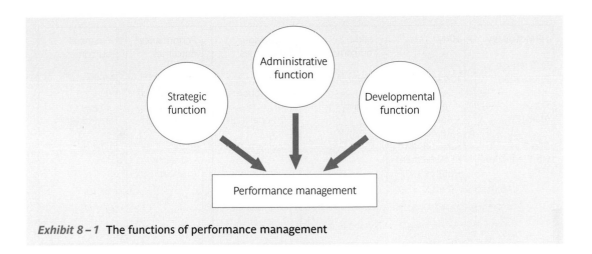

Exhibit 8 – 1 The functions of performance management

The performance management system should be able to identify whether employees' activities are meeting the organisation's goals. To do this, measurement and feedback systems are needed to identify whether this is happening. To achieve the strategic purpose, the system must be flexible. Flexibility is important as the system needs to keep pace with the changing goals and nature of the organisation. Unfortunately, many performance management systems fail to do this, and concentrate on the administrative and developmental function rather than the strategic.

Administrative function

Many organisations use performance management to make decisions about salary, promotions, retention, redundancies and recognition of individual performance. Unfortunately, many managers often see performance management as purely a box-ticking exercise rather than a motivational tool that can improve performance.

Developmental function

The developmental function of performance management should enable managers to identify when staff are not performing well and how they can improve. Unfortunately, the performance appraisal system often focuses only on an employee's poor performance when it can also be used to develop employees to enable them to progress through the organisation.

To be effective, performance management systems need to link employee activities with the organisation's strategic goals. When this is done effectively competitive advantage can be achieved.

Models of performance management

Roberts (2001) suggests setting organisational, departmental, team and individual objectives, and cascading down the strategic objectives to a meaningful set of targets for each individual. The appraisal system is linked with appropriate reward strategies, training and development feedback, communication and coaching, individual career planning and mechanisms for monitoring the effectiveness of performance management. This makes it part of the day-to-day management function rather than a specific HR function.

Guest (1997) suggests that HRM practices result in HRM outcomes, and these in turn result in employee behaviour that links to the financial outcome of the organisation, as illustrated in Exhibit 8-2. This suggests that performance is linked to every level and at different levels of the organisation (such as individual and group) as suggested by De Nisi (2000).

Exhibit 8 – 2 Linking HRM and performance
Source: Guest (1997).

However, the problem with Guest's model is the logical distance between the different elements in the model, which can make it difficult for managers to see the whole picture. Measuring and testing this process could be difficult.

Den Hartog (2004) makes the following suggestions.

■ Most performance management practices are facilitated by line management. Therefore line managers will have an impact on how employees perceive performance management initiatives.

■ HRM and performance management practices, when implemented by managers, may affect employee perceptions and evaluations (for example, they may be seen as an attempt to increase production and as a form of manipulation).

■ Employee behaviour will have an impact on organisational performance. Contextual factors can constrain the impact individual performance has on organisational-level outcomes.

■ Reversed causality plays a role. If organisational success is seen as high there could be more willingness from management to invest in HR practices, which in turn will improve employees' commitment, trust and motivation.

■ Organisational contextual factors – both internal, such as capital intensity, and external, such as union activity in the sector – and employee characteristics such as age, gender, level of education, and preferences such as job type and level of autonomy, may constrain the proposed relationships between HR practice and organisational performance.

Den Hartog's model (see Exhibit 8-3) recognises that when senior management can see improved organisational performance they are more likely to invest in HR practices. The result of such investment is improved organisational motivation and commitment. Therefore enhancing performance is important not only from an HR perspective but also from a management perspective.

HR managers have identified the following as important aspects of enhancing performance.

■ **Leadership development.** This includes succession of current leaders, as well as the succession profile for up-and-comers.

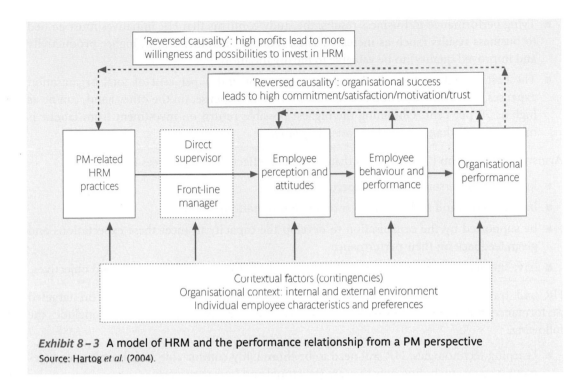

Exhibit 8 – 3 A model of HRM and the performance relationship from a PM perspective
Source: Hartog *et al.* (2004).

■ **Performance management.** Few respondents have an online performance management system, defined in the survey as a system that is used by HR to understand what employees need to develop the required skills and expertise – this is not a once-a-year review procedure.

■ **Workforce planning.** What are the skills and abilities the organisation needs, and who has them? HR and organisations have far to go in tracking this information; as one HR manager noted, 'We typically know more about an employee's laptop than we do about them.'

■ **Training and development.** How does the organisation train current employees so they can be recruited internally for positions of ever increasing responsibility?

Research by Averbrook and Spirigi (2005) has noted that HR is only moderately successful in creating and executing joint people management strategies. For example, it may be that the HR and training departments do not share common data on all employees. One major obstacle to effective performance management is lack of process and systems integration, leaving HR unable to tie together data or provide executive access to information. Silos of data make it difficult to integrate your investments in workers with business performance, or to illustrate a meaningful return on investment from performance management programmes.

Other questions raised ask: Does performance management drive learning? Is learning measured in terms of increased sales or higher performance?

■ Assessing skills and **competencies**: there is a strong link between training, knowledge and performance, Averbook and Spirigi (2005) noted. This places HR in a position to move beyond core services by redeploying and 're-skilling' talent. In most organisations, they add, there is a 'lack of understanding of skills that the organisation possesses'.

competencies
The skills and abilities a person has to do a job.

- Tying performance to business results: the study confirms that HR initiatives must be tied to business results (such as increased sales, reduced customer churn, higher productivity and improved quality) to be valuable to the organisation.

- The cost for HR is typically between 0.5 per cent and 1 per cent of total organisation expenses, say Averbrook and Spirigi (2005). Labour expense, on the other hand, can be as high as 70 per cent. Obtaining the highest possible return on investment from labour is more effective than cutting HR costs, they note.

Armstrong and Baron (2004) suggest that, to manage effectively, employees need to:

- know and understand what is expected of them
- have the skills and ability to deliver on these expectations
- be supported by the organisation to develop the capacity to meet these expectations and given feedback on their performance
- have the opportunity to discuss and contribute to individual and team aims and objectives.

HR and training systems need to be better integrated and collaborate more on targeted performance management initiatives. Skills that HR professionals will need include the following.

- Learning technologies: HR will need to be thoroughly comfortable with learning management systems, including how they are structured and how they work.

- Workforce-facing tools: HR will need to see the employees as learners, anticipating what they need to improve and what managers need to manage. In fact, learning will be embedded in work, and the organisation will need to have the technology to bring it all together.

- Marketing: many programmes are plagued by lacklustre employee participation, largely because organisations have developed technology without changing management initiatives accordingly.

Performance management needs to be incorporated into all aspects of the organisation. It should not be seen as a one-off event but rather as a continuous process that allows people the freedom to develop in line with the organisation's goals.

According to the CIPD (2004), performance management is not easy to implement as everyone in the organisation should be encouraged to have ownership of the process. However, CIPD surveys suggest that, where performance management systems focus on development, then they prove popular. Where they are linked to performance-related pay, then they are more likely to be viewed with suspicion.

The main criticisms of performance management schemes are that they can be very bureaucratic, with a constant process of form filling. There may also be ambiguity as to what performance is, as well as the issue of ensuring employees have been trained in how the system will work.

According to the CIPD (2004), the keys to the successful introduction and application of performance management are:

- being clear about what is meant by performance
- understanding what the organisation is and needs to be in its performance culture
- being very focused on how individual employees will benefit and how they can play their part in the process

- understanding that it is a tool for line managers and its success will depend on their ability to use it effectively.

Often, the starting place for performance management is through the performance appraisal system, which is discussed below.

Performance appraisal

Performance appraisal is the process of measuring and evaluating employees' performance. The performance appraisal can be a useful tool for employee development. Many employees find the idea of an appraisal daunting, but if handled correctly it can be a positive experience.

---

performance appraisal
The process of measuring and evaluating employees' performance.

To be effective, performance appraisal systems need to be job related; there should be a rationale for performance and managers must discuss required improvements with employees.

Traditionally, performance appraisal has been seen as an annual ritual performed by managers as a means of managing employee performance. Often it can be a negative form-filling exercise, where managers collect only negative information and then, because they prefer to avoid conflict, spend very little time on giving employees feedback. The result is that many managers and staff dislike the performance appraisal process.

The performance appraisal process should establish employees' goals and be linked to the organisation's strategic goals. Carried out correctly, the performance appraisal process should:

- tell top performers that they are valued by their organisation
- ensure that all employees doing similar jobs are evaluated using the same standards
- help an organisation identify its strongest and weakest employees
- legally justify HRM decisions such as promotions, bonuses, discipline and redundancies
- encourage collaboration and co-operation.

Exhibit 8-4 demonstrates the uses of performance appraisal information.

How successful an organisation is in achieving the aims of its appraisal system depends on its ability to link this with business objectives. When performance appraisals are integrated with strategic objectives managers are more able to link the goals of an individual with those of the organisation. The process should also provide a means of measuring the contribution of each work unit and each employee. A good appraisal system should also enable decisions to be made that will enhance the organisation's future performance, such as assessing skill levels and identifying training needs.

Many managers do not understand the importance of performance appraisal. This is more often apparent in departments with a specialism, such as marketing or accounting, where managers have spent time developing their subject specialism but have neglected the people side of management. The issue is to help managers understand that effective performance appraisals can help managers meet their targets by having a better developed workforce.

Managing performance appraisals should be seen as a partnership where the HR professionals, managers and employees work together to ensure that they are effective and fair to everyone. An example of how to achieve this can be seen in Exhibit 8-5 below.

An appraisal system that is aligned with the organisation's goals ensures that the employees in an organisation are able to build on and share their knowledge. An example of how staff can develop and improve their performance can be seen in the 'International perspective' box.

Between-person evaluation
Salary administration
Recognition of individual performance
Identification of poor performance
Promotion decisions
Retention and termination decisions
Redundancies

Within-person development
Performance feedback
Identification of individual strengths and weaknesses
Determination of transfers and assignments
Identification of individual training needs

Systems maintenance
Development of individual corporate goals
Evaluation of goal attainment by individuals, teams and strategic business units
Human resource planning
Determination of organisational training needs
Reinforcement of authority structure
Identification of organisational development needs
Human resource system auditing

Documentation
Documentation of HR management decisions
Meeting of HR management legal requirements
Criteria for validation research

Exhibit 8 – 4 Uses of performance appraisal information
Source: Cleveland *et al.* (1989).

Dealing with poor performance

Sometimes, regardless of the performance development processes in place, poor performance may still exist.

According to the CIPD (2004), managers can identify problems of poor performance when they have employees who:

- require constant supervision
- do work that frequently requires rectification or completion
- cannot be trusted to do work that, reasonably, should be within their ability
- avoid unpleasant tasks
- cause bottlenecks due to a work rate lower than that which could reasonably be expected
- exercise judgement, initiative or willingness at a level below that which it is reasonable to expect
- avoid their fair share of work

Electronic performance support systems (EPSS): do they offer solutions?

'EPSS is an integrated, computer-based environment that provides workers with immediate access to a full range of information, tools and training, often as part of the same automated information system with which workers do their jobs.'

It is easy to see the potential attractions, as training can be linked with performance, therefore avoiding time out for learning, and it can be delivered in bite-sized chunks.

These solutions appear attractive on paper. However, the reality could be very different.

In considering EPSS, it is important to distinguish between two concepts. The first is what might be called the 'technological tools of the trade' and the second is the more general applications, delivered through a portal, where staff can access e-learning opportunities on their PC.

One excellent example of EPSS can be found in use with US coastguards. They are responsible for inspecting fishing vessels and, in the past, boarding officers were required to attend a one-week course on the intricacies of enforcing hundreds of pages of federal regulations. Technology has allowed a more efficient approach. Each officer now has a hand-held personal digital assistant (PDA) that they take on board. This presents them with 16 questions about, for example, vessel length, type of vessel or type of engine. Based on answers to these questions, the PDA generates a customised checklist of safety requirements. Officers then check whether equipment is satisfactory. The PDA can also be used to automatically generate the required paper report.

Another example is fast-food chain McDonald's. According to recent reports, it is testing small hand-held devices that will record faults. If a large number of failures are identified, the device will alert the local manager by ringing her/his mobile phone.

Tools of the trade, however, are different from generic portals. My moment of doubt about portals came when a well-known US business school demonstrated its performance support tool. The example chosen went as follows. Here is Susan's portal. She is about to attend a negotiating session. She types in 'negotiations' and her portal is changed. Here are a series of articles, exercises and checklists.

Sounds fine – but does it work like this in practice? Let me call on my experience as a training manager in financial services. If Susan was entering a negotiation session with no prior experience, the first question to be asked is how the organisation had allowed this situation to develop. If she then came to me as a training manager, I'd buddy her with an experienced negotiator or bring in a trusted external trainer for coaching.

All this comes back to two central questions: 'How do people learn?' and 'How can we help people learn?' We need to answer these in our organisations before we move on to consider the role of technology. Learning comes first; technology second.

Source: Adapted from M. Sloman, 'Fishing for compliments', *People Management*, 13 January 2005, p. 44.

Discussion questions

1 Do you think EPSS is an effective method for improving performance?

2 Can you think of examples when EPSS could demotivate rather than improve performance?

international perspective

Line managers	Human resource professionals	Employees
Work with HR professionals and employees to develop business-relevant criteria for appraisals	Work with line managers and employees to develop criteria for appraisals	Work with line managers and HR professionals to develop criteria for appraisals
Develop an understanding of how common appraisal errors can be avoided	Co-ordinate the administrative aspects of the appraisal process	Maybe praise the work of other employees
Fill out appraisal forms carefully and conscientiously	Train everyone who provides appraisal information on how to avoid errors in appraisal	Maybe appraise personal performance
Give constructive and honest feedback to employees	Train line managers to give feedback	Seek and accept constructive and honest feedback
Seek and accept constructive feedback about personal performance	Support line managers in efforts to keep the performance management system going	Strive to improve personal performance
Use performance information for decision-making		

Exhibit 8 – 5 The performance appraisal partnership
Source: Adapted from Schuler and Jackson (1996).

- refuse to co-operate
- have an unacceptable attendance, sickness or punctuality record
- cause conflict in their relationships with other employees, suppliers, customers, and so on.

The problem for managers is doing something about it, as management action can often create an even more negative work environment.

The main reasons for employee under-performance are listed in Exhibit 8-6. This also includes reasons and possible actions a manager can take.

The difficulty lies in encouraging employees to improve by using positive behaviour rather than sanctions. One method can be through setting performance objectives and standards that can be measurable.

Objectives and performance standards

It is important to set goals or objectives, however these should be Specific, Measurable, Achievable, Relevant and Timebound (SMART).

SMART
Objectives that are Specific, Measurable, Achievable, Relevant and Timebound.

'I need to reduce scrap material waste by 10 per cent, avoid a reduction in product quality, and increase production by 5 per cent. This must be done in one month' is an example of a concise decision-making criteria statement. Decision-making criteria should be *Specific:* 'I will increase productivity by 5 per cent', not just 'I want to increase productivity'. Second, they should be *Measurable:* Saying you want to increase employee morale is not as good a criterion statement as saying that you will increase employee morale as indicated by a 4 per cent reduction in absenteeism over the next three months. Third, to gain commitment to meeting criteria, there should be sufficient time, resources and expertise available to make them *Achievable*. They must also be *Relevant*: it is no good introducing a system of childcare to increase staff morale, if none of the employees has children. They must also be *Timebound*: that is, achieved within a time limit. This helps when measuring targets and also ensures that a problem does not linger on indefinitely.

Once objectives have been set then managers need to give feedback so that employees know how they are performing.

Feedback

Whether as part of the day-to-day management of employees or as a more formal appraisal system, managers need to be able to give constructive feedback. Good-quality feedback can not only improve performance but also improve working relationships and increase motivation.

Often, managers are apprehensive about giving feedback, as there is a fine balance to be struck between being perceived as negative or constructive. The better a manager's interpersonal skills, the more able they will be to provide good-quality feedback.

The main problems with feedback can be as follows.

- **Apathy** – managers hope the problem will go away on its own. This can lead to lower standards, which can spread to the rest of the team, leaving them feeling resentful.

- **Inability to praise** – some managers think that giving praise is unnecessary, as employees are expected to do a good job, which they are paid for. The problem here is that good behaviour is not acknowledged.

- **Maintaining the status quo** – by doing nothing conflict may be avoided. However, managers who do nothing often lose all credibility.

- **Fight or flight** – the thought of causing conflict can cause some managers to either take on a fight response by being over-critical or a flight response by diluting what has been said. The result is that the employee is more concerned with their treatment than the message.

- **Unclear communication** – feedback may be given in vague subjective terms, such as 'you need to do better', rather than precise objective terms, where performance measures can be used.

It is extremely important for managers to develop good feedback skills, as poor feedback has either no effect or a negative effect on performance, while the development of good feedback skills can have a positive effect.

Developing positive feedback skills

Most people enjoy positive attention and the more positive the attention the more likely they are to respond with improved performance.

Managers need to ensure that feedback is used regularly so that employees know how they are performing. It is used as part of a constructive experience. The feedback is clear and unambiguous and can, where possible, be measured.

Reason for under-performance	What to look for	What to do
1 They do not know what you want them to achieve	Past performance acceptable Performance on other tasks acceptable Current deterioration of performance coincides with new task Frequency with which staff member checks with manager is relatively high No record of role clarity having been established	This is a **communication** problem; clarify their performance expectations and agree objectives
2 They know what you want them to achieve but lack the competence to achieve it (a) Lack of ability	Performance on other tasks acceptable Task is new to employee No record of training or coaching on this task	This is a **learning** problem; train and/or coach them
(b) Lack of aptitude	Performance on other tasks acceptable Task is new to staff member Performance below required standard despite training or coaching	This is a **person/task fit** problem; consider redeploying the person or reallocating the task, but speak to your manager and personnel first
3 They know what you want them to achieve and have the ability to achieve it but lack control over significant factors affecting their performance	Performance on other tasks acceptable Staff member usually responds to new tasks Staff member dependent on other people for all or part of task Task or procedures changed recently	This is an **interference** problem; find out what the problem is and tackle it

4 They know what you want them to achieve, have the competence and control to achieve it, but do not want to achieve it; this could be because:		
(a) they do not understand why it is important	Performance on other tasks acceptable No record of role clarity having been established Behavioural evidence of lack of understanding	This is a **communication** problem (see suggested action above)
(b) they hold views, values or beliefs contrary to those necessary for effective performance	Behavioural evidence of contrary views, values or beliefs	This is an **attitude** problem; check to see if they can perform acceptably under close supervision – if they can, but subsequently revert to the lower standard, you have confirmation of the cause: poor attitude They don't want to perform! Counsel them, point out the consequences of under-performance and let them try again
(c) they are suffering problems outside work, which they cannot help but 'bring to work' with them	Past performance acceptable Performance deterioration happened relatively quickly	This may be a **personal** problem; seek skilled assistance from the personnel department

Exhibit 8–6 Reasons for under-performance (CIPD, 2004)

Source: Browell (2003).

Poor communication skills are often one of the reasons that feedback can be seen as negative. Try the 'Stop and reflect' exercise and see if you can rephrase the sentences in a more positive light while still getting your message across. Some of them are not easy, but then neither is feedback.

Stop and reflect

How could you rephrase the following sentences to produce the desired improvement in performance without causing offence?

Problem	Desired feedback to solve the problem
You are always late.	
Your work is rubbish.	
Your absences add up to ten days in the last six months.	
You need to get on better with your colleagues.	
You are lazy at work.	
You have a body odour problem and it's offending your colleagues.	
You need to do some training.	

(*You may want to think of some other problems that you have come across as part of an appraisal.*)

360-degree feedback

The idea of **360-degree feedback** stems from the 1990s. It consists of using feedback from a variety of sources; these can include colleagues, line managers, subordinates, customers and suppliers, as well as self-assessment.

360-degree feedback

Consists of using feedback from a variety of sources; these can include colleagues, line managers, subordinates, customers and suppliers, as well as self-assessment.

According to Wilson (2005), 360-degree feedback can give a more rounded view of a person's performance than a straightforward appraisal, which is often carried out by a line manager.

However, 360-degree feedback is not easy to implement as there is a fine line between improving performance and demotivation, as illustrated in the case of Lloyds TSB in the opening vignette. To avoid pitfalls, the process needs to be managed carefully, as, for some people, the feedback can come as an unwelcome shock. This is why, during the debriefing process, managers need to frame negative issues in the more positive light of potential development.

Wilson (2005) suggests that the organisation has a responsibility to invest in consistent structures and applications, while individuals have the responsibility to give and receive honest appraisal. This builds an upward spiral of organisational trust that, over time, establishes protocols and develops confidence. This, in turn, informs and constantly refreshes the organisation. The ultimate goal for 360-degree feedback is to facilitate honest conversations.

'Male views stuck in 1970s'

According to Schein (2005), negative stereotypes of female managers have remained virtually unchanged since the 1970s and, without sex discrimination legislation, women would have struggled to make progress.

'The male managers of today hold similar attitudes to those of male managers in the 1970s. Over the course of three decades, men continue to perceive men as more likely than women to possess the characteristics necessary for managerial success. Without government pressures on equality, these views would have gone unchecked.'

Schein has spent the past 30 years researching gender stereotyping in the USA. More recently she expanded this to cover the UK, Germany, China and Japan.

She examined the extent to which managers were perceived to have characteristics associated with men rather than women, using her 'Schein descriptive index'. This involved asking male and female managers to list the characteristics that make a good manager, along with the characteristics they perceived as being typical of a man and of a woman.

'Progress has been slow because there remains a deeply held belief that management positions are for men and men only,' Schein said. She quoted statistics compiled by the International Labour Organization in 2004, which found that, while there had been some increase in women's share of managerial positions, progress was uneven.

For any real change to take place, Schein said there needed to be a complete re-examination of management structures. She stressed that attitudes to working time also needed to change.

'Performance is still assessed on how late you stay or whether you work on Saturdays. It doesn't allow for the extra responsibilities of many women. The expectations of working hours must change.'

Schein argues that many of the assumptions about successful managers are incorrect and suggests the following as an attempt to redress the diversity balance.

- Consider which management activities are part of the 'old order' and which are valid to the business today.
- Avoid the necessity for last-minute meetings, appointments and overnight trips through more forward planning.
- The expectations of working hours should be changed. Do not assess performance on how late someone works.
- Examine the relationship between how time is spent and how performance is evaluated. Longer hours should be seen as a sign of poor performance.
- Organisations should consider offering paid-for executive childcare services.

Judy Geevy from Centrica also recognises the importance of valuing diversity: 'It is depressing that it still isn't appreciated that female managers bring a lot to the workplace. Having a diversity of styles brings creativity to an organisation. When people think of management they often think of a paternalistic approach. But the skills needed to manage people today are different from those of ten years ago, especially as we move into more modern, flexible ways of working.'

While Dianah Worman of the CIPD suggests that, 'The findings are not particularly surprising. Even though there are more female managers and more effort is being made to accommodate individuals, attitudes haven't changed much in the past 30 years. There are strong arguments for valuing different styles of leadership, particularly those involving a more consensus-based approach. Businesses need to learn to give and take over working time – that is the only way to erode existing issues.'

Source: adapted from C. Edwards, 'Male views stuck in 1970s',
People Management, 27 January 2005, p. 7.
Reproduced with permission of *People Management*.

Discussion questions

1   In your experience, do you think male views of diversity are 'stuck in the 1970s'?

2   How can the workplace change to measure quality of output rather than time spent at work?

Staff retention strategies

Staff retention is about attracting and keeping good-quality staff, while accepting that some staff will leave and, when they do, ensuring the separation is as positive as possible.

Replacing staff is a cost to the organisation. Browell (2003) suggests that employers should ask themselves the following questions.

- What is the value of good staff?

- How do you define good or key members of staff – knowledge, expertise, high performance, commitment, loyalty, creativity, qualifications, talent and/or technical competence?

- Do staff have the skills and abilities that the organisation wants and needs? If the answer is yes, then they probably need to be retained.

- Who are your most valuable and vulnerable employees, who might be attractive to head-hunters and competitors?

Retaining staff is of considerable importance for the HR professional. The CIPD (2004) report into HR trends and indicators reported that 31.7 per cent of employers expect difficulty with staff retention, with larger organisations expected to find it even more difficult. If this is the case then the HR professional needs to think about strategies that can be used to keep existing staff. The benefits of staff retention are listed in Exhibit 8-7.

Therefore, staff retention should begin when staff join the organisation. This means that the image an employee has of an organisation before they start work should match their expectations once they start work.

- Reduces costs of recruitment, selection and training of new staff
- Easier to recruit new staff
- Keeps skills and knowledge in the organisation
- Improves performance, productivity and profitability
- Improves customer loyalty and satisfaction
- Can increase sales and aid competitiveness
- Less costly than replacing staff

Exhibit 8–7 Benefits of staff retention
Source: Browell (2003).

Organisations that fail to keep their staff often have fundamental problems and, according to Schmit and Allscheid (1995), are also likely to have problems retaining customers and investors. Therefore, a link can be made between job satisfaction and retention, and its relationship to organisational performance.

There are several reasons why employees may leave an organisation and some may be unavoidable, such as leaving the area or career progression, but there are reasons that employees choose to leave an organisation that could be preventable. These can often be linked to job satisfaction. Job satisfaction happens when an employee feels fulfilled by their job and it allows them to have a sense of achievement. When this does not happen, job dissatisfaction may result. Causes of job dissatisfaction can be seen in Exhibit 8-8.

One organisation that treats staff retention as a serious issue is Kwik-Fit Financial Services. Here, staff turnover has fallen from 52 per cent to 29 per cent and staff satisfaction surveys have highlighted a positive working environment. The reasons for improved retention are down to improved communication systems, where staff views feed into improving the working environment, as well as a flexible benefits scheme. Although Kwik-Fit Financial acknowledges that its turnover is still too high, it feels that by showing that it listens, not only do staff want to stay but they are also more motivated and therefore more productive. Exhibit 8-9 lists reasons why staff may stay. However, if mismanaged, these could also be the very same reasons why staff leave.

When employees are dissatisfied with their jobs they may go through a process of withdrawal, which is likely to have an impact on their performance. At first, an employee who is becoming dissatisfied may well try to do something about it. They may approach their line manager to discuss issues; if this fails to resolve the problem then they may leave the organisation. If they stay with the organisation they may psychologically disengage: in other words, they are still doing the job, but their minds are elsewhere. This can manifest itself in poor performance as they feel their job is unimportant. This in turn makes them harder to motivate and means they are unlikely to be committed to the organisation.

Recent staff absence surveys have shown that, in the UK, staff absences have risen to 7.2 days per year. A survey of 500 firms found that ten million days were lost to absence, a cost that could run into billions. With absence linked to poor morale, employers should not be complacent. It is the manager's role to identify the reasons for poor morale before it becomes detrimental to the organisation.

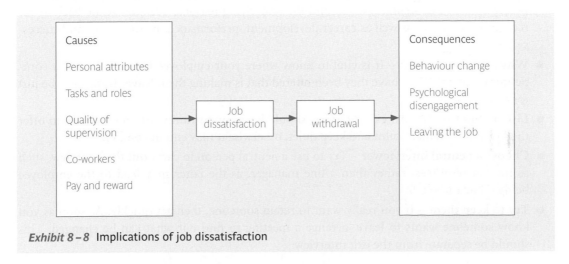

Exhibit 8–8 Implications of job dissatisfaction

- Organisational policies, procedures, culture, values, size and structure
- Recruitment and selection
- Induction
- Training and development
- Job satisfaction and motivation
- Appraisal, feedback and recognition
- Career development and promotion
- Talent management
- Money, rewards and benefits
- Stress
- Management and supervision
- Relationships with others, including team working
- Work environment
- Personal, health and domestic
- Communication, decision-making and involvement
- Innovation and creativity
- Work/life balance
- Job design
- External (e.g. strong economic climate, abundant job opportunities, headhunters)

Exhibit 8 – 9 Reasons why staff stay
Source: Browell (2003).

Alternatively, employees may decide to leave the organisation. Trying to find out the reason why can be done through exit interviews. Garrett (2003) suggests the following strategies.

- **Target all leavers** – This includes those employees you are glad to see the back of, as it probably means you had the wrong people in the wrong job, which will link back to your recruitment strategies. The questions can be delivered through interviews or questionnaires.

- **Set rules of engagement** – Make it clear that the questions will remain confidential and what will happen to feedback given.

- **Keep it structured** – The objective is to find out why the employee is leaving. Explore their perceptions of the organisation to find the underlying reasons. This can relate back to the recruitment process as well as career development, performance measurement and succession planning.

- **Why are they leaving?** – It is vital to know where your employee is going. Is it to a competitor or client? What have they been offered that is making them leave? It may not be just for more money.

- **Listen, don't react** – An exit interview should be an opportunity for an employee to offer their opinion. Remain calm and keep quiet, otherwise it may end in conflict.

- **Choose a neutral interviewer** – Try to use a neutral person to carry out the interview, such as human resources, rather than a line manager, as the latter may lead to the employee being reluctant to talk.

- **Try to keep them** – If you really want to retain someone, then act quickly. As soon as you know someone wants to leave, arrange a meeting to find out what can be changed. This should be separate from the exit interview.

- **Publicise it** – This is a positive move, as it sends a clear message to staff that you are a listening organisation.

- **Act on the data** – Information from the exit interview can be useful in looking for trends, but it can also be useful for taking immediate action if a specific problem is highlighted.

Possible causes of dissatisfaction could be down to the personal attributes of the individual, such as their character and personality. However, they could also be due to personal problems such as a family crisis. If a manager is aware of this then she/he can offer the necessary support to enable the employee to re-engage. The task and roles, such as boring and repetitive jobs with little personal control over work design, can be another reason why a worker may be dissatisfied, as can the quality of supervision and the relationship an employee may have with co-workers. Research by Cotton and Tuttle (1986) confirmed that there are many reasons why employees may decide to leave an organisation. These range from employee support, through the type of remuneration and reward, to the organisation meeting the employee's expectations. Sheridan (1992) also found that organisational culture could have a profound effect on whether an employee stays or leaves.

However, McEvoy and Cascio (1985) have shown that job enrichment has been able to reduce turnover. Huselid (1995) also suggests that, by linking work to high-performance work practices, turnover and absenteeism can be reduced.

Finally, pay and reward should also be considered. Although not necessarily a motivator, this is an indication of status and self-worth, and is therefore of vital importance when it comes to retention.

The internal labour market

Effective management of the internal labour market can also help to ensure that employers retain their staff. In the past it was quite common for organisations to only recruit to the most junior or trainee positions. The organisations would then ensure that new employees were trained and able to progress in the organisation. Often, this training would be organisation specific, which meant that the skills were suitable only for where they worked and could not be transferred to other organisations. This would be ideal for employers as it meant that employees had to stay with the organisation, which cut down on retention problems and gave employees an identifiable career structure. A lot of this changed with the economic decline in the late twentieth century, organisational delayering and the move to short-term contracts rather than jobs for life. However, research by White (2004) has identified the re-emergence of career paths. Employers are beginning to recognise that short-term contracts do not encourage company loyalty and that, by offering career paths and flexible benefits, employees are more likely to stay with the organisation.

Not all people leave jobs because they are unhappy with the work environment. Some jobs are more likely to attract part-time or temporary workers if this is what fits in with their lives. Tesco is one such company that has recently developed retention strategies to encourage students to stay with them. One scheme, known as the 'Debut Pass', offers students flexible working hours to fit in with their studies. Another offers to help reduce their student debt (Higginbottom, 2003). These strategies stem from Tesco's recognition that, by 2008, there will be a 5 per cent increase in 16–24 year olds and that, by offering younger employees a chance to earn while they learn, Tesco will also benefit.

Although the changing nature of work means that it may no longer be possible to offer long-term employment contracts, it is important to retain good-quality staff. It is quality rather than quantity that is important. This is why it is important that staff retention is linked to the human resource functions of recruitment, selection, training and development. If these connections are in place then staff are more likely to remain in the organisation.

Staff retention and the management of knowledge

Reducing staff retention turnover not only reduces the costs associated with recruitment and selection, but also helps to reduce problems with the creation of knowledge.

Knowledge in this context refers to the tacit knowledge that an employee has, which, according to Harrison and Kessels (2004), is the property of individuals and cannot be wrested from them. This means that, when people leave an organisation, they take this knowledge, which is inside their heads, with them and therefore it is lost to the company.

One way of lessening the effects of losing knowledge is to build networks within the organisation, where knowledge is shared. This means that, if staff do leave, disruption should be minimal.

Some organisations, such as McDonald's, accept that they will have a high turnover of staff, as jobs are low skilled, monotonous and tend to be used by students as a means of earning money while studying. Other reasons for high staff turnover, such as low morale, low pay rates and the job market in a particular geographic location, have been discussed above.

The question that needs to be asked is why people stay in an organisation. The Chartered Management Institute (CMI) suggests that this could be down to training and personal/professional development, the possibility for career development within an organisation, and the wish of many professionals to have a well-respected organisation on their curriculum vitae. Paying attention to knowledge management can have a direct and dramatic impact on staff retention levels.

Areas for action

The CMI (2004) suggests that, to maintain and increase the level of knowledge in an organisation, it needs to be able to directly make use of knowledge, and encourage staff commitment and loyalty. Examples of how the CMI suggests organisations should deal with knowledge retention are detailed in Exhibit 8-10.

Empowerment

A generation ago, managers began to discover the motivational power of empowerment. True, some managers have always been 'empowering' people by delegating considerable autonomy, providing ample information, and backing projects that showed creativity or initiative. Likewise, many individuals have learned over the years to be self-motivated and self-empowered – they seize opportunities to make their work more meaningful and are willing to make choices, to experiment and to have an impact on the organisation. However, until the term *empowerment* entered the manager's vocabulary, little was done to encourage the practice as a conscious way to promote self-motivation, innovation and system-wide continuous improvements.

According to Conger and Kanungo (1998), **empowerment** describes conditions that enable people to feel competent and in control, energised to take the initiative and persistent at mean-

empowerment
Describes conditions that enable people to feel competent and in control of their work, energised to take the initiative and to persist at meaningful tasks.

Make sure that you have effective practices to share knowledge (particularly tacit knowledge) across the organisation

Ensure that people work in cross-departmental teams, particularly for project work. This will benefit the project as new perspectives will be brought in if you have, say, a person from marketing directly involved in the team responsible for developing a new product, but will also help share knowledge by the action of people working together. If you have one person who is a specialist at what they do, ensure that they are responsible for passing on that knowledge by taking on someone as a part-time apprentice or by writing documentation for what they develop

Spend some time helping networks to develop within the organisation

Although you cannot micro-manage networks as these grow organically, you can foster network building by, for example, company social events, effective communication technology, a directory of who's who and their particular areas of expertise. This is especially important if not all of your staff are in the same location

Build the reputation of your organisation as an Important knowledge generator in its field

Consider what knowledge you can safely give away – either because it is protected legally by patent or copyright, or because it would be too difficult for others to copy. Publicise this information widely, by putting it on your website, encouraging publication by staff in their own name, including it in company bulletins and newsletters

Reward staff for sharing knowledge

Make sure this is a known organisational value

Ensure that you personally take an interest in the learning and development of other people and that you set a good example by asking questions and developing your own personal knowledge

Top up your training budget and make sure that your HR policies are geared towards learning and development

Exhibit 8 – 10 How organisations can foster knowledge retention
Source: Chartered Management Institute (2004).

ingful tasks. Empowerment is a multifaceted and highly personal motivational force. It can come from within the individual, from peers or from a manager. As suggested by its definition, empowerment aspires to bring about positive self-perceptions (self-concept, self-esteem and self-efficacy) and task-directed behaviours. Exhibit 8-11 portrays these forces graphically, and the following text describes some of the interplay among them.

Managers encourage empowerment by designing jobs to promote self-reliance, providing challenging goals and meaningful rewards, and exerting considerable leadership. Other people are empowering if they are accepting, provide a model for others to be self-motivated performers, and exert the patience to be mentors.

Bandura (1988) suggests that changed self-perceptions are an important manifestation of empowerment. Your **self-concept** is how you think about yourself, or see yourself in a role. Self-concept changes as you shift roles – say, from friend to student to employee. **Self-esteem** is how you generally feel about your own worthiness – your self-acceptance that you are worthy

self-concept
How we think about ourselves or see ourselves in a role.

self-esteem
How we generally feel about our own worthiness – our self-acceptance.

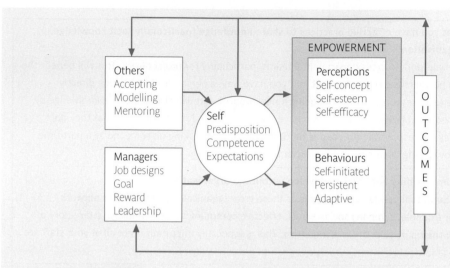

Exhibit 8–11 Empowerment grows out of self-perceptions and behaviour

---

self-efficacy

Our self-perceptions about our ability to perform certain types of task.

---

of self-respect. A specific aspect of self-esteem is self-efficacy, a concept closely linked to empowerment. **Self-efficacy** is an individual's self-perceived ability to perform a certain type of task. Your feelings of self-efficacy are important because they influence performance and give a sense of personal well-being.

Gist and Mitchell (1992) argue that individuals develop a sense of self-efficacy based on past experience with actual or similar tasks, comparisons with others and feedback from others. A person's self-assessment of ability (knowledge and skills), general physical and emotional condition, and personality (including overall self-esteem) all influence his or her feeling of task-specific self-efficacy. How skilfully and with how much effort an individual approaches tasks also influences personal performance and the subsequent feeling of self-efficacy. Empowering conditions help strengthen self-efficacy.

Self-initiated empowerment

An individual can initiate personal actions to bring about self-empowerment and greater feelings of self-efficacy. People who are intrinsically motivated internal attributors usually initiate personal efforts to expand the nature of their jobs and their power. They are willing to take on additional responsibilities and/or work creatively on ways to improve organisational processes or products. Self-empowering people are, in effect, entrepreneurs who work actively to alter the organisation in ways that make them proud of their results.

Empowerment by others

Colleagues and co-workers have a significant impact on work-related self-perceptions. Peers who promote empowerment influence how individuals within a group feel about themselves and the group itself. Within groups, people feel empowered when they are respected and treated as professionals, encourage co-workers to accept responsibility and have the sponsorship of a personal mentor. Individuals are empowered when peers seek their advice, confide in them, and include them in projects from which they can learn and make contact with others that might help their careers.

Empowerment by managers

The most talked-about source of empowerment is the behaviour of managers or leaders in interacting with staff. The empowering manager actively gives power to individuals and enables them to be self-motivated. This is done by changing employee expectations so they believe they are in control of their destiny and can shape their work and make it meaningful within their organisation. Empowering managers also share information so people can perform their jobs more accurately and confidently. Information technology and systems that allow employees to have on-demand access to whatever information they need is by itself seen as a major empowering factor.

As a management practice, empowerment also means managers open communications, delegate power, share information and cut away at the debilitating tangles of corporate bureaucracy. The manager who deliberately works to empower his or her employees gives them the licence to pursue their visions, to champion projects, and to improve practices consistent with the organisational mission and goals. The manager who shares responsibilities with subordinates and treats them as partners is likely to get the best from them.

The results of empowerment

The empowered person undergoes two types of personal change. One is *motivational enhancement*, especially when the source of empowerment is positive change initiated by a manager. Empowered people usually intensify their task focus and are energised to become more committed to a cause or goal. They experience self-efficacy, which stimulates motivation by enabling people to see themselves as competent and capable of high performance.

Empowerment also is manifested in active *problem-solving behaviours* that concentrate energy on a goal. The empowered person is more flexible in behaviour, tries alternative paths when one is blocked, and eagerly initiates new tasks or adds complexity to current ones. Behaviour becomes self-motivated when the individual seeks to carve out greater personal autonomy in undertaking tasks without the manager's help, or to draw support from team members.

Empowerment expectations

Although managers often set the stage for empowerment by promoting initiative and relaxing bureaucratic obstacles, ultimately the individual decides whether to act in an empowered way. Thomas and Velthouse (1990) suggest that, because empowerment depends in part on how people perceive reality, not everyone on a team responds the same way to empowerment opportunities.

For example, Naomi, a market analyst, has self-confidence and self-esteem because she believes she can influence organisational outcomes. According to Bandura (1986), this occurs in part because her manager enthusiastically supports her reports and allows her to present them to top management. Such repeated experiences lead to a personal belief that she is truly competent, which positively influences her expectations about future events. Naomi believes her competence transfers across situations, and she looks forward to challenging assignments. By contrast, Scott, her accounts receivable colleague, generally sees himself as weak in analytical reasoning and persuasion skills. He has low self-efficacy associated with learned helplessness in these areas. His manager audits his work, points out deficiencies and hounds him for faster turnaround times. Scott avoids situations that he expects will require analytical or persuasion skills.

Expectancy motivation comes into play in empowerment whenever a person raises questions about himself or herself and the task at hand. Managers help bring about empowerment when they encourage their people to diminish such bureaucratic thoughts as 'It's not my responsibility' or 'It's beyond my control' or the classic, 'It wasn't invented here'. One way to overcome self-deluding excuses is to have people identify the customers served by their work, even if those customers are other departments within the firm. This shifts the focus away from thinking of one's tasks as trivial 'busywork' towards perceiving one's importance in the flow of interdependent tasks.

Coaching

A recent survey by the CIPD (2004) found that 79 per cent of organisations are now using some form of coaching. Coaching is becoming a widespread development tool, which can be used to improve individual performance, deal with under-performance and improve productivity.

Coaching, according to the CIPD, is now seen as a means of developing people within an organisation in order that they perform more effectively and reach their potential. There still tends to be a lack of precise definition but coaching should encompass the activities listed in Exhibit 8-12.

coaching

A means of developing people within an organisation in order that they perform more effectively and reach their potential.

This means that coaching can be seen as a holistic process and, although aimed at improving performance in the workplace, it can also impact on a person's behaviour outside of work.

Coaching has become popular due to the following factors, identified by the CIPD (2004).

- **A rapidly evolving business environment**: targeted development interventions have become popular in helping individuals adjust to workplace changes.

- **The structural features of modern organisations**: organisational downsizing and flatter structures mean that newly promoted individuals often have to quickly fit into the higher performance requirements of their new roles. Coaching can support individuals in achieving these changes.

- **The need for targeted, individualised, just-in-time development**: the development needs of individuals can be diverse and, in smaller organisations, there are often too few

---

- Coaching is a fairly short-term activity
- It consists of one-to-one developmental discussions
- It provides people with feedback on both their strengths and weaknesses
- It is aimed at specific issues/areas
- It is timebound
- It focuses on improving performance and developing/enhancing individuals' skills
- It is used to address a wide range of issues
- Coaching activities have both organisational and individual goals
- It works on the belief that clients are self-aware and do not require a clinical intervention
- It focuses on current and future performance/behaviour
- It is a skilled activity
- Personal issues may be discussed but the emphasis is on performance at work

Exhibit 8 – 12 What is coaching?
Source: CIPD (2004).

individuals with specific development needs to warrant the design of a formal training programme. Coaching offers a flexible option that can be delivered 'just in time' to strengthen underdeveloped skills.

- **Financial costs of the poor performance of senior managers**: there is a growing acceptance of the costs associated with poorly performing senior managers/executives. Coaching provides an opportunity to undertake pre-emptive and proactive interventions to improve their performance.

- **Improved decision-making by senior employees**: for senior-level executives it can be 'lonely at the top' as they have few people they can confide in, develop ideas and discuss decisions and concerns with. A coach can be used as a 'safe and objective haven' to discuss issues and provide support.

- **Individual responsibility for development**: there is an increasing trend for individuals to take greater responsibility for their personal and professional development. Coaching can help individuals identify development needs, plan development activities and support personal problem-solving.

- **Support for other learning and development activities**: coaching offers a valuable way of providing ongoing support for personal development plans, especially in assisting the transfer of learning in the workplace.

- **A popular development mechanism**: people enjoy participating in coaching as they get direct one-to-one assistance and attention that fits in with their own time frames and schedules. There is the potential to see quick results.

Coaching is more often the tool used for developing managers rather than operative staff and, more often than not, is delivered by the HR department rather than external consultants.

Since coaching can have a variety of definitions, it is important that the HR department takes a strategic role in the design and implementation of coaching within an organisation. The HR department needs to ensure that training is available for the appropriate coaches, whether they are line managers or HR specialists. The HR department also needs to identify whether coaching is the best option when compared with other methods of training and development and, if they do decide on coaching, then they also need to consider the most appropriate tools to identify issues.

Summary

- Performance management is an important part of a manager's role and needs to be linked to the strategy of the organisation.

- Performance appraisal is part of the performance management process and needs to be seen as a constructive and fair process that can enable both the people and the organisation to develop.

- Managers also need to be able to understand and manage poor performance and be prepared to bear the consequences of their actions, however unpopular these may be.

- Objectives and performance standards are one of the methods used to ensure that objectives are Smart, Measurable, Achievable, Relevant and Timebound (SMART).

- Many managers have problems with giving feedback to staff. To be effective, managers need to understand the consequences of poor feedback and develop positive feedback skills.

- The method of 360-degree feedback uses feedback from a variety of sources and is able to give a more rounded view of an employee's performance.

- Retaining good staff is important to the organisation, as this ensures that knowledge is retained.

- Empowerment enables people to develop autonomy in their work. The development process can enable this to happen by giving employees the competence that enables them to feel energised and in control.

Personal development

1 **Understand why it is important to manage performance.** As a manager it is important to be able to manage not only your own performance, but also the performance of others. To do this effectively would you be able to set targets, link performance to the needs of the organisation, and demonstrate the link between individual performance and organisational performance?

2 **Recognise the role of performance appraisal in the workplace.** Performance appraisal is about establishing individual goals and linking them to the organisation. How would you ensure that the appraisal system is fair? What would you do about the weaker performers and how would you reward the stronger performers?

3 **Identify and remedy poor performance.** Could you identify what causes poor performance? What management strategies would you put in place to remedy the situation? How would you ensure that, when taking action, you are fair and objective?

4 **Develop positive feedback skills.** Positive feedback shows that you are interested in a person's performance. How could you use feedback to improve performance? Do you have the communication skills to provide feedback, especially on sensitive issues?

5 **Understand how empowerment can improve performance.** To become empowered you need to be able to understand yourself. What is your self-concept? Is low self-esteem holding you back? How do you view your self-efficacy? Is there anything you need to change to become empowered?

6 **Recognise the role of coaching.** Coaching can be seen as a useful management tool. What skills would you identify as necessary for a coach? Do these skills differ from other developmental techniques? Would coaching be the best option in your self-development?

❓ Discussion questions

1 Why is performance management not easy to implement?

2 What are the consequences of poor performance?

3 How would you develop an appraisal system that could measure and evaluate employees' performance effectively and link the performance to the organisation's goals?

4 What strategies could a manager use to deal with poor performance?

5 How could a manager develop a 360-degree feedback system that would be objective and positive for the organisation?

6 The results of empowerment are motivational enhancement and active problem-solving behaviours. What strategies do managers need to use to bring about empowerment?

7 Discuss the implications of coaching as a management tool. Is it a worthwhile tool or a new management fad that will soon be forgotten when the next fashion comes along?

8 What are the characteristics of a learning organisation?

9 To avoid confrontation, managers often send mixed messages to employees about their performance. How could this inhibit learning in an organisation?

10 How could a manager develop learning organisation?

🔑 Key concepts

performance management, *p. 253*	empowerment, *p. 272*
competencies, *p. 257*	self-concept, *p. 273*
performance appraisal, *p. 259*	self-esteem, *p. 273*
SMART, *p. 262*	self-efficacy, *p. 274*
360-degree feedback, *p. 266*	coaching, *p. 276*

Individual task

Imagine you are appraising a staff member and you have a disagreement about an employee's performance. The employee thinks their performance is excellent, yet you think it has been only average.

The discussion is getting heated. The employee wants a good rating as it is linked to performance-related pay. As a manager you feel that to give in to the employee will make a mockery of the appraisal system and discourage good performance.

1 What tools do you have available to demonstrate that the employee has not met the required performance?

2 What can you do to reduce the building tensions?

3 How can managers manage appraisals effectively?

Team task

Purpose To identify problems with appraisal interviews.

Time 60 minutes

Procedure Divide your group into groups of three, comprising one appraiser, one appraisee and one observer. Each appraiser and appraisee should read their role-play scenario (see below) and prepare notes before they carry out the interview. Think about how questions can be asked and how the discussion can be managed effectively.

The appraiser: Mr Bruno

You are the food and beverage manager of the Shilton Hotel, a luxury five-star hotel. You have worked for this hotel for five years and have been in your current management position for one year. You have now been asked to carry out appraisals on your waiting staff.

One of your waiters is Miguel, who although competent does not have the charismatic personality expected of someone who may want to progress to the role of restaurant manager.

You are concerned, as you are unsure what to say to say to him. His technical competence makes him a useful member of the team; he tends to be quiet but is nevertheless methodical in his work.

As a manager, you also have to ensure that he develops his skills, but Miguel already has recognised professional qualifications, albeit a bit dated, and he may not be keen to develop further.

Miguel also tends to keep apart from other members of the team: he does not socialise with them out of work, neither does he involve himself in workplace chatter – in fact, he can be rather solitary. This seems to make him quite unsuited to his job, which usually attracts more gregarious personalities who enjoy interacting with others.

The appraisee: Miguel

You are a waiter in the restaurant of the Shilton Hotel, a luxury five-star hotel. You have worked here for three years. You are about to have an appraisal interview with the food and beverage manager, Mr Bruno, who has been at the hotel for five years, but was promoted only to his current position one year ago.

You think you work well. You turn up on time, you carry out all the tasks asked of you and you ensure that your section runs smoothly. You like working for the company as the conditions are good and the surroundings pleasant.

You are not looking forward to your performance appraisal. You are naturally quiet and shy. You believe that, providing you get on with the job and nobody complains about you, then everything should be OK. You don't see why you should have to join training programmes; you know your job and, although promotion would be useful for the extra money, you feel you already have the competence required.

You know you are quiet, as you lack confidence and prefer to leave the talking to other people. You also have a young family and find it difficult to make ends meet, which means that sometimes you work as a taxi driver between shifts.

Although you think you get on all right with your team members, you tend to find them a bit irresponsible. They are all free and single, and don't have the responsibilities you have.

The interview (20 minutes)

After you have read through your relevant roles, the appraiser should start the interview with the appraisee.

The observer should read both roles beforehand too, to help them understand the different viewpoints.

The following checklist may be useful for the observer.

- How does the appraiser open the interview?
- Is the appraiser constructive in bringing up issues?
- How are negative points dealt with?
- Is it a discussion or an interrogation?
- Does the appraisee have a chance to respond?
- How would you feel as the appraiser and as the appraisee?

The debrief (10 minutes)

In your group of three, identify any issues. It may be useful to refer back to the observer's checklist.

Whole-group discussion

After the debrief, bring the whole group together and share the issues that have arisen.

You may want to discuss strategies you could use for a successful appraisal, and strategies you would avoid.

Case study: **TNT UK Ltd**

TNT UK Ltd, the express and logistics delivery service, employs over 9500 staff working throughout the UK and Ireland. The majority of these employees work at one of over 60 major depots as drivers or operational loaders, servicing both the UK and international markets. The delivery and logistics industry is heavily monitored to ensure that the flow of parcels can be tracked, but also for security reasons.

TNT believes in 'growing your own timber' – promoting staff from within the company (several depot general managers started out as drivers or indoor sales executives). It is therefore important to TNT that staff have a meaningful development path. One of the challenges has been to change the attitude of line managers from 'my job is getting parcels out' to 'my job is to develop my staff to do their jobs better'.

Unusually for an organisation employing mainly blue-collar staff, all staff, from drivers and loading bay operators to general managers and directors, have annual appraisals.

Promoting the development culture

TNT is committed to Investors In People (IIP) and has won awards for its training and development. The company firmly believes that individual learning, rather than directive training, is critical to business success. To quote from one of the managers, Dave Spong, depot general manager,

Barking: 'Training, developing and empowering your people gives you the freedom and the confidence to make changes quickly, affect your business positively and achieve results.' The benefits of this culture can be seen in better delegation, succession planning and in reducing staff turnover – crucial when there is a national driver shortage.

This view is articulated and promoted through the production of a people development charter. This one-page document is displayed prominently throughout all offices and depots, and is highlighted as part of the induction process. The charter outlines what is expected from senior managers, line managers and staff in the following terms.

All TNT managers will:

- remain actively committed to the development of TNT people
- work to build a company culture that encourages and supports learning
- lead by example in developing people
- recognise and respect the valuable contribution of our people.

Your line manager will:

- actively encourage your personal and professional development
- provide you with regular feedback on your performance
- help you to continuously improve your skills and knowledge
- ensure your learning is linked to the success of your team and the company.

You should:

- take responsibility for your own development and learning
- apply new skills and knowledge at your workplace
- know that whatever your job, wherever your location, you have the opportunity to develop.

Supporting and auditing training and learning

A team of eight regional training officers, managed by a regional training manager, supports and audits the systems in place for training and learning. They must ensure that 'what is promised' happens. Their responsibilities include: monitoring and supporting line managers at depots; carrying out IIP internal audits; and checking personnel files and appraisal forms.

Line managers undertake appraisal training as part of their management training and carry immediate responsibility for ensuring all their staff have meaningful appraisals. The regional training officers support line managers but also check that appraisals take place annually and that any training needs that have been identified are met.

One of the key reasons for the success of TNT's training and learning interventions is its evident alignment with the culture and practices of the organisation. Regular performance indicators on the training and learning efforts (for example, appraisal forms completed and training requests met) are produced and discussed at management meetings. As Ruth James, head of people development, says, 'It's imperative that our line managers take their people management responsibilities seriously to enable them to develop their staff for success. The regional training officer's role is to support and encourage line managers in their people management responsibilities as well as to report on and assess how they perform against target.'

Source: Adapted from www.investorsinpeople.co.uk.

Discussion questions

1 How has TNT managed to change the attitudes of its managers?
2 What is the role of TNT's regional training officer?
3 How can training and learning be linked to the culture and practices of the organisation?
4 How has TNT ensured that its appraisals are meaningful?

WWW exercise

According to the International Coach Federation:

> Coaching is an ongoing relationship which focuses on clients taking action toward the realisation of their visions, goals or desires. Coaching uses a process of inquiry and personal discovery to build the client's level of awareness and responsibility and provides the client with structure, support and feedback. The coaching process helps clients both define and achieve professional and personal goals faster and with more ease than would be possible otherwise.

Look at the organisation's website at www.coachfederation.org, then answer the following questions.

1 What is the International Coach Federation's advice to coaches?
2 What is a coach?
3 How can an organisation select a coach?
4 What are the coaching core competencies?
5 What are the ethical guidelines the organisation advises coaches to follow?

LEARNING CHECKLIST

Before moving on to the next chapter, check that you are able to:

☑ understand the role of appraisal systems in the management of performance
☑ examine the importance of participation and involvement
☑ recognise the role of empowerment and its relationship to performance
☑ understand the concept of a learning organisation.

Further reading

Garvin, D.A. (1993) 'Building a learning organization', *Harvard Business Review* 71(4), pp. 78–91.

Kofman, F. and Senge, P. (1993) 'Communities of commitment: the heart of learning organizations', *Organizational Dynamic*, Autumn, pp. 5–23.

Peters, T. (2000) 'Visions 21: what will we do for work?', *Time*, 22 May, pp. 68–71.

Porras, J.I. and Robertson, P.J. (1992) 'Organizational development: theory, practice, and research', in M.D. Dunnette and L.M. Hough (eds) *Handbook of Industrial and Organizational Psychology* (2nd edn), Vol. 3. Palo Alto: Consulting Psychologists Press, p. 734.

Solomon, C.M. (1994) 'HR facilitates the learning organization concept', *Personnel Journal* 73(11), November.

References

Armstrong, M. and Baron, A. (2004) *Performance Management: The New Realities.* London: Institute of Personnel and Development.

Averbrook, J. and Spirigi, H. (2005) 'How do workforce performance management initiatives rank in terms of your overall human capital management priorities?', IHRIM's HRMS Strategies 2005 Conference, Reno, NV.

Bandura, A. (1986) *Social Foundations of Thought and Action.* Englewood Cliffs, NJ: Prentice-Hall.

Bandura, A. (1988) 'Self regulation of motivation and action through goal systems', in V. Hamilton, G.H. Bower and N.H. Frijda (eds) *Competence Considered: Perceptions of Competence and Incompetence Across the Lifespan.* Dordrecht, Netherlands: Kluwer Academic Publishers, pp. 37–61.

Baron, A. and Armstrong, M. (1998) 'Out of the box', *People Management* 23, pp. 28–41.

Browell, S. (2003) *Staff Retention.* London: Chartered Management Institute/Hodder & Stoughton.

CIPD (2004) 'Performance management', factsheet. London: Chartered Institute of Personnel Development.

Cleveland, J.N., Murphy, K.R. and Williams, R.E. (1989) 'Multiple uses of performance appraisal: prevalence and correlates', *Journal of Applied Psychology* 74, February, pp. 130–135.

CMI (2004) *Managing Staff Turnover and Retention.* London: Chartered Management Institute.

Conger, J.A. and Kanungo, N. (1998) 'The empowerment process: integrating theory and practice', *Academy of Management Review* 13, July, pp. 471–482.

Cotton, J.L. and Tuttle, J.M. (1986) 'Employee turnover: a meta-analysis and review with implications for research', *Academy of Management Review* 11, pp. 55–70.

Den Hartog, D.N., Boselie, P. and Paauwe, J. (2004) 'Performance management: a model and research agenda', *Applied Psychology: An International Review* 53(4), pp. 556–569.

De Nisi, A.S. (2000) 'Performance appraisal and performance management: a multi-level analysis', in K.J. Klein and S. Kozlowski (eds) *Multilevel Theory, Research and Methods in Organizations.* San Francisco: Jossey-Bass, pp. 121–156.

Garrett, J. (2003) 'Crash course in exit interviews', *Management Today*, 30 June, p. 14.

Gist, M.E. and Mitchell, T.R. (1992) 'Self-efficacy: a theoretical analysis of its determinants and malleability', *Academy of Management Review*, 17 April, pp. 183–211.

Guest, D.E. (1997) 'Human resource management and performance: a review research agenda', *International Journal of Human Resource Management* 8, pp. 263–276.

Harrison, R. and Kessels, J. (2004) *Human Resource Development in a Knowledge Economy.* Basingstoke: Palgrave Macmillan.

Higginbottom, K. (2003) 'Tesco seeks mountain of youth', *People Management*, May, pp. 32–35.

Huselid, M.A. (1995) 'The impact of HRM practices on turnover, productivity, and corporate financial performance', *Academy of Management Journal* 38(3), pp. 635–672.

McEvoy, G.M. and Cascio, W.F. (1985) 'Strategies for reducing employee turnover: a meta-analysis', *Journal of Applied Psychology* 70(2), pp. 342–353.

Roberts, I. (2001) 'Reward and performance management', in I. Beardwell and L. Holden (eds) *Human Resource Management: A Contemporary Approach* (3rd edn). Edinburgh: Pearson, pp. 506–508.

Schein, V. (2005) BPS Division of Occupational Psychology Annual Conference, reported in *People Management*.

Schmit, M.J. and Allscheid, S.P. (1995) 'Employee attitudes and customer satisfaction: making theoretical and empirical connections', *Personnel Psychology* 48, pp. 521–536.

Schuler, R.S. and Jackson, S.E. (1996) *Human Resource Management: Positioning for the 21st Century.* New York: West Publishing.

Sheridan, J.E. (1992) 'Organizational culture and employee retention', *Academy of Management Journal* 35, pp. 1036–1056.

Thomas, K.W. and Velthouse, B.A. (1990) 'Cognitive elements of empowerment: an "interpretive" model of intrinsic task motivation', *Academy of Management Review*, 15 October, p. 673.

White, C. (2004) *Assessing Connexions: Qualitative Research with Young People.* London: Department for Education and Skills.

Wilson, J. (2005) 'Whose round is it?', *People Management*, 24 February, p. 46.

Chapter **9**

Employee relations, participation and involvement

LEARNING OUTCOMES

After studying this chapter, you should be able to:

- ☑ **understand** the theoretical perspectives of employee relations
- ☑ **understand** strategies for employee participation and involvement
- ☑ **define** and describe the conflict process
- ☑ **recognise** symptoms of conflict
- ☑ **identify** sources of conflict and appropriate conflict management strategies
- ☑ **understand** the role of negotiation and bargaining.

In recent months the Royal Mail has gone from a making a loss to making a profit. The opening vignette shows what can happen when managers start communicating and showing their trust in staff.

The Royal Mail way

The Royal Mail Centre in Chester opened just over five years ago, but from the start it was plagued by productivity and performance problems.

'Two years ago the place looked 300 years old, not three,' says Eddie Douglas, mail centre manager. There were problems with basic housekeeping, even graffiti. Now it's one of Royal Mail's best-performing units, serving as a blueprint for changes planned at seven more offices this year and, eventually, the whole network of 71.

The office is piloting 'The Royal Mail Way'. Based on lean manufacturing, the approach means asking the workforce to develop and implement their ideas on how to improve performance and service to customers.

'That never would have happened before – postmen and women changing an idea that managers and union reps had agreed? Unheard of,' Douglas says. 'But the past few months have helped us to understand that the people who work here care as much as managers do about the business.'

Douglas has been at Royal Mail for 25 years and says the culture was always one of command and control. Changing to 'The Royal Mail Way' has meant improving communication between managers and employees through regular meetings, and encouraging employees to map their work processes to look at waste-reduction opportunities.

Each area now has a 'communications cell' where meetings are held at the start of each shift and performance data is shared. Discussing upcoming problems with staff rather than trying to deal with them later has made a big difference to how managers cope with changes.

'Simply briefing people at the start of the shift can dictate productivity and the way people approach the rest of the shift,' Douglas says. 'A lot of our managers have been trained in running around putting out fires, but they can now share that responsibility with the rest of their team, letting them know: "We've got a big challenge today. I really need you to help me pull it out of the bag."'

It's a big change in style for many managers, says Patrick Keefe, people and organisational development adviser and the HR business partner for the area covering Chester and Shropshire.

'We realised managers wanted to manage in a different way, but many of them have only ever worked at Royal Mail and hadn't seen different ways of doing things,' he says. 'We've taken them to other companies to see their management styles, and given them the tools, support and coaching to operate in a different way.'

Keefe likes the simplicity of the idea. 'In the past, maybe we've been guilty of being too sophisticated or of over-intellectualising,' he says.

But it hasn't been easy to convince staff suffering from change fatigue. Improving the credibility of management was vital, according to Douglas. 'In the past, if we'd asked them to undertake this they would have seen it as a cost-cutting exercise rather than a way of getting them involved in efficiency,' he says.

Managers built credibility by spending a small amount on the work environment, sorting out issues that had made life difficult for employees, as well as communicating more. Just over a year ago the office advertised for post workers who wanted to become managers. Only 16 people applied. This time there have been almost 80. 'People said the way the company is starting to treat its people has made them want to become a manager,' Keefe says.

Kirk Perry, a Royal Mail worker for the past 22 years, says: 'Management is much more

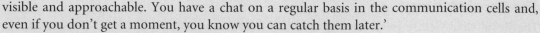

visible and approachable. You have a chat on a regular basis in the communication cells and, even if you don't get a moment, you know you can catch them later.'

Perry believes there is a stronger feeling that everyone is pulling together, but he adds: 'There have been so many changes in the past that were introduced with a big fanfare and then faded out after a year and a half. The management is still enthusiastic about this idea, but only time will tell.'

Source: Adapted from Z. Roberts, 'Back in black', *People Management*, 2 June 2005, p. 24.
Reproduced with permission of *People Management* and Zoe Roberts.

Discussion questions

1 Why is it important to have good employee relations?

2 What is the importance of good communication in managing people?

Employee relations

According to Gospel and Palmer (1993) one definition of **employee relations** is 'an economic,

employee relations
The economic, political and social relationship between the employer and the employee.

social and political relationship in which employees provide manual and mental labour in exchange for rewards allotted by employers'. This implies that there is a relationship between the employer and the employee and, as with all relationships, there are various characteristics. These characteristics are summarised by Rose (2004) as follows.

- **Conflict issues** – how workers define their interests can be crucial and problematic for the employer. Often, employers and employees have different economic interests, which can result in industrial disputes.

- **Inequality** – workers are in a subordinate position to employers, which is formalised through contracts of employment and reliance on the employer for financial reward and fair treatment.

- **Dynamic relationships** – employers have the right to redefine employees' obligations and duties in relation to the division of work.

- **Power relationship** – employees can exert their power through collective groups such as unions in the workplace, which enables them to meet the employer on more equal terms. However, the employer can also use his/her power to force employees to comply with requests. Misuse of power can result in conflict.

- **Contractual relationship** – an employee's behaviour is often governed by their contract of employment, and issues concerning grievance, discipline, redundancy, and so on.

Therefore employee relations is concerned with:

- the rule-making process
- interaction between employers and employees
- informal and formal communication
- informal and formal employee representation.

The role of the human resource manager is, therefore, to manage the employment relationship in the context of the organisation.

According to Rose (2004), this means the HR manager needs to:

- develop the talents and capacities of individual employees
- communicate with employees
- negotiate reward packages that reflect an individual's skills, experience, effort and performance
- encourage employees to make a larger contribution to decision-making and participation in the workplace
- provide employees with the opportunity to influence and negotiate their own terms of employment.

This moves away from the collective agreements of industrial relations from employee representation towards more individual agreements aimed at engaging and encouraging participation of the employee in the workplace.

Employee representation
Trades unions

Traditionally, many employees have been represented by trades unions and yet many unions are now seen as being in decline. At its peak in the 1970s union membership stood at 13 million; now only about 7.5 million employees belong to a union (Metcalf, 2005). The result is that where, in the past, unions provided employees with a representative voice, now employees communicate directly with management and each other through team meetings and problem-solving groups.

According to Metcalf (2005), the reasons for the decline and fall of unions can be attributed to:

- alterations to the composition of workforce and jobs – the decline of manufacturing, fewer full-time male workers, and changing attitudes
- the business cycle – low inflation, steady wage growth, and the changed structure of the workforce
- the role of the state – removal of the 'closed shop', promotion of share ownership, privatisation of public utilities and decentralisation of public-sector workers
- the attitudes of employers – they no longer need to recognise a single union; instead a simple recognition of employees' right to be represented is required
- the reactions of individual employees to trade unionism – less need is seen for a union and there is disenchantment with union practices
- the strategic approach and structures of the unions themselves – decentralisation meant the loss of a national voice; many saw unions as only representing men, and female priorities were not seen to be addressed.

The main reasons to belong to a union were that historically unionised workplaces received better pay and therefore financially it made sense. With the decline of union representation this is no longer seen as the case, although UNISON (the main UK public-sector union) claims that its members do have a wage premium over non-members (Blanchflower and Bryson, 2003).

However, from a management perspective, unions have been seen to reduce productivity through restrictive work practices and an adversarial style of industrial relations, resulting in a loss of trust and low co-operation between management and unions. Yet research by Card and Freeman (2004) has demonstrated that where management and unions can work together, then productivity can increase.

Changing values

Although past government legislation had a major impact on loosening the control of the unions, other factors were also at work. The high unemployment of the early 1980s sparked the development of the enterprise economy and unions, with their collective processes, were seen as a threat to individual endeavour. Tough economic conditions also meant that organisations have had to recognise the business sense of good employee relations and that managers can seek competitive advantage by working with their employees and not against them.

Work was moving away from manufacturing to a knowledge-based economy. This meant that in many organisations the skills, knowledge, experience and ideas of individual workers could help develop a competitive edge. This also meant that managers had to move away from a focus on controlling workers to one of gaining commitment. The different approaches to employee relations are illustrated in Exhibit 9-1.

Non-union organisations
Guest and Hoque's typology

Guest and Hoque (1994) identified a classification of non-unionised establishments. Their typology identifies the consequences of belonging to a particular type of organisation and the HRM performance outcomes. They referred to these as the 'good, bad, ugly and lucky' faces of non-unionisation.

Guest and Hoque based their typology on two dimensions:

1 whether firms have a human resource strategy, and

2 the nature of the HR policy and practice.

This includes employee involvement and participation.

Investment approach	Cost-minimising approach
■ Partnership arrangement with trades union/employee representatives	■ Adversarial relationship with union(s), non-recognition or de-recognition
■ Job security	■ Job insecurity/hiring and firing
■ Longer-term policies	■ Ad hoc/firefighting employee relations policies
■ More selectivity in recruitment, higher pay, investment in training	■ Casual approach to recruitment, low pay, little investment in training
■ More sophisticated/two-way communications	■ One-way communication (if any) from management
■ Application of procedures	■ Procedures not implemented, 'macho' management

Exhibit 9–1 Approaches to managing employee relations
Source: Marchington and Parker (1990).

Guest and Hoque's typology of four non-union types is as follows.

- **Type 1** – Establishments have a clear HRM strategy, encouraging and achieving high levels of employee involvement and commitment, and representing the 'good' face of non-unionism. This type is more formally labelled the full utilisation, high-involvement model.

- **Type 2** – Establishments have a clear strategy but they do not make much use of HRM practices, providing at best only minimum levels of employee rights. There may be a deliberate strategy to deprive employees of many of their traditional rights, including a voice of any sort. These represent the 'ugly' face of non-unionised workplaces and are more formally called efficiency-driven models.

- **Type 3** – Establishments not having a clear HRM strategy, but that nevertheless have adopted many innovative HRM practices, which they have, fortunately for them, stumbled on by accident. Management in these establishments often implements the latest fad without much thought for the consequences. These are known as the 'lucky' face of non-unionism and are more formally opportunist.

- **Type 4** – Establishments have no HRM strategy and a low uptake of human resource management practices. They are characterised by poor management practices that do not adequately consider human resource issues and represent the 'bad' face of non-unionism. They may be labelled benevolent bureaucrats.

Good establishments are likely to have more favourable HRM outcomes, with commitment of staff at every level of the organisation, good quality of staff employed, good-quality work produced, and flexible and enthusiastic employees who are willing to move to different positions in the organisation. The good establishments were also seen as having the best dispute resolution procedures and an increased competitive advantage through enhanced performance.

Employee participation and involvement

Employee participation is defined by Hyman and Mason (1995) as follows:

employee participation
Initiatives that promote the collective rights of employees in organisational decision-making.

> state initiatives which promote the collective rights of employees to be represented in organisational decision-making, or to the consequences of the efforts of employees themselves to establish collective representation in corporate decisions, possibly in the face of employee resistance. This definition would include collective bargaining over terms and conditions of employment.

Employee involvement is defined by Hyman and Mason (1995) as follows:

employee involvement
Policies and practices that allow employees to influence the decision-making process on matters that affect them.

> practices and policies which emanate from management and sympathisers of free market commercial activity and which purport to provide employees with the opportunity to influence and where appropriate take part in the decision making on matters which affect them.

Participation usually arises from collective employee interests supported by government initiatives. Employee involvement is usually a management initiative that encourages employee involvement in order to produce a flexible workforce and to enable it to achieve competitive advantage.

Exhibit 9-2 illustrates the similarities and differences of employee participation and involvement.

Participation and involvement should mean working in partnership with employees. According to the TUC, this means:

■ a shared commitment to the success of the organisation

■ a recognition of legitimate interests

■ a commitment to employment security

■ a focus on the quality of working life

■ openness

■ adding value.

Partnerships need to add value to both parties in order to be successful, and both parties need to see such benefits, otherwise motivation is likely to suffer.

Employee consultation

Consultation involves willingness by the employer to exchange information and views with employees or stakeholders, and to give full consideration to the other parties' proposals, while reserving the right to implement a decision without such agreement. It is better, as a starting point, to consult with employees rather than negotiate, as consultation asks for comments rather than agreement. However, sometimes managers are put in a position when a

Employee participation	Employee involvement
Mainly pluralist	*Mainly unitarist*
■ Inspired by government and/or workforce with some control delegated to workers	■ Inspired and controlled by management
■ Aims to harness collective employee inputs through market regulation	■ Orientated towards encouraging individual employee inputs through market regulation
■ Collective representation	■ Directed to responsibilities of individual employees
■ Management and organisational hierarchies chain of command broken	■ Management and organisational structures flatter, but hierarchies undisturbed
■ Active involvement of employee representatives	■ Employees are often passive recipients of information and decisions already made
■ Decision-making at higher organisational levels	■ Decisions tend to be task based
■ Plurality of interests recognised and machinery for their resolution provided	■ Assumes common interests between employer and employees
■ Aims to distribute strategic influence beyond management	■ Aims to concentrate strategic influence among management

Exhibit 9–2 Essentials of employee participation and involvement
Source: Hyman and Mason (1995).

consultation exercise does not produce the desired response and they are left with no alternative than to negotiate. The headings in the 'Stop and reflect' exercise may give you ideas for areas of consultation rather than negotiation.

Stop and reflect

What do you think should be included in the rules under the following headings?

Timekeeping and absence

Health and safety

Use of organisation facilities

Discrimination, bullying and harassment

Gross misconduct

Write down your ideas and compare them with those of a colleague.

European Works Councils

The EU Directive on establishing a **European Works Council** was finally implemented into UK law in January 2000.

European Works Council
A council of workers in organisations, who are involved in the decision-making process.

The directive covers organisations employing workers across the European Union who have more than 150 workers in more than one EU country.

The benefits of setting up a European Works Council (EWC) identified by many organisations are as follows:

- greater awareness of business strategies and priorities
- improved understanding of operating in different countries
- encourages the development of higher standards in training, in communication and in consultation
- clear focus for employee involvement, complementing national structures
- facilitates change and rational decision-making
- increased trust and enthusiasm of participants
- helps ensure that local consultation is carried out effectively.

According to the IPA (2005):

> The success or failure of EWCs in practice is dependent on the commitment of senior management, the knowledge and experience of representatives, the quality of the agenda and the dynamics of the group . . . A good EWC is one which rarely if ever needs to refer back to these regulations once it has been set up and has started to function.

The IPA suggests that EWCs work best if numbers are manageable, they meet at least twice a year, and where there is senior management commitment to engage actively in a real process of information sharing and dialogue.

EWCs are not seen as effective when there is:

- lack of management commitment – lip-service
- turnover of reps – many only ever attend one or two meetings
- language and other issues of transnational understanding, e.g. different industrial relations cultures
- lack of communication between participants between meetings
- skill level of participants (especially noticeable among non-union reps from the UK).

An example of how employee consultation works in practice can be seen in the 'International perspective' box .

Dealing with conflict

Conflict is a disagreement between two or more parties – for example, individuals, groups, departments, organisations, countries – who perceive that they have incompatible concerns. Conflicts exist whenever an action by one party is perceived as preventing or interfering with the goals, needs, or actions of another. Rahim (1992) suggests that conflicts can arise over multiple organisational experiences, such as incompatible goals, differences in the interpretation of facts, negative feelings, differences of values and philosophies, or disputes over shared resources. As defined above, conflict sounds pretty negative. However, in some cases, it can actually stimulate creative problem-solving and improve the situation for all parties involved.

conflict
A disagreement between two or more parties who perceive that they have incompatible concerns.

Perspectives of conflict

The unitarist perspective of conflict

The unitarist perspective of employee relations recognises that management has the power, and argues that when one party has control over work practices then conflict will be reduced. This is the traditional view that sees conflict as undesirable, destructive and to be avoided at all costs. In organisations it is assumed that everyone is on the same side, working towards the same goals; any differences are assumed to be the result of poor leadership, poor communication or some agitators looking for trouble. This simplistic view fails to see that difference of interest or opinion can be perfectly normal. Drucker (1984) identifies with this view in his writings about organisations, where he suggests that everyone should work together to fulfil a common goal. Morgan (1986) also acknowledges that it is popular with managers as it emphasises teamwork and anyone who questions a manager can be discredited.

The pluralist perspective of conflict

An organisation is seen as a collection of different groups, all with their legitimate aims to pursue, and therefore a degree of conflict is normal. Pluralists propose the idea that conflict is natural and therefore procedures need to be in place to handle it so that it does not disrupt the organisation as a whole. This is the widely accepted view of conflict but from a critic's view-point it ignores the wider cultural issues of conflict.

Germany – is it too set in its ways?

Germany has a history of employee consultation that seeks to balance the interests of company owners with those of other stakeholders. In Germany, there is political commitment to a social market economy and social partnership. In practice, this means highly influential and centralised employers' organisations and unions, both of which influence HR policies.

The German economy developed later than that of the UK and has therefore had less advanced capital markets. Banks have been more important in supplying capital and have tended to develop long-term relationships with companies. Such relationships have led to a longer-term view of financial objectives.

Another feature of the German economy is the set of employee relations institutions that developed out of the need for industrial peace during post-war reconstruction. Perhaps the most important element is the system of 'peak bargaining', whereby wages and conditions for each sector are negotiated by employers' associations and trades unions. Wage bargaining is taken out of the workplace, so reducing tension. Employee representatives sit on the supervisory board of companies, and Works Councils have the right to information, consultation or joint decision-making on many HR issues. One such example of consultation led to the German law of the 1994 Working Time Statute, which establishes an eight-hour working day, although, subject to an average of eight hours per day over a six-month period, employers may extend the day up to ten hours. However, variations to this can be negotiated between employers and unions for a company or sector.

Wages and working hours are also determined by unions and employers' associations. Employee relations matters are often subject to negotiation through Works Councils. Personnel departments focus on Works Councils and rarely have a strategic role. So, personnel managers play little part in developing communication about strategic objectives.

However, such practices may be at the expense of both flexibility and employment levels, and there is evidence that the constraints within European economies using the German model have caused companies to take a longer-term view and to invest in both skills and equipment as an alternative approach to flexibility.

Germany is seen to be a key player in leading Europe in employee consultation; however, culture also needs to be taken into consideration. One aspect is the difference in the understanding of managerial work in Germany when compared to the UK. The Anglo-American notion of management as a set of skills that is separable from its context is not shared in Germany. While a senior manager from industry might be recruited into a senior role in a bank in the UK, this would be considered bizarre in Germany.

It will be interesting to see how other countries, which may not have such a strong culture of employee consultation, develop such a system.

Source: Adapted from Mark Fenton-O'Creevy, 'HR practice: vive la difference',
Financial Times, 26 November 2001, p. 6.

Discussion questions

1 Do you think the German system is too rigid to enable organisations to be competitive?

2 Employee consultation is seen as the way forward for Europe. How could it be implemented in the UK?

The Marxist perspective of conflict

This is derived from the Marxist perspective and suggests that organisational conflict reflects the conflict in the wider society between the capitalist owners and the workers. This perspective takes into account the wider social view but views conflict as vertical and managers as the instruments of the owners; therefore it fails to acknowledge that managers may also have different views. It also fails to recognise that conflict can occur between people at the same level in an organisation.

The interactionist perspective

This view, proposed by McKenna (1994), sees conflict as neither good nor bad but simply inevitable. It is not too different from the pluralist perspective. It recognises that, when there is conflict, much of the organisation's energy will be channelled into its resolution, to the detriment of pursuing other goals, but it also recognises that when there is no conflict, there is unlikely to be creativity and this will lead to complacency. This means there should be an optimum level of conflict that needs to be identified to enable the organisation to develop. The problem is finding the optimal level and learning how to manage the conflict effectively.

The traditional view of conflict assumed that it was undesirable and led to negative outcomes like aggression, violence and hostility. This **dysfunctional view of conflict** implied that managers should determine the causes of conflict and eliminate them, and make sure that future conflicts were prevented. However, there is also a **functional view of conflict** because of its potential to stimulate the creative resolution of problems and corrective actions, and to keep people and organisations from slipping into complacency. Perhaps it should not matter if individuals don't like conflict. If it increases performance and is beneficial to the group or organisation as a whole, it is functional.

dysfunctional view of conflict
Conflict between groups in the same organisation that hinders the achievement of group and organisational goals.

functional view of conflict
Conflict between groups that stimulates innovations and production.

This outcome of the conflict is the criterion for determining if it is functional or dysfunctional – that is, whether it has positive or negative outcomes for the decision-making group (e.g. department, organisation, stockholders). Perhaps the most appropriate attitude towards conflict is that it is inevitable and has the potential to be dysfunctional but, if managed constructively, conflict can be functional and enhance performance.

Exhibit 9-3 provides an overview of the conflict management process. The first thing a manager needs to do is determine what stage the conflict is in. Then the source of the conflict

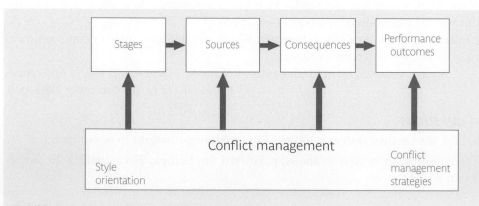

Exhibit 9–3 The conflict management process

has to be established. Next, the manager can examine the consequences and performance outcomes of the conflict. Finally, the manager needs to decide which conflict style orientation and specific strategies to apply in order to most productively manage the conflict. The next section of this chapter will focus on the first two parts of the conflict management process: the stages and sources of conflict.

The stages of conflict

Thomas (1992) suggests that a conflict does not exist until one party perceives that another party may negatively affect something that the first party cares about. The development of antecedent conditions (the sources of conflict) marks the start of the process. Pondy (1967), as shown in Exhibit 9-4, has identified five stages through which conflict can progress.

Stage 1: latent conflict

When two or more parties need each other in order to achieve desired objectives, there is

interdependence

The degree to which interactions between parties must be co-ordinated in order for them to perform adequately.

potential for conflict. Other antecedents of conflict, such as interdependence, different goals and ambiguity of responsibility, are described in the next section. They do not automatically create conflicts, but when they exist, they make it possible. Latent conflict often arises when a change occurs. Conflict might be caused by a budget cutback, a change in organisational direction, a change in a personal goal, the assignment of a new project to an already overloaded workforce, or an expected occurrence (such as a salary increase) that doesn't happen.

Stage 2: perceived conflict

This is the point at which members become aware of a problem. Incompatibility of needs is perceived and tension begins as the parties begin to worry about what will happen. At this point, however, no one feels that anything they care about is actually being overtly threatened.

Stage 3: felt conflict

Now the parties become emotionally involved and begin to focus on differences of opinion and opposing interests, sharpening perceived conflict. Internal tensions and frustrations begin to

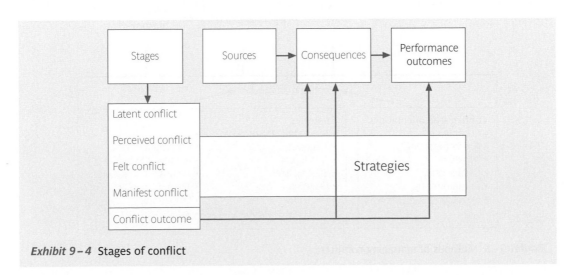

Exhibit 9–4 Stages of conflict

crystallise around specific, defined issues and people begin to build an emotional commitment to their particular position. Kuman (1989) suggests that the type of emotion felt is important because negative feelings produce low trust and negative perceptions of the other party's position, which can result in destructive win–lose tactics. More positive feelings, on the other hand, can contribute to a more balanced view of the situation and more collaborative endeavours. In either case, the result is a defining of what the conflict is actually about, which will determine the alternatives available for later resolution.

Stage 4: manifest conflict

The obvious display of conflict occurs when the opposing parties plan and follow through with acts to achieve their own objectives and frustrate the other. Glasl (1982) identifies actions that can range from minor disagreeing, questioning and challenging, at one end of the conflict-intensity continuum, to verbal attacks, threats, ultimatums, physical attacks and even efforts to destroy the other party at the other end.

Stage 5: conflict outcome

The interactions of the conflicting parties in the manifest conflict stage result in outcomes that can be functional or dysfunctional for one or both parties. As conflict proceeds through the stages, functional resolution becomes more difficult. The parties become more locked into their positions and more convinced that the conflict is a win–lose situation. It is usually easier to achieve positive collaboration and win–win outcomes when the conflict is recognised early, before frustration and other negative sentiments have set in.

Managing conflict

The first part of this chapter has shown how conflict can have negative and/or positive consequences for individuals, groups and organisations. The major variable that determines its outcome is how the conflict is managed. Exhibit 9-5 summarises conflict style orientations and conflict management methods.

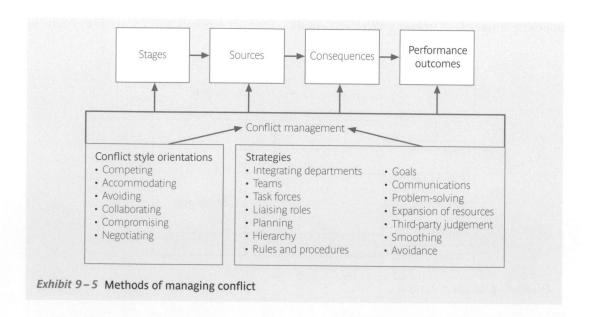

Exhibit 9–5 Methods of managing conflict

Conflict management styles

Parties engaged in a conflict usually have two main concerns: getting what they want for themselves, and maintaining the kind of relationship they want with the other party. When people are primarily concerned for themselves, they are assertive in trying to satisfy their own needs. When they care about the other party and want to maintain a positive relationship, people are co-operative and concerned about making sure the other's needs are satisfied.

conflict management styles
The different combinations of assertiveness and co-operation that people emphasise when in a conflict situation.

Rahim (1992) and Thomas (1992) suggest that the different degrees of emphasis that people place on these two basic concerns can be expanded into five specific **conflict management styles**: competing, accommodating, avoiding, collaborating and compromising. These are shown in Exhibit 9-6.

Competing

Competing is assertive and unco-operative behaviour, embodied in the parties' pursuit of their own concerns at others' expense. Competing behaviour is often used by power-orientated people, who will use every technique available to win their point or defend their position.

Competing can be beneficial when quick, decisive action is vital, as in emergencies. It is also useful when unpopular actions, such as discipline or cost-cutting, must be implemented. Finally, competing is sometimes necessary to protect against people who take advantage of non-competitive behaviour. If you are too competitive, however, you may find yourself surrounded by yes-men who have learned that it is unwise to disagree with you, which cuts you off from sources of important information.

Accommodating

Accommodating is the opposite of competing. It consists of unassertive and co-operative behaviour. Accommodating people frequently neglect their own concerns to satisfy the needs of others in order to maintain a positive relationship.

Accommodating is an appropriate strategy when the issue at stake is much more important to the other person. Satisfying another's needs as a goodwill gesture will help maintain a co-operative relationship, building up social credits for use in later conflicts. Accommodating is

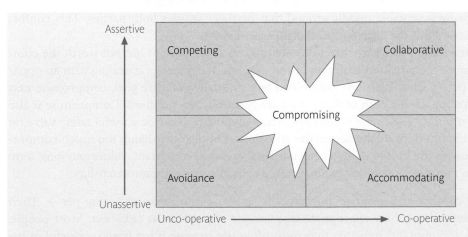

Exhibit 9-6 Interpersonal conflict management styles
Source: Adapted from Thomas (1976).

also appropriate when a manager wishes to develop subordinates by allowing them to experiment and learn from their own mistakes. Too much accommodation, however, can deprive others of your personal contributions and viewpoint.

Avoiding

Avoiding is unassertive and unco-operative behaviour. People with this conflict management style pursue neither their own concerns nor those of others. To avoid conflict altogether, a person might diplomatically side-step an issue, postpone it or withdraw from the threatening situation.

Avoiding is appropriate when the issue involved is relatively unimportant to you. In addition, if you have little power or are in a situation that is very difficult to change, avoiding may be the best choice. Similarly, avoidance may be wise if the potential damage from confronting a conflict outweighs its benefits or you need to let people cool off a little in order to bring tensions back down to a reasonable level. On the other hand, you should not let important decisions be made by default or spend a lot of energy avoiding issues that must eventually be confronted.

Collaborating

Collaborating is the opposite of avoiding; it consists of both assertive and co-operative behaviour. It involves working with the other person to find a solution that fully satisfies both parties. This is a joint problem-solving mode involving communication and creativity on the part of each party to find a mutually beneficial solution.

Collaborating is a necessity when the concerns of both parties are too important to be compromised. Collaborating merges the insights of people with different perspectives. It allows you to test your assumptions and understand those of others, to gain commitment by incorporating others' concerns, and to work through hard feelings. Not all conflict situations, however, deserve this amount of time and energy. Trivial problems often do not require optimal solutions, and not all personal differences need to be worked through. It also does little good to behave in a collaborative manner if others will not.

Compromising

Compromising falls somewhere between assertive and co-operative behaviours. The objective is to find a mutually acceptable middle ground that partially satisfies both parties. This conflict management style splits the difference and makes concessions.

A compromise is appropriate when goals are moderately important but not worth the effort of collaboration or the possible disruption of competition. If a manager is dealing with an opponent of equal power who is strongly committed to a mutually exclusive goal, compromise may be the best hope for leaving both of them in relatively satisfactory positions. Compromise is also wise when a temporary settlement needs to be achieved quickly. It can be a useful safety valve for gracefully getting out of mutually destructive situations. On the other hand, too much compromising might cause you to lose sight of principles that are more important, values and long-term objectives. Too much compromise can also create a cynical climate of gamesmanship.

None of these conflict management approaches is better or worse than any other per se. Their effectiveness depends on how appropriate they are for any particular situation. Most people, however, have a 'dominant' style that they most often use because it has been successful in the past and they are comfortable with the required behaviours. If their dominant style is not appropriate or does not work, people revert to 'back-up' styles in attempting to resolve conflicts. This involves stepping out of the comfort zone of your favourite style and adapting to the situation with a more appropriate style.

If it is important to you to resolve a conflict in a way that enhances your relationship with the other party, collaboration or compromise is far more effective than avoidance or competition. It is also necessary to recognise the importance of effective communications and constructive feedback as a way of supporting more collaborative efforts and working through any confrontations that may develop. It is also necessary to be flexible and able to negotiate and bargain with the other party.

Negotiation

Negotiation is the process that occurs when stakeholders in an organisation accept that an agreement is necessary before a decision is made or some kind of change implemented. Negotiation implies that there are some initial differences between the parties and that there needs to be a process in which, by the use of argument, persuasion and compromise, they seek to resolve these differences in order to achieve a mutually acceptable solution.

negotiation

A form of problem-solving where two groups with conflicting interests exchange things in order to reach a mutually agreeable resolution.

Therefore, negotiation involves an element of power, as each party involved in negotiation will want to exert some influence or pressure on the other. This is not always obvious until there is a problem.

Effective negotiation

Effective negotiation has four main phases:

1 setting objectives
2 preparing a case
3 the bargaining process
4 reaching agreement.

In each phase there also needs to be a contingency plan to deal with possible breakdowns in negotiation.

Setting objectives

This is the first and most vital step of the negotiation process, as without clear objectives neither party will have an understanding of what is required. It is also a good idea to decide possible levels of acceptance. These range from the ideal level, to the realistic or most probable level, to the minimum level of acceptance. This information does not, however, need to be communicated to the other parties involved.

Preparing the case

Once the objectives have been defined it is a good idea to prepare the case using a mix of facts, logic, interests, fear and pride. This involves a considerable amount of preparation, as for each objective a detailed case needs to be prepared. It is also vital to have an understanding of the other party's viewpoint since this can help in the preparation of arguments for the required proposals. It is also a good idea, if possible, to practise the presentation to ensure that all angles have been covered.

The bargaining process

The process usually begins with each side setting out its objectives, followed by each side testing the strength of the other's position. It is important at this stage not to be concerned with initial offers or rush into preliminary agreements. It is also important at this stage to be in complete agreement as to what is being negotiated, as without such agreement no negotiation can succeed.

The following strategies can be useful during the bargaining stage.

- Use adjournments to consider new points; this also gives time for reflection and allows emotions to cool.

- Make full use of questions when probing the other party's comments.

- Ask for arguments to be rephrased to achieve a better understanding; this can help identify weaknesses in the other party's argument.

- Encourage the other party to talk and listen carefully. This may help to reveal the other party's lack of an argument.

- Maintain emotional detachment, keep tempers cool and, most importantly, do not antagonise the other party as this can only make negotiations more difficult.

- If agreements cannot be reached on the detail, then put it aside for a while and move on to something else.

Reaching agreement

This is the final phase and it is important to tread carefully as, by this stage, there may well be emotional attachment to a particular outcome. In complex and difficult negotiations this may be where there is a search for common ground and care needs to be taken with the use of language to ensure there are no misunderstandings. The following tactical measures can be useful at this stage.

- Summarise each stage where an agreement has been reached before moving on to the next stage.

- Ask for views on issues without pressing for a formal response. Rephrase issues to make them more acceptable.

- Encourage the other party to see the benefits of accepting a proposal. This can help the other party to save face and maintain their pride.

- Aim for a win–win solution, where both parties feel positive about the outcome. Win–lose solutions are rarely acceptable and often leave an underlying feeling of resentment.

Once an agreement has been reached then it needs to be finalised immediately. This will prevent any second thoughts from surfacing.

Bargaining strategies

The success of your negotiations depends on the bargaining strategies that you and the other party choose to apply. There are two general approaches to negotiation: distributive bargaining and integrative bargaining.

Distributive bargaining

You see a used car advertised for sale in the newspaper. It appears to be just what you have been looking for. You go out to see the car. It's great and you want it. The owner tells you the asking

distributive bargaining
The negotiating process whereby two parties negotiate over different aspects of an issue.

price. You don't want to pay that much. The two of you then negotiate over the price. The negotiating process you are engaging in is called **distributive bargaining**. Its most identifying feature is that it operates under zero-sum conditions – that is, any gain I make is at your expense, and vice versa. Referring again to the used car example, every pound you can get the seller to cut from the car's price is a pound you save. Conversely, every extra pound he or she can get from you comes at your expense. Thus the essence of distributive bargaining is negotiating over who gets what share of a fixed pie. Appropriate conflict style orientations for distributive bargaining start with compromise, to be followed by competition and accommodation, depending upon the relative importance to you of getting more of what you want versus maintaining a positive relationship with the other party.

Stagner (1967), as also depicted in Exhibit 9-7, advanced a distributive bargaining strategy, which contains a bargaining zone of mutual acceptance. Let us assume that you and another party represent the two negotiators. Each of you has a *target point* that defines what you would like to achieve. Each of you also has a *resistance point*, which marks the lowest outcome

settlement range
The area between resistance points where there exists a point where two parties can each meet their aspirations.

that is acceptable – the point below which you would break off negotiations rather than accept a less favourable settlement. The area between these resistance points is called the **settlement range**. As long as there is some overlap in the aspiration ranges, there exists a settlement area where each of your aspirations can be met.

When engaged in distributive bargaining, your tactics should focus on trying to get your opponent to agree to your specific target point or to get as close to it as possible. Examples of such tactics are: persuading your opponent of the impossibility of getting to his or her target point and the advisability of accepting a settlement near yours; arguing that your target is fair, while your opponent's isn't; and attempting to get your opponent to feel emotionally generous towards you and thus accept an outcome close to your target point.

integrative bargaining
Where the parties assume it is possible to create a win–win solution.

Integrative bargaining

The collaborative conflict style orientation results in **integrative bargaining**, where the parties assume that it is possible to create a win–win solution. If successful, the result is satisfaction and

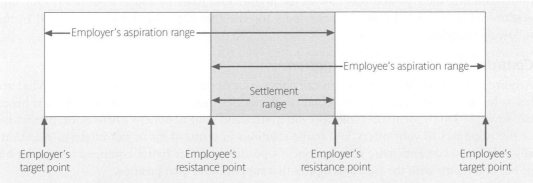

Exhibit 9–7 Distributive negotiation bargaining zone
Source: Adapted from Robbins and Hunsaker (1996).

positive long-term relationships. The following sales-credit negotiation provides an example of integrative bargaining in action.

Assume a sales representative for a women's sportswear manufacturer has just closed a £15,000 order from a small clothing retailer. The sales representative calls in the order to her firm's credit department. She is told that the firm cannot approve credit to this customer because of a past slow-pay record. The next day, the sales representative and the firm's credit supervisor meet to discuss the problem. The sales representative doesn't want to lose the business; neither does the credit supervisor, but he also doesn't want to get stuck with an uncollectable debt. The two openly review their options. After considerable discussion, they agree on a solution that meets both their needs: the credit supervisor will approve the sale, but the clothing store's owner will provide a bank guarantee that will assure payment if the bill isn't paid within 60 days.

Many experts in negotiation have concluded that integrative bargaining is generally preferable to distributive bargaining. This is because the former builds positive long-term relationships and facilitates working together in the future. It bonds negotiators and allows each to leave the bargaining table feeling that he or she has achieved a victory. Distributive bargaining, on the other hand, leaves one party a loser. It tends to build animosities and deepen divisions between people who have to work together on an ongoing basis.

If this is the case, why isn't there more integrative bargaining in organisations? The answer lies in the conditions necessary for this type of negotiation to succeed. These conditions include openness with information and frankness between parties, sensitivity on the part of each party to the other's needs, the ability to trust one another, and willingness by both parties to maintain flexibility. Unfortunately, many organisational cultures and interpersonal relationships are not characterised by these conditions. In these cases, too much openness and information sharing when trying to collaborate can make you vulnerable because the other party has more information and may use it against you. This can be very costly if the other party does not reciprocate, giving him or her more power to leverage a better deal. So, even if one party begins integrative bargaining by collaborating and attempting to establish trust, if the other party fails to reciprocate, the original collaborating party will usually shift to a distributive win–lose bargaining strategy for self-protection.

Guidelines for effective negotiating

During the actual negotiation process, the behaviours of the parties involved are very influential in determining the type and outcome of the negotiation. Robbins and Hunsaker's (1996) suggestions about the most essential behaviours for effective negotiation are summarised in the following guidelines.

Consider the other party's situation

Acquire as much information as you can about your opponent's interests and goals. What are his or her real needs versus wants? What constituencies must he or she appease? What is his or her strategy? This information will help you understand your opponent's behaviour, predict his or her responses to your offers, and frame solutions in terms of his or her interests. Additionally, when you can anticipate your opponent's position, you are better equipped to counter his or her arguments with the facts and figures that support your own position.

Have a plan and concrete strategy

Your chances of obtaining a favourable negotiation outcome increase if you plan and set goals before the action starts. Treat negotiation like a chess match. Expert chess players have a plan and a strategy. They know ahead of time how they will respond to any given situation. How strong is your situation and how important is the issue? Are you willing to split differences to achieve an early solution? If the issue is very important to you, is your position strong enough to let you play hardball and show little or no willingness to compromise? These are questions you should address before you begin bargaining.

Begin with a positive overture

Establish rapport and mutual interests before starting the negotiation. Then begin bargaining with a positive overture – perhaps a small concession. Concessions tend to be reciprocated and lead to agreements. A positive climate can be developed by reciprocating your opponent's concessions, also. But keep in mind that, although concessions enable parties to move towards the area of agreement, establish good faith and provide information about the relative importance of various negotiation concerns, the meaning of making concessions does vary from culture to culture. For example, Russians typically view concessions as a sign of weakness, while Chinese negotiators generally pull back when other parties change from their initial positions.

Address problems, not personalities

Concentrate on the negotiation issues, not on the personal characteristics of your opponent. When negotiations get tough, avoid the tendency to attack your opponent. If other people feel threatened, they concentrate on defending their self-esteem, as opposed to solving the problem. It's your opponent's ideas or position that you disagree with, not him or her personally. Separate the people from the problem, and do not personalise differences.

Maintain a rational, goal-orientated frame of mind

Use the previous guideline in reverse if your opponent attacks or gets emotional with you. Do not get hooked by emotional outbursts. Let the other person blow off steam without taking it personally, while you try to understand the problem or strategy behind the aggression.

Pay little attention to initial offers

Treat an initial offer as merely a point of departure. Everyone has to have an initial position. These initial offers tend to be extreme and idealistic. Treat them as such. Focus on the other person's interests and your own goals and principles, while you generate other possibilities.

Emphasise win–win solutions

Bargainers often assume that their gain must come at the expense of the other party. As noted with integrative bargaining, that need not be the case. There are often win–win solutions. However, assuming a zero-sum game means missed opportunities for trade-offs that could benefit both sides. So, if conditions are supportive, look for an integrative solution. Create additional alternatives, especially low-cost concessions you can make that have high value to the other party. Frame options in terms of your opponent's interests and look for solutions that can allow your opponent, as well as yourself, to declare a victory.

Create a climate of trust

Of course, neither side is going to make themselves vulnerable by sharing information in an attempt for a collaborative agreement if they do not trust the other party. Consequently, you want to avoid words and phrases that may irritate the other party or cause mistrust. Skilled negotiators do not make exaggerated statements, absurd opening offers, or renege on commitments. They listen, ask questions and try to empathise with the other party, while being patient and avoiding defensiveness if the other party tests them in the beginning.

Insist on using objective criteria

Make your negotiated decisions based on principles and results, not emotions or pressure. Agree upon objective criteria that can aid both parties in assessing the reasonableness of the alternatives. Do not succumb to emotional pleas, assertiveness or stubbornness if the other party's underlying rationale does not meet these criteria.

Be open to accepting third-party assistance

When stalemates are reached, consider soliciting the help of a neutral third party. The two most common forms of third-party assistance are mediation and arbitration. *Mediators* can help parties come to an agreement, but they do not impose a settlement. Companies like Texaco have used ombudsmen to mediate conflicts in areas such as racial discrimination allegations, in an attempt to maintain a positive and trusting environment. *Arbitrators* hear both sides of the dispute and then impose a binding solution. They are often utilised in the final stage of union grievance negotiations.

Which approach is best depends upon the specific conflict situation. Mediation provides the greatest potential for employee satisfaction when dealing with minor conflicts because it allows the parties more responsibility in determining the outcome. When the parties are at a definite stalemate, however, arbitration is usually most appropriate because its structured rules and processes provide the best sense of fairness.

Grievance and discipline

According to Acas, discipline is:

> about maintaining standards of behaviour and performance. The best way to do this is to: agree standards and make sure all staff know what these are; have rules and procedures in place to enable you to deal with unacceptable behaviour and unsatisfactory performance within the workplace. The emphasis is on maintaining standards, not punishment.

According to Acas, grievance is:

> a problem or concern somebody may have about their work, working conditions or relationships with colleagues. Therefore, it is important that you have a procedure in place to handle it. There is also a statutory definition of grievance, which we will look at later.

Although it is a good idea to solve grievances informally it is also sensible to have a grievance procedure. This makes it clear to employees that there is a course of action they can take if they feel they have a problem, and gives both the employer and employee a procedure that enables them to deal with grievances fairly and quickly. It also helps to guide all those involved through the actual process.

You should encourage everybody to try to resolve a grievance informally as this enables a speedy resolution to the problem and works well where there is a good relationship between manager and employee.

Quite often, grievances are just the result of a misunderstanding. For example, Sue complains that she is being given too much work to do and that she can't complete it on time. She puts in a formal grievance to you. However, you are aware that the previous person had no such problem and you feel the problem lies with Sue and not the job. When you meet you find that Sue is using a different computer program than her predecessor. As an employer you could agree to an upgrade and then monitor the situation. You may also need to ask yourself why this had to be part of a grievance process; managers who communicate efficiently with their staff would have been aware of the problem.

Seasoned greetings

With some innovative policies for recruiting and retaining women, ethnic minorities and older people, Hallmark Cards is aiming to go beyond motivation to engagement.

No one could accuse Hallmark of not practising what it preaches. The company was founded in 1910 by US entrepreneur J.C. Hall, who believed that making great works of art accessible to ordinary people in the form of greetings cards would enrich their lives; 95 years later, Hallmark, which in the UK alone produces around 2 billion greetings cards every year and enough wrapping paper to stretch three times round the world, still sees itself as improving people's quality of life.

Its mission statement is 'Enriching lives and relationships'. But, as a predominantly family-owned business, Hallmark aims to live out its values in the workplace too.

In 2000, five disparate Hallmark companies in the UK were combined into one, a challenge made even more difficult by the need to meld two diametrically different cultures – the traditional hierarchical, dictatorial, manufacturing-based culture of the northern companies, and the softer, more inclusive, more modern culture typical of southern businesses.

The group headquarters was switched from the south to Bradford and, in the first five months after the reorganisation, it recruited 450 staff. It took another year to standardise systems and contracts and to induct the new recruits.

'The focus during the first two years was to get bums on seats in order to keep the business running, and, at the same time, to transform an old-fashioned personnel department into a proper HR function,' says HR director Anna Farmery.

By January 2002, 80 per cent of headquarters employees were either new to the business or new to their role – many people didn't relocate – and the emphasis of the HR policies and procedures was on complying with statutory requirements. But, once the building blocks were in place, the company started to look at enhancing the provision it made for staff, in keeping with the corporate ethos.

It began the process by benchmarking Hallmark against *The Times* Top 100 Organisations – 'not to imitate them, but to give us a standard we could improve upon,' says Farmery. 'We wanted to engage individuals rather than just motivate them, and that became a question of how we could make it easy for people to work here. Improving maternity provision was one of the obvious first steps.'

Hallmark now provides three months' fully paid maternity leave and one week of fully paid paternity leave, a practice mirrored in its policy on adoptive leave. New parents get a baby bag

managing diversity

▶ (or its equivalent for older children) containing £50 worth of clothes, toys and an aromatherapy bath kit for new mothers. Returning mothers are helped back into the business through a range of different flexible working options.

The opportunity to work flexibly has now been extended to all staff, with options including four-day weeks, home working, job shares and compressed hours.

'Flexible working is slightly more difficult to arrange in a production environment where people work shifts to keep the operation running. But even on the factory floor we are as flexible as possible,' says Rebecca Hemingway, HR business partner, operations. 'On the operations side, we tend to get requests for fixed shifts [standard shifts rotate] so that parents can share childcare.'

Hallmark is also keen for its HR policies and procedures to reflect and use the diversity of its workforce and the local community.

About 26 per cent of its staff is made up of ethnic minorities, 2 per cent higher than the proportion in Bradford as a whole. It has prayer rooms with nearby washing facilities and storage space for prayer mats, and offers 'grab bags' in the canteen so that people of different religions can eat after they have fasted. Hallmark provides leave flexibility around feast days, and has tailored its training to its diverse workforce.

One of the facilitators on its Investors in Excellence personal development programme, which is open to everyone in the company, is Muslim. 'He has helped us adapt the course slightly so that it doesn't contravene Muslim beliefs,' says Nadine Maggi, HR business partner, trading. 'For example, the course encourages people not to be shy of wanting to earn money. This is slightly at odds with the Muslim religion, which encourages people to share money with the local community and the mosque. So we now highlight the fact that the community and the mosque can benefit from people progressing in their careers.'

Maggi has just begun working with local organisations, such as the Bangladeshi Community Society, to establish how Hallmark can help with their education and careers and, ultimately, to promote the organisation as an employer of choice.

'It is about building relationships and bridges, and establishing credibility,' she says. 'We had to work out what diversity meant to us internally. Now we can turn our attention to getting people to join us.'

The company now has around 3200 staff, a supportive union, and sales last year were £187 million – and rising too. J.C. Hall's philosophy seems to hold as true today as it did all those years ago when he explained: 'We simply feel that doing a little better by our people than they expect not only gives us great satisfaction but is good business sense as well.'

One of the most innovative employment practices at Hallmark is its 'run-down scheme', designed to help workers acclimatise to retirement by gradually reducing their working hours in the run-up to retirement. The scheme kicks in four months before retirement, allowing staff to work four days a week for two months and three days a week for two months on full pay.

Hallmark does not force staff to retire at 65. This year two of its employees will celebrate 50 years with the company, and one of them intends to carry on working.

'More and more staff are choosing to extend their working lives, and we are very happy for them to do that,' says HR director Anna Farmery.

'Statistics and our own evidence show that older people are often more committed, loyal and enthusiastic than their younger colleagues. What's more, employees aged between 40 and 65 are increasingly going to represent the biggest talent pool, and we need to pay closer attention to how to attract and retain people in that age group. We recently attended a recruitment fair specifically targeting the over-40s, for example,' she adds.

Around 40 of the company's staff, including some managers, are currently over 65. Yet Farmery believes the more senior people are, the more likely they are to retire early, and she recognises the need to address this issue. 'People have lots of ideas and lots of life still ahead of them at 55, not to mention lots of valuable experience. We need to work out how to tap into that, and find ways of engaging older managers for longer,' she says.

They have made some progress. Pat Gardiner, the 49-year-old company secretary, is to train to become an Investors in Excellence (a quality standard) facilitator. 'We know our investment will pay back,' says Farmery. 'Pat will be here in ten years' time, but would a 25 year old?'

Source: Jane Simms, 'Seasoned greetings', *People Management*, 19 May 2005, p. 36.
Reproduced with permission of *People Management* and Jane Simms.

Discussion questions

1 How has Hallmark developed and implemented its flexible working strategies?
2 How does encouraging diversity improve business?

Summary

- Employee relations is the economic, social and political relationship between an employer and employee.

- Trades unions have been the traditional method of employee representation. However, union membership is on the decline with the move from collective to individual representation.

- Employee consultation enables employees to participate in the decision-making process of organisations. European Works Councils are one approach used to enable employee involvement in the workplace.

- Conflict can arise when there is a disagreement between parties. Different theoretical perspectives have different views as to the effects of conflict.

- Conflict can progress through different stages, and managers need to develop strategies to manage conflicts and achieve desired outcomes.

- Negotiation enables different stakeholders to discuss their differences and seek solutions.

- Bargaining strategies can influence the success of chosen outcomes. These can include distributive bargaining and integrative bargaining.

- Grievance and discipline are issues that can cause conflict in an organisation and employers need to have clear strategies and guidelines with regard to procedures.

Personal development

1 **Identify the development of employee relations theory.** Theory can help us understand our past and guide our actions in the future. An understanding of the theoretical perspectives can help us develop strategies relating to employment issues.

2 **Develop consultation techniques.** Consultation is about asking people for opinions and advice. It is not about imposing management decisions. Managers who consult effectively with employees will create a more committed workforce.

3 **Recognise the nature of the conflict.** Conflict is natural to any relationship and it can never be completely eliminated, nor should it be. If not managed properly, conflict can be dysfunctional and lead to undesirable consequences like hostility, lack of co-operation, violence, destroyed relationships and even company failure. Nevertheless, when managed effectively, conflict can stimulate creativity, innovation and change, and build better relationships.

4 **Identify the sources of conflict.** Conflicts can arise for a large variety of reasons, such as incompatible goals, differences in the interpretation of facts, negative feelings, differences in values and philosophies, or disputes over shared resources.

5 **Use the most appropriate style orientation for managing a specific conflict.** Each of us has a preferred style orientation for handling conflicts. Nevertheless it is important to be flexible and vary our conflict management style response according to each specific situation. Know when it is most appropriate to draw upon each of the five conflict style orientations of avoidance, accommodation, forcing, compromise and collaboration when attempting to resolve dysfunctional conflicts.

6 **Empathise with the other conflict parties.** Your chances of success in managing a conflict will be greatly enhanced if you can view the conflict situation through the eyes of the conflicting parties. Determine who's involved in the conflict, what interests each party represents, and each player's values, personality, feelings and resources.

7 **Have a plan and concrete strategy.** Your chances of obtaining a favourable outcome increase if you plan and set goals before the action starts. Ask yourself questions, such as how strong your position is, how important the issue is to both yourself and the other party, and whether you are willing to negotiate and split differences.

8 **Address problems, not personalities.** Concentrate on the issues, not on the personal characteristics of your opponent. It's your opponent's ideas or position that you disagree with, not him or her personally. Separate the people from the problem and do not personalise differences.

9 **Maintain a rational, goal-orientated frame of mind.** Do not get hooked by emotional outbursts. Let the other person blow off steam, without taking it personally, while you try to understand the problem or strategy behind the aggression.

10 **Emphasise win–win solutions.** In conflict situations it initially appears that our gains must come at the expense of the other party. However, that need not be the case, and there are often win–win solutions. Nevertheless, assuming a zero-sum game means missed opportunities for trade-offs that could benefit both sides. So, if conditions are supportive, look for an integrative solution.

11 **Create a climate of trust.** Neither side is going to make itself vulnerable by sharing information in an attempt for a collaborative agreement if it does not trust the other party. Consequently, avoid words and phrases that may irritate the other party or cause mistrust. Listen, ask questions, and try to empathise with the other party, while being patient and avoiding defensiveness if the other party is competitive in the beginning.

Discussion questions

1 What are the major flaws in the unitary, systems and pluralist perspectives of employee relations?

2 Why do you think trades union membership has declined in recent years?

3 Review the major factors that cause intergroup conflicts. Now, think of a group to which you currently belong. How do these factors influence your behaviour and feelings towards other groups with which your group interacts?

4 Describe situations from your personal experience in which conflict was functional, and situations where it was dysfunctional.

5 Discuss the mechanisms for resolving conflicts between students and faculty on your campus. Are they effective? Why or why not? What mechanisms do you suggest to better resolve such conflicts?

6 Explain this statement: 'An organisation can experience too little or too much conflict.'

7 Suggest the appropriate conflict reduction strategies for a collective bargaining stalemate in which both management and union groups have a record of hostility and non-co-operation. Could such potential conflict be prevented by the design chosen for a new industrial organisation? How?

8 What is your dominant conflict management style? How did you develop it? When does it work best for you? When doesn't it work?

9 Do you think it is more important for managers to consult or negotiate?

10 What is the difference between discipline and grievance?

🔒 Key concepts

employee relations, *p. 288*	interdependence, *p. 297*
employee participation, *p. 291*	conflict management styles, *p. 299*
employee involvement, *p. 291*	negotiation, *p. 301*
European Works Council, *p. 293*	distributive bargaining, *p. 303*
conflict, *p. 294*	settlement range, *p. 303*
dysfunctional view of conflict, *p. 296*	integrative bargaining, *p. 303*
functional view of conflict, *p. 296*	

Individual task

Look at the following list of offences and think about how you would classify and deal with them under the following headings of minor, serious or gross misconduct. Place a tick in the relevant column in each case.

Offence	Minor misconduct	Serious misconduct	Gross misconduct
Poor timekeeping			
Poor attendance			
Falsification of clock card			
Refusal to carry out required duties			
Unauthorised possession of company property			
Unauthorised possession of a fellow employee's property			
Theft of company property			
Theft outside the company			
Violence to a client or customer			
Fighting in a public area			
Fighting in a non-public area			
Smoking in a public area			
Smoking in a non-public area			
Leaving work position unattended			
Sleeping on duty			
Poor work performance			
Drunkenness on duty			
Indecent behaviour			
Sexual harassment			
Obscene language in a public area			
Obscene language in a non-public area			
Breach of confidential information			
Failure to follow company procedures			
Conviction on drug charges			
Threatening behaviour			
Failure to submit a medical certificate			

Team exercise

Win as much as you can

Goals

1 To diagnose and manage a potential conflict situation within an organisation competing with another organisation.

2 To provide opportunities for practising negotiation skills.

3 To explore trust building and collaboration in a potential conflict situation.

Time The total exercise can last from 50 to 75 minutes depending on how much time is allocated for the following activities. Preparation takes from 10 to 15 minutes. The exercise takes 35 minutes for seven rounds. If you drop round 2, six rounds will take about 30 minutes. The debriefing time depends upon how much depth you go into, so it can vary from 10 to 25 minutes.

Divide the class into two or more organisations. Then divide each organisation into four one-person to five-person departments. The four departments in each organisation should be far enough apart from each other so that members of each department can communicate without being overheard by other departments.

The exercise consists of seven rounds of decision-making in which each department selects either P (profit) or Q (quality) based on its prediction of what the other departments in its organisation will do and the pay-off schedule. Winnings or losses depend on what is negotiated and what the other departments decide to do.

Procedure

1 Each player invests £1.00 in his or her company (gives the money to the instructor). If any student is uncomfortable risking a pound, or if it is a very large class, one option is to have each department assign an observer to help the instructor (a) collect and announce decisions; (b) observe internal and intergroup dynamics; (c) handle negotiations; (d) lead department debriefing; and (e) lead class debriefing.

2 Participants study the pay-off schedule, the scorecard and the profit distribution matrix (see below). (5 minutes)

3 There is to be no talking between departments, only within departments, except during negotiations.

4 There are opportunities to negotiate with other departments before the rounds with bonuses – that is, after rounds 2, 4 and 6. Departments must direct requests to negotiate to the instructor (or observer), and other departments can agree or refuse. If departments agree to negotiate, one representative from each department meets with one from another department in a private place. Negotiators are not allowed to show their scorecards to each other. Departments pick different members to negotiate with each of the other departments so that all get a chance to negotiate. Actual decisions for the next round can be made only through consensus of department members after they return from negotiations.

5 Departments have 10 minutes to get organised and determine their goals and strategy. Each decision round is three minutes. Each negotiation period is 5 minutes.

6 **Scoring** Departments keep their own cumulative scores on their scorecard. The instructor or observer duplicates a scorecard for each organisation on the board and keeps total organisation scores for each round (i.e. sum of scores for the four departments in each organisation).

7 **Pay-off schedule directions** At the beginning of each of the seven successive rounds, choose either a P to maximise profit margin or a Q for highest quality. The pay-off for each round depends on the pattern of choices made by other departments in your organisation. The pay-off schedule, scorecard and profit distribution summary are included on the decision tally sheet. Scores can be kept on this sheet in the book, but it should be duplicated and passed out to participants separately for easier use.

Profit distribution At the end of the seven rounds of play, add up the cumulative organisation and department scores. Write these on the board and distribute the total pot as follows:

- the organisation with the largest balance gets 40 per cent (equally distributed among the four departments)
- the department with the largest balance gets 30 per cent (can be either the winning or losing organisation)
- the department with the second-largest balance gets 20 per cent
- the department with the third-largest balance gets 10 per cent
- if there is no positive pay-off for either organisation, there will be no distribution, even if departments have positive balances. The instructor keeps all the money.

Discussion questions

1 How would you describe the behaviour of the departments in your organisation?
2 How would you describe your own behaviour?
3 Is this real-life behaviour?
4 How do you feel about the way you played the game? How do you feel about how the other departments played the game?
5 What did you learn about yourself? About others?

Decision tally sheet

Directions At the beginning of each of the seven successive rounds choose either a P to maximise profit margin or a Q for highest quality. The 'pay-off' for each round is dependent upon the pattern of choices made by other departments in your company.

Pay-off schedule

4 Ps: Lose £1.00 each
3 Ps: Win £1.00 each
1 Q: Lose £3.00
2 Ps: Win £2.00 each
2 Qs: Lose £2.00 each
1 P: Win £3.00
3 Qs: Lose £1.00 each
4 Qs: Win £1.00 each

Scorecard
Profit distribution

- Company with largest balance gets 40 per cent (equally distributed).
- Department with largest balance gets 30 per cent.
- Department with second-largest balance gets 20 per cent.
- Department with third-largest balance gets 10 per cent.
- If no positive pay-off for any company, there will be no distribution.

Round	Your choice (circle)	Group's pattern of choices	Your pay-off	Cumulative balance
1	P Q	___ Ps ___ Qs		
2	P Q	___ Ps ___ Qs		
3	P Q	___ Ps ___ Qs		
Bonus (×3)				
4	P Q	___ Ps ___ Qs		
5	P Q	___ Ps ___ Qs		
Bonus (×5)				
6	P Q	___ Ps ___ Qs		
7	P Q	___ Ps ___ Qs		
Bonus (×10)				

Source: Adapted from DeVito (1982) and Pfeiffer and Jones (1974).

Case study: **Patak's – not just spicy**

This case demonstrates how working together can improve discipline and grievance procedures.

Patak's is renowned in the UK for its range of Indian pickles, chutneys, stir-in cooking sauces and curry pastes. Established in the 1950s by the father of the current owner, Kirit Pathak, the business has transformed itself from a family-run business operating out of a tiny north London kitchen into a multinational business with an estimated value of £50m.

Having undergone rapid expansion over the years, the business currently occupies four sites throughout the UK and employs around 660 staff.

Its largest factory and headquarters are based in Wigan, an area with a low ethnic minority population.

Morale and working conditions are generally reported to be good at Patak's. Both the Acas adviser and a Patak's employee confirmed its reputation as a good employer in the area. Management operates an 'open door' policy and makes an effort to listen to and address staff concerns. There are regular forums for employees to communicate with managers through employee representatives and monthly lunches with the managing director, to which staff are invited.

Discipline and grievance was one area where it was felt management would benefit from practical training. In 2003, the Group HR Manager decided to address this issue and asked Acas to assist.

The primary intention behind the training was to ensure that all line managers were consistent in adopting best practice by refreshing them on correct disciplinary procedure. Past experience had indicated that managers were uncertain of their role in enforcing disciplinary matters, lacking the confidence to handle discipline and grievance situations in an appropriate manner. Moreover, they were not always clear about the distinction between their role and the role of HR in handling such situations; in some cases, they were too keen to pass discipline and grievance cases straight to HR. Thus the desired outcome of the training was to empower managers in this aspect of their role by equipping them with the necessary information and skills.

Managers realised it was important to get an independent third party to run the training on discipline and grievance. The Group HR Manager at Patak's was already familiar with the services that Acas provided and had attended network meetings hosted by Acas on employment issues. She felt that Acas's impartial approach to employment relations made it ideal to conduct this training on their behalf. Moreover, Acas was an organisation that was familiar and trusted by staff, and this would help to portray the training in a positive rather than negative light.

Acas advisers agreed a training programme with Patak's that was based around the company's existing policy and procedures on discipline and grievance. The training took the form of half-day workshops, which line managers and supervisors were invited to attend. A trades union representative also took part, as did a member of HR. Acas ran three of these workshops, with up to 12 delegates in each session. Senior managers at Patak's recognised the benefits of adopting a joint working process that involves management and union representatives working together. The principle behind Acas joint working is to encourage people from all levels of an organisation to explore and understand issues from different perspectives.

The workshops covered the following key areas.

■ The reasons for discipline: why it is a requirement and how it can be viewed as a positive way of setting standards and expectations within an organisation.

■ Best practice: the correct procedures to follow when handling discipline and grievance situations.

■ Delegating work using real-life scenarios from organisations in similar sectors.

■ Role-play exercises gave managers an opportunity to put into practice what they had learnt.

■ Guidance on handling awkward or difficult situations: the need to view situations from an objective standpoint and deal with them accordingly, while avoiding conflict and personality clashes.

Managers reported feeling much more positive and confident about their ability to handle discipline and grievance situations following the workshops. It was felt that Acas had created an environment in which staff felt comfortable with discussing difficult issues. The combination of techniques that the Acas advisers used also helped to make it a productive and enjoyable process.

As a result of undertaking the training, Acas was able to provide suggestions to HR staff about making small alterations to their policy on discipline and grievance in order to ensure it matched best practice and ironed out areas open to misinterpretation. Once HR had made the suggested changes, it consulted the trades union for its opinion and the section on discipline and grievance in the employee handbook was revised accordingly.

In the period since the training, absenteeism has dropped and the Group HR Manager feels that more general improvements in morale have occurred. Though this is not directly attributed to the training, it was felt that the training was among other factors that have helped contribute to a more stable workforce.

Source: Adapted from a case study by acas.org.uk and Turnstone Research and Consultancy. Reproduced with permission of Philly Desai, Turnstone Research and Consultancy, Acas and Patak's.

Discussion questions

1 How do you think Acas contributed to the success of the programme?

2 What are the advantages of using an impartial organisation such as Acas?

3 How did Patak's ensure that employees also bought into the process?

4 Why is it important to have clear discipline and grievance procedures?

WWW exercise

The Involvement and Participation Association (IPA) is the only UK organisation to specialise in assisting both unionised and non-unionised organisations to develop effective information and consultation processes and workplace partnerships, leading to:

■ greater competitiveness

■ increased profits and productivity

■ more efficient services

■ improved employee relations

■ higher-quality performance

■ enhanced ability to manage change effectively

■ better staff morale and motivation.

Follow the link to: http://www.ipa-involve.com.

1 How can the IPA help managers to develop employee involvement and participation?

2 In the section on partnership and participation follow the links to 'case studies'. What do these suggest about the importance of employee participation?

LEARNING CHECKLIST

Before moving on to the next chapter, check that you are able to:

- ☑ understand the theoretical perspectives of employee relations
- ☑ understand strategies for employee participation and involvement
- ☑ define and describe the conflict process
- ☑ recognise symptoms of conflict
- ☑ identify sources of conflict and appropriate conflict management strategies
- ☑ understand the role of negotiation and bargaining.

Further reading

Addison, J.T. and Schnabel, C. (eds) (2003) *International Handbook of Trades Unions*. Cheltenham, England, and Northampton, MA, USA: Edward Elgar.

Cannell, C. (2005) 'Trades unions: a short history', factsheet, CIPD.

Dunlop, J. (1958) *Industrial Relations System*. South-Western College Publishing, Thomson Learning.

Hollinshead, G., Nicholls, P. and Tailby, S. (2003) *Employee Relations* (2nd edn). Financial Times, Prentice Hall.

Legge, K. (1995) *Human Resource Management: Rhetorics and Realities*. London: Macmillan.

Marchington, M., Wilkinson, A. and Ackers, P. (2001) *Management Choice and Employee Voice*, research report. London: Chartered Institute of Personnel and Development.

Purcell, J., Kinnie, N. and Hutchinson, S. (2003) *Understanding the People and Performance Link: Unlocking the Black Box*, research report. London: Chartered Institute of Personnel and Development.

Rahim, M.A. and Magner, N.R. (1995) 'Confirmatory factor analysis of the styles of handling interpersonal conflict: first-order factor model and its invariance across groups', *Journal of Applied Psychology* 80(1), pp. 122–132.

Stagner, R. and Rosen, H. (1965) *Psychology of Union–Management Relations*. Belmont, CA: Wadsworth, pp. 95–96, 108–110.

TUC (1997) *Partners for Progress: Next Steps for the New Unionism*. London: TUC.

Webster, F. (2005a) 'Information and consultation of employees regulations', factsheet, CIPD.

Webster, F. (2005b) 'European Works Councils', factsheet, CIPD.

References

Blanchflower, D.G. and Bryson, A. (2003) 'Changes over time in union relative wage effects in the UK and US revisited', in J.T. Addison and C. Schnabel (eds) *International Handbook of Trades Unions*. Cheltenham, England, and Northampton, MA, USA: Edward Elgar.

Card, D. and Freeman, R. (2004) 'What have two decades of British economic reform delivered?', in R. Blundell, D. Card and R. Freeman (eds) *Seeking a Premier League Economy*. University of Chicago Press for NBER.

DeVito, J.A. (1982) *The Interpersonal Communication Book* (6th edn). New York: HarperCollins.

Drucker, P. (1984) *The Practice of Management.* London: Heinemann.

Glasl, F. (1982) 'The process of conflict escalation and the roles of third parties', in G.B.J. Bomers and R. Peterson (eds) *Conflict Management and Industrial Relations.* Boston: Kluwer-Nijhoff, pp. 119–140.

Gospel, H.F. and Palmer, G. (1993) *British Industrial Relations.* London: Routledge.

Guest, D. and Hoque, K. (1994) 'The good, the bad and the ugly: employment relations in new non-union workplaces', *Human Resource Management Journal* 5(1), pp. 1–14.

Hyman, J. and Mason, B. (1995) *Managing Employee Involvement and Participation.* London: Sage.

IPA (2005) *The UK Experience of European Works Councils – IPA Response to DTI Consultation.* London: Involvement and Participation Association.

Kuman, R. (1989) 'Affect, cognition and decision making in negotiations: a conceptual integration', in M.A. Rahim (ed.) *Managing Conflict: An Integrative Approach.* New York: Praeger, pp. 185–194.

Marchington, M. and Parker, P. (1990) *Changing Patterns of Employee Relations.* Hemel Hempstead: Harvester Wheatsheaf.

McKenna, E. (1994) *Business Psychology and Organizational Behaviour.* Hove, UK: Erlbaum.

Metcalf, D. (2005) *British Unions: Resurgence or Perdition?.* London: The Work Foundation.

Morgan, G. (1986) *Images of Organization.* Beverly Hills, CA: Sage.

Pfeiffer, J.W. and Jones, J.E. (eds) (1974) *A Handbook of Structured Experiences for Human Relations Training* (rev. edn). Vol. III. California: University Associates.

Pondy, L. (1967) 'Organizational conflict: concepts and models', *Administrative Science Quarterly* 12, pp. 296–320.

Rahim, M.A. (1992) *Managing Conflict in Organizations* (2nd edn). Westport, CT: Praeger.

Robbins, S.P. and Hunsaker, P.L. (1996) *Training in Interpersonal Skills: Tips for Managing People at Work* (2nd edn). Upper Saddle River, NJ: Prentice Hall, pp. 244–245.

Rose, E. (2004) *Employment Relations.* Harlow: Prentice-Hall.

Stagner, R. (1967) *Psychological Aspects of International Conflict.* Belmont, CA: Brooks/Cole.

Thomas, K.W. (1976) 'Conflict and conflict management', in M.D. Dunnette (ed.) *Handbook of Industrial and Organisational Psychology.* Palo Alto, CA: Consulting Psychologists Press, pp. 889–935.

Thomas, K.W. (1992) 'Conflict and negotiation processes in organizations', in M.D Dunnette and L.M. Hough (eds) *Handbook of Industrial and Organizational Psychology,* Vol. 3 (2nd edn). Palo Alto, CA: Consulting Psychologists Press, pp. 651–717.

PART 4

Effective human resource management

Part contents

10 Health, safety and employee well-being   *323*

11 Equal opportunities and managing diversity   *361*

12 Strategic human resource management   *399*

13 Current issues and new developments   *435*

Chapter 10

Health, safety and employee well-being

Margaret May and Edward Brunsdon

LEARNING OUTCOMES

After studying this chapter, you should be able to:

- ☑ **understand** the importance of health, safety and employee well-being in the workplace

- ☑ **understand** the development of statutory and regulatory requirements concerning health and safety at work

- ☑ **understand** the operations of the UK health and safety agencies, the Health & Safety Commission (hereafter HSC) and the Health & Safety Executive (hereafter HSE)

- ☑ **be aware of** current developments in the provision of employee health and care.

The opening vignette gives an insight into the thankless role of the health and safety officer at VM engineering.

The health and safety officer

With the synchronised beep of a thousand incoming emails, another of Nigel Ward's missives touches down in the inboxes of the hapless employees of VM Engineering. Sitting in his office, Ward smiles, a job well done. He glances at the recently sent memo with paternal pride – it's a masterpiece of clarity: there is no mistaking its message, or its importance.

Yet few will read Nigel's note. Anyone with IT experience long ago marked nigel.ward@vmengineering.co.uk as spam; and even those who haven't will likely delete it unread. Of the company's 1000 employees, 50 will probably open it. And, of those, 49 will

▶ scratch their heads and say: 'Doesn't he have anything more important to do?' The sole exception to this unanimous disregard is Karen, Nigel's PA and staunchest ally. For reasons unclear – and that do not bear close examination – Nigel, in all his V-necked glory, is her hero.

Anyhow, no, he doesn't have anything more important to do. For Nigel is the head of health and safety at VM Engineering, chief enforcer of the thousands of minor rules and petty regulations 'that exist for your own good'; in the parlance of the water cooler, he's 'the safety Nazi'.

Nigel hails from the Health & Safety Executive, where he worked variously in railways, petroleum and food. Before his arrival, VM's record in this area hadn't been all it should be and the thinking was that, by bringing in an outsider, the company would soon be up to muster. Nigel has succeeded spectacularly, though not perhaps in the way the board might have hoped. As one lucky line manager recently commented: 'It's like having a health and safety inspection every single bloody day.'

Nowhere is this more visible than when Nigel 'walks the values' with one of his periodic sweeps for those recidivists who treat his exhortations with cavalier disregard. Those new to VME often find themselves in one of those officious set pieces where they discover the true meaning of frustration. Even the security guards – who after 9/11 discovered how empowering it could be to check the passes of VM lifers eight times a day – have nothing on Nigel. A typical newbie encounter starts with Nigel asking them to rectify a minor problem; they turn it into a joke; he counters with 'This is no joking matter', words that will probably be his epitaph. Nigel always wins in the end – he has the law on his side and the hierarchy, albeit reluctantly, have to back him up.

Nigel's punctiliousness is no respecter of rank. After he'd reproached the CEO over the plugging in of unchecked electrical appliances in his office, the boss proposed to the board that they put Nigel on one of their crack negotiation teams; no one could argue for long against that kind of leaden pedantry, said the CEO.

Of course, there is nothing wrong with Nigel and his mission to 'make safety "job one"'. Accidents can be a real problem, particularly in the engineering sector. Even though the VME board fought tooth and nail against their introduction, they'll admit that measures preventing workers from falling into machines are probably a plus – especially with relatives so litigious these days. The problem is that Nigel, with his hardwired regulatory mindset, enforces the diktats concerning hot drinks with the same zeal as those governing the use of 250-tonne presses.

But even though he is the man of the minutiae, the jobsworth everyone loves to hate, and possibly the last person you'd want to go for a beer with, it's difficult to pick holes in Nigel's real accomplishments. VME is now one of the safest firms in its class: in the whole of the last financial year, there was but one accident, and that a minor one. When congratulated by the CEO, Nigel replied: 'That's still one too many.'

Source: 'The H&S officer', *Management Today*, London, December 2005, p. 80.
Reproduced with permission of Haymarket Direct.

Discussion questions

1 Why do you think so many employers and employees disregard the issue of health and safety?

2 How can health and safety be embedded in the work culture?

Introduction

Health, safety and employee well-being is an expanding domain of HR management. In part, this is a consequence of the growth in UK and EU legislation, regulation, **guidance** and codes of practice, covering a widening field of

---
guidance

Safe methods of work applied to particular industries.

---

work activities and generating additional employer responsibilities for safety. But it is also the outcome of voluntary interventions on the part of employers seeking to enhance the safety and well-being of their staff. The case for both regulatory and volitional activity in health and safety is not difficult to make: one has only to look at the latest statistics concerning fatalities, injuries and illnesses emanating from the workplace to see why they are needed. While 2004/2005 was by no means an exceptional year, there were still 220 workers and 361 members of the public killed in work-related accidents. There were approximately 151,000 non-fatal injuries to employees and 2 million people were suffering from an illness that they believed was caused or exacerbated by their current or past work; 35 million working days were lost (1.5 days per worker), 28 million due to work-related ill health and 7 million due to workplace injury (HSE, 2006).

The consequences of these injuries and illness take many forms. For employees, there is the:

- pain and suffering, and
- possible loss of earnings.

For the employer, there are a wide variety of potential ramifications, including, according to Foot and Hook (2005: 366):

- lost time, lost skills and production delays
- the costs of replacing the absent staff and training their temporary replacements
- compensation payments
- the costs of investigations into the causes of illness or accidents
- the payment of fines, or even imprisonment, if they are considered responsible for not protecting their workforce against injury or illness
- higher insurance premiums if their organisation is considered to have poor injury or illness records
- poor morale developing within the workforce
- the loss of contracts and business reputation, and
- people leaving and others not applying to work for organisations because of their poor health and safety record.

Conservative estimates suggest that the loss of working days through injury and ill health costs employers between £3.3 and £6.5 billion per annum in the UK (HSE, 2006). While not all employers will consider cost as the sole reason for their legal compliance and/or their wellness interventions, it should be clear that ignoring their statutory duty or failing to address issues of well-being can be very expensive. In the words of one chief executive: 'In addition to our moral and legal duties, no company can in today's competitive climate afford the financial losses associated with ill health and accidents at work' (Bob Baty, South West Water, in HSE, 2006). There is, in other words, a strong business case to be made for health and safety that treats it as a core procedure and a valuable investment, even in highly competitive sectors with tight cash flows and small profit margins.

It is not just in this country that health and safety is an issue, as can be seen in the case of UAB Constructus in Lithuania, in the 'International perspective' box.

international perspective

UAB Constructus, Lithuania: managing the health and safety of subcontractors

Many large construction firms employ subcontractors to do some of the work for them, and the question for many is how to implement an effective health and safety plan and, in particular, use the tender stage of a contract to secure health and safety competence and the good practice of contractors.

The problem

UAB Constructus is a construction project management company. It was engaged on a project to construct the new municipal centre for the city of Vilnius. This was a major project, which included the construction of a 20-storey building, two additional buildings of three and five storeys, and an underground car park. It therefore needed to plan and manage health and safety from the beginning of the project to minimise the occurrence of risks during the construction phase. A major responsibility of the principal contractor of any construction project is to put in place a health and safety plan. This should cover:

- arrangements for selecting subcontractors to ensure that they are competent in health and safety
- the establishment of site rules
- procedures to secure co-operation between contractors on health and safety matters.

The solution

During the planning stage, experts from UAB Constructus worked with the architects to prepare the technical design for the project, so they were able to ensure that health and safety was considered during the design phase of the project.

UAB Constructus was responsible for selecting competent subcontractors, and this included ensuring that they had competence in health and safety. The first stage in this process is to set out the health and safety conditions that the contractor must meet, identifying the procedures associated with the job and ensuring that they are included in the contractor's specification. The process should cover checking the company's experience, policy, procedures, working arrangements, training and competence, and supervision arrangements for health and safety. Working methods, equipment to be used and risk assessments for the actual work should be provided and discussed with the principal contractor before contracts are finalised. UAB Constructus established health and safety requirements that subcontractors had to address as part of the tendering process. The bids could then be assessed against these requirements. Contractors also had to prepare their own health and safety work plan and procedures.

Health and safety arrangements and procedures for contractors were prepared in advance and included in the contracts, as were penalty clauses for health and safety infringements. The site safety rules and procedures, together with instructions for the subcontractor's staff, were included as an annex to the contracts, in the form of an 'information folder'. Subcontractors were also provided with lists of chemical substances that either were not to be used on the project or whose use was restricted.

In the information folder UAB Constructus included details of work hours, general information on the organisation of work (periodicity of meetings with subcontractors, provision of time schedule, handover of works, and so on) and the main contact telephone numbers in case of accidents, fire and the like. It also included safety requirements concerning work clothes, collective and personal means of safety, warning signs and posters, workplaces, fencing, scaffolding, main safety rules, and so on.

Within their safety plans, principal contractors must establish arrangements for ensuring health and safety, including arrangements for: directing and co-ordinating subcontractors; ensuring that subcontractors and their staff receive information; meetings to discuss health and safety with subcontractors; checking that those on site have received relevant training; and monitoring.

The arrangements covering subcontractors established by UAB Constructus included:

- inclusion of health and safety in all the co-ordination activities between UAB Constructus and the subcontractors – for example, in the work schedules supplied by subcontractors
- common arrangements to control the storage and use of materials
- arrangements for ensuring who was on site, and that only authorised personnel could enter the site
- arrangements for the entry of visitors, including permissions, their accompaniment by a member of UAB Constructus staff, and provision of personal protective equipment
- daily health and safety discussions between contractors and the construction site manager
- a weekly production meeting between UAB Constructus staff and representatives from each subcontractor
- arrangements for reporting accidents and near misses, and arrangements for investigating them; arrangements for the provision, maintenance and safe use of equipment by subcontractors
- arrangements for checking the safety performance of contractors on a regular basis; any problems spotted during the inspections to be raised at the weekly meetings with the contractors
- standardised forms for making inspections and checks.

Results

The project was carried out in a well-planned, structured way with significant benefits for the management of occupational safety and health.

Planning is crucial in achieving good standards of safety and health. Projects will also benefit from the increased likelihood that they will be completed on time, and within budget and quality requirements. However, when putting plans into operation it is important to ensure that they do not simply result in a set of rules for workers to follow, but involve the workers in a co-operative process.

Source: http://agency.osha.eu.int/publications/reports/108/gp_booklet_2004_web_en.pdf.

Discussion questions

1 How can organisations ensure that subcontractors adhere to health and safety policies?
2 What other benefits, apart from safety, can a good health and safety plan have for an organisation?

This chapter focuses on two key threads of the health and safety literature: health through safety and health through well-being, as illustrated in Exhibit 10-1.

These are not mutually exclusive, but their pragmatic division does allow the recognition of different points of emphasis and different change drivers.

- **Health through safety** focuses on the protection of workers from the risks, hazards and diseases of the workplace. While there is some recognition of the voluntary activities of employers, the main drivers are the EU and UK Government legislative agendas, and their implementation by the HSE and the HSC.

- **Health through well-being** concentrates on the promotion of health through occupational services and benefits. The drivers here are 'good practice' interventions encouraged by government exhortation and/or employers' voluntary strategies, more than legislation and regulation.

Health through safety
Health and safety legislation: a brief history

The legislation on health through safety at work developed in a somewhat uneven way during the nineteenth and twentieth centuries. Most of the legislation in the nineteenth century was piecemeal, designed to address particular problems in specific industries and/or for particular work groups (Stranks, 2003), as is illustrated in Exhibit 10-2.

The 1802 Health and Morals of Apprentices Act is a case in point. It applied to the work of children in textile mills. It limited their working day to 12 hours, prohibited night work, required minimum standards of accommodation, and expected factory owners to provide some elementary education, and to attend to and report infectious diseases. The 1819 and 1825 Cotton Mill and Factory Acts similarly focused on the length of the working day of child labour in the cotton industry. It prohibited children under the age of nine from working in cotton mills, limited the hours of work and the length of the working day, and specified the time that should be allowed for breakfast and lunch breaks. Employer compliance with these Acts was to be monitored by justices of the peace.

It was the failure of employers to adhere to this legislation that led to the 1833 Mills and Factories Act. As well as insisting on younger children (under nine) attending school for two hours per day, it gave powers for the appointment of factory inspectors who, by law, were permitted to enter factories at any time and examine the health and welfare of the children in the labour force. The 1834 Chimney Sweeps Act saw attention shift from the cotton mills and factories to

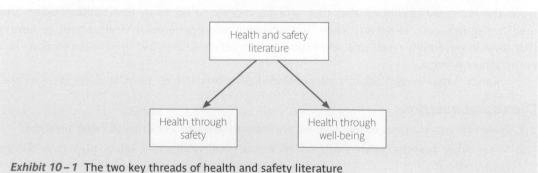

Exhibit 10 – 1 The two key threads of health and safety literature

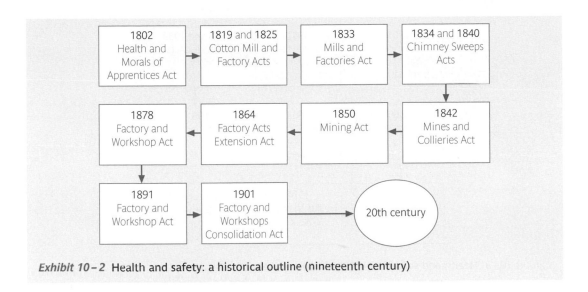

Exhibit 10–2 Health and safety: a historical outline (nineteenth century)

the age of apprentices and children sweeping chimneys. It forbade children under ten becoming apprentices, and children under 14 being employed unless apprenticed or on trial. It was the lack of **enforcement** of this Act that led to further legislation. The 1840 Chimney Sweeps Act prohibited any child under 16 being apprenticed and any person under 21 being compelled or knowingly allowed to ascend or descend a chimney or flue for sweeping, cleaning or coring.

enforcement
Ensuring that laws and regulations are adhered to.

The 1842 Mines and Collieries Act saw mining in the public eye. This was the product of a preceding Royal Commission that had revealed the terrible working conditions in the industry. The Act prohibited women and children under ten from working underground and provided for the appointment of mine inspectors to ensure that this was implemented. An 1850 Mining Act provided for more inspectors, and required mine owners to maintain plans of each of their mines and to notify fatal accidents to the Secretary of State. It was not until the 1864 Factory Acts Extension Act, however, that these inspection powers were extended to the pottery and matchmaking industries and, with the 1878 Factory and Workshop Act, to other forms of manufacturing. The 1891 Factory and Workshop Act engaged in further consolidation by extending safety and sanitary conditions **regulations**. It also transferred the inspection responsibilities of some factories and workshops to local authorities and raised the minimum age of employment in factories to 11.

regulations
Rules that need to be followed in order to comply with the law.

The early decades of the twentieth century saw a steady growth in the coverage of health and safety legislation, as can be seen in Exhibit 10-3. Although industry-specific laws continued, they were accompanied by an increasing number of statutes that sought to expand the governance of workplace safety by co-ordinating and incorporating pre-existing Acts within new laws while also adding new regulations. The 1901 Factory and Workshops Consolidation Act is an illustration. It drew together five other statutes passed since 1878 and enabled the Secretary of State to make more extensive regulations covering a wider range of relatively dangerous work processes and practices across a number of industries. It was, nonetheless, still limited in its scope to people employed in factories and workshops. It did not apply to shops, offices, laboratories, hospitals, local government buildings and schools. The Act remained the dominant piece of legislation until the Factories Act of 1937, which again sought to consolidate pre-existing

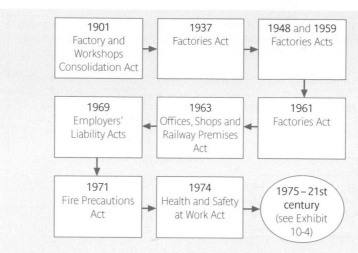

Exhibit 10–3 Health and safety: a historical outline (twentieth century)

measures while adding new regulations, in this case, as regards working age and specific safety conditions concerning stairs, working space and access to the premises.

The subsequent Acts of 1948 and 1959 added new provisions but offered no fundamental changes to the scope and pattern of the legislation. That did not happen until the 1961 Factories Act, which extended the term 'factory' to any premises in which two or more persons were employed to undertake manual labour for economic gain. In this enlarged range of manufacturing environments, the Act established minimum standards for cleanliness, revised specifications for workspace, working temperature, lighting and ventilation as well as protective guards for dangerous machinery, the provision and maintenance of washroom facilities and a statutory reporting system for accidents and industrial diseases.

Health and safety protection was not extended to non-factory premises until the Offices, Shops and Railway Premises Act of 1963. Explained by the rise in service-sector employment and the growth of white-collar trades unionism, this Act afforded similar statutory support to people working in these premises as the Factories Act had done for manufacturing in 1961. Further legislation of the 1960s and early 1970s had general application across the manufacturing/non-manufacturing divide but it did so primarily with regard to particular workplace contingencies. For example, the aim of the Employers' Liability (Compulsory Insurance) Act 1969 was to ensure that employers had adequate insurance cover should employees make claims for injury and disease suffered during work. That of the Employers' Liability (Defective Equipment) Act 1969 was designed to encourage employers to do everything practicably possible to maintain equipment provided for work purposes so that it would not cause injury. The Fire Precautions Act 1971 specified premises that required fire certificates and the conditions under which these would be granted (e.g. that sufficient preventative work had been undertaken, that, in the event of a fire, there were adequate means of raising the alarm, fighting the fire, evacuating the building, and fire training had been provided for the occupants).

In spite of this growth in coverage and consolidation, the Conservative Government of the early 1970s, under pressure from the trades unions, decided that the health and safety legislation of the time was both cumbersome and ineffective. The number of industrial accidents was not decreasing, and several million workers (e.g. those in hospitals, education and road haulage) were still not protected by safety legislation. The Robens Committee was established in

1970 to review the provision made for the safety of people in the course of their employment and its report formed the basis of the 1974 Health and Safety at Work Act (hereafter the HSW Act).

The Act was the first piece of UK legislation that sought to protect all working people – as well as members of the public who might be affected by workplace activities. It also heralded a new participative approach to health and safety in the UK, shifting the vision away from the 'careless worker' to a 'shared responsibility' viewpoint (Bratton and Gold, 2003: 152). It was a sophisticated piece of legislation whose principal aims were to:

codes of practice
Practical examples of good practice and methods of performing safe work practices.

- provide a framework within which past legislation, regulation and **codes of practice** could be incorporated and streamlined, and on which future legislation could be based
- specify the general principles of health and safety compliance
- describe the general duties employers have towards employees and members of the public
- outline the duties employees have to themselves and to others as active participants in the health and safety process (Hutter, 1993), and
- establish the HSC and HSE.

duty of care
This means that employers need to ensure the health, safety and welfare of their employees 'so far as is reasonably practicable'.

Under the Act, employers have a basic **duty of care** to ensure the health, safety and welfare of their employees 'so far as is reasonably practicable'. Within this, they are expected to:

- provide and maintain safe plant and safe systems of work
- ensure safe use of articles and substances
- provide information, training and supervision as necessary
- ensure the workplace is maintained in a safe condition
- provide and maintain a safe working environment and adequate welfare arrangements
- prepare and revise as necessary a written statement of safety policy, bringing it to the attention of all employees
- consult with safety representatives, and
- form a safety committee if requested to do so by (two or more) safety representatives.

Employees are expected to:

- take responsibility for their own health and safety, and for any health and safety problems that might be caused to colleagues by their actions, or their failure to act
- avoid misusing machinery, equipment or processes, and
- co-operate with employers in health and safety initiatives.

This last duty is but one aspect of the shared responsibility agenda introduced by the legislation. As Hutter indicates: 'Prior to the Act, the well-being of the workforce had been largely the preserve and responsibility of employers. This [statute] gave employees responsibilities and expected them to contribute to decisions about their own well-being' (1993: 452). Apart from their day-to-day conduct, that contribution was primarily to be conveyed through safety representatives and at safety committees. This safety system began operating in 1978; the representatives are selected by their trades unions or, where there are no trades unions, by the workforce.

Their main role is to consult with the employer on health and safety matters but they are also expected to investigate hazards or potential hazards, and to carry out workplace inspections. Safety committees are seen by the Act as promoting co-operation between employer and employees in developing a safer working environment. They can be instigated at the request of two safety representatives, but most organisations see it as useful to have a standing site-wide committee to which issues can be taken and at which audits, inspectors reports, accidents and notifiable diseases figures, health and safety promotions, and safety training can be discussed (Foot and Hook, 2005: 376).

The health and safety regulations that followed in the rest of the 1970s and throughout the 1980s (see Exhibit 10-4) were developed within the framework of the HSW Act. The most notable of these was the 1988 Control of Substances Hazardous to Health Regulations (COSHH). Its importance rests not simply with the attempt to convey that there are potentially hazardous substances in all workplaces, nor with the 19 regulations and four approved codes of practice backing up that message, but with the introduction of the practice of risk assessment, which employers are expected to undertake. Employers are required to:

- carry out assessments of the risks to their employees and others who might be affected by the hazardous materials used in the workplace
- identify and introduce appropriate precautions
- inform and train employees in the use of these hazardous substances, and
- regularly monitor the health of those employees using these materials.

The next major legislative intervention came via the 1989 EU Framework Directive (89/391/EEC). EU directives are binding on member states; the only discretionary areas concern *how* (and, in a few instances, *when*) they are translated into domestic law. In the case of the UK, it is usually in the form of regulations. In this instance, the directive led to the Management of Health and Safety at Work Regulations 1992 and five further sets of regulations implemented that year (together they're known as the 'six pack'). The directive combined general principles of how health and safety should be managed and monitored, promoted the conception of shared responsibility between employers and employees, added to their respective duties, and specified key areas for improvement. These included: provision and use of work equipment; personal protective equipment; display screen equipment; and manual handling. Inevitably with changes in raw materials, work skills and technology, all the regulations have required subsequent amendment and updating (see Exhibit 10-4). The most significant of these appeared in the UK as the Management of Health and Safety at Work Regulations 1999. This sought to re-specify the principles of the Directive and further enhance the duties of employers and employees described in the HSW Act. The main duties for employers in these regulations are that they should:

- undertake and record assessments of health and safety risks to employees and the public
- plan and take action to deal with these risks
- train and educate the workforce with regard to the risks
- inform employees and workforce representatives of the risks
- encourage participation from employees in dealing with the risks
- if they are not currently present, establish emergency procedures
- appoint a competent person (or team) to be responsible for preventative and protective measures

Health & Safety Inquiries (Procedure) Regulations 1975

Employer's Health & Safety Policy Statements (Exemptions) Regulations 1975

Health & Safety (First-Aid) Regulations 1981, covers requirements for first-aid provision

Control of Substances Hazardous to Health Regulations (COSHH) 1988 (amended 2002), requires employers to assess the risks from hazardous substances and take appropriate precautions

Noise at Work Regulations 1989, requires employers to take action to protect employees from hearing damage

Electricity at Work Regulations 1989, requires people in control of electrical systems to ensure that these are safe to use and maintained in a safe condition

The Health and Safety Information for Employees Regulations 1989, requires employers to display a poster telling employees what they need to know about health and safety

Workplace (Health, Safety and Welfare) Regulations 1992, covers a wide range of basic health, safety and welfare issues, such as ventilation, heating, lighting, workstations, seating and welfare facilities

Personal Protective Equipment at Work Regulations 1992, requires employers to supply appropriate protective clothing and equipment for their employees

Manual Handling Operations Regulations 1992, covers the moving of objects by hand or bodily force

Health and Safety (Display Screen Equipment) Regulations 1992, sets out requirements for work with visual display units (VDUs)

Reporting of Injuries, Diseases and Dangerous Occurrences Regulations 1995 (RIDDOR), requires employers to notify fatal accidents, certain occupational injuries, diseases and dangerous events to the HSE or local authority

Provision and Use of Work Equipment Regulations 1998, requires that equipment provided for use at work, including machinery, is safe

The Working Time Regulations 1998, implements the provisions of the EU Working Time Directive 1993

The Management of Health and Safety at Work Regulations 1999, requires employers to undertake risk assessments to both employees and the public, make arrangements to implement necessary measures, appoint competent people, and arrange for appropriate information and training

Working Time Amendment Regulations 1999, 2001, 2002 and 2003, amend the 1998 regulations

Revitalising Health and Safety Strategy 2000, seeks to give the government's health and safety programme a fresh impetus. Following a detailed consultation with stakeholders, it identified areas for improvement, established goals and specific targets, and an action plan for attaining them

Securing Health Together 2000, a complementary long-term strategy focused on good health and safety practice, and continuous improvement through networking and partnerships

Merchant Shipping Regulations 2002 and 2003, introduce working time regulations for merchant shipping personnel

Civil Aviation Working Time Regulations 2004, introduces working time regulations for civil aviation personnel

Health, Work and Wellbeing Strategy 2005, dovetails with the strategies published in 2000 to propose the establishment of a new network of bodies, entitled the National and Local Stakeholder Councils. Overseen by the newly appointed National Director of Occupational Health (2005) and working closely with the HSC/E, they will be responsible for promoting workplace health and social care

Exhibit 10–4 Key UK legislative, regulatory and strategic health and safety developments post the 1974 Act

- establish emergency procedures, and
- co-operate with other employers who may share the same work site.

For employees, they are to:

- take reasonable care of their own health and safety, and that of others who may be affected by what they do or do not do
- use machinery and safety devices correctly
- inform the employer or safety representatives of dangers to health and safety in the workplace, and
- co-operate with the employer to ensure that health and safety measures are implemented correctly and working conditions are safe.

Running in tandem with these changes was a further family of regulations emanating from the EU Working Time Directive 1993. Initially opposed by the British Conservative Government of the time, it was accepted by the majority of EU member states and became part of UK domestic law in 1998 under the qualified majority voting scheme (Geyer, 2000). The directive argued that the organisation of working time was an extremely important feature of economic growth and competitiveness, but that it 'should not have negative repercussions [for] the health and safety of workers'. To avoid such consequences 'it was essential for the EU to regulate certain elements of working time' (Geyer, 2000: 87). Its main specifications were:

- a maximum weekly working time of 48 hours on average (including overtime)
- at least four weeks' paid annual leave
- a minimum of 11 hours' rest between finishing work one day and returning to work the next, and one day each week
- a rest period if the working day is longer than six hours
- a maximum of eight hours' night work, on average, in each 24, and
- regular health assessments for night workers.

The directive excluded workers in air, road and rail transport, fishing and other work activities at sea, and doctors in training (on the grounds that their work conditions and environments necessitated distinct consideration). It allowed for the average working week to be calculated over a four-month period (or up to 12 months by collective agreement), and gave member states some leeway in defining terms such as 'rest period' and 'night work' in their domestic legislation. The regulations have subsequently been amended or supplemented on an almost annual basis by further directives, which have been speedily incorporated into UK law by a more compliant Labour Government. The amendments have primarily involved bringing the excluded work groups within the working time framework through the Working Time Amendment Regulations (1999, 2001, 2002 and 2003), the Merchant Shipping Regulations (2002 and 2003) and the Civil Aviation Working Time Regulations (2004).

Post-2000 health and safety initiatives from the British Government have largely centred on its Revitalising Health and Safety Strategy 2000. This was launched by the HSC and Deputy Prime Minister John Prescott, and seeks by 2010 to:

- significantly reduce the incidence of work-related ill health
- assist those not currently in work due to illness or disability to return to work, and
- use the work environment to help people maintain and improve health.

As with all legislation since the HSW Act 1974, it views the attainment of these goals as a social compact arrangement in which government, employers, employers' associations, trades unions and workers work together. At the heart of the strategy are a series of targets for the UK's health and safety system. These are:

- to reduce the number of working days lost per 100,000 workers from work-related injury and ill health by 30 per cent by 2010
- to reduce the incidence of fatal and major accidents by 10 per cent by 2010
- to reduce the incidence rate of cases of work-related ill health by 20 per cent by 2010
- to achieve half the improvement under each target by 2004.

Supporting these targets are a ten-point strategy statement, which sets the direction of the health and safety system, and a 44-point action plan (DETR, 2000). So far (2006), the government and HSC look to be on their way to reaching their 2010 targets. On current interim figures, the HSE's Statistics Branch is claiming that a 15 per cent reduction in working days lost per worker and a 10 per cent reduction in the incidence of work-related ill health have both 'possibly' been met, although the sought decline in the number of fatal and major injuries has not been achieved (HSE, 2006).

Stop and reflect

Employees are expected to take responsibility for their own health and safety and for any health and safety problems that might be caused to colleagues by their actions, or their failure to act.

Are some health and safety issues more important than others? Look at the following scenarios.

You are working in a restaurant and see the following incidents. What would you do?

1 The waiter drops some food on the floor, puts it back on the customer's plate and serves them with it.

2 The chef returns from the toilet without washing his hands and starts cooking.

3 The guard on the mixer is left off as it is easier to add ingredients that way and not likely to cause serious injury.

4 Food that is past its sell-buy date is served to customers.

5 The guard on a meat slicer is broken, but you need to cut some meat urgently.

6 The chef is drunk again and becoming abusive.

Proposed legislation that is complementary to this strategy includes the reform of the law on corporate manslaughter involving the creation of a new criminal offence of 'corporate killing' (likely to reach the statute book in late 2006), a Health Bill that contains proposals to ban smoking in all enclosed public spaces and workplaces (implementation is proposed for the summer of 2007), and a Work and Families Bill. This last looks to extend paid maternity leave (to nine months), increase paternity leave, allow parents to decide how they will share their leave, and give carers the right to request flexible working. Dovetailing with this projected legislation is a further set of developments emanating from a cross-departmental policy document, *Health, Work and Wellbeing* (2005). As will be seen later in the chapter, this proposes the establishment of a new network of bodies, entitled the National and Local Stakeholder Councils. Overseen by the recently appointed National Director of Occupational Health and working closely with the HSC/E, they will be responsible for promoting workplace health and social care.

One such example of promoting workplace health can be seen at Deloitte in the 'Managing diversity' box.

Implementing the health and safety legislation and regulations
Health and safety agencies

Established by the HSW Act, the HSC and HSE have key roles to play in implementing, supporting and enforcing the UK legislation and regulations. The HSC is responsible for:

- health and safety policy
- recommending new legislation, regulations, standards and procedures
- conducting research
- supplying information and advice, and
- maintaining the Employment Medical Advisory Service (EMAS), which provides advice on occupational health matters (HSE, 2003).

managing diversity

Deloitte

Levels of obesity have tripled in England over the past two decades. Most adults are overweight and 20 per cent are obese, according to the National Audit Office. Its 2001 study found that obesity accounted for 18 million days of sickness absence a year and estimated that the resulting loss in productivity cost the wider economy £12 billion annually.

The government is running a two-year, £1.5 million research programme aimed at establishing what changes can be made in and around the workplace to improve people's health.

At Deloitte in the UK, they are already working to improve the health choices of staff. Deloitte believes that exceptional client service can be delivered only by exceptional people and it is people that will make Deloitte a success with its clients.

'This generation of employees has a different perspective on work/life balance and is more focused on health. I believe that employers need to support this,' says Jane Lucien-Scholle, partner in human capital at Deloitte.

'A suggestion from our employee focus group, which provides ideas aimed at improving the workplace, resulted in the "health pod" at our UK headquarters. It is open four days a week and provides stress management, massage and various beauty treatments at a favourable price. We're planning to extend this to offer health-related treatments such as cholesterol tests and body mass index ratings.

'At break times in staff meetings, we provide five-minute massages, fresh juices, yoghurts and other healthy snacks.'

Source: Adapted from K. Hope, CIPD annual conference newspaper,
in *People Management*, 28 October 2005, p. 18.
Reproduced with permission of *People Management*.

Discussion questions

1 Should it be the responsibility of employers to ensure that workers are fit and healthy?

2 What else could employers do to encourage employees to become fit and healthy?

Appointed by the Secretary of State for Transport, Local Government and the Regions, the Commission consists of a chairperson and nine other people drawn from bodies representing employers, employees, local authorities and the general public.

The HSE, a body of three people, is appointed by the HSC (with the consent of the Secretary of State). The Executive has approximately 4000 staff members, which include health and safety inspectors, policy advisers and technologists, as well as scientific and medical experts (HSE, 2003). It advises and assists the Commission in its functions but also has its own statutory responsibilities, which include:

- the enforcement of health and safety law (a role shared with local authorities)
- conducting research, and
- supplying the Commission with policy, technological and professional advice.

This remit applies across industrial sectors and processes to include: nuclear installations, mines, factories, farms, hospitals, schools, offshore gas and oil installations, the safety of the gas grid, the movement of dangerous goods and substances, and railway safety. Consumer and food safety, marine and aviation safety, and pollution are not covered by the HSW Act and do not feature on the agendas of the HSC and HSE. Local authorities are responsible for the enforcement of health and safety legislation in offices, shops, retail and wholesale distribution, hotel and catering establishments, petrol filling stations, residential care homes and the leisure industry (HSC, 2002). They work closely with the HSE through a network of committees and liaison officers.

Action on health and safety: the options

Among the many factors that can prompt action from the HSC/E are changes in technologies, industries or risks; evidence of accidents or ill health; public concern and European directives. Where action is deemed necessary to supplement existing health and safety arrangements, the agencies have three main options. They can issue:

1 guidance
2 Approved Codes of Practice, or
3 regulations.

Guidance

Guidance can be specific to the particular problems of an industry (e.g. dispensing with used syringes in hospitals), to a particular process used in a number of industries (e.g. guides to the law on VDUs or manual handling) or to a particular workplace disease or illness (see the 'Team task' on stress at the end of this chapter). Its main purposes are:

- to help people understand health and safety laws through clear and concise interpretation
- to help people comply with the law, and
- to offer technical advice (HSE, 2003).

Guidance is, in effect, a notification of expected standards. It has no legal authority and employers are therefore free to take other actions. However, if they do follow HSC/E proposals and advice, they will normally be doing enough to comply with the law.

Approved Codes of Practice

'Approved Codes of Practice offer practical examples of good practice. They give advice on how to comply with the law by, for example, providing a guide to what is "reasonably practicable" ... if [for instance] regulations use words like "suitable and sufficient", an Approved Code of Practice can illustrate what this requires in particular circumstances' (HSE, 2003: 5). In law, Approved Codes of Practice have a 'special legal status': 'If employers are prosecuted for a breach of health and safety law, and it is proved that they have not followed the relevant provisions of the Approved Code of Practice, a court can find them at fault unless they can show that they have complied with the law in some other way' (HSE, 2003: 6).

Regulations

Unlike guidance and Approved Codes of Practice, regulations are laws approved by Parliament. Whether they originated as European directives or domestic initiatives proposed by the HSC, they are usually set within the framework of the HSW Act. Where appropriate, the regulations tend to specify targets, stating *what* must be achieved, leaving it to employers to decide *how* this should be done. There are instances, however, particularly in the management of hazards, when it is necessary to prescribe both the goal and the process for achieving that goal, leaving little room for employer initiative.

Enforcement

Enforcement of health and safety legislation is undertaken by HSE inspectors and, for local authorities, by environmental health officers. Both have similar powers, which include the right to:

- enter any premises where work is carried on, without giving notice
- carry out inspections/investigations
- talk to employees and safety representatives
- take equipment or materials on to the premises
- take photographs and samples
- examine company documents, and
- impound dangerous equipment and substances (HSC, 2003; Foot and Hook, 2005).

If they are not satisfied with the levels of health and safety being achieved, they have several measures for obtaining improvements. These include the following.

- **Advice or informal warnings:** typically issued for minor breaches of the legislation; they explain what the employer is doing wrong and what it needs to do to comply with the law.
- **Improvement notices:** give a specified time within which the contraventions of the law must be remedied.
- **Prohibition notices:** usually issued when inspectors think there is a risk of serious personal injury. They require an activity to be stopped immediately, or after a specified time period, unless the employer takes action to remedy the problem. Employers do have a right of appeal to employment tribunals, but the prohibition notice remains in force until the appeal is held, unless the tribunal issues a notice to the contrary.

(In 2003/2004, 17,500 (prohibition and improvement) notices were issued by the enforcing authorities, a 9 per cent decrease on 2002/2003. In 2004/2005, the HSE issued 8445 notices and, while no comparable figures have yet been published by the local authorities, they are also likely to follow a declining trend that has seen numbers drop from 26,980 in 1992/1993 to 6080 in 2003/2004 (HSE, 2006).)

- **Prosecution in the criminal law courts:** the grounds on which to prosecute are laid down in the HSC's enforcement policy statement (see www.hse.gov.uk), which suggests that:
  - enforcement action should be proportionate to the risk created
  - it should be targeted at more serious risks, and
  - it should be used where hazards are least controlled.

Prosecutions in Scotland are usually pursued in the sheriff courts, while those in England and Wales are taken to magistrates courts. Both courts can impose prison sentences and fines to a maximum of £20,000. If they think cases warrant it, they can refer them to a higher court where there is no limit to the fine that can be imposed. Balfour Beatty and Network Rail, for example, were fined £10 million and £3.5 million respectively at the Old Bailey in October 2005 for their part in the Hatfield rail disaster, which killed four people and injured 102. Transco, the gas firm, was forced by the Scottish High Court to pay £15 million after an explosion killed four members of a family in Lanarkshire in 1999.

The number of prosecutions pursued by the HSE has been fewer than 2000 cases per annum since 1995/1996. The figure stood at 1267 in 2004/2005, a decline of 26 per cent over the preceding year. The latest figures for local authority prosecutions are those for 2003/2004 in which 410 cases were pursued through the courts (an increase of 24 per cent on the preceding year). The number of convictions for the HSE has remained in the region of 75 per cent of the prosecutions over the last few years (79 per cent in 2004/2005) and, in the case of local authorities, 86 per cent for the last two years of available statistics (2002/2004). The average penalty per conviction in cases brought by the HSE was £12,642 in 2004/2005, with 20 fines exceeding £100,000, whereas for local authority prosecutions it was £4375, which includes one fine of £150,000 (HSE, 2006)

Workplace accidents that result in deaths are always formally assessed by inspectors to ascertain whether 'gross negligence' has contributed to the outcome. If the inspectors think that it has, the case is handed to the police for prosecution. However, very few prosecutions have been attempted since 1965, when companies became open to manslaughter proceedings, and only a handful of convictions have resulted. In the case cited above, for example, Balfour Beatty and Network Rail were both charged with manslaughter. The judge described the lack of track maintenance leading to the crash as 'one of the worst examples of sustained industrial negligence' (Hencke and Milner, 2005), yet he still felt obliged to dismiss the charges because of the 'controlling mind' requirement in current law (i.e. that one person in a position of control has to be directly responsible for the negligence). As indicated in the previous section, the government is looking to change this law, to introduce an offence of 'corporate killing' and new legal duties that make senior managers directly responsible for health and safety matters.

Health through well-being

So far, this chapter has focused on health through safety, and the legislative and regulatory agenda set by the EU, the UK Government, the HSC and the HSE. What the rest of the chapter addresses are the many initiatives (going beyond risk protection) that employers utilise in promoting the well-being of their staff. In one sense this is not a new development: HRM grew from early twentieth-century concerns about employee welfare (see Chapter 1) and ensuring well-being has remained an important HR agenda item. Actively encouraged by government through legislation, tax relief and other incentives (May and Brunsdon, 1999; May and Brunsdon, 2006), it nonetheless remains largely a voluntary activity that employers choose to undertake. They tailor services to their perceived needs and in terms of their resources, and this largely explains the patchwork nature of provision across the UK.

Services promoting well-being

It is this variability that makes capturing the array of workplace support a difficult task. Based on the nature of the service offered, however, a broad distinction can be drawn between seven main types of provision (see Exhibit 10-5). A further subdivision can be drawn between those designed to directly address issues of health and well-being (e.g. health and social care services) and those created for other purposes, which can have an indirect impact (e.g. an organisation's reward and training packages or recreational facilities). This section of the chapter will begin by briefly describing those services with an indirect impact before it offers a more detailed consideration of direct service provision.

Many employers reward their staff with various forms of financial benefit in addition to their pay. Though often referred to as 'perks', from an employee's perspective such assistance may enhance their disposable incomes and improve their quality of life. It may also offer protection against life-cycle contingencies. In many respects, these subventions function as a form of social security, serving either as supplements to pay or as a substitute when employees are unable to work, or face particular life events. Occupational retirement pensions are probably the best-known substitutions for pay, but employers also fund a wide range of other income-maintenance schemes, ranging from survivors' benefits to support above the statutory minimum in the event of redundancy (Armstrong, 2002; Wright, 2004).

Supplements to pay may be offered in cash or in kind, and embrace a number of different types of benefit. They range from low- or no-interest loans, financial help with transport, including company cars, car purchase schemes, parking facilities and subsidised season tickets, to the cost of renting telephones or mobile phones, assistance with home contents, car or even pet insurance, and an ever changing array of discount arrangements. Traditionally, these enabled staff to pay less for the organisation's products and services. The last decade, however, has seen a rapid expansion of voucher systems entitling employees to lower-cost retail and leisure goods purchased either from local firms or national outlets (Dennis, 2005).

Income enhancement on these lines is closely tied with other measures that may also indirectly promote employee health and well-being. Many, particularly large organisations, offer

Type of provision	Focus on employee health and well-being
Financial benefits and services	Direct/indirect
Accommodation services	Indirect
Education, training and personal development services	Indirect
Recreational and leisure services	Indirect
Community-orientated services	Indirect
Health services	Direct
Care services	Direct

Exhibit 10–5 Direct and indirect forms of UK workplace well-being services

various housing services and benefits, the most common being subsidised mortgages and assistance with relocation. Others provide training and education programmes, which, although predominantly vocational in nature, will often also incorporate opportunities for general education, and personal as well as professional development. The government-subsidised home computer scheme, with its work and non-work usages, is a case in point. There are also companies that are prepared to sponsor recreational and non-vocational learning. Ford, for instance, offers financial support for language and art classes taken by its employees.

Employers also offer other recreational services. These can range from sports or gym facilities, subsidised membership schemes and time off for staff participating in particular competitions, to free or discounted tickets and vouchers for the theatre and concerts. Conscious of the growing corporate social responsibility agenda, organisations may also encourage their staff to participate in various forms of community work. This type of enterprise welfare encompasses both corporate and active citizenship programmes and is being heavily promoted by the government. Companies might opt to fund local or other projects or support voluntary groups through donations, sponsorship or secondments. More widely, employees could be encouraged to undertake civic or voluntary roles with staff participation supported through leave or flexible working.

Exhibit 10-6 provides a more detailed overview of the indirect (and direct) forms of well-being service developed by employers. Together they constitute a significant organisational investment averaging approximately 30 per cent of organisations' salary bills and, in some cases, rising to 50 per cent (IDS, 1999; Armstrong and Stephens, 2005). It is the direct contributors to well-being, the health and social services, that are among the most costly. They are also the fastest growing, with the occupational healthcare market alone expected to grow by over 20 per cent by 2009 (*Personnel Today*, 9 August 2005: 10).

Direct provision: healthcare services and benefits

Traditionally, **occupational health** care has focused on risk minimisation in the workplace and on individuals suffering from declared health problems (IPD, 1995). Recently this reactive, illness-orientated, perspective has begun to give way to a broader, more proactive approach focused on healthy living and encompassing the whole workforce. Marked by the emergence of a host of 'wellness initiatives', it signifies a new conception of employee health and an extension of employers' responsibilities. Provision is as yet uneven and characteristic of large rather than small organisations. But the move to more comprehensive occupational healthcare is being actively canvassed by both the UK Government and the EU, and looks set to expand (DWP/DoH/HSE, 2005). In what follows we look at the main constituents of both conventional provision and the 'new' occupational health.

occupational health
Services provided by the employer to ensure the health and well-being of employees at work.

Illness services
Occupational sick pay (OSP)

Occupational sick pay (OSP) is one of the most common forms of benefit provided by employers and, from an employee's perspective, constitutes a crucial 'top up' to **statutory sick pay** (SSP). Under social security legislation, employers are responsible for administering SSP and for paying it in full for the first four weeks of absence. Thereafter some of the cost is refunded through

occupational sick pay
A benefit provided by the employer to top up statutory sick pay when employees are sick.

statutory sick pay
Money that must be paid to an employee when she or he is sick.

Form of support	Statutory	Non-statutory
Financial benefits and services	Pensions Redundancy pay	Occupational pensions (retirement; survivors; ill health retirement) Life insurance/death in service benefits Personal accident insurance Enhanced redundancy pay Professional indemnity insurance Travel insurance Interest-free loans Voluntary benefits: discounts for employee purchases (income protection insurance; leisure activities; household goods) Transport benefits: company cars; car tax/fuel/insurance; car allowances; driving lessons; season ticket vouchers/loans; free parking; free cycles/loan schemes
Accommodation services		Company housing/on-site accommodation Mortgage allowances Relocation searches Relocation expenses Bridging loans Buildings/contents insurance
Education, training and personal development	Health and safety	Above minimum H&S training Study support: tuition/exam fees; equipment, books, subsistence, travel Study leave Personal development leave (sabbaticals; career breaks) Fees/subscriptions to professional bodies Children's education assistance (fee subsidies; grants; subsidised loans)
Recreational and leisure services		Sports/social/recreational facilities Subsidised sports/recreational club membership
Community-orientated services		Corporate donations (cash/kind) Employee secondment schemes Employee mentoring schemes Employee volunteering schemes Employee fund-raising schemes

Exhibit 10–6 Forms of employee support
Source: Adapted from May and Brunsdon (2006).

Form of support	Statutory	Non-statutory
Health services	Statutory sick pay (SSP)	Occupational sick pay (OSP)
		*Private medical insurance (PMI)
		*Subsidised health care/cash plans
		Permanent health insurance/long-term disability pay
		Critical illness insurance
	Ante-natal care time off	Extended ante-natal care leave
		Fertility treatment leave
		Leave/time out for appointments/treatment (medical/dental/ophthalmic)
		Occupational health services
		Wellness services
Care services		
Personal counselling and support services		Information services
		General advice and counselling schemes
		Employee assistance schemes
		Specialist counselling schemes
Work/life balance services		
General leave	Paid holiday leave	Extended (paid) holiday leave
	Civic duties	Civic duties
'Family'-related leave		Marriage/civil partnership leave
	Maternity leave	Extended maternity leave
	Paternity leave	Extended paternity leave
	Adoption leave	Extended adoption leave
	Parental leave	Extended (paid) parental leave
	Dependant emergency care leave	Extended (paid) dependant care leave
		Foster parent leave
		Grandparent leave
	Carers' leave	Extended (paid) carers' leave
Flexible working arrangements	Right to request: parents of under sixes and disabled children up to 18	Other parents/carers/older employees
		Flexible work schemes (see Exhibit 10–8)
Financial support	Statutory maternity pay	Occupational maternity pay (plus)
	Statutory adoption pay	Occupational paternity pay (plus)
Childcare service		Information and referral services
		Advice/parentcraft services
		Provisions for employees with disabled children
		Workplace nurseries
		Subsidy/voucher schemes
		(Salary sacrifice schemes)

Form of support	Statutory	Non-statutory
Elder care/dependant adult services		Information, referral/advice services Care vouchers/assistance
Concierge services		Subsidised cafeterias; meal allowances/vouchers Housework/laundry/shopping services
Redundancy	Time off for job search/retraining	Enhanced leave/time off Outplacement/job search services (counselling; information/advice; career planning; assistance with job search/application skills/process; job search facilities; placement services)
Pre-retirement services		Flexible retirement schemes Pre-retirement planning and advice Information/referral services
Post-retirement services		'Keeping in touch'/Home visiting schemes Assistance with hospital/medical fees Respite care

* Options include: day surgery; in-hospital treatment; in-hospital maternity care; parental hospital care; convalescence; physiotherapy, chiropody; surgical appliances, hearing aids, complementary therapies – reflexology, acupuncture, osteopathy, etc.

reductions in the employer's National Insurance contributions, with the state taking complete responsibility when an employee has been absent for a continuous or linked period of 28 weeks. Provisions for reclaiming are geared to supporting smaller employers. They can recoup a higher share of the outlay than large employers, who generally meet all the costs. Nonetheless, though they are not required to further compensate employees for lost earnings, many employers also invest in OSP schemes. Recent national studies show that nearly three in five workplaces have such a scheme for most (though not all) employees (White *et al.*, 2004: 59).

The design of these schemes varies considerably in terms of the level and length of assistance provided and eligibility. The most widespread secure an individual's income by providing full pay for a set number of weeks. Other systems maintain salary at a reduced rate or offer a predetermined flat rate in addition to SSP. Many schemes also offer scaled-down support for a further period of absence. Whatever the approach, employees receive an emolument above the statutory minimum, with employers reclaiming the SSP element where possible. Some employers offer protection from the first day, others operate a qualifying period of one to several days, but usually no more than a week.

Entitlement may also be contingent on an employee's length of service, as might the maximum payment. A number of employers are still setting 'waiting periods', which range from a minimum of a week's service to up to a year for particular groups of employees. The 'speed' at which employees qualify for full OSP also differs markedly. A minority of employers offer maximum cover to all staff, including new entrants; others may confine it to those with ten or more years' service, with various grades in between (IDS, 2003a). Entitlement may also depend on an employee's status. Traditionally, many schemes offered more generous support to those in managerial or supervisory positions, and recent studies (e.g. Kersley *et al.*, 2005) suggest this tendency still prevails. Overall, SMEs are the least likely to supply OSP and, where they do, to operate the lowest benefits. The most munificent schemes are to be found in the public sector, in large corporations and heavily unionised workplaces. Public-sector OSP typically covers the whole workforce often on a '6 + 6' basis, with staff receiving full pay for the first six months and half pay for the next. These employers are also likely to extend payments while medical assessments are ongoing and/or where employees need a slightly longer recovery time. Similar schemes exist in large corporations, though with variations between employment groups.

For all employers, however, managing sick leave and pay is becoming an increasingly expensive process and, as with occupational pensions, there are signs that organisations are beginning to revise their provision. Many are now offering tighter, less generous, support (IDS, 2003a) and placing emphasis on preventative services (see below). But it is not just the rising cost of OSP that is causing concern. A number of employers are also beginning to see the benefit as counterproductive and open to abuse, with some staff off work for longer than necessary or just 'taking a sickie'. This has prompted some organisations – Tesco and the Royal Mail among them – to stop OSP for the first three days of absence. The CIPD indicates that 15 per cent of the sample in its absence management survey (2005a) pursue this strategy, and many run their management of sick pay in tandem with organisational attendance and rehabilitation policies.

Insurance-based medical and after-care services

One of the tools deployed by some organisations to expedite the return to work is the use of medical and health insurance schemes to fund diagnosis and treatment costs. The most common form of this is private medical insurance (PMI), which is employed to fund diagnoses and treatment costs, and typically covers consultation, hospitalisation, day surgery, physiotherapy, radiology and other elective treatments, usually but not necessarily undertaken in private hospitals and clinics. From an employer's perspective, PMI secures fast-track treatment scheduled at business-convenient times and may also speed up after-care services in emergency cases. For employees it brings further benefits. The size of company-paid PMI frequently means pre-existing conditions are usually covered, and spouses or partners and dependent children may also be protected (IDS, 2003b). However, to contain rising premiums, cost limits are often placed on some treatments, which may also have to be sought at specified hospitals.

medical and health insurance
Insurance provided either by the employer or taken out by the employee to provide cover for illness or accidents.

Employers are the major purchasers of PMI in the UK, providing for two-thirds of those with such protection (Baggott, 2004). Around 10 per cent of employees are eligible for PMI, most of whom are in senior or key positions (CIPD, 2005b). Partly in response to recent changes in NHS provision, employers have also developed wider-based forms of assistance and begun to purchase other insurance products. Some, for instance, support employee-paid PMI through group discounts; others offer similarly reduced healthcare cash plans, both of which may now be used for dental, ophthalmic and chiropody as well as medical treatment.

Occupational healthcare facilities

In spite of this increase in the range of insurance-based products, the main source of employer support for staff healthcare remains workplace health services. Those in 'high risk' industries and services and large corporations have provided on-site or local healthcare services over a long period of time. Originally established to advise on workplace safety and deal with accidents or staff taken ill at work, they now additionally provide advice and support in managing both short- and long-term ill health absence. Similar services exist across the public, private and voluntary sectors, where provision depends largely on the size and nature of the workplace. The CIPD's survey (2005a) found 46 per cent of its respondents operated an in-house service, run either by a dedicated unit, a specialist nurse or a company doctor. Of those outsourced to external agencies, 26 per cent of the sample brought in professional help as and when necessary.

Internal and external providers play a key role in pre-employment medicals and investigating and advising on cases of recurrent short-term absence. They are also widely deployed in overseeing provisions to enable those with prolonged illnesses or needing lengthy treatment to return to work. Their responsibilities here range from organising or undertaking medical assessments and counselling, and advising on specialist help or aftercare, to maintaining contact with staff and overseeing their return. CIPD data suggest that nearly three-quarters of employers enable employees to access occupational healthcare services (CIPD, 2005a). The quality of the service offered, however, is highly variable (DWP/DoH/HSE, 2005: 16).

Rehabilitation and return to work services

Occupational health services usually form part of a broader absence management policy covering rehabilitation and return to work (Bevan, 2003; IDS, 2005). In the case of both short- and long-term absence, for instance, employees are often required to attend return to work interviews. In the case of short-term absence, its purpose is to welcome and resettle staff and avoid repeat absences by ensuring that their cause(s) do not recur. For longer-term absentees, the aim is to keep in regular contact and subsequently ease individuals back into their jobs. To this end organisations may run extensive rehabilitation programmes. They may arrange phased return with reduced hours or responsibilities and (in accordance with disability discrimination legislation) adaptations to equipment or the workspace. Where continuing with the previous post is not feasible, alternative employment may be offered. Redeployment depends on both the individual's circumstances and past roles and the openings available; it also has pay implications. Policy and practice in these respects vary markedly. Some large firms offer graduated re-entry from long-term absence for all returnees, whereas SMEs tend simply to adjust initial hours (Silcox, 2005a). Some, mainly large, organisations offer preserved salaries for the first year or two of redeployment and for phased returns, whereas SMEs, not surprisingly, may lack the necessary resources to make such provision.

Ill-health retirement, permanent health, critical illness and disability insurance

Having considered the available options it may be necessary to terminate an individual's contract on the grounds of ill health. To aid individuals unable to continue working, employers have developed a number of income replacement measures. Until recently the most generous were discretionary ill health or medical pensions available to companies with final salary pension schemes. Though little discussed, recent large-scale closures of these schemes are jeopardising this form of assistance. The main alternatives are permanent health insurance (PHI) or disability benefit insurance products. These enable employers to fund pensions for individuals with a long-term illness or disability for a specified time period, usually until the normal retirement age. Critical illness, or 'dread disease', insurance offers a further form of income protection, which some employers also purchase.

With premiums costing up to 2 per cent of payrolls, only a few organisations currently offer PHI and then primarily to senior personnel (IDS, 2003a). Whether companies moving to money purchase pensions will buy alternative private incapacity benefits is unclear, as is the outcome of the Turner Commission. It is widely recognised, however, that the cost-effective

wellness services
Services targeted at all employees to raise awareness and provide support for health issues.

way forward is to invest in preventative rather than curative healthcare (IoD, 2002; ABI/TUC, 2003). This step-change is now under way and is marked by the spread of wellness services targeted at all employees rather than those with overt health problems.

Wellness services

In developing these new interventions, employers have followed general health promotion practices and have also drawn on organisational change and diversity management programmes to tailor provision to particular organisational concerns and workforce profiles. At their core are a number of key services; Exhibit 10-7 provides a summary of these. Not all employers offer the same services, of course, and organisations diverge quite markedly in their use of in-house and external suppliers. Many wellness programmes are time-limited and project-based, with health education activities in particular characterised by a cycle of initiatives.

While wellness management is still evolving, with only around a third of employers running health promotion and other programmes (Silcox, 2005b), it is nonetheless moving up the

Service	Examples
Screening and diagnostic services	Periodic single factor screening (e.g. body weight, blood pressure, cholesterol, cardiac risk assessments; chest X-rays; sight, glaucoma, hearing, dental checks); personal profiling and risk assessments/feedback; specialist tests (e.g. cancer screening); general wellness tests (e.g. health risk appraisals; lifestyle audits)
Health counselling	Stress management/sleeping/diet/exercise/lifestyle strategies; advice on sources of specialist help
Health education/promotion	Workplace health care 'champions'/'ambassadors'; healthy eating/smoking cessation/alcohol care/healthy hearts/lifestyles/healthy ageing/fitness campaigns ('special events'/weeks; health fairs; workshops, courses; leaflets; posters; electronic bulletins; desk drops; advice material in in-house journals); mental health awareness campaigns
Preventative healthcare	Lifestyle coaching: stress management/emotional health workshops/courses; healthy catering/vending machines; 'free fruit' days; nutritional events; workplace smoking; alcohol policies; fitness/vitality programmes/facilities (on-site/personal fitness trainers/coaches/exercise classes/sessions/competitions; 'walk/cycle more' campaigns/sponsorships; 'stair prompts'/free pedometers; on-site/subsidised sports facilities/gyms; 'activities' events); complementary medicine facilities (on-/off-site: aromatherapy, reflexology; massage; yoga, pilates)
Specialist services	Alcohol/substance abuse counselling/support services

Exhibit 10–7 The main wellness services offered by UK employers

well-being agenda. Its increasing significance is evident in the formation of umbrella groups such as the European Health and Performance Management Community and Business Action on Health, both of which want to see health audits and promotional activities included in companies' annual reports. Barclays Bank and the Royal Bank of Scotland have taken a lead by adding 'health and wellbeing managers' to their HR directorates while BT and Prudential have both invested heavily in healthy living and working programmes. BT runs a 'workfit' scheme in which it offers health risk assessments, advice and, where necessary, rehabilitation assistance. On a slightly different tack, Prudential's wellness focus (introduced in 2004) addresses four key health issues: muscle pain (which it estimates costs the company 4000 lost days annually), pressure, skin cancer and healthy eating. A 'floor walker' scheme provides for checks on posture and workstation usage, and offers neck massage and exercise advice. A programme of stress checks, awareness and advice events, supported by therapies such as head massage and promotional literature, are in place; a parallel skin cancer prevention campaign has also begun, along with 'healthy options' in staff restaurants and 'lunch and learn' promotions (Paton, 2005). Similar schemes are being introduced across the public sector largely, but not exclusively, in response to the government's drive to modernise work practices and reduce levels of absenteeism. 'Invest to spend' projects establishing proactive occupational health systems are being instigated in Whitehall departments, the prison service, local government and police authorities, while the UK's largest employer, the NHS, operates its own Improving Working Lives Standard (DoH, 2000; Cabinet Office, 2004, 2005).

Care services

personal counselling
Its main purpose is to offer advice and assistance to employees with 'personal problems', stemming either from their 'non-work' circumstances or from relationship issues in the workplace.

Like wellness services, workplace care is a fast-growing aspect of employee well-being. The long-established industrial social work has given way to a wide range of **personal counselling** services to which employers have added new types of intervention, frequently summarised in the phrase 'work/life balance services'. Such services are geared to employees' changing work, caring and personal development needs, and offer more flexible leave, career, location, working- and learning-time arrangements (see Exhibit 10-8).

Personal counselling services

Workplace counselling services vary in terms of their provenance, modes of delivery and the types of support they offer. Their main purpose is to offer advice and assistance to employees with 'personal problems', stemming either from their 'non-work' circumstances or from relationship issues in the workplace. In the employer's eyes the service is particularly pertinent where problems are considered to affect employee work performance or conduct, and where counselling can provide a cost-effective way forward. Who supplies the service is subject to marked variation. In large commercial organisations, it is likely to be an in-house or externally contracted occupational health specialist or a trained member of the organisation's HR unit. In SMEs, the mantle of counsellor is more likely to be taken by the line manager – who may or may not be trained (Kiefer and Briner, 2003). As with other areas of employee well-being, it is public-sector services that are likely to provide a more consistent provision and make it available to all members of their workforce.

employee assistance programmes
Viewed by many organisations as the preferred form of support for troubled staff.

This is certainly the case with the more specialist **employee assistance programmes** (EAPs) – viewed by many organisations as the preferred form of support for troubled staff. An American

Contractual provisions	(Permanent) part-time; fixed-term; temporary; consultancy/project
Flexible working times	Staggered hours; flexitime; variable hours; annualised hours; compressed hours; shift work/adjustable shifts; self-rostering; term-time work; part-time work; job-sharing (overtime)
Leave arrangements *Annual leave* *'Family'-related leave* *Civic leave* *'Personal development leave'* *Breaks*	Statutory/non-statutory; paid/unpaid (see Exhibit 10–6) At/above statutory minimum/enforcement of Ante-natal leave; maternity leave; paternity leave; adoption leave; fostering leave; parental leave; carers' leave; dependant/emergency leave; bereavement leave; compassionate leave Civic duties; voluntary and community activities Study leave; sabbaticals; career breaks Duvet leave
Flexible careers	Returner schemes; slow-tracking; decruitment
Flexible retirement	Decruitment; reduced hours; phased retirement
Locational flexibility/flexi-space	Home working/teleworking
Working/learning time accounts/banks	See text

Exhibit 10–8 Work/life balance: flexible working services

import, it has now been taken up by much of public-sector and corporate Britain. A programme of some description is now offered by around a third of companies (Zneimer, 2005). It was initially devised in the 1970s to deal with alcohol-related problems in the workplace. Today, it has a much broader remit and employees can receive expert assistance with relationships, sexual and domestic problems, and with anxieties and fears arising from divorce, bereavement and caring responsibilities. Some employers offer further advisory services (on legal and housing matters, debt management, and financial and retirement planning) as well as support for victims of domestic violence or crime (Overell, 2005).

As with personal counselling, EAPs can be designed and managed in-house through HR or occupational health services or, given the required expertise and confidentiality, contracted out to specialist agencies. In some instances, both sources are used with general counselling and advice provided in-house and the more particular personal issues met by the outside providers. Though individuals can be referred by their managers, most EAPs operate on a self-referral basis. Trained counsellors offer information and advice through the use of casework techniques, helping individuals to 'work through' their personal concerns. The support time varies, but employees are usually offered a predetermined number of counselling sessions (normally three to five) and/or a telephone helpline service (IDS, 2002).

Work/life balance (WLB) services

The workplace counselling discussed in preceding paragraphs is often accompanied by services aimed at enhancing well-being through a better balance between work and other responsibilities and interests. Provision here has partly been driven by EU and UK legislation on working time, holiday and parental leave, and flexible working arrangements. But the government has also invested in a stream of measures to persuade employers to move beyond the statutory minima. In particular, it has actively promoted the business case for a range of **WLB** schemes, sponsoring research, building up a supportive evidence base, and showcasing examples in national and regional campaigns.

WLB

Work/life balance strategies to enable employees to balance their home and work life, taking into account caring responsibilities.

As these illustrate, UK employers have developed an abundance of schemes designed to help some or all staff combine paid employment with other aspects of their lives (see Exhibit 10-8). Typically these originated with 'family friendly' measures targeted at working parents (particularly mothers), but leading-edge employers have now extended their support schemes way beyond this remit to include: staff caring for dependent adults, and 'gap' leave and flexible working for those wishing to take time out or pursue a particular interest. They have also launched various forms of flexible retirement. To facilitate this, some organisations are using salary sacrifice systems; others have developed a conception of 'time banks' along the lines piloted in Australia. In these, employees are allowed to purchase extra leave. Their reduced pay is spread across the year but their pensions and other contributions are maintained at the full amount (Neagle, 2003; IPPR, 2006).

The distribution of WLB services follows a similar pattern to the supply of other well-being services. Some are universally available; others, such as holiday entitlements, are subject to status and/or length of service, or individual circumstances. Again, public-sector employees are offered the more comprehensive packages, while larger non-statutory organisations have a higher level and range of schemes than smaller ones (Taylor, 2002a, 2002b). But it is still the case that significant numbers of commercial employers (in companies of all sizes) are limiting themselves to the minimalist position of simply complying with the statutory regulations. Opportunities for flexible working have undoubtedly increased (Woodland *et al.*, 2003; Kersley *et al.*, 2005) but whether employers do not accept the business case for WLB, or significant numbers of (male) employees feel constrained by career concerns and do not participate in initiatives, is not clear. For many observers, WLB provision has yet to make an impact on Britain's long-hours culture, the processes making for work intensification, or the resultant pressures on people's non-working lives (Bunting, 2004).

Future scenarios: the well-being debate

From an HRM perspective these disparities raise several issues that are not easily reconciled. The first centres on the appropriate balance of responsibility between employers, individual employees and the state. Debate here overlaps with broader discussions over corporate social responsibility (see Chapter 6). The other dilemmas centre more on the role of the HR adviser and the practicalities of well-being service management.

In terms of responsibility for employee well-being, opinion is divided between two conflicting schools of thought.

1 Analysts who, like Friedman (1963) and Henderson (2001), hold that businesses have 'one and only one social responsibility', that of profit maximisation and hence wealth creation, and that employee well-being is a matter of individual not corporate responsibility. (Others similarly oppose employer-based schemes, but do so on the grounds that this entails unwarranted intrusion into employees' personal lives.)

2 Those who contend that employer provision is insufficient and should be expanded. Pointing to the uneven development of health and well-being services, and their differential distribution between employees, some proponents favour a move towards more comprehensive schemes. Others are concerned that employer provision tends to focus on the symptoms rather than what they see as the prime sources of 'diswelfare' in the workplace. Alongside greater investment in counselling, wellness and other services, they call for improvements in the quality and design of work, greater job security and increased employee involvement (Coates and Max, 2005).

Concern over the unevenness of employer provision is shared by the government, which has launched a series of initiatives to secure further action. As already noted, new legislation to extend paid leave and rights to flexible working is already in progress, along with a renewed campaign to promote WLB arrangements. Equally importantly, the government is committed to developing a Scandinavian-style system of national occupational health geared to prevention. Its plans have been laid out in the strategy documents from the HSC and HSE discussed earlier and, for England, by the Department of Health (DoH, 1999). A series of policy documents have embellished them (notably, Wanless, 2002; Cabinet Office, 2004; DoH, 2004; DWP, 2005; DWP/DoH/HSE, 2005). With similar schemes for Wales and Scotland, they collectively foresee a 'new, innovative and far-reaching strategy' to revamp public health around work and expand employer healthcare (DWP/DoH/HSE, 2005: 8). The main pillars of this are:

- the establishment of a National Director of Occupational Health
- a Charter for Health, Work and Well-being
- the development of an Investors In People 'healthy business assessment' and health standard
- a National Stakeholder Council, Network and Summit
- local Stakeholder Councils
- the Framework for Vocational Rehabilitation
- NHS Plus (enabling NHS occupational health support and advice for external employers)
- Workplace Health Connect (an advisory service for SMEs)
- a national workplace health award system
- encouragement for companies to report occupational health and safety as part of their business performance reporting (using the HSE's Health and Safety Performance Indicator or its SME equivalent).

In presenting these, the government has also spelt out the case for more comprehensive provision, pointing in particular to:

- the need to boost productivity and plug the gap between the performance of UK workers and their counterparts in the USA and elsewhere
- the associated need to both maximise employment levels and cultivate high-performance working
- the economic and fiscal drain on government and organisations alike arising from absenteeism and ill health among those of working age, and the associated costs of incapacity benefit claims
- the health-maintenance issues posed by an 'ageing' workforce and pressures for longer working lives

- the manifold difficulties of funding the NHS
- the cost-effectiveness of preventative healthcare
- the utility of the workplace as a venue for preventative healthcare
- the business gains arising from workplace interventions
- the benefits of work-based well-being and wellness services for employers, employees and the wider society.

In the government's eyes these imperatives are self-explanatory. Hence its strategy is to raise employer awareness of the plans and pledge infrastructural support rather than offer fiscal or regulatory incentives. Recent HSE research, however, has cast doubt on the level of awareness among employers, most of whom still do not calculate the business costs of work-related health problems (HSE, 2005). Looking at these findings and the prevalence of low-cost, high-visibility health promotion rather than radical preventative action, others feel a legislative steer will be needed (Coates and Max, 2005).

Either way, both employer-led and governmental concerns presage an expanding set of responsibilities for HRM advisers. Some observers even predict that well-being and wellness management will replace HRM as a business function (Phillips, 2006). Less radically, others foresee the emergence of a 'new type of people manager', one who 'prioritises employee health as highly as good management systems' (Mancocha, 2004). Such forecasts may seem far-fetched but they do highlight the dilemmas and practical problems that come with this growing remit. In its bid for organisational authority, the profession has tended to distance itself from its welfarist function (Goss, 1994; Bratton and Gold, 2005). Currently this is manifest in the popularity of what Ulrich has termed the 'business partner' model (Ulrich, 1998). Pressure to expand health and well-being may, however, bring other roles to the fore and contribute to the remodelling of these along the lines outlined elsewhere by Ulrich and Brockbank (2005).

At a practical level, HR advisers face a further set of issues. In particular, they will need to consider how to develop an employee well-being strategy that:

- meets the overall aims of the business
- has clear, measurable goals
- offers a clear return on investment
- is benchmarked against key competitors' positions
- has board-level support
- maximises management support at all other levels
- aligns with other HR activities, particularly reward and absence management
- is affordable
- is cost-effective
- is tax-efficient, capitalising on tax relief and other government support
- is based on consultation with employees and an analysis of employees' needs and views
- allows for variations in employee needs
- is based on an evaluation of the relative merits of 'core' and 'optional' services, including their place in any flexible benefits package
- is communicated effectively
- is subject to regular monitoring and updating.

Summary

- This chapter has focused on health through safety and health through well-being.

- It has looked at the protracted and incremental development of health and safety legislation in the UK, the current statutory and regulatory framework, and the powers and responsibilities of the main health and safety agencies.

- It has also considered the key tools developed by employers to deal with employee sickness and ill health.

- In the process the chapter has pointed to the factors shaping change and the current redirection of health, safety and well-being policy and practice.

- Opinion is clearly divided over these developments and their implications.

- What is clear is the growing significance of this arena for both the discipline of HRM and its practitioners.

Personal development

1 **Understand how health and safety legislation has evolved.** In what ways did the Health and Safety at Work Act 1974 herald a new approach to health and safety? What were the main duties imposed on employers and employees by the Act? How have they subsequently been amended?

2 **Identify the importance of a healthy workforce.** What is the business case for extra-statutory safety and well-being provision? Why is European law important for the development of UK health and safety?

3 **Identify who enforces health and safety legislation.** What are the main agencies charged with enforcing health and safety legislation? What are their respective duties?

4 **Recognise how legislation is implemented in organisations.** Are you aware of the health and safety policy of the organisation for which you work or at which you study? What are its main provisions?

5 **Identify the role of the health and safety officer.** Using a workplace with which you are familiar, find out who is responsible for health and safety and how they perceive their role. If there is a health and safety representative, try to find out how they undertake their role. What is an EAP?

6 **Understand the importance of work/life balance.** What are the main constituents of organisational work/life balance policies? You have been asked to provide a briefing paper for line managers on the advantages of introducing a wellness service. What arguments would you present? Many writers argue that health, well-being and lifestyle decisions are individual responsibilities, not those of the employer. On what grounds would you defend/oppose this view?

Discussion questions

1 Why did it take so long for the UK to establish comprehensive health and safety legislation covering all workplaces and employees?

2 What impact has membership of the EU had on workplace health, safety and well-being policies in the UK?

3 What are the main bodies responsible for implementing UK health and safety legislation and regulations? What are their responsibilities? What enforcement powers do they have?

4 What are the grounds for criminal prosecution in cases of health and safety?

5 How likely is the HSC to reach the 2010 targets set by the Revitalising Health and Safety Strategy 2000?

6 The phrase 'as far as reasonably practicable' is employed in the Health and Safety at Work Act 1974. What factors do you think should be considered in deciding whether a particular safety activity is 'reasonably practicable'?

7 How would you account for the spread of work/life balance provision in UK organisations? How effective is this?

8 Should the right to flexible working be extended to all employees?

9 How would you characterise a 'healthy organisation'?

10 In a letter to *Personnel Today* (4 October 2005) it was suggested that: HR people often couch their arguments in nineteenth-century notions such as 'we're here to help people'. The letter went on to argue 'No we are not. That's what unions are for. HR managers are here to help employers run a business' and 'If you are not about what helps business, don't be in business. Go and do voluntary work.' To what extent would you endorse this conception of HRM?

🔓 Key concepts

guidance, *p. 325*	statutory sick pay, *p. 341*
enforcement, *p. 329*	medical and health insurance, *p. 345*
regulations, *p. 329*	wellness services, *p. 347*
codes of practice, *p. 331*	personal counselling, *p. 348*
duty of care, *p. 331*	employee assistance programmes, *p. 348*
occupational health, *p. 341*	WLB, *p. 350*
occupational sick pay, *p. 341*	

Individual task

Purpose To consider alternative penalties for health and safety offences.

Time 60 minutes

Procedure Prosecution is the main means by which the HSE and local authorities hold to account those who have committed serious breaches of health and safety law. There are currently few sentencing options for the court, and conviction usually results in a fine. What alternative penalties would you consider for health and safety offences? Check out the discussion on this topic on the HSE website at www.hse.gov.uk.

Team task

Purpose To assess the case for legislation on stress.

Time 45 minutes

Procedure The HSE defines stress as 'the adverse reaction people have to excessive pressure or other types of demand placed on them'. It estimates that about half a million people in the UK experience work-related stress at a level they think is making them ill. In the UK there is considerable pressure from the TUC for a specific set of regulations or an Approved Code of Practice on stress. At EU level, there is similar pressure from the ETUC for a directive on stress.

The management pressure group, the CBI, maintains that due to its multicausal nature and the fact that work and non-work causes can overlap, stress does not lend itself to a legislative solution. What is needed is practical guidance from the HSC/E, on what is the best way forward.

What do you think? Discuss this in your group.

Sources: www.cbi.org.uk; www.etuc.org; www.hse.gov.uk; www.tuc.org.uk.

Case study: **Beware the gathering storm**

How far employers can go on insisting employees work in unsafe countries is being tested in the courts. Round one has gone in the employee's favour.

On 15 December, Richard Gizbert, a former news correspondent, was found to have been unfairly dismissed for refusing to work in Iraq.

Gizbert was the first journalist to use UK legislation protecting dismissal on health and safety grounds to claim unfair dismissal because of concern for his personal safety. The tribunal had to decide whether the principal reason for dismissing Gizbert was his refusal to go to war zones, as he claimed, or cutbacks at his workplace, as his employer maintained.

The tribunal's decision may have been influenced by Gizbert's employer, ABC News Intercontinental, part of the Disney Group, having signed up to an industry 'code of practice' drawn up to safeguard journalists working in dangerous environments. The code, established in 2000 by a number of news organisations including the BBC, CNN and Reuters, states that 'unwarranted risks in pursuit of a story are unacceptable and must be strongly discouraged. Assignments to war zones or hostile environments must be voluntary and should involve only experienced newsgatherers and those under their direct supervision.' A tribunal would expect any employer signatory of such a code to comply with it.

It is easy to see why a court might accept that sending an employee to Iraq could endanger that person's safety, and the circumstances in the Gizbert case could arise for any employer that sends employees to potentially unsafe territories. Many developing markets are in unstable states and this case could be used by employees who are unhappy about travelling to such places. To minimise the risk of claims, employers should consider implementing aspects of the code. It states that all staff must have access to safety training and retraining, be provided with efficient safety equipment and personal insurance, and be encouraged to use a counselling service to deal with their fears.

It would also be sensible for employers to carry out risk assessments in potentially hostile environments and report back to employees so they can make an informed decision on whether to work there. The basic rule under the Health and Safety at Work Act 1974 remains that if an employer is aware a job has an inherent risk to employees' health and safety, and it cannot prevent the risk, it must inform the employee of all relevant details, even if this results in the employee refusing to take the job.

It is now clear that dismissing employees who refuse to travel to such a location would be unfair, possibly even if they were originally recruited for that role but have since changed their minds. An employer must try to redeploy the employee to another part of the business if possible. The Gizbert case potentially has wider ramifications in the area of discrimination. For example, there is a possibility that Jewish employees may refuse to work in certain Muslim countries, in view of the beheading of US journalist Daniel Pearl in Pakistan in 2002. Similarly, a gay employee could refuse to work in a country where homosexual activities were illegal. Forcing employees to work in such hostile environments, or failing to promote them because they refuse to go, could result in a successful race or sexual orientation discrimination claim combined with a constructive unfair dismissal claim. A possible defence to such a claim could be the presence of an employee in a certain country being essential to that person's job, or a promotion being conditional on an employee obtaining training in that country.

Source: E. Clark, 'Beware the gathering storm', *People Management*, 26 January 2006, p. 20.
Reproduced with permission of *People Management* and Emma Clark.

Discussion questions

1 Have employees' rights now gone too far?

2 Should employers still be liable if an employee had agreed to work in an unsafe area?

3 What type of training should an employee be given to help them deal with dangerous work environments?

4 What are the wider implications of this court ruling?

WWW exercise

Search the DoH website for the *NHS Improving Working Lives* standard document. How is this being implemented? What lessons might you draw from it for other organisations?

www.doh.gov.uk

Specific web exercise

Visit the CIPD website. What advice does it provide on the role of HR advisers with regard to health, safety and well-being at work?

www.cipd.co.uk

In addition to the HSE website, visit the DTI and DWP websites. Look at the examples of company best practice in workplace health and care. What are the main provisions that they offer?

www.hse.gov.uk
www.dti.gov.uk
www.dwp.gov.uk

Look at the Business in the Community website. What arguments can you find in support of wellness interventions?

www.bti.org.uk

Look at the coverage of health and safety issues on the CBI and TUC websites. What are their respective health, safety and well-being concerns?

www.tuc.org.uk
www.cbi.org.uk

You could also visit the website of the European Foundation for the Improvement of Living and Working Conditions. This will give you an insight into the range of research into the area of health and safety, and debates and developments in other EU countries.

www.eurofound.eu.int

Other activities

Have a look at the articles by Silcox (2005a, 2005b and 2005c) for illustrations of current corporate initiatives in wellness, particularly the case of Vyelife.

LEARNING CHECKLIST

Before moving on to the next chapter, check that you are able to:

- ☑ explain the importance of health, safety and well-being in the workplace
- ☑ outline the development of workplace health and safety legislation in the UK
- ☑ summarise the current legal framework
- ☑ list the responsibilities and powers of the main UK health and safety agencies
- ☑ describe the main forms of well-being services offered by employers
- ☑ evaluate current governmental and organisational developments in health, safety and well-being provision.

Further reading

Department of Health (1999) *The NHS Plan.* London: DoH.

Department of Trade and Industry (DTI) (2005) *A Short History of the Working Time Directive to January 2005* (accessed at www.dti.gov.uk).

Dunn, C. and Wilkinson, A. (2002) 'Wish you were here: managing absence', *Personnel Review* 31, pp. 228–246.

Health & Safety Commission (2005) *Health & Safety Statistics 2004/05.* London: National Statistics (also available at www.hsc.gov.uk).

Useful websites

Official bodies

Health and Safety Commission: www.hse.gov.uk

Health and Safety Executive: www.hse.gov.uk

Industrial Injuries Advisory Council: www.iiac.org.uk

Pressure groups

British Safety Council (BSC): www.britishsafetycouncil.co.uk

Business Action on Health: www.bitc.org.uk (Business in the Community website)

Confederation of British Industries: www.cbi.org.uk

Employers and Work-Life Balance (EaWLB): www.employersandworklifebalance.org.uk

Occupational and Environmental Diseases Association: www.oeda.demon.co.uk

Royal Society for the Prevention of Accidents (RoSPA): www.rospa.com

Trades Union Congress: www.tuc.org.uk

Professional bodies

CIPD: www.cipd.co.uk

Employee Assistance Professional Association: www.eapa.org.uk

Institute of Occupational Safety and Health: www.iosh.co.uk

References

ABI/TUC (2003) *National Rehabilitation Action Plan.* London: ABI/TUC.

Armstrong, M. (2002) *Employee Reward* (3rd edn). London: CIPD.

Armstrong, M. and Stephens, T. (2005) *Employee Reward Management in Context.* London: CIPD.

Baggott, R. (2004) *Health Care in Britain* (3rd edn). Houndmills: Palgrave Macmillan.

Bevan, S. (2003) *Attendance Management.* London: The Work Foundation.

Bratton, J. and Gold, J. (2003) *Human Resource Management* (3rd edn). Basingstoke: Palgrave Macmillan.

Bratton, J. and Gold, J. (2005) *Human Resource Management: Theory and Practice.* Basingstoke: Palgrave Macmillan.

Bunting, M. (2004) *Willing Slaves: How the Overwork Culture is Ruling Our Lives.* London: Harper-Collins.

Cabinet Office (2004) *Managing Sickness Absence in the Public Sector.* London: Cabinet Office.

Cabinet Office (2005) *Ministerial Taskforce on Health, Safety and Productivity One Year On Report.* London: Cabinet Office.

CIPD (2005a) *Absence Management: A Survey of Policy and Practice.* London: CIPD.

CIPD (2005b) *Reward Management: An Annual Survey Report.* London: CIPD.

Coates, D. and Max, C. (2005) *Healthy Work: Productive Workplaces.* London: The Work Foundation.

Dennis, S. (2005) 'Voluntary benefits: saving in the workplace', *IRS Employment Review* 818, February, pp. 27–31.

Department of Health (1999) *Saving Lives: Our Healthier Nation.* London: The Stationery Office.

Department of Health (2000) *The NHS Plan: A Plan for Investment, A Plan For Reform.* London: The Stationery Office.

Department of Health (2004) *Choosing Health: Making Healthier Choices Easy*, Public Health White Paper. London: DoH.

Department of the Environment, Transport and the Regions (2000) *Revitalising Health and Safety.* London: DETR.

Department of Work and Pensions (2005) *Department of Work and Pensions Five year Strategy: Opportunity and Security Through Life.* London: DWP.

Department of Work and Pensions, Department of Health and the Health and Safety Executive (2005) *Health, Work and Well-being – Caring for Our Future.* London: The Stationery Office.

Foot, M. and Hook, C. (2005) *Introducing Human Resource Management* (4th edn). Harlow: FT/Prentice Hall.

Friedman, M. (1963) *Capitalism and Freedom.* Chicago: Chicago University Press.

Geyer, R.R. (2000) *Exploring European Social Policy.* Cambridge: Polity Press.

Goss, D. (1994) *Principles of Human Resource Management.* London: Routledge.

Health & Safety Commission (2002) *The Health and Safety System in Great Britain* (3rd edn). London: Health and Safety Commission.

Health & Safety Executive (2003) *Health & Safety Regulation: A Short Guide.* London: HSE.

Health & Safety Executive (2005) *Perceptions of the Cost Implications of Health and Safety Failures,* HSE Research Report 403. London: HSE.

Health & Safety Executive (2006) hse.gov.uk/statistics/index.htm, accessed 14 January 2006.

Hencke, D. and Milner, M. (2005) 'Hatfield victims and unions call for new corporate killing law', *Guardian,* 8 October.

Henderson, D. (2001) *Misguided Virtue: False Notions of Corporate Social Responsibility.* London: IEA.

Hutter, B.M. (1993) 'Regulating employers and employees: health and safety in the workplace', *Journal of Law & Society* 20, pp. 452–470.

IDS (1999) 'Benefits, costs and values', *IDS Study Plus,* July. London: IDS.

IDS (2002) 'Employee assistance programmes', *IDS Study Plus,* Winter. London: IDS.

IDS (2003a) 'Sick pay schemes', *IDS Studies* 761, November. London: IDS.

IDS (2003b) 'Private medical insurance', *IDS Studies* 745, March. London: IDS.

IDS (2005) 'Absence management', *IDS HR Studies* 810. London: IDS.

Institute of Directors (2002) *Health and Wellbeing in the Workplace: A Director's Guide.* London: IoD.

IPD (1995) *Managing Occupational Health.* London: IPD.

IPPR (2006) *The Citizen's Stake.* London: IPPR.

Kersley, B., Alpin, C., Forth, J., Bryson, A., Bewley, H., Dix, G. and Oxenbridge, S. (2005) *Inside the Workplace: Findings from the 2004 Workplace Employment Relations Survey.* London: DTI.

Kiefer, T. and Briner, R. (2003) 'Handle with care', *People Management,* 23 October, pp. 48–50.

May, M. and Brunsdon, E. (1999) 'Commercial and occupational welfare', in R.M. Page and R. Silburn (eds) *British Social Welfare in the Twentieth Century.* Houndmills: Macmillan, pp. 271–298.

May, M. and Brunsdon, E. (2006) 'Occupational welfare', in M. Powell (ed.) *The Mixed Economy of Welfare.* Bristol: Policy Press.

Mancocha, R. (2004) 'Well-adjusted', *People Management,* 28 October, pp. 6–9.

Neagle, H. (2003) *A New Organisation of Time over Working Life.* Dublin: European Foundation for the Improvement of Living and Working Conditions.

Overell, S. (2005) 'Where do you stand on health?', *Personnel Today,* 25 October, pp. 26–32.

Paton, N. (2005) 'The health of nations', *Personnel Today,* 25 October, pp. 30–31.

Phillips, A. (2006) 'How to sustain higher performance and enable employees to enjoy life even more – wellness management', CIPD Central London Branch Wellness Management event leaflet, 30 March.

Silcox, S. (2005a) 'Absence essentials: phased returns to work', *IRS Employment Review* 828, July, pp. 18–21.

Silcox, S. (2005b) 'Spend to save on employee health and productivity', *IRS Employment Review* 828, July, pp. 22–25.

Silcox, S. (2005c) 'Health promotion works', *IRS Employment Review* 828, July, pp. 26–32.

Stranks, J. (2003) *Health & Safety at Work* (7th edn). London: Kogan Page.

Ulrich, D. (1998) 'A new mandate for human resources', *Harvard Business Review*, January–February, pp. 124–134; and 'HR with attitude', *People Management*, 23 August, pp. 36–41.

Ulrich, D. and Brockbank, W. (2005) 'Rolecall', *People Management*, 16 June, pp. 24–28.

Taylor, R. (2002a) *Britain's World of Work – Myths and Realities*. Swindon: ESRC.

Taylor, R. (2002b) *The Future of Work–Life Balance*. Swindon: ESRC.

Wanless, D. (2002) *Securing Our Future Health: Taking a Long Term View, Final Report*. London: HM Treasury.

White, M., Hill, S., Mills, C. and Smeaton, D. (2004) *Managing to Change? British Workplaces and the Future of Work*. Houndmills: Palgrave Macmillan.

Woodland, S., Simmonds, N., Thornby, M., Fitzgerald, R. and McGee, A. (2003) *The Second Work–Life Balance Study*. London: DTI.

Wright, A. (2004) *Reward Management in Context*. London: CIPD.

Zneimer, A. (2005) 'Time for a helping hand', *Benefits Report*, July, pp. 29–32.

Chapter 11

Equal opportunities and managing diversity

Gil Robinson

LEARNING OUTCOMES

After studying this chapter, you should be able to:

☑ **define** what is meant by equal opportunities and managing diversity

☑ **have** an understanding of anti-discrimination legislation, and approaches to workplace equality and diversity

☑ **understand** how equal opportunities and managing diversity are issues in HR practice

☑ **outline** the development and functions of equal opportunities and managing diversity

☑ **have** an appreciation of the challenges involved in developing and delivering equality and diversity in organisations

☑ **evaluate** approaches to equality and diversity in organisations.

The opening vignette is an example of good workplace practice with regard to equality and diversity. The NHS is beginning to recognise that achieving diversity can be healthy for the organisation.

Improving working lives: tackling racial harassment in the NHS

The NHS has a long tradition of employing people from all racial and ethnic backgrounds, so when its employees experience racial harassment or feel that their careers are being held back because of their colour, it takes it extremely seriously. The development of local and regional black and minority ethnic networks has been encouraged, with start-up funding being provided by the Department of Health.

'The starting point and the reason we have a range of programmes and initiatives to tackle racism is that it is acknowledged as unacceptable,' says Lutfur Ali, head of equality and diversity in NHS employment policy at the department. 'We recognise that there are inequalities in society and these can permeate into the NHS, but we also need to recognise that this challenge can't be overcome overnight. We have made significant strides in encouraging local NHS organisations to see challenging racism as central to service delivery. If staff are not valued, respected and treated fairly they will not be able to give their best.' An acknowledgement that cultural change is required from the ground upwards underpins Positively Diverse, a development programme that aims to encourage NHS organisations to develop their own ways of promoting equality and diversity. Some 170 NHS organisations are currently taking part in the national programme, with ten lead sites exploring, developing and disseminating practical ways of managing diversity in the NHS for the benefit of both staff and patients.

The West Yorkshire black and minority ethnic network was established two years ago with a grant from Positively Diverse. The network provides career and leadership training as well as mentoring support for black and minority ethnic people working within NHS trusts and primary care trusts across West Yorkshire. 'When black or minority ethnic people move up in an organisation it can be very lonely and it is good to have someone to give support and advice,' says Pam Samuel, assistant director of equality and diversity at Bradford Teaching Hospitals NHS Trust and a former chair of the network. 'Plus there is a lot of evidence that many people are overqualified for the jobs they are applying for and our network helps push them to achieve their maximum. The network holds regular meetings, at which members are encouraged to give presentations, take turns in chairing meetings, and generally develop their presentation and management skills. We acknowledge that we don't have many black and minority ethnic people at senior level and this is enabling them to get there. Our approach is very positive. It is not about moaning but looking at the skills we have and what we want to achieve.'

Positively Diverse programme director Maroline Lasebikan says, 'We try to get NHS organisations to give diversity management a status just as they do other management areas, such as human resources or IT, and then go ahead to make change happen.' Lutfur Ali also sees Positively Diverse as the ideal medium through which to tackle the issue of harassment. 'Harassment and bullying are both unacceptable and unlawful, but the way we deal with these issues has to be left to local organisations because there will be different approaches required for different needs. Although there is no compulsion for organisations to take part in the project, the department is currently examining ways in which the good work it has fostered can be spread more widely. We are looking to cultivate environments for spreading best practice and to ensure that staff have the capacity to create workforces that reflect their communities.' Its starting point is the fact that people working in the NHS know what works best. 'We will be looking at the department's role in bringing good practice together and spreading it nationally, possibly through developing networks or using the existing human resources network. We want to improve co-ordination and ensure that best practice is communicated widely. We are also looking into equality and diversity issues in the medical workforce, and the possibility of nurses and midwives taking advice from the General Medical Council and the British Medical Association. A good number of black and minority ethnic people apply to work in the NHS but for some reason they are not getting through and when they do we need to ensure they are achieving their full potential. We need to look at the reasons why this should be and are consulting the community about this.'

The department is clear that an effective equality and diversity strategy reflects the overall health of an organisation. 'Successful organisations are successful in many areas, not just diversity. To talk about equality and diversity is basically to talk about effective management and patient-centred services,' according to Lutfur. Pam Samuel believes that initiatives such as the West Yorkshire network provide black and minority ethnic people with the chance to make the very best of the opportunities they have. 'I was an enrolled nurse when I joined the NHS but I moved forward and I say to others that they can do it too. I acknowledge that there are problems, but the Positively Diverse strategy allows black and minority ethnic people to share best practice and celebrate diversity so we can all benefit. There are strong role models within the NHS and people should look at them and say "they have achieved something so why can't we?"'

Source: Adapted from Sarah Person, *Improving Working Lives – Tackling Racial Harassment in the NHS* (http://www.nhs.uk/nhsmagazine/archive/sep03/feat11.asp).

Discussion questions

1 Why do you think a positively diverse strategy would be good for business?

2 What can organisations do to ensure that diversity is reflected at all levels of the organisation?

In this chapter the aim is to explore some of the issues and problems that arise for organisations (employers, employees and managers) in developing and applying human resources policies with the intention of promoting fair treatment and the recognition and management of different social categories of people in the workplace. In Chapter 1 the focus was on how organisations, through the human resources manager, implement policies and practices that 'serve' the needs of the organisation, while at the same time 'nurture' and develop the most valued commodity: its employees. In doing so, it set a clear pattern for the fair treatment of employees. Approaches to the fair treatment of all employees are informed by two main principles: equal opportunities and managing diversity. Some theorists see managing diversity as an extension of equal opportunities while others see it as a new **paradigm**, as illustrated in Exhibit 11-1. Kandola and Fullerton argue that 'Diversity is understood as being different from **equal opportunities**' (2002: 169).

Since the 1970s there has been a commitment to equal opportunities in the UK, especially the public sector. This has been brought about by successive governments introducing anti-**discrimination** legislation to address the inequalities that exist in work organisations. The stated aim of the various legislation is to reduce disadvantage for particular social categories of

paradigm

Similar to a frame of reference, with implicit assumptions or beliefs about what sorts of things make up the world, how they act, how they hang together and how they may be known (Weick, 1995).

equal opportunities

The idea that everyone can be treated equally and should be given the same opportunities as those who have traditionally held power.

discrimination

Discrimination is about differential treatment and then the consideration of whether or not the difference is justified or lawful (Banton, 1994).

regulatory

The regulatory approach specifies rules of conduct for individuals and institutions, and is usually concerned with procedures and processes . . . because beneficial consequences are assumed to flow . . . Practices are based on the prohibition of certain specified forms of behaviour . . . and are essentially a policy of control (Young, 1993).

diversity

Recognising that people are different and that these differences should be valued and used to enhance the workplace.

social justice

Organisations, through their managers, have a moral obligation to treat employees with fairness and dignity, while ensuring that management decisions are made with due regard to prejudice and stereotypes (Beardwell *et al.*, 2004).

business case

The business case is concerned with fair treatment making good business sense because it is better for human resources, it leads to a wider customer base, it creates a wider pool for recruitment and selection, and it leads to a positive company image (Beardwell *et al.*, 2004).

people. This approach, which is seen as **regulatory**, was informed by the action of successive governments in the USA, in its attempt to ameliorate the clear social injustices that spawned the development of the civil rights movement in the late 1950s and 1960s.

Who manages diversity?

The public sector has largely regarded itself as leading the way in the progression of equal opportunity policies. However, managing **diversity** strategies are now overtaking equal opportunity practices. Within the public sector, however, the process is more likely to be underpinned by a **social justice** rationale, although recent events suggest this can also be driven by a **business case** argument. This has led to a huge debate about the form and content of equality and diversity approaches, particularly where policies contain a collaborated traditional equality initiative alongside a business case-driven diversity objective. Although most UK organisations declare themselves equal opportunity employers, it is currently rather a topical issue to discuss the 'diversity organisation'. This is particularly a result of managing diversity as a strategy being at an early stage in its development in the UK. It is also important to reiterate the huge variance in the practice of such policies by employers, as research by Cully *et al.* (1999) verifies that there is low integration between policy and practice to the extent that there is no equal opportunity employer. To date, there is no evidence of any organisation making the claim to be a 'diversity organisation'.

Most equality policies and diversity strategies focus on the key functions of human resource management. Monitoring and auditing are relatively common means of collecting information on different parts of the workforce to aid in analysing and evaluating the success of policy and strategy levers. Even though the public sector had equal pay for

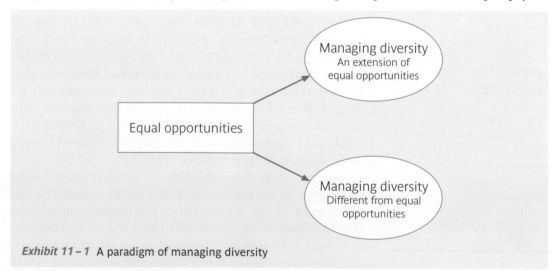

Exhibit 11 – 1 A paradigm of managing diversity

equal work and equal access to pensions (Equal Pay Act 1970), reasonable maternity leave schemes and positive action for women (Sex Discrimination Act 1975), discrimination on the basis of race, ethnic origin and nationality was outlawed, and positive action for racialised groups encouraged (Race Relations Act 1976), such activism did not prevent unequal pay for women, sex segregation and race discrimination. Neither did the legislation limit restrictions to managerial positions for women, racial groups and other social categories of people. However, as can be seen below, these are still major problems for certain social categories of people and it should be pointed out that they exist in other areas as well, which will be discussed later.

The problems with policies

The problems identified earlier in this chapter illustrate that neither equal opportunity policies nor managing diversity strategies are able to combat action that leads to disadvantage and discrimination against certain social categories of employees in the workplace. Higher education institutions (universities) are regulated by legislation to carry out certain specific duties; however, the evidence suggests that there is a big divide between expected practice and actual outcome. There are concerns about pay and the **glass ceiling** that is in evidence for people from racial groups employed in universities. It is important for HR managers to understand the structures and organisational culture in which people work so that the potential of such people can be released and rewarded. The evidence provided from the research conducted does suggest that there is a shortfall between rhetoric and reality in the higher education sector.

glass ceiling
An invisible but very real career progression barrier that exists in organisations for discriminated-against social categories.

It seems that universities, in general, especially those employees at the top of such organisations, such as vice chancellors, do demonstrate naivety about disadvantage and discrimination in relation to certain social groupings, when they argue, 'they just don't apply'. Even if they applied and were successful would they be made visible? The evidence from research carried out in other areas of the public sector does suggest that there are similar patterns existing elsewhere. For example, Creegan *et al.*, in their research, reveal an 'intersection of race and gender' where 'a spectrum of opinion emerges underpinned by evidence of a significant association between ethnicity among both men and women, and between opinion and gender' (2003: 626–627) with regards to the implementation of race equality policies in a local authority in London. This, and other research, suggests that there is a perception of failure by equal opportunity policies to deliver anti-discriminatory practices. The moral arguments, along with social justice and the present legislation, are not enough to engender among employers and their human resource managers the fair treatment required for all the social groupings that exist in the workplace. These and other arguments have created a compelling case for a new strategy – that of the 'business case for diversity' – in the search for answers in achieving equity and fairness in contemporary organisations, although others see a combination of equality and diversity as the way forward. As can be seen in the opening vignette, the NHS has already recognised that good workplace practice leads to improved organisational effectiveness.

Stop and reflect

Identify and describe actions that organisations with which you are familiar can take to pass their diversity health check.

Definition of equal opportunities and diversity

In order for any organisation to address the issue of disadvantage and discrimination in its work practices in a systematic way, it has to be guided by a policy framework. Many organisations are creating equal opportunity policies in order to guide human resource and line managers in decision-making. Contemporary organisations argue that there is clearly a business-case argument in developing equality policies and diversity strategies, and that there is a social and moral argument to do so. In some quarters there is no support for the moral and social basis for such policies to exist within the business environment. Nevertheless, organisations are increasingly adopting such policies or strategies, although these may vary in their make-up from one organisation to the next. The ten-point plan reproduced later in this chapter (see Exhibit 11-4) is from the UK's Equal Opportunity Commission (www.eoc.org.uk) and the Commission for Racial Equality (www.cre.gov.uk). It typifies the recommended good practice that organisations setting up their own policies are encouraged to adopt.

Beardwell *et al.* (2004) suggest that there are four types of categorisation of equal opportunity organisation: the negative, the minimalist, the compliant and the proactive (Exhibit 11-2). The latter practises equality using all the guidelines and might even go beyond them. The negative organisation will not even contemplate or make any claim of being an equal opportunity employer. The minimalist makes some claim to be an equal opportunity employer but is not guided by a policy framework, while the compliant will have a written policy and will comply with good practice guidelines as recommended.

Jewson and Mason (1986) have conducted probably the best-known research on equal opportunity practices. They theorised: 'The theory and practice of equal opportunities: liberal and radical approaches.' In their research, a contrast was made between the approaches to equal opportunities policies; in doing this, they were able to formalise a framework within which literature on equal opportunities could be analysed.

According to Jewson and Mason (1986), they derived their liberal approach from the political ideals of classic liberalism and liberal democracy. The basis of their argument is around the rights of the individual to be provided with universally applicable standards of justice and citizenship (Webb, 1997, in Kirton and Greene, 2000). Accordingly, 'equality of opportunity exists

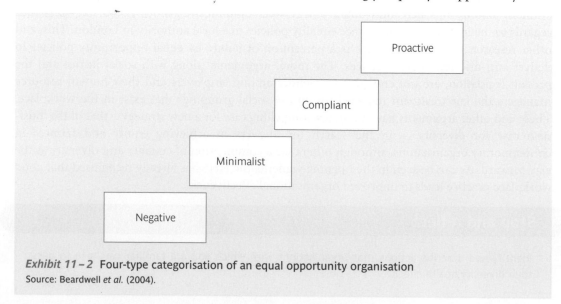

Exhibit 11 – 2 Four-type categorisation of an equal opportunity organisation
Source: Beardwell *et al.* (2004).

when all individuals are enabled freely and equally to compete for social rewards' (Jewson and Mason, 1986: 307). The liberal model of equal opportunities is based on principles of 'sameness' – that is, people ought to have access to and be assessed in their workplaces as individuals, irrespective of their social category. Here, the attention is focused on the individual, 'where people are required to deny, or attempt to minimize, differences and compete solely on the grounds of individual merit' (Liff and Wajcman, 1996, in Kirton and Green, 2000).

The most efficient means of achieving a fair distribution of resources in the workplace is with policies based on the individual being seen as neutral. The context of such practices should be within a free market philosophy. According to Kirton and Green, practice within the liberal framework of equal opportunity 'has a grounding in theories of free market competition' (2000: 101) and draws reference from the neoclassical explanation of occupational segregation. The neoclassical view takes the position that discrimination is neither 'an inherent or intrinsic feature of the capitalist labour market, but ... a distortion of an otherwise rational market' (Kirton and Green, 2000: 101). The philosophical tenets of the free market are instrumental to the liberal approach of equal opportunities in organisations and, as such, the liberal approach utilises the activities available within positive action. Positive action is usually a combination of activities whereby attempts are made by organisations to remove, as far as is possible, obstacles to the operation of the free labour market and meritocracy. (For more on positive action, see below.)

radical approach
An approach of intervention in order to achieve equality of opportunity, such as positive discrimination.

The **radical approach** to equal opportunities suggests intervention wherever it is necessary in order to achieve equality of opportunity (the 'rules of the game', according to Jewson and Mason (1986)), as well as equality of outcome. The objective is to achieve through fair procedures, fair distribution of rewards. The radical approach aims to highlight the fact that although individuals experience discrimination and disadvantage, this can only really be identified at the group level. The view that everyone is equal irrespective of his or her social category ought to be reflected in how workplaces distribute their rewards. The lack of fair distribution of rewards is enough evidence to suggest that unfair discrimination is taking place. The radical approach to equal opportunities highlights the use of 'positive discrimination' (Jewson and Mason, 1986) and is in evidence where practices in employment are manipulated, specifically to ensure the fair distribution of rewards for those in social categories that are deemed to experience disadvantage and discrimination in the workplace.

The outcome of the radical approach is the politicisation of the decision-making process, while from the liberal approach we get bureaucratisation of the decision-making process. In the case of the radical approach to equal opportunity policies and practices, organisations may impose quotas or targets for groups experiencing disadvantage and discrimination, based on the demographic profiles of the catchment area from which they recruit and select the majority of their employees. Such strategies, especially quotas, are deemed to be unlawful in the UK. Nevertheless, practices encouraging the radical approach do form parts of existing legislation, and there are organisations whose policies on equal opportunities do reflect the radical approach. For example, both the Sex Discrimination Act 1975 and the Race Relations Act 1976 advocate the use of Genuine Occupational Qualifications (GOQs) for use in certain specific areas of employment practice and situations.

positive action
Where measures are actively taken to encourage people who are usually under-represented to apply for positions (such as women MPs).

Positive action measures under the Sex Discrimination Act 1975 may include Training (S47) and Encouragement (S48). The Equal Opportunities Commission suggests that:

> Before deciding to introduce positive action training, organisations need to assess whether within the previous 12 months women have been under-represented in the kind of work for which training is envisaged. It is important to note that, in order for positive action training to be of benefit to black and ethnic minority women, organisations will also need to look at the representation of black and ethnic minority people in the kind of work in question.

(For more information on Positive Action on Race, contact the Commission for Racial Equality.) Positive action may include:

- courses to develop confidence or assertiveness
- retraining for women whose skills have become rusty or out of date
- training that is based on job sampling, work experience, 'taster' days with employers, work shadowing experience
- training in a skill (e.g. carpentry, computer programming, social work)
- training in a technique (e.g. interviewing, managing or supervision)
- management training to encourage women to apply for management positions
- career counselling and guidance for women returning to work or those in work
- retraining in areas of skills shortage – especially suitable for women returners who did not previously have the opportunity to obtain these qualifications.

Encouragement under the act suggests that:

> Nothing ... shall render unlawful any act done by an employer in relation to particular work in his employment, being an act done in, or in connection with
>
> - affording his female employees only, or his male employees only, access to facilities for training which would help to fit them for that work, or
> - encouraging women only, or men only, to take advantage of opportunities for doing that work, where at any time within the 12 months immediately preceding ... there were no persons of the sex in question among those doing that work ... or the number of persons of that sex doing the work was comparatively small. (SDA, 1975 S 48)
>
> (Adapted from
> www.eoc.org.uk/cseng/advice/managing_successful_positive_action.asp)

The EOC recommends that the easiest way of becoming an equal opportunities employer is first to formulate a written equal opportunities policy. This focuses attention on your commitment and allows it to be expressed publicly, in line with your objectives. The policy should make clear your intention to develop and apply procedures and practices that do not discriminate on the grounds of sex or marriage, and that provide equality of opportunity for all job applicants and employees. Most policies will include the points listed in Exhibit 11-3.

Exhibit 11-4 shows the CRE's ten-point plan to help employers promote equality of opportunity in their organisations. *These are guidance points only and employers should seek further details about each of the areas listed.*

The long and short agenda advocated by Cockburn (1989, 1991) shows how some organisations adopt equal opportunity initiatives through their managers who are only taking the short-term view into consideration. These may include reacting to the external agenda, problem-solving in the short term, even attempts at promoting equity to service users and clients alike. These activities do not take into consideration initiatives that may lead to more

Most equal opportunities policies will include:

■ a definition of direct and indirect sex and marriage discrimination, victimisation and sexual harassment

■ a statement of the organisation's commitment to equal opportunities

■ the name(s) of the employee(s) responsible for policy

■ details of the structure for implementing the policy

■ an obligation upon employees to respect and act in accordance with the policy

■ procedures for dealing with complaints of discrimination

■ examples of unlawful practices

■ details of monitoring and review procedures

■ a commitment to remove barriers to equal opportunity

■ details of how the information provided by the monitoring process will be analysed

Exhibit 11–3 Promoting equal opportunity
Source: www.eoc.org.uk/EOCeng/EOCcs/Advice/guidelines.asp.

1	Develop an equal opportunities policy, covering recruitment, promotion and training
2	Set an action plan, with targets, so that you and your staff have a clear idea of what can be achieved and by when
3	Provide training for all people, including managers, throughout your organisation, to ensure they understand the importance of equal opportunities. Provide additional training for staff who recruit, select and train your employees
4	Assess the present position to establish your starting point, and monitor progress in achieving your objectives
5	Review recruitment, selection, promotion and training procedures regularly, to ensure that you are delivering on your policy
6	Draw up clear and justifiable job criteria, which are demonstrably objective and job related
7	Offer pre-employment training, where appropriate, to prepare potential job applicants for selection tests and interviews; you should also consider positive action training to help ethnic minority employees to apply for jobs in areas where they are under-represented
8	Consider your organisation's image: do you encourage applications from under-represented groups and feature women, ethnic minority staff and people with disabilities in recruitment literature, or could you be seen as an employer that is indifferent to these groups?
9	Consider flexible working, career breaks, providing childcare facilities, and so on, to help women in particular meet domestic responsibilities and pursue their occupations; consider providing special equipment and assistance to help people with disabilities
10	Develop links with local community groups, organisations and schools, in order to reach a wider pool of potential applicants

Exhibit 11–4 The CRE's ten-point plan
Source: www.cre.gov.uk/gdpract/eop.ht.

long-term achievements in dismantling disadvantage and discrimination, which will only occur when there is long-term action to change organisation structures and processes. Cockburn welcomes the short-term action of managers, as she suggests that it enables bias, which results from certain practices, to be eliminated. However, it is essential to consider the long agenda. This arguably is a strategy that challenges organisational cultural practices, and will enable transformation through changes to processes, attitudes, roles, relationships, norms and values.

Cockburn states that the above can only be achieved through dismantling

> the processes by which the power of some groups over others in institutions is built and renewed. It acknowledges the needs of disadvantaged groups for access to power ... [and] also looks for change in the nature of power, in the control ordinary people of diverse kinds have over institutions, a melting away of the white male monoculture.
>
> (Cockburn, 1989: 218)

While Cockburn's suggestions are laudable, they raise certain problems of people in positions of power relinquishing any of their power and/or dominance. This is highly unlikely, as the actions that the long agenda demands will ultimately lead to change in the way managers carry out certain organisational practices. Such changes mean a diminution of power for managers, which they are unlikely to surrender without a struggle. This brings the activists (employees) who are pursuing the long agenda into conflict with those in positions of power. Resolving the issues usually involves political intervention, especially with regard to furthering and ensuring an equality agenda, which may include actions such as monitoring of employment targets for certain social categories (e.g. women, minority groups, people with a disability, and so on). Political intervention tends to usurp the liberal approach of fair treatment regardless of social category. The differential treatment that results incorporates aspects of the radical approach, as it is seen as creating tangible links with disadvantaged and discriminated-against social categories, and so becomes irrelevant with regard to meritocracy and the 'free' labour market.

In attempting to define equal opportunities, there are many difficulties, as practice within organisations is not streamlined and sometimes the agenda emerges as the process is developing. This prompts Kirton and Green to conclude, 'EO policy is symptomatic of the ambiguous nature of [the] traditional conceptualisation of EO' (2000: 104). Furthermore, 'organisations which are proactive on equality issues have stretched and re-interpreted the equal treatment model in a number of ways' (Liff and Wajcman, 1996: 82). Not surprisingly, Jewson and Mason (1986) found in their research that social categories that are disadvantaged and discriminated against will from time to time invoke various aspects of both the liberal and radical approach, whenever they feel it necessary, in order to satisfy the immediate need. Similarly, Cockburn (1989) observed that sometimes those involved do interpret equal opportunity policies in organisations differently, and interpretation is based on expectation and desired outcomes from the policies. Often the conceptualisation, interpretation and practices in organisations around equal opportunity stem from confusion and misunderstanding, as well as, sometimes, deliberate acts designed to mislead and mystify those who are not fully cognisant with the practice. A good example of the above is Kirton and Green's (2000) interpretation of how Cockburn sees the various interest groups' views of equal opportunity in the retail sector:

> ■ The shareholders had a strong commitment to equal opportunities
> ■ The executive team saw equal opportunities as a profit sharing policy
> ■ The lawyers wanted equal opportunities to avoid employment tribunals [for] cases of discrimination

- The personnel managers saw equal opportunities as part of wider management trends
- The line managers were only concerned with equal opportunities if it did not conflict with maintaining work discipline and cost budgeting.

(Adapted from Kirton and Green, 2000)

The lack of an overall agreement across the various employment sectors on how equal opportunity policies should be developed and practised prompts the following statement: 'The confused and contradictory deployment of different conceptions of equal opportunities policies can constitute an important aspect of the struggle for control of resources, deference and legitimacy at work' (Jewson and Mason, 1986: 302). Taking into consideration the foregoing, it is probably wise not to attempt a definition of a subject matter that is open to many different interpretations.

An understanding of the aim of the legal framework on inequality in the UK provides insight into the intentions of the law, which is to ensure anti-discrimination within the labour market based on age (forthcoming), criminal convictions, disability, race, religion and beliefs, sex and sexuality. It also reinforces the concept of equal treatment through the removal of prejudice, while supporting meritocracy. The above suggests that inequality in the labour market can be interpreted as 'actions that lead to discrimination against people on grounds that are irrelevant to the jobs they are doing or for which they are applying' (Chryssides and Kaler, 1996: 89). Perhaps by interpreting inequality, a better comprehension of what equal opportunity policies are setting out to do becomes clearer; whether it achieves its objectives through the intervention of the law, or in some cases going beyond the law (as demonstrated earlier) is open to debate.

Naturally, there are inevitable criticisms of equal opportunity policies. Some see equal opportunity policies as worthless and of little, if any, consequence to the organisation's bottom line. In certain organisations, equal opportunity policies are claimed to demonstrate the positive image of the organisation, when in effect very little is carried out or achieved within or through the policy initiative. The suggested basics of a policy such as monitoring or reviewing how vacancies in organisations are advertised, recruited, selected and/or promoted are neither put in place nor adhered to. In such situations, the policy is in existence in name only.

Another criticism levelled at equal opportunity policies in organisations, despite attempts to formalise procedures and practices, is that there are no guarantees that fairness for all social categories will be achieved. Research conducted by Liff and Dale (1994) demonstrates how the equal opportunity policy can be cynically side-stepped by managers. Another study demonstrates collusion between line and human resource managers (Collinson *et al.*, 1990). A further study, by Creegan *et al.*, shows how through the perception of the workforce, a local authority's equal opportunity policy 'performance, ownership and efficacy' (2003: 617–640) were questioned through the organisation's performance in areas such as delivery of its race action plan, tackling of racism, opportunities for promotion and methods of dealing with employee grievance. The following quote from a visible minority employee demonstrates the state of play in this particular organisation:

Managers manage these [grievance] procedures rather than personnel ... people who are raising a grievance find that they are intimidated before it gets off the ground. And the climate is one of constant restructuring, therefore constant loss of jobs, and people have pointed out instances where managers have got rid of people who have raised a grievance. Managers can intervene, can slow it [the grievance procedure] down and, even though they're not supposed to, can intimidate you.

(Adapted from Creegan *et al.*, 2003)

Other criticisms emanate from the weakness of the legislation in practice, which allows both direct and indirect discrimination to persist (Collinson *et al.*, 1990). There is also evidence within the UK labour market of segregation against certain social categories. Such criticisms have focused on the lack of strength of the legislation to curb discrimination as well as the struggle for power by human resource managers in organisations. Human resource departments are commonly seen as the departments responsible for the implementation of equal opportunities within organisations. The 'sameness' approach suggests that people should be treated equally, irrespective of social categories. It leaves organisational structures, values and practices in place, and allows the prejudices and stereotypes to go unchallenged, reproducing inequalities – hence the criticism of 'ineffectiveness' (Rees, 1998).

Finally, because equal opportunity policies are externally driven and 'focus on rights and procedures not outcomes they stand as attempts to treat the symptoms of disadvantage and discrimination rather than the causes' (Kirton and Green, 2000: 108). Despite over 30 years of equal treatment legislation and equal opportunity policies, social categories, which traditionally experience disadvantage and discrimination, have not witnessed any changes to the system, structures and hierarchies that presently exist in organisations, and there is no vision of fair treatment leading to a lack of discrimination on the horizon. Rather these social categories in organisations are expected to suppress their own identity and differences, in order to assimilate into an organisational monoculture that is predominantly white, able-bodied, heterosexual and male. These prevailing conditions have energised those who are interested in achieving equity and fairness for employees to examine new possibilities. This strategy for managing diversity will now be discussed.

Managing diversity

The management of diversity attempts to shift the emphasis from social categories (groups) experiencing disadvantage and discrimination in organisations to managing individual differences in the workplace. The arguments for a managing diversity strategy in organisations stems from research conducted in the USA by Johnston and Packer (1987), which showed that by the year 2000 white males would be in the minority of those entering the labour market. It highlighted for the first time a significant shift in an already changing demographic space. Furthermore, it forced human resource practitioners to sit up and take notice. Subsequently, a paper followed by Thomas (1991), which suggested that there was a different way to deal with issues of disadvantage and discrimination in organisations other than the equal opportunities paradigm; this approach he labelled 'managing diversity'. In the UK, there was also a shift taking place. This involved a move towards flexibility, new managerialism, human resource management and deregulation (Webb, 1997). Moreover, the sameness debate of equal opportunities prompted commentators in the UK to examine the managing diversity arguments and, in some cases, embrace them. Synonymous with managing diversity is the debate on difference, leading to various claims, which suggest that 'diversity is understood as being different from equal opportunities' (Kandola and Fullerton, 2002: 169). Others suggest that it is: a 'sophistication of the EO approach' (Rubin, in Overell, 1996); a repackaging of EO (Ford, 1996); a sanitised, politically unthreatening and market-orientated notion (Webb, 1997); a 'comfort zone', allowing employers to avoid actively fighting discrimination (Ouseley, in Overell, 1996) (as cited in Kirton and Greene, 2000; 109). The above views tend to suggest that 'managing diversity means different things to different people' (Kandola and Fullerton, 2002: 6). Having reviewed a number of definitions of managing diversity, Kandola and Fullerton produced their own, which they argue is a 'central theme' in the conceptualisation of the subject matter. It is as follows:

> The basic concept of managing diversity accepts that the workforce consists of [a] diverse population of people. The diversity consists of visible and non-visible differences which will include factors such as sex, age, background, race, disability, personality and workstyle. It is founded on the premises that harnessing these differences will create a productive environment in which everybody feels valued, where their talents are being fully utilised and in which organisational goals are met.
>
> (Kandola and Fullerton, 2002: 8)

They contrast managing diversity with a 'mosaic', suggesting that 'differences come together' (2002: 8) to form 'a whole organisation in the same way that single pieces of a mosaic come together to create a pattern' (2002: 8), with all the pieces having a value towards the whole. Kandola and Fullerton imply that people should be treated differently in organisational practices rather than adopting the sameness view expressed in the equal opportunity discussions. However, there is 'a stark contrast between an approach that encourages differential treatment for individuals and one that emphasises neutrality through "sameness" of treatment to provide fairness in workplace decision-making' (Foster and Harris, 2005: 124). Exhibit 11-5 lists the differences between managing diversity and equal opportunities.

There is evidence that managers interpret managing diversity practices in organisations inconsistently. Furthermore, Foster and Harris show how 'the lack of common understanding of managing diversity contributes to the frequent variance in what is intended in a policy statement on diversity and what happens in practice' (2005: 119). Foster's (2003) research identifies misunderstandings of the term managing diversity, suggesting that it means different things to people in different work settings and contexts, which is similar to the way equal opportunities has been interpreted. Notwithstanding the various interpretations, there is evidence of consensus over the principles and characteristics of an approach to managing diversity. On closer examination of some of the definitions, one is able to observe that there are some key tenets that inform managing diversity strategies. For example:

- the valuing, recognising and harnessing of a wide range of individual differences

Managing diversity	Equal opportunities
■ Ensures all employees maximise their potential and their contribution to the organisation ■ Embraces a broad range of people – no one is excluded ■ Concentrates on movement within an organisation, the culture of the organisation and the meeting of business objectives ■ Is the concern of all employees, especially managers ■ Does not rely on positive action/affirmative action	■ Concentrates on discrimination ■ Is perceived as an issue for women, ethnic minorities and people with disabilities ■ Concentrates on the number of groups employed ■ Is seen as an issue to do with personnel and human resource practitioners ■ Relies on positive action

Exhibit 11 – 5 Differences between equal opportunities and managing diversity
Source: Kandola and Fullerton (2002: 167).

- a recognition that business advantages do stem from recognising individual differences
- a recognition that there are benefits to be gained in the employment relationship from responding to individual needs.

Moreover, those who advocate the implementation of managing diversity indicate that organisations should recognise all the numerous ways in which people differ, and not just those differences highlighted by anti-discrimination laws. For example, Thomas (1991) posits that managing diversity should also consider the needs of white males in organisations, because they are employees whose interests were not served by past equal opportunity policy initiatives. Other differences that should be recognised include age, personal work styles, and personal and corporate background. These differences may be seen as characteristics that are 'visible and non-visible' (Kandola and Fullerton, 2002: 8), or as primary (gender, age, race and disability) and secondary (class and sexuality) (Wilson and Iles, 1999, cited in Foster and Harris, 2005). Defining differences in the ways described above calls for vigilance, as people do possess a number of characteristics that can be both visible and non-visible.

The business case for managing diversity utilises a number of reasons for its promotion in organisations' human resources practices. These are suggested to be:

- a maximisation of the resources available in the labour market
- a maximisation of the potential of all employees in the organisation
- a creation of business opportunities by employing a diverse workforce; this diversity will enable new insights to be gained into customers' markets not previously accessed, while at the same time appealing to a wider customer base
- sustainability of the organisation in different cultures – especially if the organisation is operating globally.

In terms of what is achievable by human resource practitioners, some commentators suggest that managing diversity strategies will lead to more commitment from employees, since employers will be seen as more committed to the development of their individual differences. This may contribute to a reduction in labour turnover and absenteeism among employees. Once such practices are known, employers will inevitably become 'employers of choice' (Cox and Blake, 1991), enabling them to recruit the most talented workers available within the labour market. Evidence of visible diversity within the workforce may also contribute to the organisation's bottom line, through the widening of its customer base, emanating from a greater sensitivity to different customers' needs through the services or products that are on offer. Further benefits that may be derived from managing diversity practices include the generation of better ideas and solutions to problems, stemming from the heterogeneity of the workforce. Organisational policies are also likely to become more flexible, as a result of recognising the variety of different needs among employees.

The guiding principle behind managing diversity policies seems to be that of 'special treatment according to individual needs' (Noon, 2004: 247, cited in Beardwell *et al.*, 2004). Some argue that managing diversity actually goes further and sees policy 'as being about more than just conventional HR issues' (Foster and Harris, 2005), in that it is alleged to improve 'organisational resilience by creating new customer segments aided by developing a diverse workforce that is representative of . . . customers' (Foster and Harris, 2005).

Criticisms of managing diversity

Despite the positive initiatives reported about managing diversity, there are also criticisms. Among those criticising such strategies is past chairman of the Commission for Racial Equality, Sir Herman Ouseley, who argues that 'employers are using diversity approach as a "comfort-zone" to protect them and act as an alibi for avoiding the responsibility of addressing the unfairness which characterizes many employees' experiences' (Overell, 1996, cited in Kirton and Greene, 2000: 113). There are also dangers in using differences to emphasise practice, in that such differences that exist may be utilised to assert stereotypes and issues surrounding discussions of inferiority and/or superiority, leading to the marginalisation and exclusion of social categories (groups) as employees in the workplace.

A further criticism of managing diversity is that its emphasis on individuals enables employers to 'divide and rule', as there isn't the collective focus and/or group support to be gained from social categories (groups) in the workplace who may be experiencing disadvantage and discrimination. Hill-Collins argues that 'diversity ... renders the experiences of people of colour and of non-privileged white women and men invisible. One way to dehumanise an individual or group is to deny the reality of their experiences' (2000: 563).

Another criticism facing the diversity model is that, by focusing exclusively on individual differences, it is evidently forcing the realities of inequality issues to be avoided (i.e. discrimination, prejudice and unfair treatment). According to Prasad *et al.* (1997), diversity programmes, whether in their simplest form or otherwise, have not proved to be effective in eliminating workplace disadvantage and discrimination. The managing diversity framework is therefore called into question, due to the fact that the diversity literature ignores the reality of white anger, hostility and foul play. Thus, the managing diversity framework continues to demonstrate an underestimation of 'organisational monoculturalism and the related issue of institutional resistance' (Kersten, 2000: 235–248). Moreover, the managing diversity model depicts an emphasis on a 'relational rather than a structural' approach, by focusing on the mobility of people within organisations and therefore excluding the more fundamental issues of 'structural inequality and accountability' (Kersten, 2000: 235–248).

Kandola and Fullerton comment that managing diversity is about 'recognising that prejudices exist and then questioning them before acting' (2002: 12) and that this is realistic. However, to then suggest that it is not about 'removing them', is rather nonsensical, especially if they are in the conscious mind. The mere fact that managing diversity fails to remove or challenge the prejudices (the attitudes that lead to discrimination), allows room for 'stereotyped discretion' (Kirton and Greene 2000: 113). The important thing, then, is to recognise that prejudices and negative views on different social categories do exist, however then 'not to challenge and aim to remove them' is a dereliction of duty by the organisation and a weakness with regard to the managing diversity strategy. As a result of this weakness, even where managing diversity efforts have been implemented, the 'painful experiences of exclusion, conflict, harassment, marginalization and problematization' (Nkomo, 1992: 487–513) continue throughout organisational life, enabling the realities of disadvantage and discrimination to become 'trivialised and minimised' (Kersten, 2000: 235–248) and therefore the policy is silenced. Moreover, within the very label it claims to represent (i.e. difference), managing diversity ultimately diverts attention through its own rhetoric. It then attempts to replace the painful voices of injustice, oppression and exploitation of social categories with silence. Evidence suggests that the impatience of 'superior' groups is often the cause of discrimination (see Frankenburg, 1993); therefore, it is important to take cognisance of the nature of 'structural, economic, ideological and rhetorical tensions in order to resolve ... inequalities which diversity management is designed to contain, restrain and obscure' (Kersten, 2000: 235–248). Linstead *et al.* (2004) suggest that 'managing diversity initiatives to increase productivity might find [themselves] following research and development or marketing, which ignores and ultimately damages the interests' (2004: 67) of others. Furthermore, 'fully developed diversity, it seems, is a difficult goal to achieve'.

Notwithstanding that, Thomas and Ely (1996) warn that seeing managing diversity only in terms of business benefits is unlikely to prevent problems such as racism and other behaviour resulting from prejudice from being tackled as part of the diversity initiative. Finally, as diversity management continues to 'neutralise race and gender' (Acker, 1992: 248–260) and other forms of discrimination, through a denial of 'race, racism and the racial biases of organisational culture', it has led much of the conflict on discrimination on gender and race and other forms of discrimination in organisations to be forced underground. Although the tensions have temporarily been absorbed, it will be only a matter of time before the continued struggle for meaningful equality and change will resurface.

The legal framework

The right to **equal treatment** is considered a taken-for-granted universal human right. As such,

---

equal treatment

A requirement under equal opportunities legislation where people must receive equal treatment in the workplace; in other words, you cannot discriminate in favour of one gender over another, for example.

---

laws made in the UK, and directives and regulations from the European Union, guide both equal opportunity policies and managing diversity strategies. As EU law overrides UK law, EU directives and regulations have to be adhered to by the UK; therefore, organisations in the UK and elsewhere in the EU ought to subscribe to them. Failure to fully implement EU directives and/or regulations effectively, as a member state, can lead to individuals seeking redress from the European Court of Justice. Taking the above into consideration would suggest that equal opportunities and managing diversity in the workplace are both founded on the premise that human beings do have human rights.

In the UK, the Sex Discrimination Act 1975 set up the Equal Opportunities Commission (EOC), the Race Relations Act 1976 set up the Commission for Racial Equality (CRE) and the Disability Rights Commission Act 1999 set up the Disability Rights Commission (DRC). The EOC's intention is to remove unlawful discrimination and ensure equal opportunities for all members of society, whereas the CRE's role is to ensure that there is no unlawful discrimination on the grounds of race, nationality and/or ethnicity. The DRC's role is to provide advice and promote equality to employers with the aim to ensure that people with disabilities are treated fairly. It also has within its functions investigative and enforcement powers, similar to those of the EOC and CRE. The presence of the three commissions listed above means that individuals in the UK are protected by legislation against discriminatory practices by employers based on their disability, gender, marital status, nationality, race, ethnicity, religion and skin colour. There are other EU regulations, introduced in the UK in 2003, that outlaw discrimination, harassment and victimisation in employment and vocational training on the grounds of sexual orientation, and religion or beliefs.

Another area of discrimination that is thought to be common in employment practices in the UK is age. Walker believes that age discrimination 'creates a series of barriers to the achievement of individual potential' (1999: 7). Other evidence suggests that the UK workforce is an ageing one and it is estimated that, by 2015, nearly 50 per cent of UK workers will be aged 50 years or over. Such statistics caused the government of the day to take note and, in 1999, it published the *Code of Practice on Age Diversity in Employment*. The Code addressed ageism and age-related discriminatory practices in recruitment, selection, promotion training, development, redundancy and retirement. However, there is evidence to suggest that the problem needs more than a voluntary code of practice to reduce the levels of discrimination based on age within employment practices. The comments listed in the mini case on ageism support this view.

The evidence shown in the mini case and cited in an EU directive has led to the government indicating that legislation on age discrimination will be forthcoming in 2006. Notwithstanding the present position in the UK on age, see the mini case on IKEA for evidence of good practice by some employers.

The legislative framework in the UK surrounding anti-discrimination matters has developed in a fragmented way, mainly as a result of a series of laws dating back to 1944, when the government of the day drafted legislation on disability. Later there was legislation on race, protecting the early settlers from discrimination in certain areas (e.g. housing). In later years legislation on equal pay, gender and race permitted individuals who felt that unfair treatment had taken place to seek redress through the industrial (now employment) tribunal system. Presently in the UK there is no overarching legal rights legislation that guarantees equal treatment for all as there is in other countries (e.g. the USA and Canada). There is the intention, however, in Protocol 12 of the European Convention, for individuals to be provided with a free-standing right not to be discriminated against.

History has shown that equality laws in the UK are informed by three principles: neutrality, individualism and promotion of autonomy (Fredman, 2001: 154). The aim of neutrality is to ensure that people are treated in the same way (sameness). Neutrality features in most anti-discrimination legislation in the UK, and appears to be of major importance in the goal of achieving consistency of treatment. Individualism supports the position of meritocracy, and suggests that people should be judged based on their talents and abilities, not their social

---

Mini case: A view of ageism in the UK

'My first general point is that we are living in an overwhelmingly ageist society, and that view permeates all the evidence that we received. It is a society that has not adjusted to increased life expectancy.... In the private sector, there is ageism in job applications. Many firms simply have an arbitrary age limit when considering applications. We would like to believe that the new European directive will put an end to that, but it must be closely monitored, otherwise it will be ignored.

'Of course, there is ageism when it comes to retirement. People are not judged on their merits but are made to leave firms when they are perfectly capable of doing jobs, and want to do so, because they have reached the so-called leaving age. Having said that in criticism of the private sector, the public sector seems to us far worse as regards not only retirement but also recruitment. We are told that the government has moved towards flexible employment practices, but for the most part, that seems to be asymmetric. It is flexible when it comes to certain hiring practices to do with short contracts, but very inflexible when it comes to such matters as mandatory retirement ages' (Lord Preston, 2004).

Source: Adapted from a speech made in the House of Lords debate on the Economics of an Ageing Population (www.agepositive.gov.uk/newsdetail.cfm).

Mini case: **Evidence of good practice on age at IKEA**

All advertisements mention that we seek our employees from all backgrounds, students, people returning to work and those on a pension who wish to supplement their earnings or just have time to spare and would like a further interest. So our equal opportunity and human resource policies include age, and state our aims to offer opportunity and responsibility regardless of the employee's age. IKEA is working closely with employment agencies to reach as wide a variety of prospective employees as possible. We believe that this benefits IKEA as a business and brings a balanced working environment. The broad and varied experience of our older workforce provides a complement to other employees who are just starting their careers. Their interpersonal skills, gained through their life experiences, help to enhance our relationship with our customers.

As employee diversity rapidly moves up its business agenda, IKEA has been working to ensure that staff in its flagship Cardiff Bay store fully reflect the diversity of its customer base. 'Before we could open for business, we needed to recruit around 500 staff,' says Gay Gwinnitt, IKEA's HR manager. 'We wanted to be sure that we were attracting a truly diverse workforce by reaching everyone in the community, including older people.'

IKEA held special coffee mornings for prospective employees aged over 50. The events were publicised by adverts in the local paper, in-store and elsewhere. The people who attended met with similarly aged employees and IKEA management, who were prepared to share their experiences with them. IKEA has continued to work closely with specialist diversity managers from JobCentre Plus, which is examining all our current recruitment methods and refining processes to make employing a more age-diverse workforce easier. This action has helped IKEA to achieve the right balance among the workforce in Cardiff.

Source: Adapted from www.agepositive.gov.uk/newsdetail.cfm.

groupings. Furthermore, they should not be treated less favourably on the basis of certain characteristics (e.g. gender, race, disability, religion and beliefs). Promotion of autonomy concerns the right of the individual to make choices of his or her own. Another feature of legislation in the UK is the provision of negative rights – that is, the right of the individual to not be discriminated against. Negative rights enabled organisations not to promote the positive rights of staff in aiming to achieve equality of opportunity in the workforce; however, this position was reversed by the Race Relations (Amendment) Act 2000. This Act's feature is a positive duty placed on public-sector organisations to promote racial equality. It is commonly thought that this change was brought about as a result of the proven case of **institutional racism** against the Metropolitan Police Service by the Macpherson Commission (1999) findings. Key legislation on equal opportunities and managing diversity is listed in Exhibit 11-6.

institutional racism

The collective failure of an organisation to provide an appropriate and professional service to people because of their race, culture or ethnic origin. It can be seen or detected in processes, attitudes and behaviour which amount to discrimination through unwitting prejudice, ignorance, thoughtlessness and racist stereotyping, which disadvantages minority ethnic people (Macpherson Report, 1999).

Diversity awareness

So far, this chapter has discussed some of the complex and even contradictory issues with regard to equal opportunities policies and managing diversity strategies. In discussing awareness about these subject matters, one must first understand the processes of what equality and diversity are attempting to do – that is, comprehend the process of discrimination in

The acts and regulations	Date	Areas covered by the acts
Equal Pay	1970	Men and women to get equal pay for work of equal value, like work or equivalent work
Rehabilitation of Offenders Act	1974	An individual does not have to reveal a criminal offence if the conviction is deemed spent
Sex Discrimination Act	1975	Gender and marital status, positive action and genuine occupational qualification
Race Relations Act	1976	Race, colour, nationality, ethnic origin, positive action and genuine occupational qualification
Data Protection Act	1984 and 1998	Protection of data and its usage, and its extension
Disability Discrimination Act	1995 and 1999	People with disabilities and the Disability Rights Commission
Public Interest Disclosure Act	1998	Protection for whistle-blowing (providing information on unlawful action)
Employment Rights (Dispute Resolution) Act	1998	The reformation of the industrial tribunal system
National Minimum Wage Act	1999	The enforcement of the national minimum wage
Working Time Directive	1999	The maximum number of hours to be worked in a week
Employment Relations Act	1999	Unfair dismissal claims, maternity leave, trades union representation and employment tribunals
Human Rights Act	1999	Protection of individual human rights
Race Relations (Amendment) Act	2000	For public authorities to eliminate unlawful racial discrimination; promote equality of opportunity and good race relations; racial equality schemes
Employment Equality (Sexual Orientation) Regulations	2003	Protects against unlawful discrimination in employment practices on sexual orientation
Employment Equality (Religion and Beliefs) Regulations	2003	Protects against unlawful discrimination in employment practices on religion or beliefs grounds

Exhibit 11–6 Equal opportunities and managing diversity: the key legislation

organisations, so that policies and practices can be developed to remedy the outcomes. Exhibit 11-7 illustrates the process of discrimination in an organisation.

Noon (2004) suggests that pivotal to the process of discrimination is the basis of policy and practice, and consideration of whether this is fair.

Fairness may be judged on a number of different issues – for example, selection, promotion, performance appraisals, and so on. A range of other variables influence assessment of the issues. These variables Noon calls 'personal influences (beliefs, values and political agenda), external pressures and organisational pressures' (2004: 251).

prejudices

Opinions and actions, usually negative, that may be expressed about other people not belonging to the same culture or social group.

stereotypes

Placing people into categories, often as a result of misunderstandings about different cultural and social groups.

Personal influences will in turn be influenced by the manager's individual experiences and values, including **prejudices** and/or **stereotypes** about social categories. Moreover, political agendas, both organisational and individual, will inform the decision-making of managers. Added to these personal influences will be external pressures – for example, legislation and issues with customers and clients, suppliers and the like. The issues of why organisations adopt equality policies and diversity strategies are varied and may influence what managers see as part of the external pressures. Organisational pressures are usually internal ones, and are influenced by the plural nature of organisations and the different interest groups involved. Nonetheless, organisations are political institutions by nature and the issue of power and its variables will always tend to complicate matters with regard to organisational pressures.

These multiple influences and pressures will inform and even influence the decision-making about policies and practices within the organisation. Those pressures and influences with regard to equality and diversity are likely to be about sameness (equal treatment) and/or differences (special treatment) between dominant groups and other social categories (groups). The other

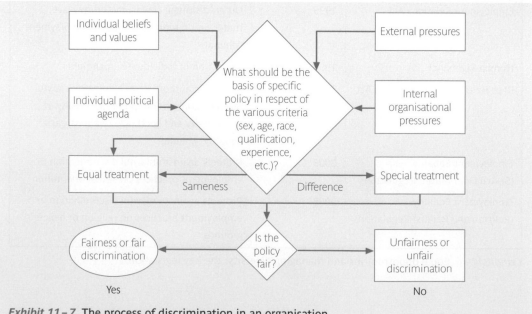

Exhibit 11–7 The process of discrimination in an organisation
Source: Noon and Blyton, in Beardwell *et al.* (2004).

social categories (gender, race, disability, etc.) are members of the workforce who, as a result of analysis of information about organisational practices, are seen as experiencing disadvantages and discrimination.

The competing forces in decision-making

The results from mapping the process of discrimination in organisations illustrate that there are competing forces at play with regard to the decisions made by managers. These forces are employees who are either for or against the decisions made, some seeing them as fair while others will see them as not justifiable. The positions taken by employees, with regard to the decision-making, and therefore the issue of fairness or lack of it, will, suggests Noon, 'vary according to the circumstances and [are] likely to reflect whether they are directly involved with, or affected by, the outcome' (Noon, 2004). Equal opportunities and managing diversity are more about making choices, taking into consideration various courses of action. The decisions reached are usually based on whichever of the competing points of view is prevailing at the precise moment. However, this does not mean that, at that particular point in time, there is a correct or incorrect method. It seems, according to Noon, that it 'is about judgement and conscience' (2004).

If, as Noon suggests, equality and/or diversity is about individual judgement and conscience, what awareness is required by these individuals and what should their roles be in ensuring equality and diversity? Kandola and Fullerton suggest that, 'it is necessary to understand the issues that minorities face at work' (2002: 96), as illustrated in Exhibit 11-8. Other matters of importance that individuals will need to understand are stereotyping and how this influences perceptions. If negative (and stereotypes usually are), they may lead to negative views and treatment of employees by those in positions of power and influence. In her seminal work, Kanter (1997) identified how women in a minority position experienced the organisation (cited in Kandola and Fullerton, 2002: 97):

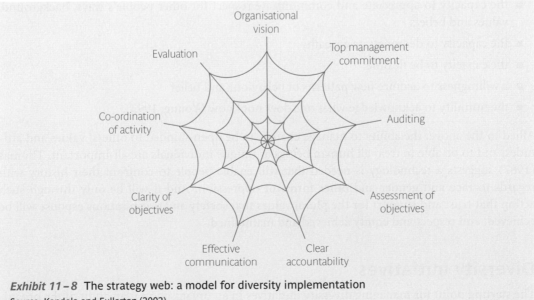

Exhibit 11-8 **The strategy web: a model for diversity implementation**
Source: Kandola and Fullerton (2002).

■ certain behaviours, particularly those related to poor performance, are noted more readily than those in the majority

■ there is a tendency to focus on areas of difference between groups and to magnify and exaggerate them; the differences therefore become larger than they really are

■ behaviour is misinterpreted or misattributed, which then enables people to maintain their stereotypes.

Kanter (1977) shows how tokens (minorities) are treated with double standards, made to feel aware of their differences; they are visible, yet do not participate in decision-making, or policy development, and 'lose their individuality behind stereotyped roles' (1977: 239). Equal opportunities practices and diversity strategies have attempted, through legislation to engender colour and gender blindness, to proclaim 'racelessness' and 'sexlessness'. Accordingly, Thomas (1987) suggests that there are 'taboos' that are 'deeply embedded in feelings and practice, and people . . . enact the system of mistrust and devaluation that shapes relations between the races' (1987: 200), and that diversity strategies and equal opportunities practices may actually strengthen the **taboos** that don't allow people and organisations to examine the impact of gender and colour on our interactions with each other.

> **taboos**
>
> A taboo is a system or the act of setting a person or thing apart as sacred or accursed (*Oxford English Dictionary*, 1991). Thomas (1987: 192–193) suggests that taboo 'operates on two levels. They forbid action, but they also forbid *reflecting* on what is forbidden . . . and they operate out of awareness.'

Confronted by such issues as those mentioned above, managers working in the diverse workplace will require competencies and skills that will enable those experiencing disadvantage and discrimination to feel valued. Such competencies and skill are seen as:

■ the capacity to accept the relativity of one's own knowledge and perceptions

■ the capacity to be non-judgemental

■ a tolerance for ambiguity

■ the capacity to appreciate and communicate respect for other people's ways, background, values and beliefs

■ the capacity to demonstrate empathy

■ the capacity to be flexible

■ a willingness to acquire new patterns of behaviour and belief

■ the humility to acknowledge what one does not know (Young, 1993).

Allied to the above, the ability to manage change, to be open-minded to others' values and attitudes, and to be able to treat all human beings as unique individuals are all-important. Thomas (1987) suggests a technology is needed that will enable people to confront their history with regards to race and gender and other forms of oppression. And it will be only through such action that trust and support for the plural values that society and organisations espouse will be achieved, and respect and equity achieved and maintained.

Diversity initiatives

The starting point for managing diversity initiatives in an organisation is an audit of the organisation's practices and policies (for models of managing diversity, see Exhibit 11-9). The aim of

Process model of managing diversity (Thomas, 1990)	Process and content models of managing diversity (Harrington, 1993)
■ Clarify your motivation ■ Clarify your vision ■ Expand your focus ■ Audit your corporate culture ■ Modify your assumptions ■ Modify your systems ■ Modify your models ■ Help your people pioneer	■ Top management support and commitment ■ Open attitude to new ways of working ■ Distinguish between three approaches to managing diversity

Exhibit 11–9 Models of managing diversity
Source: Kandola and Fullerton (2002).

this audit is to examine any practices taking place that could impact on certain social categories (women, disabled people, racial minorities, etc.) susceptible to disadvantage and discrimination. In order to audit the organisation, information should be collected on the make-up of the workforce, the organisational culture, its systems and the procedures in operation. The information collected will be utilised in checking how the organisation is performing in relation to achieving diversity objectives. The information given in the mini case on ensuring successful diversity implementation is an adapted extract from Linda Wirth (2004, International Labour Organization) and suggests practices that ought to be in place if the organisation is to ensure that its managing diversity strategy is successful.

Mini case: Ensuring successful diversity implementation and support

Thomas and Ely (1996) argue that previous corporate approaches to managing diversity have prevented organisations from capitalising on their diversity assets. They maintain that companies should adopt a holistic approach, designed around the framework of a 'learning and effectiveness' paradigm. This paradigm should emphasise integration in order to enhance organisational effectiveness. It does so by incorporating employees' varied perspectives into the main work of the organisation. Certain preconditions have to be satisfied by employers in organising around the learning effectiveness paradigm, in their attempts to fully leverage workforce diversity.

To ensure a corporate culture that fully utilises and values workforce diversity, senior executives must take responsibility for engendering cultural change through the entire organisation. Organisations finding success with diversity initiatives are typically led by CEOs who elect to spearhead the organisation's diversity initiative, by ensuring the requisite resources are available alongside their high-level support.

Similar to other HR initiatives, if the managing diversity strategy is to be successful, it has to be firmly rooted in the senior management ranks of the organisation. Research has argued consistently that diversity measures attempting to short-circuit these key principles and practices are not likely to be successful. Furthermore, there is evidence to suggest that diversity is not self-managing and that senior managers must take a more proactive stance towards their own involvement with employees in order to drive the managing diversity strategy.

Source: Adapted from: http://www.workinfo.com/.

In achieving a successful managing diversity strategy for the organisation, there needs to be clear accountability and effective communication by senior managers. Furthermore, there needs to be training in diversity awareness and/or diversity skills. Such activity will have to be co-ordinated and managed effectively if it is to be successful. Some writers on the subject, like Cox and Blake (1991), suggest that 'diversity champions' will be required at lower levels in the organisational structure to ensure employees' participation and the implementation of the managing diversity strategy. The employees who play the role of diversity champions are there to gain information and opinions on diversity practices as well as to draw attention to areas that may need improvement in terms of how the diversity strategy has been implemented. The diversity champion's role should be clearly communicated and they should be well known and have the support of senior managers in the organisation. The example in the 'International perspective' box demonstrates how Citigroup, a global organisation, ensures implementation of its managing diversity strategy. Notice the role of senior managers and other HR specialists.

Earlier, it was mentioned that an audit of the organisation's policy and practices ought to be carried out as part of implementing a managing diversity strategy. Kirton and Greene (2000) state that recruitment and selection, training and development, and terms and conditions of service are prerequisites of any effective managing diversity strategy in organisations and, as such, should come under scrutiny when auditing and the collection of information are being conducted. For example, the formalisation of recruitment and selection procedures and practices will lead to the objective requirements of the job being identified, and can lead to clearer decision-making with regard to the selection of suitable candidates. Training and development can be utilised to ensure understanding of issues such as prejudice and stereotyping, which are integral to discrimination and segregation taking place in organisations.

Moreover, training and development in recruitment and selection have been known to enhance the diversity of the workforce, as it enables those who appoint staff to take cognisance of practices that may have contributed to the disadvantage and discrimination of certain social categories that are susceptible. Terms and conditions of employment are areas where discriminatory practices often occur – for example, in terms of differences in pay between men and women employees, and also in terms of the promotion of women, disabled people and people who are from a minority background, in comparison with white males, leading to experiences of the 'glass ceiling' by the former groups mentioned. It is therefore necessary that fair and equitable conditions of employment be applied to all employees in the workforce. By auditing this area of organisation practice, other strategies can be implemented to ensure that disadvantage and discrimination do not occur to those social categories in organisations that are most likely to be vulnerable. Here, the scrutiny of conditions of employment can show up under-representation in certain areas of the workforce and lead to positive action measures (already discussed) being taken to remedy such shortfalls. The collection and auditing of such information, and the justification of such practices for the purpose of achieving equity and diversity in organisations, will be discussed in the next section.

Measuring diversity

The evidence which suggests that diversity is not self-managing is clear. This and other reasons are why the previous section identified the function of auditing, especially when initially setting out a managing diversity strategy for the organisation. Here, the role of monitoring is of fundamental importance. The auditing function conducted at the outset of the implementation of

Diversity in action: across the globe with Citigroup

At Citigroup, diversity is a source of strength for our people and our businesses. In 2003, our company's senior leaders enhanced their commitment to diversity by fostering inclusion through training, mentoring and networking initiatives, often becoming personally involved in the effort; 2003 was the first year that we linked progress in diversity to the performance of our senior managers.

We communicated leadership standards by which all senior managers throughout the organisation will be reviewed. The standards – which address four broad areas: business results, client focus, people, and the way we do business – are described in general terms, except for diversity, where we provide explicit standards on accountability, talent, development and our work environment.

We continued to promote diversity through our diversity councils, in which business leaders and employees from various levels and functional groups develop and execute diversity strategies for their businesses. Citigroup has 21 diversity councils globally, the newest of which was formed in Japan. Citigroup's primary cross-business Diversity Operating Council, chaired by global workforce diversity director Ana Duarte McCarthy, consists of senior diversity directors and human resources leaders representing our major businesses and regions. The council meets twice a month to review diversity policy and share best practice.

The councils operating within the businesses have fostered a greater awareness of diversity. For example, the Fixed Income diversity council in the Global Corporate and Investment Banking Group designed a 'blueprint message' as part of its diversity strategy to highlight the importance of diversity in everyday management behaviour. It was communicated to all Fixed Income managing directors in the USA.

Source: www.citigroup.com/citigroup/citizen/diversity.

Discussion questions

1 How would issues for diversity differ depending on which country the organisation is in?
2 Could one diversity policy 'fit all' in a global organisation?

international perspective

the managing diversity strategy enables those charged with the responsibility of implementing the managing diversity strategy to have a starting point. The data collected through auditing illustrate where the organisation is in terms of achieving its aims and objectives for managing diversity. As such, the data can then be used to evaluate and monitor diversity implementation and any improvements made over time. Monitoring and evaluation of the diversity practice is not only good practice for the organisation, it is in line with the traditions of measuring organisation performance against set aims and objectives. Monitoring is therefore 'a process of systematically collecting and analysing data on the composition of the workforce, particularly with regards to recruitment and selection and promotion' (Noon, 2004: 240) and the conditions of employment afforded to employees. It should also include analysis of data on grievance, disciplinary and performance appraisals, and any other area of practice in the organisation where data can be utilised to demonstrate whether discrimination is taking place within the organisation.

Organisations practising in this area should measure the outcomes from the implementation of the managing diversity strategy by developing monitoring and evaluation mechanisms. The practice of measuring diversity through monitoring and evaluation is important, according to Kirton and Greene, because it makes good business sense and produces the 'evidence required to justify and to plan any further action and initiatives' (2000: 191) in the future. In terms of the business case, diversity monitoring and evaluation enables the organisation to be familiar with the resources available and how they are being utilised. Having access to information of this nature will enable those responsible for organisational objectives and outcomes to make the necessary connections between business objectives, their outcomes and the managing diversity strategy. The success of the organisation in achieving its 'bottom line' can therefore be positively linked to practices in relation to the implementation of the managing diversity strategy, especially where this is transparent.

Earlier on in this chapter, equal opportunity policies and managing diversity strategies were criticised for various reasons. If the incidence of prejudice and discrimination is to be eradicated from organisations' practices and procedures then monitoring and evaluation to ensure equity and social justice ought to be enforced. Noon suggests that the rationale for monitoring 'is that it is impossible for managers to make an assessment of what action to take (if any) unless they are aware of the current situation' (Noon, 2004: 240). The arguments for and against monitoring of equal opportunity policies and managing diversity strategies are set out in Exhibit 11-10.

In examining the outcomes of research conducted in organisations, Creegan *et al.* (2003) demonstrated that employees, especially those from social categories that often experience disadvantage and discrimination, have little confidence in organisational practices with regard to either equal opportunity and/or managing diversity implementation. And, when organisations that practise equality and/or diversity examine employees' opinions through surveys and/or other mechanisms (i.e. monitoring) that provide data on perceptions of the outcomes, this

The case in favour of equal opportunity and managing diversity monitoring	The case against equal opportunity and managing diversity monitoring
■ It allows an organisation to demonstrate what it is doing and identify particular problem areas so that it can take action ■ It encourages managers to think creatively about positive action initiatives; it removes the need for robust legislation such as quotas (positive discrimination) ■ The data can be kept confidential, just like any other information ■ It provides useful information to help management decision-making ■ Organisations conducting their activities in line with legal requirements have nothing to fear ■ The costs are modest ■ It is good business practice	■ It stirs up trouble and discontent, and can create problems that would not otherwise arise ■ It puts undue pressure on managers, and might encourage them to lower standards or appoint for the wrong reasons; it is positive discrimination by the back door ■ It is an invasion of privacy and open to abuse ■ It creates the requirement to collect information that is unecessary ■ Organisations with no problems regarding equal opportunities do not need this burdensome bureaucratic mechanism ■ It is an unnecessary expenditure ■ The business needs to focus on its commercial activities

Exhibit 11–10 The case for and against monitoring equal opportunity and diversity
Source: Adapted from Noon (2004).

often leads to opportunities for expressing dissatisfaction and claims of institutional discrimination, which widens rather than narrows the implementation gap with regard to equal opportunity and/or managing diversity.

Implementing diversity strategy

Demographic changes, increasing global competition and the movement of people across national borders have convinced many CEOs of the necessity to implement diversity as an essential part of their business strategy. Accordingly, many organisations have developed specific efforts to manage the diverse employee population that now makes up the workforce. Practices that are common to some of these organisations include: continuous monitoring of recruitment and selection, promotions, grievance, disciplinary, performance appraisals and other HRM procedures; organisational commitment to flexibility; diversity linked to the business case, as well as strategic vision; systems and procedures that support the development of managing diversity strategies, and the underpinning of valuing and utilising diversity and difference within the workforce.

Bearing in mind the above practices, organisations are increasingly being challenged to manage programmes in order to find ways to help the diverse workforce achieve the business 'bottom line'. The main barriers to achieving managing diversity can be seen as organisational and individual. Many have already been identified – such as discrimination, discomfort with people who are different, prejudice, stereotyping, racism, sexism and bias. Some of the individual barriers will include lack of career planning, failure to understand the organisation and its culture, low self-esteem and poor self-image. Factors that will influence diversity initiatives will include demographic changes, globalisation, a diverse customer base, legislation, and the fact that people are more comfortable about being different.

To facilitate this 'mosaic' (Kandola and Fullerton, 2002), organisations ought to develop education and training programmes for awareness, skills and teamwork as part of employee development. Other issues to be taken into consideration are organisational policies that encourage career and succession planning programmes, mentoring and coaching, use of performance management systems and ethics.

The importance of senior management support for managing diversity programmes, as already mentioned, will be of crucial importance. Other factors necessary will include embedding diversity in all the organisation's procedures and functions, and the creation of an organisational culture that will support the diversity initiatives. Managing diversity in organisations is a complex matter and will require the use of various strategies, as there is no one strategy and/or activity that will facilitate its development and embeddedness in the organisation.

Finally, the need to audit, monitor and evaluate is essential, as these procedures provide data on performance in both the short and long term. The short-term effects of diversity can be used to provide useful information on issues such as change in organisational culture and employee attitude to managing diversity. Performance measurement systems may include the assessment of diversity competence as part of achieving rewards. Such practices will ensure the reinforcement of diversity in management and employee behaviour.

The future envisaged for organisations includes globalisation, with employees' cultural backgrounds and other social and cultural factors being evident in the workplace, making it even more diverse. These and other factors will contribute to an ever increasing global labour market in which there will be diverse work teams, and progressively more of senior management's responsibilities and time will involve issues on managing diversity. This will be brought about by the realisation that managing diversity will effectively enable their organisation to secure the leading edge over competitors. Managing diversity will also be seen as creating competitive advantage and as being good for business. Even the present government is convinced by these sentiments, and is merging the three commissions (the EOC, CRE and DRC) into one body to be called the Commission for Equality and Human Rights (see the 'Managing diversity' box).

Rights here, rights now: the case for a new diversity commission

The Commission for Equality and Human Rights will deliver an equality guarantee for all and put diversity at the top of the HR agenda: that's the view expressed by Jacqui Smith, deputy minister for women and equality.

The government wants a society where every individual is able to achieve their potential, free from prejudice and discrimination. Every person is entitled to respect and dignity in the course of their daily lives, and that applies particularly to the workplace. The government has been working in partnership with business on tackling all discrimination at work, be it based on race, sex, age, disability, religion, belief or sexual orientation. By tackling the prejudice that prevents individual success, we benefit not only the individual, but also the employer and society as a whole. That is why we are bringing forward a bill to establish a Commission for Equality and Human Rights (CEHR). It will, for the first time, draw together in one body the three pillars of law and social policy: equality, human rights, and the promotion of good relations between different groups. It will have the power and authority to deliver an equality guarantee for all.

The new commission will bring specific benefits to employees and will work closely with employers to advance equality and human rights. Businesses already recognise that they cannot afford to cast on to the scrapheap some of our most experienced, skilled and valuable people on grounds of prejudice – whether deliberate or through a lack of understanding. The CEHR will help employers to better understand discrimination law and the business benefits of diversity, through expert advice covering all areas of the law. Equally, employers will be able to help the CEHR to understand the pressures and needs of business.

The government has made progress across a range of equality and diversity issues, and has introduced new laws that address discrimination. We have worked with businesses to place work/life balance issues at the centre of the debate on work and caring, and have kick-started a dialogue between government and business, employer and employee, on flexible working. Combining work and caring responsibilities is now at the top of the HR agenda and is used by good employers to recruit and retain the best people.

On race, through the Race Relations (Amendment) Act, we have introduced laws placing a duty on public bodies to promote equality and to foster good relations between different racial groups. On disability, we introduced new legislation last October outlawing discrimination by employers against disabled people in all aspects of employment. We have also extended protection to employees against discrimination on grounds of sexual orientation, religion and belief. And, with a rapidly ageing population, we are working towards legislation to outlaw age discrimination in employment and vocational training.

The government is very proud of the progress made, but there is more to be done. Much has changed in Britain since the 1970s, when the first race and equality laws were introduced to make race and sex discrimination unlawful. And significant challenges lie ahead. The minority ethnic population accounts for 8 per cent of the total UK population and is rising. By 2014, there will be more people over 65 than under 16 in the UK. There are more than 10 million disabled people still working to secure full rights in education, employment, transport and services, and we will all still be struggling to balance the demands of work and family. But we need to remember that it is discrimination that is the issue, not the communities who face it.

For these reasons, we need a new, authoritative and independent voice against discrimination and for social justice. But the CEHR cannot tackle these issues alone. It must harness the expertise already present in industry, and share and encourage best practice. The new equality body needs to develop close partnerships with business and employers. It will help business to attract and retain employees from diverse backgrounds. It will also bring equality and diversity into the mainstream of working practice, placing it firmly at the top of the HR agenda.

Source: Adapted from Jacqui Smith, *People Management*, 24 February 2005, p. 23.
Reproduced with permission of *People Management*.

Discussion questions

1 Do you think that uniting all the issues concerning equity and diversity under one commission will be beneficial in terms of reducing levels of discrimination?

2 Isn't such a strategy in danger of producing hierarchies of discrimination?

Legal aspects

'Common law upholds the principle of freedom of contract and the concept of discrimination is not recognised ... The complaints based system of anti-discrimination law in the UK is founded in the Acts of Parliament, which overrides common law' (Johnson and Johnstone, in Kirton and Greene, 2000: 131). The law on discrimination provides rights for people who may be refused employment and/or other services because of disability, gender, race, marital status, age (forthcoming), sexual orientation, and religion or belief.

The law on discrimination outlaws the following practices.

- **Direct discrimination** – treating people less favourably than others on grounds of disability, gender, race, marital status, age (forthcoming), sexual orientation, and religion or belief.

- **Indirect discrimination** – applying a provision, criterion or practice that disadvantages people due to their disability, gender, race, marital status, age (forthcoming), sexual orientation, religion or belief, which is not justified as a proportionate means of achieving a legitimate aim.

- **Harassment** – unwanted conduct that violates people's dignity or creates an intimidating, hostile, degrading, humiliating or offensive environment.

- **Victimisation** – treating people less favourably because of something they have done due to or in connection with gender, marital status, race, disability, age (forthcoming), religion or belief, and sexual orientation (e.g. made a formal complaint of discrimination or given evidence in an employment tribunal case).

Lustgarten suggests that the UK is 'walking backward with our faces to the future, as if determined to ignore the evidence of our eyes and to exacerbate the inequalities and divisions within our society' (in Hepple and Szyszczak, 1992: 455). This is in relation to discrimination law particularly pertaining to race. Further argument that discrimination law is hampered in many different ways by 'individuation', is suggested by Lustgarten and Edwards, who state that 'this individuation is partly explicable in terms of managerial rationality, the need to keep litigation manageable in a judicial system that has minimal support services for judges and relies exclusively on oral presentation of evidence and legal arguments' (in Braham *et al.*, 1992: 274).

The outcome of unlawful discrimination, as can be expected from a system based on complaints, is compensation for the victim who suffers the discrimination. So, in order to avoid complaints of unlawful discrimination and therefore compensation awards against them, employers should adopt policies and practices in employment and service delivery that support equality and/or diversity. For this reason, employers need to examine carefully their employment policies and practices to make sure they do not discriminate, irrespective of the fact that there is no legal requirement to review practices in employment. A further matter to be considered by employers is the avoidance of legal liability. Here, employers must ensure good record-keeping and the implementation of formal procedures in the recruitment and selection process. Previously, in any allegation of discrimination, the burden of proof was on the employee to prove that discrimination did take place; it was up to the employer to rebut such allegations of discrimination. However, a recent judgment by the courts has clarified the ambiguity regarding burden of proof for employers in discrimination cases. The judgment makes it clear that, after an individual has proved facts, which suggest that they have been treated unfavourably because of discrimination, employers are expected to provide detailed evidence to prove that they did not discriminate. This new requirement forces employers to provide evidence to show that their actions were in no way connected to an employee's sex, race, disability, religion or beliefs, and sexual orientation. Only when such evidence can be produced, will employers be able to refute allegations of discrimination by employees. This action by the courts was greeted with universal acclaim from the three commissions.

All three commissions (the EOC, CRE and DRC) have produced codes of practice. Although these are not legally binding documents, they do recommend good practice. Any breach of the recommended guidelines in any of the codes (specific to the alleged discrimination) may be utilised by a person making an allegation of discrimination as evidence. In such cases the employment tribunal may well take the breach into consideration when passing judgment. Under Section 41 of the SDA 1975 and Section 32 of the RRA 1976, employers may also be deemed liable for discriminatory action 'in the course of employment' by fellow employees. Because the commissions do not have recourse to challenge the law in the area of institutional discrimination, it is up to individual complainants to take such action and criticism has been voiced by others with regard to such weaknesses in the law (e.g. Lustgarten and Edwards, 1992). The SDA 1975 and RRA 1976 allow for positive action, which includes activity such as monitoring, training for under-represented groups, development of strategies to combat under-representation and also methods for evaluating the success of the aforementioned strategies. Another area of allowable practice is the setting of targets in the area of recruitment, and the promotion of employees from social categories that are deemed to experience discrimination under the law.

The Human Rights Act 1998 incorporates the European Convention of Human Rights into UK law. This incorporation will have an impact in the area of discrimination, as it requires all public authorities to observe the rights and obligations set out in the Convention. The Convention actually supports the right of every individual to equality on grounds of race, colour, sex, religion, political or other opinion, language, national or social origin, birth or other status. The principle of equality enshrined in the Convention is internationally recognised as a fundamental human right.

Summary

- Throughout this chapter an attempt has been made to critically analyse the implementation and practice of equal opportunity and managing diversity in organisations. In doing so it is evident that organisations implement both equal opportunity policies and managing diversity strategies differently, to support their own needs. In the same way that there is diversity in policy implementation, there is also diversity in the social categories that experience disadvantage and discrimination as a result of organisational practices. These diversities should be recognised, and policies developed that are sensitive to the different experiences of disadvantage and discrimination of the various social categories.

- Organisations and their leaders often develop strategies to prevent discrimination. Often these strategies are based around either social justice or business-case needs, or indeed both. Perhaps it is time that organisations and their leaders take full cognisance of the moral and the business-case arguments to pursue equity for all employees and silence the critics, who argue that profit (where applicable) should be the sole motive for organisations' practices. As such, both the business case and the moral arguments can form powerful alliances to ensure equality of outcome for all social categories that experience disadvantage and discrimination in organisations.

- For both equal opportunities policies and managing diversity strategies to be effective, they need to pursue positive action initiatives. This will ensure the levelling of the playing field for all social categories, and enable practices like auditing, monitoring and evaluation to assess the initiatives over both short- and long-term periods. In this way, practices that are found to be effective can be utilised in the long term and those that are found to be detrimental can be revised.

- Some writers (e.g. Kandola and Fullerton, 2002) and some practitioners in the field see managing diversity as a different paradigm. In certain instances, it presupposes that the organisation is already diverse in terms of its representation. This position is not always correct, and it is for this reason that positive action is advocated for use in practices for both equal opportunity policy and managing diversity implementation.

- An important concept for managers to come to terms with in organisations is that treating an individual the same and/or differently could lead to unfair treatment and discrimination. It is therefore incumbent upon organisations and their leaders to be sensitive to both similarities and differences when developing policies and strategies around disadvantage and discrimination.

- The concept of institutional discrimination is used to describe practices, policies and procedures that are unquestionably discriminatory in their outcomes. As suggested in the Macpherson Report (1999), these may be unwitting, and are often not recognised. These practices, policies and procedures are often embedded in the culture and structure of the organisation. In order to eradicate them, the organisation may need to revert to actions that are deemed 'radical' (Jewson and Mason, 1986) in terms of an equal opportunity stance. Similar radicalism may also be needed for managing diversity strategies. By taking actions such as those mentioned, organisations will be increasing their chances of reducing unfairness, as well as providing burden of proof in cases of alleged discrimination by employees.

- Discrimination as a process is evident in a mixture of personal, external and internal pressures on organisational leaders in their decision-making choices. For example, in connection with the selection of staff, promotion of employees, how work is allocated, those selected for training and development opportunities, when assessing performance in the workplace using performance management systems, and many other areas, especially when considering sameness and difference. Employees' perception of disadvantage and discrimination, and therefore unfairness, results from their expectations and management decision-making. When observed from this standpoint, decision-making in organisations can be vulnerable to allegations of unfairness. This is of course dependent on the perspective of the employee(s) concerned, especially with regard to issues like the criteria used for the decision-making and whether the treatment is acceptable or not to the employee(s) concerned.

Personal development

1 **Recognise differences.** Think about your own values and how they differ from those of your friends, family, neighbours, colleagues. What is it that you value about yourself and others? Can you relate this to valuing diversity?

2 **Value differences.** Has there ever been a time when you have had to repress your differences? What was the outcome? How did you feel afterwards? Do you think it was worthwhile or should you have spoken out?

3 **Develop ways to respond to diversity.** By acknowledging and responding to diversity issues we can develop the ability not only to manage ourselves but also to manage others. Think about strategies you could use for dealing with the sort of conflict that can arise from a lack of understanding of others.

4 **Develop leadership skills.** These should be the sort of leadership skills that enable you to respond to diversity. As a manager you will need to recognise that people come from diverse backgrounds, and have different perspectives and approaches to work. How can you develop this positively to get results?

5 **Communicate strategy.** Think about how you can influence others with regard to issues of equality and diversity. Sometimes it is very hard to challenge other people's stereotypes without causing conflict. What could you do when someone makes an unfair statement?

6 **Aim to do well and to do good.** This means treating others as you would like to be treated. Think about your intentions when you make a decision that affects others. Could the decisions you make harm anyone? Managers often have to make decisions for the greater good. How do they know if they will get it right?

❓ Discussion questions

1 Define what is meant by equal opportunities and managing diversity.

2 Describe the approaches to implementing anti-discrimination legislation.

3 What are the different approaches to implementing policies on workplace equality and diversity?

4 How could the HR manager take responsibility for equal opportunities and managing diversity?

5 Outline the development and functions of equal opportunities and managing diversity.

6 What are the challenges in developing and delivering equality and diversity in organisations?

7   Evaluate approaches to equality and diversity in organisations.

8   What do we mean by diversity management?

9   Women and ethnic minorities are still under-represented in top management. How could you redress the balance?

10 What is meant by the 'glass ceiling'?

🔓 Key concepts

paradigm, *p. 363*	radical approach, *p. 367*
equal opportunities, *p. 363*	positive action, *p. 367*
discrimination, *p. 363*	equal treatment, *p. 376*
regulatory, *p. 364*	institutional racism, *p. 378*
diversity, *p. 364*	prejudices, *p. 380*
social justice, *p. 364*	stereotypes, *p. 380*
business case, *p. 364*	taboos, *p. 382*
glass ceiling, *p. 365*	

Individual task

Uncovering stereotypes

Purpose To examine how we develop stereotypes about others.

Time 30 minutes

Procedure Using the chart below, complete the 'First thought' column and then write a judgement about the different groups. Rate each judgement as either positive (+), negative (−) or neutral (0). In the last column indicate your sources for each judgement.

Category	First thought/judgement	Rating (+, −, 0)	Source of judgement
Working mother			
Female prime minister			
Smoker			
HIV positive			
Trainspotter			
Spectacle wearer			
Hijab wearer			
Tattoo and piercings wearer			

Discussion questions

1 How have you developed your stereotypes? Was it through your family, the media, friends or experience?

2 How many of your stereotypes were positive, negative or neutral?

3 Working as a group, see how your stereotypes compare to those of others in your class.

Team task

Purpose To examine how the media can influence our opinions and reinforce stereotypes.

Time 40 minutes

Materials A selection of newspapers and magazines, such as the *Telegraph*, *The Times*, the *Independent*, the *Guardian*, the *Sun*, the *News of the World*, the *Daily Mail*, *The Economist* and *Newsweek*.

Procedure Divide into groups and examine one of the above, or similar, publications.

- What group of people is the newspaper aiming at?
- How does it refer to different sectors of society (e.g. race, religion, gender)?
- What messages of cultural values and stereotypes does it convey?
- What about the advertisements, do these reflect stereotypes?

As a whole class, think about the following questions.

- What influence do the media have on establishing cultural stereotypes?
- How do you think the media could play a part in helping us to value diversity?

Case study: **A case of 'older and wiser'**

It is now widely accepted that the financial sector's problems during the economic recession of the early 1990s were exacerbated by the policy – also common in other industries – of shedding older workers in previous downturns. The result was a lack of managers with knowledge of the whole business cycle and, consequently, less well-informed lending decisions. In recognising this loss of 'corporate memory', Barclays Bank, for one, has recently instigated a range of policies to attract and retain older employees. Its efforts have been recognised with an award for outstanding achievement from Age Positive, the government-backed organisation that helps employers to combat age discrimination.

By changing recruitment policies to attract older candidates, encouraging people to stay with the company through long-service awards, allowing employees to work beyond the normal retirement age, and other initiatives, the organisation has increased the number of staff over the age of 55 by nearly 400 in two years, and there are now more over-50s than under-21s. 'We aim to ensure that our policies are leading edge,' says Barclays' equality and diversity deputy director. 'We have introduced recruitment policies and campaigns specifically targeting the over-60s and have given employees the option to work until the age of 70.'

Barclays was one of the first organisations to see the benefits of employing older workers – along with other financial services businesses. This interest is largely prompted by the twin spectres of legislation on age discrimination, which the UK is due to introduce in accordance with

European law in 2006, and the relaxation of rules on pension ages, expected at about the same time, in response to the pensions 'time bomb'. The risk of heavy compensation payments for non-compliance is enough of a business case for action for many employers, but there is also evidence that organisations are responding to the falling birth rate by drawing on a wider pool of workers in a genuine attempt to address the shortfall in 'young and dynamic' workers.

While it is important to recognise that any legislation will outlaw bias against youth as much as against experience, the main focus appears to be on recruiting and retaining older workers. The CIPD adviser on diversity agrees: 'The impact of demographic changes on the size of the labour market means that employers are going to have to engage with more mature workers.'

One such organisation is Nationwide. Its head of corporate personnel says that the company estimates that it saves about £5.5 million a year by having lower staff turnover rates through encouraging a wider age range of employees. The company, which has won awards for its commitment to customer service, has seen a strong correlation between length of service and customer satisfaction. 'There is a strong link with how much experience employees have, not only of products, but of life generally.'

Convinced that customer satisfaction has a big impact on profit, the firm sees employing older workers, as well as the younger ones it has traditionally recruited, as a key factor in improving profit. However, it is acknowledged that taking such a step involves overcoming some myths. For instance, it is widely thought that older people are absent from work more often than younger workers, but Nationwide has found the opposite to be true. Similarly, rather than being under-performers, most over-50s have a better overall performance rate than under-50s. And while staff turnover among over-50s is less than 6 per cent, it is more than 9 per cent among younger workers.

These initiatives show that older workers are, for example, as productive as their younger counterparts, and other sectors that are already facing a shortfall in younger staff will start to see the business case. After all, by taking on a wider range of recruits and giving them the chance to stay longer, employers will be less susceptible to the sort of war for talent that caused such problems at the height of the dotcom boom.

Source: Adapted from an article by Roger Trapp, *People Management*, 23 December 2004, p. 40.
Reproduced with permission of *People Management* and Roger Trapp.

Discussion questions

1 Why has the policy of shedding older workers in the past caused such problems?

2 How can organisations retain older workers?

3 What is the legal obligation of the employer to older employees?

4 What policies would you develop in order to promote diversity to all people in your organisation?

WWW exercise

Fairplay South East is an organisation that promotes equality of opportunity in education, employment and the community in the south-east of England. It offers information, training, advice and research on issues relating to people potentially disadvantaged by gender, race, disability or age.

Visit its website at http://www.fairplayse.org.uk/.

1 What issues does it cover?

2 What advice can Fairplay give to employers and employees in organisations?

3 How does it define issues of diversity and equal opportunity?

LEARNING CHECKLIST

Before moving on to the next chapter, check that you are able to:

- ☑ define what is meant by equal opportunities and managing diversity
- ☑ understand anti-discrimination legislation and approaches to workplace equality and diversity
- ☑ understand how equal opportunities and managing diversity are issues in HR practice
- ☑ outline the development and functions of equal opportunities and managing diversity
- ☑ appreciate the challenges involved in developing and delivering equality and diversity in organisations
- ☑ evaluate approaches to equality and diversity in organisations.

Further reading

Crace, J. (2004) 'We remain almost invisible', *Guardian*, 14 December.

Hawkins, J.M. and Allen, R. (1991) *The Oxford Encyclopaedic English Dictionary*. Oxford: Clarendon Press.

Hill-Collins, P. (1993) 'Towards a new vision – race, class, and gender as categories of analysis and connection', in T.E. Ore (2000) *The Social Construction of Difference and Inequality: Race, Class, Gender, and Sexuality*. California: Mayfield Publishing.

Leopold , J. (2005) *Human Resources in Organisations*. London: FT Prentice Hall.

Lustgarten, L. (1992) Cited in B. Hepple and E.M. Szyszczak (eds) *Discrimination: The Limits of the Law*. London: Mansel.

Smith, J. (2005) 'Rights here, rights now', at www.peoplemanagement.co.uk/pm/articles/rightshere.

References

Acker, J. (1992) 'Gendering organisational theory', in G. Kirton and A. Greene (2000) *The Dynamics of Managing Diversity – A Critical Approach*. Oxford: Butterworth Heinemann.

Age Positive (2004) www.agepositive.gov.uk/newsdetail.cfm.

Banton, M. (1994) *Discrimination*. Buckingham: Open University Press.

Beardwell, I., Holden, L. and Claydon, T. (eds) (2004) *Human Resources – A Contemporary Approach*. Harlow: Prentice Hall.

Braham, P., Tattansi, A. and Skellington, R. (eds) (1992) *Racism and Anti-racism*. London: Sage.

Chryssides, G. and Kaler, J. (1996) *Essentials of Business Ethics*. Maidenhead: McGraw-Hill.

Cockburn, C. (1989) 'Equal opportunities: the long and short agenda', *Industrial Relations* 20, Autumn, pp. 213–225.

Cockburn, C. (1991) *In the Way of Women: Men's Resistance to Sex Equality in Organisations*. Basingstoke: Macmillan.

Collinson, D.L., Knights, D. and Collinson, M. (1990) *Managing to Discriminate*. London: Routledge.

Commission for Racial Equality (CRE) www.cre.gov.uk/gdpract/eop.ht.

Cox, T. and Blake, S. (1991) 'Managing cultural diversity: implications for organisational competitiveness', *Academy of Management Executives* 5(3), pp. 45–56.

Creegan, C., Colgan, F., Charlesworth, R. and Robinson, G. (2003) 'Race equality policies at work: employee perceptions of the "implementation gap" in a UK local authority', *Work, Employment and Society* 17(4), pp. 617–640.

Cully, M., Woodland, S., O'Reiley, A. and Dix, G. (1999) 'Britain at work as depicted by the 1998 Workplace Employee Relations Survey', in J. Leopold, L. Harris and T. Watson (eds) (2005) *The Strategic Managing of Human Resources*. Harlow: Prentice Hall.

Equal Opportunities Commission (EOC) www.eoc.org.uk/cseng/advice/managing_successful_positive_action.asp.

Ford, V. (1996) 'Partnership is the secret of progress', *People Management* 2(3), pp. 34–36.

Foster, C. and Harris, L. (2005) 'From equal opportunities to diversity management', in J. Leopold, L. Harris and T. Watson (eds) (2005) *The Strategic Managing of Human Resources*. Harlow: Prentice Hall.

Foster, J. (2003) *Essays on the Evils of Popular Ignorance*. Kessinger Publishing.

Frankenburg, R. (1993) *The Social Construction of Whiteness – White Woman, Race Matters*. London: Routledge.

Fredman, S. (2001) 'Equality: a new generation?', *Industrial Law Journal* 30(2), pp. 145–168.

Harrington, L. (1993) 'Why managing diversity is so important', *Distribution* 92(11), pp. 88–92.

Hepple, B. and Szyszczak, E.M. (1992) *Discrimination: The Limits of the Law*. London: Continuum International Publishing Group.

Hill-Collins, P. (2000) *Black Feminist Thought: Knowledge, Consciousness, and the Politics of Empowerment* (2nd edn). New York: Routledge.

Jewson, N. and Mason, D. (1986) 'The theory and practice of equal opportunities policies: liberal and radical approaches', *Sociological Review* 34(2), pp. 307–334.

Johnston, W.B. and Packer, A.E. (1987) *Workforce 2000: Work and Workers for the 21st Century*. Washington, DC: US Department of Labor.

Kandola, R. and Fullerton, J. (2002) *Diversity in Action – Managing the Mosaic*. London: CIPD.

Kanter, R.M. (1997) *Men and Women of the Corporation*. New York: Basic Books.

Kersten, I. (2000) 'Diversity management: dialogue, dialectics and diversion', *Journal of Organisational Change* 13(3).

Kirton, G. and Greene, A. (2000) *The Dynamics of Managing Diversity – A Critical Approach*. Oxford: Butterworth Heinemann.

Liff, S. and Dale, K. (1994) 'Formal opportunity, informal barriers: black women managers within a local authority', *Work, Employment and Society* 8(2), pp. 177–198.

Liff, S. and Wajcman, J. (1996) ' "Sameness" and "Difference" revisited: which way forward for equal opportunity initiatives?', *Journal of Management Studies* 33(1), pp. 79–95, in G. Kirton and A. Greene (2000) *The Dynamics of Managing Diversity – A Critical Approach.* Oxford: Butterworth Heinemann.

Linstead, S., Fulop, L. and Lilley, S. (2004) *Management and Organisation – A Critical Text.* Basingstoke: Palgrave Macmillan.

Lustgarten, L. and Edwards, J. (1992) cited in P. Braham, A. Rattansi and R. Skellington (eds) *Racism and Antiracism – Inequalities, Opportunities and Policies.* London: Sage.

Macpherson Report (1999) *Report from the Stephen Lawrence Inquiry.* London: HMSO.

Nkomo, S. (1992) 'The emperor has no clothes: rewriting "Race in organisations" ', *Academy of Management Review* 17(3).

Noon, M. (2004) 'Managing equality and diversity', in I. Beardwell, L. Holden and T. Claydon (eds) *Human Resources – A Contemporary Approach.* Harlow: Prentice Hall.

Person, S. (2003) 'Improving working lives – tackling racial harassment in the NHS', at http://www.nhs.uk/nhsmagazine/archive/sep03/feat11.asp.

Overell, S. (1996) 'Union calls for law to stop bullying at work', *People Management* 2(16), pp. 9–10.

Prasad, P., Mills, A.J., Elmes, M. and Prasad, A. (eds) (1997) *Managing the Organisational Melting Pot – Dilemmas of Workplace Diversity.* London: Sage.

Rees, T. (1998) *Mainstreaming Equality in the European Union: Education, Training and Labour Market Policies.* London: Routledge.

Thomas, D.A. (1987) 'Mentoring and irrationality: the role of racial taboos', in L. Hirschhorn and C.K. Barnett (eds) *The Psychodynamics of Organizations.* Philadelphia: Temple University Press.

Thomas, D. and Ely, R. (1996) 'Making difference matter: a new paradigm for managing diversity', *Harvard Business Review* 74(5), pp. 79–90.

Thomas, R. (1990) 'From affirmative action to affirming diversity', *Harvard Business Review* 68(2), pp. 107–117.

Thomas, R. (1991) *Beyond Race and Gender.* New York: Amacom.

Walker, A. (1999) 'Breaking down the barriers on ageism in the professional manager', in L. Maund (2001) *An Introduction to Human Resource Management – Theory and Practice.* Basingstoke: Palgrave Macmillan.

Webb, J. (1997) 'The politics of equal opportunity', *Gender, Work and Organisation* 4(3), pp. 159–177, in G. Kirton and A. Greene (2000) *The Dynamics of Managing Diversity – A Critical Approach.* Oxford: Butterworth Heinemann.

Weick, K.E. (1995) *Sensemaking in Organizations.* Los Angeles: Sage.

Wilson, E. and Iles, P. (1999) 'Managing Diversity – an employment and service delivery challenge', *International Journal of Public Sector Management* 12(1), pp. 27–48, in J. Leopold, L. Harris and T. Watson (eds) (2005) *The Strategic Managing of Human Resources.* Harlow: Prentice Hall.

Wirth, L. (2004) 'International Labour Organization practice', at www.workinfo.com/.

Young, K. (1993) 'The space between words: local authorities and the concept of equal opportunities', in R. Jenkins and J. Solomos (eds) *Racism and Equal Opportunity Policies in the 1980s.* Cambridge: Cambridge University Press.

Chapter 12

Strategic human resource management

LEARNING OUTCOMES

After studying this chapter, you should be able to:

☑ **understand** the development of strategic management

☑ **understand** the role of strategy in human resource management

☑ **evaluate** the models of strategic management and strategic human resource management (SHRM)

☑ **recognise** the importance of SHRM in gaining competitive advantage.

The opening vignette demonstrates how the National Trust needed to change in order to move into the twenty-first century. A change in management brought with it a change in strategy.

Strategic thinking at the National Trust

With more than three million members, 612,000 acres of land and 600 miles of coastline, the National Trust is the very image of a venerable British institution. But while its 109-year history is impressive, certain ways of working had become ingrained, and the Trust needed to refresh its approach to remain at the cutting edge and ensure it fulfilled its vital conservation role.

The arrival of Fiona Reynolds as director-general in January 2001 provided the leadership for implementing the organisational review commissioned by her predecessor. The process led to the creation of a new management board and regional structure, and the redesign of over 200 roles, affecting more than 1000 staff.

▶ 'The organisational review was about making sure we could punch our weight in the twenty-first century,' explains Paul Boniface, director of human resources and legal services. 'On the face of it we were phenomenally successful, but we felt we were not doing all we could for conservation. We needed to look externally to influence government and opinion-formers on some of the big threats facing conservation, and start to make people realise that we are not just about looking after rural mansions and the countryside.'

Boniface was originally appointed as director of personnel and organisational development in 2000 to lead the changes, and effectively became project director, with 90 per cent of his job related to the review.

The first phase was structural and looked at how the organisation, which combines visitor attractions with heritage and conservation work, needed to be reorganised to deliver its services more effectively. The management board was reshaped to achieve a better balance of operations, specialist functions and internal services, and the number of management regions was reduced from 15 to 11, better reflecting the boundaries of the organisations that the Trust seeks to partner or influence, such as the government's regional development agencies.

This naturally gave rise to changes in some office locations, including the merger of the Trust's four national offices into two – one in Swindon, due to open next year, and a small London base.

'In some ways, the decision to establish a new central office in Swindon was the most painful element of the changes, as it affected large numbers of staff,' says Boniface. 'But we concluded it was necessary to the success of the organisational review. We believe it will create an exciting and creative centre for the Trust.'

Once the new structure was decided, the staff structures underneath had to be changed to fit the new principles. But instead of relying on external management consultants, employees were asked to suggest the best way forward – a move that helped ensure a high level of staff buy-in.

Eight project teams, representing seven newly structured departments, plus an additional one on behavioural change, were set up. Each team of between 12 and 15 employees reported to Boniface and was led by an internal client.

The project groups developed ideas on what the new structures should be, including job roles and duties, which were then put to the management board for consideration.

'This is a passionate organisation and people really care about it. Our staff were truly interested in what the structures should be to serve the organisation best. If employees get the proper lead and facilitation, they will come up with fantastic thoughts and ideas,' says Boniface.

One idea suggested by the customer services project team, a new department created in the restructuring, was to call visitors 'customers' – a term that the Trust had previously been uncomfortable about using.

'We are trying to introduce more commercial principles, while not losing the basic ethos of the Trust,' says Boniface. 'We have to provide the right customer experience in order to make money to mend a leaky roof, for example. But some staff did not see a direct link between conservation and customers. This change recognises that essentially we do provide a service.'

With the new structure agreed, the organisation embarked on a two-year implementation period. Changes to the HR department, which moved to a shared service centre model, were made last so that it was able to lead the process in all other departments.

Boniface admits this was an emotional time for the Trust, particularly as it was not used to large-scale change: 'This process affected 1300 of our 5000 employees, who all had to go through the worry of what it meant. Lots of people had to be interviewed for jobs and we lost 200 staff. The majority of these were voluntary, and many were a result of the closure of some of our regional offices.' To ensure this was a fair process, staff representatives were elected for consultation with the Trust.

Once the structural elements of the change programme were largely complete, the second and perhaps more key part of the review could begin: the behavioural change programme. The project team for this was led by the director-general herself, reflecting its importance to the review's success and the fact that it was one of the longer-term aspects of the change.

The team came up with a number of observations about the Trust. Among these were that it should hold on to its tolerance of eccentricity, but that it consulted too much, was too 'nice', had a meetings culture and was not fast enough on its feet. It also identified the aspects of the organisation's culture that shouldn't be changed.

From this, Reynolds and her team developed a set of values and ways of working. The management board, in turn, agreed a list of actions to prove its commitment to these, including sharing good practice via the intranet and engaging more managers in 'back-to-the-floor' experiences.

An innovations fund of £500,000 was introduced to recognise good ideas. This allows departments to bid for money internally instead of going to a local authority to seek funding – so, for example, a property can 'win' money to produce brochures for a nature walk.

The most important outcome of the behavioural change process was that, for the first time, the Trust ran a programme for all 5000 permanent staff on the new ways of working. This one-day course also explained the structural changes in the context of history, demonstrating that the Trust has always responded to changes in the demands placed on it. The organisation is now running a second one-day programme for staff on improving performance. It is also overhauling its performance and development review (appraisal) system.

'Conservation is about the management of change, such as coastal erosion. It was important to get across the message that change is a continuous process and part of what the Trust is about in this broader context, as there was a school of thought saying that "now we've got through the organisational review, we can settle back down again",' says Boniface.

Later this year, the Trust will begin to review the success of the new changes. Boniface is already confident that this will show the organisation is able to respond better to the pressures of a fast-changing world, but he admits that 'the behavioural aspect of the changes will go on for some years'.

How was HR affected?

The National Trust decided to move to a shared service centre model to reduce HR time spent on routine queries and improve employees' awareness of their benefits.

At the end of April, an intranet site containing information on employee benefits and a service centre to answer personal queries on benefits for all 5000 permanent employees and 4500 seasonal staff went live.

HR services manager Christina O'Donovan-Rossa says the new system saves time: 'If the service centre cannot answer a query, it is then escalated to a regional HR director. But it means HR does not get bogged down with straightforward queries. We now have time for succession planning and to look after teams in the field.'

Internet access is not available in many of the Trust's locations, but the organisation overcame this problem by sending information out on CD-Rom. The service centre also opens at weekends and early mornings to suit staff hours.

O'Donovan-Rossa says staff awareness of benefits and their eligibility for these has improved. 'We are an independent charity so do not offer stacks of money or golden handshakes, but employees now know what we offer as an employer in terms of the whole deal,' she says.

Other departments, including finance, are now keen to follow HR's lead, and in the longer term the service centre will be linked to the new payroll system.

Staff consultation

Historically, the National Trust has not had a relationship with trades unions, but this changed during the organisational review.

In the early stages, elected employees were consulted on the proposals, but the Trust also decided to establish longer-term processes for staff consultation. To help ensure the right model was chosen, other organisations, such as John Lewis, were invited to speak to staff about how different models work. With the help of independent election services provider Electoral Reform Services, staff were then balloted on whether they wanted a staff association, full union recognition, a negotiating committee comprising union and non-union members, or a consultative committee of elected staff members and representatives from the management board.

The staff voted for trades union recognition and, in April 2003, Prospect signed a recognition agreement with the Trust, giving the union responsibility for negotiating terms and conditions, and representing the interests of all permanent staff.

Prospect is now working with the Trust on the move to the central office in Swindon.

Source: Katie Hope, *People Management*, 2 September 2004, p. 32.
Reproduced with permission of *People Management*.

Discussion questions

1 How has the National Trust implemented strategy through its people?

2 To ensure that people accepted change, what procedures did the National Trust follow?

3 Do you think its strategy will be successful?

Introduction to strategic human resource management (SHRM)

All organisations have an aim or a reason for being, whether it is to provide a service or make a profit. To enable organisations to achieve their aim, it is necessary to have a strategy. The example given in the opening vignette demonstrates that charitable organisations such as the National Trust, who are there to give a service, still need to think strategically in order to maximise resources.

Organisations when they do business also need to think about maximising profits, reducing costs and how best to deploy their resources, whether these are financial, material resources or people. The **strategy** of an organisation may be obvious in that it is clearly defined and laid down for all to see, but in many businesses it is not obvious as it is

strategy
From the Greek word *strategia*, refers to generalship in the art of war.

embedded in the organisation and implemented through the behaviour of management and staff. Mintzberg (1994) recognised that strategy is an evolutionary and political process, moulded by events rather than through systematic calculations.

Organisations employ people and in an attempt to act strategically HR managers often have

---
strategic choices

The planned choices an organisation implements in relation to its strategy.

---

a set of **strategic choices**. In other words, HR managers need to know the strategy of the organisation and link it to the HR functions of recruitment, selection and development of employees. The opening vignette illustrates that, in implementing its strategy for change, the National Trust realised the impact that this would have on the HR function and acted accordingly to ensure that employees were kept informed and were able to share their views.

This chapter introduces a definition of strategic management and shows how strategic management can be linked to strategic human resource management (SHRM).

Strategic management

The literature on **strategic management** is wide and diverse. This is not helped by the word

---
strategic management

The process of addressing the competitive challenges an organisation faces, through planning.

---

strategy having different meanings for different people. Sometimes it is used to make managers feel more important; to others it is a plan of action; and for another group strategy is seen as vital in an attempt to gain competitive advantage. Strategic management does not take place in isolation and managers have to

manage strategically in the daily confines of the work environment. Mintzberg (1989) recognised this difficulty and identified that most managers have a multiplicity of tasks to perform as part of their daily activities. To be successful, strategic management is about taking action. It is about gathering information on which to base decisions that will lead to the desired actions.

Aspects of strategy

For a practical application of strategy Macmillan and Tampoe (2000) have identified the following 10 aspects.

1 **Strategy as a statement of ends, purpose and intent** – this is a definition of purpose, which can form part of the vision and mission of the organisation.

2 **Strategy and a high-level plan** – this develops strategy into a plan and should answer such questions as who, when, where, how and what.

3 **Strategy as a means of beating the competition** – this links strategy with achieving competitive advantage.

4 **Strategy as an element of leadership** – development and implementation of strategy needs strong leadership. When leaders change strategy may also change.

5 **Strategy as positioning for the future** – this is about planning for the future and developing strategies for dealing with uncertainty.

6 **Strategy as building capability** – this can be related to the HR function. Strategies are developed to build the skills, knowledge and capabilities of an organisation's people to encourage flexibility and react to changes.

7 **Strategy as a fit between capabilities and opportunities** – creating a fit between what the business is capable of and the opportunities available.

8 **Strategy as a result of deep involvement with the business** – in other words, those who are involved in the business should also be involved in strategy formulation. It should not be seen as an abstract exercise.

9 **Strategy as a pattern of behaviour resulting from embedded culture** – culture influences strategy as well as other aspects of the organisation, and depending on the culture this can create success or failure.

10 **Strategy as an emerging pattern of successful behaviour** – strategy needs to be constantly re-examined to identify success and develop these successes into planned actions.

As can be seen from Macmillan and Tampoe's (2000) list, strategy is applied to all aspects of an organisation.

Exhibit 12-1 helps illustrate how effective HRM strategies can impact on other areas of the organisation and help meet the overall business strategy.

generic strategy
Non-specific strategies that can be applied to organisations, such as cost differentiation or focus.

Generic strategy is only a small part of strategic management. There is also a need to develop strategies for achieving organisational goals in the current environment. This means that managers need to make choices when faced with demands from the various stakeholders, such as employees, customers, shareholders, and so on. Therefore, strategic management is not only a process for analysing an organisation's competitive system but also a means of developing strategic goals, devising a plan of action and allocating resources, which can be human, financial and physical, in such a way as to achieve the strategy and goals. To do this the HR manager needs to be aware of the competitive issues an organisation is dealing with and think strategically about how best human resources can respond to the issues.

Often HR managers are accused of not being strategic enough. A recent survey of organisations found that while 34 per cent of organisations felt they had moved beyond the basic administrative role, only 12 per cent felt they were now playing a more strategic role.

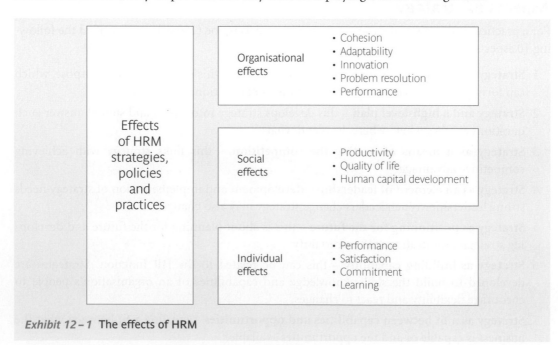

Exhibit 12 – 1 The effects of HRM

Some ways in which employers were seen as moving HR to a more strategic role were by:

- improving or upgrading HR operations
- implementing talent planning initiatives
- implementing self-service technology
- integrating companies from mergers and acquisitions
- implementing global workforce plans.

However, with more of the functions of HR being outsourced, HR managers will need to have a more strategic focus just to survive. Recently the BBC decided to move a number of its services to Capita in its quest for value for money. A BBC spokesperson argued that: 'Value for money is a big part of the reality of the BBC and rightly so . . . This deal offers substantial savings, but every bit as important is the deal that allows us to repurpose BBC people as a function that can deliver strategic advantage in years ahead.'

The BBC has decided that its strategic advantage can be achieved by outsourcing its services and this could be the reality for many organisations. Therefore, HR needs to move away from the functions and focus on a more strategic approach.

Christensen (2006) suggests a 'road map' for HR that moves from the basic HR function to specific tools for making HR more attuned to business needs. This is illustrated in Exhibit 12-2.

Christensen suggests that the HR manager should be seen as the 'organisational architect', who although she/he should be competent in the functions should also be able to develop a detailed HR plan that is linked to the business goals.

Hammonds (2006) criticises HR managers for their lack of strategic and leadership ability and, although he argues that HR has the greatest potential as a key driver for organisational change, he says that it consistently under-delivers. The problem is that many HR managers, although competent at the administrative functions, lack basic business acumen. Hammonds

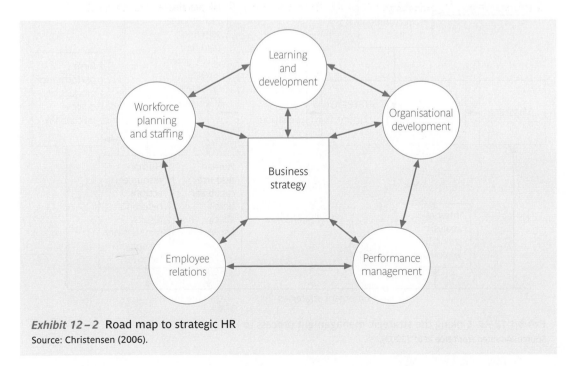

Exhibit 12–2 Road map to strategic HR
Source: Christensen (2006).

suggests that for HR managers to be strategic they need to be able to answer the following questions.

- Who is your core customer?
- What challenges do they face?
- Who is the competition?
- What do they do well?

The best HR professionals are proactive. An example is Libby Sartain at Yahoo!, who regularly liaises with senior management from other departments and makes sure that talent is always top of the agenda. Other organisations that have seen the link between people management and competitive advantage include Procter & Gamble, Goldman Sachs and General Electric. Unfortunately, there are many others that could do more. As Nelson (2006) suggests: 'Product markets and financial markets will still matter, but the centre of gravity for value creation and capture will inexorably migrate to global talent markets.' Therefore managers need to link business strategy to human resource practices.

A model of how the strategic management process can be linked to HR practices can be seen in Exhibit 12-3.

SWOT analysis
An assessment of an organisation's Strengths, Weaknesses, Opportunities and Threats.

As can be seen from Exhibit 12-3, strategy is formulated from the mission and goals of the organisation. These are the reasons for the existence of the organisation. The strategy choice is often the result of a **SWOT analysis**, which analyses the internal

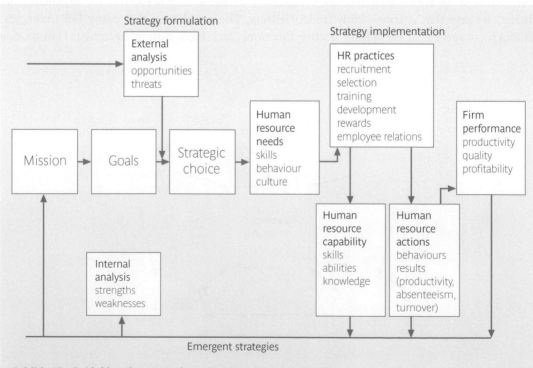

Exhibit 12–3 Linking the strategic management process to HR
Source: Adapted from Noe *et al.* (2003).

Strengths and Weaknesses of an organisation, and the external Opportunities and Threats (hence SWOT).

The HR manager needs to ensure that the human resource needs of skills, behaviours and culture are developed to enable the organisation to fulfil its objectives. In other words, the HR practices, capabilities and actions form part of the strategy implementation process and a strategic human resource manager will need to ensure that these are appropriate to enable the organisation to perform. Writers on strategic HRM suggest that there are four different approaches that can help managers become more strategic.

Perspectives of strategic human resource management

The four perspectives of strategic human resource management identified in the literature are universalist, contingent, configurational and contextual. These are illustrated in Exhibit 12-4.

The universalist perspective

This is the simplest approach to human resource management. Researchers using this model identify the best human resource practices, which according to Becker and Gerhart (1996) are characterised by their ability to:

- demonstrate a capacity to improve organisational performance
- be generalisable.

best practice
The practices that are most effective for the organisation to enable it to create a high-quality and high-productivity environment.

high-performance work systems
Systems designed to ensure that workers possess high levels of skills, competence and motivation.

As is illustrated in Exhibit 12-5, this perspective concentrates on how certain isolated HR practices are linked to organisational performance. It also may look for one **best practice** as an attempt to identify **high-performance work systems**. It does not look at the interdependence or integration of practices. Martin-Alcazar *et al.* (2005) argue that the result is that the idea of combining different patterns of practices to achieve strategic fit is ignored. This perspective tends to focus on practices that reinforce employees' abilities, recruitment and selection, comprehensive training or performance appraisal, although, according

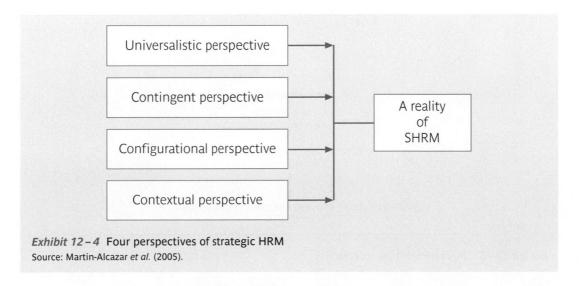

Exhibit 12 – 4 Four perspectives of strategic HRM
Source: Martin-Alcazar *et al.* (2005).

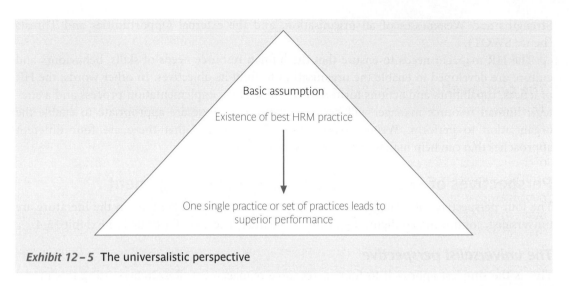

Exhibit 12 – 5 The universalistic perspective

to Youndt *et al.* (1996), there has been a recent shift towards teamwork and job redesign. The approach is based on observations of workers rather than any theoretical underpinning.

The contingency perspective

This model starts with the assumption that there is a relationship between variables in the workplace, as illustrated in Exhibit 12-6. Researchers suggest that the approach used depends very much on the context and culture of the organisation.

According to Martin-Alcazar *et al.* (2005), contingency relationships can be grouped into three generic categories:

1 strategic variables
2 organisational variables
3 external environmental factors.

Contingency models are based on two theoretical frameworks. The first is described in the work of Miles and Snow (1984) and Jackson and Schuler (1995), whose behavioural theory looks for

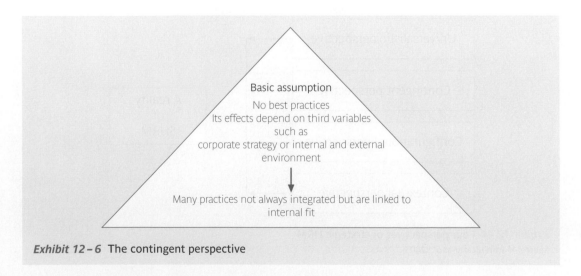

Exhibit 12 – 6 The contingent perspective

a fit between business strategy and human resource management. The second framework concentrates on the resources and capabilities of the firm, and looks for a strategic fit between people and organisational strategies (Boxall, 1998).

The configurational perspective

This perspective helps to explain how the functions of human resource management can be integrated. According to Martin-Alcazar *et al.* (2005), 'the HRM system is defined as a multidimensional set of elements that can be combined in different ways to obtain an infinite number of configurations'. This is illustrated in Exhibit 12-7.

This approach suggests that the relationship between the elements of HR and organisational performance is not linear. It suggests also that the HR function can be analysed as a complex and interactive system. It acknowledges the importance of the contingency approach but recognises that different combinations of policies and practices can help the organisation achieve its goals. To apply the configurational approach, managers need to look at the elements that build the HR system and see how they work in different combinations for the best fit to the business strategy.

The contextual perspective

The contextual approach proposes an important shift in how strategic human resource management should be analysed. It introduces a broader model, which highlights the need to look at the peculiarities of different geographical and industrial contexts. This is illustrated in Exhibit 12-8.

Brewster (1999) suggests that the concept of **strategic human resource management** (SHRM) needs to be expanded to offer a more complex explanation of how the internal functions and workings of an organisation can achieve its business goals. This model reconsiders three aspects of SHRM: the nature of human resources; the level of analysis; and the actors implied in this organisational function. It is also important to consider external environmental factors that can impact on the business environment, such as the influence of society, government and culture. According to Brewster (1999), this means that the function of HRM should no longer be the preserve of a few specialists but should be extended to all managers in the organisation.

strategic human resource management
Planned deployment of the human resource to enable an organisation to achieve its goals.

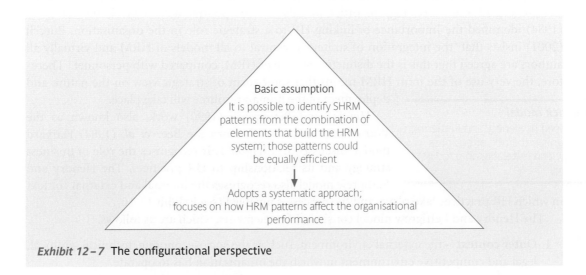

Basic assumption
It is possible to identify SHRM patterns from the combination of elements that build the HRM system; those patterns could be equally efficient

Adopts a systematic approach; focuses on how HRM patterns affect the organisational performance

Exhibit 12 – 7 The configurational perspective

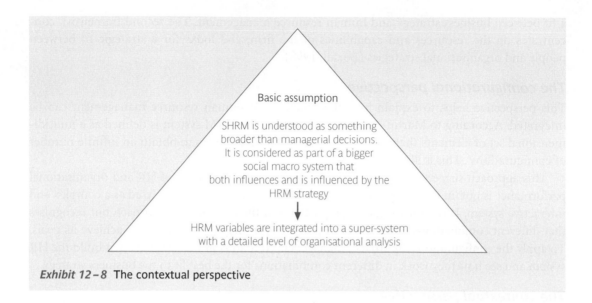

Basic assumption

SHRM is understood as something
broader than managerial decisions.
It is considered as part of a bigger
social macro system that
both influences and is influenced by the
HRM strategy

HRM variables are integrated into a super-system
with a detailed level of organisational analysis

Exhibit 12–8 The contextual perspective

The contextual approach also recognises the importance of external and internal stakeholders and that they can be influenced by strategic decisions. Therefore, all impacts of all interested parties need to be explored if the organisation is to maintain its competitive advantage.

The different perspectives of the universalistic, contingency, configurational and contextual approach do not need to be considered in isolation but can complement each other. They all have different contributions to make as well as some limitations. These are illustrated in Exhibit 12-9.

The attempt to develop strategic human resource management and link it to business strategy through the policies and practices can be seen in the development of strategic human resource management.

The development of SHRM

Strategic human resource management developed as an attempt to link HR policies and practices to organisational strategy in order to enhance competitive advantage. Fombrun *et al.* (1984) identified the importance of linking HR to a strategic role in the organisation. Purcell (2001) insists that 'the integration of strategy is central to all models of HRM and virtually all authors are agreed that this is the distinctive feature of HRM, compared with personnel.' Therefore, the very use of the term HRM means that some form of strategic view on the nature and deployment of the human resource will take place.

Warwick model
Developed by Hendry and Pettigrew, it recognises the role of business strategy and its relationship to HR practices.

Hendry and Pettigrew's (1990) work, also known as the **Warwick model**, extends from the Beer *et al.* (1984) Harvard model, discussed in Chapter 1. It recognises the role of business strategy and its relationship to HR practices. The Hendry and Pettigrew model also recognises the internal and external context in which HR practices take place, and the processes involved (see Exhibit 12-10).

The Hendry and Pettigrew model consists of five elements, which are as follows.

1 **Outer context** – the external environment, such as the socio-economic, technical, political, legal and competitive environment in which the organisation has to operate.

Universalistic	Contingent	Configurational	Contextual
Contributions	Contributions	Contributions	Contributions
• Demonstration of the importance of the human factor in organisations • Use of statistics as proof	• Consideration of third variables that mediate the relationship between HRM and performance • Strong theoretical basis	• Internal analysis of the HRM system • Consideration of synergy and interdependence among the different elements of the system • Consideration that different HRM configurations can be equally efficient	• Introduction of the social dimension of HRM • Integration of the HRM system in a macro social context • Reconsideration of manager's autonomy of decision • Large series of data
Limitations	Limitations		
• Deficient theoretical foundations • Narrow objectives • Mechanistic and rational explanations • Conceptual limitation in the establishment of causal relationships • Performance measures based exclusively on financial indicators • Does not explain strategic change • HRM considered a 'black box'	• Limited use of statistics • Excessive emphasis on 'fit' issues • No consideration of political variables • HRM considered a 'black box'	Limitations • The definition of management patterns is a simplification of reality • Limited empirical evidence	Limitations • Deficient empirical treatment • Based mainly on descriptive statistics • Based mainly on the UK approach to industrial relations

Exhibit 12 – 9 The contributions and limitations of the universalistic, contingent, configurational and contextual approach

2 **Inner context** – the internal environment of culture, organisational structure, the politics and leadership issues inside the organisation, the technology and business outputs.

3 **Business strategy content** – the organisation's objectives, the product market, and the organisational strategy and tactics that will be the practical application of the organisation's mission.

4 **HRM context** – the role and definition of HRM in the organisation, the organisation of the HR role and the HR outputs.

5 **HRM content** – this includes the HR functions of HR flows, work systems, reward systems and employee relations.

The Hendry and Pettigrew model links the external environment (outer context) and internal environment (inner context) to the business strategy and HRM context. It also links the business strategy content and HRM context to the HRM content. The model proposes that, when external and internal contexts are aligned, businesses are more likely to obtain competitive advantage.

SHRM recognises the need to have HR activities aligned with the organisational goals. This means that HR managers need to understand organisational design and to involve themselves with the organisational goals. This should help them to recognise the capabilities of their employees and develop a strategic approach to ensure that the deployment of the human resource will meet the overall company objectives.

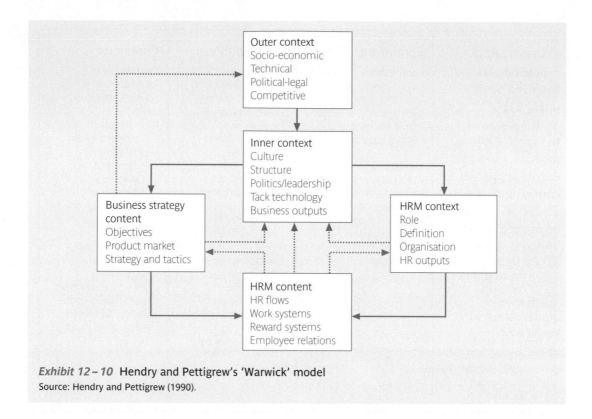

Exhibit 12–10 Hendry and Pettigrew's 'Warwick' model
Source: Hendry and Pettigrew (1990).

One of the arguments put forward is that there is very little difference between HRM and SHRM. Hendry (1994) argues that strategy is a dominant theme in HRM, but that few managers can actually identify the individual strategies. Hendry attributes much of this to a lack of understanding about the nature of strategy in general on the part of HR theorists.

A study by Rothwell *et al.* (1998) compared traditional HR with strategic HR. They argued that traditional HR managers:

■ do not have enough 'working knowledge of what business is all about or of the strategic goals of the organisations they serve'

■ lack leadership ability

■ are seen as reactive rather than proactive

■ are unable to lead in 'establishing a vision for change and garnering the support necessary to lead change'

■ are seen as following the latest fad; they 'drop them in place without taking into account the unique business objectives, corporate culture, organisation-specific politics, and individual personalities of key decision-makers found in their organisational settings'.

These are the same criticisms made against personnel management. Rothwell and colleagues view traditional HR as the same as personnel management, and set out strategic HR as the way forward.

One of the problems with HR is the lack of measurement. Managers need to know if their decisions are effective. One way of doing this is through a system of human resource accounting.

HR accounting and its impact on strategy

HR accounting has its roots in financial accounting, and attempts to measure the impact of people on organisational functions. According to Sveiby (1997), this can prove difficult, as there is a need to measure not only the tangible assets of an organisation, such as people, but also intangible ones, such as skills and knowledge.

HR accounting consists of a set of both financial and non-financial techniques, which are thought to provide a more balanced measurement of performance. One method used to measure these assets is Wyatt's 'Human Capital Index', developed as a diagnostic influence to enable organisations to measure and benchmark their HR health against that of others. The emphasis of the Human Capital Index is on the measurement of knowledge and intellectual capital, as this is thought to link to competitive advantage and improve the profitability of organisations (Toulson and Dewe, 2004).

Other tools available include those that measure economic value-added, the balanced score-card and intellectual capital. Bontis *et al.* (1999) suggest that all these approaches focus on the idea that the value-added capacity relates to the knowledge and capabilities of its people.

In practice many companies do measure their human capital but do not include it in their annual company reports, as they see this as not in keeping with accounting conventions, or because it gives away too much information (Sveiby, 1997). However, there is a movement towards reporting human capital, with some Swedish companies taking the lead and issuing a statement of their human resources in their annual reports.

According to Flamholtz (1999), HR accounting has three main roles:

1 to provide organisations with objective information about the cost and value of human resources
2 to provide a framework to guide HR decision-making
3 to motivate decision-makers to take an HR perspective.

The importance of HR accounting has increased as more employers are realising the important role that employees have in an organisation and their role in gaining competitive advantage.

Toulson and Dewe (2004) have identified some common themes that have led to some academics and practitioners changing their views. These are:

- the changing structures of organisations
- the importance of communications and the impact of technology
- the need for continuous learning and the emergence of the knowledge worker
- the rise of the notion of the importance of intangible assets and intellectual capital
- the globalisation of competition, where competing through cost is no longer enough
- the idea that sustainable growth comes from the organisation's ability to develop its people
- the changing nature of management, where managers become 'facilitators'.

According to Toulson and Dewe (2004), HR managers need to recognise the distinction between measurement as a strategic decision-making tool and an accounting tool. HRM is about measuring the value and worth of an organisation's most valuable assets and, although financial techniques can be useful, HR should not just be about costs but also be about added value.

One way of measuring performance can be through the balanced scorecard, which can be customised to each organisation.

The balanced scorecard

The balanced scorecard is a framework applied by managers that uses a range of performance indicators to measure company performance and its relationship to vision and strategy. The balanced scorecard differs from traditional measures by emphasising that critical indicators should be contingent on individual organisations' strategies, and should be customised and developed as strategies change. This means that for each organisation the scorecard would be different.

The scorecard also needs to be communicated to all employees, as this provides a framework that enables them to see the goals and strategies of an organisation, how they are measured and how they, as employees, influence critical indicators.

According to Ulrich (1997), the balanced scorecard should be used to:

- link human resource management activities to the company's business strategy
- evaluate the extent to which the HRM function is helping the organisation meet its strategic objectives.

The measures used usually relate to productivity, people and process, and are demonstrated in Exhibit 12-11.

Pfeffer (1998) suggests that using the balanced scorecard can help to build high-performance work systems. Pfeffer uses a model of the high-performance work system that includes seven key factors.

1 **Employment security** – employees will be more committed to an organisation if they know that their jobs are secure. This freedom from fear of job loss means that employees are free to focus on the long-term goals of the organisation.

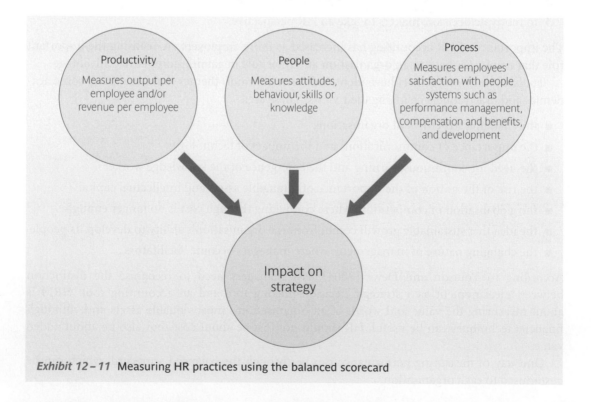

Exhibit 12–11 Measuring HR practices using the balanced scorecard

2 **Selective hiring** – HR needs to ensure that the right people are recruited to the right place at the right time. This means identifying the critical skills and ensuring employees have the required competencies.

3 **Self-managed teams and decentralised decision-making** – this advocates the move to flatter, leaner structures, where the team manages itself and is responsible for meeting organisational targets.

4 **High compensation contingent on organisational performance** – employees are rewarded for improved company performance. This can be linked to gainsharing plans, share plans or bonuses. The importance of such a system is that employees are able to see that their contribution to performance has a direct link with competitive advantage.

5 **Training** – is proactive rather than reactive. Employees are given the skills to enable flexibility and for them to compete with other organisations.

6 **Reduction of status differences** – by moving to a flatter organisational structure managers become facilitators rather than authoritative and controlling figures. This means that employees take responsibility for managing performance.

7 **Sharing information** – communication is the key in creating a high-performance work organisation. This means that there should be transparency within the organisation, with a sharing of financial information to enable employees to plan and organise their work and remove distrust.

Continuing from high-performance work systems, Richardson and Thompson (2001) suggest that the development of human resource strategies should include three main approaches as follows.

1 The 'best practice approach', which leads to improved organisational performance. This is based on Pfeffer's (1998) framework, discussed above.

2 The 'best fit approach', which is based on the belief that HRM policies and practice are contingent on the context and culture of the organisation and need to be adapted accordingly.

3 The 'configurational approach', which focuses on the need to achieve horizontal and internal fit. MacDuffie (1995) explains this by bundling HR and development practices together. This identifies which practices are interrelated and bundles them together with the idea that this will improve performance. (This will be explained in more detail later in this chapter.)

Other research, by Purcell (1999), indicates that three factors are important in the link between people and performance and, as such, HR should influence strategy at both senior and operational level. The three factors identified during the research by Purcell (1999) are as follows.

1 Most companies have a vision that is understood and accepted by everyone.

2 Companies put their idea into practice through the integration of different functional specialists and unifying measures of success, thus attempting to overcome organisational divides and rivalries.

3 Team working, where people belong to more than one team and hence share ideas and facilitate innovation, problem-solving, professional development and the transfer of tacit knowledge (CIPD, 2001).

Implementation of HR strategies

Once an organisation has made a strategic choice, this will become a part of the day-to-day workings of the organisation. The chosen strategy will have implications for the HR manager, as can be seen from Exhibit 12-12.

An organisation has several choices with regard to how to structure itself, and much of this is dependent on the product or service the organisation is offering. The success of strategy implementation is affected by variables such as the organisation's structure, task design, information systems, reward systems, and the selection, training and development of people. The HR manager has primary responsibility for the task design, reward systems, and selection, training and development of people. However, for an organisation to be successful, the HR manager should also input into the structure and information, and decision-making processes. An example of the need for strategic HR is illustrated in the 'International perspective' box.

Resource-based SHRM

resource-based

Looks beyond the industrial-based economics view of strategy and examines how organisations can sustain competitive advantage.

The **resource-based** view of HRM looks beyond the industrial-based economics view of strategy and examines how organisations can sustain competitive advantage. To become competitive Chan *et al.* (2004) suggest that organisations need to be able to 'continuously identify, upgrade, rejuvenate and reinvent valuable resources'. Organisations also need to 'create an environment in which they can be self-reinforcing and enhancing in value and strength'. It is the people who are more likely to be able to do this when the environment is changing rapidly.

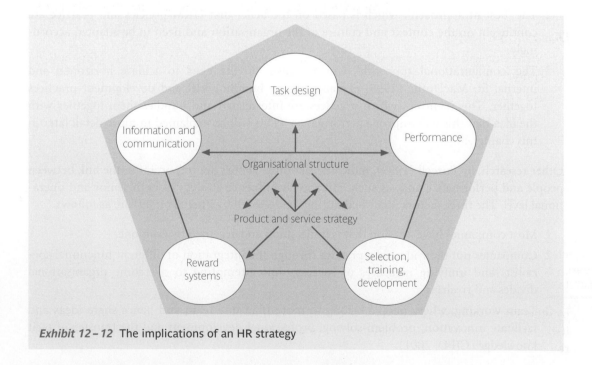

Exhibit 12 – 12 The implications of an HR strategy

Global expansion 'needs strategic HR'

Business advisers William O'Keefe, vice-president of American consultancy Caliper, and Hsu O'Keefe, university professor of international economy at Fairleigh Dickinson University, USA, told delegates in a session on human resources in China, that HR must learn about cultural differences in order to be effective.

'There are many opportunities for HR – in China,' said William O'Keefe. 'But you need to sit down and learn about the Chinese and get to know their behaviours.

'In an HR role, you need to think about the behaviours and attitudes of team members from your own company,' he said.

The O'Keefes researched differences and similarities in characteristics in China, Brazil and the USA over two years, looking for those that might affect the HR sector and business in general. For example, while Brazil and the USA scored high for levels of 'sociability', at 74 per cent and 68 per cent respectively, the Chinese were average at 45 per cent.

William O'Keefe said: 'There might be frustration in business dealings because of the different bases that exist for a business relationship in each country.'

The research also showed that the Chinese and Brazilians were not good at empathy nor at adjusting their behaviour in response to others. They both rated low at 26 per cent and 32 per cent, while the USA's score was 50 per cent. The research found that similarities could cause problems too. It discovered that common traits were high levels of urgency and working well alone.

William O'Keefe said there was great potential for chaos unless there were agreed procedures and shared goals that were frequently reaffirmed, as well as good performance management and clear guidance to keep everyone aligned.

Because of these challenges, Hsu O'Keefe said, early HR involvement was essential: 'HR must be part of the strategic team from the beginning. It can help to prepare people.'

Source: Julie Griffiths, The World Federation of Personnel Management Associations' 10th World HR Congress in Rio de Janeiro, 2 September 2004, p. 13.

Discussion questions

1 What strategic decisions would an HR manager need to make when operating in another country?

2 How can the HR manager prepare people to be part of the organisation's strategy?

international perspective

According to Youndt *et al.* (1996):

> Numerous researchers have recently noted that people may be the ultimate source of sustained advantage since traditional sources related to market, financial capital, and scale economies have been weakened by globalisation and other economic changes.

competitive advantage
A means of gaining or maintaining market share in industry.

Barney (1991) also takes the view that, to sustain **competitive advantage**, an organisation needs a superior resource. The resource-based view is that a superior resource needs to be valuable, rare and difficult to imitate, so that it cannot be reproduced by other organisations. However, the organisation also needs the ability to change and reinvent itself rapidly. One of the key resources of organisations that are able to do this are human resources.

high-performance HR system
A work system that maximises the fit between the organisation's social systems and technical system.

Guest *et al.* (2004) argue that a **high-performance HR system** 'should be designed to ensure that workers possess high skills and competence, a high level of motivation and the opportunity to contribute discretionary effort'. Research by Guest *et al.* (2004) suggests that 'bundles' of HR practices can enhance job performance and employee satisfaction. Although Guest *et al.* recognise that their research was limited, they propose that priority should be given to the follow practices:

- team working
- job design
- training and development
- performance appraisal
- employee involvement
- equal opportunity
- information provision.

This is probably not such a surprise to HR professionals. In fact, previous research by MacDuffie (1995) found that organisations that produced both high productivity and high quality used 'HRM best practices', with the emphasis placed on recruitment and selection, reward tied to performance, low levels of status differentiation, high levels of training throughout the organisation, and employee participation through team working and problem-solving groups. Huselid (1995) also identified higher levels of productivity from organisations with systems in place that included selection, testing, training, appropriate pay structures, employee participation and information sharing.

Stop and reflect

How strategic are you?
Look at the questions that follow and, for each one, circle the number you feel relates to you the most: 1 = not at all, 2 = not really, 3 = sometimes, 4 = mostly, 5 = definitely.

1 Do you have a vision of where you want to be in five years' time?		1 2 3 4 5
2 Have you a plan to help you achieve your vision?		1 2 3 4 5
3 Is your plan achievable?		1 2 3 4 5
4 Have you the resources to implement your plan?		1 2 3 4 5
5 Have you communicated your plan to the people who can support you?		1 2 3 4 5
6 Do you ask for feedback to improve your performance?		1 2 3 4 5
7 Do you act on the feedback to improve your performance?		1 2 3 4 5
8 Do you re-evaluate your goals and check on progress?		1 2 3 4 5
9 Do you have alternative courses of action, if problems arise?		1 2 3 4 5
10 Do you add to your skills to improve your competitive advantage?		1 2 3 4 5

Add the numbers together. The higher the result the more strategic you are likely to be.

Creating competitive advantage

Most companies want to be competitive as this means that they will be able to either maintain or gain market share in their industry. Even non-profitmaking organisations such as charities need to be concerned with competitiveness, as they need to maintain market share when they are raising funds.

Competitiveness and company effectiveness often go hand in hand. If an organisation satisfies its stakeholders then it can be seen as being effective. These stakeholders are not just the investors, who want a return on their money, they are also the customers and employees. If customers are not satisfied then they will go elsewhere and if employees are not satisfied they will not perform well and are also likely to leave. Organisations that are unable to meet their stakeholders' needs are unlikely to have competitive advantage over other organisations wanting the same market share.

The need to think strategically is in line with today's business thinking. To create or maintain competitive advantage an organisation needs to link strategy to the functions of HR. Effective HR practices support the organisation's goals and objectives. In other words, effective HRM practices are strategic. Delaney and Huselid (1996) suggest that effective HRM can enhance an organisation's performance by adding to employee and customer satisfaction, innovation and development.

The challenge for the HR manager is to link the strategic direction of an organisation with the day-to-day functions. Ulrich (1998) identifies the activities of HR as 'people versus process'. However, the HR functions can be linked to strategy, as is demonstrated in Exhibit 12-13.

Ulrich (1998) demonstrates that the roles involved in the management of strategic human resources, the management of the firm's infrastructure, the management of transformation and change, and the management of employee contribution need to be considered along with the functions of HR.

However, Halcrow (1988) provided the following questions for an organisation to ask itself to determine if HRM is playing a strategic role in the organisation.

1 What is HR doing to provide value-added services to internal clients?

2 What can the HR department add to the bottom line?

Exhibit 12–13 HR functions and strategy

Source: Ulrich (1998: 24). Reprinted by permission of Harvard Business School Press from *Human Resource Champions* by D. Ulrich. Boston, MA 1998, p. 24. Copyright © 1998 by the Harvard Business School Publishing Corporation, all rights reserved.

3 How are you measuring the effectiveness of HR?

4 How can we reinvest in employees?

5 What HR strategy will we use to get the business from point A to point B?

6 What makes an employee want to stay at our company?

7 How are we going to invest in HR so we have a better HR department than our competitors?

8 From an HR perspective, what should we be doing to improve our marketplace position?

9 What's the best change we can make to prepare for the future?

To maintain competitive advantage, HR managers should consider the above questions otherwise it is unlikely that the organisation will have the ability to deal with maintaining its current position, let alone gaining competitive advantage. This would also help with the implementation of high-performance work systems. It should also be remembered that, in order to maintain competitive advantage, employees cannot be ignored. As the EU expands so the workforce may become more diverse. This is illustrated in the 'Managing diversity' box.

managing diversity

What are the implications for HR with the expansion of the EU?

Nick Isles, an associate director of The Work Foundation, takes a look at accession and migration in the expanded European Union and what it means for the HR department.

On 1 May 2004, 10 new countries joined the European Union. These countries – Poland, Malta, Cyprus, Czech Republic, Estonia, Hungary, Latvia, Lithuania, Slovakia and Slovenia – have added 75 million people to the EU population, bringing it up to 450 million. The EU is now the world's third-largest labour market after India and China.

Never in European history have so many been bound by common conditions of peace, democracy and the rule of law. In short, 1 May was a momentous day deserving of celebration. Yet, far from celebrating the accession of these countries, the debate in western Europe has been dominated by one subject: mass migration.

For many people, including many in the HR profession, the spectre of mass economic migration from accession countries to the West is a fearful prospect. To allay such fears, many western EU countries have implemented strict controls over migration from the accession countries for the first two years following accession. After that, the rules will be reviewed and extended for up to five more years.

In the case of the UK, having first decided to keep borders open, the government belatedly introduced a registration scheme, whereby individuals from all the accession countries, except for Malta and Cyprus, will have to pay £50 for a Home Office certificate confirming their eligibility to work in the country. This will lapse if they lose their job within the first year of work, and if they find a new job they will need to renew their registration. After 12 months of continuous employment, such individuals will be able to work in the UK without any restrictions, and access job-seeker benefits if they become unemployed.

However, many of the migrants most likely to move to find work are already here. In 1998, there were 900,000 citizens of central and eastern European countries living and working in the 15 EU states. It is therefore arguable that much of the expected economic migration has already occurred.

Demographics plays a part. Both the existing 15 EU countries and the accession countries share similar demographic profiles. In fact, the accession countries have lower fertility levels and higher death rates, creating even more opportunities for the more highly educated and the highly skilled in particular to find good jobs in the countries of their birth.

The transfer of resources for economic development, increased trade and inward investment flows have all accompanied accession. As happened with Spain, Ireland and, to a lesser extent, Portugal and Greece, accession to the EU is making 'catch up' economic development speed up considerably.

There is little evidence to show that existing citizens of countries in the EU have been on the move, migrating away from their countries of origin. For example, Portugal is welcoming back a net figure of around 13,000 nationals each year. We have not seen mass migration from Madrid to Manchester, or from Lisbon to Liverpool.

For those who do make the journey to the UK, what are the implications for HR professionals? Will these new migrants make good workers? It is important to split such migrants into two broad groups: the highly skilled and the rest. All the existing economic evidence shows that people tend to move to places where sectors are offering jobs that match their existing skills. With 500,000 job vacancies at any one time and employment reaching record levels of more than 28.3 million people in work, the government and employers would welcome a new influx of relevant skilled workers. For the UK to continue moving up the productivity ladder, it needs to train and attract the brightest and the smartest. Low-value, low-productivity industries and jobs are yesterday's story.

For example, construction workers are in relatively short supply with the recent return of so much Irish labour to Ireland. The government's proposed housing expansion in the south east and other parts of the country will provide a magnet for low-skilled workers from eastern Europe and elsewhere, and the employers among the construction industry keen to employ them. And London's service sector already enjoys the labour of many eastern Europeans, whether it be waiting at tables or offering affordable childcare to the capital's dual-income households.

However, in preparing for job enquiries from workers from the accession countries or in setting up operations in accession countries, HR professionals need to be aware of several broad requirements.

Rules for employment

The first is registration of accession country workers. It is the responsibility of the HR professional to make sure the person they hire registers within a month of taking up the job. Successful registration needs to be kept on file. Failure to register and monitor will result in a £5000 fine.

HR responsibilities

- To ensure that any workers that are hired are registered within one month of taking up the job. HR must check and make copies of passports, work permits, birth certificates, certificates of naturalisation or registration certificates.

- A more diverse workforce will require the development and adoption of inclusion strategies.

■ Ensure compliance with EU directives including those on Works Councils, data protection and working time.

■ Be aware of the EU Services Directive, due to be operational in 2007, which will make it easier for service businesses to set up throughout the expanded EU.

The new Europe is an exciting place: bigger, more diverse, with more opportunities for UK business to expand east and recruit to the west. That will be good for these countries, and it will be good for us.

Source: Nick Isles, *Personnel Today*, 4 May 2004, at PersonnelToday.com.

Discussion questions

1 What impact could the expansion of the EU have on the diversity strategy of an organisation?

2 How will the HR functions need to be developed to ensure that they comply with EU directives?

High-performance work systems

High-performance work systems (HPWS) are the result of the linking of HR strategy and business performance. Applebaum *et al.* (2000) and Batt (2000) popularised the term HPWS and, according to these authors, HPWS involve work systems and employment models that include a mix of key practices such as rigorous selection and better training systems to increase ability levels. They also encourage comprehensive incentives such as employee bonuses and internal career ladders to encourage motivation and participation with the use of self-managed teams and quality circles.

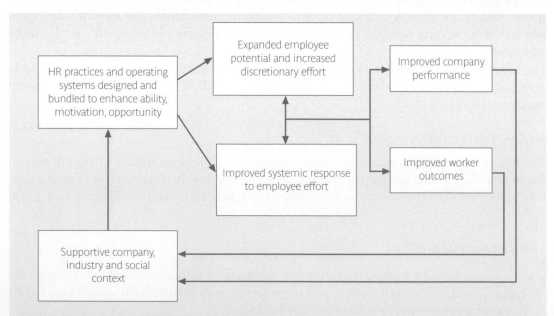

Exhibit 12 – 14 High-performance work systems

Source: Boxall and Purcell (2003), *Strategy and Human Resource Management*, Palgrave Macmillan. Reproduced with permission of Palgrave Macmillan.

Boxall (2003) suggests that frameworks help to identify the nature of the links between competitive strategies and HR strategies, and argues that organisations may have several different segments and strategic groups depending on which particular customers' needs they are seeking to meet. He suggests the use of benchmarks to enable a comparison to be made in similar industry sectors. Research into different industries has identified different strategies in the same industries, depending on which market the organisation is aiming at. For example, Batt (2000) identified that within low-end call centres where cold calling was used, for example, to sell double glazing, the strategies used focused on control, with set scripts, and so on. At the high-end call centres, employee interactions relied more on skill and discretion. This meant that at the low-end call centres employees were expected to deal with far more calls than at the high end.

Batt (2000) makes the following comments about the differences in the contours of HR strategy across the different market segments of the telecommunications industry:

> Implementation of high involvement work practices varies systematically, according to the demand characteristics of the customer segment served, with the use of these systems more likely in higher value-added markets. Work practices that correlate with customer segment include the type of interaction with the customer; the extent to which technology is used as a control device versus a resource input; the skill requirements of jobs; discretion to influence work methods and procedures; and types and levels of compensation.
>
> (Batt, 2000: 555)

The same type of differentiation strategies have been found in other industries and have been developed into a typology by Herzenberg et al. (1998) and summarised by Boxall (2003). These are shown in Exhibit 12-15.

The framework, shown in Exhibit 12-15 demonstrates that at one end of the scale work is controlled by managers and involves little or no discretion by employees, while at the other end employees have a high degree of flexibility with regard to the performance of work tasks. In the middle are labour-intensive, less skilled jobs lacking management systems, and semi-autonomous jobs that do not allow for a high amount of employee discretion yet are moderately supervised.

Another typology can be seen in Exhibit 12-16. This links back to strategic management and Porter (1985), discussed earlier in this chapter.

Boxall (2003) argues that differentiation does not necessarily lead to sustained competitive advantage. In his typology (see Exhibit 12-16) he suggests that Quadrant C represents the standard picture of perfect competition suggested by economists. Organisations will tend to pay the market wage and are unlikely to exceed it, as pay is a significant cost that could affect the organisation's profitability.

Quadrant A suggests that organisations that identify new markets or are innovative enjoy increased profits but, as others jump on the bandwagon, profits fall back to Quadrant C.

Quadrant B describes an organisation with resource-based advantage, which is either protected or hard to imitate. An example would be the Royal Mail before changes in the law to allow competing companies to deliver mail.

Quadrant D identifies organisations with niche markets but without superior performance.

Boxall (2003) argues that, for an HR strategy to lead to high-performance work systems, it is important for organisations to identify the correct mix of HR practices. In doing so, this will enable improved performance and competitive advantage; however, these will differ not only in different industries but also within the different market segments for each industry.

Work systems	Tightly constrained	Unrationalised, labour intensive	Semi-autonomous	High skill autonomous
Examples	Telephone operators, fast-food workers, cheque proofers	Some nurse's aides, domestics, long-distance truck drivers, childcare workers, clerical home workers	Clerical and administrative jobs with relatively broad responsibilities, low-level managers some sales workers, delivery drivers	Physicians, high-level managers, laboratory technicians, electricians, engineers
Markets served	High volume, low cost; standardised quality	Low cost, high volume; often low or uneven quality	Volume and quality vary	Low volume (each job may differ); quality is often in the eye of the beholder
Task supervision	Tight	Loose	Moderate	Little
Formal education of workers	Low to moderate	Low to moderate (skill often unrecognised)	Moderate	High
On-the-job training	Limited	Some informal, unrecognised learning from other workers	Limited to moderate	Substantial

Exhibit 12 – 15 A typology of work systems
Source: Abridged from Herzenberg *et al.* (1998) in Boxall (2003).

Identifying bundles of HR practices

MacDuffie (1995) suggested that a combination of HR practices could be integrated to form a 'bundle' in order to generate a high-commitment, high-performance work organisation. To MacDuffie, an HR bundle is the equivalent of an HR system, and the key to improved performance is linking the system to other systems to fit what he calls the 'organisational logic'.

MacDuffie argues that, in order to succeed, bundles of HR practices need to be consistent with bundles of organisational practices, and these need to provide the 'best fit' for the organisation.

MacDuffie suggests that: 'It is the combination of practices in a bundle, rather than individual practices, that shapes the pattern of interactions between and among managers and employees' (1995: 200).

The implications for managers are that HR practices work better when bundled together, and managers need to identify the various HR practices and understand how these link to organisational practices, while also recognising the importance of variables that can affect competitive advantage.

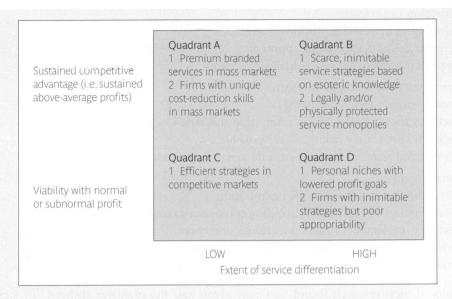

Exhibit 12–16 A typology of competitive strategies and business outcomes in services
Source: Boxall (2003) 'Human Resource Strategy and competitive advantage in the service sector', *Human Resource Management Journal* 13(3), p. 11. Reproduced with permission of Blackwell Publishing.

Guest *et al.* (2004) argue that, although MacDuffie clearly identifies a bundle as an HR system with how this links to flexible production and a distinctive work system, which in turn leads to a high-commitment HR system, the measurements he uses are limited and therefore, Guest *et al.* argue, it is unclear what should or should not be included in a system and the best practice for identifying and measuring such bundles.

MacDuffie (1995) does, however, suggest three methods of identifying and measuring bundles once they have been identified in organisations.

1 **A measure of reliability** – which tests that the measurements are consistent with one another and therefore can be seen to be reliable.

2 **A factor analysis** – which identifies the different factors that make up a bundle, such as the development of skills, abilities or practices of motivation.

3 **A cluster analysis** – this starts at the organisational level and clusters organisations on the basis of a set of variables, such as HR practices.

Guest *et al.* (2004) suggest using a statistical method known as a sequential tree analysis to overcome the problems of how to identify and measure bundles or systems of HR practices.

The use of a tree analysis helps to reveal the interrelationships between variables so that hierarchical patterns are identified, which reflect the use of different HR practices. This means that a direct link can be seen with the use of an HR practice and performance.

To identify which practices were most likely to link to high performance, Guest *et al.* (2004) measured 14 HR practices, which they divided into the four areas described below (Guest *et al.*, 2004: 85).

■ Competence of the workforce:
 – use of psychometric tests in selection
 – extensive opportunities to update skills through training and development.

- Motivation to perform:
  - employees involved in workplace decisions
  - regular use of performance appraisal
  - part of pay related to individual performance.

- Opportunity to participate/perform:
  - keeps employee well informed
  - actively tries to make jobs as interesting and varied as possible
  - actively uses team working where possible
  - conducted a company-wide attitude survey in the past two years.

- Commitment:
  - try to fill vacancies within the organisation
  - stated policy of deliberately avoiding compulsory redundancies
  - actively implements equal opportunities practices
  - has a range of family-friendly practices in place
  - has a Work Council or consultative process is place.

The results of their research found that only about half the practices showed any significant effect. Therefore, the other practices may not be important for improved performance but may well be necessary to comply with legislation or for administrative reasons. The practices that had the most impact on performance were those that enhanced competence, encouraged motivation and promoted employee contribution. Therefore, Guest *et al.* (2004) suggest that priority should be given to team working, job design, training and development, performance appraisal, employee involvement, equal opportunity, and communication systems.

Summary

- Strategic management originated in the USA in the 1960s and develops the idea that strategy formulation is an important role for managers.

- Strategic management has been criticised as being too concerned with economic goals and ignoring the sociological and psychological aspects of work.

- Strategic HRM attempts to link HR strategy to organisational strategy and is seen as a means of enhancing competitive advantage.

- There are four different perspectives of SHRM, which can complement each other.

- The Hendry and Pettigrew model recognises the role of business strategy and its relationship to HR practices. The model proposes that, when the external and internal contexts of business are aligned, businesses are more likely to obtain competitive advantage.

- Resource-based HRM looks beyond the industrial economics view of strategy and suggests that, for an organisation to sustain competitive advantage, it needs a superior resource.

- To create competitive advantage the HR manager needs to link strategy to the HR functions. Ulrich (1998) demonstrates how these links can be forged.

- High-performance work systems link HR strategy and business performance. This involves a mix of development practices to increase ability levels.

Personal development

1 **Understand the principles of strategic thinking.** When you start out in your career you may have a view of where you want to be in five or ten years' time. What type of strategy do you need to develop to achieve your goals? What resources do you have that you can utilise (this could be time, money, education etc.)? What is your plan and how will you evaluate it?

2 **Understand the role of strategy in HRM.** If you work for an organisation, can you identify its strategy? How has it linked it to the people? Even small organisations may have a people strategy, although it is unlikely to be written down.

3 **Recognise the implications of resource-based HRM.** Can you identify any organisations that use a resource-based approach to HRM? How do they develop their people to become a superior resource? As a result, is the workforce more productive and more motivated?

4 **Focus on your own sources of competitive advantage.** What can you offer that other people may not be able to? Can you build on your strengths and reduce your weaknesses? Strengthen your sources of competitive advantage through self-reflection and self-appraisal.

5 **Develop high-performance work systems.** Can you identify organisations that may adopt such practices? Would you like to be part of such an organisation? What type of motivational practices would you expect from such an organisation?

❓ Discussion questions

1 What does the word strategy mean for an organisation?

2 How can a SWOT analysis be used in the HR department to enable it to become more strategic?

3 Why do you think non-HR line managers are becoming more involved in developing and implementing HRM practices?

4 Explain why HRM should become more strategic, or why not.

5 How can an HR manager develop the skills to become more strategic?

6 How does the Macmillan and Tampoe (2000) view of the application of strategy fit in with the functions of HR?

7 According to Hendry and Pettigrew (1990), HR managers need to develop a strategic approach to ensure the human resource meets overall company objectives. How can an HR manager do this?

8 How can an HR manager implement resource-based HRM?

9 Discuss how effective HRM can lead to competitive advantage.

10 Are high-performance work systems just another method of getting more from employees? Explain your answer.

🔒 Key concepts

strategy, *p. 402*

strategic choices, *p. 403*

strategic management, *p. 403*

generic strategy, *p. 404*

SWOT analysis, *p. 406*

best practice, *p. 407*

high-performance work systems, *p. 407*

strategic human resource management, *p. 409*

Warwick model, *p. 410*

resource-based, *p. 416*

competitive advantage, *p. 417*

high-performance HR system, *p. 418*

Individual task

Purpose More and more jobs in HR require strategic thinking. Below is an example of an actual job advertisement. You think you have the necessary skills for the job but need to demonstrate the ability to act strategically.

Time 40 minutes

> A leading financial services organisation requires an interim senior business partner. The position has the scope to become permanent. You will work closely with the HR director in implementing HR strategy into business through a team of HR managers and client groups. You will have a firm understanding of all HR issues, including grievance and disciplinary, compensation and benefits, and systems.
>
> You will be an accomplished professional with a breadth of experience gained from across a range of industry sectors. You will also have proven experience in delivery of a comprehensive HR service within a complex, matrix management organisation.

Procedure As an experienced HR practitioner, who is now looking for a promotion, you have decided to apply for the job. Your CV is prepared but you have to write a personal statement demonstrating your ability to think and act strategically.

Prepare a response to the advert, which you could include with your application.

Team task

Planning a strategy

Purpose This exercise enables teams to develop skills for strategic thinking in an HR environment, and link it to HR practice.

Time 40 minutes

Procedure The following SWOT analysis has been carried out by external consultants on your organisation, the well-known fast-food chain Gut Busters. Summaries of the findings can be found below.

Strengths	Weaknesses
High gross profit margins on food	High staff turnover
Central locations	Shortage of trained staff
Well-known brand	Poor management practices
Established products	Poor attendance record
	Stock losses
	Customer dissatisfaction

Opportunities	Threats
Large potential labour pool	Industrial action by staff
More people eating out	Employment tribunals
Expansion of opening hours	Customer defection due to poor service
Competitive pricing	Increased competition

Divide into teams of eight.

You are the senior executive team of Gut Busters and, looking at the SWOT analysis, have realised that you need to develop a more strategic approach to your management of people. In the past the HR department has dealt mainly with contracts of employment and payroll issues. It has not involved itself in the development of staff; as the labour pool has been plentiful and as the majority of staff are part-time students, training has been minimal. The lack of staff development and general poor morale are now affecting the business.

Develop a strategy to link the HR function to maintaining competitive advantage.

In your group you may like to each choose a different role, such as HR director, finance director, marketing director, training manager. Think about how strategy can be different depending on your role in the organisation.

Debriefing Report the outcome of your discussion to the rest of the class. How do the strategies compare?

Case study: **British Airways under fire**

Another bank holiday and another threatened strike from the workers at BA. This time 10,000 baggage handlers, check-in and ground staff threatened strike action over the imposition of a new absence policy.

In this competitive world it seems that no one has told the management and staff at BA that they are no longer a nationalised industry and now need to compete in the real world. But someone must have known they were privatised, as who was it that had the strategic vision to introduce new working practices? It must have come from somewhere.

BA has every right to bring about efficient working practices – other airlines have. It seems, though, that it is how it is going about it that is the problem. BA has had its nose put out of joint on several occasions over the last few years. Virgin took it to court over uncompetitive trading practices, then the budget airlines sprang up and BA had to compete with the likes of easyJet and Ryanair. This it did with the introduction of GO, which it sold to easyJet after criticism of subsidising the airline. Then September 11th stopped America and many other parts of the world travelling, and the following Gulf War also had an impact on trade. However, it is not the only airline in such circumstances.

Change was definitely needed, but maybe the planning and implementation of the cost-cutting measures should have been considered as part of strategy implementation. Changes to work practices are nearly always difficult and dangerous to negotiate. If changes introduced involve the introduction of 'time cards' or other measures, then it tends to indicate that poor management may have been an issue anyway as, if staff had been monitored, poor timekeeping and attendance problems could have been resolved. Managers responsible for the implementation of new working practices should have factored into the strategy from the start that a change in working practice could cause problems for industrial relations.

Instead what has happened is that BA management has given its workers the upper hand, forced unions into a win–lose situation, lost more money than could be recovered from the efficiencies of a time-card system and wrecked its public image, which has meant that all the money spent on PR and advertising in the last year is now down the drain. Not only that, it has probably also endangered its future and, sadly, cost jobs.

In the end the strike was averted, but this was not the end of the problem: planes were still cancelled and flights delayed, this time due to poor workforce planning.

A spokesperson for the Transport and General Workers Union (TGWU) put forward the view that 'BA will have to consider its staffing levels and ask itself how it wasn't able to plan for one of the busiest times of the year. Our view at the union is that staffing levels are too low.'

BA has denied that it has cut staff. Instead it blames high staff turnover, lack of new recruits and delays in gaining staff security clearances. It does seem that there is a complete lack of vision and leadership at the top. What is Rod Eddington, BA Chief Executive, doing? There is obviously a failure to grasp the basics of industrial relations, and with a cut in 900 routes just announced in the media, 'the world's favourite airline' may soon be in the past tense.

Source: www.gategourmet.com, www.bbc.co.uk, www.unison.org.uk.

Discussion questions

1 Comment on the strategic approach taken by BA.

2 How would you link a cost-cutting strategy to people management?

3 How could a SWOT analysis help the organisation to develop a strategy?

4 Looking at the example from BA, how could changes in working practices have been implemented without staff shortages and threats of strike action?

WWW exercise

The John Lewis Partnership is a retailer that believes in sharing its success with its partners, which is the name it uses for its employees. The principles of the organisation can be found on its website at www.johnlewis.com. Follow the links at the bottom of the web page to 'corporate information'.

1 How are the principles of the John Lewis Partnership demonstrated in its people management?

2 How does it link people development to its business strategy?

3 If you were to apply for a career with John Lewis, how would you expect it to develop in five years? Ten years?

LEARNING CHECKLIST

Before moving on to the next chapter, check that you are able to:

☑ understand the development of strategic management

☑ understand the role of strategy in human resource management

☑ evaluate the models of strategic management and strategic human resource management

☑ recognise the importance of SHRM in gaining competitive advantage.

Further reading

Ansoff, K.R. (1965/1987) *Corporate Strategy* (rev. edn). London: Penguin (first published by McGraw-Hill, 1965).

Chandler, A.D. (1962) *Strategy and Structure*. Cambridge, Mass.: MIT Press.

Drucker, P. (1955) *The Practice of Management*. Oxford: Butterworth Heinemann.

Guest, D. and King, Z. (2004) 'Power, innovation and problem solving: the personnel manager's three steps to heaven?', *Journal of Management Studies* 41(3), May, p. 401.

Miles, R.E. and Snow, C.C. (1978) *Organizational Strategy, Structure and Process*. New York: McGraw-Hill.

References

Applebaum, E., Bailey, T. and Berg, P. (2000) *Manufacturing Advantage: Why High Performance Systems Pay Off*. Ithaca: ILR Press.

Barney, J. (1991) 'Firm resources and sustained competitive advantage', *Journal of Management* 17(1), pp. 99–120.

Batt, R. (2000) 'Strategic segmentation in front-line services: matching customers, employees and human resource systems', *International Journal of Human Resource Management* 11(3), pp. 540–561.

Becker, B.E. and Gerhart, B. (1996) 'The impact of human resource management on organizational performance: progress and prospects', *Academy of Management Journal* 39(4), pp. 779–801.

Beer, M., Spector, B.A., Lawrence, P.R., Mills, Q. and Walton, R.E. (1984) *Managing Human Assets*. New York: Free Press.

Bontis, N., Dragonetti, N.C., Jacobsen, K. and Roos, G. (1999) 'The knowledge toolbox: a review of tools available to measure and manage intangible resources', *European Management Journal* 17(4), pp. 391–401.

Boxall, P. (1998) 'Achieving competitive advantage through human resource strategy: towards a theory of industry dynamics', *Human Resource Management Review* 8(3), pp. 265–288.

Boxall, P. (2003) 'HR strategy and competitive advantage in the service sector', *Human Resource Management Journal* 13(3).

Boxall, P. and Purcell, J. (2003) *Strategy and Human Resource Management*. Basingstoke and New York: Palgrave Macmillan.

Brewster, C. (1999) 'SHRM: the value of different paradigms', *Management International Review* 20(6), pp. 4–11.

Chan, L.L.M., Shaffer, M.A. and Snape, E. (2004) 'In search of sustained competitive advantage: the impact of organizational culture, competitive strategy and human resource management practices on firm performance', *International Journal of Human Resource Management* 15(1), February, pp. 17–35.

Christensen, R. (2006) *Roadmap to Strategic HR*. AMACOM.

CIPD (2001) *The Case for Good People Management: A Summary of Research*. London: Chartered Institute of Personnel and Development.

Delaney, J.T. and Huselid, M.A. (1996) 'The impact of human resource management practices on perceptions of organizational performance', *Academy of Management Journal* 39, pp. 949–969.

Flamholtz, E.G. (1999) *Human Resource Accounting: Advances in Concepts, Methods and Applications*. Boston: Kluwer Academic Publishers.

Fombrun, C.J., Tichy, N.M. and Devanna, M.A. (1984) *Strategic Human Resource Management.* New York: John Wiley & Sons.

Guest, D., Conway, N. and Dewe, P. (2004) 'Using sequential tree analysis to search for "bundles" of HR practices', *Human Resource Management Journal* 14(1), pp. 79–96.

Halcrow, A. (1988) 'Survey shows HR in transition', *Workforce*, June, p. 74.

Hammonds, K.H. (2006) 'HR "is still not strategic enough"', *People Management*, 23 March, p. 13.

Hendry, C. (1994) 'The single European market and the HRM response', in P.S. Kirkbride (ed.) *Human Resource Management: Perspectives for the 1990s.* London: Routledge.

Hendry, C. and Pettigrew, A. (1990) 'Human resource management: an agenda for the 1990s', *International Journal of Human Resource Management* 1(1), pp. 17–43.

Herzenberg, S., Alic, J. and Wial, H. (1998) *New Rules for a New Economy: Employment and Opportunity in Postindustrial America.* Ithaca: ILR Press.

Huselid, M. (1995) 'The impact of human resource management practices on turnover, productivity and corporate financial performance', *Academy of Management Journal* 38, pp. 635–672.

Jackson, S.E. and Schuler, R.S. (1995) 'Understanding human resource management in the context of organisations and their environments', *Annual Review of Psychology* 46, pp. 237–264.

MacDuffie, J.P. (1995) 'Human resource bundles and manufacturing performance: organizational logic and flexible systems in the world auto industry', *Industrial Labour Relations Review* 48(2), pp. 197–221.

Macmillan, H. and Tampoe, M. (2000) *Strategic Management.* Oxford: Oxford University Press.

Martin-Alcazar, F., Rumero-Fernadez, P.M. and Sanchez-Gardey, G. (2005) 'Strategic human resource management: integrating the universalistic, contingent, configurational and contextual perspectives', *International Journal of Human Resource Management* 16(5), pp. 633–659.

Miles, R.E, and Snow, C.C. (1984) 'Designing strategic human resource systems', *Organisational Dynamics*, Summer, pp. 26–52.

Mintzberg, H. (1989) *Mintzberg on Management.* New York: Free Press.

Mintzberg, H. (1994) *The Rise and Fall of Strategic Planning.* London: Prentice Hall.

Nelson, J. (2006) 'Contours for a new business strategy', *New Zealand Management*, February, p. 48.

Noe, R., Hollenbeck, J., Gerhart, B. and Wright, P. (2003) *Human Resource Management – Gaining a Competitive Advantage* (4th edn). McGraw-Hill Irwin.

Pfeffer, J. (1998) *The Human Equation: Building Profits by Putting People First.* Boston, Mass.: Harvard Business School Press.

Porter, M. (1985) *Competitive Advantage: Creating and Sustaining Superior Performance.* New York: Free Press.

Purcell, J. (1999) 'Best practice and best fit: chimera or cul de sac?', *Human Resource Management Journal* 9(3), pp. 26–41.

Purcell, J. (2001) *Human Resource Management: A Critical Text.* London: Routledge.

Richardson, R. and Thompson, M. (2001) *The Impact of People Management Practices on Business Performance: A Literature Review.* London: Institute of Personnel Development.

Rothwell, W.J., Prescott, R.K. and Taylor, M.W. (1998) *The Strategic Human Resource Leader: How to Prepare Your Organization for Six Key Trends Shaping The Future.* Palo Alto, CA: Davies-Black Publications.

Sveiby, K.E. (1997) *The New Organizational Wealth: Managing and Measuring Knowledge Based Assets.* San Francisco: Berrett-Koeler Publishers, Inc.

Toulson, P.K. and Dewe, P. (2004) 'HR accounting as a measurement tool', *Human Resource Management Journal* 14(2).

Ulrich, D. (1997) *Measuring Human Resources: An Overview of Practice and a Prescription.* Boston, Mass.: Harvard Business School Press.

Ulrich, D. (1998) *Human Resource Champions.* Boston, Mass.: Harvard Business School Press.

Youndt, M.A., Snell, S.A. Jr, Dean, J.W. and Lepak, D.P. (1996) 'Human resource management, manufacturing strategy, and firm performance', *Academy of Management Journal* 39(4), pp. 836–866.

13

Current issues and new developments

Michael Flagg

LEARNING OUTCOMES

After studying this chapter, you should be able to:

- ☑ **understand** the changing nature of work
- ☑ **recognise** the impact of globalisation on all organisations
- ☑ **be aware of** the reasons for outsourcing both facilities and expertise
- ☑ **understand** the implications of relocating personnel according to HRM requirements
- ☑ **acknowledge** the consequences of change involving downsizing and mergers
- ☑ **recognise** the impact of technological innovation and virtual organisations.

The opening vignette illustrates how a traditional City of London organisation can develop practices to improve work/life balance.

Flexible working at Cushman and Wakefield, Healey and Baker

Cushman and Wakefield, Healey and Baker is an international real estate firm operating in the City of London, where many City institutions would in the past have frowned upon flexible working. Below are examples of how two members of staff were able to maintain a better work/life balance.

In order to combine her career with her private-life responsibilities, Sue Stephens, partner at Cushman and Wakefield, Healey and Baker, has been working reduced hours since becoming a mum in 2000.

▶ 'The firm had very little experience of its professional employees/partners wanting to work part-time or indeed flexible hours in 2000. However, it was not only receptive to the concept, the firm was very positive in making it work for both me, clients and my colleagues. I work four days per week, Monday through to Thursday, with three being based in the London office and one working from home.

'Working part-time has helped enormously. Commuting into the London office takes me over an hour each way, so having to do that only three days a week is not so arduous and tiring. Combining work and motherhood is hard work, and anything that supports me is beneficial. I have an office at home and I am fully wired up with a separate telephone and fax line and a computer, which links into the office network. This has proved to be essential. It also means I can work in the evening if required.

'Communication and a degree of flexibility on the side of both parties are essential, too. Being available to clients is also key. Even though I do not work on Fridays all my clients and colleagues know they can call me at home or on my mobile if it is really necessary. Most clients have been very supportive, as have my colleagues. I think that it has benefited both parties: I have been able to continue my career, and Cushman and Wakefield, Healey and Baker has retained someone highly experienced.'

Julia McClelland, floating secretary, was offered the opportunity to work part-time within Cushman and Wakefield, Healey and Baker, and has been working flexibly since 2001. When she joined the firm in 1998 she worked full-time as an equity partner's secretary. After she returned to work from maternity leave she took up her full-time position again, but soon realised that it was not for her: 'I came back to work full-time for another 18 months and found it too much, so I approached my human resources manager to ask if I could reduce the number of days I worked. She was very supportive and offered the possibility of joining the "floating secretary" team, working as part of a job share with another lady who only works two days so we both make up a whole week.

'I now work 24 hours a week. Mainly I do 8.30 am to 5.00 pm, or if I need to take my daughter to school in the morning I do 10.00 am to 6.00 pm with 30 minutes' lunch break instead of an hour. Sometimes I need to change my working hours or I require to swap days due to my personal responsibilities, but that is never a problem as long as I notify our human resources department beforehand,' says Julia.

Operationally, business dictates that we must provide service to our clients during core working hours. However, Cushman and Wakefield, Healey and Baker recognises that an employee may wish to work flexibly, therefore we offer different flexible working options to guarantee a healthy work/life balance. Altered hours, part-time working and home working are among the flexible working arrangements that may be considered and are being enjoyed by a number of our female professionals.

Source: Adapted from *Business in the Community*, at www.bitc.org.
Reproduced with permission of BITC.

Discussion questions

1 What in your view could be the major causes of absenteeism from work?

2 What do you think are the major reasons for opposition to flexible working arrangements in organisations?

The opening vignette illustrates that many employers are developing flexibility in order to meet the requirements not only of EU directives and legislation, but also the expectations of their employees. Flexible working is just one of the many issues facing HR managers today. This chapter highlights the current issues that human resource managers should be aware of, as illustrated in Exhibit 13-1. Many of the current issues, such as flexible working, have been discussed in earlier chapters and you are referred back to these chapters where appropriate. Some of the issues in this chapter are unrelated; however, what they have in common is that they show how the workplace is changing. This chapter aims to highlight these changes and suggest ways in which HR professionals can deal with these new challenges.

Much has been written on issues encouraging changing work patterns in employment. Recently, the Institute of Employment Research (2002) cited that one in eight people in Britain are now carers for more than 50 hours per week. Sickness and absence in 1988 cost the UK £10.2 billion, or 8.5 working days, per employee. Could this primary cause of absence be due to workplace stress and the many domestic responsibilities that are making significant demands on employees' time? Or is it that, with employment of women now at its highest ever rate (68.9 per cent), female employees might have to be away from work more often due to a sick child or elderly relative? Not only that but today the proportion of families headed by a lone parent has also increased from 8 to 20 per cent over the last 30 years. This means that flexible working and work/life balance have become buzz words for governments, as discussed in Chapter 3. However, it is not only flexibility that is an issue: employment costs are often the largest cost an organisation incurs and therefore managers need to think about how to improve the efficiency of their workforce, which is not only a major expense but also a major asset.

Employment costs

The oil crisis of 1974 set off a wave for change in organisations' employment costs. Prior to the discovery of North Sea oil, a cartel of oil-producing countries set high oil prices, dramatically raising industrial costs, which were largely dependent on oil at that time. Manufacturing firms

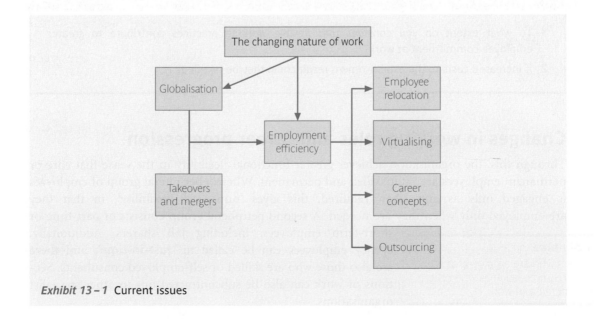

Exhibit 13–1 Current issues

therefore had to focus on greater efficiency in the use of all their resources and their attention turned especially to highly priced labour resources, where they sought to reduce costs, in order to remain both competitive and viable.

The requirement to manage employment costs is as important in the early twenty-first century as it was in the 1970s. This quest for greater efficiency and cost reduction led to company restructuring or downsizing in manufacturing industry in the later 1970s, which spread to service industries in the 1980s. The underlying economic argument was to address greater competition from international competitors, who had lower costs. This coincided with developments in new technology and instant access to business performance. This capital-intensive resource enabled performance monitoring through up-to-the-minute information, or 'just-in-time' or immediate correction, to improve efficiency where targets were not being met.

learning organisation
An organisation which supports the continuous self-development of its members which enables them to respond to change.

Theory Z
A theory put forward by Ouchi, based on a traditional Japanese system of employment.

New technology requires higher-level skills that either have to be recruited into the firm or developed through existing employees in a **learning organisation**. The idea has been developed by Ouchi *et al.* (1978) with their **Theory Z**. Ouchi *et al.*'s research adapted Japanese management practices and applied them to the American workplace, where they were used in such organisations as IBM and Hewlett-Packard. The characteristics of Z organisations include an emphasis on inter-personal skills and group work; however they stop short of the Japanese practices of group decision-making, leaving decisions to individuals. Theory Z also places greater emphasis on informal democratic relations based on trust, which HRM professionals are keen to emphasise. Theory Z viewed people as whole human beings rather than a production tool, and many of the ideas on flexible organisations have been developed from Ouchi *et al.*'s ideas. The 'Stop and reflect' box will help you develop ideas on the implementation of flexible work practices.

Stop and reflect

1 To what extent do you consider that flexible working practices contribute to greater employee commitment at work?

2 If increased costs to the establishment result could they be justified?

Changes in working roles and career progression

Through this, the organisation achieves greater functional flexibility in the sense that core or permanent employees are multiskilled and permanent. Where a peripheral group of employees is engaged only as and when required, this gives 'numerical flexibility', in that they are employed only when they are needed. A second peripheral group consists of part-time or short-term employees, including job sharers. Additionally, agency employees can be called in 'just-in-time', and there are also those who are skilled or self-employed consultants. Sections of work can also be subcontracted out to other specialist organisations.

just-in-time
Workers who are employed as and when required, such as when there is an increase in work.

This is becoming more common with some administrative HR functions, such as payroll, recruitment and selection, which can also help reduce employee costs for the organisation. Many people are therefore having to change their whole notion of a job for life or career progression in the same firm. Often, these temporary or short-term personnel are required to make their own social security contributions and pension payments, either individually or through their employing agencies.

Changes in career paths

The changes in working practices, career paths and styles of working can be seen to have had a sizeable impact on the modern organisation and also on the individual employee. Some commentators have labelled this **career pandemonium** and this is discussed below.

career pandemonium
The idea that uncertainties in organisations can play havoc with traditional career paths.

Brousseau *et al.* (1996) have acknowledged that the uncertainties that cause change in organisations also play havoc with traditional notions of career paths. The results of downsizing, delayering and outsourcing have changed the notion of progression up a corporate ladder in order to 'get ahead'. The onus is now on the individual to plan their own career in that they not only develop their portfolio of skills but also might be engaged in a multi-employment situation. Such people should be ready to go anywhere where opportunities take them and should not feel committed to one function or job, or even one employer. This does not necessarily mean a total lack of stability and commitment but would probably lead to an increase in what has been described as pandemonium. This may also result in a situation that enables a pluralistic strategy, whereby some core personnel individual growth and development take place within the same firm alongside the non-permanent or peripheral personnel: in other words, the workforce is made up of 'core personnel' versus the 'transient peripheral'.

The notion of permanent jobs, dating back to the Industrial Revolution, could soon, in effect, be obsolete. Storey (1995) argues that, where previously in accordance with structured functionalism work was organised into specific tasks performed by individuals or groups, it is now distributed to clusters, who operate in general fields in the absence of any fixed tasks or even duties. Consequently, it is not possible to deliver in what Waterman and Collard (1994) have described as an unspoken covenant between employee and employer that consists of a promise of permanent employment in return for performance and total loyalty where a hierarchical structure no longer exists. In its place is a teamwork organisation where team members share expertise and are required to deal with different tasks at different times, or even at the same time. This change in the psychological contract has a major impact on how careers are perceived and how employees relate to the organisation. This clearly also has a significant impact for HR professionals. Young people entering the workforce – known as **generation X** – no longer have loyalty to one organisation, instead HR professionals need to develop their loyalty to the task and the team, which may be temporary in nature. This means a rethink in terms of the types of reward and incentive on offer.

generation X
The changing values that the next generation can have on an organisation. They often question their purpose and role in life.

Generation X and the 'career-resilient workforce'

There are other cultural shifts that, it has been argued, also affect the working environment. The concept of a generation X describes twentysomething people entering the workforce who want to explore and do different kinds of work for their individual self-development. Such a generation is difficult to manage since they are not motivated by the idea of doing a specific task in a particular way or because they are told to. Hearsey and Blanchard (1996) suggest that ideas have to be 'sold' to them and that the work must have meaning. Such a requirement means that organisations must be more creative in their procedures, and that may mean unorthodox methods.

A picture begins to emerge of shifting sands, where older and bewildered disenfranchised employees search for stability in the midst of continuous change. A change whereby the ascendancy of a career pathway is cut short and converted to an interdisciplinary autonomous team in which young employees seek meaning but lack commitment. Again, this generational split in the workforce can contribute to the idea of 'pandemonium'. A situation emerges in which individual survival is dependent upon reliance on no one else, just on one's own capabilities.

Waterman *et al.* (1980) take another perspective, coining the idea of a 'career-resilient workforce'. This means that the individual does not cling to one job or company, or one career path. Employees need to be dedicated to the idea of continuous learning and reinvention of oneself in order to keep pace with change, and the onus is often on them to do just that. In the long term, this means a greater diversification of individual capabilities, together with an improved ability to cope with change.

One needs to consider how this might change an organisation. First, there would need to be enough people who are emotionally suited to constant change, in that they have the confidence to deal with any situation that might occur. Employees that prefer stability might therefore lose out against their more flexible colleagues.

Second, there is the question of expertise and highly specialised training. In a knowledge- and information-based economy, skills and knowledge would be replaced with physical and financial capital in which there is no investment in highly sophisticated skills. Here we enter the realm of the 'Jack of all trades' – meaning that the employee must master a number of different skills. By extension, this means that there are fewer and fewer expert employees specialising in specific areas of expertise.

Third, as we have already seen, this change in employment conditions also results in reduced loyalty to a company and its ideals. Without special ties to the organisation, employees may not even have an emotional stake in long-term company goals. This sense of feeling alienated might mean that employees are prone to opportunism and apathy. It is clear, then, that these issues have serious implications across the whole business – from job design to motivation – and in dealing with career development and promotion.

A new perspective: linear, expert, spiral and transient employees

The previously monolithic organisational solution assumed there was no need to develop alternatives, but the new change-orientated approach is arguably more suitable for coping with business environmental turbulence (Ansoff, 1984). From another perspective it is argued also that, although there might be turbulence at times, at other times some stability may prevail. Therefore a pluralistic approach, or a combination of the two, might be a better bet on the path to employee development. An organisation that takes a 'pluralistic approach' might retain certain core competencies and organisational leadership but have a more dynamic and less structured process to deal with external change. The debate continues with the perspective that the pluralistic approach enables opportunities for different career perspectives. This may mean that a more flexible organisation could emerge that can cater for a diverse workforce and could develop a style that would minimise the possibility of pleasing one group and alienating another. This system could manage to approach both career management and personal development.

Four career concepts

Brousseau *et al.* (1996) advocate four different patterns of career experience that in themselves can offer 'hybrid concepts'. Different motives underlie the four concepts, as illustrated in Exhibit 13-2.

The linear concept

This refers to an upward movement to achievement and power. People with strong linear career concepts often bring numerous motives to their careers. Chief among these motives are power and achievement. Basically, 'linears' are motivated by opportunities to make important things happen.

The expert concept

This requires lifelong commitment and requires becoming more skilful in a chosen speciality, whether in terms of technical competence or security and stability.

The spiral concept

This breaks away from the traditional linear and expert in that the best career depends upon making regular moves into occupational areas and specialisms, but the 'spiral' may not achieve mastery in all of them. The essence is the 'seven-year itch'.

The transitory concept

This is sometimes defined as 'consistent inconsistency' in that the person, every three to five years, goes to a very different or totally unrelated job. Individuals would not consider themselves as having careers, but seek a broad range of experience that could loosely be defined in terms of 'variety is the spice of life'.

Where previously those with both expert and linear concepts have looked forward to achieving their goals on the move upward, this would be a less amicable situation for the spiral and transitory concepts of career development. Burns and Stalker (1994) suggest that, as organisations before were more organic and less structured, here the rigid boundaries between jobs are reduced and therefore are more appropriate for spiral and transitory employee pathways. The linear pathway prospects of moving up have diminished as have the opportunities for specialised skills. This is also happening at a time of the demographic bulge of the mid-career baby boomer, born in the 1960s, who traditionally should be in middle or senior management by now; instead many have abandoned their careers in search of more meaningful work. This has meant, for some employers and employees, that the concept of linear and expert pathways is

	Linear	Expert	Spiral	Transitory
Direction of movement	Upward	Little movement	Lateral	Lateral
Duration of stay in one field	Variable	Life	7–10 years	3–5 years
Key motives	Power achievement	Expertise Security	Personal growth Creativity	Variety Independence

Exhibit 13–2 Four career concepts: key features and motives

becoming obsolete. Consequently the argument that the pluralistic approach is more attractive to organisations in the twenty-first century, where employees are seeking a spiral or more transitory career pathway, means that HR managers need to be aware of this as part of their planning process.

According to Brousseau *et al.* (1996), organisations might not simply be concerned with linear and expert employee ambitions. Some organisations might be more dependent upon the spiral or the transitory. Alternatively, at certain times a mixture of all four may be required – in other words, a 'pluralistic' career culture could be most sensible. The behavioural competencies linked to each career concept are listed in Exhibit 13-3.

Brousseau *et al.* (1996) therefore propose a particular mix of competencies at any one time. This in turn requires that organisations have pluralistic management practices, so that the different mixes can be adopted.

The writers then go on to argue that organisations have variable needs for the four listed career concepts and motives, and that they should vary this mix in accordance with these needs. However, the move is away from the monolithic structure and towards multiple career structures, or a shift away from what has been called the 'promotion culture' of the past in organisations. In this situation, the culture of the organisation needs to change as well, as is demonstrated in Exhibit 13-4: away from explicit and implicit career management requirements. In future, the idea that moving up the hierarchy is a good thing, and that the best people are those that can and do get promoted to the highest levels, may no longer be current. Instead employees need to have the flexibility to move to different tasks either within the organisation or with different organisations and, as we have already seen, the responsibility for career development rests with the employee.

Pluralism does not mean that those who are technically brilliant are necessarily the most ready for promotion, especially where all posts are currently filled. It might, however, mean that the experts are more likely to be rewarded. In fact, it may be possible to tailor the style to the focus of the organisation and its goals.

Brousseau *et al.* (1996) suggest that a

> Spiral culture would better support a strategy calling for creativity and diversification. An Expert culture would better support a strategy aimed at maintaining the organization's position based on high quality and high reliability products and services. A Transitory culture would suit a strategy of exploiting new opportunities by getting into new markets quickly with highly innovative or easy to use products or services.

Linear	Expert	Spiral	Transitory
Leadership	Quality	Creativity	Speed
Competitiveness	Commitment	Teamwork	Networking
Cost-efficiency	Reliability	Skill diversity	Adaptability
Logistics management	Technical competence	Lateral co-ordination	Fast learning
Profit orientation	Stability orientation	People development	Project focus

Exhibit 13–3 Career motives and associated behavioural competencies

	Linear	Expert	Spiral	Transitory
Structure	Tall pyramid Narrow span of control	Flat Strong functional departments	Matrix Self-directed, interdisciplinary teams	Loose amorphous structure Temporary teams
Valued performance factors	Leadership Efficiency Logistics management	Quality Reliability Stability Technical	Creativity Teamwork People development	Speed Adaptability Innovation
Rewards	Promotions management Perquisites Executive bonuses	Fringe benefits Recognition awards Continuing technical training	Lateral assignments Cross-training Creative latitude	Immediate cash bonuses Independence and autonomy Special temporary assignments Job rotation

Exhibit 13-4 Organisational career cultures

Certainly, to be effective there needs to be a link between organisational strategies and career cultures, as is demonstrated in Exhibit 13-5.

Contracts

Brousseau *et al.* (1996) also make reference to a dual career ladder that has been in operation in some organisations for some years: first, for those orientated to a linear-style managerial or executive pathway and, second, a pathway for an expert or technical specialist. This dual progression is often used in technology industries, where it is important to retain technical

Strategic direction	Strategic advantage	Organisational career culture
Growth Deeper market penetration	Low price High volume/low cost	Linear
Maintain position	Quality Reliability	Expert
Diversification	Creativity Innovation	Spiral
Entrepreneurial opportunity New market creation	Speed Novelty Ease of use	Transitory

Exhibit 13-5 Linking organisational strategies to career cultures

personnel – such as programmers, software developers and other highly specialised employees – alongside a more traditional management structure. In the 'Managing diversity' box, we look at a company that has developed this kind of 'pluralist' approach. It has a flexible structure and can therefore accommodate these different styles of work. However, it is important to consider whether taking on the diversity of pluralism in some organisations would be difficult unless the culture becomes more flexible. It might be readily acceptable in small organisations but it could be resisted in some large organisations that have bureaucratic structures. Consequently, newer approaches, such as 'cafeteria-style career management', in which employers pick and mix their managers depending on which particular skills they need at that time, might be premature.

Globalisation and international human resource management

Now we turn to another issue facing HR: the wider change in the business environment of **globalisation**. Many companies are now multinational organisations, increasing competition in the marketplace and placing a new emphasis on the availability of human resources with appropriate skills. To examine this issue, it is at first interesting to look at different cultures and to examine how their economies have become so successful. Porter (1990) questioned why a particular nation might achieve international success in a particular industry, while Holden (1999) questions the reasons for the international success of both Switzerland and Japan. Switzerland is the world leader in chocolate, pharmaceuticals, banking and specialised machinery. However, it is not only landlocked but has a high cost of labour and few natural resources. Similarly Japan, although lacking in natural resources, became a major and formidable economy. As Porter states, this illustrates how the human resources function has increased the development of competency through systems of training and education to enable competitive advantage. A positive HRM issue is investment in training and in individual development. Political, economic, sociological and ecological issues also have a systemic effect on all industries worldwide in terms of commodity supply systems and pricing. (This has already been mentioned when we looked at the work of Brousseau *et al.* (1996).) The importance of resourcing, or the deployment of human resources in terms of expatriate managers and managerial systems, is highly significant to multinationals. Successful overseas operations are critically dependent upon the efficiency and effectiveness of their HRM systems.

globalisation

When an organisation starts to operate on an international level, either across countries or boundaries.

Holden (1999) further debates the growing interest in international human resource management (IHRM) and the lack of clarity about what it actually implies. It cannot be considered in the absence of contextual variables. As Boxall (1995) states, where international human resource management of multinationals in foreign subsidiaries can be known simply as HRM 'on a wider scale', of wider significance is comparative HRM, which was initially perceived in Anglo-American terms. This approach is useful when comparing different organisations, cultures and countries. It is known as a comparative approach and is useful for highlighting the important managerial and cultural differences (Clark, 1996) that contribute to success and failure in different countries. Using a comparative approach may ultimately help managers decide whether to use convergence or divergence criteria when managing the HR function globally.

International comparative HRM: convergence and divergence

When considering managing HRM on a global scale, academics have used various philosophies and academic disciplines to categorise four main areas (Holden, 1999). These can help

The tide turns

Within Laboratoires Boiron, nobody speaks of 'older' or 'senior' workers. Those over 55 have the same rights to continuing training and promotion as other members of the workforce of this well-known French manufacturer of homeopathic medicines. Yet they can also scale down their working hours.

The firm's management realised as early as 1976 that most workers had a rough time when they retired and suddenly found themselves without an occupation. A scheme called 'Preparation for retirement' was therefore introduced and, for the past 25 years, has regularly been renegotiated with workers' representatives.

The scheme is optional and covers all full-time and part-time employees. About six years before they retire – which, depending on the individual, might be at 60, 63 or 64 – employees with at least five years' service are invited to discuss their end-of-career plans. If they wish, they can progressively reduce their work time in preparation for retirement without any significant salary reduction, and most take up this option. They have to reduce their work time by at least three hours per week in the first year, and after six years work about a half to two-thirds of their previous work time.

This transition between employment and full retirement gives employees longer periods of rest and recuperation from work, and a chance to reorganise their free time and get more involved in voluntary or family activities. The scheme also allows for better management of skills and jobs, and facilitates the transmission of knowledge and company culture from older to younger workers through an informal tuition system. Indeed, the firm insists on age diversity as one of the keys to a balanced and healthy team spirit.

For most of us, our life cycles have also radically altered in recent years. The organisation of life into three age-based vertical periods – training, work, retirement – is gradually giving way to a horizontal arrangement where we train, work, bring up families, spend our leisure time and retire in ways that are different to those of the past. Continuing training and lifelong education are becoming an accepted part of life and work.

We are staying young and in good shape for many more years, and most people are no longer 'old' at 60 or 65. Many of us 'age actively', performing voluntary and family activities that are essential for our communities. Surveys also show that there is a strong need for a transition between full-time work and full-time retirement. People retiring today – and even more so in the coming years and decades – are very different from current retirees, many of whom started their working lives very early, often in difficult physical circumstances.

Of course, age management is not only about introducing part-time work. It also includes career planning, continuing vocational training and lifelong education, ergonomics and mobility, seniority wages, pension regulations, anti-age discrimination and codes of practice.

Career planning and training are, of course, crucial to external or internal mobility. In banks and insurance companies, where workers often still have a 'career job', employees can change functions.

But who would wish to work beyond 60? Diversity and fairness are important factors. Workers enter the labour market at different ages, in different work circumstances and with a wide range of life expectancies. The retirement age should therefore be in part a reflection of the arduousness of work. However, job mobility needs to be developed, especially for workers performing difficult, physical or stressful work. If working longer will soon be unavoidable, then flexibility in relation to a higher retirement age needs to be encouraged. At the same time, an earlier exit must also remain a possibility, especially for manual workers or those performing psychologically demanding tasks.

Source: G. Reday-Mulvey, 'The tide turns', *People Management*, 30 June 2005, p. 36.
Reproduced with permission of *People Management*.

Discussion questions

1 Why is career management just as important for younger people as older people?
2 Work/life balance affects all employees, not just those with families. How would you develop work/life balance policies?

managers gain an understanding of the approach they could use when expanding globally or when synchronising operations acquired through takeovers and mergers. One such approach is through the convergence of operations.

Convergence

One way of streamlining operations is through the convergence approach. One explanation, given by Kerr *et al.* (1960), argues that the case for technological change produces similar industrial systems, due to the requirements for similar structures and work forms. Such similarity in organisational structures over time is known as *convergence theory*. This implies that, as organisations reach a certain size and scale, functional specialisation becomes a necessity. The maintenance of organisational control requires co-ordination through rules, regulations and hierarchies, as in Fordism, discussed below. The result would account for global similarities in operational practices through the same technologies and production systems. This argument has been extended from work processes to payment systems and the globalisation of markets.

convergence theory
Where organisational structures come together over time to form one system.

Such convergence has become known as *McDonaldisation*: the requirement for homogeneity in product and in service, which leads to efficiency, predictability, calculability and control through the substitution of non-human for human technology, a situation in which the work culture in one region will be indistinguishable from the culture in any other. However, this is not only technology driven, since the globalisation of markets leads to regional legislation as in the European Union. Using such a system often leads to the de-skilling of employees, which has the advantage for management of reducing labour costs.

McDonaldisation
The term used to encapsulate the idea of standardised products and systems that can be replicated across countries and regions.

Braverman (1974) focuses on the relationship between management and employees in such issues as control over the workforce, de-skilling through the introduction of new technologies, and flexible working practices.

Fordism
The start of mass production systems which brought standardised products to the masses.

This is illustrated in **Fordism** up to the 1960s and 1970s, as the predominant organisation for the creation of western capital, being dependent upon mass production industries such as car manufacturing, hence the name Fordism. An alternative approach to global operations is highlighted by the cultural approach.

The cultural approach

The cultural approach identified by Hofstede (1980) sees no convergence of different cultures into a global culture. Significantly, they are an important factor in employee behaviour in different organisations. Hofstede found that technology produces only superficial similarities, and his research into IBM in 66 different countries in terms of managers and employees in the four dimensions of what are referred to as power distance, uncertainty avoidance, individualism and masculinity, was highly significant. Similar studies by Trompenaars (1996) also examined cultural differences globally with the use of the following dimensions, each with an opposite or polarised value.

- **Universalism versus particularism** – describe the preference for rules and regulation rather than personal trust. UK and US cultures tend to reflect these ideas.

- **Achieved status versus ascribed status** – whether we can achieve status through hard work or through family connections and position.

- **Neutral versus emotional** – considers how much we show our emotions. UK culture is often seen as lacking emotion compared with Latin cultures.

- **Communitarianism versus individualism** – whether a culture works better as a group or as individuals. Again, US and UK cultures tend to be more individualistic, whereas Asian cultures are more group based.

- **Diffuse versus specific cultures** – considers how much we become involved in what is happening around us.

- **Human–time relationship** – the preference for doing things fast in the shortest possible time or the synchronisation of efforts so that completion is co-ordinated. The ability to multitask.

- **Internal versus external orientation** – how far we can influence what goes on around us, or whether we are controlled by our environment.

Using these approaches, Lane (1995) examines the relationship between social settings and organisational forms. The similarities or differences indicate either convergence or divergence.

Although each approach has its limitations, all are useful as a basis for the interpretation and comparison of the employment relationship in international terms, as has been discussed in earlier chapters.

Child (1981) claims evidence for both convergence and divergence, which highlights the evolutionary nature of both managerial and HRM development with culture as a contextual variable over time but dwindling in importance. It could be argued that this is the result of globalisation.

Outsourcing

As mentioned before, focus on reducing costs in areas not essential to core business interests resulted in the UK in **downsizing** in the 1970s and 1980s. One example of this is National Health Service Trusts seeking to contract out their catering and gardening to companies or individuals who are specialists in these areas. Contract catering was already a well-established practice, which had started in the reign of Charles II. This contract or 'industrial catering' developed rapidly, particularly in large factories, and in banking, insurance and oil companies such as Shell and BP, after the First World War. More recently, the operation of a franchise or management contract is a form of **outsourcing** and has been a growing practice for 30 years. The main attraction for the 'parent company', or organisation contracting out, is that it can reduce employment costs in the areas of National Insurance and company pension schemes. Furthermore, the argument is that professionals in these specialisms can benefit from economies of scale and can provide a more efficient service more cheaply. This frees the parent company to concentrate on its core business.

Outsourcing can cover a range of activities, from mail and refuse collection to road maintenance and cleaning, as it does in the UK. However, the efficiency and appropriate means of outsourcing are under scrutiny. Many state-funded organisations, such as the NHS, outsource to private contractors who may make a profit at the expense of the taxpayers. Therefore, to be effective, organisations need to ensure that they have a competitive tendering procedure in place, which ensures that quality service is provided at a competitive price. This is equally

downsizing
A reduction in staff numbers through reorganisation.

outsourcing
Where support activities are given to outside specialists allowing the organisation to concentrate on its core business.

important for the outsourcing of HRM operations such as payroll, recruitment, selection or training, whether for a multinational or a state-funded institution.

HR managers need to think about how the HR function could be outsourced. In any outsourcing agreement, control by the parent organisation becomes indirect and this could have implications for legislative employment issues and the corporate strategies of parent companies. Not only that, but when the decision has been made to outsource operations, HR needs to offer support in the form of a specific HRM plan. Decisions also need to be made as to whether a **phased approach** or a **clean break approach** should be used (see below).

---

phased approach

Where changes in business organisations are done gradually.

clean break approach

Where changes in organisations are done immediately.

Employers need to consider their legal and moral obligations, especially in areas such as discrimination, ethical standards, workplace communication, consultation and co-operation. They also need to consider how they will protect company secrets when the workers in their organisation are employed by an outsourcing company.

Of greater significance to HRM is ensuring accurate records are kept that can form a data trail, whether by the organisation or its outsourcing provider. Procedures also need to be clear about what happens if the outsourcing contract is terminated, to ensure that records are returned to the original owner after use by a contractor and not destroyed by them.

On the plus side as far as small businesses are concerned, there are advantages in outsourcing personnel or HRM business. A dedicated HRM organisation, which has excellent resources, such as an appropriate database of HRM specialists and proven expertise it can offer for a fee, can provide a small business with the knowledge and experience advantages of a large company. Although initially more expensive for small firms, this could lead to greater benefits or cost savings in the longer term through improved efficiency and the freeing up of managers' time for other core business activities.

Outsourcing is also useful when specialists are required for short-term contracts. There is a crucial requirement in the twenty-first century for specialists at short notice for specific projects. Having a database of tested and tried personnel reduces the element of risk of incorrect personnel selection.

Often, redundancy follows outsourcing, especially if the service provider does not take on the existing employees. In the interests of fairness, all employees should be fully consulted on matters directly affecting them, including codes of conduct.

It is suggested that, in order to implement an outsourcing plan effectively, it is necessary to have a staffing profile. This would include details of number of employees, cases for compensation and availability of employee skills. Resources would need to include a dedicated and well-trained project team. There is also a need for support services in areas such as training, re-training and consultancy, and appropriate and suitable resources to deal with resignations, redeployment advice and assistance, together with the calculation of benefits.

A dynamic communications strategy is needed for consultation purposes, explaining the roles and responsibilities of the project team members. Also required are outlets for communication, such as bulletin boards and newsletters, together with support services to staff.

Flexibility is required in meeting the needs of the differing work groups affected through outsourcing procedures. This might be through industrial relations, superannuation, taxation, job placements or financial counselling, even preparation for further job interviews, CVs, interview skills and, in some cases, language skills.

Much of the outsourcing in the UK has moved to India, where graduates fluent in English are keen to take on jobs often seen as unskilled in the UK at a fraction of the pay. These companies have been criticised for 'stealing jobs'; however, what is clear is that corporate users in most countries are increasingly turning to offshore providers as a means of cutting costs. Outsourcing is used by organisations whose areas of operation range from home construction to security and information technology. The procedure advocated for success is a step-by-step approach. There is a growing demand for computing and managed services, and an example of how outsourcing impacts on the Indian economy can be seen in the 'International perspective' box.

Outsourcing to India

Business process outsourcing (BPO) is the latest mantra in India. As the current sources of revenue face slower growth, software companies are trying new ways to increase their revenues. BPO is top of their list. IT services companies are making a quick entry into the BPO space on the strength of their existing set of clients.

The philosophy behind BPO is specific: do what you do best and leave everything else to business process outsourcers. Companies are moving their non-core business processes to outsource providers. BPO saves precious management time and resources, and allows focus while building upon core competencies. The list of functions being outsourced is getting longer by the day. Call centres apart, functions outsourced span purchasing and disbursement, order entry, billing and collection, human resources administration, cash and investment management, tax compliance, internal audit, payroll . . . the list gets longer every day. In view of the accounting scandals in 2002 (Enron, WorldCom, Xerox, etc.), more and more companies are keen to keep their investors happy. Hence, it is important for them to increase profits. BPO is one way of increasing profits. If done well, BPO results in increasing shareholder value.

Typically, a customer calls the call centre (usually on a freephone number). After pressing numerous numbers (1 for English, 2 for Spanish, 3 for bank balance!) the operator will answer your query by accessing the database. Call centres are used in areas such as sales support, airline/hotel reservations, technical queries, bank accounts, client services, receivables, telemarketing and market research.

If a bank shifts the work of 1000 people from the UK to India it can save about £10 million a year due to the lower costs in India. According to McKinsey, pharmaceutical firms can reduce the cost of developing a new drug, currently estimated at between £400 million and £700 million, by as much as £200 million if development work is outsourced to India.

Benefits for organisations from outsourcing can include:

- productivity improvements
- access to expertise
- operational cost control
- cost savings
- improved accountability
- improved HR
- opportunity to focus on core business.

Outsourcing is not new – it has been a popular management tool for decades. One can safely say outsourcing has evolved as follows:

- 1960s – time-sharing
- 1970s – parts of IT operations

international perspective

- 1980s – entire IT operations
- 1990s – alliances/tie-ups
- 2000s – IT-enabled services.

India has one of the world's largest pools of low-cost English-speaking scientific and technical talent. This makes it one of the obvious places to which to outsource. Dell, Sun Microsystems, LG, Ford, GE and Oracle have all announced plans to scale up their operations in India. Others, like American Express, IBM and British Airways, are leveraging the cost advantage India has to offer while setting up call centres. Several foreign airlines and banks have also set up business process operations in India. Indian revenues from BPO are estimated to have grown 107 per cent to £400 million and in 2002 this particular area employed 35,000 people.

What about the employees, though?

As in the UK, retention of staff is a problem. The staff turnover rate is 35–40 per cent and as employees need to be fluent in English, they tend to be well-educated graduates; yet the work does not require graduate skills. Exit interviews have shown that the following reasons may contribute to high staff turnover:

- no growth opportunity/lack of promotion
- for higher salary
- for higher education
- misguidance by the company
- policies and procedures are not conducive
- no personal life
- physical strains
- uneasy relationship with peers or managers.

Yet, compared to many employers in India, call centres also provide several benefits not often expected in other industries, such as medical care, a higher than average salary, bonuses, and so on. However, as elsewhere, the emerging workforce is developing very different attitudes about its role in the workplace. Today's employees place a high priority on the following:

- family orientation
- quality-of-life issues
- autonomy.

Smart employers are beginning to realise that, to hold on to your people, you have to work counter to prevailing trends affecting staff retention. Smart employers make it a strategic initiative to understand what their people want and need – then give it to them.

Source: adapted from www.BPO.org.

Discussion questions

1 What do you think are the issues when outsourcing to India?

2 What are the benefits to the organisation and the placement country of outsourcing?

Outsourcing and ethical standards

There is a need to establish a common basis for undertaking and managing business activities. Participants should be required to adhere to a code of practice. The success of outsourcing is also dependent upon HRM issues and will in turn be dependent upon the acceptance of agreed guidelines. However, such guidelines will need to be flexible enough to respond to changed circumstances. Furthermore, transparency is required in order that employees can make informed opinions.

Organisations need to realise that outsourcing to developing countries with poor employment protection practices can adversely affect their standing. This was highlighted recently in the case of Nike, which was found to be using child labour in India.

Managing the outsourcing contract

As previously stated, the agency outsourcing a particular business activity will be responsible for the maintenance of a predetermined service standard, together with priorities for service delivery, such as computer maintenance or cleaning.

In terms of employment contracts these can be either 'phased' or 'clean break' approaches. Each has both advantages and disadvantages.

The 'phased' approach

This enables the establishment of a more permanent employment status both in terms of the agency co-operating in recruitment but also to encourage the continuation of specific individuals in the longer term. This is also important where specific skills or experience are in short supply. It is crucial that it enables a smoother change to a new service provider and also reduces the possibility of employees receiving redundancy payments in addition to new job offers. The 'phased' approach will not necessarily mean redundancies but could lessen them, especially in cases where employees refuse to take up new job opportunities.

The 'clean break' approach

This is simpler to operate and can be viewed as an incentive in that employment can be continued with the outsourcing agency until a new provider takes over. The main advantages of using the 'clean break' approach are that it is an administratively simpler process for agencies and it can be implemented within a reasonably short time period. The benefits available to employees under the 'clean break' approach can also be used as an incentive to ensure that affected employees continue in employment with the outsourcing agency until the new provider takes over the function. As there is no attempt to broker jobs with the new service provider, negotiations can be much less protracted than under the 'phased' approach, thereby minimising the potentially heavy resource requirements that may need to be devoted to the process.

The disadvantages of the 'clean break' approach include the cost in terms of redundancy payments and/or redeployment costs for employees who have been performing the function. There may also be risks to the continuity of service delivery if, as a result of this approach, the new service provider is unable to recruit employees with sufficient experience and skills to perform the necessary work, particularly on handover. Both the outsourcing agency and the new service provider may be uncertain about the number and skills of employees who will take up job offers with the new service provider at the commencement date of the outsourced arrangements.

In the case, for instance, of HRM outsourcing it is essential to avoid difficult issues such as conflicts of interest or the misuse of inside information sources.

Due to the increase in trade between nations that previously had trade barriers, outsourcing internationally is developing continuously. For example, Chinese companies seek expertise in overseas companies by sending their work abroad. The Sino-India Cooperative Office is currently trying to attract Indian software developers such as Wipro, Infosys and Satyam. The Indian phone company Bharti has outsourcing arrangements with IBM, Siemens and Ericsson. This does not necessarily mean a threat to the job market in the home country since, although some move overseas, others flow in.

Outsourcing enables risk reduction in that the organisation is no longer responsible for the employment costs of the outsourced organisation. It also enables senior management to concentrate on core business activities. Therefore, outsourcing could feature as an essential part of long-term strategy. Not all areas should be outsourced and contracts should be flexible for specific periods of time. The potential for the twenty-first century is enormous in that specific expertise can be sought at any time and anywhere in the world.

More recent developments have included the exploitation of information technology, which is leading to a 'virtualising' of the workplace.

Whether a virtual organisation or using outsourcing providers, the main business reason for such developments is to cut costs and create greater efficiency.

Virtualising

Developments in technology have enabled the development of the concept of 'virtual management'. This operates on the basis of an intelligent network to reduce costs and improve efficiencies for the achievement of business objectives. Consequently the network sets out to add specific value to the company. In turn this can be achieved only by focusing on the company's core business in order to gauge the most effective means of achieving the highest competitive advantage. Email access is the starting point for this virtuality due to the fact that it can be accessed from a number of locations at the same time. However, companies have also recognised the need to consider security of information.

The advantage of the virtual organisation is that, instead of having office space to centralise a team, it makes sense to support a diversely spread infrastructure. Central to virtuality is the ability to enhance the competitive strength of the company. This is best provided by means of a strategic core focus, instantly online and well maintained. The foundations for a successful virtual network are security based with intellectual property access controls, together with quality of service delivery. Users have access to resources and the network is also virtualised in terms of management and maintenance.

Virtualisation is already well advanced due to email access, even though this was not originally regarded as a vehicle for it. Often, virtualisation develops through gradual implementation, perhaps starting with a specific department or service as a first step. Virtualising a team can be achieved on a worldwide scale via a high-speed link, enabling access to all records essential to job performance, including human resource data. One of the obvious advantages of this is the saving that can be made in terms of office space costs. Setting up an internal accounting department, for instance, often involves a large capital investment. Accounting resources often have to be widely spread and scarcity of expertise and staff turnover can be problematic.

In the UK, the approach currently used by independent financial advisers, for example, allows for access to appropriate expertise as and when required and on a global scale, and can also be used to support outsourcing operations. As a consequence, this would facilitate the employment of competent individuals, including – and more importantly, perhaps – those with physical disabilities or domestic responsibilities that prevent them from undertaking the journey to a workplace.

Companies such as INET Finance (see Exhibit 13-6) regard outsourcing as a strategic issue, not just a quick fix. In this way, some capital investment can be avoided, with senior management free to concentrate on core business.

Virtualisation sets out to meet the requirements of service industries that are focused on the customer and the customer's perception of added value. Other advantages as far as organisations themselves are concerned include contribution to or involvement with specific projects of either long- or short-term duration.

One of the main advantages of virtual offices is that employees from different geographically spread locations, or in different time zones, can be involved in an information or problem-solving exercise together, using technology to link them together.

Of course, home working, or mobile working, enables the continuous development of virtualisation and interaction with people who might not be able to participate in a physical capacity. Thus, as previously stated, it enables organisations in the twenty-first century to capitalise on the skills of a much wider range of people on a global basis, who may or may not belong to a physical organisation.

This prompts Thomson and Mabey (1994) to question how performance management and performance development can take place. The virtual management aspect is that it is organisational outputs that are measured, rather than 'presenteeism' (the employee's physical presence at a desk).

Another advantage of virtualising, according to Price (2000), is that teams can be dissolved and can reappear at a later stage in a different form. They may meet physically at a conference or may interact through videoconferencing. What emerges from this is that virtual organisations create new problems for HRM in terms of management at a distance and differential contracts of service. There are also the requirements for professional integrity, regulation and accountability.

The extent of virtualisation of organisations can vary from specific aspects of the job through to an entire organisation. Bradt (1998) suggested that organisations could be ranged along a continuum of virtuality ranging from 1 to 4, as outlined below.

1 Conducted by means of linked partners.

2 Distributed geographically and connected through technology, thereby viewed as a single organisation.

1 Less time lost in engaging and training both full- and part-time staff
2 Only the amount of time spent on the business is actually charged
3 Expertise available from a wide range of professionals globally
4 More adaptive to business demand patterns, high and low
5 Enhanced credibility with banks and advisers
6 Control of costs and cash flow
7 Continued access to updated information

Exhibit 13 – 6 INET benefits summarised

3   No visible structure through high-street branches, but a network of call centres via the tele-phone.

4   Totally virtual (e.g. Amazon.com, which holds few books in stock, but sources them from warehouses as and when required).

Most businesses have started down the path of virtualisation (see the section on this, later in the chapter) without realising it. For example, email access is ubiquitous. Users can access their email from home, desk or the road using a variety of methods.

Companies have recognised how important email is to driving business, and have imple-mented the application, security and user-access methods necessary for any time, anywhere access.

One benefit of moving towards virtualisation is that it can be implemented incrementally. The focus might be on a specific department or specific job roles. In this model, virtualisation would be a vertical implementation, starting with a review of the physical level and wrapping up with identifying the core applications needed within that group. The next step in virtualising could be providing support for a team to access intellectual property from anywhere on the globe. This could be through connections to company resources through a high-speed link, wired or wireless; they would be able to access everything needed to perform their job, but be limited only to the information necessary to this specific role. By using usernames and pass-words, an intelligent network is created. This allows human resources to access personnel information but not financial information or any other departmental information.

A further step would be to ask whether paying for office space would be the best use of company resources. The money spent on leasing and maintaining office space might be better used to build and support the intelligent infrastructure needed to support employees around the globe. This is especially the case where specialisms are needed, as many businesses only want the brains – therefore, there is no need to acquire bodies too!

Whereas outsourcing a process only shifts responsibility for supporting a particular activity, virtualisation emphasises the use of an intelligent networked infrastructure to enhance the busi-ness's competitive position. It forces the decision-makers to focus on the core business, and the applications and processes that drive the growth of the business.

Employee relocation

The impact of globalisation can also mean that there are new issues that arise regarding relocat-ing employees. In our global working world, HR managers may need to become involved in moving an organisation's skilled staff to a new location.

The main reasons for relocation are that specific expertise is required elsewhere and this in itself is driven by market needs and business changes. It may also be done to transfer knowledge to local staff for a specific time period, with the aim in the long term of setting up a new spe-cialised department. The total costs for relocation are borne by the company seeking to make the transfer, although there are major differences between companies as to what actual costs might be included. These costs not only cover the airfare, car rental and temporary accommo-dation for the company employee, but also for their spouse and family. Relocation is not a new phenomenon and well-established firms that have experience over time are aware of the requirements dictated through cultural differences.

Arkin (1994) questioned whether it was cheaper to manage relocation in-house or seek the services of consultants. He acknowledged that employment relocation was never easy due to legal and financial issues; first, in terms of property sale and purchase and, second, due to the stress experienced by all family members. Arkin (1994) cited this as the most complex activity outside of core business. This led to the use of relocation companies in the 1980s as a means of reducing employment costs. Prior to this, the CBI Employee Relocation Council and accountants Ernst & Young, had the previous year completed a survey of 577 employers and concluded that one-fifth at that time had employed external relocation advisers for domestic moves and one-third had appointed advisers for international moves, largely due to assumptions about the growth potential of relocation companies as a result of expected reductions in company in-house human resource functions.

The reasons for outsourcing relocation activities had wide variations in that some employers favoured guaranteed price schemes in order that employees would sell their homes more quickly and thereby reduce the cost of bridging loans. The Finance Act 1993 was instrumental in promoting house purchase schemes that were operated by relocation companies, but had a limit of £8000 on tax-free relocating expenses, with the relocating company acting as an agent for the employer in buying the property to house the employee. Thus employees now received the same favourable tax treatment whether they transferred the beneficial interest in their home to their employer, or directly to a relocation company. From the Ernst & Young survey, it appeared that this was the preferred option since employees could distance themselves from property sales issues. Much of this was highly contentious on house price differentials and often led to arguments – a further reason for it being taken outside of the company. Employers were not always pleased with relocation companies, especially when dealing with estate agents. Others commented that although it was a good idea to deal with the whole thing outside of the company itself, it sometimes meant that the employees had to drop their asking price. Midland Bank at that time did the opposite and set up an internal relocation unit in 1991 with a staff of just four people. It did save £8 million pounds and achieve high levels of satisfaction in those 200 average managers relocated per year. Prior to 1991, staff relocated had to be responsible for their own move and the bank provided them with an interest-free bridging loan. The services of the relocating company were offered by the bank, which included a guaranteed price for the employee's property where this property was difficult to sell. At that time the director of Hambro Countrywide Relocation stated that savings with in-house relocation were only possible if 30–40 were undertaken per year. Hence the counterargument for a contractor that has economies of scale, good negotiating networks, together with long experience in the field. This led to US company Pricoa Relocation providing a service for Goldman Sachs, which relocated some 200 employees per year within the European Union.

Organisations with less locating experience might choose to engage the services of professional relocation agents. Such bodies are well versed in the needs of both individuals and their families who are being moved, and can guarantee a smoother move in terms of knowledge of contacts, accommodation, utilities services, education and leisure facilities – not forgetting the all-important training required to gain acceptance in different cultural areas. Agents already well experienced in these issues will enable an employee to settle in more quickly and consequently achieve more efficient productivity. Building up this knowledge is expensive, however, especially if relocation is sporadic, and is a further reason for seeking the services of a well-established agent.

The role of the relocation company is therefore to act as co-ordinator through the human resource management department in terms of counselling on employee objectives and expectations, expenses to be paid by the company, and agreeing finance such as deposits for property or a lease. This external agent would deal with such aspects as searching for suitable accommodation and ensuring utilities are provided. The main advantage of using a reputable external agent would be their knowledge database. Individuals who wish to relocate might also take this advantage and receive pre-travel support, accommodation, education, personal development potential, etc. Specific packages can be designed for individuals or for families, for long- or short-term moves – hence the term used in the United States, 'destination service provider', for a person or service fully conversant with a specific destination area. This has become a growth area for freelance consultants, who are able to market their expertise to a wide range of organisations. Such a person is well focused on housing, facilities and schools, and the lifestyle needs of communities. Of course, a large amount of information for databases can be sought and marketed online through a 'virtual organisation', provided that confidentiality and privacy can be guaranteed. Agents that deal with employees and families on the move reduce the pressure on company human resource departments. Therefore, their fees are justified if savings are made by reducing the number of nights needed to be spent in hotels, or through providing reduced rental charges.

Problem issues

One reason for relocation is mergers and acquisitions. One relocation specialist, however, suggests that between 50 and 80 per cent of mergers, acquisitions and alliances fail within the first five years. This is despite the fact that international mergers are growing continuously in China. Most companies concentrate on making deals, such as return on investment, that may be in conflict with people issues, which seem to be at the expense of culture in terms of the different mindsets of emerging companies (KPMG study, Mergers and Acquisitions, 2003). According to Dr Anne Copeland of the Interchange Institute, a five-year study has identified several problems with relocation, such as spousal adjustment, which had an adverse effect on employees' productivity, lack of cultural training and changes in flexible working and work/life balance due to the changing work culture.

Employment relocation covers outsourced and in-house relocation management. It recognises that both leaving a job and going to a new home can be a stressful experience both for employees and their families. The limitations of trying to strike a balance and controlling costs need to be considered. The decision for employers is how far they can themselves deal with relocation or hand over to external specialists.

To implement relocation effectively, managers need to think about the management of relocation activities in the following terms.

- How it is to be communicated to employees and how it is to be evaluated.

- What type of relocation package will be offered, such as obtaining temporary accommodation, support for family members together with the leavers.

- Whether to deal with relocation in-house or use the services of a relocation management company.

Often, employee relocation is a result of takeovers, mergers and acquisition, and HR managers need to consider the impact that wider organisational issues can have on their employees.

The role of HRM in takeovers and mergers

So far in this chapter we have looked at a number of issues facing HR professionals in our changing times: the change in working practices, including flexible working, changes in career pathways and their implication for HR practice, the globalisation of modern businesses, and issues such as outsourcing and relocation. We are now going to examine the problems that can be faced if a company is involved in a merger or acquisition. This momentous change can result in a number of specific issues, which need to be carefully considered by the HR function.

mergers
When two or more businesses come together to form one organisation.

acquisitions
The purchase of another organisation. It can be a similar or diverse product type.

Research by Kristjanson-Love (2000), examined 44 Canadian organisations active over the previous 20 years in the areas of **mergers** and **acquisitions**. The idea of the research was to identify the key issues involved, in order to assist HRM practitioners in understanding, with greater clarity, what were considered to be 'vague people problems' that led to the failure of mergers and acquisitions. A common reason appeared to be a reduction of the workforce within two months of an acquisition, particularly in the case of hourly paid employees. This contributed to an 81 per cent failure rate in mergers and takeovers, although for technical and professional employees this was 100 per cent. Failures were common in the case of unanticipated turnover in managerial, technical and professional employees, especially if restructuring the acquired firms was undertaken within six months after acquisition. However, failures were also enhanced due to a reduction in physical structure or plant closure. As might be expected, any change that is gradual or incremental contributes to a higher probability of success, especially where companies have avoided radical integrated approaches early on that were not based upon criteria seen to be both fair and consistent.

Shrivastava (1986) has suggested that two-thirds of acquisitions and mergers do not produce the rewards anticipated. This is applicable to 90 per cent of cases according to Buono and Bowditch (1989). In addition, 30 per cent of acquired firms are sold off within five years. This is, in the main, attributed to lack of clear management understanding of human resource issues, which are sometimes regarded as superfluous to strategic planning (Napier, 1989). A seven-step approach to comprehending these all-important human resource problems (Marks and Mivis, 2001) can be useful for HR managers. Five steps are in the pre-merger and the other two in the post-merger stages.

Pre-merger and strategic planning

This is at the very first stage of deciding the type of merger approach, including the development of the mission statement and how to achieve the corporate objectives.

It also includes the procedure and decision on the creation of a specific team for the facilitation of the entire merger process. Highly significant was that the research indicated that corporate executives failed to include and integrate the crucial human resource aspects – an essential factor that could largely be due to lack of knowledge about the establishment of an effective management of change strategy, or ignorance of the negative effects of change on employees. This was probably due to emphasis being placed upon financial and legal concerns, which dominated the pre-merger stage. This is a crucial issue that undermines the importance of human resource managers participating as corporate decision-makers in the core strategic team – the very people who are likely to be more conversant with the capabilities of the original firm's employees and possess the essential skills that are necessary for the survival of the new company. Apart from corporate decision-making, Walsh (1989) emphasises the importance of retaining a qualified management team as a crucial element for success.

Analysis and offer

This is another crucial stage in obtaining the 'best fit' of the two firms. It is dependent upon financial, business and organisational strengths: the success of the merger depends upon all these being present. The organisational fit must include human resources, and take account of the fact that the two organisational cultures can be integrated successfully. However, if the differences are wide, then the desired level of integration will be difficult to achieve.

Post-merger: transition and integration

This focuses upon the management required to ensure both a stabilising influence and encourage a climate for change. Schweiger *et al.* (1987) highlight factors that cause uncertainty, anxiety, anger and frustration. In other words, 'a delicate balance'. Early voluntary leavers have indicated their reasons to be based upon negative factors such as psychological withdrawal and family disruption as a result of job relocation, as well as job insecurity and anxiety. The employee's perception of the threat, their feeling of confusion and of being powerless to counteract it, are highly contributory factors in the failure of mergers and acquisitions. There is a tendency for the firm taking over to dominate through centralising and controlling the functions of the acquired firm. Often, surviving managers feel a loss of their autonomy; this results in a situation that contributes to higher levels of absenteeism and lower productivity in the longer term, in the new operation.

Similar issues might occur in the case of downsizing, which might sometimes be perceived by employees to be based upon unclear criteria, but this is often due to poor communication (Schweiger *et al.*, 1987). Fombrun *et al.* (1984) noted that organisations making cuts without communicating their proposals actually put employees in a fight for personal survival – a situation that results in a vicious cycle of disintegration and low morale. The role of HR is to ensure that employees are consulted and included in any discussions.

Other problems, in the specific case of acquisitions, found that they tended to under-pay and under-reward seniority in the firms they had acquired, relative to their own personnel. Another factor was the employment fate of those with lower job seniority (Margolis, 2003).

Consequently, employees of the taken-over firm were less likely to remain for long, although those with high earnings were more likely to stay with the new entity. Significantly, these factors were found to be reflected in a model of takeovers. Margolis (2003) also raised the question as to why some firms are targets for takeover, viewed by the popular press as being motivated by the need to gain synergy, or rationalising activities that lead to some lay-offs and early retirements in order to achieve cost reductions. A further economic argument is that a firm might take over another where the net cost of takeover is inferior to the discounted value of the rents, or if firms are 'undervalued' in the market.

Mergers and acquisitions are frequently analysed by corporate finance literature. Some writers view the takeover as a procedure in which the market exerts control over management decisions considered by the market to be suboptimal, in that shareholder value is not maximised. Consequently, acquirement of the firm and dismissal of the manager can lead to efficiency gains.

It could be argued that the easiest task in management is the buying of another business, since one merely identifies the target at the price one prefers and then makes an offer. Achieving success with the actual merger might, however, be very difficult. From the start, choosing the wrong strategic objectives for the takeover is sure to lead to unsuccessful consequences. Therefore selecting the right combination of targets, and maintaining an optimistic approach throughout the merger, is vitally important in order to avoid failures. Essential in the whole procedure is the establishment and maintenance of a trusting relationship and therefore maintaining a satisfied workforce.

The model shown in Exhibit 13-7 is suggestive of the type of relationship applicable to any merger between the acquiring firm and the firm targeted. From left to right the diagram illustrates the relationship, decisions and actions representing trust in the management of the acquiring firm, as well as the number of controls imposed on the target.

As Jemison and Sitkin (1986) mention, in hostile bids the acquirer can be expected to adopt a 'hands on' approach and assert their control over the firm that is being acquired. Therefore management communication can have a serious impact on the trust that employees have of the firm taking them over, which is dependent upon the friendliness of the procedure involved. It is obvious that hostility would occur in the case of an unwanted takeover, especially if the acquirer is motivated by finance and seeks domination, as opposed to a climate of co-operation (Bastien, 1987; Schweiger and Walsh, 1990).

To achieve the objective, the first stage would be the replacement of the management of the targeted firm (Buono and Bowditch, 1989; Hambrick and Cannella, 1993; Hunt, 1990).

Communicating takeover decisions

Examples of poorly handled acquisitions are legion. Often, as a consequence of expansion, the management span of control at the top of the newly created organisation becomes much wider and this causes new strains that make successful coping even more difficult. Not only that but a lack of understanding of different organisational cultures and threats of downsizing might lead to resentments. Furthermore, delays after acquisitions, as in the example of BMW, may also ensure a non-successful outcome. Another factor is the spread of rumour and counter-rumour as reported by Stahl and Sitkin (2004) with the case of the Ciba-Geigy employees who heard

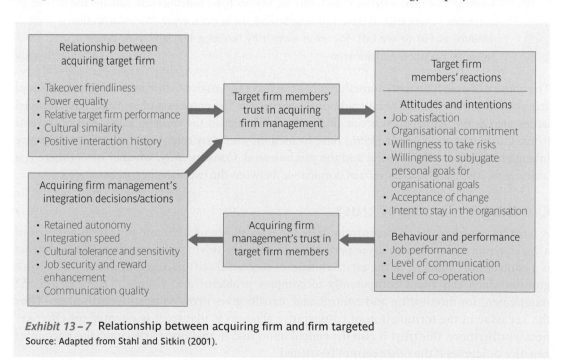

Exhibit 13 – 7 Relationship between acquiring firm and firm targeted
Source: Adapted from Stahl and Sitkin (2001).

over the radio that their company was to merge in 1998 with Sandoz, a competitor, and that large-scale reductions in the size of the workforce were to be the result. This was a totally unprompted revelation as far as the Ciba-Geigy workforce was concerned, further exacerbated through the lack of further information as to how the workforce was to be affected in the longer term. The only information provided was a vague statement that there would be a reduction of 10 per cent and that the new company name was Novartis.

Writers such as Caudron (1994) also illustrate this and similar cases, noting the resulting total lack of trust throughout an organisation. The lack of specific information can only lead to speculation and rumour, both negative and positive. Ideally such a situation would never occur because management would be expected to reveal all relevant and important details. Cartwright and Cooper (1996) defined this as the 'merger syndrome'. Such a crisis in an organisation can be viewed as occurring at three levels. First, at the personal level for employees who are due to change, experiencing a culture shock that leads to lower job performance, increases resistance to change, and encourages the spread of rumours and counter-rumours. As a consequence of this situation there is an increase in fear and betrayal, primarily in the minds of those employees who have been taken over. Second, at the organisational level, where senior management centralise decision-making that leads to a decline in communication together with reactive management. Third, from the new organisation perspective, this could increase the prevalence of culture clashes. A positive aspect in the Novartis case clearly illustrated that management had actually tried to address the problem of lack of trust. It was not that management did not recognise the importance of a climate of trust for the success of the merger – the chair of the board, Dr Daniel Vasella, had stated that:

> Trust is the most important of our values. Only in a climate of trust are people willing to strive for the slightly impossible. For people to take decisions on their own. To take the initiative and to feel accountable. Trust is the prerequisite for working together effectively and also an ally to fight bureaucracy. Among the corporate values, trust is the one that suffered most in the merger. We must fill this vacuum as fast as we can. We must earn it by 'walking the talk' with candour, integrity, openness and fairness!

The above example highlights something that can become a major factor in whether mergers and acquisitions succeed or fail. The traditional approach is the emphasis of strategic and financial issues such as the degree of 'strategic fit', or the similarities in the mission statements of the two firms. Cartwright and Cooper (1996) have focused on what they refer to as 'softer issues' that are intangible. These are the cultural and the psychological. Consequently, whether or not there is a 'cultural fit', there is also a 'pattern of dominance' between the two merging organisations.

Creating a climate of trust

A large body of research appears to indicate the importance of a climate of trust as a means of achieving more effective employee performance, problem-solving and commitment. Such trust is a contributory element in the establishment of successful self-managed or autonomous work groups, which can adapt competently to complex problems and change. Trust reduces the requirement for monitoring and control, and actually gives firms competitive advantage. Thus the key issue in the formulation of co-operative alliances is that trust is essential for effectiveness. Furthermore, this trust is also dependent upon risk, in that one party could also encounter negative outcomes if the other cannot be trusted.

At an individual level the concept of risk in the acquired firm will determine whether it will leave the organisation or remain. A further risk for managers is whether they are able to set up co-operative relationships by dispelling rumours, and consequently reduce employee anxiety. An issue of further importance is objectivity, or what is beneficial for the organisation as a whole, rather than subjectivity or the priority of self-interest. Gabarro (1978) and Mayer *et al.* (1995) postulate that, according to studies in trust in organisations, there are five critical characteristics required by the trustee. Namely:

1 competence
2 integrity
3 benevolence
4 openness
5 value congruence.

For instance, should a project team fail to meet its performance expectations after the acquisition it could be viewed from the perspective of the acquirer as incompetent overall. A lack of reliable information to the targeted firm's employees concerning job losses by the firm taking over, could adversely influence their perception of the integrity of the acquiring firm's management. The anticipated resistance to change from the perspective of the acquiring firm's managers could stimulate their distrust of the loyalty or benevolence of employees in the firm taken over. This also would affect the employees taken over as far as their perception of the openness of the acquiring managers (not forgetting organisational culture differences in terms of the manner in which problems were previously solved, risk assessment, and so on). Mistrust in these can lead to value incongruence.

In addition, the number of controls imposed upon the target should be taken into account. As Jemison and Sitkin (1986) mention, in hostile bids the acquirer can be expected to adopt a 'hands on' approach. The principal factor is the degree to which the management of the firm taking over affects the control of that being acquired in terms of communication (Bastien, 1987; Schweiger and Walsh, 1990).

More importantly, there is the trust that employees in the acquired firm hold with respect to the acquirers, together with the friendliness of the takeover. Obviously, most hostility would be shown if the takeover was unwanted, or if the takeover was motivated by finance and seeks domination as opposed to co-operation. Achieving the objective of the first stage would involve replacement of the management of the targeted firm. Buono and Bowditch (1989), Hambrick and Cannella (1993), and Hunt (1990) cite that hostility would create suspicion towards the acquirer. (See Exhibit 13-8.)

This is to do with the change in the actual distribution of power, especially if the takeover firm is larger (Pablo, 1994), in which case the employees' needs in the firm being acquired get trivialised. As the stronger party exercises greater power, the weaker one becomes more distrustful (Anderson and Weitz, 1989).

Managing integration

Takeover may actually increase motivation, however, especially if the previous management has been ineffective (Hunt, 1990). Acquisition of an under-performing firm by a more efficient one can create greater job satisfaction and job security, as well as better prospects for promotion or compensation. Conversely, poor performance might lead to a threatening of the targeted firm's managers.

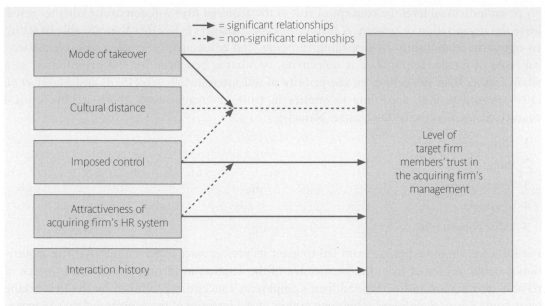

Exhibit 13–8 Hypothesised relationships and findings of a policy-capturing study
Source: Adapted from Stahl and Chua (2002).

A balanced merger can occur in practice, but more often the norm is that the firm taking over imposes control. Policy systems and culture changes are more likely, therefore, to be experienced by the acquiring firm (Hambrick and Cannella, 1993; Marks and Mivis, 2001). Removal of existing autonomy from the managers of the firm taken over can resultantly lead to feelings of hostility, helplessness and distrust (Datta and Grant, 1990).

The speed of integration, as suggested by Buono and Bowditch (1989), is through a 'window of opportunity'. This means that any changes should be implemented within the first 100 days, in order to reduce uncertainty and trauma. Conversely there is the argument put forward by Jemison and Sitkin (1986) for a slow pace. Either too quick or too slow can lead to undesirable consequences. Thus they argue the case for a moderate speed: fast enough to reduce feelings of risk or fear, but slow enough to enable effective communication to take place. They also acknowledge, paradoxically, that employees of the targeted company expect a major change shortly after takeover. That hesitation will actually increase suspicion.

Culture tolerance and sensitivity

Cultural distance might result from the growth in divergence (Kogut and Singh, 1998).

Cross-border acquisitions require a double-layered acculturation, which causes difficulty for effective integration between national and corporate cultures.

Positive interaction depends on a climate being established in the case of strategic alliances and socially embedded partnerships, which have been repeated over time (Gulati, 1995; Zaheer *et al.*, 1998). Sitkin and Roth (1993) use an analogy with romantic relationships that mature with interaction, frequency, duration and diversity of the challenges that partners face together. Such exchange and risk-taking situations collaborate together with success in achieving expectations. Therefore it is the nature of this relationship that a climate of trust is required.

This is where the takeover is seen not to have a detrimental effect on the morale of the targeted firm. The acquiring firm will be anxious to encourage and develop further that which has gone before (Chaterjee *et al.*, 1992; Pablo, 1994). However, if the acquiring firm has a unique ideology it may set out to impose this. The success of the takeover will essentially depend upon the firm's sensitivity to cultural differences, for arrogance on the part of the acquirer could significantly affect levels of trust.

Reward and job security enhancement, if seen as an outcome from the perspective of the acquired firm's employees, will obviously enhance the success of the takeover – likewise, any improvements in job satisfaction and job security. Hunt's (1990) study of Swedish acquisitions proved that there was a reduction in resistance to takeover. In this case employees perceived the outcome to be greater job security together with further opportunities for rewards and advancement. This emphasises once more that the clarity of information reduces the perception of risk and, together with trust, will lead to greater confidence in the management of the acquiring firm. Conversely, too much information may produce bewilderment, creating the opposite effect (Stahl and Sitkin, 2004).

Summary

- The increasing costs of employment and the need for greater efficiency are resulting in a more flexible workforce.

- Work/life balance enables people to choose how and when they work.

- Career pandemonium is the idea that uncertainties in the workplace can play havoc with traditional career paths, and organisations need to ensure progression opportunities are available for employees.

- Career concepts need to be flexible to take account of the new ways of working.

- HRM has an important role to play in the globalisation of business, in ensuring that employees are aware of the consequences of working in a global marketplace.

- Outsourcing is one method where organisations can relocate supporting roles to enable them to concentrate on their core business. HR can ensure that for employees the process runs smoothly.

- The relocation of employees can have an impact not only on the employee her/himself but also on their family. The HR department needs to ensure that effective policies are in place for a smooth transition.

- Virtualising means that employees may no longer be visible. Employers need to ensure that employees who work from home have the same support they would have if they were in an office environment.

- Takeovers and mergers can have consequences for employees, as these can create a time of stress and uncertainty. HR needs to ensure that communication is effective and that there are clear policies in place.

Personal development

1 **Develop a career path.** How can you develop a flexible career path that will fit in with changing employment patterns?

2 **Continually develop life planning.** Make choices about what mix of the primary aspects of your life you want: family, leisure, work, educational, social and spiritual development. Keep a check on how much time you spend on your priorities. Do you need to change anything? If so, how?

3 **Plan for work/life balance.** What are your life priorities, values and interests? What are your best skills and where do you want to use them? Decide what type of people you would like to work with and in what kind of organisation. What salary, developmental and advancement opportunities would you expect?

4 **Develop a global career.** Would you be able to work across countries and across cultures? What types of skills would you need to develop? Would you also need to develop new language skills? How could you gain an understanding of how businesses operate in different cultures?

5 **Work flexibly.** Can you update your skills regularly to ensure that you remain competitive in a fast-changing environment? Think about work skills, technical skills, managerial skills and, as you progress in your career, you will also need to develop critical, analytical and problem-solving skills.

6 **Develop technological competence.** Are you a technophobe or a technophile? The ability to use the latest technology is an advantage in today's society. The more technological competence you develop the easier it becomes. Keep abreast of new developments and learn how to use the technology effectively.

❓ Discussion questions

1 If work has to be interesting and have meaning does this mean that routine jobs will no longer get done? As a manager how would you approach this phenomenon?

2 To what extent is it possible to satisfy the career aspirations of all individuals within an organisation in the twenty-first century?

3 To what extent will the individual be responsible for the management of his or her own career pathway in organisations of the future?

4 Is it possible that all future organisations will be virtual and individuals transient in respect of career pathways?

5 State the processes and procedures that are essential to ensure that a merger or takeover is successful.

6 Discuss the key factors that lead to voluntary wastage in the first six months during the acquisition of an organisation.

7 What would you need to take into consideration before outsourcing the HR function?

8 What are the major effects of technological innovation for the HR manager?

9 What are the implications of relocating personnel for the HR manager?

10 What are the consequences of a phased and a clean break approach to relocation of the human resource?

🔑 Key concepts

learning organisation, *p. 438*

Theory Z, *p. 438*

just-in-time, *p. 438*

career pandemonium, *p. 439*

generation X, *p. 439*

globalisation, *p. 444*

convergence theory, *p. 446*

McDonaldisation, *p. 446*

Fordism, *p. 446*

downsizing, *p. 447*

outsourcing, *p. 447*

phased approach, *p. 448*

clean break approach, *p. 448*

mergers, *p. 457*

acquisitions, *p. 457*

Individual task

Purpose To identify the factors that need to be considered when offering employees international contracts.

Time 30 minutes

Procedure More and more organisations are working in global markets, which means more employees have the opportunity to work in other countries away from the home organisation. Look at the issues listed in the table below and identify:

- how important they would be to you as a manager employing staff for international operations
- what type of policies you would have in place to support overseas assignments.

Issue	Order of importance	Type of policy
Motivation		
Health		
Language ability		
Family considerations		
Resourcefulness		
Initiative		
Adaptability		
Career planning		
Financial package		

Team task

Purpose To identify problems and solutions to virtual working.

Time 40 minutes

Procedure Divide into small groups. Discuss the scenario that follows and then answer the questions below.

Your organisation is at the forefront of modern information technology. All your managers have voicemail and email, and all are networked. Many have started working from home. They have put the case to you that they are more productive at home and they don't need to waste time travelling when they could be working instead.

However, the CEO of your organisation is very traditional and thinks that if staff are not visible then they are not working. You also have some concerns as you recently discovered two employees who, although they communicate regularly by email, have never met in person. You consider the organisation as a warm and friendly place and you are alarmed by this lack of interaction.

You have now called together the team to discuss the following points.

- Is face-to-face communication important in today's workplace?
- How can we develop a plan for enhancing communication and interpersonal relations through the use of technology?
- Develop a policy for effective home working, taking into account the responsibility of an employer for the health and well-being of employees.

Case study: **Tipping the balance**

Work/life balance would appear to be a goal that no one could object to. But, in practice, employer schemes to improve work/life balance can be divisive and cause resentment. This is because of the disjunction between principles and practice.

In principle, work/life balance policies should offer all employees small adjustments to working time and employment arrangements that reduce the friction between job demands and private lives. But, in reality, most schemes are designed with a single group in mind: working parents or, more specifically, mothers of young children. These often take the shape of mother-friendly policies such as maternity leave, the right to work part-time after childbirth, time off to look after sick children, the option of working at home at times, flexible working hours, and so on.

The need for work/life balance at other stages of the life cycle, and among the childless, is usually forgotten. This narrow approach is largely due to the fact that European Commission social policy was focused for a long time on sex discrimination in the labour market, including a concern to establish minimum rights for women around pregnancy and childbirth, when many lost their jobs.

What is the effect of this? Unfortunately, it can create division because it prioritises young parents above other staff. Companies have already found that older women, who quit their jobs while their children were young, can be just as resentful as single and childless employees, and other staff who do not benefit from mother-friendly schemes.

Work/life balance policies should be redesigned to be gender-neutral and even-handed between all employees. The need to care for elderly parents can be just as onerous as the demands of young children or adolescents. People who are childless by choice now amount to around one-fifth of all adults, and their right to reconcile work and private lives is no less valid than that of parents.

In *Work-Lifestyle Choices in the 21st Century*, I argue that employer, trades union and government social policies can be redesigned to be more even-handed between all groups and types of worker. At present, there is a bias towards the interests of working women, especially young mothers. Policies need to be rebalanced to offer greater fairness in the context of workforce diversity.

This reorientation will require imagination. One-size-fits-all policies should be replaced with ones that recognise the differentiated, even conflicting, interests of workers with differing work/life balance priorities. There are already some examples to get us started.

In the Netherlands, recent legislation gave all workers the right to ask for a transfer to part-time hours, for any reason or none. The aim is to destigmatise part-time work, but also to give all employees the option of reducing their working hours to accommodate other life interests, be they further education, politics, sport, arts, community activities or leisure.

Flexible benefit schemes are popular precisely because they give all workers tangible benefits that can be spent or accumulated, and they recognise the increasing social and cultural diversity of the workforce.

All workers feel the need for work/life balance. The needs of parents have been the catalyst for changing inflexible employment practices, but the benefits of greater flexibility, in working time and in careers, should be open.

Source: Adapted from C. Hakim, 'Tipping the balance', *People Management*, 2 June 2005, p. 7.
Reproduced with permission of *People Management* and Catherine Hakim

Discussion questions

1 Give your definition of the term work/life balance. What does it mean for you?

2 As a manager, how would you design a flexible benefits system?

3 Why can work/life balance cause resentment?

4 Who are the stakeholders in ensuring the success of work/life balance policies?

WWW exercise

Employers for Work-Life Balance (EfWLB) is an organisation that aims to help all UK organisations implement and continuously improve sustainable work/life strategies that meet customer needs and corporate goals, and enhance the quality of life for individuals.

Visit its website at http://www.employersforwork-lifebalance.org.uk/.

1 What advice does it give (a) large organisations, (b) small/medium enterprises, and (c) individuals about how to achieve work/life balance?

2 What is the current legislation available to help support individuals in the achievement of work/life balance?

LEARNING CHECKLIST

Before moving on, check that you are able to:

☑ have an understanding of the changing nature of work

☑ recognise the impact of globalisation on all organisations

☑ be aware of the reasons for outsourcing both facilities and expertise

☑ understand the implications of relocating personnel according to HRM requirements

☑ acknowledge the consequences of change involving downsizing and mergers

☑ recognise the impact of technological innovation and virtual organisations.

Further reading

Atkinson, J. (1985) 'Flexible working patterns', Institute of Manpower Co-operative Research Programme, delivered at a lecture at the then Polytechnic of Central London.

Larsson, R. (1990) *Co-ordination of Action in Mergers and Acquisitions: Interpretive and Systems Approaches Towards Synergy.* Lund: University Press.

Trompenaars, E. and Hampden-Turner, C. (1999) *Riding the Waves of Culture* (2nd edn). London: Nicholas Brearly.

References

Anderson, E. and Weitz, B. (1989) 'Determinant of continuity in conventional industrial channel dyads', *Marketing Science* 8, pp. 310–323.

Ansoff, I. (1984) *From Strategic Planning to Strategic Management.* Prentice Hall.

Arkin, A. (1994) 'Employee relocation', *Personnel Management,* July, pp. 48–49.

Bastien, D.T. (1987) 'Common patterns of behaviour and communication in corporate acquisitions', *Human Resource Management* 26, pp. 17–34.

Boxall, P. (1995) 'Strategic human resource management: beginnings of a new theoretical sophistication', *HRM Journal* 2(3), pp. 60–79.

Bradt, R. (1998) *Virtual Organisations, A Simple Taxonomy.* Infothink.

Braverman, H. (1974) *Labour and Monopoly Capital: The Degradation of Work in the Twentieth Century.* Monthly Review Press.

Brousseau, K.R., Driver, M.J., Eneroth, K. and Larsson, R. (1996) 'Career pandemonium: or realigning organizations and individuals', *Academy of Management Executive* 10(4).

Buono, A.F. and Bowditch, J.L. (1989) *The Human Side of Mergers and Acquisitions: Managing Collisions between People, Cultures and Organizations.* San Francisco: Jossey-Bass.

Burns, T. and Stalker, G.M. (1994) *The Management of Innovation.* Oxford: Oxford University Press.

Cartwright, S. and Cooper, C.L. (1996) *Managing Mergers, Acquisitions and Strategic Alliances: Integrating People and Cultures* (2nd edn). Oxford: Butterworth Heinemann.

Caudron, S. (1994) 'HR leaders brainstorm', *Personnel Journal,* August, p. 54.

Chaterjee, S., Lubatkin, M.H., Schweiger, D.M. and Weber, Y. (1992) 'Cultural differences and shareholder value in related mergers: linking equity and human capital', *Strategic Management Journal* 13, pp. 319–334.

Child, J. (1981) 'Culture, contingency and capitalism in the cross national study of organisation', *Research in Organisational Behaviour* 3, pp. 303–356.

Clark, T. (1996) *European Human Resource Management.* Oxford: Blackwell.

Datta, D.K. and Grant, J.H. (1990) 'Relationships between type of acquisition, the autonomy given to the acquired firm and acquisition success: an empirical analysis', *Journal of Management* 16, pp. 29–44.

Fombrun, C., Tichy, N. and Devanna, M. (1984) *Strategic Human Resource Management.* John Wiley & Sons.

Gabarro, J.J. (1978) 'The development of trust, influence and expectations', in A.G. Athos and J.J. Gabarro (eds) *Interpersonal Behaviour: Communication and Understanding in Relationships.* Englewood Cliffs: Prentice Hall, pp. 290–303.

Gulati, R. (1995) 'Does familiarity breed trust? The implications of repeated ties for contractual choice in alliances', *Academy of Management Journal* 38, pp. 85–112.

Hambrick, D.C. and Cannella, A.A. (1993) 'Relative standing: a framework for understanding departures of acquired executives', *Academy of Management Journal* 8, pp. 2–30.

Hearsey, P. and Blanchard, K.H. (1996) *Management of Organisational Behaviour: Utilising Human Resources* (7th edn). Prentice Hall.

Hofstede, G. (1980) *Culture's Consequences: International Differences in Work Related Values.* Sage Publications.

Holden, L. (1999) *International Human Resource Management, A Contemporary Approach.* London: FT/Prentice Hall.

Hunt, J.W. (1990) 'Changing pattern of acquisition behaviour in takeovers and the consequences for acquisition processes', *Strategic Management Journal* 11, pp. 69–77.

Jemison, D.B. and Sitkin, S.B. (1986) 'Corporate acquisitions: a process perspective', *Academy of Management Review* 11, pp. 145–163.

Kerr, C., Dunlop, J., Harbison, F. and Myers, C. (1960) *Industrialisation and Industrial Management.* Boston, Mass.: Harvard University Press.

Kogut, B. and Singh, H. (1998) 'The effect of national culture on entry mode', *Journal of International Business Studies* 19, pp. 411–432.

Kristjanson-Love, C. (2000) *Mergers and Acquisitions – the Role of Success.* Ontario, Canada: Industrial Relations Centre.

Lane, C. (1995) *Industry and Society in Europe.* Aldershot: Elgar.

Margolis, D.N. (2003) 'Compensation policy, human resource management practices and takeovers', Sorbonne Economic Centre.

Marks, M.L. and Mivis, P.H. (2001) 'Making mergers and acquisitions work: strategic and psychological preparation', *Academy of Management Executive* 15, pp. 80–92.

Mayer, R.C., Davis, J.H. and Schoorman, F.D. (1995) 'An integrative model of organisational trust', *Academy of Management Review* 20, pp. 709–734.

Napier, N.K. (1989) 'Mergers and acquisitions, human resource issues and outcomes: a review and suggested typology', *Journal of Management Studies* 26, pp. 271–289.

Ouchi, W.G. and Jaeger, A.M. (1978) 'Type Z organisation: stability in the midst of mobility', *Academy of Management Review*, 3 April, pp. 305–314.

Pablo, A.L. (1994) 'Determinants of acquisition integration level: a decision making perspective', *Academy of Management Journal* 37, pp. 206–215.

Porter, M. (1990) *The Competitive Advantage of Nations.* New York: Free Press.

Price, A. (2000) *Human Resource Management in a Business Context* (2nd edn). London: Thompson.

Schweiger, D.M. and Walsh, J.P. (1990) 'Mergers and acquisitions: an interdisciplinary view', *Research in Personnel and Human Resource Management* 8, pp. 41–107.

Schweiger, D.M., Ivancevich, J.M. and Power, F.R. (1987) 'Executive actions for managing human resources before and after acquisition', *Academy of Management Review* 1, pp. 127–138.

Shrivastava, P. (1986) 'Is strategic management ideological?', *Journal of Management* 12(3), pp. 79–92.

Sitkin, S. and Roth, N.L. (1993) 'Explaining the limited effectiveness of legalistic remedies for trust/distrust', *Organisation Science* 4(3), pp. 365–390.

Stahl, G.K. and Chua, C.H. (2002) *Antecedents of Target Firm Members' Trust Following a Takeover: A Decision Making Approach.* Paris: INSEAD working paper series.

Stahl, G.K. and Sitkin, S.B. (2001) *Trust in Corporate Acquisitions*, INSEAD working paper. Fontainebleu, France.

Stahl, G.K. and Sitkin, S.B. (2004) *Trust in Mergers and Acquisitions.* University-Duke Corporation Education.

Storey, J. (ed.) (1995) *Human Resource Management: A Critical Text.* London: Thompson.

Thomson, R. and Mabey, C. (1994) *Developing Human Resources.* Butterworth-Heinneman.

Trompenaars, E. (1996) 'Resolving international conflict: culture and business strategy', *Business Strategy Review* 7(3), pp. 51–69.

Walsh, J.P. (1989) 'Top management turnover following mergers and acquisitions', *Strategic Management Journal* 9, pp. 173–184.

Waterman, R.H. and Collard, B.A. (1994) 'Towards a career-resilient workforce', *Harvard Business Review* 72(4), pp. 87–95.

Waterman, R.H., Peters, T.J. and Phillips, J.R. (1980) 'Structure is not organisation', *Business Horizons* 23(14).

Zaheer, A., McEvily, B. and Perrone, V. (1998) 'Does trust matter? Exploring the effects of interorganisational and interpersonal trust on performance', *Organisation Science* 9, pp. 141–159.

Index

360-degree feedback 266

A

ability testing
    administrative testing 156
    advantages 156–7
    aptitude testing 155
    attainment testing 155
    dexterity testing 156
    diagrammatic testing 156
    disadvantages 157
    intelligence testing 155
    mechanical testing 156
    numerical testing 156
    selection 155–7
    sensory testing 156
    spatial testing 156
    types 155–6
    verbal/communication testing 156
absenteeism, job sharing 68
academic references 149
Acas
    case study 316–17
    employee relations 316–17
accommodating, conflict management style
    299–300
accommodator, learning style 225
accounting, HR 413–15
acquisitions
    see also mergers
    defining 457
    employee relocation 456
    HR role 456–63
    relationships 458–63
activist, learning style 226–7
administration objectives, HR activity 12
administrative testing 156
advertising and recruitment consultants 127
age discrimination 80–1
    IKEA 378
ageism 377
    case study 394–5
agencies
    advertising and recruitment consultants 127
    commercial recruitment 126–7
    cyber 129–30
    executive search 128–9
    permanent employment 128–9
    recruitment 126–30
    temporary and contract staffing 127–8
agile workers, transferable skills 67

analysing HR needs, planning 50–1
analysis
    job analysis 75–6, 109–13
    needs analysis, training 230–1
    training 230–1
    work design 75–6
    work flow analysis 77–8
annual hours, flexible working 67
anticipatory control 222
application forms
    benefits 142
    limitations 142
    online 142
    selection 141–2
appointments
    contracts of employment 164
    employment particulars 164–5
    legal framework 163–5
    selection 163–5
appraisal
    interviews 280–1
    performance 259–62, 280–1
    soft HRM 21
apprenticeships 249
aptitude testing 155
artificial intelligence, gender bias 138–9
assessment centres
    complementary activities 162–3
    defining 160
    group work 161–2
    limitations 163
    presentations 162
    role-plays 162
    selection 160–3
    strengths 163
    written exercises 162
assimilator, learning style 225
attainment testing 155
avoiding, conflict management style 300

B

balanced scorecard 414–15
banks/banking
    international perspective 29–30
    offshoring 29–30
    outsourcing 29–30
    South Africa 29–30
bargaining strategies 302–4
barriers, teamwork 96
behavioural conditioning, learning 220–1
behavioural questioning, interviews 145

Belbin's team roles, work design 92–4
benchmarking, pay 184
best practice 407
  defining 407
biographical profiling
  benefits 152
  defining 151
  limitations 152
  selection 151–3
biographical questioning, interviews 145
biological approach, job design 85
bioprofiling *see* biographical profiling
bonuses 187
  defining 187
BPO *see* outsourcing
branding
  people 60
  talent 60
British Airways, strategy 430–1
broad banding 182
business case
  defining 364
  diversity, managing 364–5
business process outsourcing (BPO)
    see outsourcing
business school, Mexico, international perspective
    229–30

C
Canada, teleworking 88–91
candidate group interviews 146–7
car industry, training 215–17
care services 348–9
career concepts 440–3
career management
  diversity, managing 445
  Laboratoires Boiron 445
  WLB 445
career pandemonium 439
career paths, changes 439
career planning 51
careers, contracts 443–4
case study
  Acas 316–17
  ageism 394–5
  development 281–3
  diversity, managing 394–5
  employee relations 316–17
  health, safety and employee well-being 355–6
  hotels 134–5
  Intel Ireland 247–9
  job design 100
  O₂ 209–10
  Patak's 316–17
  police 37–8
  PRP 209–10
  recruitment 134–5
  selection 171–2
  St Lucia's secondary school 100

TNT UK Ltd 281–3
  training 247–9, 281–3
  WLB 467–8
CEHR *see* Commission for Equality and Human
    Rights
centralisation
  defining 78
  organisational structure 78–9
change
  career paths 439
  HR 5–6
change management
  National Trust 399–402
  objectives 11–12
  soft HRM 20
changing nature of jobs 79–81
changing nature of work 64–5
Chartered Institute of Personnel and Development
    (CIPD), www exercises 38
Citigroup
  diversity, managing 385
  international perspective 385
classical conditioning 220
clean break approach 448
  defining 448
  outsourcing 451–2
coaching
  defining 276
  development 276
  performance 276–7
  www exercises 283
coaching culture, talent 60
codes of practice
  defining 331
  health, safety and employee well-being 331, 338
cognitive learning 222–3
  defining 222
collaborating, conflict management style 300
commercial recruitment agencies 126–7
Commission for Equality and Human Rights (CEHR)
    388–9
Commission for Racial Equality (CRE)
  diversity, managing 366–9
  ten-point plan 366, 369
communication
  employee relations 286–8
  flexible working 68
  mergers 459–61
communication systems, soft HRM 21, 22
community sense, talent 61
competencies, performance management 257–8
competency alternative, recruitment 114–16
competency, defining 114
competency frameworks, recruitment 113–14
competing, conflict management style 299
competition
  labour supply/demand 54
  pay 183–4
  talent 61

competitive advantage 417
  creating 419–20
  defining 417
compromising, conflict management style 300–1
conditioning, behavioural 220–1
configurational perspective, SHRM 409, 411
conflict 294–301
  defining 294
  dysfunctional view 296–7
  felt 297–8
  functional view 296–7
  interactionist perspective 296–7
  interdependence 297
  latent 297
  managing 296–301
  manifest 298
  Marxist perspective 296
  outcome 298
  perceived 297
  perspectives 294–7
  pluralist perspective 294
  stages 297–8
  unitarist perspective 294
conflict management styles 298–301
  defining 299
contemporary selection 151
context
  defining 25
  economic 27
  external 26–8
  global 28
  HRM 25–8
  organisational 25–6
  political 26
  social 27
  technological 27–8
contextual perspective, SHRM 409–10, 411
contingency perspective, SHRM 408–9, 411
contingency plans 49
contracts
  careers 443–4
  individual tasks 466
contracts of employment, appointments 164
Control of Substances Hazardous to Health
    Regulations (COSHH), health, safety and
    employee well-being 332
convergence, international HRM 444–7
convergence theory 446
converger, learning style 225
corporate social responsibility (CSR), pay 176–7
corporate values, talent 60
corruption, international perspective 229–30
COSHH see Control of Substances Hazardous to
    Health Regulations
costs, employment 437–8
counselling 348–9
CRE see Commission for Racial Equality
CSR see corporate social responsibility
cultural approach 446–7

cultural sensitivity, mergers 462–3
cultural tolerance, mergers 462–3
culture, defining 27
current issues 435–70
Cushman and Wakefield, Healey and Baker, flexible
    working 435–6
CVs
  benefits 141
  limitations 142
  selection 141–2
cyber agencies 129–30
cycle, human resource, hard HRM 24–5

D
decision-making
  competing forces 381–2
  diversity, managing 381–2
  pay 183–4
Deloitte, health, safety and employee well-being 336
demand/supply, labour 52–6, 62–4
demographics, labour supply/demand 53–4
demotions, labour supply/demand 63
depth/scope, job design 85–8
development 31–2, 215–51
  see also learning; personal development; training
  advantages 218–19
  case study 281–3
  changing nature of jobs 81
  coaching 276
  defining 32
  diversity, managing 384
  performance 252–85
  SHRM 410–12
  soft HRM 19–23
  TNT UK Ltd 281–3
developments, new 435–70
dexterity testing 156
diagrammatic testing 156
diaries/logs, job analysis 110–11
differentiation, learning 223
discipline
  defining 306
  employee relations 306–7, 316–17
discrimination
  see also racism
  age 80–1
  defining 223, 363
  diversity, managing 80–1, 143–4
  dress codes 19
  JobCentre 19
  learning 223
  legal framework 376–8
  legislation 80–1, 363–5, 379
  police 143–4
  process 380
distributive bargaining
  defining 302
  negotiation 302–3
distributive justice 189

divergence, international HRM 444–7
diverger, learning style 224
diversity
    awareness 378–81
    defining 364, 366–72
    initiatives 382–4
    measuring 384–7
    monitoring 384–7
diversity, managing 361–98
    see also equal opportunities
    awareness 378–81
    business case 364–5, 374
    career management 445
    case study 394–5
    CEHR 388–9
    Citigroup 385
    CRE 366–9
    criticisms 375–6
    decision-making 381–2
    development 81, 384
    discrimination 80–1, 143–4
    dress codes 18–19
    dyslexia 237–9
    employee benefits 81
    EOC 366–9
    vs equal opportunities 373
    EU expansion 420–2
    Expedia 117
    flexible working 307–9
    glass ceiling 365
    Hallmark Cards 307–9
    implementation 382–4, 387–9
    individual tasks 393–4
    initiatives 382–4
    international perspective 385
    interpreting 373–4
    Laboratoires Boiron 445
    legal aspects 389–90
    legal framework 376–8, 379
    legislation 379
    models 382–4
    monitoring 384–7
    motivation 203
    NHS 362–3
    paradigm 363–5
    personal development 392
    police 143–4
    prejudices 380
    prisoners 62
    problems 365
    promotion 80
    recruitment 62, 80–1, 117
    redundancies 81
    retirement 81
    selection 80–1, 143–4
    sick days 203
    social justice 364–5
    stereotypes 267–8, 380
    support 382–4
    taboos 382
    team tasks 394
    Tesco 203
    training 237–9, 384, 445
    training/development 81
    WLB 445
double-loop learning 242–3
    defining 242
downsizing 447
    defining 447
    labour supply/demand 62
dress codes
    discrimination 19
    diversity, managing 18–19
    JobCentre 19
dual-factor theory 190–2
    defining 191
duty of care
    defining 331
    health, safety and employee well-being 331
dysfunctional view of conflict 296–7
    defining 296
dyslexia, training 237–9

E
EAPs *see* employee assistance programmes
early retirement, labour supply/demand 63
economic context, HRM 27
education
    business school 229–30
    defining 218
    international perspective 229–30
    vs training 218–19
educational sources, recruitment 124–5
efficiency wage theory 184
electronic performance support systems (EPSS) 261
empiricism
    defining 112
    job analysis 112–13
employee assistance programmes (EAPs) 348–9
employee benefits, changing nature of jobs 81
employee commitment, soft HRM 22
employee consultation 292–3
    international perspective 295
employee influence, soft HRM 16
employee involvement 291–2
    defining 291
employee participation 291–2
    defining 291
employee relations 32–3, 286–319
    Acas 316–17
    approaches 290–1
    case study 316–17
    communication 286–8
    conflict 294–301
    defining 32, 288
    discipline 306–7, 316–17
    employee representation 289–91
    flexible working 307–9

grievance 306–7, 316–17
  HR managers' role 289
  individual tasks 312
  personal development 310–11
  Royal Mail 286–8
  team tasks 313–15
employee relocation 454–6
employee representation 289–91
  Guest and Hoque's typology 290–1
  non-union organisations 290–1
  trades unions 289–90
employee support, forms 342–4
employment costs 437–8
employment particulars, appointments 164–5
employment references 149
Employment Rights Act 1996; 202
empowerment
  defining 272
  expectations 275–6
  by managers 275
  by others 274
  performance 272–6
  results 275
  self-initiated 274
enforcement
  defining 329
  health, safety and employee well being 329
enlarged jobs, job design 86–7
enriched jobs, job design 86–7
Enron 3–5
enterprise resource planning (ERP) 58–9
environmental pressures, hard HRM 23
EOC see Equal Opportunities Commission
EPSS see electronic performance support systems
equal opportunities 361–98
  see also discrimination; diversity, managing
  CEHR 388–9
  criticisms 371–2
  defining 363, 366–72
  vs diversity, managing 373
  individual tasks 393–4
  legal aspects 389–90
  legal framework 376–8, 379
  legislation 379
  monitoring 384–7
  personal development 392
  police 143–4
  positive action 367–8, 369
  promoting 368–9
  radical approach 367
  regulatory approach 363–4
  team tasks 394
  ten-point plan, CRE 366, 369
  www exercises 396
Equal Opportunities Commission (EOC)
  diversity, managing 366–9
  pay 204–5
Equal Pay Act 1970; 201
Equal Pay Amendment (Regulations) 1983; 202

equal treatment, defining 376
equity, pay 204–5
equity theory
  defining 188
  motivation 188–9
ergonomics
  defining 85
  job design 85
ERP see enterprise resource planning
ethics, international perspective 229–30
EU expansion
  diversity, managing 420–2
  HR implications 420–2
  strategy 420–2
European Works Councils (EWC) 293–4
EWC see European Works Councils
executive search agencies 128–9
exit interviews 270–1
expectancy theory 189–90
  defining 189
Expedia
  diversity, managing 117
  recruitment 117
experiential learning styles 223–7
expert concept, careers 440–3
external context, HRM 26–8
external courses, training 236
external labour market, planning 61–2
external recruitment 121–31
  defining 121

F

factor comparison 180–1
  defining 180
Fastow, Andrew 3–5
feedback
  360-degree 266
  performance 263–6
  positive 263–6
  problems 263
felt conflict 297–8
flexible benefits 196, 197
  defining 196
  talent 60
flexible working 67, 435–7
  agile workers 67
  annual hours 67
  communication 68
  Cushman and Wakefield, Healey and Baker
    435–6
  employee relations 307–9
  Hallmark Cards 307–9
  job design 88–91
  job sharing 68
  patterns 65–8
  planning 65–8
  real estate 435–6
  teleworking 88–91
  work/life balance 65–7

Fordism 446
  defining 446
  history 7
forecasting
  defining 50
  planning 50–1
foundations, HR activity 10–12
Fraser's five-point plan, person specifications 115
functional group roles, work design 92–4
functional view of conflict 296–7
  defining 296
functions, HR 28–33
  planning 28–30
  resourcing 28–30
  staff retention 28–30
future scenarios, health, safety and employee well-being 350–2

G

gainsharing 187–8
  defining 187
gender bias
  artificial intelligence 138–9
  IQ tests 138–9
generalisation
  defining 223
  learning 223
generation X 439–40
  defining 439
generic strategy 404
Germany, employee consultation 295
gestalt 222
Ghana, selection 153
glass ceiling
  defining 365
  diversity, managing 365
global context, HRM 28
globalisation 444–7
government agencies, recruitment 125–6
grievance
  defining 306
  employee relations 306–7, 316–17
group work, assessment centres 161–2
Guest and Hoque's typology, employee representation 290–1
Guest's model, HRM 21, 22
guidance
  defining 325
  health, safety and employee well-being 325

H

Hallmark Cards
  diversity, managing 307–9
  flexible working 307–9
hard HRM 23–5
  cycle, human resource 24–5
  defining 14
  environmental pressures 23
  management systems 24–5

Michigan model 23, 24–5
mission 24
organisation structure 24
strategic management 23
Harvard model
  defining 16
  soft HRM 16–17, 20
health, safety and employee well-being 323–60
  care services 348–9
  case study 355–6
  codes of practice 331, 338
  COSHH 332
  counselling 348–9
  Deloitte 336
  duty of care 331
  EAPs 348–9
  employee support 342–4
  enforcement 329, 338–9
  future scenarios 350–2
  guidance 325, 337
  health and safety officer 323–4
  history 328–36
  individual tasks 354
  international perspective 326–7
  legislation 328–39, 355–6
  medical and health insurance 345
  occupational health 341
  occupational healthcare facilities 345–7
  options 337–8
  personal counselling 348–9
  personal development 353
  policies 350–2
  prosecutions 338–9
  regulations 329, 338
  rehabilitation services 346
  responsibilities 335–6
  return to work services 346
  services 339–52
  subcontractors 326–7
  team tasks 355
  well-being 339–52
  wellness services 347–8
  Working Time Directive 334
  www exercises 356–7
hemispheres (brain), learning 227
Herzberg's dual-factor theory 190–2
hierarchical job analysis 112
high-performance HR system 418
high-performance work systems
  defining 407
  strategy 407–8, 422–4
history
  First World War 8
  Fordism 7
  health, safety and employee well-being 328–36
  HRM 6–10
  human relations movement 8
  late nineteenth century 6–7
  scientific management 7

Second World War 9
time line 6
war years 8–10
Honey and Mumford's learning styles 226–7
horizontal loading
defining 84
job design 84
hotels
case study 134–5
recruitment 134–5
HR accounting 413–15
HR managers
employee relations role 289
roles 28–33
skills 228
HR outcomes, soft HRM 18
HR practices, performance 424–6
human factor approach, job design 85
human relations approach, job design 82–5
human relations movement, history 8
human resource flow
defining 20
soft HRM 16, 20
hunting analogy, self-interest 3–5
hygiene factors 191
defining 191

I

IIP see Investors In People
IKEA, age discrimination 378
in-house programmes, training 235–6
incentives 196
India
outsourcing 449–50
PRP 194
individual pay 197
individual tasks
contracts 466
diversity, managing 393–4
employee relations 312
equal opportunities 393–4
health, safety and employee well-being 354
learning 245–7
pay 208–9
performance 279
planning 70
psychological contract 98
recruitment 133
selection 170
stereotypes 393–4
strategic thinking 36
strategy 429
individuals' values, talent 60
induction
defining 165
selection 165–7
INET Finance, virtualising 453
inputs, work flow analysis 77–8
insight 222–3

institutional racism 378
defining 378
police 378
insurance, medical and health 345, 346–7
integration, mergers 461–2
integrative bargaining
defining 303
negotiation 303–4
Intel Ireland
case study 247–9
training 247–9
intelligence 219–20
defining 219
testing 155
interactionist perspective, conflict 296–7
interdependence
conflict 297
defining 297
internal labour market
planning 56–8
staff retention 271–2
internal recruitment 120
international HRM 444–7
international perspective
banks/banking 29–30
business school 229–30
Canada 88–91
Citigroup 385
corruption 229–30
diversity, managing 385
education 229–30
employee consultation 295
EPSS 261
ethics 229–30
Germany 295
Ghana 153
health, safety and employee well-being 326–7
India 194
Juapong Textiles 153
Lithuania 326–7
Mexico 229–30
offshoring 29–30
outsourcing 29–30, 449–50
planning 55–6
PRP 194
recruitment 55–6, 125
selection 153
South Africa 29–30
strategy 417
subcontractors 326–7
teleworking 88–91
training 229–30
internet businesses, recruitment 117
internet, recruitment 55–6, 117
interviews
appraisal 280–1
behavioural questioning 145
biographical questioning 145
candidate group 146–7

interviews – *contd.*
   content 145–6
   delivery formats 146–7
   exit 270–1
   job analysis 111
   one-to-one 146–7
   panel 146–7
   performance appraisal 280–1
   problems 147–8
   selection 144–8
   situational questioning 145
   small group 146–7
   stress questioning 146
   structures 144–5
   tandem 146–7
   team tasks 280–1
   telephone 146–7
   videoconference 146–7
intuition 227
Investors In People (IIP) 281–3
IQ tests
   gender bias 138–9
   selection 138–9

J

Japanese attitude, training 215–17
job analysis 75–6
   defining 109
   diaries/logs 110–11
   empiricism 112–13
   hierarchical 112
   interviews 111
   limitations 112–13
   methods 110–12
   observation 111
   questionnaires 111–12
   recruitment 109–13
job classification 181
   defining 181
job descriptions, recruitment 113–14
job design 74–102
   biological approach 85
   case study 100
   defining 81–2
   ergonomics 85
   horizontal loading 84
   human factor approach 85
   human relations approach 82–5
   job enlargement 84
   job enrichment 84
   job profiles 86–7
   job rotation 84
   jobs characteristics model 83
   mechanistic approach 82
   motivational approach 82–5
   new ways of working 88
   observation 82
   perceptual-motor approach 85
   psychological contract 87–8

school 100
scientific management 82
soft HRM 20
St Lucia's secondary school 100
task depth/scope 85–8
vertical loading 84
www exercises 101
job enlargement
   defining 84
   job design 84
job enrichment
   defining 84
   job design 84
job evaluation 180–1
   defining 180
job families 183
job profiles, job design 86–7
job ranking 181
job rotation
   defining 84
   job design 84
job satisfaction 268–72
   see also staff retention
job sharing, flexible working 68
JobCentre
   discrimination 19
   dress codes 19
   recruitment 125–6
jobs, changing nature of 79–81
jobs characteristics model, job design 83
John Lewis Partnership, strategy 431
Juapong Textiles, Ghana, selection 153
just-in-time 438–9
   defining 438

K

knowledge management, staff retention 272, 273
Kolb's experiential learning model 223–7

L

Laboratoires Boiron
   career management 445
   diversity, managing 445
   training 445
labour demand 52–6
   defining 52
   strategies 62–4
labour market
   external 61–2
   internal 56–8, 271–2
labour supply 52–6
   defining 52
   strategies 62–4
latent conflict 297
learning 215–51
   see also development; personal development;
      training
   advantages 218–19
   apprenticeships 249

behavioural conditioning 220–1
cognitive 222–3
defining 219
differences 223–8
experiential learning styles 223–7
hemispheres (brain) 227
individual tasks 245–7
lifelong 228
personal development 244
self-managed learning 236–7
social learning theory 221–2
socialisation 217
styles 223–7
team tasks 247
theories 219–23
www exercises 249
Learning and Skills Council (LSC), training 233–4
learning organisation 239–43, 438
   characteristics 239–40
   creating 241–2
   defining 239, 438
   double-loop learning 242–3
   single-loop learning 242–3
legal aspects
   diversity, managing 389–90
   equal opportunities 389–90
   pay 201–4
legal context, recruitment 116–19
legal framework
   appointments 163–5
   diversity, managing 376–8, 379
   equal opportunities 376–8, 379
legislation
   discrimination 80–1, 363–5
   diversity, managing 379
   equal opportunities 379
   health, safety and employee well-being 328–39,
      355–6
   prosecutions 338–9
   recruitment 116–19
lifelong learning 228
linear concept, careers 440–3
Lithuania, international perspective 326–7
living wage 176–8
Lloyds TSB, performance 252–3
long-term consequences, soft HRM 18
low pay 204
LSC see Learning and Skills Council

M
McDonaldisation 446
maintenance roles, work design 94
management systems, hard HRM 24–5
managers
   empowerment by 275
   responsibilities 200
managers, HR see HR managers
manifest conflict 298
manpower flows, soft HRM 21

market competition 183
market, labour see labour market
market surveys, pay 184
Marxist perspective, conflict 296
mechanical testing 156
media sources, recruitment 130–1
medical and health insurance 345, 346–7
   defining 345
mergers
   see also acquisitions
   communication 459–61
   cultural sensitivity 462–3
   cultural tolerance 462–3
   defining 457
   employee relocation 456
   HR role 456–63
   integration 461–2
   post-merger transition/integration 458–63
   pre-merger planning 457–8
   relationships 458–63
   strategic plans 457–8
   trust 460–1
merit pay 186
Mexico, business school 229–30
Michigan model, hard HRM 23, 24–5
minimum wage 176–8
   National Minimum Wage Act 1998; 203–4
mission
   defining 24
   hard HRM 24
motivation
   diversity, managing 203
   equity theory 188–9
   rewards 188–201
   satisfiers 191–2
   sick days 203
   Tesco 203
   work flow analysis 78
   www exercises 72
motivational approach, job design 82–5
motivator factors 191
   defining 191
myths, pay 185

N
National Crime Squad, work design 74–5
National Learning Targets, training 232
National Minimum Wage Act 1998; 203–4
National Trust
   change management 399–402
   strategic thinking 399–402
National Vocational Qualifications (NVQs)
   defining 232
   training 231–2, 233
natural wastage, labour supply/demand 63
needs analysis, training 230–1
negotiation 301–6
   bargaining process 302
   defining 301

negotiation – *contd.*
   distributive bargaining 302–3
   effective 301–2
   guidelines 304–6
   objectives 301
   preparation 301
   reaching agreement 302
   settlement range 303
   strategies 302–4
new developments 435–70
new pay 186
new recruits, labour supply/demand 63
newsprint sources, recruitment 130–1
NHS
   diversity, managing 362–3
   racism 362–3
NHS Greater Glasgow, recruitment 105–6
numerical testing 156
NVQs *see* National Vocational Qualifications

O

O_2
   case study 209–10
   PRP 209–10
objectives
   administration 12
   change management 11–12
   negotiation 301
   performance 11, 262–3
   SMART 262–3
   staffing 10–11
   training 235
observation
   defining 82
   job analysis 111
   job design 82
occupational health
   defining 341
   health, safety and employee well-being 341
occupational healthcare facilities 345–7
occupational sick pay (OSP) 341–5
   defining 341
offshoring
   banks/banking 29–30
   international perspective 29–30
on-the-job training 235
one-to-one interviews 146–7
online application forms 142
online testing, selection 160
open system, defining 26
operant conditioning 220–1
   defining 220
operational plans 49
organisation structure, hard HRM 24
organisational design, soft HRM 20
organisational goals, defining 28
organisational planning 48–9
organisational structure 76–7, 78–9
   centralisation 78–9

   defining 76
   by division 78–9
   by function 78–9
organisational values
   defining 46
   planning 46
organisation's own resources, recruitment 121–4
OSP *see* occupational sick pay
outputs, work flow analysis 77–8
outsourcing 447–52
   banks/banking 29–30
   clean break approach 451–2
   defining 447
   ethical standards 451
   India 449–50
   international perspective 29–30, 449–50
   labour supply/demand 63
   managing 451–2
   phased approach 451
overtime, labour supply/demand 63

P

paired comparison 181
panel interviews 146–7
paradigm
   defining 363
   diversity, managing 363–5
Patak's, case study 316–17
paternalist 6–7
   defining 6
pay 32
   see also remuneration; rewards
   benchmarking 184
   competition 183–4
   CSR 176–7
   decision-making 183–4
   defining 32
   EOC 204–5
   equity 204–5
   individual 197
   individual tasks 208–9
   legal aspects 201–4
   living wage 176–8
   low 204
   market surveys 184
   merit 186
   minimum wage 176–8, 203–4
   myths 185
   new 186
   OSP 341–5
   PRP 194, 197–8, 199, 209–10
   rate ranges 184–5
   SSP 341–5
   team 198–201
   team tasks 209
   traditional 186
   transparency 204–5
pay reductions, labour supply/demand 63
pay structures, defining 180

payment concepts 185–8
payment structure 179–82
people branding, talent 60
PeopleSoft 58–9
perceived conflict 297
perceptual-motor approach
    defining 85
    job design 85
performance
    appraising 259–62
    coaching 276–7
    development 252–85
    empowerment 272–6
    EPSS 261
    feedback 263–6
    high-performance work systems 407–8, 422–4
    HR practices 424–6
    IIP 281–3
    individual tasks 279
    Lloyds TSB 252–3
    managing 252–85
    objectives 11, 262–3
    personal development 278
    poor 260–2
    reasons, under-performance 264–5
    SMART objectives 262–3
    staff retention strategies 268–72
    stereotypes 267–8
    TNT UK Ltd 281–3
    under-performance reasons 264–5
performance appraisal 21, 259–62
    defining 259
    interviews 280–1
performance management 253–9
    competencies 257–8
    defining 253–4
    functions 254–5
    models 255–9
performance objectives 262–3
    HR activity 11
performance-related pay (PRP) 194, 197–8, 199
    advantages 199
    case study 209–10
    defining 197
    disadvantages 199
    O$_2$ 209–10
permanent employment agencies 128–9
person specifications
    example 116
    Fraser's five-point plan 115
    recruitment 113–14
    Rodger's seven-point plan 115
personal counselling 348–9
    defining 348
personal development 34–5, 69, 464–5
    diversity, managing 392
    employee relations 310–11
    equal opportunities 392
    health, safety and employee well-being 353

learning 244
    performance 278
    recruitment 132
    remuneration 206–7
    selection 168–9
    strategy 427
    training 244
    work design 97–8
personal references 149
personal roles, work design 94
personality assessments, selection 158–9
personnel management vs HRM 10–14, 15
phased approach 448
    defining 448
    outsourcing 451
planning 28–30, 41–73
    analysing HR needs 50–1
    career 51
    contingency plans 49
    defining 30
    ERP 58–9
    external labour market 61–2
    flexible working 65–8
    forecasting 50–1
    individual tasks 70
    internal labour market 56–8
    international perspective 55–6
    operational plans 49
    organisational 48–9
    organisational values 46
    process 43–4, 49
    ratio analysis 51
    redundancies 41–3
    software 58–9
    St Albans Council 71–2
    standard 44–5
    strategic 46–8
    strategic plans 48
    succession 57–8
    tactical plans 49
    talent 58–61
    team tasks 71
    transitional matrices 56–7
    trend analysis 50–1
    types 44
    Virgin Atlantic 41–3
    work/life balance 65–7
pluralist perspective, conflict 294
points rating 180–1
    defining 180
police
    case study 37–8
    discrimination 143–4
    equal opportunities 143–4
    institutional racism 378
    selection 143–4
policies
    health, safety and employee well-being 350–2
    training 231–4

policy formulation, soft HRM 20
political context, HRM 26
politics, labour supply/demand 54
positive action
    defining 367
    equal opportunities 367–8, 369
positive energy, talent 61
positive feedback 263–6
pragmatist, learning style 226
predictive validity
    defining 140
    selection 140–1
prejudices
    defining 380
    diversity, managing 380
Premack principle 221
presentations, assessment centres 162
prisoners
    diversity, managing 62
    recruitment 62
    work experience 62
procedural justice 189
profit sharing 187
promotion, changing nature of jobs 80
prosecutions, health, safety and employee well-being
    338–9
PRP see performance-related pay
psychological contract
    defining 87
    individual tasks 98
    job design 87–8
    talent 60
psychological disposition
    advantages 159
    defining 157
    disadvantages 159
    selection 157–9
psychological testing
    classification 154
    defining 153
    selection 153–4

Q
quality, soft HRM 22–3
questionnaires, job analysis 111–12

R
racism
    see also discrimination
    institutional 378
    NHS 362–3
    ten-point plan, CRE 366, 369
radical approach
    defining 367
    equal opportunities 367
rate ranges, pay 184–5
ratio analysis
    defining 51
    planning 51

real estate, flexible working 435–6
recruitment 105–38
    see also selection
    activities 108–9
    agencies 126–30
    case study 134–5
    changing nature of jobs 80
    competency alternative 114–16
    competency frameworks 113–14
    consultants 127
    defining 30, 106–7
    diversity, managing 62, 80–1, 117
    educational sources 124–5
    Expedia 117
    external 121–31
    formative activities 108–9
    freeze, labour supply/demand 63
    government agencies 125–6
    hotels 134–5
    individual tasks 133
    internal 120
    international perspective 55–6, 125
    internet 55–6
    internet businesses 117
    job analysis 109–13
    job descriptions 113–14
    JobCentre 125–6
    legal context 116–19
    legislation 116–19
    media sources 130–1
    methods 119–31
    newsprint sources 130–1
    NHS Greater Glasgow 105–6
    organisation's own resources 121–4
    person specifications 113–14
    personal development 132
    prisoners 62
    sequence 108–9
    Shell 125
    soft HRM 20
    sources 119–31
    stages 108–9
    team tasks 134
    websites 136
    work experience 62
    www exercises 38, 136
redundancies
    changing nature of jobs 81
    planning 41–3
    Virgin Atlantic 41–3
references
    academic 149
    employment 149
    improving 150
    personal 149
    problems 150
    selection 148–50
    specialist 149
    types 149

reflector, learning style 225
regulations
    defining 329
    health, safety and employee well-being 329, 338
regulatory approach, equal opportunities 363–4
rehabilitation services 346
relocation, employee 454–6
remuneration 32, 176–212
    see also pay...; rewards
    defining 32, 178–9
    personal development 206–7
    www exercises 210
representation, employee 289–91
resource-based, defining 416
resource-based SHRM 416–18
resourcing 28–30
    defining 30
    strategies 64
retention, staff see staff retention
retirement
    changing nature of jobs 81
    early retirement, labour supply/demand 63
retrained transfers, labour supply/demand 63
retraining, labour supply/demand 63
return to work services 346
reward strategy 193
rewards 32, 176–212
    see also pay...; remuneration
    defining 32, 178–9
    motivation 188–201
    total 193–6
rewards systems 178–9
    soft HRM 16–17, 21
rise, HRM 10
Rodger's seven-point plan, person specifications 115
role-plays, assessment centres 162
roles
    defining 92
    HR managers 28–33
    teams 92–4
    work design 92–4
routine jobs, job design 86–7
Royal Mail, employee relations 286–8

S

safety see health, safety and employee well-being
satisfiers, motivation 191–2
school, job design 100
scientific management
    defining 7, 82
    history 7
    job design 82
    team tasks 99–100
scope/depth, job design 85–8
selection 107, 138–75
    see also recruitment
    ability testing 155–7
    application forms 141–2
    appointments 163–5

    assessment centres 160–3
    biographical profiling 151–3
    case study 171–2
    changing nature of jobs 80
    contemporary 151
    contemporary methods 151–63
    CVs 141–2
    defining 30, 107, 139
    discrimination 143–4
    diversity, managing 80–1
    Ghana 153
    individual tasks 170
    induction 165–7
    international perspective 153
    interviews 144–8
    IQ tests 138–9
    Juapong Textiles, Ghana 153
    online testing 160
    personal development 168–9
    personality assessments 158–9
    police 143–4
    predictive validity 140–1
    problems 138–40, 171–2
    psychological disposition 157–9
    psychological testing 153–4
    references 148–50
    shortlisting 143–4
    soft HRM 20
    team tasks 170–1
    testing ability 155–7
    traditional 140–1
    www exercises 173
self-concept 273–4
    defining 273
self-efficacy 274
self-esteem 273–4
    defining 273
self-interest, hunting analogy 3–5
self-managed learning, training 236–7
self-managed teams
    defining 94
    work design 94–6
self-management, contingencies 221
sensory testing 156
settlement range
    defining 303
    negotiation 303
Shell
    international perspective 125
    recruitment 125
shortlisting, selection 143–4
SHRM see strategic human resource management
sick days
    motivation 203
    reducing 203
    Tesco 203
single-loop learning 242–3
    defining 242
'sitting next to Nellie', training 235

situational factors, soft HRM 18
situational questioning, interviews 145
skills
    HR managers 228
    transferable 64–5
small group interviews 146–7
SMART objectives, performance 262–3
social context, HRM 27
social exclusion
    defining 53
    labour supply/demand 53
social justice
    defining 364
    diversity, managing 364–5
social learning theory 221–2
    defining 221
Social Security Contributions and Benefits Act 1992;
        202–3
socialisation, learning 217
society, labour supply/demand 52–3
soft HRM 14–23
    appraisal 21
    change management 20
    communication systems 21, 22
    defining 14
    development 19–23
    employee commitment 22
    employee influence 16
    Guest's model 21, 22
    Harvard model 16–17, 20
    HR outcomes 18
    human resource flow 16, 20
    job design 20
    long-term consequences 18
    manpower flows 21
    organisational design 20
    policy formulation 20
    quality 22–3
    recruitment 20
    rewards systems 16–17, 21
    selection 20
    situational factors 18
    stakeholder interests 18
    strategic integration 21
    training/development 21
    work systems 17
    workforce flexibility 22
software
    ERP 58–9
    PeopleSoft 58–9
    planning 58–9
South Africa, banks/banking 29–30
spatial testing 156
specialist references 149
spiral concept, careers 440–3
SSP see statutory sick pay
St Albans Council, planning 71–2
St Lucia's secondary school, job design 100
staff retention 28–30

benefits 268
internal labour market 271–2
knowledge management 272, 273
strategies 268–72
Tesco 271
www exercises 72
staffing objectives, HR activity 10–11
stakeholder interests, soft HRM 18
stakeholders, defining 25
standard planning 44–5
statutory sick pay (SSP) 341–5
    defining 341
stereotypes
    defining 380
    diversity, managing 267–8, 380
    individual tasks 393–4
    performance 267–8
    team tasks 394
strategic choices 403
strategic human resource management (SHRM)
        399–434
    defining 409
    development 410–12
    perspectives 407–10
    resource-based 416–18
strategic integration, soft HRM 21
strategic management 403–7
    defining 403
    hard HRM 23
strategic planning 46–8
strategic plans 48
    defining 48
    mergers 457–8
strategic thinking
    individual tasks 36
    National Trust 399–402
    team tasks 36
strategies
    bargaining 302–4
    implementation 416
    labour supply/demand 62–4
    negotiation 302–4
    resourcing 64
    staff retention 268–72
    training 235–7
    WLB 349–50
strategy
    aspects 403–4
    British Airways 430–1
    defining 21, 402–3
    EU expansion 420–2
    generic 404
    high-performance work systems 407–8, 422–4
    individual tasks 429
    international perspective 417
    John Lewis Partnership 431
    personal development 427
    team tasks 429–30
    www exercises 431

stress questioning, interviews 146
subcontractors
    health, safety and employee well-being 326–7
    international perspective 326–7
succession planning 57–8
    defining 57
supply/demand, labour 52–6, 62–4
SWOT analysis 406–7
    defining 406

T
taboos
    defining 382
    diversity, managing 382
tactical plans 49
takeovers see acquisitions; mergers
talent
    branding 60
    coaching culture 60
    community sense 61
    competition 61
    corporate values 60
    flexible benefits 60
    individuals' values 60
    managing 58–61
    people branding 60
    planning 58–61
    positive energy 61
    psychological contract 60
    values 60
    work/life balance 60
tandem interviews 146–7
task depth/scope, job design 85–8
task roles, work design 94
Taylor, Frederick 7
team pay 198–201
    advantages 201
    defining 199
    disadvantages 201
team tasks
    appraisal interviews 280–1
    diversity, managing 394
    employee relations 313–15
    equal opportunities 394
    health, safety and employee well-being 355
    interviews 280–1
    learning 247
    pay 209
    planning 71
    recruitment 134
    scientific management 99–100
    selection 170–1
    stereotypes 394
    strategic thinking 36
    strategy 429–30
    virtualising 466–7
teams
    barriers 96
    Belbin's team roles 92–4

    responsibilities 200
    self-managed teams 94–6
    work design 92–6
technician jobs, job design 86–7
technological context, HRM 27–8
technological innovation, labour supply/demand 63
technology, labour supply/demand 54
telephone interviews 146–7
teleworking
    flexible working 88–91
    international perspective 88–91
temporary and contract staffing agencies 127–8
temporary employees, labour supply/demand 63
Tesco
    motivation 203
    sick days 203
    staff retention 271
testing ability, selection 155–7
theorist, learning style 226
Theory Z 438
time line, history 6
TNT UK Ltd
    case study 281–3
    development 281–3
    performance 281–3
    training 281–3
total rewards 193–6
    defining 193
trades unions
    decline/fall 289–90
    employee representation 289–90
traditional pay 186
    defining 186
traditional selection 140–1
    defining 140
training 31–2, 215–51
    see also development; learning; personal
        development
    advantages 218–19
    car industry 215–17
    case study 247–9, 281–3
    changing nature of jobs 81
    defining 218–19
    diversity, managing 237–9, 384, 445
    dyslexia 237–9
    vs education 218–19
    evaluation 237
    external courses 236
    in-house programmes 235–6
    Intel Ireland 247–9
    international perspective 229–30
    Japanese attitude 215–17
    LSC 233–4
    National Learning Targets 232
    needs 234–5
    needs analysis 230–1
    NVQs 231–2, 233
    objectives 235
    on-the-job 235

training – *contd.*
  personal development 244
  policies 231–4
  process 230
  programmes 228–30
  self-managed learning 236–7
  'sitting next to Nellie' 235
  soft HRM 21
  steps 230–1
  strategies 235–7
  TNT UK Ltd 281–3
transferable skills 64–5
  agile workers 67
transfers, labour supply/demand 63
transitional matrices
  defining 56
  planning 56–7
transitory concept, careers 440–3
transparency, pay 204–5
trend analysis
  defining 50
  planning 50–1
trust, mergers 460–1
turnover reduction, labour supply/demand 63

U
UAB Constructus
  health, safety and employee well-being 326–7
  subcontractors 326–7
unitarist perspective, conflict 294
universalist perspective, SHRM 407–8, 411

V
values
  corporate 60
  individuals' 60
  organisational 46
  talent 60
verbal/communication testing 156
vertical loading
  defining 84
  job design 84
videoconference interviews 146–7
views, HR 5–6
Virgin Atlantic
  planning 41–3
  redundancies 41–3
virtualising 452–4
  team tasks 466–7
vision 5

W
war years, history 8–10
Warwick model
  defining 410
  SHRM 410–12

websites, recruitment 136
well-being, employee *see* health, safety and employee
    well-being
wellness services 347–8
WLB *see* work/life balance
work, changing nature of 64–5
work combining, labour supply/demand 63
work design 74–102
  analysis 75–6
  Belbin's team roles 92–4
  functional group roles 92–4
  maintenance roles 94
  National Crime Squad 74–5
  personal development 97–8
  personal roles 94
  roles 92–4
  self-managed teams 94–6
  task roles 94
  teams 92–6
work experience, prisoners 62
work flow analysis 77–8
work flow design 76–7
work/life balance (WLB)
  see also flexible working
  career management 445
  case study 467–8
  diversity, managing 445
  planning 65–7
  services 349–50
  strategies 349–50
  talent 60
  www exercises 468
work systems, soft HRM 17
workforce centred 12
workforce flexibility
  see also flexible working
  soft HRM 22
Working Time Directive, health, safety and employee
    well-being 334
www exercises
  apprenticeships 249
  CIPD 38
  coaching 283
  equal opportunities 396
  health, safety and employee well-being 356–7
  job design 101
  learning 249
  motivation 72
  recruitment 38, 136
  remuneration 210
  selection 173
  staff retention 72
  strategy 431
  WLB 468